KARL LLEWELLYN AND THE REALIST MOVEMENT, SECOND EDITION

First published in 1973, *Karl Llewellyn and the Realist Movement* is recognized as a classic account of American Legal Realism and its leading figure. Karl Llewellyn is the best known and most substantial jurist of the variegated group of lawyers known as the American Realists. A man of wide interests and colorful character, he made important contributions to legal theory, legal sociology, commercial law, contract law, civil liberties, and legal education.

This intellectual biography sets Llewellyn in the broad context of the rise of the American Realist movement and contains a brief overview of Llewellyn's life and character before focusing attention on his most important works, including *The Cheyenne Way*, *The Bramble Bush*, *The Common Law Tradition*, the *Uniform Commercial Code*, and some significant manuscripts. In this second edition the original text is unchanged and is supplemented with a foreword by Frederick Schauer and a lengthy afterword in which William Twining gives a fascinating personal account of the making of the book and comments on developments in relevant legal scholarship over the past forty years.

William Twining is the Quain Professor of Jurisprudence Emeritus at University College London and a regular Visiting Professor at the University of Miami School of Law. He was a pupil of Karl Llewellyn in 1957–58 and put Llewellyn's very extensive papers in order after his death in 1962. Twining's recent writings include *Rethinking Evidence* (2nd edition, 2006), *General Jurisprudence* (2009), and *How to Do Things with Rules* (5th edition with David Miers, 2010), all published by Cambridge University Press and recognizable as part of the Realist tradition.

THE LAW IN CONTEXT SERIES

Editors: William Twining (University College London),
Christopher McCrudden (The Queen's University, Belfast), and
Bronwen Morgan (University of Bristol)

Since 1970 the Law in Context series has been in the forefront of the movement to broaden the study of law. It has been a vehicle for the publication of
innovative scholarly books that treat law and legal phenomena critically in
their social, political, and economic contexts from a variety of perspectives.
The series particularly aims to publish scholarly legal writing that brings
fresh perspectives to bear on new and existing areas of law taught in universities. A contextual approach involves treating legal subjects broadly, using
materials from other social sciences, and from any other discipline that
helps to explain the operation in practice of the subject under discussion. It
is hoped that this orientation is at once more stimulating and more realistic
than the bare exposition of legal rules. The series includes original books
that have a different emphasis from traditional legal textbooks, while maintaining the same high standards of scholarship. They are written primarily
for undergraduate and graduate students of law and of other disciplines,
but most also appeal to a wider readership. In the past, most books in the
series have focused on English law, but recent publications include books
on European law, globalization, transnational legal processes, and comparative law.

(continued after the index)

Karl Llewellyn and the Realist Movement

Second Edition

William Twining

University College London

CAMBRIDGE
UNIVERSITY PRESS

CAMBRIDGE UNIVERSITY PRESS
Cambridge, New York, Melbourne, Madrid, Cape Town,
Singapore, São Paulo, Delhi, Mexico City

Cambridge University Press
32 Avenue of the Americas, New York, NY 10013-2473, USA

www.cambridge.org
Information on this title: www.cambridge.org/9781107023383

First published 1973
Second edition published 2012

A catalog record for this publication is available from the British Library.

ISBN 978-1-107-02338-3 Hardback

Cambridge University Press has no responsibility for the persistence or accuracy of
URLS for external or third-party Internet Web sites referred to in this publication
and does not guarantee that any content on such Web sites is, or will remain,
accurate or appropriate.

Cover photo: The photograph depicts a bust of Llewellyn by the Russian sculptor
Sergei Konenkov, who later came to be regarded as one of the leading Russian art-
ists of the twentieth century. Karl and Betty Llewellyn befriended Konenkov in New
York in 1924 and helped him to obtain commissions for busts of leading American
luminaries, including three Supreme Court Justices. (See M. T. Lampard, J. E. Bowlt,
and W. R. Salmond, *The Uncommon Vision of Sergei Konenkov 1974–1971: A Russian
Sculptor and His Times*, New Brunswick: Rutgers University Press, 2001; KLRM 421,
447.) The original of the Llewellyn bust is in the University of Chicago Law School,
and a cast is in the University of Miami Law School.

CONTENTS

FOREWORD

Frederick Schauer

I

Legal Realism is contested terrain. Whether we label the perspective *legal realism*, or *Legal Realism*, or *American Legal Realism*, there have been for at least eighty years serious disputes about just what Legal Realism is and what it claims. Moreover, the terrain is contested not merely because there are disagreements around the edges – that is, with respect to the borderline cases of what is or is not a Realist perspective.[1] Rather, the very nature of Legal Realism is contested, as we can see from the existence of widely divergent views about just what the core claims and commitments of Legal Realism are.

A sample of the various positions claiming the Legal Realist banner will make the extent of this disagreement clearer. Thus, some theorists believe that Legal Realism is centrally about the relative importance of facts in adjudication, in contrast to a traditional view allegedly holding that abstract rules are more important determinants of legal outcomes than are the facts of particular cases.[2]

---

[1] In this foreword, *Legal Realism* will be capitalized, in part to emphasize the differences between Legal Realism as a view about some or many aspects of law, on one hand, and the various forms of philosophical realism, on the other. In the fields of metaphysics and meta-ethics, for example, realist perspectives stress the existence of some external or objective reality, as opposed to the view that what we perceive as moral or physical reality is no more than the creation of human cultures or the minds of individual human beings. By stressing the mind independence of an external reality, therefore, most embodiments of philosophical realism are virtually the exact opposite of Legal Realism, at least insofar as Legal Realism in most of its forms is understood to place an emphasis on discretion, indeterminacy, non-objectivity, and the human element in legal decision making.

[2] See especially Brian Leiter, *Naturalizing Jurisprudence: Essays on American Legal Realism and Naturalism in Legal Philosophy* (Oxford: Oxford University Press, 2007);

Those who subscribe to this understanding of Legal Realism's core commitments do not, of course, saddle the traditional view with the implausible position that abstract legal rules can be applied to particular cases without regard to the facts presented in those cases. Nevertheless, an important difference remains in emphasis between a traditional view that the determination of which facts are relevant comes from preexisting legal rules, and a Legal Realist view holding that judicial and other legal decisions are made primarily on the basis of all the facts of a particular controversy that a particular judge deems relevant, without regard to whether some array of preexisting legal rules makes those facts relevant.

Closely allied with this view about the importance of the facts of particular controversies is the idea that realism is centrally about the sequencing of decision making and justification. Going back at least as far as Judge Joseph Hutcheson's famous 1929 article about the role of the hunch in judicial decision making,[3] and continuing as the primary point of Jerome Frank's *Law and the Modern Mind*,[4] theorists and commentators often designated as Legal Realists have argued that judges do not first consult the law and thereafter reach a decision on the basis of that law, as the traditional picture would have it. Rather, Hutcheson and Frank and many others have claimed, judges initially reach a decision about which party ought to prevail, often on the basis of a full range of both legal and nonlegal facts and factors, and then, and only then, do they consult the law in order to justify or rationalize a decision made substantially on nonlegal grounds.

Still another view of Realism contrasts realism with formalism, or at least something claimed to be formalism.[5] Here Realism's target

---

Brian Leiter, "American Legal Realism," in Martin P. Golding & William A. Edmundson, eds., *Blackwell Guide to the Philosophy of Law and Legal Theory* (Oxford: Blackwell Publishing, 2005), pp. 50–66; Brian Leiter, "Legal Realism," in Dennis Patterson, ed., *A Companion to Philosophy of Law and legal Theory* (Oxford: Blackwell Publishers, 1996), pp. 261–79.

[3] Joseph J. Hutcheson, Jr., "The Judgment Intuitive: The Function of the 'Hunch' in Judicial Decision," *Cornell Law Journal*, vol. 14 (1929), pp. 274–88.

[4] Jerome Frank, *Law and the Modern Mind* (New York: Brentano's, 1930).

[5] See Laura Kalman, *Legal Realism at Yale 1927-1960* (Chapel Hill, North Carolina: University of North Carolina Press, 1986). See also Theodore M. Benditt, *Law as Rule and Principle: Problems of Legal Philosophy* (Stanford, California: Stanford University Press, 1978), pp. 2–5; Brian Bix, *Jurisprudence: Theory and Context* (London: Sweet & Maxwell, 3d ed., 2003), pp. 179–80; Robert S. Summers, *Form

is said to be the view that law is often, usually, or almost always determinate, such that the law dictates a particular result, or at least renders ineligible most of the outcomes that would be otherwise eligible on moral, political, economic, or pragmatic grounds.[6] The Realist challenge to this view, a challenge sometimes described in terms of indeterminacy[7] and sometimes in terms of functionalism or instrumentalism,[8] is the view that in all, most, or many cases, especially in the controversies that wind up in court or wind up in appellate courts, the law simply does not uniquely determine a result, the consequence being that the law leaves open to the judge or other decision maker a wide range of possible results, results that the decision maker may or must select on nonlegal grounds.[9]

The foregoing forms of Legal Realist claims are all about judicial decision making, but other Realist perspectives are about academic or empirical method. What do we want to know about law, and how do we go about finding it? Thus, Legal Realism is often thought of as the empirical (and largely external) examination of law and its processes, with the aim of allowing lawyers and others to predict legal outcomes,[10] or of offering social science insights

---

and Function in a Legal System (New York: Cambridge University Press, 2006), pp. 28–9; Anthony J. Sebok, *Legal Positivism in American Jurisprudence* (Cambridge: Cambridge University Press, 1998), pp. 75–83; Brian Z. Tamanaha, *Beyond the Formalist-Realist Divide: The Role of Politics in Judging* (Princeton, New Jersey: Princeton University Press, 2010).

[6] For an analysis and qualified defense of formalism, see Frederick Schauer, "Formalism," *Yale Law Journal*, vol. 97 (1988), pp. 509–48.

[7] See Kent Greenawalt, *Law and Objectivity* (New York: Oxford University Press, 1992), p. 11; Roger Shiner, *Norm and Nature: The Movements of Legal Thought* (Oxford: Clarendon Press, 1992), p. 217; Mark Tushnet, *Red, White, and Blue: A Critical Analysis of Constitutional Law* (Cambridge, Massachusetts: Harvard University Press, 1988), pp. 191–6.

[8] Kalman, *op. cit.* note 5, pp. 29–31.

[9] See Brian Leiter, "Law and Objectivity," in Jules Coleman & Scott Shapiro, eds., *Oxford Handbook of Jurisprudence and Philosophy of Law* (Oxford: Oxford University Press, 2002), pp. 969–89.

[10] The importance of seeing law at least partly in terms of predicting legal outcomes is a major theme of Oliver Wendell Holmes, "The Path of the Law," *Harvard Law Review*, vol. 10 (1897), pp. 457–78. The Realists embraced this idea, see, for example, Karl N. Llewellyn, *The Theory of Rules* (Frederick Schauer, ed., Chicago: University of Chicago Press, 2011), pp. 55–60, but took it one step further. Holmes believed that knowledge of legal rules and legal categories would facilitate accurate prediction, but the Realists, *contra* Holmes, stressed that identifying various nonlegal factors would often make for better predictions.

or conclusions about the nature of law itself, or, more commonly, identifying the determinants of legal outcomes. And thus a common claim is that a multiplicity of different forms of social science inquiry about law and legal decision making, forms of inquiry that are to be contrasted with the close textual and doctrinal analysis that still pervade legal education and legal scholarship, constitute the preeminent contribution of Legal Realism.[11]

A more modern characterization of Realism goes in a quite different direction, focusing less on judicial decision making and more on the substance of law. More particularly, this view, which tends to see Robert Hale[12] as a central figure in the Realist tradition,[13] understands Legal Realism as the denial of law's alleged neutrality. Legal rules and doctrines, according to this critique, are traditionally thought to be natural, neutral, or both.[14] To the extent that this view exists, then the contrasting view – that legal rules or legal baselines

And thus the modern political scientists who emphasize the role of nonlegal factors in determining and predicting Supreme Court decisions are properly understood as heirs to this strand of Realism. See, for example, Saul Brenner & Harold J. Spaeth, *Stare Indecisis: The Alteration of Precedent on the Supreme Court , 1946-1992* (New York: Cambridge University Press, 1996); Jeffrey J. Segal & Harold J. Spaeth, *The Supreme Court and the Attitudinal Model Revisited* (New York: Cambridge University Press, 2004). For a valuable analysis of the relationship among prediction, Holmes, and Realism, see William Twining, "The Bad Man Revisited," *Cornell Law Review*, vol. 58 (1972), pp. 275–303.

[11] See John Henry Schlegel, *American Legal Realism and Empirical Social Science* (Durham, North Carolina: University of North Carolina Press, 1995); Brian Z. Tamanaha, *Realistic Socio-Legal Theory* (Oxford: Clarendon Press, 1997).

[12] See Robert L. Hale, "Coercion and Distribution in a Supposedly Non-Coercive State," *Political Science Quarterly*, vol. 38 (1923), pp. 470–9.

[13] Hale, an economist and lawyer, was a Columbia colleague of Llewellyn's, but Llewellyn does not list him among the Realists in Karl Llewellyn "Some Realism About Realism," *Harvard Law Review*, vol. 44 (1931), pp. 1222–64. This exclusion may or may not be telling about Llewellyn's view of the core commitments of Realism, although the exclusion of Hale may be no more dispositive than the inclusion of Edwin Patterson, whose work bears few earmarks of any Realist perspective. See William Twining, this volume, p. 410 note 33.

[14] Blackstone is a particularly common target. See Duncan Kennedy, "The Structure of Blackstone's Commentaries," *Buffalo Law Review*, vol. 28 (1979), pp. 209–382. It is not at all clear just who actually believed (or believes) that the substantive baselines of legal doctrine are either natural or neutral. Most of the standard suspects, e.g., Herbert Wechsler, "Toward Neutral Principles in Constitutional Law," *Harvard Law Review*, vol. 73 (1959), pp. 1–35, turn out on close reading and inspection to either have had more complex views or to have believed nothing of the kind.

are actually the product of political and economic choices – is, once
again, claimed to be the true version of Legal Realism.[15]

II

Each of the foregoing understandings of Legal Realism has its
adherents. Members of and sympathizers with the Critical Legal
Studies Movement, for example, tend to promote the last mentioned of these interpretations,[16] insisting that Legal Realism was
centrally about recognizing the non-neutrality and consequent
political choices implicit in substantive legal doctrine.[17] And both
the qualitative and the quantitative empirical social scientists who
study the operation of law claim to be fostering the "new legal realism," even as their methods (and home disciplines) vary widely.[18]

[15] See, for example, Neil Duxbury, *Patterns of American Jurisprudence* (Oxford:
  Clarendon Press, 1995); Barbara H. Fried, *The Progressive Assault on Laissez Faire:
  Robert Hale and the First Law and Economics Movement* (Cambridge, Massachusetts:
  Harvard University Press, 1998); Morton J. Horwitz, *The Transformation of Amer-
  ican Law 1870-1960* (New York: Oxford University Press, 1992), pp. 169–246;
  Gary Minda, *Postmodern Legal Movements: Law and Jurisprudence at Century's End*
  (New York: New York University Press, 1995). This substantive conception of
  Realism is also apparent in the Introduction, chapter introductions, and organi-
  zation (which does not get to issues of legal reasoning and decision making until
  Chapter 6) of William W. Fisher III, Morton J. Horwitz, & Thomas A. Reed, eds.,
  American Legal Realism New York: Oxford University Press, 1993).
[16] See Horwitz, ibid.; Minda, ibid.; Guyora Binder, "Critical Legal Studies," in
  Patterson, *A Companion to Philosophy of Law, op. cit.* note 2, pp. 280–90. See also
  Andrew Altman, *Critical Legal Studies: A Liberal Critique* (Princeton, New Jersey:
  Princeton University Press, 1990), pp. 106–17.
[17] It is worth noting, however, that one of the goals of Critical Legal Studies is/was
  also to continue the more conventionally understood dimensions of the Realist project, in particular the focus on law's indeterminacy and the consequent
  choices open to a judge in any particular case. See, for example, Duncan Ken-
  nedy, "Freedom and Constraint in Adjudication: A Critical Phenomenology,"
  Journal of Legal Education, vol. 36 (1986), pp. 518–62; Mark Tushnet, "Critical
  Legal Studies: An Introduction to Its Origins and Underpinnings," *Journal of
  Legal Education*, vol. 36 (1986), pp. 505–17.
[18] Compare Howard Erlanger *et al.*, "Is It Time for a New Legal Realism?" *Wisconsin
  Law Review*, vol. 2005 (2005), pp. 335–63, with Daniel A. Farber, "Toward a New
  Legal Realism," *University of Chicago Law Review*, vol. 68 (2001), pp. 279–393,
  with Thomas J. Miles & Cass R. Sunstein, "The New Legal Realism," *University
  of Chicago Law Review*, vol. 75 (2008), pp. 831–51. See also Victoria E. Nourse
  & Gregory C. Shaffer, "Varieties of New Legal Realism: Can a New World Order
  Prompt a New Legal Theory?" *Cornall Law Review*, vol. 95 (2009), pp. 61–137.

It would be tempting to dismiss as irrelevant these contrasting perspectives on the true nature of Legal Realism. The disputes, some might say, are merely contests about a label, and labels are just that – labels with no intrinsic reality. But the temptation should be resisted. Labels often make a difference in terms of how we perceive, categorize, and organize the world, or at least some part of it, and the battle over how we should understand Legal Realism and the tradition that created it is in reality a battle over ownership of the legacy of perhaps the most important strand of American legal theory, or at least the most characteristically American strand of American legal theory. Any attempt to frame or to reframe Legal Realism, therefore, is best understood as an offer or attempt to reach an understanding of a large component of the American legal tradition.[19]

Of course the various perspectives on or strands of Legal Realism need not be thought of as necessarily mutually exclusive. The importance of an external empirical study of the determinants of legal decisions, for example, is fully compatible with the view that nonlegal factors are preeminent among those determinants; and the view that nonlegal factors are of principal importance is similarly compatible with the view that the equities of the particular facts of particular cases are among the most important of the nonlegal factors. On the other hand, the view that legal rules are indeed causally important in judicial decision making, but that the rules that are causally important diverge from the "paper rules" found in law books, a view most attributable to Llewellyn,[20] is in some tension with the fact-focused particularism of Hutcheson,

[19] It is worthwhile noting here that the connections between American Legal Realism and the Scandinavian Legal Realism of Axel Hägerström, A. Vilhelm Lundstedt, Karl Olivecrona, and Alf Ross (see Gregory S. Alexander, "Comparing the Two Legal Realisms – American and Scandinavian," *American Journal of Comparative Law*, vol. 50 [2002], pp. 131–74 [2002]) are, at best, attenuated. Although, as Alexander argues, the Scandinavian Realists shared some political goals with many of the American Realists, the fundamental core of Scandinavian Realism was skepticism about the objectivity (or even the point) of morality, a view drawn from the logical positivism that flourished during the period when many of the Scandinavian Realists were writing. Some American Realists may have been similarly skeptical of the objectivity of morality, but the American Realist enterprise tended to be far removed from addressing such issues.

[20] See Llewellyn, *op. cit.* note 10; Karl Llewellyn, "A Realistic Jurisprudence: The Next Step," *Columbia Law Review*, vol. 30 (1930), pp. 431–65.

Frank, and others. Even putting such tensions aside, however, matters of emphasis are important. Consequently, the question of the true or central nature of Legal Realism persists. It was a question that very much concerned Llewellyn in "Some Realism about Realism,"[21] and it is a question the importance of which should not be easily dismissed as simply being about mere labels.

Asking about the real nature of something, however, is fraught with perils. Famously, J. L. Austin treated "real" as his primary example of what he (unfortunately) called a "trouser-word," in the sense of there being some other word, the negation, that "wore the trousers" by virtue of playing the leading role.[22] Thus, we do not really know what it is for something to be real unless we have an understanding of the particular form of unreality that the designation of something as real is intended to reject. The statement that a coat is made of real fur, for example, is an assertion that the coat is not made out of imitation fur, but it is not an assertion that the fur is not toy fur, yet in other contexts real means not a toy, as when in some contexts we talk about a real car when we mean precisely to say that it is not a toy car.

In the context of law, therefore, it is interesting to wonder just what form of unreality the various claims of Legal Realism to be real are attempting to deny. There are numerous candidates for such claimed unrealities, and each of the characterizations of Realism described here is premised on a belief that there is a certain kind of unreality that would be usefully disabused by accepting the Realist challenge. Thus, for some the relevant unreality is the belief that legal decision making is rule-intensive rather than fact-intensive,[23] for others it is the belief that judges do not decide on an outcome until after consulting the relevant legal rules,[24] for still others it is the belief that judicial opinions are an accurate description of the

[21] *Op. cit.* note 9. It is important to note, however, that Llewellyn, both in this article and elsewhere, had a decidedly non-essentialist view about the nature of Legal Realism, believing that it was more a state of mind than a program or a movement and believing that multiple and partially divergent perspectives could all properly be characterized as Realist.

[22] J. L. Austin, *Sense and Sensibilia* (G. J. Warnock, ed., Oxford: Oxford University Press, 1962), pp. 15–19, 63–77.

[23] See especially Leiter, *Naturalizing Jurisprudence, op. cit.* note 2, pp. 73–80. See also Frederick Schauer, "Introduction," in Karl N. Llewellyn, *The Theory of Rules, op. cit.* note 10, pp. 1–28.

[24] See Hutcheson, *op. cit.* note 3; Frank, *op. cit.* note 4.

thinking and reasoning processes of judges,[25] and there is also the form of unreality represented by the belief that the best way to understand law is by engaging in the largely nonempirical analysis of reported appellate opinions.[26] And so on. And thus when Holmes observed, famously, that "The life of law has not been logic, it has been experience,"[27] he not only established himself as a Realist precursor in seeking to debunk a long-held belief about the nature of common law reasoning, but emphasized that we understand legal perspectives substantially by what they seek to reject. Had there not been a tradition of treating common law development as a process of logical discovery, Holmes's quip would have made no

[25] Even outside of the Realist canon and explicit discussions about Realism, there is a normative debate about whether judges are or should be candid in their opinions. Compare David Shapiro, "In Defense of Judicial Candor," *Harvard Law Review*, vol. 100 (1987), pp. 731–50, with Scott C. Idleman, "A Prudential Theory of Judicial Candor," *Texas Law Review*, vol. 73 (1995), pp. 1307–1417. And Richard A. Wasserstrom, *The Judicial Decision: Toward a Theory of Legal Justification* (Stanford, California: Stanford University Press, 1961), distinguishes the role of law in causing legal decisions – the logic of decision – from its role in justifying them – the logic of justification.

[26] It is often said that "we are all Realists now," Gary Peller, "The Metaphysics of American Law," *California Law Review*, vol. 73 (1985), pp. 1151–1290, at p. 1151; Joseph William Singer, "Legal Realism Now," *California Law Review*, vol. 76 (1988), pp. 465–544, at p. 467, but it is far from clear that that is actually so. Obviously the truth of the claim that we are now all Realists depends on the conception of Realism that the claimant holds, but there are at least some indications that the main lines of the Realist critique remain resisted. For one example, consider the torts casebook developed by Leon Green, a central Realist figure. Green believed that the determinants of outcomes in torts cases were not formal doctrines such as foreseeability and proximate cause and reasonable care, but rather the factual situations in which claims arose. As a result, he organized his casebook not around the traditional legal categories of tort law, but instead around the factual categories of the world, such as railways and animals. Leon Green, *The Judicial Process in Torts Cases* (St. Paul, Minnesota: West Publishing Co., 1931). Yet it is noteworthy that no modern torts book takes a similar approach. Is this rejection of Green's approach based on the view that Green was empirically mistaken, and that the formal categories of tort law have more to do with outcomes in tort cases than the factual situations in which tort claims arise, or is it perhaps because there is more resistance to the core claims of Legal Realism than the common incantation of "we are all Realists now" appears to imagine? On the latter possibility, albeit with a somewhat different conception of Realism in mind, see Hanoch Dagan, "The Realist Conception of Law," *University of Toronto Law Journal*, vol. 57 (2007), pp. 607–60.

[27] Oliver Wendell Holmes, Jr., *The Common Law* (Boston: Little, Brown, 1881), p. 1.

sense. It gets its bite precisely from the existence of what it seeks to rebut. And so too with much of Legal Realism, whose enduring importance stems largely from the cluster of traditional views about legal thought and judicial decision making that it has sought, from the beginning, to challenge.

III

But if there are competing conceptions of Legal Realism, and thus competing conceptions of just which accepted belief about the nature of law and legal decision making is in need of debunking, how are we to resolve the controversy? One possibility is that there is no need to resolve it at all. If Legal Realism is more a state of mind than a concrete position, as Llewellyn long insisted,[28] then it could well be that the various positions associated with Realism are connected by nothing more than a family resemblance, a cluster of related positions sharing no common features among all. And it is also possible that the claims of Legal Realism are appropriately modified over time in order to recognize the needs and issues of the present rather than the issues that happen to have occupied a certain group of people at a particular time. Just as history, even the history of the same events, is (or must be) rewritten for each generation, maybe so too is the history, the meaning, the legacy, and the importance of Legal Realism different now than it was in the 1980s, and different in the 1980s from what it was in the 1950s, and different in the 1950s from what it was in the 1930s.

Yet, however we seek to define the task of understanding Realism, we cannot, or at least should not, avoid an inquiry that is at least in part historical. There existed real Realists, as it were. Llewellyn, Frank, Oliphant, and many others were real people who had real thoughts and who write real books and real articles. And while there might be genuine debates about whether certain figures were or were not Legal Realists – Oliver Wendell Holmes, John Chipman Gray, Benjamin Cardozo, Robert Hale, and others are often the subject of these debates – these are debates at the periphery, debates about figures whose entitlement to the Realist label is open to legitimate disagreement. But no one seriously

---

[28] Especially in "Some Realism about Realism," *op. cit.* note 12.

doubts that Jerome Frank, Karl Llewellyn, Felix Cohen, Herman Oliphant, Hessel Yntema, William Douglas, Wesley Sturges, Thurman Arnold, Max Radin, Leon Green, and Underhill Moore, among others, existed at the historical core of American Legal Realism from the 1920s to the 1940s, and an understanding of Legal Realism that does not recognize the centrality of at least most of these major figures is more usefully understood as an attempt to hijack the Legal Realist legacy than to understand or continue it.

Once we acknowledge the importance of history in understanding Legal Realism, and once we acknowledge as well the central position of a small group of principal players in defining what Realism was and remains, we are led to the importance of William Twining's magisterial *Karl Llewellyn and the Realist Movement*. It would be tempting to describe the book as a classic, but that description understates its importance. Although others have written about Karl Llewellyn,[29] and although the work of numerous scholars has illuminated Llewellyn's special role in the development of commercial law as we know it,[30] nothing even approaches Twining's book in its comprehensiveness. If nothing else, it is the definitive intellectual biography of an enduring figure in American legal theory, and the most penetrating analysis of the ideas of one of the small number of people who, from the

---

[29] See N. E. H. Hull, *Roscoe Pound and Karl Llewellyn: Searching for an American Jurisprudence* (Chicago: University of Chicago Press, 1997); Wilfrid E. Rumble, *American Legal Realism: Skepticism, Reform, and the Judicial Process* (Ithaca, New York: Cornell University Press, 1968); Brian Leiter, "Karl Nickerson Llewellyn (1893–1962)," in *International Encyclopedia of the Social and Behavioral Sciences*, Karl Ulrich Meyer, ed. (New York: Elsevier, 2001), pp. 8999–9001.

[30] See Douglas G. Baird, "Llewellyn's Heirs," *Louisiana Law Review*, vol. 62 (2002), pp. 1287–97; Ingrid Michelsen Hillinger, "The Article 2 Merchant Rules: Karl Llewellyn's Attempt to Achieve The Good, The True, The Beautiful in Commercial Law," *Georgetown Law Journal*, vol. 73 (1985), pp. 1141–84; Allen R. Kamp, "Karl Llewellyn, Legal Realism, and the UCC in Context," *Albany Law Review*, vol. 59 (1995), pp. 325–97; Gregory E. Maggs, "Karl Llewellyn's Fading Imprint on the Jurisprudence of the Uniform Commercial Code," *University of Colorado Law Review*, vol. 71 (2000), pp. 541–88; James Whitman, "Commercial Law and the American Volk: A Note on Llewellyn's German Sources for the UCC," *Yale Law Journal*, vol. 97 (1987), pp. 156–75; Zipporah Batshaw Wiseman, "The Limits of Vision: Karl Llewellyn and the Merchant Rules," *Harvard Law Review*, vol. 100 (1987), pp. 465–545.

1920s until the 1960s, were at the pinnacle of American legal thought.[31]

But the volume's title is accurate. This is a book not only about Llewellyn, but also, and perhaps more importantly, about American Legal Realism. Implicit in the title, of course, is Twining's view that one cannot understand Realism without understanding Llewellyn's thought,[32] and that Llewellyn was arguably the most important of the Realists. Others – Herman Oliphant,[33] Underhill Moore,[34] and Joseph Hutcheson,[35] as well as the more complex Holmes and Gray[36] – may have been earlier. And others – Jerome Frank,[37] Thurman Arnold,[38]

---

[31] I will not list those who I believe are the others, for fear of treating and ranking legal theorists and thinkers as if they were movie actors or centerfielders.

[32] For a similar view about the importance of biography to understanding Realism, see Roy Kreitner, "Biographing Realist Jurisprudence," *Law & Social Inquiry*, vol. 35 (2010), pp. 765–88.

[33] Oliphant's "A Return to Stare Decisis," *American Bar Association Journal*, vol. 14 (1928), pp. 71–6, as based on a speech given in 1927, and Oliphant had been active in Realist-sounding curricular reform at the Columbia Law School from the early 1920s. Kalman, *op. cit.* note 5, pp. 68–75.

[34] Moore's empirical Realism was evident as early as his 1923 "The Rational Basis of Legal Institutions," *Columbia Law Review*, vol. 23 (1923), pp. 609–17, and he too was involved in the curricular upheavals at the Columbia Law School that started even earlier. Schlegel, *op. cit.* note 8.

[35] Hutcheson's most memorable writing was in 1929, Hutcheson, *op. cit.* note 3, and the roots of his thinking and writing go back somewhat earlier. See Charles L. Zelden, "The Judge Intuitive: The Life and Judicial Philosophy of Judge Joseph C. Hutcheson, Jr.," *South Texas Law Review*, vol. 39 (1998), pp. 905–17.

[36] More complex in the sense that they are better thought of as precursors to Realism than Realists themselves. See Frederick Schauer, *Thinking Like a Lawyer: A New Introduction to Legal Reasoning* (Cambridge, Massachusetts: Harvard University Press, 2009), pp. 124–8.

[37] Especially in *Law and the Modern Mind*, *op. cit.* note 4, but also in, for example, Jerome Frank, *If Men Were Angels* (New York: Harper & Brothers, 1942), and Jerome Frank, "Are Judges Human? Part One: The Effect on Legal Thinking of the Assumption That Judges Behave like Human Beings," *University of Pennsylvania Law Review*, vol. 80 (1931), pp. 17–53. It is common to dismiss Frank as a comparatively unimportant figure in Realist thought, partly because of the infatuation with the naïve and crude version of psychoanalytic theory represented in *Law and the Modern Mind* and other early works, and partly because of his combative and flamboyant language. See, for example, Leiter, *Naturalizing Jurisprudence*, *op. cit.* note 2, pp. 17, 44–5. But Frank's views about the importance of particular facts in particular cases and about the order of decision and justification are important aspects of Realist thought, to which Frank was one of the initial contributors. See Charles Barzun, "Jerome Frank and the Modern Mind," *Buffalo Law Review*, vol. 58 (2010), pp. 1127–58.

and Fred Rodell[39] – may have produced more shock value by the boldness of their arguments, the extravagance of their prose, and the nature of their personalities. But Llewellyn (who had no need to yield to anyone with respect to colorful prose or noteworthy personal characteristics) was there at something close to the beginning, and – by virtue of his positions at Yale, and Columbia, and Chicago; of his anthropological work;[40] and of his role in the creation of modern commercial law[41] – was the pervasive presence of Legal Realism for at least thirty years. To understand Llewellyn is simply to understand Realism, and to understand Realism is to understand Llewellyn, Twining insists, and in that he is not far wrong.

Karl Llewellyn and the Realist Movement was thus when it was first written the right book on the right topic to understand Legal Realism, and it remains so forty years on. The book is comprehensive, meticulously researched, engagingly presented, and, perhaps most important, jurisprudentially sophisticated. Twining started his academic career with Hart, but very soon thereafter became immersed in Llewellyn and Realism. And Twining has continued as a substantial figure in legal theory in his own right. His work on the theory and history of evidence and proof remains definitive,[42] he has made major contributions to thinking

[38] See, for example, Thurman W. Arnold, "The Jurisprudence of Edward S. Robinson," *Yale Law Journal*, vol. 41 (1932), pp. 1282–9. See also Spencer Weber Waller, *Thurman Arnold: A Biography* (New York: New York University Press, 2005); Neil Duxbury, "Some Radicalism about Realism? Thurman Arnold and the Politics of Modern Jurisprudence," *Oxford Journal of Legal Studies*, vol. 10 (1990), pp. 11–41, and the description in Kalman, *Legal Realism at Yale, op. cit.* note 5, at pp. 136–41.

[39] See Fred Rodell, *Woe Unto You, Lawyers!* New York: Reynal & Hitchcock, 1935). And see the description of Rodell in Charles Alan Wright, "Goodbye to Fred Rodell," *Yale Law Journal*, vol. 89 (1980), pp. 1456–7.

[40] Karl Llewellyn & E. Adamson Hoebel, *The Cheyenne Way* (Norman, Oklahoma: University of Oklahoma Press, 1941). Various other works with an anthropological orientation, most published in the 1940s and 1950s, are listed in Twining's definitive bibliography of Llewellyn's published and unpublished works. William Twining, *The Karl Llewellyn Papers* (Chicago: University of Chicago Law School, 1968), pp. 47–78. See also Ajay K. Mehrotra, "Law and the 'Other': Karl N. Llewellyn, Cultural Anthropology, and the Legacy of *The Cheyenne Way*," *Law & Social Inquiry*, vol. 26 (2001), pp. 741–72.

[41] See references *op. cit.* note 29.

[42] See especially William Twining, *Rethinking Evidence: Exploratory Essays* (Cambridge: Cambridge University Press, 2d ed., 2006); William Twining, *Theories of Evidence: Bentham and Wigmore* (London: Weidenfeld & Nicolson, 1985).

about legal reasoning,[43] and in much of his recent work he has attempted, with much success, to try to understand legality in a world of highly diverse cultures and legal systems.[44] As the afterword to this edition makes stunningly clear, Twining thinks and writes about the nature of law in a way that situates him at an angle from the mainstream of contemporary analytic jurisprudence, but it would be a mistake to confuse his iconoclasm with a lack of sophistication or a lack of knowledge. When *Karl Llewellyn and the Realist Movement* was first written in 1971, Twining was very much a part of the world of jurisprudence, and it is a world with which he remains connected and one he understands well. And thus one of the things that sets *Karl Llewellyn and the Realist Movement* apart from most of the other books and articles about Llewellyn and about Legal Realism is that the meticulous and exhaustively documented historical account that Twining provides is combined with an understanding of legal theory that is evident from Twining's other work, but which in this book frames and informs his analysis of Legal Realism in unique and important ways.

V

Twining's Llewellyn and Twining's Realism are both very much informed by a particular point of view. Thus, although there are those – this author among them – who are inclined to see a substantial shift in Llewellyn's thought over the years, and who are inclined to take seriously what some think of as the more extreme claims of Legal Realism, Twining sees mostly consistency in Llewellyn's thought throughout the years, and he is at pains to emphasize that many of the seemingly more guarded conclusions of Llewellyn's later work were present even from the beginning.[45] For Twining,

---

[43] See William Twining & David Miers, *How to Do Things with Rules* (London: Butterworths, 4th ed., 1999).

[44] William Twining, *General Jurisprudence: Understanding Law from a Global Perspective* (Cambridge: Cambridge University Press, 2009).

[45] Thus, there are themes in Llewellyn's later work that are foreshadowed, and in a more understated way than in *The Bramble Bush*, in *The Case Law System in America* (Chicago: University of Chicago Press, Paul Gewirtz, ed., Michael Ansaldi, trans., 1989), originally written in German as *Präjudizienrecht und Rechtssprechung in Amerika*, published in Germany in 1933, and based on lectures that Llewellyn delivered in Leipzig in 1928.

Llewellyn was never as extreme as the opening pages of *The Bramble Bush* suggest, and never as narrowly focused on appellate adjudication as some have thought. And thus for Twining the full compass of Llewellyn's thought and contribution were there to be found by the careful reader almost from the very beginning. Similarly, therefore, a full appreciation of Realism is, for Twining, an appreciation of Realism's focus on legal culture as well as appellate adjudication, and an empirical and sensitive understanding of law's determinacies as well as its indeterminacies.

Twining's account thus takes a strong position, and that is part of its value, both for those who agree and those who disagree. For those who disagree, at least in part, Twining's accurate excavation of the origins of Llewellyn's later thought in Llewellyn's earlier writing may slight important differences of emphasis. Yes, there are connections between the Llewellyn of *The Bramble Bush* and "Some Realism About Realism" on one hand and the Llewellyn of the Uniform Commercial Code and *The Common Law Tradition*[16] on the other, but there may also be discontinuities. And this should not be surprising. Over the course of a long and complex career, Llewellyn not only grew older (and maybe wiser), but become more immersed in the world of practice and the world of law reform, and became more aware of the role of law in other cultures. It would be surprising if such a wealth of experiences over thirty years did not change the thought of someone with as curious and fertile a mind as Llewellyn, and consequently it may tell only part of the story to emphasize the undoubted continuities over time without also noting the numerous changes over the span of a long and productive career in different institutions in different places and with at least somewhat different roles and responsibilities.

Perhaps more significant, it may be important to recognize that Llewellyn at his most extreme may have been more correct than Twining and many others have recognized. Rules may not be "pretty playthings," as Llewellyn, to his regret, noted in the opening pages of *The Bramble Bush*, but the extent of their causal contribution to legal outcomes may still be exaggerated by those who make their living thinking and teaching about legal rules and legal doctrine. Indeed, although Llewellyn was insistent throughout his

---

[16]   Karl N. Llewellyn, *The Common Law Tradition – Deciding Appeals* (Boston: Little, Brown, 1960).

life that real legal rules diverged in important ways from the literal meaning of the "paper rules" that one could find in statute books and that are summarized in black letters in hornbooks and casebooks, he did subscribe to the view that the real rules were causally important in determining legal outcomes, and that various non-rule factors exercised a stabilizing and moderating influence on the operation and development of law.[47] But perhaps Llewellyn, whose admiration for the culture of real lawyers and real judges was considerable, and who respected the collective wisdom of the legal establishment (he called them "the lawmen"), overestimated, whether always or eventually, the determinacy of even law broadly conceived, and underestimated the role that ephemeral personal, psychological, political, and economic factors played in causing legal results. Perhaps, therefore, the less qualified utterances of the earlier Llewellyn, along with the even less qualified utterances of Jerome Frank, for example, and others, still have more to teach us then Twining's Llewellyn, or even anyone else's Llewellyn, or possibly even the later Llewellyn, may have imagined.

VI

That Twining's picture offers falsifiable hypotheses and strong but debatable conclusions is, of course, an unqualified virtue and not a vice. Even as originally written, this is a book that not only provides a wealth of historical detail and interstitial insight, but also stakes out a position about the meaning of Legal Realism and about the nature of Llewellyn's thought that no legal theorist or historian of American legal thought can afford to ignore. But now, with the addition to Twining's genuinely new and lengthy afterword that concludes this volume, the importance of the book is even greater. The afterword offers a series of personal insights into the conception and writing of the original book that will now become an important part of the historical record about Realism and about Llewellyn. But the afterword also situates Llewellyn and Realism within the modern jurisprudential terrain, a terrain just beginning to develop in the late 1960s and early 1970s. This is a terrain that tends, by and large, to ignore Llewellyn and to ignore Legal Realism, with most of its inhabitants remaining largely in the thrall of

[47] See especially, Llewellyn, *The Theory of Rules, op. cit.* note 10.

H. L. A. Hart's misreading of Llewellyn and misunderstanding of Legal Realism in *The Concept of Law*.[48] Moreover, it is a terrain, as Twining emphatically believes, that has achieved a degree of philosophical sophistication at the expense of the empirical Realism that was central to Llewellyn's thought, and, more important, at the expense of understanding the phenomenon of law as it exists in the world we know.

As with his interpretations of Llewellyn and Realism, Twining's concerns about the directions of modern legal theory, concerns that are very much in evidence in the afterword, will attract objections as well as agreement. But this too is to be applauded and not dismissed. In offering in the afterword new and important historical data along with crisp and challengeable claims about the nature of legal theory as it is practiced today, Twining has combined the historical with the jurisprudential in a way that is both faithful to the original book, and that makes the book and its new afterword required reading for all those who wish to understand Karl Llewellyn, Legal Realism, American legal thought, and the nature of law itself.

[48] In Chapter Seven of *The Concept of Law* (Oxford: Clarendon Press, 2d ed., Penelope A. Bulloch & Joseph Raz, eds., 1994), Hart not only ignores Llewellyn's qualifications of the early passages of *The Bramble Bush*, qualifications that Hart himself had acknowledged several years earlier in H. L. A. Hart, "Positivism and the Separation of Law and Morals," *Harvard Law Review*, vol. 71 (1958), pp. 593–629, at p. 615 note 40, and thus not only too easily brands Llewellyn as a "rule skeptic," but makes several more substantive blunders. He characterizes Realism as being concerned only with the external prediction of judicial decisions, although Llewellyn and others had long recognized the internal as well as external points of view. And he accuses the Realists of conflating the disputed edges of legal rules with all of law, although once again Llewellyn and others had explicitly insisted that their claims about legal indeterminacy were limited to litigated or appellate cases, and that litigated cases bear the same relationship to the underlying pool of disputes "as does homicidal mania or sleeping sickness, to our normal life." Karl N. Llewellyn, *The Bramble Bush: On Our Law and Its Study* (New York: Columbia Law School, 1930), p. 58. A valuable modern edition of *The Bramble Bush* is Karl N. Llewellyn, *The Bramble Bush: On Our Law and Its Study* (New York: Oxford University Press, Steven Sheppard, ed., 2009).

PREFACE

At first sight it may seem that few jurists can stake as strong a claim to singularity as Karl Llewellyn: the only American ever to have been awarded the Iron Cross; the most fertile and inventive legal scholar of his generation; legal theory's most colourful personality since Jeremy Bentham; the only common lawyer known to have collaborated successfully with an anthropologist on a major work; a rare example of a law-teacher poet; the chief architect of the most ambitious common law code of recent times; the most romantic of legal realists, the most down-to-earth of legal theorists; the most ardently evangelical of legal sceptics; the most unmethodical of methodologists; and least controvertible of claims, the possessor of one of the most exotic prose styles in all legal literature.

Yet for all his idiosyncrasies, Llewellyn was to an extraordinary degree representative of the best of his generation of American law teachers. This is partly a function of the breadth of his interests. In studying him we inevitably have to learn something of subjects as varied as commercial law, civil liberties, appellate judging, advocacy, legislative drafting, legal education, the sociology of the legal profession, the philosophy of pragmatism, semantics, functional anthropology, the *Sacco-Vanzetti Case*, empirical research into legal processes, law reform, and, of course, the American realist movement. However, Llewellyn mirrored his environment for reasons that lie deeper than the fact that he had a broad perspective and a variety of interests. He could only have been an American; he once summed up his viewpoint as being 'dominantly American, northern, urban, bourgeois, Protestant gentile, academic, liberal, "private" rather than "public" law, "office" rather than "litigation"—and, of course, contemporary'. This is a fair statement, but it says nothing of what was perhaps his most important characteristic. This was an extraordinary capacity for empathy, a Protean quality, which enabled him to project himself imaginatively into the position of other people and to assimilate and work with the atmosphere and values of his immediate milieu, whether it was the German army, the American bar, the world of commerce, or a New Mexican Pueblo. This quality is to be found both in his ability to see a wide variety of processes from the point of view of the participants, and in his sympathetic, but not uncritical, identification with the values of the common law, of the legal profession, of the American law school and of many other institutions and groups. Because of it he was sometimes criticized for being fickle or unprincipled and, perhaps with more justice, for being romantically conservative. Nevertheless it was essentially a source of strength, the basis for profound insights into a variety of institutions and processes and for the unexpectedly representative quality of his apparently bizarre writings. This is perhaps why, despite his disclaimers, he can be fairly treated as speaking not only for legal realism but also, in such works as the *Bramble Bush* and *The Common Law Tradition*, for some of the more fundamental values of the common law, and of the American law school during what may come to be viewed as its heyday.

Llewellyn's works comprise nearly 250 published items and a substantial number of unpublished manuscripts. Although there is much overlap and repetition in these writings, no single one gives a comprehensive picture of his thought. The work which most nearly approximates to this is a hitherto unpublished set of materials for a course on jurisprudence. He had planned to use these materials as the basis for a series of lectures in Germany in 1962–3, but he died before he was able to undertake the project. Even if he had lived to complete it, the available evidence suggests that it would probably not have adequately filled the need for a systematic exposition of his ideas. Indeed, the reader must not expect to find in the present work an account of a complete intellectual system, for Llewellyn did not have one. Although by mid-career he had developed a rough framework of ideas, approximating to a general theory, many of his most important contributions were more specific than general. In jurisprudence, too, the judgment of history may be that he was, for the most part, more representative than original.

My principal aim in writing this book has been to make Llewellyn's work more accessible by giving a relatively coherent interpretation of his thought and of its development, especially in the sphere of jurisprudence. In doing this I have tried to catch something of the flavour of his personality and of his environment, not only because these are interesting in themselves, but also because, I believe, jurists as well as law are best understood in context. A secondary aim has been to provide the basis for a reinterpretation of American legal realism. The subject is too large and too amorphous to be dealt with fully in a book about any single realist, but Llewellyn's formative period happened to coincide in time and place with a crucial phase in the history of realism. Some account of these matters would have been necessary in any case and I have taken the opportunity to re-tell the story of the rise of the realist movement from 1870 to 1931. If, as I believe, realism must be treated historically before it can be satisfactorily dealt with analytically, this account may help to pave the way for a more detailed history of an interesting phenomenon. The final chapter contains my personal evaluation of the contemporary significance of realism.

It has been said that Llewellyn was too volatile a subject to be capable of a definitive study. I accept this view. Although every effort has been made to give an accurate and balanced account of his thought, selection and an element of liberal interpretation have been inevitable. Llewellyn's writings are very extensive, variable in quality and often rather loosely expressed. If his work is to survive, the wheat needs to be resolutely winnowed from the chaff. I have not hesitated to express my own judgments, but, while not trying to gloss over his weaknesses, I have tried to act on his own working principle that in reading or discussing a jurist or any other type of thinker it is more rewarding to concentrate on his strengths than to dwell on his faults, and that it is usually more important to try to understand than to criticize.

Since this work cannot claim to be without bias, it may help to say a little about its perspective. As a former pupil of Llewellyn, very much in his intellectual debt, as the person who put his papers in order, and as a friend of the family I can claim the intimacy, and the prejudice, of an insider. As an Englishman observing the American scene, as a jurist who was first nurtured on the analytical work of Hart and Austin, and who has subsequently been attracted back to Bentham and Mill, and as a teacher who has spent most of his working life to date in Africa and Ireland, I have most of the disadvantages and few of the advantages of an outsider. As one who knows little commercial law and almost no German, I have been unable to do justice to these phases of Llewellyn's work. Finally, as one who is fascinated by jurisprudence, but frustrated by much of its literature, I am particularly concerned to try to break away from some of the worst aspects of its literary tradition and to try to bridge the gap between the complementary and unnecessarily polemical worlds of the English analytical and American sociological approaches. If this work can make a small contribution to this end, it will have served its purpose.

Belfast, 1971   W.L.T.

Postscript

Twenty years after the first publication of *The Bramble Bush*, Karl Llewellyn decided to abandon his attempts to make substantial revisions to the text because 'the young fellow who wrote those lectures just' isn't here any more' (below, p. 151). It is over twenty years since I began work on *Karl Llewellyn and the Realist Movement* and nearly fourteen since the manuscript was delivered to the publishers. I am naturally delighted that Weidenfeld and Nicolson has decided to re-issue it and that it will simultaneously be produced for the first time in the United States by the publishers of *The Cheyenne Way*. No doubt to the relief of both, I have decided to follow Llewellyn's example and refrain from revising the text. I have, however, taken the opportunity presented by an invitation to deliver the John Dewey Lecture at New York University Law School in October 1984 to take a fresh look at Legal Realism and to comment on some of the more interesting recent research and writing on the subject. The published version of this lecture will indicate some changes in perspective and emphasis, but I hope that it will serve to scotch suggestions of premature senility or radical changes of mind. It also makes it possible to keep this postscript quite brief.

In the period since 1970 there have been significant developments both in relevant specialized work and in the general intellectual climates of academic law in the United States and the United Kingdom. These include some publications that are directly relevant to matters dealt with in this book. Three items can be added to Llewellyn's bibliography: (i) *Recht, Rechtsleben und Gesselschaft* (ed. M. Rehbinder) was published in Berlin in 1977 by Duncker and Humblot. This was the German language manuscript on 'Law, the Life of the Law and Society', written in 1932 in connection with his visit to Leipzig (below, p. 107). It is interesting as a statement of Llewellyn's early sociological views and, in particular, of his debt to Weber and his differences with Ehrlich (see further G. Casper in 24 *U. Chi. L.S. Record* 27 (1978)). (ii) In 1981 I came across a hitherto unlisted publication by Llewellyn: 'Law in Society', in Horace Taylor (ed.), *Contemporary Problems in the United States* (1934-5 edn; Harcourt, Brace, New York), vol. 2, pp. 17-25. (iii) In 1981, Soia Mentschikoff and Irwin P. Stotzky published *The Theory and Craft of American Law* (Matthew Bender, New York), which is based on the materials for the course on 'Elements of Law' at Chicago (see below, p. 151, where I probably understated its significance. See further Gerwin and Shupack in 33 *J. Legal Education* 64 (1983).) Finally, two of Llewellyn's works have been published in paperback editions: *The Bramble Bush* (Oceana, 7th printing 1981) and *The Cheyenne Way* (Oklahoma U.P., 1983).

It would not be appropriate here to attempt to provide a comprehensive bibliography about Realism and the contributions of individual Realists published since 1971. It is, however, worth selecting a few works for brief comment. Outstanding is the as yet unfinished historical research of J.H. Schlegel on Realism and Empirical Social Science. This has already added significantly to our knowledge and understanding of the Yale Realists (see especially 28 *Buffalo L. Rev.* 459 (1979) and 29 *Buffalo L. Rev.* 195 (1980)). Robert S. Summers' fine book *Instrumentalism and American Legal Theory* (1982) is a bold attempt to reconstruct a distinctive American 'general theory about law and its use' from the writings of Holmes, Dewey, Pound and some Realists, including Llewellyn. I have reservations about aspects of Summers' enterprise, but our differences are greater than our disagreements. Reference should also be made to Alan Hunt, *The Sociological Movement in Law* (1978), G. Edward White, *The American Judicial Tradition* (1976), Bruce Ackerman, *Reconstructing American Law* (1984), and the useful series of articles by Simon Verdun-Jones in 7 *Sydney L. Rev.* 180 (1974) (Frank); 1 *Dalhousie L. Jo.* 441 (1974) (Llewellyn); 3 *id.* 470 (1976) (Arnold); 5 *id.* 3 (1979) (Cook, Oliphant, Yntema). See also the *festschrift* for Soia Mentschikoff Llewellyn in 37 *U. of Miami L. Rev.* (1984). One pleasing development has been the growth in the number of scholarly biographies and critical studies of American legal thinkers. At a more general level the burgeoning interest in both legal and intellectual history has greatly added to our understanding of the political, intellectual and institutional contexts in which Realism developed.

During the period that this book was being written, intellectual biography seemed to be considered an eccentric indulgence for an academic lawyer; jurisprudence in the United States was muted and in England, at least, Realism was thought to be discredited; both Marxism and Economic Analysis of Law had very few adherents among legal scholars in either country; such terms as critical legal studies, socio-legal, contextual, structuralism and phenomenology have all gained currency in the law-school world since then. The same period has seen major contributions to legal theory, broadly conceived, from Dworkin, Finnis, Fuller, Hart, MacCormick, Nozick, Rawls, Raz, Summers, Unger and many others; the history and theory of contracts has had a particularly rich period; legal history has blossomed and diversified; and there have been interesting developments in legal anthropology. There has also been the welcome revival of a contextual approach to the intellectual history of political thought by Skinner and others. This has strong affinities to the approach adopted in the present work.

The list could be extended almost indefinitely. The significance of these intellectual developments is that if work on this book had begun fifteen years later, it would have taken place in a substantially different intellectual climate. This would have inevitably affected one's concerns, perspectives and judgments of significance. Nevertheless, it is unlikely that it would have resulted in a major change of emphasis on the variety of Llewellyn's contributions, to say nothing of those of other Realists, or on the extent to which their concerns were directed to issues affecting the practice of legal education and scholarship far more than to more abstract questions of legal philosophy. Apart from a few minor corrections and additions, noted in the Dewey Lecture, I am prepared to stand by what I wrote. Indeed, my inclination is to be more emphatic about a number of themes: for example, the value of studying jurists and particular texts in context; the dangers of generalizing about Realism; and, above all, the perennial relevance of realist ideas to continuing attempts to develop coherent and systematic alternatives to approaches that treat the discipline of law as co-existensive with legal dogmatics. I remain committed to the view that the main, but not the only, respect in which the Realist enterprises are of continuing significance is as a brave, but only partially successful, attempt to broaden the study of law from within.

London, January 1985   W.L.T.

ACKNOWLEDGEMENTS

Work started on this book in 1963–4. It is impossible to mention all those who have contributed to it during the ensuing years through discussion, comment and advice. I hope that they will accept this general acknowledgement of my debts and that I shall be forgiven by anyone who is left out of the list that follows.

Among those to whom I am particularly indebted are Bruce Ackerman, Peter Fitzpatrick, Arthur Leff, Robert Stevens and Geoffrey Wilson, all of whom read through early versions of the manuscript and made many valuable comments. I have profited from suggestions from Gerhard Casper, Ulrich Drobnig, E. Adamson Hoebel, Clarence Morris, Claire Palley, Rudolph Schlesinger, Robert Summers and Adrian Taylor, to mention but a few. I have also learned much from interviews and discussions with many individuals and especially with students in Dar es Salaam, Yale, Belfast and the Universities of Chicago and Pennsylvania. I wish to thank Sandra Maxwell, Mary Egan and others who typed and re-typed various drafts; all those at Weidenfeld and Nicolson who helped with the production of the book; Gertrude Mittelman who compiled the index; and Alison Harris who helped with the proofs. I am grateful, too, to the Ford Foundation, the Rockefeller Foundation and the Queen's University of Belfast, for grants which enabled me to pursue my research and to the Law Libraries and the Library staff of the University of Chicago, Columbia University, Yale University and the Queen's University of Belfast for unstinting help on many occasions. Above all my thanks are due to two individuals: Soia Mentschikoff Llewellyn put at my disposal the Llewellyn Papers and her own unrivalled knowledge of her husband and his work; her support, encouragement and patience sustained me throughout the project, yet at all times she left me entirely free to exercise my own judgment. Finally, special thanks are due to my wife who acted as research assistant, editor and critic, and who, above all, by her patience and encouragement, helped to sustain my faith in the worthwhileness of the enterprise.

ABBREVIATIONS USED IN THE TEXT

AALS	Association of American Law Schools
ABA	American Bar Association
ACLU	American Civil Liberties Union
ALI	American Law Institute
KLP	The Karl Llewellyn Papers (see Bibliographical note)
NAACP	National Association for the Advancement of Colored People
NCC	National Conference of Commissioners on Uniform State Laws
NIL	Negotiable Instruments Law
NYLRC	New York Law Revision Commission
RUSA	See URSA
UCC	Uniform Commercial Code
URSA	Uniform Revised Sales Act

BIBLIOGRAPHICAL NOTE

References in the footnotes to KLP refer to the Collection of Karl Llewellyn Papers in the Law School of the University of Chicago. The method of citation follows the inventory in *The Karl Llewellyn Papers: A Guide to the Collection* by Raymond M. Ellinwood Jr. and William L. Twining (Revised edition, 1970, University of Chicago Law School Library Publications), to which reference should be made. This includes a list of the unpublished manuscripts by Llewellyn to be found in the Chicago Collection. A small number of other manuscripts (mainly teaching materials) are in the possession of the Law Library of Columbia University.

The select bibliography in the present book refers to Llewellyn's most important published and unpublished works. A full bibliography of his published writings is to be found in *The Karl Llewellyn Papers* by William Twining (University of Chicago Law School, 1968). That work also contains a description and evaluation of the Karl Llewellyn Collection in Chicago and a selection of hitherto unpublished manuscripts by Llewellyn.

PART ONE

The Rise of the Realist
Movement 1870-1931

Introduction

A common error in contemporary jurisprudence consists in treating all 'legal theories' as if they were rival attempts to answer the same question or set of questions. The most obvious form of this error is to assume that all such theories represent purported answers to the ambiguous question: 'What is law?' There can be few jurists of note who have not been subjected to criticism which either distorts or ignores what they were trying to do. This study starts from the premise that jurisprudence is not a one-question subject and that the realist movement is significant in large part because its members helped, both directly and by the responses they provoked, to shed light on some relatively neglected topics.

Despite a recent tendency towards more sympathetic treatment, a depressingly high proportion of the enormous secondary literature on American legal realism consists of superficial interpretation and unnecessary polemics. While a variety of factors, political, cultural and academic, has no doubt contributed to this state of affairs, the error of treating all legal theories as comparables is at once the most significant and the most easily avoided. It is an elementary axiom of intellectual history that the first step towards understanding a thinker is to identify the questions which worried or puzzled him. In the case of the variously defined aggregation of American jurists known as 'the realists' it is especially important to identify the main concerns of the early members of the movement and their forerunners. It is worth risking charges of over-simplification to begin by setting those concerns in a broad historical context.

Professor Max Rheinstein has suggested that three problems arising out of the American legal experience have dominated the consciousness of her jurists :[1] the problem of adapting the

common law to the circumstances of the New World; the problem of giving specific content to the broad formulas of the
constitution of 1787 and of adapting these formulas to meet
changing conditions; and, thirdly, the preservation of the unity
of the common law in a heterogeneous country with a multiplicity of jurisdictions. To this list might be added two related
problems: that of modernization of the law in the wake of the
industrial and technological revolution that swept the United
States in the period after 1870, and the problem of simplification of the sources of law, as the legal profession and the courts
became more and more swamped by the prodigious output of
legislation, regulations and reported cases. In turn, these attempts
to simplify helped to generate a reaction based on the view that
the preferred 'solutions' did not take adequate account of the
complexities of modern life.

In this interpretation, which itself reflects the perspective of
a law teacher in a leading American law school, adaptation of
law, and judicial adaptation in particular, constitute the
principal theme. The reception of the common law into the
United States involved the importation of doctrines and techniques developed in a small, homogeneous, relatively stable
aristocracy into a large, heterogeneous, fragmented, expanding
democracy.[2] The constitution of 1787 required interpretation
and reinterpretation to keep the political framework of the
Union strong, but flexible, in the face of new demands. The rapid
growth of urbanization and industrialization in the late nineteenth
century and after were seen as leading to a marked social lag—
a gap between modern needs and the capacity of established
institutions to meet them. In the case of law the problem of
adaptation was made additionally acute by certain important
inhibitions on radical legal change. Governmental power has been
both limited and widely diffused in the United States. The constitution, with its distribution of authority between the federal
government and the various states, and its system of checks and
balances, has proved to be remarkably tough and resilient. But
the diffusion of power, coupled with the dominance of special
interest groups in some state governments contributed to the result
that the various legislatures have, during some periods, been
relatively ineffectual as agencies of legal change, especially in
respect of private law, and the initiative has often passed else-

where. A large part of that initiative passed to the courts, especially in the period preceding the relatively late growth of administrative agencies. Much of the history of American public law is written in terms of the activities of the federal judiciary and especially of the Supreme Court; to a lesser but nonetheless considerable extent the state courts have a comparable place in the story of the adaptation and development of private law. Courts, in the United States as elsewhere, have been conceived first and foremost as institutions for the resolution of individual disputes. They were not designed as law-making agencies. Such a role was not easy to reconcile with the idea, enshrined in the constitution, of 'a government of laws and not of men', a phrase which suggests, *inter alia*, that judges should impartially apply pre-existing rules to the disputes before them. Moreover, because their proceedings are public, and because of the modern practice of publishing judgments of superior courts, their work is peculiarly accessible to close scrutiny. Judicial processes are among the most visible of decision-making processes.[8]

The relative importance of the courts, their visibility and the conflict between role and ideal made it almost inevitable that they should occupy a high proportion of the attention of American jurists in the twentieth century. In fact academic law in the United States has had an extraordinarily court-centred tradition, as is illustrated by the predominance of the case method in law teaching, the emphasis placed by legal historians on judicial development of the law, the enormous literature on the Supreme Court, and the concern with the nature of judicial processes in jurisprudence.

Adaptation to changed conditions has been only one of the perennial problems of law in United States history. The size of the country and its multiplicity of jurisdictions generated the further related needs of unification and simplification of law. The common law when exported abroad has proved to be sturdy, surviving to a remarkable extent translation to different climates, cultures and political systems. The preservation of a common consciousness and of a basic similarity in approach among common lawyers has been largely independent of the location of political power. The United States provides a striking example of the capacity of the common law tradition to outlive both decolonization and the subsequent diffusion of power through a federal structure.

The resilience of the common law made the problem of maintaining its unity in the United States rather less acute than the problem of adapting it to changed conditions. Despite the decentralization of political authority, especially in the sphere of private law, the common law in the various states was slow in showing distinct signs of growing apart. However, by the middle of the nineteenth century the need for something to be done about the preservation of the unity of American law began to be recognized. Since private law for the most part fell within the jurisdiction of the states, none of the major organs of the federal government—congress, the federal courts, nor the executive—was well placed to see law in the United States as a whole. The state legislatures and courts were even less well-equipped to do so. Accordingly the main burden of the task fell on non-governmental agencies, notably to the law schools and the bar.

The contribution of the leading law schools in this respect was important. Even from the early days of the Litchfield Law School,[4] many of them insisted on regarding themselves as national institutions concerned with the law of all the American jurisdictions, not just the local law, and they drew their students from all over the United States; by doing so they ensured that the leaders of the profession would have a national outlook and a shared heritage. The same perspective dominated the approach to research and writing of the leading legal scholars. Thus law schools did much to preserve and foster a high degree of uniformity in respect of education and research, thereby helping to maintain a single legal culture. But as institutions they were individualistic and so were the law teachers; schools and individuals duplicated each others' efforts, with relatively little sharing out of functions or coordination. The steady pressure of the overriding problem did stimulate various attempts to produce coordination at a national level. Institutions proliferated; some, like the National Conference of Commissioners on Uniform State Laws and the American Law Institute,[5] were especially created to deal with problems of unification and reform, some represented special interests, such as the American Bar Association and the Association of American Law Schools. Perhaps the biggest single contribution to maintaining uniformity of laws was made by the

leading treatise writers of the nineteenth and early twentieth centuries, several of whom were associated with Harvard: Story,
Williston, Beale, Gray and Thayer.[6] Their treatises, and associated
scholarly productions, helped not only to unify, but also to simplify
and systematize the common law in the United States. The prolifera-
tion of precedents and of other authoritative sources generated a
perennial need for simplification, which was made especially acute
by the very success of efforts to maintain a single legal culture.
For the state courts were prepared to pay almost as much
deference to precedents from other American jurisdictions—and
beyond—as they were to their own. The result was that from
the middle of the nineteenth century up to the present day
American lawyers and judges have had to cope with a body of
reported cases which is so vast and varied as simply to undermine
the basic rationale of a system of precedent. Thus the relative
ineffectiveness of the legislatures and the unmanageability of
the primary sources of law were among the factors which gave
American legal scholars the opportunity to play a much more
important part in their legal system than their counterparts in the
British Isles.

The American realist movement can be viewed as one phase
of the response of American jurists to the problems of unification,
systematization and modernization of American Law. Legal
realism was, in the first instance, a product of the concerns of a
number of teachers of law, nearly all of whom were based in a
few leading law schools on the eastern seaboard of the United
States. These concerns reflected the complex situation of American
academic lawyers: as teachers they were faced with the problems
of the aims, the methods and the quality of formal preparation for
the practice of law; as scholars they needed to ask: What should
be the functions and the scope of legal research? As intellectuals
of a kind they were affected by some powerful trends in contemporary American social and philosophical thought. As lawyers
they had a dual perspective in that they were called on to identify,
at least in part, with the practitioners working in the existing
legal structure, while at the same time they were particularly well
placed to see law in the United States as a single system, transcending the boundaries of the various state and federal jurisdictions.
As reformers, they were acutely conscious of a seeming lag between

legal and social change. To understand the realist movement it is important to see it in the context of these concerns.

In this perspective, the controversies between analytical and sociological jurists and between 'formalism' and 'functionalism' appear, at least in part, to reflect differences over the priorities to be given to the relatively 'static' needs of unification and systematization and the 'dynamic' need for continuous adaptation of legal institutions to changed conditions and values. In the United States the complexity of its legal system and the pace of change during the past hundred years have combined to accentuate the strain between these competing needs. The realist movement represents part of the radical vanguard who called for a 'dynamic' jurisprudence as a basis for bringing a greater sense of urgency to bear on the problems of adapting the legal system to the needs of the twentieth century.

While it is helpful to see the realist movement in the context of a broad interpretation of American legal history, this is only one aspect of the concerns of the early realists. Their general intellectual milieu is no less important. Apart from its relationship to the international literature of jurisprudence, realism can be seen as part of a general movement in American social thought which is sometimes characterized as 'the revolt against formalism'. In a useful study Morton White has pointed to the close affinities between certain leading figures in several disciplines at the turn of the century, notably John Dewey and the pragmatists in philosophy, Charles Beard and J. H. Robinson in history, Thorstein Veblen the economist and satirist, and Mr Justice Holmes in jurisprudence.[7] All of these men were innovators in their fields; all of them were eager 'to come to grips with life, experience, process, growth, context, function'.[8] All rejected the emphasis placed in their respective disciplines on deductive logic, abstraction and analogies from mathematics. Although they were instrumentalists, they tended to be anti-Benthamite, or at least to be ambivalent towards him, being particularly critical of the ahistorical approach of English utilitarians.[9] 'In their positive ideas they showed great respect for science, historical method, economic interpretation and cultural analysis.'[10] Of particular relevance to the student of realism was their insistence on the unity of truth and the logic of its discovery and a disrespect for artificial boundaries between disciplines. It is dangerous to generalize about the intellectual development of so independent-minded and diverse a group as the early realists, but it is fair to say that 'the revolt against formalism' was an important part of the general intellectual climate that fostered their approach.

The historic problems of the American legal system, the writings of men such as Dewey, Bentley, Veblen and Beard, and the whole vast heritage of European jurisprudence, especially that of England and Germany, are all an essential part of the background of American legal realism. However, especially in the early phases, the foreground is dominated to a large extent by some more immediate, specialized concerns of academic lawyers about how they should approach their tasks of teaching and scholarly research. One premise of this essay is that the rise of the realist movement is best understood by concentrating on a few individual law teachers, all of whom happened to be based on three eastern law schools, Harvard, Yale and Columbia. To some extent the ideas of these particular individuals reflected trends in other law schools and in the world outside; to some extent they were unique or idiosyncratic or path-breaking. Accordingly, the next three chapters will consist of a series of sketches, which taken together illustrate the main threads in the story of the rise of the realist movement from 1870 to 1931 and bring into focus the complex interplay of juristic, technical legal, philosophical and educational issues which lies at the root of realist thought.

I

Langdell's Harvard

The story of the development of the Harvard Law School after 1870, and of American legal education as a whole, is commonly presented as a straightforward example of charismatic leadership.[1] In that year Christopher Columbus Langdell was appointed professor and shortly afterwards was elected Dean of the Harvard Law School. He was responsible for a number of innovations, the best known being the case method of instruction. Langdell's approach was based on a coherent but simple theory of law teaching, which he applied with consistency and determination. This theory provided the basis for an educational orthodoxy which underlies much of modern American legal education. It is arguable that in the hundred years that followed Langdell's appointment there have been few radical changes in American legal education, despite numerous attempts at innovation and experiment. The fundamentals of the Langdellian orthodoxy survived to a remarkable degree periodic bouts of dissatisfied introspection on the part of law teachers, and it was only in the late 1960s that the combination of racial tension, student unrest, the war on poverty and the war in Vietnam threatened to rock the established order in some leading law schools.

Presented thus, the story does less than justice to the richness and complexity of developments in American legal education between 1870 and 1970[2] But it is useful as a device for dramatizing the conflict of ideas that underlies the realist controversy. In so far as legal realism was in the first instance a reaction against an approach to law that was characterized as 'formalism', Langdell can be treated as a leading representative of this approach. To some critics (notably Holmes and Frank) Langdell quite explicitly symbolized 'the enemy';[3] in their hands the symbol deteriorated into caricature, and this too is revealing, for it is a good example of a tendency to over-reaction on the part of some realists, which in turn made them vulnerable to charges of extremism.

The gist of Langdell's theory is to be found in two famous passages. In the preface to his casebook on contracts he stated:

Law, considered as a science, consists of certain principles or doctrines. To have such a mastery of these as to be able to apply them with constant facility and certainty to the ever-tangled skein of human affairs, is what constitutes a true lawyer; and hence to acquire that mastery should be the business of every earnest student of law. Each of these doctrines has arrived at its present state by slow degrees; in other words, it is a growth, extending in many cases through centuries. This growth is to be traced in the main through a series of cases; and much the shortest and best, if not the only way of mastering the doctrine effectually is by studying the cases in which it is embodied. But the cases which are useful and necessary for this purpose at the present day bear an exceedingly small proportion to all that have been reported. The vast majority are useless, and worse than useless, for any purpose of systematic study. Moreover the number of fundamental legal doctrines is much less than is commonly supposed; the many different guises in which the same doctrine is constantly making its appearance, and the great extent to which legal treatises are a repetition of each other, being the cause of much misapprehension. If these doctrines could be so classified and arranged that each should be found in its proper place, and nowhere else, they would cease to be formidable from their number.⁴

Fifteen years later, on the commemoration of the 250th anniversary of the founding of Harvard College, he explained the basis of his approach as follows:

[It] was indispensable to establish at least two things; first that law is a science; secondly, that all the available materials of that science are contained in printed books. If law be not a science, a university will best consult its own dignity in declining to teach it. If it be not a science, it is a species of handicraft, and may best be learned by serving an apprenticeship to one who practices it. If it be a science, it will scarcely be disputed that it is one of the greatest and most difficult of sciences, and that it needs all the light that the most enlightened seat of learning can throw upon it. Again, law can be learned and taught in a university by means of printed books. If, therefore, there are other and better means of teaching and learning law than printed books, or if printed books can only be used to the best advantage in connection with other means, – for instance, the work of a lawyer's office, or attendance upon the proceedings of courts of justice, – it must be confessed that such means cannot be provided by a university. But if printed books are the ultimate sources of all legal knowledge; if every student who would obtain any mastery of law as a science must resort to these ultimate sources; and if the /only assistance which it is possible for the learner to receive is such as can be afforded by teachers who have travelled the same road before him, – then a university, and a university alone, can furnish every possible facility for teaching and learning law. . . . We have also constantly inculcated the idea that the library is the proper workshop of professors and students alike; that it is to us all that the laboratories of the university are to the chemists and physicists, all that the museum of natural history is to the zoologists, all that the botanical garden is to the botanists.[5]

Langdell had no pretensions to being an original legal theorist. These statements are two rare examples of occasions on which he made explicit his more general assumptions. Allowance must be made for the point that the preface to a casebook and a commemorative address are not contexts which normally call for a carefully phrased statement of a theoretical position. However, these two statements, read together, are singularly revealing and several features of them call for comment. Firstly, Langdell placed great emphasis on law as a 'science', analogous to physical sciences such as chemistry and botany.[6] It will be seen later that 'the scientific analogy' also had a powerful grip on the minds of several leading realists, for example Cook and Moore; but the concept of 'science' did not have identical associations for these jurists, although their ideas had some common roots in nineteenth-century positivist thought. To Langdell 'science' conjured up the ideas of order, system, simplicity, taxonomy and original sources. The science of law involved the search for a system of general, logically consistent principles, built up from the study of particular instances. Like the scientist, the lawyer should study original sources; like the botanist, he must select, classify and arrange his specimens.[7] In the passages quoted, Langdell does not explicitly distinguish normative from descriptive propositions but confidently equates legal principles with scientific laws; he makes no mention of experimentation and empirical observation. He asserts, rather than argues, that reported cases are the only possible 'specimens' and that the law library is closely analogous to a chemist's laboratory or a botanist's garden. Each of these ideas was to be challenged in due course.

The next point to note is that Langdell's conception of law is court-centred. Only cases are explicitly mentioned as primary sources and they are to constitute the basic diet of law students. The courts are seen as the primary agencies of legal change, which itself is seen as a very slow evolutionary process. There is perhaps even a hint that the common law may be nearing the end of the process of historical growth, culminating in a final, logically complete system. However, this is not a necessary implication of Langdell's statement.

Finally, it is important to see the connection between Langdell's assumptions about law and his pedagogical ideas. The connecting link is the view that law is an autonomous science, quite distinct from other disciplines, and that legal education should be co-extensive with legal science. Law consists solely of principles or doctrines and, in law school at least, law students should study nothing but law.[8] Langdell was not necessarily a philistine and he did not deny the value to lawyers of a broad liberal education, but to provide this was not part of the function of a law school.

If Langdell's conception of law set rather narrow limits on the scope of legal education, his conception of 'science' provided the basis for a stimulating mode of instruction. In the light of experience it is easy to see that Langdell's version of 'the case method' was based on sound educational premises: it required the intensive study of primary sources; by treating cases in chronological sequence he gave both concreteness and historical perspective to the study of legal rules; the method required disciplined participation rather than passivity on the part of students; it was more sceptical and more lively than the dreary rote learning that it in large part replaced; and, in the hands of a good teacher, sustained by the competitive atmosphere of the American law school, it secured many of the values of small-group teaching in a remarkably economic fashion. Finally, the case method involved an important switch from emphasis on learning rules of law to emphasis on skill in 'legal analysis, legal reasoning, legal argument and legal synthesis'.[9]

Langdell also invoked the idea of 'science' to give academic respectability to a form of vocational training. 'If law be not a science, a university will best consult its own dignity in declining to teach it',[10] he could declare confidently in 1886, secure in the knowledge that his conception of legal science had been firmly established at Harvard. But was the study of 'legal science' consistent with the aim of preparation for legal practice? Langdell gave a glib answer. 'The true lawyer' is one who has such a mastery of legal principles as to be able to apply them with 'constant facility and certainty to the ever-tangled skein of human affairs'.[11] As a statement of the qualities and skills that go to make up a good lawyer this formulation is inadequate and misleading. At best it covers only one group of skills which are very important for some types of lawyer. It ignores other skills and qualities that might be developed by a rounded system of legal education and it assumes that there is only one type of 'true lawyer'; this assumption was not accurate in Langdell's day and over time it has probably become less and less tenable. In short, Langdell selected one lawyer-like quality and treated it as if it were the only one. This enabled him to beg one of the central questions facing contemporary legal education, namely, what other skills and qualities of lawyers can appropriately be developed in a university law school?[12] Furthermore, the distortion in Langdell's rationalization of what he was doing was subsequently reflected in a corresponding tendency to over-use the case method: one method of developing one type of skill became the predominant method of formal professional training.

The weaknesses of Langdell's theory should not be allowed to obscure his great contributions to legal education and legal scholarship. It was by no means solely because of the case method that Harvard Law School prospered under his leadership. During his time admission standards were raised, a rigorous system of examining was introduced, the foundations of a great library were laid, an outstanding faculty was recruited, and an atmosphere was generated which encouraged scholarly research and writing of a high order. In short, a great educational institution was created. In the sphere of legal research the contribution of Harvard was of particular significance. Between 1886 and 1920 Harvard scholars, notably Williston, Beale, Gray and Thayer, took the lead in writing a series of monumental legal treatises which won immediate recognition among practitioners as well as among legal scholars at home and abroad. These were truly scholarly works, more substantial than many students' textbooks and more systematic and more rigorously analytical than ordinary practitioners' reference works. The assumptions and attitudes underlying these treatises bore a close affinity to Langdell's conception of law. The approach adopted by their authors was well suited to the systematization and simplification of law in a relatively stable society. They conceived of their task as that of extracting principles from the morass of decided cases; on the surface this involved neutral analysis and exposition of the existing law, but the variety of their sources allowed for an element of choice and hence of quiet, interstitial creation. However, their work was later criticized as being static and conservative by jurists who were more concerned with the problems of adjustment to change. As Professor Max Rheinstein has said:

The American legal scholars became the preservers of the uniformity of law in the United States. They addressed themselves to this task in ways similar to those of the legal scholars of Europe during the centuries in which they had the task of preserving legal uniformity, namely through the formation of a system and elaboration of concepts. This enterprise of [men like] *Beale* and *Williston, Bogert* and *Wigmore* culminated in the Restatement of the American Law Institute. Of necessity, these people used the method of the jurisprudence of concepts as it had been brought to high perfection in stable 19th century Europe, on the continent as well as in England.

The method was unavoidable in order to achieve the systematization of the law, so urgently necessary in America. It did not stand up, however, to the dynamics of the 20th century, the least so in the country in which the legislatures have proved to be unable to adapt and develop the law, particularly the private law.[13]

Although even as late as the 1960s Harvard Law School was regarded by some as the headquarters of Langdellian orthodoxy, the situation is very much more complicated than that. Langdell was not as doctrinaire as his critics suggest, his ideas were not slavishly followed, and Harvard for the most part followed a flexible policy of recruiting to its faculty men of outstanding ability and giving them great freedom to pursue their own ideas according to their own lights. If an orthodoxy prevailed, it was never oppressive nor doctrinaire. Moreover, the first significant attack on Langdell's ideas was mounted from within.

In 1880 Oliver Wendell Holmes Jr took issue with Langdell. In a review of *A Selection of Cases on the Law of Contracts* he wrote:

Mr Langdell's ideal in the law, the end of all his striving, is the *elegantia juris* or *logical* integrity of the system as a system. He is, perhaps, the greatest living legal theologian. But as a theologian he is less concerned with his postulates than to show that the conclusions from them hang together.[14]

The Olympian figure of Holmes presides, like some brooding

omnipresence, over all discussions of American legal realism.
While it would be foolish to deny that he was its most important
forerunner, it is impossible to delineate his relationship to the
movement with precision. It is difficult in the history of ideas to
distinguish between affinity and influence and between symptom
and cause; in the case of Holmes there are other complicating
factors : he recognized that judges can and do make law, but he
was the leading protagonist of judicial restraint; he had no
systematic, integrated philosophy, his taste for paradox invited
conflicting interpretations of his ideas, and it is not always easy
to distinguish between those who were genuinely his intellectual
disciples and those who were mainly admirers of Holmes the
man, the genial patrician, the impish visionary and the courageous judge.[15] Moreover, in a juristic tradition that has been
dominated more by sages than by philosophers, Holmes was the
Supreme Sage. His Delphic aphorisms can be made to serve as
convenient catch-phrases which somehow make detailed criticism
of them appear pedantic. 'The life of the law has not been logic,
it has been experience',[16] intoned Holmes in 1881. 'What precisely
is meant by "experience" here?' asks the critic. 'Is it meaningful
to contrast "logic" and "experience"? Is it not absurd to suggest
that logic has nothing to contribute to legal thought?'[17] Such
criticisms have some force, but the aphorism survives largely
because of, rather than in spite of, its succinct and suggestive
ambiguity.

Succinctness and suggestiveness are the two outstanding
qualities of Holmes' famous paper 'The Path of the Law', which
contains in the space of a few pages an extraordinary number
of strikingly provocative statements about legal education and
law. Among these is a passage which has often been treated as
summarizing Holmes' 'Theory of Law' (whatever that may
mean):

Take the fundamental question, What constitutes the law? You will find
some text writers telling you that it is something different from what is
decided by the courts of Massachusetts or England, that it is a system of
reason, that it is a deduction from principles of ethics or admitted axioms
or what not, which may or may not coincide with the decisions. But if we
take the view of our friend the bad man we shall find that he does not care
two straws for the axioms or deductions, but that he does want to know what

the Massachusetts or English courts are likely to do in fact. I am much of his mind. The prophecies of what the courts will do in fact, and nothing more pretentious, are what I mean by the law.[18]

To understand this passage and its significance it is necessary to see it in the context not only of the 'Path of the Law' but also of the occasion on which it was delivered. In 1897 Holmes, who had been a member of the Supreme Judicial Court of Massachusetts since 1882, was invited to give an address at the dedication of a new hall at Boston University School of Law. Langdell had resigned from the deanship of Harvard two years before, but he was still teaching and his influence was not only dominant there, but had also spread rapidly to other law schools. It is quite clear that 'The Path of the Law' is directed at law students and their teachers, and that much of it is a not very indirect attack on some aspects of the new orthodoxy in legal education.

In fact Holmes spread his fire rather wide and not all the ideas that he criticized are attributable to Langdell: he warned against 'the pitfall of antiquarianism' in legal history ('for our purposes our only interest in the past is for the light it throws upon the present'),[19] he dismissed as unenlightened the practical minded who undervalued jurisprudence ('We have too little theory in the law rather than too much'),[20] he placed the study of Roman law 'high among the unrealities',[21] and he deplored the neglect of economics by lawyers ('For the rational study of the law the blackletter man may be the man of the present, but the man of the future is the man of statistics and the master of economics').[22] But Holmes' main shafts were directed against two fallacies: the tendency of students when learning law to fail to distinguish clearly between law and morality and 'the fallacy of the logical form', that is 'the notion that the only force at work in the development of the law is logic'.[23]

The device of the bad man is introduced initially to deal with the first fallacy: 'If you want to know the law and nothing else, you must look at it as a bad man, who cares only for the material consequences which such knowledge enables him to predict, not as a good one, who finds his reasons for conduct, whether inside the law or outside of it, in the vaguer sanctions of conscience.'[24] While it may be true that the 'bad man's' main interest in legal rules is as aids to predict what will happen to him rather than as guides to socially correct action,[25] the idea of prediction is unnecessary for the purpose of distinguishing between law as it is and law as it ought to be. As critics of 'the prediction theory' have pointed out, it is strange to say that advocates, judges, textbook writers or legislators are primarily concerned to *predict* judicial decisions;[26] yet from such standpoints too the distinction between law and morals is also relevant and useful.

But 'the bad man' is a neat device for dramatizing the point that there are other ways of looking at law than as a logically consistent body of rules. For the purposes of the intending practitioner there is a more realistic way of viewing the subject-matter of his studies and this is inevitably linked to the idea of prediction. In the opening paragraph of 'The Path of the Law' Holmes made clear the significance of this for legal education:

When we study law we are not studying a mystery but a well-known profession. We are studying what we shall want in order to appear before judges, or to advise people in such a way as to keep them out of court. The reason why it is a profession, why people will pay lawyers to argue for them or to advise them, is that in societies like ours the command of the public force is intrusted to the judges in certain cases, and the whole power of the state will be put forth, if necessary, to carry out their judgements and decrees. People want to know under what circumstances and how far they will run the risk of coming against what is so much stronger than themselves, and hence it becomes a business to find out when this danger is to be feared. The object of our study, then, is prediction, the prediction of the incidence of the public force through the instrumentality of the courts.[27]

This passage clearly indicates that Holmes treated his audience as intending private practitioners, who would spend much of their time as office lawyers giving advice. In advocating that they should adopt the standpoint of the 'bad man', he was presumably not intending to suggest that they should be unethical or amoral, but rather that they should be clear thinking, hard-headed and realistic and that as law students they should look at law in the same way as they would look at it in practice. This Langdell and his colleagues were patently failing to do and Holmes was expressing in a memorable way the standard criticism of the practitioner against academic law. But Holmes was careful to dissociate himself from the anti-intellectualism and narrow-mindedness of some men of affairs. Indeed he ended on a note that was visionary and idealistic:

An intellect great enough to win the prize needs other food besides success. The remoter and more general aspects of law are those which give it universal interest. It is through them that you not only become a great master in your calling, but connect your subject with the universe and catch an echo of the infinite, a glimpse of its unfathomable process, a hint of the universal law.[28]

Holmes and those who followed him in talking of law in terms of predictions of judicial decisions have been much criticized, mainly on the ground that they confused the concepts of 'prediction' and 'legal rule'.[29] When Holmes' definition, if such it was, is taken as the basis for a purportedly rounded theory of law which could accommodate a variety of standpoints, including particularly those of the judge, the legislator, the expositor of legal doctrine and the 'good' citizen who looks to legal rules as guides to conduct, then it is indeed vulnerable to such criticism. However, the critics have tended to overlook the fact that the context of the 'bad man' statements was a discussion of legal education and that Holmes is much more illuminatingly treated as putting forward an alternative philosophy of legal education to that which was prevailing at the time than as expounding a complete philosophy of law.[30]

Holmes's views on legal education are scattered throughout his many speeches, essays and letters.[31] It was obviously a matter about which he cared deeply, but he was sceptical of the value of sustained analysis of educational problems. A result was that he did not spell out in detail the implications of an approach to legal education which takes the standpoint of 'the bad man'. He did not point out, perhaps he did not realize, that its implementation would almost inevitably involve redefinition of the subject matter of study, a re-classification of its component parts, the introduction of hitherto little used or unused source materials, and the development of a new genre of legal literature, which would need, in many instances, to be preceded by extensive research. The failure on the part of Holmes and his contemporaries to realize the full implications of the kind of perspective he was advocating in 'The Path of the Law', together with the enormous practical difficulties of implementing an approach related to that perspective, must be counted among the most important reasons for the survival of the Langdellian system for many years.

One of Langdell's contemporaries, John Chipman Gray (1839–1915), is sometimes treated as the first American legal realist.[32] Gray was one of the great Harvard figures of the period. For many years the only member of the Harvard faculty to continue in legal practice while engaged in 'full-time' teaching, Gray was considered by both practitioners and scholars to be the leading property lawyer of his time. A down-to-earth, undoctrinaire individualist, a master of the magisterial lecture, and more obviously a man of affairs than most of his colleagues, Gray went his own way at Harvard and was only converted very late to 'the case system'. At a time when members of the bar were inclined to be very critical of Langdell's innovations, Gray did much to allay their suspicions, but he was never a wholehearted devotee of the case method himself.[33] Indeed he shared Holmes' distrust of Langdell's approach to law, the distrust of the practitioner for the over-logical theorist. He appears to have normally been circumspect in expressing his opinion of Langdell, but in a letter to the president of Harvard he left no doubt about his attitude:

In law the opinions of judges and lawyers as to what the law is, *are* the law, and it is in any true sense of the word as unscientific to turn from them, as Mr Langdell does, with contempt because they are 'low and unscientific', as for a scientific man to decline to take cognizance of oxygen or gravitation because it was low or unscientific. . . . Langdell's intellectual arrogance and contempt is astounding. One may forgive it in him or Ames, but in an ordinary man it would be detestable. The idols of the cave which a school bred lawyer is sure to substitute for the facts *may be much better material for intellectual gymnastics than the facts themselves and may call forth more enthusiasm in the pupils,* but a school where the majority of the professors shuns and despises the contact with actual facts, has got the seeds of ruin in it and will and ought to go to the devil.[34]

Although deeply suspicious of 'school men', Gray conformed to scholarly conventions. His most important work of scholarship, his famous *The Rule Against Perpetuities,*[35] belongs to the same genre as the treatise of Williston, Beale and Thayer. Nor do his influential six volumes of *Select Cases and Other Authorities in the Law of Property*[36] suggest a marked unorthodoxy in his ideas on legal research. His reputation as a heterodox jurist rests almost entirely on his last book, *The Nature and Sources of Law*.[37] Except as an example of his felicitous style of writing, this is not typical of his work as a legal scholar. Published in his seventieth year, it was the only substantial incursion into jurisprudence by one who was generally regarded as a down-to-earth property lawyer. Indeed, his close friend Holmes later commented to Laski: '[A]nd intimately as I knew Gray I didn't suspect him [of being a philosopher] until his book came out.'[38]

The extent of the unorthodoxy of *The Nature and Sources of Law* has sometimes been exaggerated. The one really striking idea, which has attracted much critical attention, is Gray's assertion that nothing is law until it has been declared to be so by the courts.[39] Gray drew a sharp distinction between law and sources of law and advanced the strange theory that a statute is not 'law' but is only a source of law.

In attempting to refute 'the declaratory theory' of judging (which he attributed to J. C. Carter) and to explain 'gaps' in the law, Gray was led to place great emphasis on the fact that the final authority for resolving doubtful points of law is vested in the courts and not in the legislature. He summarized his theory about the nature of law in the form of a definition:

The Law of the State or of any organized body of men is composed of the rules which the courts, that is, the judicial organs of that body, lay down for the determination of legal rights and duties.[40]

This provocative statement has already been accorded more critical attention than it deserves, for neither is it based on particularly acute analysis nor does it appear to have been widely adopted, except as a convenient Aunt Sally.[41] Indeed, it is difficult to understand in what sense this is thought to be 'realistic'.[42]

The Nature and Sources of Law for the most part reflects the conventional wisdom of the time and there is little in the book that is either original or profound. Its chief virtues are its lucidity and its homely common sense which help to make it unusually readable for a treatise on legal philosophy. Philosophically it is rather naive, the work of a learned man of affairs who wandered belatedly into the realms of abstract analysis. Its main claim to originality lies in the great, indeed the excessive, significance attached to the finality of judicial decisions. As so often happens in jurisprudence, the weakest part of the work has been the main

reason for its continued prominence. In fact Gray's ideas presented
no serious threat to the Langdellian orthodoxy. In his emphasis on
judicial law-making, and in his rather simplistic manner of testing
juristic theories to see if they 'fit the facts', Gray could be said
to have taken a step away from Austin and Langdell in the direction of realism. But in his teaching he was, if anything, pre-
Langdellian, he was an oustanding but essentially orthodox legal
scholar and as a theorist he went less far than Holmes in questioning the basic assumptions of his colleagues or in suggesting the
basis for a more empirically oriented approach to law.

Less easy to explain is the relationship of Roscoe Pound to
Langdellism and to the realist movement. As the leading prophet
of sociological jurisprudence Pound might be expected to have
been an open critic of the former and a member, or at least an
ally, of the latter. Instead, as Dean of the Harvard Law School
for twenty years, he presided with little apparent discomfort over
what many considered to be the main stronghold of Langdellian
orthodoxy, and he was one of the foremost critics of realism.

The names of Holmes and Pound are often linked. Both were
Harvard men, both were pioneers of sociological jurisprudence
in the United States, and between them they dominated American
jurisprudence for many years. They had contrasting styles:
Holmes was a patrician sage, given to aphorisms; Pound was a
savant with little of Holmes' cutting edge but unrivalled in the
breadth of his reading and in his capacity for synthesizing the
ideas of others. Some measure of Pound's achievement is indicated
by the extent to which the names of some of his better known
papers have become catch-phrases: 'The Limits of Effective
Legal Action',[43] 'Mechanical Jurisprudence',[44] 'Survey of Social
Interests',[45] 'Law in Books and Law in Action',[46] and 'The Need
for a Sociological Jurisprudence'.[47] Where Pound did not originally coin these phrases, he was largely responsible for giving them
wide currency.

Pound saw more clearly than anyone, and earlier than most,
the relevance to law of 'the revolt against formalism'. In a
famous passage, published in 1909, he wrote:

Jurisprudence is the last in the march of the sciences away from the method
of deduction from predetermined conceptions. The sociological movement
in jurisprudence, the movement for pragmatism as a philosophy of law,

the movement for the adjustment of principles and doctrines to the human conditions they are to govern rather than to assumed first principles, the movement for putting the human factor in the central place and relegating logic to its true position as an instrument, has scarcely shown itself as yet in America.[48]

This and many other similar passages could be interpreted as prophecies of the advent of realism. And, as Llewellyn later acknowledged, 'half of the commonplace equipment' of the new jurisprudence of the 1920s and 1930s had been provided by Pound:[49] the theory of interests, the idea of law as a form of social engineering, the emphasis on interdisciplinary cooperation and on the need for factual data about the law in action, concern with the nature of judicial discretion, were among the themes that were given an airing by Pound before the realist movement got under way at Yale and Columbia.

Yet somehow he seemed unable to avoid reducing such ideas to the status of bland generalities to which 'legal monks'[50] could render lip-service and continue to behave as before.[51] And Pound proved on many occasions to be remarkably unperceptive about the practical implications of his general ideas. At Harvard during his Deanship, despite continuous self-appraisal on the part of the faculty,[52] there were remarkably few changes in the style and content of the undergraduate curriculum, and the kind of innovations that might have been expected of a sociologically oriented Dean were for the most part relegated to the status of fringe activities.

Two incidents, in themselves relatively minor, illustrate the failure of America's leading jurist to realize the promise of his own teachings. In 1915 he deliberately restricted his own course on jurisprudence to postgraduates, the implication being that this subject was at best an optional extra, which might confuse, distract, or—it has been suggested—contaminate the ordinary run of intending practitioners.[53] In 1923-4 Pound was actively involved in the American Law Institute's plans for the *Restatement of Law*. In connection with this he was asked to prepare a paper on classification of law.[54] Classification was a special interest of Pound's—his first scholarly work had involved an elaborate taxonomy of Nebraskan plants[55]—and the occasion provided an excellent opportunity for him to question the prevailing mode of dividing law into a number of overlapping, ill-defined 'fields' such as contract, tort, equity, conflicts of law, and to suggest a scheme of classification which more adequately reflected sociological and economic categories. Pound's paper might well have been written by someone who had never heard of 'sociological jurisprudence'. He did little more than to provide a potted history of various theories of classification, only to reject most of them in favour of acceptance of the traditional categories of the common law: 'Our law has grown up around certain conceptions which have been developed by analogy such as Contract, Tort, Trust. We ought to use these categories as far as we can.'[56] This comforting advice was accepted by the American Law Institute.

A considerable proportion of the work of members of the realist movement can be viewed as a series of attempts to concretize sociological jurisprudence, by seeking to apply it in practice in a variety of spheres. From this point of view Pound should have been the high priest of the realist movement rather than one of its fiercest critics. It will be seen later that Pound's attacks on realism were based largely on misunderstanding and that his antipathy did not seem to be rooted in any profound intellectual disagreements.[57] Similarly, the main complaint of realists who criticized Pound, such as Llewellyn and Oliphant, was not that his ideas were wrong, but that their detailed implications had not been worked through thoroughly and in sufficient detail for sociological jurisprudence to be more than a set of vague aspirations.[58] Pound's theories were not in such a form that they could be *used* in reforming the law or legal education or legal research or by judges or practitioners in their daily work. To them Pound's weakness was that too often he was prepared to allow jurisprudence to be treated as a subject apart.

The association with Harvard of men like Holmes, Gray and Pound no doubt ensured that there was no simple victory there for a cloistered, over-logical approach to law. The scepticism of Holmes was a powerful antidote to crude dogmatism, men like Gray ensured a healthy tension between the system-builder and the practitioner, and Pound managed at least to give an aura of respectability to talk of 'sociological jurisprudence'. At a later stage the presence of a Felix Frankfurter or a T. R. Powell indicated that this was no mere temple of slumbering orthodoxy. But in the teaching and research activities of the school the spirit of Langdell more than the spirit of Holmes was in the ascendant, and, in other leading law schools, Harvard was seen more and more as the headquarters of 'legal theology'. A fairly typical picture of the law school by one who later reacted against it was painted by Thurman Arnold in his autobiography:

In the fall of 1911 I entered Harvard Law School. It was a new and exciting experience. Enough of my Western manners had rubbed off so that I was no longer lonely. The professors at Harvard, compared with the Princeton faculty, seemed intellectual giants. The narrow logic of the law, the building of legal principle on the solid basis of a long line of precedents, and the analysis of cases in class by the Socratic method were fascinating. It was also fun to have to work hard, which one never did at Princeton. But the world of the Harvard Law School was as much a world of eternal verities and absolute certainties as it had been at Princeton. The study of human society was divided into fields in which scholars could work without having to acquaint themselves with what people were doing in other fields. The principal fields were law and economics. Then there was another field called the social sciences, though real scholars were dubious about whether this field was truly a science. It was felt that only superficial scholars would be content to work in the field of sociology. The study of psychology was something no sound scholar would care to be caught dabbling in. The idea that thinking was a form of human behavior lay far beyond the horizon. The writings of Freud were completely unknown to properly educated men.

The field of law in turn was carved up into many separate fields: contracts, agency, corporations, real property, personal property, and so on. The workers in these separate fields had little to do with the workers in other fields. They were joined together at the top by the brooding omnipresence in the sky called the science of jurisprudence. Through the wise application of this science, the accidental inconsistencies of the minor fields were ironed out and the law was made into a seamless web.

Professor Thomas Reed Powell, one of the few rebels on the Harvard faculty twenty-five years later, said: 'If you can think of a subject which is interrelated and inextricably combined with another subject, without knowing anything about or giving any consideration to the second subject, then you have a legal mind.'[59]

This, it may be claimed, is a caricature. But it is fairly typical of the picture of Harvard that was prevalent among those who were seeking to develop an alternative approach at Yale and Columbia in the next two decades. Whether or not the picture was entirely fair is beside the point. In so far as the leaders of the realist movement were in revolt against prevailing attitudes to legal education and legal research, this kind of caricature of Langdell's Harvard provided the principal target.

2

Corbin's Yale, 1897-1918

In the present interpretation six individuals will be singled out as having made key contributions to the rise of the realist movement between 1914 and 1931: Corbin, Hohfeld, Cook, Underhill Moore, Llewellyn and Oliphant. All but the last of these had close connections with Yale Law School during this period. In 1931 Llewellyn and Frank compiled a list of twenty realists,[1] sixteen of whom had at some time been associated with either Yale or Columbia Law Schools, in several cases with both. Scrutiny of the names of notable omissions from this list suggests no bias in favour of the two law schools on the part of the compilers, but rather the reverse. The fact is that, at least up to 1928, the realist movement, in so far as it was a discrete phenomenon, was based on two law schools. It was in some respects analogous to the Bloomsbury Group, in that there was no defined 'membership', no shared dogma, and no concerted programme of action. Rather, the 'movement' consisted of a loosely integrated collection of interacting individuals, with a complex network of personal relationships and an almost equally complex family of related ideas, given some coherence, perhaps, by a shared dissatisfaction, not always precisely diagnosed, with the existing intellectual milieu of law in general and legal education in particular. It is immaterial, from this point of view, that some of the ideas of 'the realists' at Yale and Columbia were shared by people in other institutions, even in the formative period, just as it would not be particularly important, nor surprising, to find that there were contemporaries who had affinities with Maynard Keynes or Virginia Woolf, yet who were not members of the Bloomsbury Group. Of course, the realist movement, like the Bloomsbury Group, must also be put in a wider context. Some of this has already been sketched, but there are aspects that will require further elaboration. The point stressed here is that the *immediate* causes of the rise of the realist movement are to be found in a somewhat narrow and parochial context, although the movement both reflected much broader trends and had implications beyond the world of the American law school.

The rise to eminence of the Yale Law School is closely linked with the first phase of the realist movement. Up to 1918 the lead was taken by three individuals: Corbin, Hohfeld and Cook. In 1919 an editorial of the *Yale Law Journal* pinpointed two lines of thinking which had gained ascendancy in the law school during the preceding years:

The first of these is that the rules of human action that we know as law are constantly changing, that no system of human justice is eternal, that law forms but a part of our ever-changing social *mores*, and that it is the function of lawyers, of jurists and of law schools to cause the statement and the application of our legal rules to be in harmony with the *mores* of the present instead of those of an outgrown past. The second matter upon which emphasis has been placed, and the one perhaps which has been most obvious in recent pages of the *Journal* has been the necessity of a more exact terminology leading to a more accurate legal analysis.[2]

The chief proponents of these ideas were Corbin and Hohfeld respectively. Arthur Linton Corbin was born in 1874 and brought up on the prairies of Kansas.[3] Religious scepticism, the pioneer spirit and a grandfather who 'laughed at orthodoxies' set the tone of his early upbringing. His father was a farmer who had taken an active part in making Kansas a 'free state'; his mother was a school teacher for many years. As an undergraduate at the University of Kansas, where he studied biology, anatomy and chemistry, Corbin was deeply impressed by the theory of evolution. From Kansas he went to the Yale Law School in 1897. At the time the law school was an undistinguished institution with an unimpressive body of students. Nearly all of the instruction was given by lawyers and judges for whom teaching was only a side-line. They included some men of outstanding ability, but this merely serves to confirm the general experience that part-time teachers, however distinguished, rarely on their own make a distinguished law school.

The faculty was committed as a matter of firm policy to a uniform method of instruction, known as the 'Yale system'.[4] This represented a deliberate entrenchment of traditional methods of law teaching in resistance to the challenge of Langdell's case method, which had been introduced at Harvard in 1870–1 and which had soon spread to a number of other law schools. 'We were told', says Corbin, 'that the Case System at Harvard turned out only "case lawyers", who could not argue from "principle", but had to depend on finding a case "on all fours".'[5] The 'Yale system' consisted essentially of lectures, recitations, and the intensive study of set textbooks, such as Robinson's *Elementary Law* (a condensation of Blackstone), Jones on *Mortgages* and Cooley on *Torts*. The object was to teach '*the* principles of *the law*' and the few cases that were studied were almost exclusively used merely as examples. 'Recitations', as the name suggests, involved the examination of students by the teacher on their knowledge of the texts and cases, the standard question being framed to admit solely of a correct or an incorrect answer. Some allowance was made for classroom discussion but, as Corbin says, 'the greatest weakness in the Law School was that we were given no experience in the analysis of complex fact problems, in the comparison of decisions, or in the formation or criticism of supposed rules'.[6] This weakness was the direct result of an explicit and cherished theory as to the best way of preparing men for legal practice— a theory held by men who were themselves first and foremost practitioners and whose ability is not in question.

Corbin graduated with high honours in 1899 and went into practice at Cripple Creek, Colorado. As a student he had not felt particularly critical of the methods or the content of the teaching he had received, but he soon found that what he had been taught seemed to bear little relation to what was expected of him in practice. 'Because my law teachers gave me nothing but canned doctrine, I had to decide problems by the gut method almost exclusively, and the pleadings I drew in four years of practice were a scandal and a crime.'[7]

In 1903 Corbin was invited to join the Yale law faculty. He accepted and took charge of the first year course on contracts. As soon as he started he realized that he was inadequately equipped for the task: his years in practice had no better prepared him for teaching than his time as a law student had prepared him for practice. Now that he was embarking on a career as a teacher and a scholar his central concern was to work out a method of teaching and of exposition of legal doctrine which overcame the inadequacies of the Yale system. He found nothing in the ideas or methods of his colleagues to help him to resolve his puzzlement and so he started to try to solve the problem for himself.

It is important to grasp the nature of Corbin's concern at this time. He had only heard vaguely of Langdell and he knew nothing of Austin, so he could hardly be said to be reacting against either.[8] Critics of realism are wide of the mark when they assume that it represents a reaction against Austinian jurisprudence. Few, if any, of the realists were much concerned with the same questions that dominated the attention of Austin and his successors. Corbin provides a particularly clear example. There is practically nothing in his early writings which can be interpreted as direct criticism of Austin or Markby or Holland or Salmond. Indeed, at the end of his life he claimed that he had never read Austin and even that 'in my early teaching years I knew *nothing* of Roscoe Pound except that he talked of "sociological jurisprudence" '.[9] He showed no great interest in questions relating to the definition of 'law', the nature of sovereignty, the province of jurisprudence, the relation between law and morals, and so on. In respect of analysis and refinement of legal concepts, far from reacting against the Austinian tradition, Corbin, following Hohfeld, worked vigorously within it. But his chief preoccupation was at quite a different level : he was worried by the teaching methods and barely articulated assumptions of his teachers and early colleagues; with the almost schizophrenic way in which practising lawyers could talk about 'the law' in one way and set about handling actual problems in a manner which seemed to be largely unconnected with their talk; with the difference between the orthodox view of the judge's role, as held by nearly all lawyers and judges and the general public, and the actual function that judges seemed to him to be performing; and, to a lesser extent, with the occasional failure of judges' opinions to explain or justify their actual decisions. In other words, he was primarily concerned about a gap between 'theory' and 'practice'. But the 'theory' involved was not the articulate and comparatively sophisticated jurisprudence of Austin and Holland, but the primitive and barely articulated assumptions of judges, practitioners and laymen. The impetus to develop his own theory did not come from a detached philosophical puzzlement about certain abstract questions concerning the nature of law; it came instead from a concern to develop a method in teaching and in writing which would minimize the dichotomy of which he was so acutely aware.

Thus, like Langdell, Corbin was first stimulated largely by pedagogical problems to develop a theory of law and of legal education. Never satisfied with the conclusions of others, he began to work out his own approach by trial and error in the classroom, and gradually he evolved a theory to support it. Corbin's educational approach was similar to Langdell's in many respects (except that Corbin made a more extensive use of problems), but their ideas on law were significantly different. The fullest statements of Corbin's theoretical position are to be found in two papers that were separated by almost exactly fifty years. In 1913 an essay entitled 'The Law and the Judges' was published in the *Yale Review*, a 'lay' journal.[10] In 1964, in his 'final legal writing', entitled 'Sixty-Eight Years at Law', he restated his 'major conclusions as to legal education and the nature and growth of law'.[11] The ideas and orientation of the two papers are essentially the same and there is no evidence of a radical shift in Corbin's views during the intervening period. This is not surprising, for Corbin is a striking example of someone who fashioned for himself a basic working theory at an early stage and thereafter devoted himself single-mindedly to detailed work in a field of substantive law. Corbin will be remembered as one of the greatest of contract scholars and much of his greatness lies in the consistency, patience and rigour with which he approached his chosen field of specialization.[12]

'The Law and the Judges' is a curiously eloquent and compact paper. There are echoes of Holmes, Gray and Sumner; there are also traces of the theory of evolution. However, the paper as a whole is a forthright statement of Corbin's own views. The main topic is 'the exact part played by the judge in our social system'. There had recently been a good deal of public controversy about the position of judges. In particular it has been suggested that judicial decisions should be subject to recall by the voters. Corbin, in opposing this suggestion, directs his argument to two main conclusions: first that judges have a discretion to make law in individual cases and should accordingly be both open to criticism and ultimately accountable for their decisions; secondly, that the wise exercise of judicial discretion involves acting in accordance with the *sittlichkeit* of the time, a term which Corbin seemingly equated with the prevailing sense of justice and the mores of a community.[13] The paper ends with a statement which bears a striking resemblance to a controversial passage in Llewellyn's *The Common Law Tradition*, which was published more than forty years later:

That judge is just and wise who draws from the weltering mass the principle actually immanent therein and declares it as the law. This has always been the judicial function in all countries, and for its performance the judge must bear the responsibility.[14]

Like Holmes' 'Path of the Law', Corbin's paper is pregnant with both suggestive and controversial statements.[15] For present purposes, however, three themes are of particular relevance. The first is the great emphasis placed by Corbin on the continuous process of change:

For the growth of the law is an evolutionary process. Its principles consist of such generalizations as may tentatively be made from a vast number of individual instances. The instances change as man and society change, with the climate, with the growth of population, with the progress of invention, with social selection. And as the instances change, so must our generalizations change. So must our idea of justice change.[16]

The second theme, implicit in the last passage, is that all propositions of law must be viewed as 'tentative working rules' arrived at inductively by the examination of the facts and results of all the relevant cases. As each decision is handed down the old formulation of a rule must be re-examined to see if it fits the facts and results of the new case. If it does not, then the relevant cases must be re-examined and a new 'tentative working rule' must be formulated. Fifty years later, in a revealing passage, Corbin articulated the basis for this approach. After stating that as a student he had found reading 'Hornbooks' (students' text-books) 'a total waste of time', he continued:

I have never been able to memorize, and parrot-like to repeat, the 'rules' and doctrines and generalizations of men, often (if not always) based on quite insufficient life experience and inaccurate observation, but solemnly repeated down the corridors of time. Templin had put me through a book entitled *Inductive Logic* by that clearest minded of men, John Stuart Mill. It was only after beginning the teaching of 'law' that I fully realized that the meaning and value of any 'rule' or generalization are wholly dependent on the specific items of life experience and observation on which they are based.[17]

It is important to note here that Corbin's sceptical approach to legal rules formulated by others did not involve commitment to the idea that rules are a 'myth' or are unimportant: ' "Pared-down principles" there must of course be—"the law"; but it seldom struck me that the ones I found in print were *the ones*.'[18]

A great deal of unnecessary controversy could have been avoided if critics of 'realism' had grasped the distinction between scepticism about textbook formulations of legal rules and scepticism about the very existence of any rules or principles. The term 'rule-scepticism', coined by Frank, and indiscriminately applied by critics to Llewellyn and other realists, obscures this important distinction.[19]

A third theme in Corbin's paper, reiterated in his later writings on contract, and subsequently taken up and elaborated by Karl Llewellyn, is the idea that it is as important to study the facts of cases as to study legal doctrines.[20] Judicial decisions, Corbin suggested, are influenced by the manner in which the facts are perceived as much as by legal authorities; the good lawyer must be able to interpret the facts of his case in terms of the conditions and values of contemporary society; in this he can learn more from the law reports, as 'a mighty storehouse of facts', than from a lifetime of experience;[21] even in arguing a point of law a good lawyer studies the 'facts' of a case with great care. Corbin used Chancellor Kent as an example of a great judge who adopted this approach:

He further says that in deciding cases his practice was first to make himself perfectly and accurately master of the facts. Then he says: 'I was master of the cause and ready to decide it. I saw where justice lay and the moral sense decided the cause half the time, and I then sat down to search the authorities until I had exhausted my books, and I might once and a while be embarrassed by a technical rule, but I most always found principles suited to my views of the case.[22]

Corbin's 'Law and the Judges' is of historical interest as one of the earliest realist writings. To the modern reader it will seem, in some respects at least, dogmatic and unsophisticated and on a number of points it is clearly vulnerable to some of the criticisms that were later levelled indiscriminately at realism in general. The fact that it was addressed to a lay audience provides only a partial justification for its main defect, that of oversimplification. On certain points Corbin takes an extreme position by any standards, but people today would not be shocked, as was Professor Simeon

Baldwin, by assertions that judges make law or that the decisions of judges should be freely and publicly criticized in the same manner as those of other responsible decision-makers.[23] But in 1913 such ideas were considered heretical; the paper met with a frigid reception from Corbin's colleagues and from practising members of the legal profession, one outraged reader going so far as to suggest that he should be dismissed from Yale because of it.[24]

Corbin's theory of law, as set out in 'The Law and the Judges', reveals some sharp divergences from that of Langdell. But there were also important similarities. Both men were attracted by 'the scientific analogy', but Langdell's 'theological' conception of science contrasts sharply with Corbin's scepticism of unproven generalizations and his Social Darwinism. Their conceptions of 'induction' were also different. Both men saw the growth of law as an evolutionary process, but Corbin placed much greater emphasis on change as a continuing and vital process which needs to be always in the forefront of lawyers' minds. Both men were specialists in contract and they shared a perspective on law, that made courts the central focus of attention. Corbin was essentially a case-law scholar. He loved the law reports and he devoted the greater part of his energies to reading and analyzing them. He neither undertook nor exhibited much interest in empirical research. In this respect he was not very different from other scholars, like Langdell, who relied almost exclusively on appellate decisions for their source-material and who believed that all the law is to be found in printed books. Corbin may not have assented intellectually to the latter sentiment, but he tended to behave as if he did. But Corbin's manner of reading cases and the use he made of them were significantly different from Langdell's, as is illustrated by his emphatic rejection of the suggestion that 'the vast majority are useless, and worse than useless, for any purpose of systematic study'.[25]

On education matters the ideas of the two men were very similar. Corbin devised his own version of case-method teaching before he learned in any detail about Langdell's innovations at Harvard. Later, Corbin was largely responsible for breaking down resistance to the 'case method' at Yale. On the administrative side he played a leading role in pressing policies which ensured that the institution was built up on sound lines: the quality of the students was improved by the steady raising of admission standards and, later, by steady increase of competition for places. The library was expanded and a cadre of full-time teachers was recruited; a determined talent hunt secured the services of some outstanding individuals, including ex-President William Howard Taft (1913), Wesley Newcomb Hohfeld (1914), Walter Wheeler Cook and Thomas Swan (1916), as Dean. In so far as Yale Law School's ascent to eminence was due to the determined efforts to improve the quality of the students, staff and library, the formula for success was essentially the same as Harvard's.[26] It was mainly in respect of the prevailing attitude to law that the approaches of the two schools differed significantly.

The appointment of Hohfeld[27] in 1914 marked the next significant departure. In 1913 a hitherto unknown professor at Stanford, Hohfeld submitted to the *Yale Law Journal* an article entitled 'Some Fundamental Conceptions as Applied in Judicial Reasoning'. The editors consulted Corbin, who was so impressed that he not only advised publication but also pressed for Hohfeld's appointment to the Yale faculty. An offer was made and, according to Corbin, Hohfeld put his analysis of 'rights' to good use in negotiating terms with Yale and Stanford.[28]

In only four years at Yale, which ended in his death at the age of thirty-eight in October 1918, Hohfeld generated an extraordinary intellectual excitement which carried over for a considerable time after his death. Indeed, for many law teachers in other law schools the image of Yale Law School from about 1914 until the mid-1920s was largely associated with 'Hohfeldian analysis'. Today Hohfeld is mainly remembered for his analysis of 'legal right' and related concepts. Hohfeld showed that the term 'legal right' was used by judges in at least four different senses and he outlined a scheme of eight linked jural 'correlatives' and 'opposites' which, he claimed, could be called 'the lowest common denominators of the law ... the lowest generic conceptions to which any and all "legal quantities" may be reduced'.[29]

While Hohfeld raised some important questions and made effective use of his analytical tools to show up confusions and inadequacies in judicial reasoning, and collected together some excellent illustrative material, it is now widely accepted that his analysis was less original and has a less widespread utility than was once thought, and that he failed to substantiate his claims that reducing all legal relations to their lowest common denominators would make it possible to discuss common principles of justice and policy underlying the various jural problems involved and that it would increase 'one's perception of fundamental unity and harmony in law'.[30] But in the years following the publication of his first article in the *Yale Law Journal* Hohfeld's analysis and its variants became fashionable, in some quarters almost to the point of obsession. In particular, it made a profound impression on three leading realists, Corbin, Cook and Llewellyn.

After Hohfeld's death Cook and Corbin played a leading pàrt in keeping alive an interest in his ideas. Both adopted his analysis as a prominent part of their intellectual equipment; Cook edited Hohfeld's collected papers and the mark of Hohfeld is apparent in much of his own work. Corbin published several discussions about Hohfeld's analysis of 'right', he made repeated reference to it in his writings on contract, and he persuaded the authors of the *Restatement of Contracts* to adopt it.[31] He continued to use Hohfeld's concepts, although less obtrusively, in his later years. This persistence is understandable, for there is some truth in the saying that this type of analysis has more value in its application to contract than to most other branches of law. Karl Llewellyn was a student of Hohfeld's at Yale and, at the time, he was one of his most ardent admirers. It cannot be claimed that Hohfeld was entirely successful in training this particular pupil always to be disciplined in his use of language—and later Llewellyn was to be quite critical of his former teacher—but Llewellyn too made explicit and effective use of Hohfeldian analysis in his writings on sales, and later, less openly, in his work on the Uniform Commercial Code.[32]

The impact made by Hohfeld on these early realists is of particular significance because it established an important link between the English tradition of analytical jurisprudence and American legal realism. Hohfeld built on the work of English analytical jurists such as Holland, Markby, Salmond and above all Austin, whom he first read while he was an undergraduate at college.[33] In style he was very much in the Austinian tradition, and at first sight it may seem almost paradoxical that a disciple of Austin should have provided the early realists with some of the most powerful weapons for their onslaught on 'the formalism' and 'conceptualism' for which Austin is often blamed.[34]

The paradox is only apparent, for there is no necessary incompatibility between rigorous analysis of concepts and a realist approach. Hohfeld himself was by no means a blinkered formalist. He considered his articles on 'fundamental legal conceptions' to be only a beginning: at the time of his death he appears to have had plans for the publication of works on trusts, evidence and conflicts of laws as well as a longer work on *Fundamental Legal Conceptions*.[35] It is also clear from his address before the Association of American Law Schools in 1914 on 'A Vital School of Jurisprudence and Law' that he thought that analysis of concepts should only be part of a much more broadly conceived approach to jurisprudence.[36] Indeed, his paper can be read as an indirect attack on the narrow approach to law and to legal education which dominated most of the leading law schools and which had become further entrenched by the spread of Langdell's gospel to other schools.

Corbin and Cook used analytical techniques to challenge a picture of American law as an integrated system of abstract, relatively static, legal principles which were applied by the courts to decide cases. The object of their scepticism was an orthodoxy which was more firmly entrenched in the assumptions of academics, judges and practitioners when they talked or wrote about law, than in the articulated theories of leading jurists. And Corbin, in particular, launched his main attack in the context of discussion of specific legal concepts and doctrines. It is on the basis of his writings on contract that his achievements and limitations should be assessed. In these writings are displayed an awareness of semantic problems, a scepticism of broad formulations of principle, and an insistence on patient, minute and precise analysis of legal relations. For all of these qualities it is reasonable to give Hohfeld at least part of the credit. Cook's use of Hohfeld, it will be seen, was somewhat different: in his teaching the main target of attack was the deductive model of judicial decision-making and in general his approach was more ruthlessly iconoclastic and less constructive than Corbin's. But for both men the techniques of conceptual analysis were their main weapon in their attack on 'formalism'.

It is worth making one final point about Hohfeld. As an undergraduate he had studied chemistry and it has been pointed out that his analysis of fundamental legal conceptions bears some resemblance to chemical analysis in that it seeks to break down its subject-matter into constituent elements.[37] Hohfeld did from time to time use metaphors derived from the physical sciences and mathematics (for instance, his 'homely metaphor' about the lowest common denominators of the law), but it is only fair to add that he appears to have taken 'the scientific analogy' less seriously than some of his contemporaries.

Much more than Hohfeld and Corbin, Walter Wheeler Cook approached law with an outlook and habits of mind conditioned by training as a physical scientist.[38] Before he ever studied law he had served as an assistant in mathematics at Columbia and had read for a doctorate in physics at Berlin. Throughout his long career as a legal scholar he wandered restlessly from university to university, leaving behind him the reputation of being one of the most brilliant law teachers and one of the most difficult colleagues of his generation.

Between 1916 and 1933, as he moved from Chicago to Yale to Columbia, back to Yale again, and then to Johns Hopkins, Cook was one of the most controversial figures in the realist movement. His temperament and his background combined to make him something of a misfit among American law teachers. He was, for instance, the first person since 1891 without any experience of legal practice to be appointed to the Columbia faculty.[39] He was completely out of sympathy with the vocational orientation of the great majority of his colleagues and he subscribed to a rather dogmatic version of the conception of a university as a community of scholars devoted to the scientific advancement of knowledge. It is said that 'he was extremely sensitive and shy, and he assumed as protective armour an attitude of cold and austere intellectuality that many people found repellent. Like most men with a passion for accurate thinking, he seemed to believe that no one thought accurately but himself.'[40]

Throughout his career Cook's overriding concern was the contrast between the methods of physical scientists and the methods of lawyers of all types. The road to progress was through the application of 'truly scientific methods' to law.[41] Cook took 'the scientific analogy' far more seriously than his predecessors among American jurists. He read widely in the philosophy of science and, in his later years, wrote a number of papers on scientific method in law in which he developed a theory which drew heavily on the ideas of John Dewey. His own conclusion was that 'the same logic of inquiry used in physics and chemistry will yield useful results if applied in all fields in which intelligent inquiry can be carried on'.[42] His starting-point was a teleological conception of law, which could hardly be claimed as original, but which provided the basis for challenging the assumption that all the materials of legal science are available in printed books:

Underlying any scientific study of the law, it is submitted, will lie one fundamental postulate, viz., that human laws are devices, tools which society uses as one of its methods to regulate human conduct and to promote those types of it which are regarded as desirable. If so, it follows that the worth or value of a given rule of law can be determined only by finding out how it works, that is, by ascertaining so far as that can be done, whether it promotes or retards the attainment of desired ends. If this is to be done, quite clearly we must know what at any given period these ends are and also whether the means selected, the given rules of law, are indeed adapted to securing them.[43]

It will be seen later that Cook played a leading part in the movement to develop scientific empirical research into legal processes. At first, however, he used his understanding of modern conceptions of science as a base from which to attack the approaches of other jurists. Cook took as his main target the idea that the common law consists of 'a body of scientific principle' which can be discovered by 'induction' from decided cases and from which decisions in new cases can be 'deduced'.[44] Cook attributed this idea to his 'bêtes noires' in conflicts of laws, Story and Beale, and the editors of the *Restatement of Conflicts of Laws,* but he added that 'essentially the same ideas underlie nearly all the teaching in our law schools'.[45] For many years to destroy this mechanical model of jurisprudence seemed to be his primary aim.[46] Thus he dazzled his students at Yale with a brilliant display of dialectics as he set out to show, case by case, that the results did not necessarily follow from the judges' articulated premises and that traditional formulations of the same legal doctrine could be used to support opposing conclusions. Cook was probably unfair in attributing so simplistic a view to his adversaries, and he tended to spoil his case, when arguing at the general level, by choosing too crude a target to attack. But he had unusual powers of analysis and his detailed criticisms of specific doctrines were often devastating, the most notable example being his

critique of the territorial theory of the conflict of laws, of which
Story and Beale were the leading proponents.[47]

For much of his career Cook was content to criticise the accepted 'legal logic' from within, using analytical techniques to show
up ambiguities and confusions in the reasoning of judges and of
other jurists. Here he followed his adversaries in concentrating
almost exclusively on decisions of appellate courts. This part of
his work has much in common with that of Corbin: acute distrust
of other people's generalizations and of broadly stated legal
principles, enthusiasm for Hohfeld's analytical scheme, scepticism
of claims for 'certainty' in law, and a concern to investigate and
bring into the open the policy considerations underlying particular
legal doctrines and judicial decisions. However, he lacked Corbin's
professional orientation,[48] and his dialectical style tended to give
the impression that he was only capable of 'destructive' analysis.
Thus some of those who accepted his critique of the territorial
theory of conflicts, found his work 'sterile' in his failure to provide
an alternative theory as a basis for systematic development;[49]
along with other realists he was sometimes accused of believing
that 'talk of rules is a myth'[50] and at least once he was accused
of suggesting that one cannot draw any generalizations.[51] Cook
strongly denied all these charges,[52] but there is some truth in the
suggestion that he was at his most brilliant in attacking the
generalizations of others, without always suggesting a definite
alternative.

At some point, probably soon after he left Yale in 1919, Cook
began to emphasize the need for empirical research into the actual
operation of the legal system. This is not marked by an abrupt
break in his own approach, but it introduced an important new
element into legal realism.[53] The development is strikingly illustrated by Cook's reviews of successive editions of Williston's
treatise on *The Law of Contracts*. On both occasions Cook paid
tribute to Williston's industry and learning, but he found the
treatise profoundly unsatisfying. In his review of the first edition
he sought to rationalize his dissatisfaction by arguing that
Williston repeatedly fell into error because of his failure to adopt
Hohfeld's analysis of fundamental legal conceptions.[54] In his
review of the second edition, almost twenty years later, Cook's
dissatisfaction remained, but he shifted his ground of attack, this
time emphasizing the point that Williston's treatment was

divorced from 'empirical reality'.[55] The implications of this shift will become apparent when developments at Columbia Law School in the 1920s are considered.

As a jurist Cook was neither particularly original nor profound. His principal contribution was to explore at length the implications of 'the scientific analogy' for law in the light of contemporary ideas about the physical sciences. Many of his own ideas were derivative, for he drew heavily on the work of Holmes, Dewey, Hohfeld and writers on the philosophy of science. Moreover, there are some serious weaknesses in his attempts to transfer scientific empiricism to law. His place as an important figure in the history of realism is based on three main claims : first, in his work in conflicts, and to a lesser extent in equity, he showed up convincingly the inadequacies of some of the most widely accepted theories and suggested that their fault lay essentially in some fundamental methodological misconceptions. Secondly, Cook's theory of an empirical science of law, although rather crude, provided the basis for the first serious attempt to break away from narrow, library-bound conceptions of the proper scope and methods of research by legal scholars.[56] Finally, Cook played a leading part in trying to apply this theory in practice, first at Columbia and subsequently at Johns Hopkins.

Hohfeld died in 1918 and in the following year Cook moved to Columbia, tempted by the twin attractions of a higher salary and a distinguished Dean, Harlan Fiske Stone.[57] During the next ten years Yale Law School continued to grow in stature as an institution, but the movement for reform lost much of its impetus. There is little doubt that Columbia was the main centre of the realist ferment between 1920 and 1928. Accordingly, in the next phase the scene shifts to Columbia, but we shall later return briefly to Yale to review developments there.

3
Columbia in the 1920's

Between 1919 and 1933 Columbia was the focal point of the
ferment that marked the next stage in the history of the realist
movement. Although new ideas were being aired in other law
schools there was a greater concentration of energetic and radical
jurists at Columbia than anywhere else; furthermore the implications of some of the new ideas that were being bandied about
were given focus by becoming the subject of sharp controversy
both within and outside the law school. A series of spectacular
events, notably the curriculum discussions of 1926–8, the deanship
crisis of 1928, and Llewellyn's debate with Pound in 1931, dramatized the jurisprudential issues and helped to make them a matter
of public concern among academic and practising lawyers. It was
during this period that the existence of a new movement began
to be recognized and that, almost at the same time as it became
visible, the movement split in two.

The story can be said to begin with the appointment of Walter
Wheeler Cook to the Columbia faculty in 1919. At the time
Columbia Law School was considered by many to be second only
to Harvard in prestige. It was larger than the Yale Law School
and had a longer and more distinguished tradition. The famous
legal scholar James Kent had been Professor of Law at Columbia
from 1793 to 1797 and from 1823 to 1846.[2] He had added
distinction to the university, but had done little to develop the law
school as an institution. However, from the time of the appointment of Theodore Dwight as Professor and Dean in 1858 the
school had been blessed with a succession of outstanding personalities who had built up a fine tradition. Under Dwight the battle
to establish the respectability of university legal education had
been won relatively early; in 1891 Keener, a pupil of Langdell's,
had successfully introduced the case method and thereafter there

had been a steady increase in the standards of instruction and the quality of the students. From 1910 the school had continued to prosper under the distinguished leadership of Harlan Fiske Stone, a man who combined a strong professional orientation with a broad and progressive vision of the educational needs of intending lawyers.

At the time of Cook's arrival the school was not radically different from the Langdellian model, but it was not a mere carbon copy of Harvard. Columbia had been the first American university to establish chairs of international law and diplomacy (1891) and legislation (1917), there was an established tradition of close contact with the School of Political Science, and in Stone's public pronouncements there were signs of awareness of a need for a broad approach to legal study. However, in 1919 the Columbia curriculum was fairly conventional and there was little evidence of any great demand for innovation.

The arrival of Cook was soon to change that, for he joined forces with William Underhill Moore in attempting to introduce a new approach to law teaching at Columbia. Their first major coup was to secure the appointment of Herman Oliphant. This was particularly significant, for shortly after Oliphant's arrival Cook himself returned to Yale, and it was Moore and Oliphant who became the key figures in the events that followed. William Underhill Moore (1879–1949) was educated at Columbia College and Columbia Law School.[8] His family included some distinguished lawyers and from an early age he was exposed to the atmosphere of legal practice. After practising in New York from 1902 to 1908 he took up law teaching, first at Kansas and then subsequently at the University of Wisconsin and the University of Chicago. After eight years of teaching in the mid-west Moore returned to Columbia Law School in 1916, where he remained for thirteen years.

At the time of his return Moore had a growing reputation as a commercial lawyer, especially in the field of bills and notes. He was also known to be an exceptionally demanding teacher, highly individualistic and impatient of any signs of intellectual sloppiness. Although he was reputed to be something of a polymath, who read avidly in many areas of the physical and social sciences, in the first years after his return to Columbia few people could have anticipated the almost fanatical espousal of 'scientific

COLUMBIA IN THE 1920S   43

research' which was ultimately to mark him as the most un-compromising, and most 'extreme', of legal scientists. Rather, his teaching at this stage was distinguished as much as anything by analytical exactness and by his refusal to allow the traditional classification of fields of law to obscure the way in which problems presented themselves in legal practice. Thus, it is reported, when Moore was teaching, 'a class in sales is likely to consider and dis-cuss problems conventionally included in mortgages, suretyship or insurance'.[4] His research during the first half of his career mainly consisted in the painstaking accumulation of notes on thousands of cases on negotiable instruments and allied topics. Thus up to about 1922 Moore appeared to be a tough minded commercial lawyer, with a practical bias, widely read, but sceptical and scorn-ful of vague theorizing.

At some stage during his time as professor at Columbia he became converted to a different approach. It is not clear how suddenly this happened, nor to what extent it was due to his association with Cook and Oliphant, or to his espousal of the behaviourist psychology of Watson,[5] or to a combination of these and other factors. When the break came it appears to have been sharp and complete. The story is told that a student one day found Moore in his office 'cursing most frightfully' as he threw out the contents of his bulging filing cabinets. On being asked what he was doing, he is reported as replying: 'It's my life work, all the notes I have taken in a lifetime of research—and it's all wrong.'[6] Having concluded that he had been proceeding on false premisses, Moore decided to start afresh and thereafter, for the rest of his career, he concentrated on 'pure' research into the effects of laws on human behaviour.[7] Having started as a relatively conventional academic lawyer, he became, after his conversion, the most un-compromising of the 'scientists'.

Moore's ideas on classification had a direct bearing on events at Columbia in the 1920s. His refusal, in his teaching, to be confined within the boundaries of conventionally defined fields of law was merely one aspect of his more general scepticism of the adequacy of existing legal concepts for categorizing in a mean-ingful way the 'facts' of reported cases. Instead he advocated the search for 'significant type fact situations' as a basis for classifying circumstances giving rise to legal problems. This idea was taken up by others, especially Oliphant, when the attempt was made at Columbia to reclassify the whole curriculum along functional lines.[8] The same idea probably stimulated two of Llewellyn's most important ideas—the quest for narrower categories[9] and the concept of 'situation sense'.[10]

Moore's friend and ally, Herman Oliphant (1884–1939) embarked on the study of law relatively late.[11] Until the age of twenty-seven he had been teaching English at a small college in Indiana. A promising career in philology was beginning to take shape when, at some considerable personal sacrifice, he decided to change direction and enrolled as a law student in the University of Chicago in 1911. He gave a revealing summary of his intellectual concerns at an AALS symposium in 1928:

I left Comparative Philology and entered Law School, hoping thereby to get in touch with something more closely allied to life. I completed the Law School course with a pretty keen feeling as to law's detachment from life. At that time, in 1914, as I emerged from the confusion of an undergraduate course of three years of law, I heard one voice that sounded a clear note in that confusion, and that was Dean Pound's counsel that the supreme need of the situation was socializing our jurisprudence.

I have been trying ever since that time to address my spare time and thinking to devising ways and means for making that aspiration a reality.[12]

Oliphant was appointed as an instructor in the Chicago Law School immediately on graduation and it was only at the end of his career, after he had made his main academic contribution, that he engaged in full-time practice (as General Counsel for the Department of Treasury 1935–9). Like Cook, who also had never practised law, Oliphant was out of sympathy with the vocational emphasis of American legal education. However, unlike Cook and Corbin, he had a literary rather than a scientific background; nevertheless, he espoused the 'scientific analogy' just as enthusiastically, and during the 1920s he was one of the most articulate and vehement spokesmen for the study of law as a social science. It is interesting to note that, like so many 'realists', Oliphant's principal fields of specialization were contracts and commercial law.

Oliphant was a lively teacher and an able man, and some of his writings are still quoted, notably an article on 'A Return to Stare Decisis';[13] but he was perhaps not in the same intellectual class as Cook or Underhill Moore, while sharing their tendency to overstatement and extremism. His principal significance in the history of realism is as a collaborator, and acolyte, of Walter Wheeler Cook, and as the chief protagonist of the latter's ideas during the Great Debate at Columbia in the 1920s. It is to these events that we now turn.

It was the aim of Cook and Moore to make the approach to law at Columbia more 'scientific' and to bring about a closer integration between law and the social sciences. They were less than tactful in their first attempts at innovation. It is said that they used 'aggressive tactics' to secure the appointment of Herman Oliphant in 1922 and they were suspected of conspiring to recruit a clique of sympathizers and of trying to get hold of certain key courses, such as Personal Property, the better to convert their students.[14] Cook was an abrasive character, and after a number of clashes with Dean Stone and other colleagues he resigned in 1922 and returned to Yale at an even higher salary. However, Oliphant immediately took over where Cook left off and during the next six years he promoted with rather more tact, but no less energy, ideas almost identical to those of Cook.

For a time 'the radicals' found a powerful ally in Nicholas Murray Butler, President of Columbia. In his report for 1922 Butler included a remarkable passage on legal education which looked very much like a thinly veiled attack on the policies of Dean Stone.[15] This may well have contributed to Stone's decision to resign a year later. In his report Butler criticized American law schools generally for being too narrow and technical in their approach and for having failed to cultivate more vigorously relations between law, ethics and social science. He suggested that there was an urgent need for a thoroughgoing critical examination of all aspects of legal education. This must have given encouragement to Oliphant and Moore. A year after his arrival Oliphant prepared a plan for far-reaching reforms of the law school, in which he argued that the institution should become a community of scholars concentrating on research into law as an aspect of social organization.[16] He sent a copy to Butler, who advised him to postpone formal action until the time was more propitious, but meanwhile to develop and promote his ideas by informal means. Butler dropped a broad hint that Oliphant might in due course become Dean.[17] Oliphant seems to have followed Butler's advice, with some success.

In 1922–3 Oliphant and Dowling gave experimental courses,

which excited some interest among their colleagues, not least because they cut across the traditional boundaries of subjects. Oliphant's course on illegal combinations, which was soon re-christened trade regulation, threatened to take over a substantial part of what was normally subsumed under torts. It included, for instance, such topics as intimidation, inducing breach of contract, and disparagement of goods; the course also trespassed on several other traditional courses, especially contract, corporations and criminal law. Dowling's course on industrial relations also cut across traditional boundaries, for it overlapped with constitutional law, contract, torts, agency and equity, in a fashion now familiar to students of labour law. These courses in time became a regular part of the curriculum of most law schools. In fact 'neither course originated in Columbia's hotbed of discontent',[18] for in this instance Harvard had taken the lead. At Columbia they attracted attention partly because they were recognized as filling important gaps, but also because of Oliphant's response to charges of trespass. Problems of overlapping are perennial in discussions of curriculum, but Oliphant added a new dimension by maintaining that it was the traditional courses that need revision on the basis of a completely reconstituted scheme of classification along functional lines. By the time that the next major move towards reform was taken a fair number of Oliphant's colleagues were at least prepared to think seriously about ways of reorganizing the subject-matter of legal studies.

During the period 1923–6 Oliphant and Moore no doubt found that most of their colleagues did not fully share their ideas; they were supported by some younger members of faculty, notably Karl Llewellyn, Hessel Yntema and William O. Douglas, but others were, for the most part, sceptical. However, no concerted opposition to their efforts developed at this stage. Stone, Jervey and Smith, who occupied the deanship in succession, were all much more professionally oriented than Cook, Moore and Oliphant, but none of them was unsympathetic to innovation nor to attempts to try to broaden the curriculum. Their attitude was epitomized by Smith, who in a letter to Stone in 1921 had written: 'Their radical ideas constitute an excellent tonic for the intellectual liver, but as a steady diet they are simply impossible.'[19]

In the spring of 1926 the Columbia faculty acted on President Butler's suggestion that a critical re-examination of legal education should be undertaken. The exercise was conducted with exceptional enthusiasm over a period of two years. Forty years later it could probably still be described, in Currie's words, as 'the most comprehensive and searching investigation of law school objectives and methods that has ever been undertaken'.[20] The whole faculty participated. Approximately a hundred memoranda, some substantial, were prepared and discussed and thousands of man-hours were spent in committee. Differences were temporarily patched up and nearly every member of the faculty devoted a considerable amount of time to the exercise. Leon C. Marshall, a distinguished economist and an expert on business education, came from the University of Chicago as visiting professor in 1927 specifically to act as chairman. Marshall had been a colleague of Oliphant at Chicago and in 1923 Oliphant had dedicated his *Cases on Trade Regulation* to him. It is some indication of the spirit in which the discussions began that it was Young B. Smith, a moderate, sceptical of Oliphant's enthusiasms, who formally proposed that an economist, such as Marshall, should be invited to assist in the discussions. This proposal was made in a long statement in which Smith outlined the case for revising the whole curriculum in order to achieve a closer integration between law and the other social sciences, especially economics.[21]

Although Smith made the first formal moves at a faculty meeting, undoubtedly Oliphant was the chief architect of the enterprise. He had pressed for reform as early as 1923, his course on trade regulation and his general ideas had stimulated, without always converting, many of his colleagues; together with Moore and Marshall, he played a leading part in the discussions. At the end he was relieved of all his other duties for the spring session of 1928 in order to prepare a report.

The chief value of the discussions lies in their concreteness. A genuine attempt was made to think through in considerable detail the problems of reorienting each part of the curriculum. At an early stage in the discussions a working scheme of classification was agreed.[22] Substantive law was shared out between three major categories: political relations, business relations and familial relations. A fourth category, law administration, covered, *inter alia*, the courts and other dispute-settlement mechanisms, and the rules of procedure and evidence. This scheme seems to have been largely the brain child of Oliphant. The thinking behind it is illuminating. Dissatisfaction with the existing divisions of law was the starting point: contracts, torts, equity, agency and corporations, for example, were open to a number of objections:

Any classification of law requires abstraction, but our present classification embodies unnecessarily broad abstractions. Many of them are antiquated partly because they were made in terms of a procedural set-up long since obsolete and partly because made prior to the industrial and financial revolutions and prior to the beginning of the present marketing revolution. Our present classification is pretty much out of touch with life. Among the things which we need to do is to come to study law from points of view more intimate than the abstractions of our present classifications permit and more significant than their age makes possible. [23]

Furthermore, the old divisions tended to obscure the social purposes of rules of law and also to put up unnecessary barriers between lawyers and social scientists. They further promoted unreality by sharpening the dichotomy between substantive law and procedure, so that legal problems tended to be considered in isolation from the processes of adjudication and enforcement.

The problem of finding an alternative basis for classification was well stated by Oliphant:

[T]he practical effects of rules of law upon life can be thrown into sharper relief, by classifying substantive law in categories closely related to modern social life. But social living has an indefinite number of aspects. It can be thought of, for example, as involving a homogeneous mass of human relations, human activities, human motives, human ends, etc. If law is to be classified in terms of the life which it affects, what aspects of that life shall be chosen as the bases of classification? [24]

Oliphant's answer is interesting. Because a prime need was to make use of the skills and findings of the social sciences, the most useful division for this purpose would be one which corresponded with areas of specialization in the social sciences. This line of argument is suggestive, even if the final scheme is a little disappointing. The major division that was settled on was (1) business relations, (2) familial relations, and (3) communal-political relations, roughly reflecting (1) political economy and business economics, (2) sociology, and (3) political science. The fourth category, law administration, served as something of a catch-all. It may be pointed out that this exhausts neither the social sciences nor the traditional subject-matter of legal studies. Moreover, in the discussions and in Oliphant's report a disproportionate amount of attention was devoted to business relations. This, according to Currie, 'was attributable not to any hypothetical orientation of the Columbia law school toward Wall Street, but to the undoubted orientation of Marshall and Oliphant toward the University of Chicago School of Business'.[25]

The contrast between the old and the new scheme of classification has sometimes been characterized as the replacement of 'legal' by 'functional' concepts. Thus trade regulation, industrial relations, risk bearing, security, business units, the family and credit have all at some time been described as 'functional'. It seems that the term is not being used precisely, if it can be applied indiscriminately to all these categories. For example 'security', 'trade regulation' and 'risk bearing' can be said to relate directly to functions (in the sense of social and economic purposes), but 'the family' refers to an institution, which may be analysable in functional terms, but is not itself a function. Conversely, equity— of which Lasswell and McDougal later asked : 'What useful purpose is served by putting this rag-bag of stuff between two covers?'[26]—can be said to have originated principally in order to perform a 'function', i.e. to mitigate the rigidities of the common law. The answer is that 'functional' has sometimes been used loosely in respect of categories in rather the same way that the term 'non-legal' has been used in respect of materials. It normally implies that the basis of classification is either the purposes which a rule or collection of rules is meant to serve or else some socially significant group of 'type-fact situations'. Since the purposes of legal rules are almost infinite in number and since there are no established criteria of social significance, 'functional' in this usage is generally a rather vague term.

During the curriculum discussions much of the detailed work was done by small committees. These for the most part reflected the agreed general scheme of classification. For instance, a committee on business relations was first established and this soon recommended the subdivision of the area into marketing, business organizations, labour relations and financial credit, with possible further categories of risk-bearing and production. Subcommittees were then instituted to deal with each of these topics, except production. Individuals as well as committees and subcommittees prepared memoranda, which were collated by Marshall and

Oliphant. In the end it was thought worthwhile to give Oliphant leave of absence to enable him to prepare a report for publication. The end-product was Oliphant's *Summary of Studies in Legal Education*, which remains to this day one of the most stimulating published discussions on this complex subject.[27]

Although the curriculum discussions foundered as a result of a split between two factions, there was a basic consensus among the participants about the general approach. Currie puts the matter as follows:

The fundamental thesis which emerged was this: Since law is a means of social control, it ought to be studied as such. Solutions to the problems of a changing social order are not implicit in the rules and principles which are formally elaborated on the basis of past decisions, to be evoked by merely formal logical processes; and effective legal education cannot proceed in disregard of this fact. If men are to be trained for intelligent and effective participation in legal processes, and if law schools are to perform their function of contributing through research to the improvement of law administration, the formalism which confines the understanding and criticism of law within limits fixed by history and authority must be abandoned, and every available resource of knowledge and judgment must be brought to the task.

A drastic retooling would be required to convert the facilities of legal education to such an effort. Two basic requirements were announced to the law school world with seismic effect: First, the formal categories of the law, shaped by tradition and by accident, tend to obscure the social problems with which law deals, the purpose which is the vital element of principle, and the actual working of legal processes; they constitute a framework which forces artificiality in perspective and development; they must be revised along lines of correspondence with the types of human activity involved. Second, an understanding of the social structure in which law operates can no longer be taken for granted or regarded as irrelevant; law students – and hence law teachers – must acquire that understanding, and must somehow learn to take into account the contributions which other disciplines and sciences can make to the solution of social problems.[28]

This is an excellent summary of the points of general agreement between the participants in the discussions. The significance of the exercise was that it was a serious attempt to work out rigorously and in detail the implications of sociological jurisprudence for law school activities. There was a general sympathy with the approach to law that had been made popular at a general level by Holmes and Pound. There seems also to have been agreement on the need to expose law students to much more 'non-legal' material and on the value of reclassifying the subject-matter of study. It was further recognized by many that a great deal of research would be needed before much of the relevant 'non-legal' material would be available for use in teaching. But a serious division of opinion emerged as to the priority to be given to such research. The issue was joined in respect of the objectives the law school should pursue.[29] Some, led by Oliphant, argued that the school should have as its principal objective scientific research into law as an aspect of social organization; it should devote itself 'primarily to the non-professional' study of law, in order that the function of law may be comprehended, its results evaluated and its development kept more nearly in step with modern life.'[30] The school would become a genuine 'community of scholars', and such teaching as would be done would be directed towards training in scholarship. This was essentially the policy which had been advocated by Oliphant in 1923, and less explicitly hinted at by Cook even earlier.

Opposed to this was the view that professional training should continue to be the school's principal function, albeit by means of a radically different approach. In Oliphant's *Summary* the objective is expressed in terms of 'providing an adequate scientific preparation for public service in law'; this formulation takes into account graduates 'who serve society in capacities other than those of the practising attorney'[31] and stresses the 'public' nature of 'private' practice, but it was probably not intended to suggest any major divergence from the traditional aim of preparation for practice at the bar. The meaning of 'scientific' in this context is obscure.

Oliphant's *Summary* states that no formal decision was taken on this issue and that the discussions proceeded on the basis that Columbia should pursue both objectives simultaneously, perhaps by setting up a 'research school' alongside, but independent of, the 'training school'.[32] Although such a compromise was the best that Oliphant might have hoped for in the circumstances, this statement glosses over both the importance of the division of opinion and the strength of feeling it engendered. The supposedly rational structure of the proposals for reform was uneasily perched on the shaky base of an unresolved disagreement about competing objectives. That these objectives were felt to be incompatible was dramatically illustrated by the deanship crisis, which had unfortunate consequences for the law school and perhaps for the development of American legal education generally.[33]

During much of the period of the curriculum discussions Dean Jervey had been ill. His resignation in February 1928, after a relatively short period in office, precipitated a crisis over the appointment of his successor. The faculty formed into two factions, one supporting Oliphant, the other Young B. Smith. Legally the power of appointing the Dean was vested in the Trustees of the University on the recommendation of the President, but on the last occasion members of the faculty had been invited to propose a nominee. This time, however, knowing that the faculty was deadlocked, President Butler acted on his own. Although he had up to this point given every encouragement to Oliphant, he accepted the advice of a number of outsiders, including ex-Dean Stone, and decided in favour of Smith. Without even going through the form of consulting the faculty he announced that unless he was persuaded to change his mind before Monday 7 May 1928, he would recommend Smith's appointment to the trustees. Butler's action was strongly resented. The official *History of Columbia Law School* continues the story as follows:

President Butler's announcement created an immediate uproar. Many members of the Faculty, particularly those who supported Professor Oliphant's candidacy, felt that Butler's action was autocratic and in flagrant disregard of what they conceived to be the Faculty's traditional prerogatives. A plenary session of the Faculty was convened at the Men's Faculty Club on 117th Street to protest the action; absent members were summoned from as far away as Virginia. The Faculty sat all day Sunday, May 6, and well into the night. The meeting was stormy. Many proposals were discussed, but a majority could not be secured for any of them. After hours of argument, the only resolution upon which anyone could agree was the self-evident proposition that any individual member of the Faculty was free to present his views to President Butler in private if he so wished. The great meeting of protest thus broke up without accomplishing anything. Some individual protests seem to have been conveyed to the President, but they did not affect his decision. On April 30, 1928, therefore, Huger W. Jervey's resignation became effective and on May 7, 1928, the Trustees made Young B. Smith Dean.[34]

Dean Robert M. Hutchins of Yale and Walter Wheeler Cook, who was in the process of establishing a research institute at Johns Hopkins University, exploited the dissatisfaction of Oliphant and his supporters. Oliphant and Yntema resigned to join Cook at John Hopkins. With them went Leon C. Marshall, who had been a visiting professor, but who might have stayed on; William O. Douglas went to Yale, where he was joined not long afterwards by Underhill Moore, who had refused an invitation to go to Johns Hopkins, on the ground that the venture was unsound.

Thus from one incident, at a crucial point in its history, Columbia Law School lost some of its most able and lively scholars, including the three leading participants in the curriculum discussions. That a vacancy for the deanship should have occurred at that particular moment was unfortunate, for there seems to have been an excellent prospect for a compromise, if only because it would almost certainly not have been feasible for the law school to have abdicated its professional training function. A substantial number of members of the faculty, probably a majority, were opposed to the idea; the alumni, a powerful pressure group in a private university by virtue of their financial contributions, would almost certainly have been outraged; and there were other influential outsiders, like ex-Dean Stone, who were known to be against any such move. Moreover, as Oliphant acknowledges in his *Summary*, it was unlikely that it would have been possible to have financed a research school from university funds;[35] the loss of alumni support and a reduction of revenue from students' fees would have increased the financial difficulties.

But for the deanship crisis, or if Oliphant (or someone more personally acceptable than Smith) had become Dean, Columbia might well have decided to continue to teach prospective attorneys, and to establish a large institute specializing in research 'into law as an aspect of social organization'. If this had happened the potential of the curriculum discussions might have been more fully realized. This is, of course, mainly a matter of speculation — but not entirely. It will be seen that a valiant effort was made by those who stayed to implement the plans for reform, with at least partial success. It will be seen that those who left went off in directions which, in the judgment of their contemporaries, turned out to be blind alleys. It can be argued that those who stayed had balance and common sense, but lacked either a clear vision of the implications of what they were doing or a complete dedication to the cause of reform. Most of those who left had the vision and the dedication, but were inclined to let enthusiasm outrun good

judgment. But for the crisis a major split in the realist movement
might have been averted, Columbia might have given a higher
priority to empirical research, and the enthusiasms of the
'Scientists' might have been restrained by their more moderate
colleagues. On the other hand, it is quite possible that differences
of opinion and personality conflicts would have continued to
disrupt the faculty; as it turned out the one clear benefit that was
derived from the departure of the dissidents was a distinct lessen-
ing of tension.

Anyone familiar with academic politics will know how chance
factors in a situation—such as individual character, personal
relationships, financial opportunity or accidents of timing—can
complicate or obscure genuine differences on issues of principle.
The events of 1928 had their share of such factors. Nevertheless
a profound difference underlay the split and it is important to see
this issue sharply, even at the risk of some simplification of history.
For present purposes its main significance is that it sheds light on
the nature of realist jurisprudence and of the split within the
realist movement.

Karl Llewellyn sometimes divided legal theory into three
branches: legal philosophy (concerned mainly with values, and the
ends of law), legal science (concerned with empirical description)
and jurisprudence, or 'prudentia iuris' (the study of the machinery
of law government and the methods and techniques of the personnel of the law—the law crafts).[86] These categories may not
provide a suitable basis for classifying individual jurists, let alone
'schools' of thinkers, for a rounded theory of law encompasses all
three aspects, but they suggest convenient labels for the two
factions at Columbia: those who resigned after the deanship crisis,
i.e. Oliphant, Moore, Douglas, Yntema and Marshall, may be
referred to as 'the Scientists', while those who stayed on may be
referred to roughly as Prudents (or Prudentes) by virtue of their
concern with professional training. Cook should be added to the
former group for obvious reasons.

Although the classification is a rough one, certain patterns are
apparent in respect of each group. Four of the Scientists, Oliphant,
Yntema, Cook and Marshall, had never practised law (Marshall
was an economist with no legal qualifications) and they lacked
the professional orientation of most of their colleagues or their
sense of commitment to professional training. They all had in

common a clear perception of the need for 'scientific' research as a precondition for progress in integrating law and the social sciences; they all expressed an interest in contemporary problems and were concerned with improving legal institutions. Thus they were not advocating 'pure' research, but research as a preliminary to the solution of social problems and to the improvement of professional training. In this Underhill Moore differed from the others by taking a longer view of needs and priorities. His later research projects at Yale, especially his parking studies, were designed to test out concepts and techniques rather than to lead to immediate practical reforms.

Those who stayed behind, and the new recruits to the faculty during the next few years, formed a more variegated group than the Scientists. Yet some relatively clear patterns can be seen in their attitudes and behaviour during the period 1928–37. They accepted the professional ethos of the law school, but they would have emphatically rejected any suggestion that it should be content to be a 'trade school' or a gymnasium for 'clever chess-players'. Dean Smith was forever proclaiming a social science version of the liberal ideal of university education.[37] There is little to suggest that his faculty was not behind him on this. More-over, their concern with 'prudentia' was more in respect of *transmission* of legal skills than in the systematic *study* of juristic method (Llewellyn's interest in this was a later development); but stimulated by the curriculum discussions they were as a group considerably more self-conscious about what they were doing than members of any other leading law school of the day. Like most American law teachers they took teaching seriously. As academics the Prudents had no option but to claim an interest in research; the philosophy professed by Dean Smith implied acceptance of the need for empirical research, but with relatively few exceptions they remained to a remarkable degree library bound. Perception of the relevance of fact-gathering was not matched by a corresponding commitment to doing it. This was the crucial difference between the Prudents and the Scientists, a difference which is more clearly brought out by examining the actions of the members of the two groups in the immediate aftermath of the crisis.

4
The Aftermath of the Split

THE PRUDENTS

In the long run the traumatic events of 1928 affected the direction
rather than the quality of Columbia Law School. Smith continued
as Dean until 1952. Throughout this period Columbia continued
to grow in size and stature and more than held its own as one
of the great law schools. Smith soon rebuilt an outstandingly
strong team: the survivors included Dowling, Goebel, Medina,
Michael, Patterson and Llewellyn, a nucleus of which most law
schools would be envious. A number of distinguished scholars
from other parts of the university maintained a close association,
notably Robert Lee Hale, the economist, John Dewey, the philosopher, and two distinguished international lawyers, Charles C.
Hyde and Philip C. Jessup.[2] New recruits in the next phase
included Adolf A. Berle, Elliott Cheatham, John Hanna, Milton
Handler, Walter Gellhorn and Herbert Wechsler, now familiar
names in American law. All of these men were positively in
favour of a contextual approach to law, but they did not have,
for the most part, a commitment to sustained empirical research.

From 1928–33 Smith succeeded in maintaining much of the
momentum of reform. Wisely, piecemeal revision and continuing
review were preferred to a dramatic break with the past. A
major part of the effort was concentrated on editing 'teaching
materials'. In his report of 1933 the Dean was able to point out
that in the previous three years his colleagues had published fourteen course books and that a further fourteen sets of materials
had been prepared in connection with revision of the curriculum. By 1937 'of the forty courses other than seminars offered
at Columbia Law School, thirty-six were being taught from books
and materials prepared by members of the Faculty; twenty-six

case books adapted to the new conception of legal education had been published and eighteen other collections of materials were in use in mineographed form.'³

The compilation of casebooks and teaching materials is a form of editorial work that has been elevated to an art by American academic lawyers. English reviewers of this art form often miss the point when they dismiss American casebooks as mere 'scissors-and-paste'. It is an arduous, time-consuming activity, involving more skill than first impressions might suggest. It reflects, more-over, the seriousness with which the American academic lawyer tends to view his role as teacher. But to the outsider it seems to stretch ordinary usage to include this activity under 'research'. In recent years even American law teachers have begun to question whether the casebook tradition has encouraged the most worth-while deployment of talent. The judgment of history may well be that, for all its virtues, the American casebook tradition has been a major brake on progress in American law schools, by absorbing energies which might otherwise have been more fruitfully employed.

The Columbia faculty between 1928 and 1937 were faithful servitors of this tradition. A shift from the Langdell model of case-book was symbolized by a change in title: 'Cases on X' was replaced by 'Cases and materials on Y'. The 'materials' were often culled from 'extra-legal' sources; exceptionally they were the fruits of original research by the compiler. Also, in some instances, 'Y' was a hitherto unused category, like business organ-ization or security, representing a revised taxonomy of the subject-matter of study. There was in fact considerable variation in the extent to which the Columbia course books were genuinely 'adapted to the new conception of legal education'. Some, like Goebel's *Cases and Materials on the Development of Legal Institutions* and Llewellyn's *Cases and Materials on the Law of Sales* were clearly novel, but the majority did not diverge radically from the traditional model.⁴

It was not only editorial work that diverted the Columbia law teachers from providing an adequate research basis for their educational reforms. The law school had for a long time had an admirable tradition of involvement in public affairs.⁵ The New Deal led to a sharp increase in the extent of this involvement. Under the Roosevelt administration intellectuals were invited to participate in American government and politics to an extent that has only since been equalled in the Kennedy era. During the New Deal law teachers were in particular demand, and there is a high correlation between those law teachers who were New Dealers and those who were associated with the realist movement. Columbia and Yale were as much Roosevelt's recruiting ground as Harvard was for Kennedy. In 1933, for example, Berle, Déak, Dowling, Handler and Hanna from the Columbia Law School all worked for the United States government.[6] From outside Columbia Jerome Frank, Felix Frankfurter, William O. Douglas, and Thurman Arnold were among the new wave of jurists who were prominent New Dealers.[7] Dean Smith well knew that the calls of public service were a threat to the implementation of his educational plans, but there were compensating advantages, and the pressures for participation in public affairs were in any case almost irresistible.

It would be churlish to say that no research was done by a faculty which between 1930–3 produced, *inter alia*, such outstanding works as Berle and Means' *The Modern Corporation and Private Property* (1932), Michael and Adler's *Crime, Law and Social Science* (1933), Llewellyn's *Praejudizienrecht und Rechtsprechung in Amerika* (1933), as well as the course books already mentioned, and an impressive list of other books and articles. Nor could it be said that no empirical research was undertaken after 1928. Francis Déak, Michael and Adler, Albert Jacobs, Adolf Berle, and Richard Powell were among those who ventured outside the library, while Karl Llewellyn made a somewhat abortive attempt to investigate the workings of the New York divorce courts.[8] But the amount done was very small in relation to the total need that had been pinpointed during the curriculum discussions, or to what might have been done if there had been a different order of priorities. Talking about research was almost as popular as doing it. The library and the armchair were still more attractive than the market place and the courts. The postgraduate programme, developed in this period under the chairmanship of Edwin Patterson, was also to a high degree library-bound.[9] This was, perhaps, the area in which a breakthrough would have been relatively easy to accomplish. Columbia in this phase had what was probably the most highly regarded and vigorous graduate programme in the country and the law school attracted a number of very promising young scholars who were sympathetic to the idea of interdisciplinary cooperation. The programme paid little more than lip service to the idea, perhaps because insistence on high standards inhibited experiment at graduate level.

During the late 1930s a strong sense of disillusion set in at Columbia and elsewhere. It is barely disguised in Dean Smith's reports during the period 1935-9. 'Nowadays' wrote Brainerd Currie, 'the phrases "functional approach" and "integration of non-legal materials" are, to a number of law teachers, trite symbols of frustration.'[10] In a sober appraisal of the Columbia experiment Currie examined at length how far the disillusion was justified and what was behind the relative failure of the integration movement. His basic conclusion is that substantial advances did result, but that:

... in the light of twenty-five years of experience, the Columbia studies are not – at least, not yet – to be classed as epoch-making. A turning-point there was, but the new era has not arrived. . . . The main stream of legal education flows on much as before. The typical casebook, although its banner now reads 'Cases and Materials', is essentially like its predecessors. There are still courses in Contracts, Torts, Property, and Trusts, retaining their old names and shapes; and even in those courses which have been revamped and re-named the appellate decision is the focus of study still. Law and the social sciences remain unintegrated.[11]

It is hard to disagree with this judgment or with the diagnosis: of the many reasons for failure, Currie found the principal one to be that 'the movement faltered under the staggering weight of the problems of execution it entailed'.[12] This is in accord with one of the central themes of the present study, *viz.* that realism is hard work.[13] Making due allowance for other factors, such as shortage of funds, the lure of the New Deal and the reaction against the realism of the early 1930s, one must conclude that a major reason for the disappointing outcome of 'the Columbia experiment' was a failure to perceive with sufficient clarity that extensive research was a precondition of the kind of educational reform that was being tried. In so far as there was perception of need, it was not backed by the will to do enough about it. The break with tradition was not sharp enough and the promise of a new era turned sour.

THE SCIENTISTS

After they left Columbia all five of the Scientists tried to practise what they preached by embarking on empirical research. The Johns Hopkins Institute for the Study of Law, which Oliphant, Marshall and Yntema joined, can be viewed as an attempt to put into practice the theories of Walter Wheeler Cook.[14] The institute was founded in June 1928, shortly after the deanship crisis at Columbia, with Cook as Director. Cook's plans had been maturing for some time and he was fortunate to have been able to recruit such a talented team so simply. Johns Hopkins University had an established tradition of research in applied science and Cook's plans for an institution devoted to the scientific study of law in action fitted well with this tradition. The institute was autonomous and was given a free hand to develop its own work.

The first statements about the programme of the institute contained few surprises. Its professed philosophy rested on three familiar ideas: 'scientific method', 'social engineering' and 'community of scholars'. The principal function was to be research, training being ancillary and directly related to the major objectives of the institute. The clearest statement of education aims was expressed in negative terms: 'It seems clear that the Institute must not now (and, so far as we can now see, should never) commit itself to maintaining an orthodox professional school for training of practitioners.'[15]

The rationale for the first programme of research states the gist of the institute's philosophy:

In general, it is appropriate that the selection of research projects should be influenced by considerations of (a) the availability of personnel, (b) the social significance of subject-matter, and (c) the scientific significance of methods and techniques.

The relevance of the availability of personnel is obvious, although it may be worth emphasizing that scarcity of competent personnel will more frequently be a limiting factor than might at first thought be supposed. The personnel problem seems likely to be one of the major problems of the Institute.

The relevance of the social significance of subject matter is equally obvious, when it is remembered that the Institute is vitally interested in the study of the human effects of law. Any final judgment concerning the most promising areas of study from this point of view may well await further investigation, but even at the present confidence may be placed in the current, widespread, persistent and informed opinion that research is needed in such matters as the cost and delay of litigation, the defects in legislative policies and practices, the defective recruiting and discipline of the bar, the cultural lag of social institutions including law, and the 'prevention of disease' in our social relationships.

The relevance of the scientific significance of methods and techniques is immediately apparent, once it is recognized that judgments on social and legal questions should rest, as far as reasonably may be, upon objective data rather than upon unanalyzed subjective attitudes. Clearly, there should be a constant effort: to keep the work of the Institute in close contact with the actual affairs of life; to gather and to use greater and greater quantities of objective data which are comparable and dependable; to make actual experiments in the use of different devices in social control wherever possible; and generally to seek continuously to improve the existing methods and techniques used in research. Necessarily, fruitful research in this field will seek to integrate the scholarship of law with that of allied fields.[16]

The first programme listed an impressive collection of projects under five heads: (a) projects lending themselves readily to realistic treatment and to keeping close to practical affairs; (b) projects looking towards making available greater quantities of dependable comparable data; (c) projects involving the use of the experimental approach; (d) projects looking toward the improvement of existing techniques; and (e) projects looking toward a greater integration of law with the other social sciences.[17]

By no means all of this programme was in fact implemented. During 1928–9, whilst plans were still being worked out, the work of the institute reflected the interests of individuals. The four senior members concentrated for the most part on completing work they had begun before they had joined the institute. An official account of the institute's plans for 1928–9[18] states that Cook intended to develop his ideas on 'problems of method in the study of law and other social sciences' and to continue the work which culminated in his well known *The Logical and Legal Bases of the Conflict of Laws*.[19] Marshall, in addition to his own work on 'the structure of the economic order', was to collaborate with Oliphant on legal and economic problems of business management. Oliphant was also to study 'legal and economic problems in the social control of marketing' and Yntema planned to investigate 'the development of remedies in the common law'. All of these studies were broadly conceived, but not radically so, and the majority resulted in competent and interesting publications.[20] For the most part they involved little or no field work.

There was a radical change in the next phase. Empirical work was begun on a large scale when the institute concentrated most of its resources in the area of judicial administration. An ambitious series of linked studies of the operation of the courts in Maryland, Ohio and New York was undertaken. Particular emphasis was placed on the improvement of the systems of judicial statistics in these states, and there were numerous subprojects connected with such matters as divorce litigation in Ohio (Marshall), delay in court in New York (Oliphant), and detailed analysis of the work of selected courts.[21]

The early promotional literature of the institute and those parts of the first programme that were in fact implemented suggest a distinct bias towards the contemporary and the utilitarian. This was probably due very largely to the nature of the financing of the institute. It was dependent on continuing support from an uncomfortably large number of sources rather than from university funds or from a major foundation. Law firms and professional organizations were major contributors; some of the projects were sponsored by official agencies. Inevitably this led to pressure to emphasize the immediate practical utility of the institute's work and to seek quick returns. Much more serious, however, was the fact that the institute was completely defenceless against the effects of the Great Crash and the Depression. Before the completion of even the first series of projects, which represented a fraction of the first programme, funds ran out and the institute was forced to close.[22]

Two of the 'Scientists' did not join Cook's team at Johns Hopkins: William O. Douglas, after resigning in protest at the manner of Smith's appointment as Dean, moved directly to Yale. Underhill Moore stayed on at Columbia for a further year, emulating Achilles in his tent, until he too was wooed to New Haven.[23] At this time the Yale Law School was moving in a direction similar to Columbia's although the highly individualistic approach of Yale law professors did not give so much scope for coordinated planning and teamwork. In 1927 the appointment of Robert Maynard Hutchins as Dean, at the age of twenty-eight, marked the start of a period of renewed efforts to integrate law and the social sciences. In 1929 a substantial endowment was raised, largely through the efforts of Hutchins, for the establishment of an Institute of Human Relations with the aim of bringing together scholars of several disciplines 'to correlate knowledge of the mind and body and of individual and group conduct and to study further the interrelations of the many factors influencing human actions'.[24] Members of the law school played a particularly prominent part in the work of the institute in this period and it was under its auspices that the most important empirical research projects relating to law were conducted. Douglas collaborated with a sociologist, Dorothy Thomas, and others to study the causes of business failures in the District of New Jersey;[25] Charles E. Clark and others investigated judicial administration in Connecticut;[26] and Dean Hutchins explored the bearings of psychology on the law of evidence.[27] Of the 'Scientists' at Yale, Underhill Moore showed the greatest stamina. For nearly twenty years, until his retirement in 1947, he soldiered on, resolutely, grappling with the problem of applying scientific method to the empirical study of law. He first sought to develop methods for predicting judicial decisions through intensive studies of certain banking situations (debiting of direct discounts and orders to stop payment of cheques);[28] later, in a search for greater precision and objectivity, he embarked on a protracted and laborious investigation of the effects of police notices on the parking behaviour of drivers in New Haven.[29]

Moore's parking studies were considered by many to be the *reductio ad absurdum* of 'scientism' and they were the target of a great deal of unsympathetic criticism and even ridicule. Today this project and the Johns Hopkins venture are sometimes referred to as examples of 'naive realism' and are written off as failures.[30] This judgment has not been confined to unsympathetic critics of realism. For instance, Karl Llewellyn, who had collaborated closely with the 'Scientists' up to 1928, was sharply critical of them in an address in 1956:

Hopkins and Yale – was it about 1929? – got huge grants and with drums and trumpets put the grants into circulation. I doubt whether in all of the quest for social science there has ever been such hastily considered, ill-planned, mal-prepared large-scale so-called research as was perpetrated by Cook and Oliphant at Hopkins. But it was at Yale that the nadir of idiocy was achieved when Underhill Moore 'tested out' whether law has mystical operation by an elaborate observation, metering and statisticking of the noneffect on the parking practices of New Haveners of a change in the official regulations which he had arranged to keep carefully from coming to the knowledge of any trafficker.

The Hopkins ebullition and its partial counterparts at Yale had a single notable effect. For twenty-five years, they pretty thoroughly choked off foundation interest in such research in law as quested beyond doctrine.[31]

The principal reason for these abberations, in Llewellyn's view, was that too few academic lawyers had been interested enough to perform the role of a critical audience for the 'Scientists', restraining overenthusiasm and debunking half-baked ideas. 'Only in *old* research fields can technicians be trusted on their own.'[32] The result was that the 'Scientists' allowed themselves to become victims of their own fads:

Take Moore first: he fadded into pure behaviorism in regard to the effects of men's behaviour on appellate decision. His base-approach, on this, sounds almost insane and was certainly perverse. Moore was so set against taking the impact of words of authority as being in themselves solely determinative that he insisted on studying behaviour without reference to the words and configuration of pre-existing rules of law at all, and even without reference to whether any knowledge of the supposedly relevant behaviour was brought home to the judges whose deciding was under inquiry; and he insisted on further assuming that these unknown patterns or semi-patterns or non-patterns of often obscurely technical lay-behavior could have significantly measurable and provable determinative impact on the appellate decisions.

As for Oliphant, with Marshall's help he counted and counted among the court records of Baltimore and of Ohio. I read all the results, but I never dug out what most of the counting was good for. Some things were revealed about time-lapse in litigation and the like, for instance, which I think a few intelligent newspaper reporters could have developed with about equal significance and adequacy at an outlay of ten or five per cent or less of the time and money spent. Certainly among the major sins were inquiry running wastefully beyond clear hypothesis, unnecessary large-scale work where careful and shrewd sampling would have sufficed, heavy quantifying where it did not pay, and slowness to correct poor leads.

What irritates particularly about the work of both Moore and Oliphant, however, is the failure to build toward theories either of deep basic utility or of availability to large numbers of workers elsewhere who would be laboring unblessed by dollars in the hundred thousands or the tens. Moore's hypothesis would have been basic enough, indeed, if usable; it merely, at least for the next century or so, is silly.[33]

Llewellyn hints at other factors behind his disapproval: there was too much institutional rivalry and no 'sense of a trusteeship of experiment and technique for the general legal public'.[34] Of this both the 'Scientists' and their opponents, for instance at Harvard and Michigan, were equally guilty. Moreover, the desire for quick returns and for instant prestige prompted the sacrifice of pilot projects and cautious advance.

There is some sense in Llewellyn's analysis, but it is at best incomplete and unfair. It makes no allowance for the methodological concerns of Moore, who had in any case anticipated most of Llewellyn's criticisms in his rather ponderous introspection about his research; the purposes of several of Oliphant's studies of the courts in Maryland and Ohio, such as those concerned with improved systems of judicial statistics or delay in court, were either expressly stated or apparent on their face—is it absolutely necessary to spell out the reasons for studying delay in court? Furthermore, it is strange that Llewellyn should have picked out for special praise Charles Clark's studies in judicial administration in Connecticut. These were contemporaneous with the Johns Hopkins studies and concerned with similar, and to some extent overlapping, subject-matter. What was the difference between the studies and whether the alleged superiority of Clark's work was in respect of conception or execution or both is not made clear by Llewellyn.

Llewellyn was normally a balanced, even generous, critic and the strongly emotive language of his criticism is especially surprising in view of his early sympathies.[35] But it is not unrepresentative of a generally hostile attitude to the 'Scientists'. Typically, Moore's work is dismissed as absurd. The Johns Hopkins Institute had many enemies at the time of its collapse and contemporary discussions have a strikingly similar emotional aura. Most subsequent references to the institute *assume* that it was a fiasco, and many imply that it was inevitably doomed to be one. Those studies of judicial administration that were completed have been, for the most part, ignored.[36]

Whatever the motives of their detractors, there is little doubt that the failure of the first efforts of the 'Scientists', if failure it was, must have been convenient for many law teachers. The image of Underhill Moore sitting on a camp stool in Bermuda shorts in the streets of New Haven solemnly counting cars could more easily be made a symbol of the ridiculous and expensive pursuit of trivia by the highly talented. As such it could be a comforting excuse for defensive hilarity by any innumerate law professor, fearful of statistics, or anxious for a more glamorous occupation. Add to this the equally comforting quarter-truth that field work is necessarily expensive and the excuse for staying in the office or library was almost cast-iron for all but the most tender conscience. At first sight a camp stool is less cosy than an armchair. Yet what American legal scholar has been closer to the spirit of scientific enquiry than Moore in his disdain for facile solutions and quick results in preference to the patient but passionate pursuit of the truth?

A thorough and informed post mortem, comparable to Currie's articles on the Columbia experiment, is still awaited.[37] Among the points awaiting clarification are the following: how far can the espousal of 'the scientific analogy' by Cook and Moore be treated as valid in the light of modern developments in the philosophy of science? Were Moore's methodological postulates sound? What were the differences in conception and method between the Johns Hopkins studies in judicial administration and other studies in the area, contemporaneous and subsequent? What are the grounds for maintaining that the Johns Hopkins studies were in some sense inferior? To what extent, if at all, can the 'failure' of these studies, if they were a failure, be attributed to defective basic conceptions and faulty planning as opposed to poor execution and chance factors such as the economic situation and the personalities of the participants? Was the Johns Hopkins 'failure' relative not only to inflated expectations of a quick breakthrough but also to a more sober assessment of what might reasonably have been expected of a pioneering effort? All of these questions are to some extent matters of opinion: nevertheless, it would be instructive to set the detached appraisal of an informed expert armed with the wisdom of hindsight against the impressionistic and heated judgments of the Scientists' contemporaries.

Finally, the 'failure' of these first projects served further to obscure the issues that were at the root of the Columbia crisis. Can a contextual approach to law *teaching* make much progress *before* a great deal of relevant research has been completed? Can this kind of research be satisfactorily combined with professional training or will they, at best, be uneasy companions? In short might there not have been more in the Scientists' case than they were given credit for? Forty years later these questions were still awaiting answers.

THE DIFFUSION OF REALISM

After 1928 the realist movement lost such coherence as it ever had. Not only did the Columbia Prudents and Scientists go off in different directions, but 'realist' ideas became widely diffused and from 1931 realism became the subject of confused and confusing controversy. The Yale Law School is generally regarded as the headquarters of realism after 1928. While it was by no means the only institution at which changes were taking place, it was certainly exceptionally lively. Some of the atmosphere is evoked by Thurman Arnold in his typically free-wheeling autobiography. After describing some of the work of the Institute of Human Relations and Charles Clark's efforts to make procedure 'the centre of the Yale curriculum', he continues:

Needless to say, Yale was an exciting place in the days of the Depression. Harvard represented, to us at least, the conventional attitude toward the law, the traditional forces dividing the law into separate fields and the lack of emphasis on procedure. We at Yale were busy tearing up the old courses and devising new ones that we thought were far better adapted to the realities of judicial institutions. Wesley Sturges was writing his books on credit transactions, which threw together the conventional fields of bills and notes, mortgages, real property, corporate law, and so on. His attention was centered not on legal theory, but on what happened when financial credits were involved. William O. Douglas had abandoned the conventional course on corporate law and was writing on business units, and including the law of corporations, partnerships, bankruptcy, receivership, and so forth, all rolled into one course which gave the students a picture of what happened in corporate enterprise. Walton Hamilton, an economist who had never been graduated from law school, was examining cases that related to the operation of a competitive market place in a free-enterprise society, using materials that might ordinarily come under a course on the antitrust laws, constitutional law, or administrative trade regulations. I was giving a course on the psychological basis for the law with that brilliant professor of psychology at Yale, Edward Robinson. Out of this course came my two books *The Symbols of Government* and *The Folklore of Capitalism*. The conservatives charged that we were not operating a law school, but instead were denizens of a cave of the winds. Today even the Harvard Law School offers courses in psychiatry. I like to think, though I am probably overstating the case, that it all started at Yale.[88]

Of course Arnold was overstating the case, for men like Hutchins, Clark and Moore were building on the work of the pioneer realists. But Yale in the 1930s was a different place from Columbia in the 1920s. There was a greater interest in psychiatry and psychology, more emphasis on procedure and process, a decidedly more political orientation, especially at the time of the New Deal, and less concern for the niceties of scholarship. Whereas Dean Hutchins represented a lofty and idealistic form of liberal humanism, the brash irreverence of men like Arnold, Sturges, Douglas and Rodell was more typical of the 1930s and made the efforts of the pioneer realists look staid by comparison. The rumbustuous iconoclasm of some of their writings, which were often more journalistic than scholarly, helped to give realism in general an exaggerated reputation for nihilism.

While the atmosphere at Yale in this period was undoubtedly stimulating, it was not entirely compatible with the development of an approach to research which required the patient investment of enormous labour with no promise of spectacular returns. Probably more pioneering empirical studies were done at Yale in the 1930s than at any other law school, but the end-product of their enthusiastic efforts was somewhat fragmented. The presence of Underhill Moore served to underline the difficulty of reconciling the ideal of objectivity in science with the quest for insights of immediate practical application. At Yale, as elsewhere, there was a loss of impetus as time went on: Dean Hutchins left in 1929 to become Chancellor of the University of Chicago; the Institute of Human Relations, although initially better endowed than the Johns Hopkins Institute of Law, also suffered badly from the effects of the Depression, and the New Deal seduced two of the most able Yale men, Arnold and Douglas, away from academic life. But more important than these specific events was the loss of the coherence that had characterized the early phases of the realist movement. Of course, some of the sense of disillusion that accompanied the loss of impetus in the middle and late 1930s is attributable to the very fact of success as 'realist' ideas were at least partially assimilated into law school culture and began to be taken for granted.[89] The lack of coherence was also in part a symptom of the times: The 1930s were not uneventful years in American life and some of their brashness, vigour and turmoil is reflected in juristic literature. There is more than a grain of truth in C. K. Allen's suggestion that the jazz age produced a jazz jurisprudence.[40]

5

The Realist Controversy,
1930-1

Up to 1929 the ferment at Yale and Columbia was neither expressed nor interpreted in terms of 'legal realism'. A number of theoretical papers had been published by Hohfeld, Corbin, Cook, Oliphant
and Moore, but most of these dealt with particular topics and only
one or two invited interpretation as a call for a new brand of legal
theory. The developments at Yale, the Columbia curriculum discussions and the deanship crisis, the establishment of the Johns Hopkins
Institute and the Yale Institute of Human Relations, had all attracted attention, at least among academic lawyers, but they had for the
most part developed pragmatically and at a relatively down-to-
earth level. The first general discussion of 'legal realism' as a
distinct form of jurisprudence was a paper by Karl Llewellyn, which
appeared in the *Columbia Law Review* in 1930. Llewellyn had been
a pupil of Corbin, Hohfeld and Cook at Yale and, as a relatively
junior member of the faculty, he had participated in the events at
Columbia between 1924 and 1928. In 1929 Llewellyn was invited to
give a paper on 'Modern Concepts of Law' at a Round Table on
Current Trends in Political and Legal Thought. This was published
in the following year under the title 'A Realistic Jurisprudence—
The Next Step'.[1] Although his own contribution to developments
at Yale and Columbia had been relatively insignificant up to this
time, Llewellyn was particularly well qualified to identify some of
the new trends, to place them in the context of their intellectual
history, and to suggest possible lines for future development. In
this first round of the realist debate he missed the opportunity.
Instead he wrote a loosely organized paper which starts with the
rejection of a general definition of 'law', explores perceptively some

of Pound's limitations as a theorist, mixes in some quasi-Hohfeldian ideas about remedies and rules, and ends with a plea for an inter-disciplinary approach to legal research, with human behaviour as an important focus. A *pot pourri* of interesting ideas, some of them as yet only half formed, this paper represented a definite step in Llewellyn's development as a theorist, but it is not to be recom-mended to someone who seeks a coherent introduction to realism. Historically its chief significance is that it gave currency to 'legal realism' as a label of somewhat indeterminate reference. In his paper Llewellyn had been careful not to make rash generalizations about the ideas of others; subsequent commentators did not always follow his example.

Although Llewellyn's paper contained some controversial state-ments and had been quite critical of him, Roscoe Pound wrote a warm letter of congratulations. Llewellyn was delighted and may even for a time have been under the impression that Pound looked on him with special favour. If this is so, he was sharply disillusioned in the following year, when 'realism' became the focal point of a bitter and protracted controversy.

In 1930 Llewellyn's *The Bramble Bush* and Frank's *Law and the Modern Mind* were published in quick succession. Both books were eminently readable, both were provocative, in time both proved to be the least balanced and the most widely read works of their respective authors, prompting the thought that in jurisprudence it pays to strike extreme postures if one wishes to attract attention or make money. Of the two, *Law and the Modern Mind* was the more extreme and attracted the greater attention. Frank, who was an alumnus of the University of Chicago Law School, was at that time practising at the New York bar and he lacked the scholarly inhibitions which, at least until that date, had restrained even the most radical jurists at Columbia and Yale.[2] He had, moreover, a significantly different orientation from most academic lawyers, as is evidenced especially by his greater interest in the fact-finding processes of lower courts than in the resolution of points of law by upper courts, a concern which still dominated the attention of library-bound academics.[3] *Law and the Modern Mind* is a polemic, written in the style of a well read journalist: with bold overstate-ment and engaging wit Frank attacked on a broad front and in a sweeping fashion 'the basic myth of legal certainty'. While his most stinging barbs were directed against legal reactionaries, represented by Joseph Beale of Harvard,[4] Frank was sufficiently damning of revisionists like Pound[5] and Cardozo[6] to invite a response from within the citadels of sociological jurisprudence. Only Holmes, 'the completely adult jurist', was accepted as a model.[7] This dual challenge to the values of the Harvard Law School as exemplified by Beale, and to moderate sociological jurisprudence, not surprisingly provoked a response from Roscoe Pound, who was the Dean of the former and the doyen of the latter.

The March 1931 number of the *Harvard Law Review* celebrated the ninetieth birthday of Mr Justice Holmes. Pound's contribution was an article entitled 'The Call for a Realist Jurisprudence';[8] it comes between some conventional eulogies and some scholarly examinations of different phases of the Justice's work. This halfway position is not inappropriate, for the article is scholarly in conception but unscholarly in execution. As Pound later admitted, it was written in haste at a time when he was burdened with administrative duties, not least his work as a member of the National Commission on Law Observance and Enforcement.[9] The gist can be summarized in four propositions: there is a new school of young law teachers who are calling for a realist jurisprudence; we should try to understand them sympathetically; there is a widespread tendency among members of the school to make certain elementary errors; a relativist realist jurisprudence should follow my seven-point programme. The views attributed to this school are convincingly shown to be erroneous or exaggerated, but no subscriber to these views is mentioned by name; the seven point programme is a typical Poundian hotch-pot—a list of quite sensible, but only vaguely related suggestions.[10]

Pound repeatedly emphasized that his intentions were not polemical: 'It is much more important to understand than to criticize',[11] he wrote, and in a letter to Llewellyn he congratulated himself on his long record of abstention from polemical jurisprudence.[12] Nevertheless the core of the article consists of sweeping criticism of a number of ideas that he attributed to juristic realism.[13] In the circumstances it is hardly surprising that he provoked a strong reaction.

Since Frank's *Law and the Modern Mind* and Llewellyn's *Bramble Bush* and 'A Realistic Jurisprudence—The Next Step' had been published in the previous year, the authors naturally interpreted Pound's article as a covert attack on them and a particularly unjust one. Llewellyn was keenly disappointed, because of Pound's earlier encouragement.

When Pound's article 'The Call for a Realist Jurisprudence' appeared in the March Harvard Law Review, Jerome Frank and I were distressed. We felt that Pound was mistaken as to the views of the 'realists' and as to their significance for his own thinking. We felt that his criticisms were in the main well taken, if anyone held the views criticised; but we knew of hardly anyone whom one might fairly suspect of holding any of the views criticised. And as to every pertinent criticism we thought we recalled one or more 'realists' who had anticipated Pound in print. We thought that a canvass of the literature and the placing of the results of such a canvass, point by point, against Pound's article, would greatly clarify the situation.[14]

At first they encountered resistance to their plan. The *Harvard Law Review* refused to grant them space for a reply until pressure was brought to bear on the Editor by members of the Harvard faculty, including Pound himself.[15] Pound, however, when challenged to name individual realists, vaguely mentioned Bingham and Lorenzen, exonerated Charles E. Clark and then retreated behind the excuse of pressure of work.[16] Llewellyn and Frank had to compile their own list of possible 'realists'. It will be seen later that this above all else has been a source of confusion about realism. For this reason the basis for the list needs to be considered in some detail.

WHO WERE THE REALISTS?

Criteria for membership of a group of thinkers may be of different kinds: most commonly the criterion takes the form of acceptance of one or more propositions; for example, 'a positivist is one who accepts that there is no necessary connection between law and morals'.[17] Adherence to one or more particular propositions may be a necessary condition of membership of a group or school, or a sufficient condition, or both, or neither. There are, of course, other kinds of criteria. A group of thinkers may, for example, be characterized by their acceptance of the intellectual leadership of a particular person (e.g. Thomists) or by their historical or geographical relationship (e.g. the Vienna Circle or the Bloomsbury Group), although it is unlikely that the criteria of identification of any group of thinkers would entirely exclude a reference to their acceptance or rejection of certain ideas. Thinkers and ideas tend to resist neat classification, with the result that the historian of thought, and others who wish to make such classifications, are faced with a recurring dilemma: insistence on precise criteria of membership of a group may result in the exclusion of individuals who may fruitfully be considered in relation to members of the group; lack of such precision is a potent source of error.

That Llewellyn was well aware of these difficulties is shown by his repeated denial that there was a school of realists and by his warnings about the dangers of making generalizations about the amorphous collection of trends that he characterized as a 'movement'.[18]

The term 'realism' itself has been of very limited assistance in identifying 'realists'. Outside the sphere of jurisprudence the word has several usages. Realism in art is not necessarily the same as realism in philosophy; a realist may be contrasted with a romantic, with a nominalist or with an idealist; to philosophers the question 'What is reality?' is as perplexing as the question 'What is truth?' In jurisprudence the term 'legal realism' has also been controversial, but the literature supports Rumble's conclusion that 'logomachy over "legal realism" is a cul-de-sac'.[19] Llewellyn used the term fairly consistently, if not very precisely. Although he did not provide a complete definition, the following formulation would seem to be consistent with his normal usage: 'A realist is one who, no matter what his ideological or philosophical views, believes that it is important regularly to focus attention on the law in action at any given time and to try to describe as honestly and clearly as possible what is to be seen.'

Several points about this definition should be noted. First, it approximates to common-sense 'realism', in the sense of 'actual recording of things as they are', and has no necessary connection with realism in the philosophical sense.[20] Secondly, the belief incorporated in the definition is hardly a matter for sharp controversy. Few jurists are likely to *believe* otherwise than that realistic observation of the law in action is a valid and valuable activity, although not all jurists will *act* on this belief.[21] Thirdly, 'realism' is not confined to study of judicial processes, but 'it applies to anything'.[22] Fourthly, the definition, taken by itself, is vague and begs a lot of questions, some of which are or might be controversial. What is encompassed within the concept of 'the law in action' (or 'the institution of law')? To what extent can description be detached from the observer's desires or values? How important for what purposes is description of what? For any given purpose, what is the most appropriate method for arriving at an adequate description? And so on. Llewellyn's usage of 'realism' was deliberately divorced from his own personal views on such issues and from the views of other members of the American realist movement. Accordingly, the term 'realism', so defined, is as uninformative as it is uncontroversial and it is a rather tenuous basis for classifying a group of thinkers, since few lawyers are not 'realists' in this sense. In interpreting the American realist movement, belief in 'realism' in the broad sense might be a necessary, but could hardly be a sufficient, criterion of membership.[23]

In *Some Realism about Realism*, Llewellyn and Frank were obliged to identify as realists a number of named individuals in order to test out the validity of Pound's allegations about the so-called 'realist school'. Although some commentators have compiled their own lists,[24] Llewellyn's 'sample' of twenty, which is set out here, is the one most commonly used as a means of identifying 'the realists' by those who have bothered to be specific.

The criteria employed by Llewellyn and Frank were somewhat artificial. They took as their starting point certain attributes mentioned by Pound. The principal ones were as follows: (i) Younger teachers of law;[25] (ii) insistence 'on beginning with an objectively scientific gathering of facts'; (iii) interest in the psychology of rationalization; (iv) 'looking at precepts and doctrines and institutions with reference to how they work and fail to work and why'; (v) open recognition of the non-rational elements in judicial behaviour.[26] 'If these were the attributes of the "new realists", we knew who they were.'[27] But it was by no means clear who held the views attacked by Pound. Accordingly the net was cast wider and three further criteria were employed in choosing 'the sample': '(i) they must include the leading figures in the new ferment; (ii) in order that we may turn up most passages supporting the items we challenge, the men chosen must include all who are reputed to have taken extreme positions; (iii) a wide range of views and positions must be included.'[28]

These criteria may have been appropriate for the debate with Pound, but they are seriously inadequate as a basis for interpreting realism as a form of legal theory or as an historical phenomenon. If realism is to be treated analytically, it is artificial to restrict the

LLEWELLYN'S 'SAMPLE' OF REALISTS

Name	Date of Birth	Law degree(s) from	Occupation in 1930–1
1. W. Bingham	1878	University of Chicago	Professor of Law, Stanford
2. C. E. Clark	1889	Yale	Dean, Yale Law School
3. W. W. Cook	1873	Columbia (LL.M.)	Johns Hopkins Institute
4. A. L. Corbin	1874	Yale	Professor of Law, Yale
5. W. O. Douglas	1898	Columbia	Professor of Law, Yale
6. J. Francis	1890	University of Chicago (J.D.), Yale (J.S.D.)	Professor of Law, Oklahoma 1921–8
7. J. Frank	1889	University of Chicago	Practising Attorney, N.Y.
8. L. Green	1888	LL.B. (Texas), Hon. M.A. (Yale)	Dean, Northwestern University Law School
9. J. C. Hutcheson	1879	Texas	1931. Judge of USCA Fifth Circuit
10. S. Klaus	Circa 1900	Columbia	Practising Attorney, New York City*
11. K. N. Llewellyn	1893	Yale	Professor of Law, Columbia
12. E. G. Lorenzen	1876	Cornell, Göttingen	Professor of Law, Yale
13. W. U. Moore	1879	Columbia	Professor of Law, Yale
14. H. Oliphant	1884	University of Chicago	Johns Hopkins Institute
15. E. W. Patterson	1889	Harvard (LL.B. S.J.D.)	Professor of Law, Columbia
16. T. R. Powell	1880	LL.B. (Harvard)	Professor of Law, Harvard†
17. M. Radin	1880	LL.B. (N.Y.U.) Ph.D. (Columbia)	Professor of Law, University of California (Berkeley)
18. W. A. Sturges	1893	LL.B. (Columbia) J.D. (Yale)	Professor of Law, Yale
19. L. A. Tulin	1901	LL.B. (Yale)	Associate Professor of Law, Columbia
20. H. E. Yntema	1891	B.A. (Oxford) S.J.D. (Harvard)	Johns Hopkins Institute

* Taught at Columbia until 1928. † Taught at Columbia 1911–25.

term to people who happened to be younger law teachers in 1931 : Holmes, Gray, Cardozo and Pound himself were, in some respects, closer to the leaders of the ferment than were several of the people included in the sample.[29] Furthermore, it is rather quaint to seek for shared characteristics among a group deliberately selected for its diversity.

There are other features about the selection of the sample which deserve comment. The institutional connections of those included are of interest. Only Powell and Patterson could be called Harvard men; few people would regard them as the leaders of the ferment.[30] Sixteen out of the twenty had at that time close connections with either Yale or Columbia, or in some cases with both. Of the four exceptions, only Frank and Bingham could be said to have made significant contributions.[31] Moreover, several notable omissions from Llewellyn's list were also connected with Columbia or Yale.[32] The same is true of a high proportion of individuals who came into prominence later and who have been identified as 'realists' by one or more commentators.[33] Thus, for example, in Llewellyn's later paper, 'On Reading and Using the Newer Jurisprudence' (1940), works by several people not on the original list are considered. Accordingly we must conclude that Llewellyn's sample of realists cannot today provide a satisfactory basis for either an historical or an analytical treatment of American legal realism.

In 1931 Frank and Llewellyn circulated a questionnaire to the individuals on the list. All those who replied agreed that if Pound had intended to refer to them he had badly misrepresented their ideas. One or two doubted the wisdom of a public response. Several expressed surprise at being labelled 'realists' and others disclaimed membership of a 'school'. From the replies it was quite clear that Frank and Llewellyn had no mandate to act as spokesmen for anyone but themselves.[34] Undeterred, they set to work to analyse a selection of the writings of the persons on their list. In the end Llewellyn did most of the work, including the drafting of the article and, on Frank's insistence, it was published under his name alone.[35]

The reply to Pound appeared in the June number of the *Harvard Law Review* under the title 'Some Realism about Realism'. In form it was a model for disciplined polemics. In Part One Pound's article was treated on the analogy of an indictment. His criticisms of 'the realist school' were broken down into thirteen specific charges and a representative selection of the published writings of each of the twenty people on the list was combed for evidence that they held the views attributed to them.[36] The sole question considered was whether the writers in question in fact held certain views; the question whether such views were erroneous or misguided was not put in issue. In all, approximately a hundred published pieces were canvassed. The findings were convincing:

Of eleven points on which evidence in support could be diagnosed and counted, we find such evidence as to seven – but how much? We can adduce some support for *one* point from *three of our twenty men,* for each of four further points from two of our twenty, for each of two further points from one of our twenty. *One of our twenty men* offers some support *for three of the eleven points,* three offer some support each for two of the eleven points, four offer some support each for one point. *In no instance is the support offered strong, unambiguous, or unqualified,* even on the printed record.[37]

What this amounted to was that nearly all of Pound's general accusations against 'the realist school' were completely unwarranted; at most a few individuals in a few passages, for the most part unrepresentative, had made vulnerable remarks. Far from understanding the 'school', Pound had badly misrepresented it.

Llewellyn's analysis showed that Pound had been guilty of two unscholarly practices. First, he had committed an elementary fallacy:

A believes a and is a member of group R

B believes b and is a member of group R

∴ all members of group R believe a and b.

Secondly, by failing to identify any particular individuals as realists, let alone specific passages in which they had committed the alleged errors, he had failed to produce evidence in support of his allegations and had made disciplined discussion of them difficult, if not impossible. Llewellyn's exposure of Pound was so effective that it is disappointing that some of Pound's accusations continued to be levelled against 'the realists' and that the pernicious practice of indeterminate attribution of views also continued.

Having shown convincingly what realism was not, Llewellyn proceeded to try to analyze what, if anything, it was. Part Two of the article is an inquiry into the extent to which it is possible to generalize about realism. Llewellyn was emphatic that there was no school or group of realists, sharing a single credo or pursuing a single programme. Rather there was an amorphous movement[38] of individuals who shared some common points of departure, but who were working independently in different specialized fields and with a variety of orientations. Realism was, at this stage, a 'mass of trends in legal work and thinking'.[39] Apart from a copiously documented survey of some of these trends, the most striking feature of Part Two is the famous passage in which he listed nine 'points of departure' common to the movement:

The common points of departure are several.

(1) The conception of law in flux, of moving law, and of judicial creation of law.

(2) The conception of law as a means to social ends and not as an end in itself; so that any part needs constantly to be examined for its purpose, and for its effect, and to be judged in the light of both and of their relation to each other.

(3) The conception of society in flux, and in flux typically faster than the law, so that the probability is always given that any portion of law needs reëxamination to determine how far it fits the society it purports to serve.

(4) The *temporary* divorce of Is and Ought for purposes of study. By this I mean that whereas value judgments must always be appealed to in order to set objectives for inquiry, yet during the inquiry itself into what Is, the observation, the description, and the establishment of relations between the things described are to remain *as largely as possible* uncontaminated by the desires of the observer or by what he wishes might be or thinks ought (ethically) to be. . . .

(5) Distrust of traditional legal rules and concepts insofar as they purport to *describe* what either courts or people are actually doing. Hence the constant emphasis on rules as 'generalized predictions of what courts will do.' This is much more widespread as yet than its counterpart: the careful severance of rules *for* doing (precepts) from rules *of* doing (practices).

(6) Hand in hand with this distrust of traditional rules (on the descriptive side) goes a distrust of the theory that traditional prescriptive rule-formulations are *the* heavily operative factor in producing court decisions. This involves the tentative exploration of the theory of rationalization for what light it can give in the study of opinions. It will be noted that 'distrust' in this and the preceding point is not at all equivalent to 'negation in any given instance.'

(7) The belief in the worthwhileness of grouping cases and legal situations into narrower categories than has been the practice in the past. This is connected with the distrust of verbally simple rules – which so often cover dissimilar and non-simple fact situations (dissimilarity being tested partly by the way cases come out, and partly by the observer's judgment as to how they ought to come out; but a realist tries to indicate explicitly which criterion he is applying in any particular instance).

(8) An insistence on evaluation of any part of law in terms of its effects, and an insistence on the worthwhileness of trying to find these effects.

(9) Insistence on *sustained and programmatic attack* on the problems of law along any of these lines. . . .[40]

In the chapters which follow the meaning and significance of each of these propositions should become clear. It should also become apparent that whereas Part One of 'Some Realism about Realism' is exceptionally effective in showing what twenty named jurists did not believe, Part Two is less satisfactory as an account of what they did believe and why. Its principal defect is that Llewellyn, somewhat uncharacteristically, attempted to analyse the ideas of a rather variegated selection of people without reference to the relevant historical background, the institutional context, or the specific issues that had agitated them. Neither Pound's paper nor Llewellyn's reply gives any indication of the significance of the Columbia curriculum discussions; even more surprisingly the split between the Scientists and the Prudents is glossed over. Ironically, despite Llewellyn's insistence that there was no 'school' of realists, his use of the term 'realism' and the debate with Pound helped to establish the idea of a new unitary -ism in jurisprudence, shortly after the realist movement had split in two and had lost such coherence as it ever had.

Of all legal subjects jurisprudence is most susceptible to controversy: juristic controversies are prone to be inconclusive and unsatisfactory; of juristic controversies that surrounding realism has had more than its share of slovenly scholarship, silly misunderstandings and jejune polemics. In 1931 public discussion of 'realism' got off to a bad start from which it never fully recovered. Whereas Part Two of 'Some Realism about Realism' has often been treated as the basic text for interpreting the realist movement, the lessons of Part One were not always taken to heart. This was doubly unfortunate. Some of Pound's accusations continued to be levelled against 'the realists' and the unscholarly practices of indeterminate attribution of views and of unfounded generalizations about realism continued. The following are some examples of such statements:

'The realist cosmos is centred on the judge. Law is what the judges decide.'[41]
'The realists . . . assert that all that is ever needed is to examine what judges do, rather than what they say they do.'[42]

'Realists . . . share the view that law consists of the pronouncement of the courts.'[43]
'[The realists support] the view that a judge can decide a case as he pleases.'[44]
'There is a more or less complete skepticism as to the systematic character of official action as a quality of the legal order . . .'.[45]
'In this school, there is recognition only of the factual reality and a complete disregard for the normative content of all law.'[46]
'The attempts of the realists to deal with legal science as if it were identical with natural science was bound [in the view of Kantorowicz] to fail. . . . The realists confused explanation with justification.'[47]
Some realists (the rule-skeptics) believe that 'talk of rules is a myth'.[48]
Many of the realists insist that the rational element in law is an illusion.'[49]
And the realists, by their own preference, bypassed the ought of law as 'irrelevant to legal science'.[50]

So many views have been loosely attributed to 'realism', so many people have at one time or another been labelled 'realists' that it would be laborious, tedious and almost certainly unrewarding to attempt a comprehensive analysis of who believed what. However, Karl Llewellyn is the one jurist who accepted the title 'realist' without reservations and, in the course of considering his works, it will become apparent that none of the views quoted above ever represented his position and that several are almost the exact contraries of what he believed. It should also be clear that whether or not it is possible to point to passages in the writings of others which lend support to such interpretations, by and large the statements quoted above give a seriously misleading picture of the realist movement.

It is not difficult to show that Llewellyn and some of his contemporaries have often been misunderstood and misrepresented. It is not easy to explain why this should be so. A partial explanation is to be found in the unsatisfactory nature of the first exchange between Pound and Llewellyn. Failure to identify who were 'the realists' has been the most fruitful source of error. But other factors contributed to the confusion: the principal defect of most interpretations of the realist movement, including those of Llewellyn and Pound, has been that they represent attempts to deal with the ideas of 'the realists' analytically without reference to their historical context. To make matters worse the timing of the first round of 'the realist controversy' has sometimes been ignored. This occurred in 1931, *after* the realist movement, as an historical phenomenon, had started to disintegrate, but relatively early in the juristic careers of the two individuals who are most often treated as the two leading realists, Llewellyn and Frank. It is quite misleading to treat the writings of these two jurists up to 1931 as representative of their work as a whole. Similarly, some of the more controversial writings that have been sometimes, but not always, associated with 'realism', such as Thurman Arnold's *The Folklore of Capitalism*, Rodell's *Woe unto You, Lawyers*, Robinson's *Law and the Lawyers*, and the writings of Lasswell and McDougal, were published after 1931 and really belong to a new, or even a post-realist, phase marked by a whole range of new concerns and influences. In discussing 'realism' it is of crucial importance not only to identify who is being categorized as a realist but also what period is under consideration.

To conclude: the main thesis of this essay has been that it is meaningful to treat 'The realist movement' up to 1928 as a discrete phenomenon, but thereafter the activities and ideas associated with 'realism' became too diffused and diversified to warrant a single label. The unifying element was the attempt to work out an alternative to the 'orthodox' approach to legal education and legal research that was symbolized by the popular images of Harvard and of Langdell. But the ideas of even the six realists that have been treated here as key figures up to 1931, Corbin, Hohfeld, Cook, Moore, Oliphant and Llewellyn, are too diverse for worthwhile treatment under a single '-ism'. Add Frank, and generalization is made even harder. Add Green or Arnold or Douglas or Hutchins, to say nothing of Lasswell and McDougal, and almost any generalization of substance is liable to be dangerously misleading, if not downright inaccurate. In short, it is safer to treat the realist movement as an historical phenomenon than to treat 'realism' analytically as a kind of legal theory. Yet members of the movement did contribute much of significance to jurisprudence. In this respect there is no alternative to the detailed study of the contributions of particular individuals. In my judgment of all those who have at some time or other been labelled 'realists', Karl Llewellyn is the one with the best claim to be treated as a major jurist in his own right. Part Two of this book can be read as a case study of realism, in that an attempt will be made to explore the relationship between Llewellyn's major works (especially *The Cheyenne Way, The*

Uniform Commercial Code and *The Common Law Tradition*) and the ideas that he associated with 'realism'. But to see Llewellyn's works solely in these terms would be oversimple; for, as has already been stressed, 'realism' is too uninformative and incomplete a label by which to characterize the work of any jurist.

PART TWO

The Life and Work of Karl Llewellyn: A Case Study

6

The Man

CURRICULUM VITAE[1]

Karl Nickerson Llewellyn was born at Seattle, Washington on 22 May 1893. His father, William Henry Llewellyn, was a first generation American of Welsh ancestry, as his name suggests. His mother, whose maiden name was Janet George, came from a New England family which claimed descent from Elder Brewster of the Mayflower and which had settled in Oregon. Contrary to popular belief, Karl Llewellyn was not of German descent on either side. The name Karl, it is said, was suggested to his parents by a character in *The Student Prince*.

Llewellyn's parents had contrasting personalities. William Llewellyn was an easy-going, perennially optimistic businessman of varying fortunes. There were times when he could claim to be wealthy, but he was more than once in serious financial difficulties. Karl maintained affectionate relations with his father, who was by all accounts an engaging person, but their relationship does not seem to have been very intimate. Karl, who was fond of comparing people he liked to trees, categorized his father as 'a cherry tree type', beautiful but not very solid.[2] It seems that Karl's mother was the more dominating character and exerted a greater influence on him. Janet Llewellyn married young. Her formal education did not match her intelligence. Her strict puritan upbringing, her energy and her brains made her a formidable crusader on a number of fronts. Described by her son as 'conservatively acting, radically thinking',[3] she was an ardent evangelical congregationalist, a Daughter of the American Revolution, and a stalwart feminist. According to one story she patrolled the docks of Brooklyn in order to obstruct the prostitutes;[4] as a boy Karl was made to march in parades on behalf of suffragettes and against the evils of drink. Those who knew both Karl and his mother maintain that he took after her in respect of his

brains, his evangelical ardour, his religious concern, and more submerged, a strong, sometimes crippling, puritan conscience.

Thus Llewellyn's background was protestant, with a tradition of
militant non-conformism on his mother's side. He tended to be
acutely conscious of being different from other people and he associated this with his non-conformist ancestry:

> Queerness of view and action seems to be in my blood. My great-grand-
> mother in her eightieth year became a Seventh Day Adventist, and every
> Sunday, seated in blazing sunlight in her parlor window, jaw set and
> knitting needles flying, rebuked the unenlightened as they passed to
> church. My grandfather lent help and countenance to the then looked down
> upon Salvation Army, and was a woman suffragist in the 'seventies. My
> mother reads Ellen Key, works for birth control, votes for Debs, and
> distributed peace leaflets at the Democratic convention in New York.
> Through college I conformed so little that I did not discover until after
> graduation what a Big Man was; my uncut thatch became a byword in my
> law school days; and the canons of etiquette which I have left unbroken
> include few things but eating with the knife. My views have been, and are,
> as curious as my clothes. With a few more years, and more experience, I
> have gained some respect for most of the accepted ways of action, but little
> respect indeed for most of the accepted ways of thought about such action. [5]

Although few details survive of Llewellyn's religious education as
a child, it is reasonable to infer from the available evidence that he
was treated to heavy doses of hell fire, bible reading, puritan ethics
and anticlericalism. As a schoolboy and at college he was active in
the YMCA and when, in his twenties, he acted as counsellor at a
boys' summer camp in Maine he showed his familiarity with the
Bible by producing Llewellynesque versions of the Old Testament
stories. [6]

At some stage during his adolescence he rebelled against his
religious upbringing and in Germany he at least professed to be an
atheist. From his undergraduate days he moved in an intellectual
milieu in which the ideas of thinkers like Sumner, Freud, Veblen,
Holmes and Dewey challenged any conscious remnants of a Calvin-
istic morality. For all of his adult life Llewellyn was a professed ethical relativist; he was sceptical of all dogma, tolerant in respect of sex
and religious belief, a Democrat in politics, and a fighter for civil
liberties, taking up cudgels for the oppressed and the underdog—
Sacco and Vanzetti, Blacks, American Indians, and litigants in need
of legal aid. In short, in respect of his professed beliefs on matters of

politics and morality he was not untypical of liberal intellectuals of his generation, except that he had little sympathy with socialists or communism. If, as seems probable, a strong puritan conscience and a deep religious need survived from his childhood, on the whole they worked beneath the surface.[7]

While Karl was still a baby, his father went bankrupt after the panic of 1893. Not long afterwards the family moved to Brooklyn, where Karl spent most of his childhood and adolescence and where he went to school. Few details survive concerning his childhood and early education. His time at the Boys' High School in Brooklyn does not appear to have been particularly remarkable, except that, such was his intellectual promise, by the time he was sixteen the school had nothing to offer him academically. He was too young to enter Yale College and his father decided that he would benefit from a period in Germany. Eventually, through a chance conversation between his father and Heinrich Musaus, a German-American resident of Brooklyn, a place was found for Karl in the Realgymnasium at Schwerin in Mecklenburg.[8] Here he spent three happy years, boarding with relatives of Heinrich Musaus and participating fully in the life of the school. Before his arrival he spoke good German and by the time he left he was bilingual as well as fluent in the local dialect, 'Mecklenburger Plattdeutsch'. Later he was to publish a book and several articles on law[9] in German; indeed, two distinguished jurists, Kocoureck and Ehrenzweig, were to comment that they preferred Llewellyn's German to his English prose style.[10]

Llewellyn probably did not work especially hard at the Realgymnasium, but he passed his 'Abitur' (school-leaving examination) in the spring of 1911. He did particularly well in mathematics and science, and rather less well in languages. His most remarkable teacher was Herr Lachmund, whose classes on Shakespeare increased his enthusiasm for the English language. He was fond of remarking that he had to go to Germany to learn to appreciate Shakespeare.

Llewellyn led a full life during his stay in Mecklenburg. Accounts of his contemporaries give the impression that he was a member of a close-knit group of friends who discussed politics, art, love and life with an intensity which was characteristic of intelligent German adolescents of the time.[11] It is reported that 'politically they tended to the left, in sexual matters to free love and in religious matters to atheism'.[12] If Llewellyn ever in fact professed such views, it was not for long, and may only have been a pose; for most of his life the opinions he expressed were more compatible with his love of tradition, his puritan background and his intensely religious nature. Llewellyn's contemporaries describe him as being highly intelligent, quiet, modest and thoughtful, with 'titanic energy' and 'fanatic ambition'. His school fellows, in a half-serious projection of his future career, prophesied that, after practising as an attorney, he would in time be elected mayor of New York and later president of the United States; in this capacity he would 'solve the problem of the negroes which had been an impediment to the development of America and attack the trusts with all his energy.... Under his government the People's Party will soon increase and will soon become the mightiest in the whole United States.'[13]

Llewellyn never lost his attachment to Mecklenburg. Whenever he was in Germany he tried to revisit Schwerin. When an old boys association was formed he sent a gift of money 'to settle his moral debts to his old school'.[14] He participated in a speech day in 1932 and for a long time maintained contact with several of his school friends. In 1960 the Lachmunds informed him that the authorities were threatening to destroy the medieval churches of Wismar on the Baltic Sea, north of Schwerin.[15] Llewellyn's response was immediate. He persuaded a number of prominent people to sign a petition to the East German authorities pleading for their preservation. Shortly before his death it was announced that it had been officially decided to restore one of the churches and to preserve the tower of the second one, but the news reached the United States too late for Llewellyn to learn of the success of his campaign.[16]

Llewellyn left Schwerin at Easter, 1911. Before returning to the United States he attended the University of Lausanne for a brief time and then, in September 1911, he entered Yale College as a freshman.[17] Llewellyn's first two and a half years at Yale are not well documented. Some personal papers drop hints of a regular clique of college friends, acute shortage of money, a variety of girl friends, some attempts at writing poetry and short stories, and a generally enthusiastic but not especially prominent involvement in the life of the college.[18] Until 1914 Llewellyn rarely featured in the *Yale Daily News*, a most informative journal, except that his name appeared regularly in the honours lists for academic work. The *History of the Class of Nineteen-fifteen* lists, somewhat cryptically, his principal achievements:

He received a Philosophical Oration, and won a Berkeley Premium, the Donald Annis Prize [for English and German] ... and the second L. F. Robinson Latin Prize. He took part in the Ten Eyck competition, and was interested in boxing and tennis. Deutscher Verein. Society for the Study of Socialism. Phi Beta Kappa. Beta Theta Pi.[19]

In short, for the first three years of his time at Yale the available evidence suggests an excellent academic record, fraternity life, a fair range of activities, but a prominence restricted to academic achievements. This did not satisfy Llewellyn. His contemporaries at Schwerin had already noted his 'fanatical ambition'. At Yale he found himself at a bit of a disadvantage: he was conscious of coming from a less well-to-do background than some of his colleagues; he was small and not particularly athletic; he was aware that he had a good brain, but this was not such a source of prestige as success at sport or in other extracurricular activities. He took up boxing with great vigour and with some success.[20] But this was not enough. He later confessed that he had awaited with dread the summer of 1914 when a small elite from his class would be chosen for membership of one of the prestigious secret societies.[21] Then a way out presented itself. His friend, Hans Lachmund, had passed a semester at Paris and wrote enthusiastically about the courses on sociology of Charles Gide, and on the sociology of law of René Worms. He urged Llewellyn to follow his example, if only for a term.[22] Llewellyn decided to accept the advice, mainly because, by his own confession, he would avoid the ordeal of the fraternity tapping ceremony.

Thus in the spring of 1914, for not entirely honourable reasons, Llewellyn spent four months at the Sorbonne studying Latin, law and French. He was still in Paris when war broke out. There followed the episode which has since become a legend and which survives in a number of versions. Briefly the facts were as follows: on the outbreak of hostilities Llewellyn made his way to Germany and tried to enlist. Although he had not officially joined up, he attached himself to the 78th Prussian Infantry, and he accompanied the regiment to the western front. He was wounded near Ypres in November 1914 and spent nearly three months in a military hospital at Nürtingen. Shortly before he was discharged in February, 1915 he was awarded the Iron Cross (second class). He arrived back in the United States in March and returned to Yale. (A full account of this episode is set out in Appendix A.)

Llewellyn's second period at Yale College, after his return from the war, was very different from the first. He was now 'a big man on campus' and was accorded a lot of attention and publicity. He was much more self-confident and he had matured in a number of ways. In particular, he seems to have started to take his studies very much more seriously. About this time he decided that he wanted to pursue an academic career, but it was far from clear what he would teach. One of his teachers, E. P. Morris, had stimulated a passing interest in Latin and this was for a time his favourite subject.[23] However, at this point Llewellyn fell under the spell of William Graham Sumner, who had been a dominant figure at Yale in the latter part of the nineteenth century.[24] He had died in 1910, before Llewellyn entered Yale College, but his ideas were still kept alive by his writings and by his devoted disciple, A. G. Keller.[25]

Sumner's best known work, and the one most frequently cited by Llewellyn, was *Folkways*.[26] Although it is now in many respects outdated, this book is still very readable and quite capable of making a profound impact upon an impressionable mind. Using as his main source a wide range of anthropological writings about preliterate societies, Sumner set out to document the relativity of social practices and beliefs and the powerful influence for both conservation and change of the 'folkways' and 'mores' of each society. Both of these last-mentioned concepts refer to patterns of individual behaviour which by constant repetition have taken on the character of mass phenomena. The behaviour of the individual is in the first instance a response to some felt need; life in society consists of satisfying these needs or 'interests', which are based on the 'four great motives of human action':[27] hunger, love, vanity and fear. In response to a stimulus the individual proceeds by trial and error until a reasonably satisfactory adjustment is made and noticed; when a distinct pattern of behaviour by many individuals in response to similar stimuli becomes discernible, a 'folkway' has arisen. 'The Folkways are unconscious, spontaneous, uncoordinated. It is never known who led in devising them, although we must believe that talent exerted its leadership at all times.'[28] When members of a society have become convinced that a particular folkway is indispensable to the welfare of that society, it has become part of 'the mores'. 'The mores are the folkways, including the philosophical and ethical generalizations as to societal welfare which are suggested by them, and inherent in them, as they grow.'[29] Social institutions develop out of 'the mores'. This analysis of the process of the growth of social institutions fitted in comfortably both with fashionable theories of social evolution and with Sumner's personal brand of extreme economic individualism.[30]

Although it has been said that *Folkways* was neither systematic nor original,[31] it is generally regarded as one of the seminal early works of American sociology. It is not easy to state with confidence in what particular respects it attracted Llewellyn. It is hard to believe that he ever shared Sumner's extreme individualism or that he espoused for long such a simplistic form of Social Darwinism. Llewellyn is said to have been notoriously fond of the term 'mores' during his time at Yale Law School; but he was later to criticize it, along with 'custom', as being inadequate as a tool of social analysis.[32] His interests in 'primitive' societies may have been aroused by Sumner's writings, and some of Sumner's favourite concepts—'life conditions', 'ritual', 'dogma', 'inertia', are examples—became part of Llewellyn's vocabulary; 'law-ways' was, no doubt, adapted from 'folkways' and Llewellyn's analysis of the concept of 'institution' appears to have been derived partly from Sumner, partly from an article by Walton Hamilton.[33] Llewellyn also shared Sumner's dislike of professional philosophy and philosophers,[34] but how far such similarities can be attributed to 'influence' is uncertain. In acknowledging his debt to Sumner, Llewellyn did not usually lay much stress on the value of Sumner's ideas and theories, which must in time have come to seem rather crude and oversimple. Rather he acknowledged a general gain in perspective. A similar claim is sometimes made for the study of anthropology in general: that by studying other societies comparatively one can learn to look at one's own with some of the detachment of the scientist, and with an awareness that its institutions and codes of conduct are not the only possible ones, nor necessarily the most appropriate for its circumstances. Sumner, Llewellyn claimed, curbed and re-channeled his inherited tendency to crusading radicalism:

As I grow older, I grow no less a rebel, a freak, a non-conformist. But for the early and deep-cut influences of Sumner's writings, I should by now hold some obnoxious fighting faith and be stump-speaking a vigorous progress into jail. As things have turned, however, I study social science, not for any love of things that are, or belief in their rightness, but because attempted change seems useless until one finds the laws of change – what can be changed, and how, and with what result?[35]

Having fallen under the spell of Sumner before he reached law school, Llewellyn came to the study of law with a predisposition to see law as a social institution embedded in its surrounding culture, with a sympathy for comparative work, and with the scepticism of the ethical relativist about conventions and ideals.

Llewellyn remembered his days at Yale College with fondness, and he attended reunions of the class of 1915 fairly regularly. But his memories were mainly social and, apart from Sumner, his studies did not fully engage him until he entered Yale Law School in 1915. In a typically free-wheeling summary of his intellectual development in one of his jurisprudence lectures he dismissed his undergraduate days rather curtly: 'I am an autodidache [i.e. largely self-taught] if I may say so; I learned in college Palaeontology, Latin and a few things like that. None of the things that I use in my professional life did I learn from anybody except [in] books and I'm proud of it....'[86] He is similarly succinct about the next step: 'On graduation I had become clear that I wanted to teach, but had gotten no further towards picking a field than a general interest in Latin. My father's urging got me into law, and my own inclinations got me back into teaching.'[87]

Llewellyn entered Yale Law School as a student in 1915, at a time when the school was in the middle of a period of transition.[88] The influence of Corbin and Hohfeld had begun to make itself felt, resistance to Langdellian ideas on legal education had been largely broken down, but the faculty still contained some survivors of the days of the old 'Yale System', notably Simeon Baldwin and the Dean, Henry Wade Rogers.

Shortly before Llewellyn's arrival Hohfeld's first article on 'Fundamental Legal Conceptions', his paper on 'A Vital School of Jurisprudence and Law', and Corbin's 'Law and the Judges' had been published in quick succession. These three essays first brought into prominence the ideas that formed the basis of a 'new approach' which gained ascendancy in the law school during the next few years. Thus Llewellyn's introduction to the law coincided with a crucial phase in the history of the Yale Law School and of the realist movement. The arrival of Walter Wheeler Cook in 1916 further stimulated the intellectual ferment that set the tone of Llewellyn's time as a law student.

Llewellyn's legal education was exceptional in another important respect. After America's entry into the war, Yale Law School lost

more than half of its students and a similar proportion of its faculty
(but not Corbin, Hohfeld or Cook). The result was that instead of
finding himself a member of an elite group of law students who
would be to a large extent educating themselves and each other in
a highly competitive atmosphere, Llewellyn got little competition
or stimulus from his fellows. A letter to a friend in 1918, just after
he had graduated, reveals his attitude towards the survivors:

... there are some hopeless homeless souls still here. Some, like me, aren't in
service because they can't get in. With me it's German Army service; with
others it's physical difficulties. Still others are here because they've dodged
getting in, one way or another. Still others are too old, or married and provided with dependent families or aliens, or taking part in S.A.T.C. work on
the side. But altogether they don't amount to much in respect of quality.
And the best men are gone.[39]

However, the war had its compensations, for it brought Llewellyn
into unusually close contact with some of his teachers, especially
Corbin and Hohfeld. It may well be that the reduction in size of the
law school helped to make their approach more coherent and more
visible than might otherwise have been the case. Certainly Llewellyn
subsequently interpreted his experience of law school largely in
terms of his contact with Corbin and Hohfeld and, to a lesser extent,
Cook, Rogers and Taft.

After he graduated Llewellyn often referred to Corbin as his
'father in the law' (and in fact addressed him in private as 'Dad'),
and there can be little doubt that in his career as a jurist he owed
more to him than to any other single person. Ironically Llewellyn
did not attend Corbin's classes on contracts, for he had taken a
course on contracts at Michigan under W. M. Page in the summer
before he entered Yale Law School;[40] He was probably taught by
Corbin in two minor courses, quasi-contracts and suretyship; their
closest contact came outside the classroom where they worked together on the *Yale Law Journal* during Llewellyn's period as Editor-
in-Chief.[41] A remarkable intellectual empathy developed between
the two, reinforced over the years by an affectionate life-long
friendship and a deep mutual admiration. The fact that they
specialized in cognate areas of substantive law further strengthened
the bond. A fundamental harmony in their jurisprudential thinking persisted right up to Llewellyn's death, so that in December 1960
Corbin was able to write of *The Common Law Tradition*: '...
never before have I found within two covers so many of the

thoughts that I approve, so much of the judgment I confirm—all weighed by experience and supported in detail.'[42]

When Llewellyn's writings are considered in detail the affinity between ideas and attitudes of the teacher and his pupil will become apparent. In particular, it will be seen that 'The Law and the Judges' anticipates a number of ideas in *The Common Law Tradition*.[43] How much credit should be given to Corbin for Llewellyn's achievements must naturally remain largely a matter of speculation. The pupil was to prove to be a much more articulate and sophisticated jurist than his teacher. In time their paths diverged. Llewellyn developed broader interests and was less single-minded than Corbin, who continued unremittingly to work in the single field of contracts. In temperament and in style they were profoundly different, but their basic similarity of outlook and ideas remained to the end. In particular in their love of case law and their sense of identification with the ordinary private practitioner of law and in their emphasis on constant evolutionary change within a relatively stable tradition, they retained an essential affinity which overshadowed the differences between them.

Llewellyn's close relationship with Corbin prompts one suggestion which can at best be treated as speculative. Corbin's most striking characteristic was the patient relentlessness of his scholarship. 'Craft' and 'craftsmanship' became important concepts for Llewellyn and he often used Corbin as an exemplar of his ideal of 'the legal craftsman'. In 1918–9, at a crucial stage in Llewellyn's intellectual development, the two of them worked closely together on the *Yale Law Journal*, writing over half the comments and case notes between them. It would be hard to devise a more rigorous apprenticeship in legal scholarship than writing a number of case notes with Corbin. Llewellyn's fondness for praising what he would refer to as 'good, clean, solid work' must have seemed strange to those who saw him as a volatile genius, bubbling over with brilliant insights, but slapdash in execution. But much of Llewellyn's work is marked by painstaking efforts of careful scholarship which seem out of character with some of his more freewheeling writings. It may not be implausible to suggest that there was in Llewellyn a tension between his spirited and imaginative insight and the 'craftsmanship' that he so much admired in Corbin, between his own inclination and his scholarly ideal. Indeed it is possible that his contact with Corbin led Llewellyn to internalize his image of the 'craftsman' to such an extent that it acted as a sort of conscience to which he made himself accountable in all his legal work and which he probably found it difficult to satisfy.[44]

If Corbin was in the long run the most influential of Llewellyn's teachers, up to 1918 Hohfeld was his hero of the moment. Like Langdell, Hohfeld's initial attempt to introduce a new approach in the classroom had met with fierce resistance from students.[45] But by the time that Llewellyn began to take his courses, opinion, at least among the better students, had shifted from bitter complaint to a combination of awe and evangelical enthusiasm.

Llewellyn's obituary notice of Hohfeld,[46] written when he was editor-in-chief of the *Yale Law Journal*, bears eloquent testimony to this enthusiasm, which was no doubt heightened by the emotional atmosphere that surrounded Hohfeld's last illness and death at the early age of thirty-eight. Hohfeld's supporters saw him as a prophet tragically cut off in his prime and Llewellyn, who was by then one of his most ardent admirers, was among the leaders. In addition to writing his obituary, he organized his fellow students to continue Hohfeld's course on conflicts and even for a short period arrogated to himself the role of unofficial literary executor.[47]

In praising him, Llewellyn stressed the breadth of Hohfeld's learning and his vision of the law as a whole more than the more prosaic virtues of clarity and precision. He found these qualities particularly in his work on conflicts.[48] In his own teaching Llewellyn used to insist that Hohfeld's distinctions between the four meanings of 'right' should be part of the elementary equipment of every law student,[49] and he was always careful to observe them. In the Uniform Commercial Code these distinctions were also observed, but his terminology was not followed;[50] Llewellyn learned from Hohfeld to be sceptical of abstract legal concepts like 'ownership', 'possession', 'master and servant', and he consciously adopted the technique of 'narrow issue thinking', using it to particularly good effect in his analysis of 'title' in sales.[51] But as time progressed his enthusiasm for Hohfeld visibly waned; he became increasingly conscious of the limitations of the usefulness of the scheme of jural correlatives and opposites, and he also expressed a number of reservations about the details of the analysis and even of Hohfeld's understanding of logic.[52] There remains, moreover, the obvious fact that the two men were of quite different cast of mind. In his German schooling, in his classical studies, and in law school,

Llewellyn was repeatedly exposed to teachers who emphasized the twin values of verbal precision and rigorous conceptual analysis. Their outlook left its mark on his thinking, as did Korzybyskian semantics,[53] but they never subverted his more basic desire to express himself in flexible and figurative language. He tended to prefer vague but suggestive concepts to precise ones, often deliberately refusing to define his terms. A Hohfeldian style and 'situation-sense', 'life situation', 'law-stuff' and 'right reason' are hardly compatible. Hohfeld was one of the young man's heroes, but his legacy was primarily a vision of law from a mountain peak, the technique of narrow issue thinking and an understanding of the differences between 'must', 'may' and 'can'.

Both personally and intellectually Llewellyn was closer to Hohfeld and Corbin than he was to Cook. Llewellyn acknowledged Cook's influence on his ideas about judicial reasoning and he recognized his analytical brilliance, but he never sympathized with Cook's anti-professional orientation and he was later to be highly critical of his attempts at 'scientific research'.[54] Subsequently Llewellyn and Cook were colleagues at Yale for a time and appear to have been on good terms, although not close to each other.[55]

Two more of Llewellyn's teachers deserve brief mention. Dean Henry Wade Rogers gave him first-hand experience of the old 'Yale system' of instruction.[56] Between 1913 and 1916 Rogers combined the deanship of the law school with his position as a Judge of the United States Circuit Court of Appeals. He was clearly a relic of an older tradition and he appears to have epitomized for Llewellyn much of what was under attack by the younger teachers at Yale. On one occasion, after a scathing attack on Rogers, Llewellyn commented sarcastically: 'I rate Henry Wade Rogers' effect on me as being one of the really vital stimulating pieces of my legal education'.[57] This was probably Llewellyn's first contact with one of the supposed 'enemies' of realism.

In a more subtle way ex-President Taft also unwittingly made an impression.[58] Taft, who taught constitutional law, was often cited by his former pupil as a prime example of a man who was 'almost without consciousness' of the techniques he actually used in practice.[59] His teaching was old-fashioned and formalistic, with a 'correct interpretation' for each decision. He would often break off from exposition and tell anecdotes full of practical insights drawn from his experience in politics, on the bench and as an administrator, but he made it clear that he thought that these were digressions and not part of the subject-matter of the course. Llewellyn was fond of telling how Taft complained about him to the Dean of the Yale Law School for 'criticizing the Supreme Court'. Taft in expounding doctrine would at times accept happily the pure language of the court as laying down the *ratio decidendi* of its decision, but at other times, without any apparent consciousness that he was using a different technique, he would with consummate skill whittle down the opinion to a very narrow holding. When Llewellyn imitated Taft's whittling technique to produce a narrower interpretation than the language of the court suggested on some cases which Taft had never felt the need to distinguish, Taft interpreted this as impertinent and uncalled for criticism and reported him to the Dean. Analysis by a student amounted to criticism, analysis by Taft was the way to find the true holding.

In many respects Llewellyn's legal education reflected the prevailing orthodoxy. The curriculum was conventional and oriented towards private practice, with a heavy emphasis on property, commercial law and procedural subjects. He studied Roman law, but not jurisprudence. Because of the war there were few optional courses. There was little emphasis on history or on statute law or administrative law. Although Cook, Corbin and Hohfeld were all emphasizing in different ways the divergence between law in books and law in action, their approach was analytical, appellate cases were almost exclusively the subject of attention, they were concerned to find the 'real rules' behind the decisions and they had not turned to dealing systematically with questions of policy or social facts.

Llewellyn graduated easily top of his class in 1918 *magna cum laude*. In his final year his lowest mark was 88 per cent. He was elected to the editorial board of the *Yale Law Journal* in 1916, and, because of the crisis in the law school occasioned by the war, he remained as an editor for over three years, a much longer period than usual. In 1918, after he had graduated, he was invited to stay on as Editor-in-Chief to keep the journal going with a depleted editorial staff. During the academic year 1918–9 Llewellyn in fact had a triple role: he was Editor-in-Chief of the journal; he was a student, reading for the Connecticut Bar examination (admitted 1919) and for the J.D. degree (which he obtained in 1920); and he was also a part-time instructor in the law school.[60]

Llewellyn's first opportunity to teach was occasioned by the illness of John Edgerton, the Professor of Commercial Law. In the spring of 1919 Llewellyn took over Edgerton's course on bills and notes. In the summer he gave a course on partnership and in the following academic year he taught bills and notes, partnership and sales. Thus it was chance rather than choice that led him to become a specialist in commercial law.[61] It remained, together with jurisprudence, his principal area of interest for the rest of his life. At first sight it might seem paradoxical that so prosaic and technical a subject should have attracted someone with poetic tendencies and a strong sociological bias. The paradox is only apparent. The world of commerce had an enduring fascination for Llewellyn. In it he found both aesthetic and intellectual satisfaction. At one level he had a romantic vision of the vast canvas of human activity connected with the gathering of raw materials, their processing, manufacture and distribution through the multifarious channels of trade; at a different level he was unceasingly curious about the details of the way things are done; he would take an intense interest in the minutiae of even the most mundane transactions and he would enthusiastically praise as 'lovely' or 'beautiful' examples of deftness or of neat solutions to technical problems. His vision of the world of commerce accommodated not only 'Quinquereme of Nineveh from distant Ophir', but also the functional 'beauty' of mill-race and turbine.[62] Secondly, Llewellyn also claimed that he found a distinct similarity between the world of commerce and preliterate societies in that each contained relatively simple, homogeneous groups, which could be studied 'in the round'. Where the context is relatively simple, and especially where the same values are widely shared, the study of the relationship between legal rules and processes and the context of their operation is made easier.[63]

To start with, Llewellyn enjoyed teaching commercial law for quite a different reason. The course on bills and notes was built around the Uniform Negotiable Instruments Law, the chief characteristic of which was its technical complexity. At first, Llewellyn took great pleasure in the quasi-mathematical challenge that it offered, a challenge to cleverness rather than insight. However, it was not long before he became dissatisfied with such 'verbal chess games':[64]

I hadn't been in it for more than a year and a half when it became clear to me that the things I was finding in the cases had very little indeed to do with what was going on in practice. That came home to me when I started giving courses to the American Bankers Institute, an outfit that used to train bank clerks in the law of their subject at night; and when you give courses to bank clerks, if you are any good, and above all, if you believe in discussion, you develop shortly a large body of questions that have to do with the things that have been coming up during the last week and you discover that the law you are supposedly teaching them, which is derived largely from the cases, has absolutely or almost nothing to do with the problems that are crossing their desks. It became clear to me, therefore, that there was no hope for me to make any headway at all in the investigations I was interested in, unless I found out what was going on de facto in practice. . . .[65]

Accordingly Llewellyn decided to gain some practical experience of his subject before settling down to an academic career. He secured a position in the legal department of the National City Bank and in September 1920 he moved to New York, where he remained for the next two years. Soon after he joined it, the National City Bank dissolved its legal department and transferred its legal business to the Wall Street law firm of Shearman and Sterling.[66] Llewellyn was also transferred and he continued to work almost exclusively on the bank's business. Once again he was fortunate. At Shearman and Sterling he worked directly under the supervision of William W. Lancaster, who at the age of forty-six was already recognized as being a leading authority on banking law.[67] Llewellyn worked closely with Lancaster and subsequently he used to talk of him with gratitude and affection. Not only was Llewellyn apprenticed to an almost ideal master, but he also happened to start in practice at a particularly interesting and busy time. The National City Bank was going through a period of rapid expansion; in the international sphere there was a flood of suits from Russian refugees who had deposits at the bank's branch in Petrograd at the time of the revolution and who from 1919 began to bring suits in New York to recover the dollar value of their ruble deposits at a rate of exchange which greatly favoured them; the collapse of the sugar industry in Cuba and the depression of 1921 in the United States also brought in a great deal of varied, non-routine work:

Work boomed. The banks were busy on the legal side due to the losses and credit tie-ups of the depression. A great number of practices which had seemed safe while things were good, required revamping in the light of difficulties. Hence the number of matters that came across a man's desk was very large, although the opportunity to dig up the law was correspondingly limited.[68]

Llewellyn was almost entirely concerned with office work, writing opinions on points of law, advising on whether or not to accept a particular draft, drafting various kinds of documents, writing letters, and doing a certain amount of 'creative' work, such as devising new standard forms. Accordingly, during his time in practice he was usually faced with situations where the facts were not in dispute; typically his role was to advise on the safest course of action on the basis of a prediction of how a court might decide on the law if the particular facts came before it. On one occasion he gave Lancaster a memorandum in which he presented an ingenious and carefully rehearsed legal argument; he was rebuked for wasting his time and for not concentrating on finding a simple way of ensuring that the matter never reached the courts.[69] It is likely that Llewellyn's relative inattention to the problems of fact-finding (as contrasted with Frank) and his instinctive identification with the standpoint of the office lawyer stem from the nature of his experience in practice.

Llewellyn thoroughly enjoyed this period. However, after two years he decided to return to teaching, despite a financially attractive offer from his law firm. For a long time he had been interested in teaching and an academic career had the added attraction '[that] no other branch of law work seems to give a man time to stay with a thing until he gets to the bottom of it'.[70] So in 1922 he returned to Yale with the rank of assistant professor and began his career as a full-time teacher of law.

Llewellyn did not stay long at Yale. In 1923 he was promoted to the rank of associate professor and he looked set for a long and distinguished career in New Haven. However, on 23 February 1924 he married his first wife, Elizabeth Sanford, of Freeport, Illinois, who was at that time a graduate student in economics at Columbia University. In order to accommodate his wife's desire to remain in New York, Llewellyn moved to Columbia Law School, first as visiting lecturer in 1924, and then with the substantive rank of associate professor in the following year. For a time he commuted between New Haven and New York, teaching in both law schools, but in 1925 he reluctantly severed his formal connection with Yale and settled in New York, where he stayed until 1951. He continued to be a frequent visitor to New Haven and he always retained a warm affection for both Yale College and the law school. More than once he was invited to return as professor of law but, somewhat surprisingly, he declined on each occasion.[71]

Although personal reasons prompted Llewellyn's move to Columbia, his transfer had important jurisprudential consequences. One result was that he became the only leading realist to have had first-hand experience both of Yale at the critical period from 1914-8 and of Columbia during the eventful years between 1922 and 1933. At Yale, as a student, he was at most an enthusiastic disciple of the pace-setters; at Columbia he was more actively involved, but, at least up to 1929, he was not counted among the leaders. During the curriculum discussions he was a member of two of the most important committees, (business relations and methodology) and he also served with Moore as a subcommittee on finance and credit and with Oliphant as a subcommittee on marketing. He participated energetically in the work of these bodies and he also submitted a number of memoranda of his own on general issues.[72] He was in substantial agreement with Moore and Oliphant in their approach to the reorganization of courses in the area of 'business relations' and he clearly learned much from them. Indeed, there is little to suggest that he made at this stage any more significant contribution than might be expected from a lively and interested junior colleague working closely with his seniors. However, Llewellyn's marginal annotations of his personal copies of some memoranda show that he was far from being an uncritical disciple of the ideas of Moore and Oliphant, particularly in relation to 'scientific' research.[73] It is also clear that he was in no doubt that preparation for practice should continue to be the main function of the undergraduate law degree, the issue on which the discussions foundered.

Llewellyn's posture during the deanship crisis is less clear. Yntema recollected that he played 'a minor, but vacillating role';[74] Corbin could not remember discussing it with him;[75] the Llewellyn Papers offer little help and the Columbia archives are closed to outsiders. Yntema's memory appears to be substantially correct. The indications are that Llewellyn was probably somewhat ambivalent. He opposed Smith's appointment, he protested to President Butler over his manner of handling the affair, but he decided to stay on.[76] His failure to resign is said to have alienated Underhill Moore, but the reasons for this are obscure.[77] Llewellyn's motives are also not entirely clear: according to Corbin he said that it was because the law school needed him more than ever. However, there is no evidence that he had any offers from elsewhere at this time;[78] it is quite possible that he was approached by Yale, but it is highly improbable that he would have been willing to join Cook and Oliphant at Johns Hopkins. Llewellyn was not a supporter of Smith, with whom he maintained an uneasy relationship for more than twenty-five years, but neither before nor after the crisis of 1928 did he show himself to be a particular admirer of Oliphant. He learned much from the theoretical ideas of Cook, Moore and Oliphant, but he never espoused their 'scientism'; in view of his strong sense of identification with the legal profession, it is virtually unthinkable that he would have supported any move to convert Columbia into a research institute. Thus at the time of the crisis Llewellyn was faced with a dilemma: jurisprudentially he was closer in some respects to the dissidents, but educationally he was on the other side. Whatever his motives, Llewellyn stayed on at Columbia, whereas Oliphant, Moore, Marshall, Yntema and Douglas left.

The curriculum discussions, the deanship crisis and the split between the Scientists and Prudents constitute the more spectacular aspects of the background of Llewellyn's early years at Columbia. He had joined the faculty in 1924 as a specialist in commercial law. During the next five years this area absorbed most of his energies. With the exception of a graduate seminar in 'Law and Society', a cooperative exercise shared with several colleagues, all of his teaching was in commercial subjects. In 1926 he was appointed a Commissioner on Uniform State Laws, a position he held until he moved to Chicago. In the same year he became draftsman of the Uniform Chattel Mortgage Act and the Uniform Trust Receipts Act.[79] Legislative drafting and the preparation of teaching materials were his two principal extracurricular activities between 1925 and 1930 and during this period he published relatively little.

Until 1929 jurisprudence came a poor second to commercial law. Although as a student Llewellyn had been in close contact with teachers who were trying to pioneer new methods of legal analysis, his early work is not characterized by any sharp break with tradition. Indeed his development as a commercial lawyer between 1918 and 1930 is a good example of the difficulty of breaking away from a tough taught tradition of doctrinal analysis. Even before he started teaching he had been conditioned by Sumner and Corbin to be dissatisfied with the tradition, yet he found himself playing 'clever chess games' with the negotiable instruments law in his first courses. His two years in practice, undertaken in part as an antidote to this tendency, did not completely cure him, for in drafting the Uniform Trust Receipts Act he adopted, apparently without being conscious of it, a style of drafting which he later considered to be unnecessarily complex.[80]

During the 1920s Llewellyn made slow and painful progress in evolving a different approach.[81] From 1927 to 1930 his main courses were contracts and sales of personal property, two solidly 'traditional' subjects. The principal arena for his struggle towards a different approach was his casebook on sales. It reveals clearly that Llewellyn's break with formalism was the outcome of hard labour rather than of sudden conversion. 'Five years of struggle gets one hand free to wave for help.'[82] Corbin had only taken him part of the way.

Meanwhile his interest in jurisprudence continued to grow, in part independently of, in part in conjunction with, his work in commercial law. In fact he published relatively little before 1930, and a high proportion of his first publications were of a general nature. In 1925 a paper on 'The Effect of Legal Institutions on Economics' presaged his interest in interdisciplinary cooperation. In 1928-9 he published articles on legal education, legal research and law enforcement and between 1923 and 1929 a series of book reviews reveal his concern with new trends and approaches to legal education, legal research and law in general. Today these pieces are mainly interesting as indicia of the state of Llewellyn's intellectual development. Taken on their own they could be misleading, for several of his most promising lines of enquiry had not yet been worked up into publishable form.

During the 1920s Llewellyn's work in jurisprudence developed slowly along three main lines. First, he kept alive his interest in anthropology and sociology—the Sumnerian strand—through his participation in a graduate seminar on law in society. Manuscripts from this period show him struggling towards a general sociological theory of law, but this remained for the time being the least developed aspect of his thought. Secondly, from about 1927 he began to take a sustained interest in the nature of the appellate judicial process and of case law. He had been in close contact with the pace-setters in this field from the time he was a law student: Corbin's 'The Law and the Judges' had been seminal for him; Cook had been his teacher; Cardozo's Storrs Lectures on 'The Nature of the Judicial Process' were delivered while Llewellyn was still closely associated with Yale; the implications for the analysis of judicial processes of the ideas of Freud and Dewey and behaviourist psychology were beginning to excite a number of law teachers. Llewellyn could hardly avoid becoming involved. Rather it is a little surprising that his interest developed so late.

The third main strand of Llewellyn's theoretical concerns in the late 1920s arose out of his involvement in the curriculum discussions and their aftermath. Here he matured most quickly, as ideas about interdisciplinary cooperation, realism and legal education interacted and were submitted to the arduous discipline of applying them in an area of substantive law which he had already gone a long way to mastering.

Llewellyn's first project to fall squarely within the area of jurisprudence developed out of an invitation to spend a semester at Leipzig as a visiting professor in 1928–9. He chose as his subject for a series of lectures the operation of case law in the United States. Five years later an expanded version of these lectures, together with some illustrative material, was published under the title of *Praejudizienrecht und Rechtsprechung in Amerika*.[83] Although it was intended as an introductory work, the book presented an unusually bold and sophisticated account of the practical functioning of American case law. It contained in elementary form a number of ideas that Llewellyn was subsequently to develop at great length in *The Common Law Tradition*. The ideas were not so much new as a reminder of the neglected obvious;[84] they excited some considerable interest among German scholars, but the political climate of the time probably prevented the book from making a greater impact.[85]

This project marked an important stage in Llewellyn's intellectual development. For the first time he moved out of a single field of law to look at one phase of the operation of the legal system as a whole; he began to be interested in the processes and techniques of judicial decisions, as well as in the doctrines that could be extracted from them and he began to realize how much general jurisprudential writing was based on the selective use of examples rather than on the disciplined testing of the hypotheses against the facts of daily practice.[86] He had taken his first major step as a legal theorist.

Llewellyn was invited to return to Leipzig in 1931. Once again the prospect of speaking to foreign audiences stimulated him to move away from the detailed treatment of technical subjects onto a broader plane. On this second visit he lectured on a variety of general topics and, while he was still in Germany, he began to expand one of these lectures into a full-length book, entitled *Recht, Rechtsleben und Gesellschaft* (Law, the Life of the Law and Society).[87] Llewellyn's aim was to follow in the tradition of Ehrlich and Weber: 'Ehrlich remains unclear; Max Weber, in spite of the depth and the wealth of his experiences, is extraordinarily inaccessible and regards the sociology of law merely as a less important branch of research.'[88]

He tried to have the book published in Germany in 1932, but without success. This work represents Llewellyn's first sustained attempt to develop a sociological theory of law. He returned to the subject again and again; some of his ideas in this area appeared in print, but he never completed for publication a full statement of his 'whole view', as he called it. The context for the most fully developed version of this aspect of his work was the course on 'Law in our Society', which will be considered in chapter 9. Llewellyn had arranged to return to Germany in 1962, almost exactly thirty years after his last visit, and he had planned to give a series of lectures in publishable form which would contain a final statement of his position. Unfortunately he died before he was able to execute this project.

During his time in Germany Llewellyn had close contact with a number of distinguished German scholars, of whom Nussbaum, Kantorowicz, Koschaker, Jahrreis and Mitteis are perhaps the best known outside Germany. He was on intimate terms with Franz Exner, who was then a young professor of criminal law at Leipzig, and with a sociologist, Freyer. There is evidence to suggest that his first thorough reading of Ehrlich and Weber may have been undertaken during his first visit to Leipzig. He took a general interest in German civil law and he also made plans for two research projects, a study of the handling of precedent by the *Reichsgericht* (the supreme court of the German Reich) and, jointly with his former school-friend Hans Lachmund, an analysis of German civil procedure. Neither project was ever completed. In 1931 Llewellyn had been invited to act as a consultant to the International Institute for the Unification of Law in connection with their project for the unification of the law of sales. He attended one session of their deliberations at Rome in March 1932. (His comment was: 'Interesting, laborious, unpractical.')[89] On both visits to Germany Llewellyn gave lectures at a number of universities, mostly on broad theoretical themes. These lectures were, for the most part, very well received and helped to strengthen his excellent reputation among German scholars.

Llewellyn's German schooling and his subsequent connections with Germany have not surprisingly prompted speculation about the extent of German influence on his character and thought. It has been pointed out that some of his ideas have a close affinity with those of Weber, Ehrlich, Nussbaum and, to a lesser extent, the *Freirechtslehre* (free law theories) of Fuchs, Isay and again of Ehrlich.[90] There are features of the Uniform Commercial Code that will be recognized by lawyers trained in the civil law; Llewellyn and Ernst Rabel had similar approaches to the law of sales.[91] Others have found 'Germanic' traits in Llewellyn's character, his prose style, and his cast of mind.

In this context it is naturally much easier to point to affinity than to prove influence. That Llewellyn had much in common with German legal scholars of the early twentieth century is not to be doubted, just as it is obvious that he had many American traits. However, so far as his general method of approach is concerned the evidence tends to suggest that he only began to study German legal and sociological literature seriously in the late 1920s, by which time the main patterns of his concerns and ideas had been settled. This is corroborated by Llewellyn's autobiographical accounts of his intellectual development in which he placed relatively little stress on his connections with Germany. A more likely explanation of the affinity is that American sociological jurisprudence, through Carter, Gray, Holmes and, above all, Pound, had already assimilated much from German jurists of the nineteenth century, before Llewellyn took up the subject. It is perhaps significant that several reviewers of *Praejudizienrecht* criticized Llewellyn for not paying sufficient attention to German writings on the jurisprudence of interests, fact research in law, and the 'free law' theories of judicial deciding.[92] Almost all Llewellyn's references were to American works. However, it was the stimulus of having to interpret American law to foreign audiences that led him to take a sustained look at the system as a whole from the outside and prompted his first two substantial works of general theory. These works, written in German, while he was in close contact with German scholars and German literature, mark the start of his original contributions to jurisprudence. From now on he was no longer merely an acolyte of Corbin, Hohfeld, Cook and Moore, but a fully fledged jurist in his own right.

The remainder of Llewellyn's career is largely a story of the development of his ideas through the medium of his teaching and writings and such projects as the Uniform Commercial Code. Most of the relevant details are best considered in later chapters in connection with particular works. However, it may be useful to complete this account with a brief survey of the principal events of Llewellyn's life between 1929 and 1962.

Nineteen hundred and twenty-nine marked another important turning-point in Llewellyn's career. At the beginning of the academic year 1929–30 he delivered a series of introductory lectures to first-year law students which were published in the following year under the title of *The Bramble Bush*. In the same year he was appointed the first Betts Professor of Jurisprudence at Columbia. Not long afterwards the realist controversy broke on the academic legal world and Llewellyn was in the thick of it. Whereas *Cases and Materials on the Law of Sales*, published in 1930, excited admiration among commercial law specialists, his articles on realism, notably 'A Realistic Jurisprudence, The Next Step' and 'Some Realism about Realism', when taken with *The Bramble Bush,* gave him a reputation, together with Jerome Frank, of being iconoclastic and somewhat intemperate as a jurist.

During the ensuing nine years the formerly unproductive Llewellyn suddenly became enormously prolific. During the 1930s he published three major books, over twenty substantial articles and numerous lesser pieces. The great majority of published and unpublished works were concerned with the sociology of law, contracts and commercial law. This burst of energy coincided with a period of intense personal unhappiness. His first marriage ended in divorce in 1930 after his wife left him for another man. During the ensuing years Llewellyn had to struggle continually with alcoholism and it may well be that the enormous energy which he put into his professional activities was his way of fighting the unhappiness of his private life. In an effort to get away from his personal problems he revisited Leipzig as a guest professor in 1931–2. Before returning to the United States he made a further tour of Germany, giving lectures. In 1931 Llewellyn also published privately a book of poems entitled *Put in His Thumb* and a companion pamphlet of lyrics entitled *Beach Plums*.

In June 1933 he first met a young anthropologist, E. Adamson Hoebel, who was to collaborate with him on a number of studies of American Indian law, and in the same month he married Emma Corstvet who was at that time an assistant professor of sociology at Yale and an associate of Underhill Moore. The marriage was not a very easy one and it ended in divorce in 1946.

Llewellyn was also quite active in public affairs during this period. From 1927 to 1935 he was involved in the furore surrounding the Sacco-Vanzetti case: he organized a petition and broadcast on behalf of the accused, served as a member of the executive committee of the Sacco-Vanzetti National League, and after the execution in 1927 he did a considerable amount of preparatory work on a book about the case, which was never completed.[93] Thereafter Llewellyn was associated with a number of 'liberal' causes: he gave assistance to the NAACP and, according to one unconfirmed report, he was one of the first to advocate a strategy of litigation through test cases as a means of advancing the position of Negroes;[94] in 1934 he made an abortive entry into politics, running as a candidate for 'the Knickerbocker Democrats' against the incumbent, James J. Hines, for membership of the Democratic State Committee (11th District); his platform was 'clean up Tammany Hall', but although he was the subject of a certain amount of publicity, he did not make much headway and, before polling day, he was persuaded to stand down in favour of a candidate with a similar platform.[95] During the 1930s Llewellyn was also associated with the American Civil Liberties Union, especially in connection with a campaign to liberalize laws relating to sedition.[96] On more than one occasion at Columbia he clashed with the university authorities when speakers were banned from the university campus. After the 1930s he continued to write and speak occasionally on civil liberties, but he was less actively involved with liberal causes.[97] There was one major exception to this : his efforts to make legal services more accessible to the poor and to the lower middle class. In this area he made a significant contribution, and since they are intimately connected with some of his juristic ideas, his activities will be described in detail below.[98]

The years 1936–40 were particularly eventful. In collaboration with Hoebel he completed a study of the Cheyenne Indians which was published in 1941 as *The Cheyenne Way*.[99] This was immediately recognized as a major contribution to the anthropological study of primitive law; the project also stimulated some crucial advances in Llewellyn's ideas about the sociology of law. In 1937 he became involved in the campaign for the enactment of a Federal Sales Act and this led on directly, via work on the Revised Uniform Sales Act, to the project for a Uniform Commercial Code, which was to take up a large part of his energies for the next fifteen years.[100] During the same period, 1936 to 1940, Llewellyn published a notable series of articles on the law of sales, which further consolidated his reputation as one of the leading commercial lawyers of his day.[101] A third major interest, the judicial process, was also revived at this time. Borrowing the concept of 'period style' from architecture he applied it to the study of American state appellate courts in two series of lectures, one at the University of Chicago on 'The Good, the True and the Beautiful in Law',[102] (1941) and the prestigious Storrs lectures at Yale on 'The Common Law Tradition' (1941). It was not, however, until twenty years later, in 1960, that these ideas were fully developed in print in his jurisprudential *magnum opus, The Common Law Tradition: Deciding Appeals*.[103]

These three sets of interests blossomed into three major projects which took up most of Llewellyn's energies, outside teaching, during the last twenty-two years of his life (1940–62): The Uniform Commercial Code, *The Common Law Tradition*, and the development of a general sociological theory of law.

Although the 1940s were dominated by the Code project Llewellyn continued to write on a variety of subjects. During this period he published articles on jurisprudence, legal education, the legal profession and commercial law. In 1944 he was chairman of an Association of American Law Schools committee on curriculum which produced a notable report on the place of skills in legal education.[104] In the same year, again in collaboration with Hoebel, he embarked on another study of American Indians, this time the Pueblos of New Mexico. Llewellyn spent much more time doing fieldwork on this project than he had done in the case of the Cheyennes, but the study was never completed. During his visits to New Mexico he became actively involved in Pueblo affairs; he drafted codes for some of the Pueblo councils, he acted in a number of cases, and ultimately his interest in Indian affairs led to his appointment to the Commission on the Rights, Liberties and Responsibilities of the American Indian (1956).[105]

By 1949 nearly all the work on preparing the first draft of the total Code had been completed and Llewellyn had begun once more to direct his attention to jurisprudence. In that year he was invited as visiting professor to Harvard, and in addition to teaching commercial law he took this as an opportunity for developing a new course on jurisprudence.[106] This course, which he continued to experiment with during the last twelve years of his life, was the vehicle for developing his general sociological theory. During the 1940s too Llewellyn was increasingly called on to participate in the affairs of the AALS and after a spell on the executive he was installed as president in December 1949.[107]

During his latter years at Columbia Llewellyn's relations with some of his colleagues, and sometimes with his students, had deteriorated. His work on the Code was exhausting and although he did continue to publish a number of scholarly articles, they did not compare in either originality or quality with much of his work of the previous decade.

In 1946, after a divorce, he married Soia Mentschikoff, who had been his student, research assistant and Associate Chief Reporter on the Code. During the period 1941–8 she had established a reputation as an outstanding commercial lawyer in her own right and in 1947 she had the honour of being the first woman ever to be invited to teach at Harvard Law School.[108] Llewellyn resigned from Columbia in 1951, after he and his wife had accepted a joint appointment at the University of Chicago Law School. His main reason for moving to Chicago was that he thought that the law school, under Dean Edward Levi, whom he greatly admired, promised to become the first in the mid-west seriously to challenge the dominance of the great schools of the eastern seaboard.[109]

The move to Chicago was a success and some of Llewellyn's old intellectual vigour which some thought he had lost in the 1940s was recaptured during his last ten years of teaching. Although he was still officially Chief Reporter on the Uniform Commercial Code, after 1952 his main contribution to that project had been made, and he devoted most of his attention to jurisprudence. Llewellyn died of a heart attack on 13 February 1962. In an obituary Dean Levi gave this account of his final period:

Karl's many-sidedness was reflected in the radius of his influence at Chicago. He had done much of the pioneering work on the relationships between law and sociology and law and economics. At Chicago he gave the protection of his boldness to the law and behavioral science program and the guidance of his insights gained from his seminal study of the creative power of the sense of justice reflected in the law ways of an Indian tribe. He had played a leading role in the great disputes on legal realism. His *Bramble Bush* was a classic. The students at Chicago received from him a more sophisticated and mature view of law but with the same fire and poetry. When he came to Chicago, his knowledge of commercial law was prodigious; his major task of fashioning the Uniform Commercial Code was near completion. His influence was strong for instruction in draftsmanship. His concern for instruction in the skills of the craft produced the course in advocacy, which he taught, and gave impetus to student work in moot court and legal aid. Karl was interested in the organizations of the bar. He was interested in many law schools. I think it is right to say he was in love with Chicago. He was enormously stimulated by the exciting atmosphere of the school close to the bar and judiciary and yet so much an integral part of a university with an unparalleled tradition and practice of interdisciplinary research . . .
. . . In the last year of his life, his book *The Common Law Tradition: Deciding Appeals* was published. It was the great work which he knew he had in him. Before his death he had been told the book had been voted the Henry M. Phillips prize given by the American Philosophical Society. Eight days before his death he had finished the preface to a collection of his essays since published under the title *Jurisprudence: Realism in Theory and Practice*. His last year of law teaching was perhaps his best. The barrier between teacher and student was low; the creative power of the teaching was strong. He did not regard his work as finished. He still had before him a work on law in society.[110]

Llewellyn had been invited to lecture in Germany in 1962, and he had planned to make this the occasion for a final statement of his juristic views. His untimely death left a serious lacuna in that there is no single published piece, either by Llewellyn or anyone else, which sets out his basic ideas as a reasonably coherent whole. To meet this need is one of the aims of the present work.

THE MAN AND HIS WORK

This bare résumé of Llewellyn's career conveys little of his personal qualities. In fact he imprinted his personality on everything he did, and even if it were desirable, it would be virtually impossible to exclude the strong flavour of the Llewellynesque from any study of his work. Few people could be indifferent to Karl Llewellyn. He frequently stimulated admiration and enthusiasm, but there were also non-enthusiasts. There is some consistency in the respective reactions of those who were definite Karlo-phobes or Karlo-philes. The former tended to consider him a vulgar exhibitionist, sometimes brash and insensitive, sometimes perverse, lacking in self-discipline and too erratic to be taken seriously. His admirers tended to emphasize his combination of humanity and brilliance: warm-hearted, gay, tolerant, uninhibited and vital as a person, stimulating and inspiring as a teacher, perspicacious and wise as a thinker. Taken together such judgments suggest a volatile genius. There is truth in this image, but on its own it is too facile.

There is a strange aura about Llewellyn's writings which is unique in juristic literature. It fascinates some readers, repels others and perplexes most. This strangeness is often attributed to his prose style, which at its best is picturesque and memorable, but is often mannered, irritating and obscure. His use of language is idiosyncratic but it is quite clear that by itself Llewellynese does not explain the Llewellynesque. It is beyond my competence to try to emulate the brave biographer who seeks to give a rounded account of the relationship between the personality and the ideas of his subject. The pitfalls are too many and this study is, in any event, not intended to be in any sense a 'complete' biography. However, there are two aspects of Llewellyn's private life which have a direct bearing on his work as a jurist: his supposed 'artistic' qualities and his personal credo. Before these are considered, it may be of interest to quote from some personal impressions that I recorded of Llewellyn on the basis of my experience of him as a pupil in 1957–8 and when I put his papers in order in 1963–4:

English friends who had been to the United States had emphasized the bizarre: the only American ever to have been awarded the Iron Cross; joint organizer of a verse competition for law students; histrionics in the class-room; eulogies of the 'beauty' of the letter of credit. First impressions did not quite fit this picture; a stocky man with fierce eyebrows and a limp; traces of a parade-ground manner (trying to frighten me?); primarily interested in how much of his work I had read; embarrassing questions about negotiable instruments. Not quite the reception that an Oxford man expects. We exchanged writings. I gave him my proposals for a very ambitious research project. He gave me a bundle of his articles and teaching materials and sent me away. I scampered over rather than through these, selected the first paragraph of one and wrote several pages of detailed analytical notes, mostly in the form of questions about his use of language. About three days later I returned rather pleased with myself to Llewellyn's office. He was surprised to see me. Had I read *all* that he had given me? Indeed, and here were some critical comments. A few probing questions showed up the extent of my incomprehension. I was sent back to re-read the assignment. Shortly afterward my pieces were returned, covered with annotations which were in some instances longer than the original text. Expletives, enthusiastic praise for points which had seemed to me so obvious as to be hardly worth mentioning and, repeatedly, questions challenging rigid dichotomies, precise boundary-drawing and all-or-nothing assertions.* My main concern had been with language; Llewellyn met my challenges head-on with a precision and a linguistic sophistication which, in my arrogance, I had not anticipated.

At our next meeting he diagnosed sympathetically, but with devastating accuracy, exactly what had been going wrong. He then produced some photographs. The first series depicted carvings made with the help of only one tool, the adze. They were crude, but powerful and expressive – works of art by men who were masters of their medium. The second series also depicted carvings – less crude, but obviously inferior as works of art. These, said Llewellyn, were by craftsmen working in the same tradition shortly after the introduction of the chisel. In their enthusiasm for the new, more refined tool, they had jettisoned the adze completely with most unfortunate results. What lessons could I learn from this which would be applicable to jurisprudence? After some discussion, he summed up with a statement that I can render almost *verbatim*: 'Son, you've been staking all your savings on a horse that is not yet even ready to start. Let him alone for a while and go back to him later.' Both diagnosis and prescription proved to be sound. Throughout my contact with him Llewellyn revealed these same qualities as a teacher; pains taken over marking written work; interest in his students as individuals; an uncanny capacity to spot intellectual strengths and weaknesses and to build on the strengths; and the use of vivid metaphor or analogy to make a point unforgettable. That my experience was by no means unique is confirmed by the testimony of many of his former pupils and by the heavily annotated student papers which are to be found in the collection.

In his lectures on jurisprudence Llewellyn's spectacular side was more in

---

* Cf. ' "And–Not" is bad Jurisprudence. In observation of any social scene, the complexity of material makes any *exclusively* single attribute or sequence highly improbable. "And–not" is the traditional bane of sound Jurisprudence (and of lay thinking in general): "Because it is A it is therefore *not* B" presupposes a thoroughly explored, exactly defined area of discussion, divided accurately and exhaustively into A and not A – which the current social scene almost never is.' Llewellyn, *Law in Our Society* (unpublished course materials), p. 35.

evidence. He pounded the table with his fist, he employed rhetorical devices, he insisted on being well supplied with colored chalk, and he imported into the classroom flowers and Gothic spoons and photographs of cathedrals as visual aids. However his reputation for histrionics had been much exaggerated, and, in this course at least, he was far from being the 'strutting player' that some students had depicted. Indeed his lectures were rambling discourses, delivered for the most part in a dry tone and notable as much for satirical touches as for rhetorical flourishes; a large part of my notes consists of provocative aphorisms, copied down *verbatim*, of which the following are examples:

When you stood around when Cicero made a speech you said: 'No mortal man is so eloquent.' When you stood around when Demosthenes made a speech, you said: 'WAR!'

Traditional jurisprudence is the only known pursuit of man from which both sides invariably emerge victorious.

The last thirty-five years of jurisprudence have made clear the quantum of leeway to too many lawyers who will become judges. The last thirty-five years have not, in Law School, made clear the narrow limits of the leeway.

The whole history of the English constitution could be written in terms of pressure of work.

Doctrine brittle and neat is the tool of tender minds in pursuit of policy that can be embraced without using one's intellect.

Technique without ideals is a menace; ideals without technique are a mess.*

Jurisprudence was one of his most successful courses. Early on Llewellyn would make the startling claim that he considered it to be 'the best bread-and-butter course' and 'the one with the most immediate practicality' of any course in Law School. 'This is an arrogant position which I sustain without hesitation and loudly.' 'It is also in my opinion the deepest theoretical course . . . and that is because it is the only course given in this school, which reaches for simplicity, consistently and essentially. . . . And the deepest theory, at least in matters of law, is the deepest simplicity.'† Philosophy as 'contemporaneous polysyllabic professionalized academic discipline' had no place in the course; 'in contrast what is here sought is old-fashioned non-professional "philosophy": general serviceable life-wisdom about some body of material and its homely but basic meaning for life and for man.' § A student's failure to grasp this provoked the only outburst of anger by Llewellyn that I ever witnessed. We were required to do a weekly paper 'on anything to do with the course'. One member of the class

* This was one of Llewellyn's favorite aphorisms. Cf., e.g., 'The Adventures of Rollo', *U. Chi. Law School Record*, Vol. 2, No. 1, pp. 3, 23 (1952).

† The exact words are taken from the transcripts of Llewellyn's Jurisprudence Lectures of 1956, § I, pp. 5–7.

§ *Law in Our Society, op. cit.*, n. 3, p. 8.

had submitted a paper on the Kantian distinction between the 'is' and the 'ought,' a fairly conventional topic. Llewellyn exploded. 'What the hell,' he thundered, 'has Kant to do with *my* course on Jurisprudence?' And, as the class sat in shocked silence, he ranted and raved for several minutes at the poor student, without giving him a chance to defend himself. If this was not genuine rage, it was certainly a convincing performance.

Llewellyn made a further claim: 'I hold that what we do here is not only of application in your professional life, which it is most vigorously, but in your daily life.'* A fundamental objective of the course was to get students to relate their thinking about law to their thinking about life in general. To this end he encouraged them to draw continually on their own experience for material for the weekly papers. For example, one assignment was to take his theory of the function of law ('the law jobs' theory),† which is really a theory about the nature of human groups in general, and to test it out against any group, family, school, boys' camp, submarine, of which the writer of the essay had had firsthand experience. Married students were encouraged to draw analogies between problems of regulating their family life and similar problems in society as a whole. I found myself writing, *inter alia*, about beehives, a self-help scheme in East Africa, and walking in the Lake District, and in the process rediscovering a lot of things that I knew already and for the first time ever relating them to my thinking about law. An impressive number of students who experienced this course have testified to its lasting influence on them, and several have acknowledged that it was indeed the most 'practical', in the sense of having the most direct application to their daily work as lawyers, of all the courses that they took in Law School.

All Llewellyn's courses were unorthodox, and in all he was essentially trying to teach a way of approaching lawyers' problems. But the roles in which he cast himself varied: in Elements he was inclined to be the stern taskmaster, particularly emphasizing the need for solid craftsmanship as a basis for any work in law; in Sales he was more the scholar who had managed to combine deep learning with a firm grasp of the realities of business practice; at almost any time the evangelist might take over, at his best infecting his audience with some of his enthusiasm for the law and his concern for decency and justice. . . .[110a]

THE HALF-WAY ARTIST

'The law', said Holmes, 'is not the place for the artist or the poet. The law is the calling of thinkers'.[111] Lawyers seeking a simple explanation of the strange phenomenon in their midst were inclined to say of Llewellyn: 'Oh well, he's a poet'; this, if facile, is not

---

* *Op. cit.*, § II, p. 18.
† See, e.g., *The Cheyenne Way* (1941), ch. xi.

entirely misleading. But it is not enough. Other successful lawyers have written poetry or have been accomplished musicians or connoisseurs of the arts or have contributed to literature even when writing about law. They may have been unusual; Llewellyn was unique.

Llewellyn's interests and activities gave colour to the image of him as a poet or artist. At one time or another he applied himself with his usual enthusiasm to writing stories, science fiction, plays for children, satire, self-parody, ballads and verse of varied style and quality.[112] In 1931 he published two collections of poems; during the rest of his life he continued to write occasional light verse about cats and colleagues and camping and trees and jurisprudence and judges and many other subjects. After his death a poem entitled 'Njal Invokes Justice',[113] written in both German and English, was found among the papers on his desk; in most of his legal books he included at least one specimen of his verse; he enlivened gatherings of law teachers by leading singing sessions, which often included one or two Llewellyniana – the best known being his ballad in praise of 'The Common Law Tradition'.[114] At one period he took up clay modelling and wood carving, at another he dabbled in painting. He had some facility as a cartoonist. His insatiable curiosity led him to take an interest in many of the arts, but only in respect of Gothic architecture could he have made any serious claim to expertise.

Llewellyn did not take himself very seriously as a poet. He wrote verse rather than poetry and put most of it in the category of 'art-for-fun'. In the preface of *Put in His Thumb* he spoke of 'ballads that creak, sonnets that sacrifice music to meaning, meaning sometimes buried in obscure expressions'.[115] An early lyric repeats the theme:

BARRIER

I would make you songs, lady
        make your heart sing,
songs sweet as peach blossom,
        fragrant as spring.

I would make you songs, lady
        each little while –
laughing lilting little lays,
        would make your eyes smile.

I would sing you the heart of things,
    winnow away the chaff –
I would make you songs, lady –
    but you would laugh.[116]

Many of his lighter verses and songs concerned law:

LAMENT ON WHAT'S WRONG WITH OUR LAW

(Tune: Unidentified but sad)
It's A is the source of the trouble
It's A is the guy who gets me
And not till I die will I ever see why
The courts don't give judgment for B.

It's A is the man with the offer
The 'master' of 'promise for act'
And then he revokes with his loud and lewd jokes
In time to keep out of the pact.

When 'A says to B', B's in trouble
You ought to feel sorry for B
B won't catch him ever, old A is too clever –
And meanwhile he's out rooking P.

For A has 'apparent authority'
And A goes on hogging the swag
While poor trusting P, just a fellow like me,
Is always left holding the bag.

You'll find A indicted for thieving,
For murder, for crimes about sex
But he gets the breaks with the bad law he makes
Along with his buddy, that X.

Our law could be perfect tomorrow
Our law could be better today
If every last court of final resort
Would just put the skids under A.[117]

These examples may help to give some perspective to the idea of
Llewellyn as a poet. He was capable of writing pleasant pieces, but
no great talents await discovery.

    Llewellyn's prose also exposes both his potentialities and his
limitations as an artist. He laboured, perhaps too self-consciously,

to write well. The results were only occasionally successful; sometimes they were disastrous. Indeed, no other aspect of his work is more likely to swell the ranks of the Karlo-phobes, especially if the variety of his styles is overlooked. The most striking feature is the vocabulary: there is an uninhibited use of slang and neologisms; terms, not always elegant, are freely minted ('jurisprude', 'law-stuff', 'situation sense', skelegal'); nouns are transformed into verbs ('to lawyer'; 'to poultice'), there is frequent resort to metaphor, sometimes mixed, often vivid, but equally often somewhat imprecise; rigid dichotomies are eschewed; the grammar is sometimes idiosyncratic.[118] He shared Holmes' taste for aphorism and Carlyle's for hyphenated words. Indeed, Llewellyn's style is sometimes compared with that of Thomas Carlyle.[119] The comparison is apt, but dangerous. What Woodward said of Carlyle is applicable to some works, like *The Common Law Tradition*: 'His English style had many of the faults which he attributed to Parliaments. It was verbose, egoistical, noisy, full of repetition and overstatement.'[120] Yet the writings of both authors are exceptionally quotable, abounding with pithy epigrams and striking phrases. The outcome is a disorderly profusion, richness not matched by a corresponding discipline and sense of form. That Llewellyn is reminiscent of Carlyle is not entirely a coincidence. At college he had admired *Sartor Resartus* and *On Heroes and Hero-Worship*;[121] as an adult, when he wanted to step beyond conventional bounds of juristic propriety, he adopted the pseudonym of Carlyle's creation, Teufelsdrockh, the Philosopher of [the] Clothes.[122] The original Teufelsdrockh provided his creator with a convenient outlet for self-parody and semi-serious fantasy; the character of Diogenes Jonathan Swift Teufelsdrockh performed a similar function for Llewellyn. In each case, too, the device seems to have misfired in that the conscious humour proved heavy and awkward, while the self-parody sometimes cuts deeper than the author probably intended.

In fact Llewellyn had not one style, but several. In some works, especially those which began as lectures, such as *The Bramble Bush*, the sentences tended to be short and crisp, sometimes without a verb. Some such passages, deprived of the gestures and variations in tone which accompanied their delivery, may seem awkward to the reader, but others are effective and memorable. The 'oral style' is usually quite easy to understand. This is not true of some of the serious jurisprudential writings, in which too often long sentences meander learnedly through provisos and dependent clauses, inappropriately decked in metaphors and colloquialisms—an unhappy marriage between a German pedant and a vulgar Brooklyn floozy. Llewellyn's touch seems to have been surer when he wrote on commercial subjects; here he often successfuly combined cool professionalism with flashes which are vivid and amusing. Unfortunately the manner of presentation is not a reliable indicator of the quality of the substance, for some of Llewellyn's most important thoughts appear in some of his least readable writings.[123] In short, his prose style was as complex and as varied as his character.

Llewellyn's writings do not suggest unfaltering judgment and taste in literary matters. He disclaimed any such thing:

I am a barbarian, a primitive, in my tastes in art. *The Everlasting Mercy* is my idea of poetry, especially the fight-part and the passages where Saul Kane thinks of youngsters. Action and directness and simplicity: almost a folksong. And I like drama; that's a primitive taste, too. O'Neill's *Hairy Ape* and the heroic exaggerations of Shakespeare – *Macbeth* more than *Hamlet*. And stories: the Volsung Saga, and Samson, and Treasure Island (I read that over every birthday); and adventure and detective yarns when not too badly written. All that, I take it, shows a paleolithic taste, a taste sound enough as far as it goes, but unrefined, crude, savage. Shelley doesn't thrill me, nor Swinburne; nor Villon, very much. So that if I should speak of drama in the large, you would understand that my opinions, even if based on vastly wider reading, would be notably lop-sided. But I claim that their very bias makes them sound, when applied not to grown-ups (God pity them), but to other kids. If my development in literature and every other art has been stunted at the kid stage, so much the more authority to my views on art for kids.[124]

This passage appears in an unpublished essay on producing plays for children. The context may explain the exaggerated note of self-deprecation, but the confession is basically convincing. Llewellyn was not especially well-read for an intellectual and he had a decided taste for the folksy, not only in literature. In philosophy he preferred Ben Franklin to Hegel; he liked orchards and village craftsmen and Maine fishermen and sages like Will Rogers and Mr Dooley. His humour tended to be earthy and unsophisticated.[125]

If Llewellyn's performance as a poet or *litterateur* need not be taken too seriously the artistic side of his nature should not be ignored. It affected his approach to almost everything. In this context 'artistic' refers not only to his emotional intensity and general volatility, but also to his cast of mind. He seemed to work at least as much by intuition and imagination as by conscious reasoning and analysis. He thought, says Soia Mentschikoff, in 'Gestalts'; some of the less disciplined passages in his writings give the impression that the author is proceeding by free association. He would react with excitement to seemingly obvious ideas and he would give to even the most mundane of transactions an aura of romanticism; he rhapsodized about the 'beauty' of the letter of credit, praised judgments for their loveliness, and his vision of the world of commerce was often more in the spirit of Masefield's 'Cargoes' than of *The Wall Street Journal*. Who else would have been so quick to recognize a certain deftness in the Cheyennes' handling of conflict or, having done so, would have concluded a work of anthropological scholarship with what has been aptly termed 'almost a prose poem in praise of the Cheyenne juristic method'?[126] To many lawyers such romanticism may seem inappropriate, even distasteful; but for Llewellyn it was a natural way of seeing law and commerce as part and parcel of his general world view.

Of all Llewellyn's 'artistic' qualities, the most highly developed was his capacity for quick intuitive perception. In personal relations he was able to attain immediate rapport with a wide variety of people—small town lawyers, leaders of the bar, painters, bankers, students,—although on occasion he could also be quite insensitive to the feelings of others. His rapport with American Indians was quite remarkable. He was fascinated by human institutions and transactions and he had an uncanny capacity for getting the feel for the point of view of ordinary participants and their ways of going about their work.[127] His well-known grasp of business practice was based partly on his insatiable interest in the details of the subject (always with an eye for the significant pattern) and partly on this capacity for intuitively sensing what was not fully articulated.[128]

It is easy to see how Llewellyn got the reputation for being an artist abroad in the law. He was interested in the arts, not only as a dilettante spectator, but also as an enthusiastic if not entirely successful performer, and he had qualities which are commonly associated with an artistic temperament. The unusual feature was that he gave an extraordinarily free rein to his interests and temperament in his legal work. He frequently resorted to analogies from the arts in his legal writings; concepts such as 'style' and 'craft' played an important part in his jurisprudence and he even expounded a theory of legal aesthetics. Idiosyncratic prose, bursts of uninhibited enthusiasm, a tendency to self-dramatization, and a romantic imagination do not fit in well with the stereotype of the lawyer, conservative, unemotional, cautious, and generally prosaic. Small wonder, then, that some have been tempted to add to the assertion 'he's a poet', an assumed corollary, 'not a lawyer'. They have been mistaken. For Llewellyn was at least as much a lawyer as he was an artist. He loved the law, he was learned in it, he identified himself with the legal profession to a marked extent, he had outstanding grades as a law student, his record in practice was excellent, and he became one of the leading commercial lawyers of his time.[129]

To conclude: applied to Llewellyn Holmes' dictum pinpoints a puzzle, but fails to resolve it. 'He was a poet, not a lawyer' suggests a false antithesis, implying that intuition, imagination and depth of feeling have nothing to contribute to law, and are inconsistent with the qualities which go to make a good lawyer. This is as foolish and misleading as the discredited idea that imagination and intuition have no part to play in science. In so intellectualized and tough a milieu as law they are not easily accommodated; for this very reason they have the additional value of scarcity. Llewellyn approached most subjects on a number of different levels simultaneously and this helps to explain some of the strangeness about his work. It must be admitted that he was not always successful and the results were sometimes awkward; but it must equally be admitted that such success as he had was in no small part due to his 'artistic' qualities.[130] Furthermore, his highly personal style gives more scope for differences of taste than do most juristic writings. He had in almost equal measure the capacity to excite and to repel. One of the problems of making a sober appraisal of his contribution to juristic thought is to discount as largely irrelevant excesses of enthusiasm and revulsion stemming from the differing tastes of Karlo-philes and Karlo-phobes.

RELIGION AND IDEOLOGY

Llewellyn's non-conformist upbringing and his adolescent reaction to it have already been noted. For most of his adult life his religious views probably reflected some inner conflict. He believed in God, but he had a marked antipathy towards organized religion; he was suspicious of dogmas and was a professed relativist in ethics, yet for over thirty years he flirted with Natural Law, emotionally attracted by it, yet intellectually sceptical.[181] At various times he gave serious consideration to becoming a member of the Roman Catholic or the Russian Orthodox Church. He felt a strong need 'to join up', as he put it, but equally strongly he wanted no human machinery interposed between himself and God. At some time in the early 1940s he had a religious experience, 'a direct intimation of God'.[182] In 1943 he tried to sort out his ideas on paper and came to the conclusion that he wished 'to have a Catholic connection without paying a right Catholic price'.[183] He did not 'join up' on this occasion, nor thereafter, but he continued to be preoccupied with religious questions, especially just before his death.

Llewellyn never resolved his religious dilemmas. In his later years in Chicago he moved even closer to Roman Catholicism: he took to questioning Catholics about their beliefs, St Thomas featured more prominently in his jurisprudence course, he tried to convert some of his friends, and a few days before he died he began to draft a circular letter to Roman Catholic law teachers taking them to task for poor public relations in spreading the message of their faith.[184] But he never reached the stage of seeking formal instruction preparatory to being received into the Roman Church and there is little evidence to suggest that his views had changed sufficiently from 1943 to make such a step feasible or even credible. His distrust of dogmatism, his ethical relativism and his general attitude to human institutions and human authority would have been formidable, if not insurmountable, obstacles. Perhaps the crux of the matter is a paradox: as a student of institutions, he was especially attracted to Rome through his admiration for the Catholic Church as an institution—the whole apparatus of organization, personnel, skills, ritual and even dogma—yet, like Shaw's St Joan, he could not accept any intermediary between himself and God.

Llewellyn's attitude to religion changed several times during his lifetime; his position on social and political issues was probably more constant, but he appears to have created a widespread impression that he tended to be ambivalent or indifferent to such matters. At first sight there does appear to be a pattern: for example, in the first world war he was prepared to change sides;[185] although an active supporter of the NAACP and the ACLU until about 1940 and a professed opponent of racial segregation, his friends were surprised by his lukewarm reaction when an attempt was made within the AALS to attack racial discrimination in southern law schools;[136] during the New Deal he appeared to sit on the fence, when many of his friends and colleagues (including several realists) committed themselves wholeheartedly to the cause; some of his academic colleagues who worked with him on the Uniform Commercial Code felt that he was too ready to compromise on issues relating to consumer protection;[137] and others, including his collaborator Hoebel, found it difficult to see how he could reconcile his enthusiasm for the 'authoritarian gerontocracy' of the Pueblos with the image of an 'American liberal democrat'.[138] Finally, while only the most imperceptive and ignorant of critics could seriously accuse Llewellyn of being indifferent to values in his jurisprudence or of believing that Might is Right, some thoughtful scholars have found it difficult to identify precise principles to which he was prepared to commit himself wholeheartedly, and they could point out that in articulating goals he tended to take refuge in notoriously vague terms—justice, wisdom, decency and fairness. In short, it may be asked, was Llewellyn as truly 'liberal' as he professed to be?

While this doubt cannot be completely resolved, it is possible to argue that Llewellyn's reactions to political or ideological issues were really quite consistent for so emotional and intuitive a person.[139] First, allowance must be made for his strong antidoctrinaire tendencies. Like Holmes and Dewey he preferred to leave his ultimate values 'unstressed and implicit',[140] and his reasons for doing so were very similar to theirs. Some of the examples cited in the last paragraph could be used as an index of sophistication rather than of caprice: it can be pointed out that on the issue of racial discrimination in legal education he advanced some practical reasons for being doubtful about the proposed measure, while expressing his general sympathy with the cause;[141] that in his approach to the Uniform Commercial Code and the problems of the Pueblos he clearly saw the presence of conflicting interests; that scattered throughout the Uniform Commercial Code are a number of starting points for the judicial development of doctrines favouring consumers;[142] that he worked actively to introduce certain basic civil liberties (such as the concept of a fair hearing) into the traditional Pueblo system;[143] and that his attitude to Natural Law was sympathetic, subtle and consistent over time.[144] In short it can be argued that Llewellyn was usually intellectually consistent in his suspicion of broad abstract formulas and in his refusal to be dogmatic, while being emotionally constant in his sympathy for the underdog and in his loyalty to his basic ethos.

What was that ethos? Llewellyn's 'liberalism' was the old-fashioned liberalism of John Adams or of some of the leaders of the New York bar, such as C. C. Burlingham. He believed deeply in certain basic liberties (especially equality of opportunity, freedom of speech and association, and procedural due process),[145] but equally in the responsibility of the individual to make the most of his opportunities ('Give a man a chance and then it is up to him'). He was opposed to what he considered the sentimental liberalism of those who acted as if the underdog is always right, and to the paternalism of some of the welfare-minded New Dealers and of those who wanted to impose the American way of life on the 'American' Indians. He was also much concerned with efficiency: no measure, however well-intentioned, was worth fighting for unless it had a good prospect of working. Thus he was prepared to hold back, where others might feel that he was being 'unprincipled', because he did not believe in ignoring considerations of feasibility in his pursuit of what he considered to be desirable.[146] Thus, in this view, during his working life Llewellyn was a pragmatic, old-fashioned, American liberal, whose most important operative values were equality of opportunity, individual responsibility and efficiency.

CONCLUSION

A Chicago colleague once referred to Llewellyn as 'that extraordinary piece of radio-active material abroad in the Law School world for over forty years'. This is a better summary than most, if any summary is possible. The aim of this chapter has been to provide little more than an introductory sketch of Llewellyn's life and character and to pin-point certain features that may have had a direct bearing on his approach to jurisprudence and to law. In the chapters which follow there will be further glimpses of Llewellyn in action, in the campaign for the Uniform Commercial Code, in his dealings with American Indians, and in the class-room; frequent quotations from his writings will be a constant reminder of the man, but from now on it will be his ideas rather than his personality that will be the centre of attention.

Like any other thinker of substance, Llewellyn's ideas developed and changed over the years. However, his most important works

were written after the main lines of his thought had been settled.[147]
Some commentators notwithstanding, *The Common Law Tradition*
(1960) marks no sharp break from *The Bramble Bush* (1930). There
is a difference of mood and style, but no significant *volte-face*.
Since Llewellyn tended to have several projects going simultaneously, it would not be sensible to attempt to deal with them in a
strictly chronological order. However, the most important advances
in his thinking will be indicated.

Wherever possible, in order to avoid repetition, Llewellyn's ideas
on a particular topic are dealt with thematically in connection
with a single work. For instance, his miscellaneous writings on precedent and case law are treated together in the chapter on *The
Common Law Tradition*. Five works have been given special
prominence: *Cases and Materials on the Law of Sales, The
Cheyenne Way*, the Uniform Commercial Code, *The Common Law
Tradition*, and the manuscript of *Law in Our Society*. The chapters
on these, and the shorter sections on other particular works, such as
The Bramble Bush, have been written as largely self-contained
essays, in the hope that this may facilitate their use as introductory
guides to the originals.

7

Two Early Works

The interdependence of teaching and research is an article of faith for many university teachers. In practice the conjunction of the two activities can act either as a brake or as a stimulus to the advancement of learning or the interaction can be more complex. Karl Llewellyn was a dedicated teacher, especially during the first part of his career. Apart from his verse, his first three books were all ostensibly addressed to students. In each case, however, this fact had curiously different results. *Cases and Materials on the Law of Sales* is a remarkable example of an undergraduate course book which is based on learning and insight worthy of a major treatise. In *The Bramble Bush* Llewellyn threw aside scholarly inhibitions in an attempt to excite the interest of first-year students, only to find that he had thereby attracted an unwelcome amount of so-called 'scholarly' attention. His German book on case law in America looks more like a book of materials for a course (and this was in part its origin) than a scholarly monograph, yet it was published for the benefit of, and was probably mainly read by, established German scholars.

Llewellyn's ideas on case law are best considered in connection with *The Common Law Tradition*. In this chapter *Cases and Materials on the Law of Sales* and *The Bramble Bush* will be discussed in turn. Each in its way marks an important stage in the development of his thought, but in both instances the author's educational objectives determined the manner of the presentation of his ideas.

CASES AND MATERIALS ON THE LAW OF SALES

Llewellyn's first work of substance, *Cases and Materials on the Law of Sales*, grew directly out of the Columbia curriculum discussions.

It was preceded by a series of reviews of casebooks, in which he tried to develop his ideas about what constituted suitable materials for the study of law. It is fitting that what might be called his first articulation of a realist position is to be found in the last of this sequence, a review of Campbell's *Cases on Mortgages of Real Property*.[1] The passage shows clearly the connection between Llewellyn's concern about problems of teaching and his jurisprudential ideas:

The reviewer holds that the time has passed when the study of law could profitably be centered on legal doctrine. At the present juncture the only serviceable focus of law study is law-in-action; law-in-action not only in the sense of Dean Pound's well known article: what the courts and all quasi-judicial bodies actually do; but also in Ehrlich's sense: the actual ordering of men's actions.

I do not wish to be misunderstood on this point. I do not say that the study of legal doctrine should be discarded. Doctrinal formulas, even when patently untrue to the cases, repeatedly influence results. Concepts – which are but summaries of doctrine – repeatedly produce decisions, sometimes in the teeth of good sense. Received formulas, good or bad, therefore need study. The traditional patterns of the law – such as 'mortgage' – now block growth, now direct its course; the lawyer needs to know this, and to be familiar with the patterns. But I do say that the role of such doctrines and concepts is vastly less important than our current teaching would suggest. Holmes has long made us familiar with the proposition that a rule is merely a prediction of what a court will *do*. Courts are continually arriving at results 'unsound on principle' – but pretty sane on the facts. Even more often, they are arriving at results we approve, in cases which 'might better have been put on other grounds'. Meantime psychologists have been arguing that men decide matters first – on emotional grounds – and rationalize them afterwards – in opinions. Doctrine, if it is to mean – or lead to – accurate prediction, must be in terms of what courts *do*; and of what they *say* only so far as a connection is demonstrated between what they say and what they do. And when all allowance has been made for judicial conservatism, for the technical ritual of the law, for judicial ignorance, the fact remains that everywhere, and especially in the business field, what courts have *done* and will *do* is, in the main, understandable only in terms of what *men* do. The results of cases tend to follow the practice of men. The practice of lawyers, in dealing with the results of cases, tends even more strongly to follow the practice of men. *Mortgage* is a legal concept; that concept, in all its phases, is important. *Mortgage* is also a security device. That fact, in all its phases, is even more important. The legal concept is empty, without its application. The history, the steady changes of the concept, are unintelligible except in the light of the strains successively put on the concept by men's needs and men's actions. The present meaning of the concept, its future course, are not less unintelligible without that light.

Lawyers when writing textbooks seem curiously blind to this. But the same lawyers, when preparing documents, or trials, or briefs, become vividly alive to it – within the limits of the particular situation before them. Under pressure of a client's interest, principles hitherto regarded as firmly settled take on elasticity or sudden limits. Under pressure of regulating the multitude of situations never settled in court, the business lawyer is recognizing the practical need of a lawyer's being trained to see his law against the facts of men's lives, and the practical fact that law not thus seen is not truly seen at all. Doctrine, then, we must have, first. But doctrine alone is vacuous, an illusion. Doctrine plus knowledge of the uses to which legal institutions are being put, is the only doctrine with meaning. Given the two together, one approaches the question of whether doctrine will expand to meet a new need, equipped for persuasion – and without false hopes as to the certainty of the outcome.[2]

It is worth noting that Llewellyn, while finding illumination in the views attributed to Holmes and behaviourist psychologists, does not commit himself wholeheartedly to their acceptance. Furthermore he is careful to stress that it is the treatment of doctrine *in vacuo*, not doctrine itself, which he is criticizing; just as he is careful to state in another part of the review that, to argue that a lawyer needs a reasonable knowledge of the economics and sociology of business as a basis for understanding mortgages, does not involve commitment to the view that a lawyer is a social scientist. Rather, Llewellyn asserts, 'He is a craftsman. He is a specialized technician.'[3] Thus, even as early as 1926, Llewellyn was careful to avoid some of the extreme views of which realists were later to be accused; he was also more concerned with *prudentia* than with science.

The review of Campbell was published during the early stages of the preparation of the casebook on sales. By the time the book was complete Llewellyn had further developed his ideas about teaching tools and in the thirteen-page introduction he set them out at a great length. Rarely, if ever, has the author of a legal treatise, let alone the compiler of a casebook, tried to rationalize and articulate so exhaustively 'the aims and method of the book, and the theoretical base on which it rests'.[4] It dwarfs even Langdell's famous preface. A similar self-consciousness is a feature of a number of casebooks in the 'realist' mould.[5]

Llewellyn devoted almost as much thought to the organization of the book, to the choice of source materials and their manner of presentation, and even to the elaborate indexes, as he did to its substantive content. Ironically the enormous labour expended on the book contributed to its partial failure to achieve its main objective, that is to say, to be a usable teaching tool. It was nearly 1,100 pages long, with many passages in small print, and much of the material condensed. It was quite clearly a work of profound scholarship and originality. A book so long, so meaty and so novel appeared formidable to the ordinary student and almost equally so to teachers accustomed to a more straightforward and traditional approach. Llewellyn used the book in his own courses, with conspicuous success with better students, but most other teachers of sales, even those who greatly admired it as a work of original scholarship, felt that it was too hard to inflict on students, and its normal fate was to be used as a teacher's desk book. It was not a commercial success.

The fact that Llewellyn's *Cases and Materials on Sales* was not widely used in teaching did not deter others from using it as a model.[6] In fact it is generally recognized as a landmark in the history of the American casebook, being the first of a series of works that departed from the traditional model of Langdell.[7] It would be easy to give an exaggerated impression of its uniqueness unless it is set in the context of other activities that were going on at Columbia Law School at the time. In particular it must be remembered that between 1930 and 1933 members of the Columbia Faculty published fourteen course books, most of which involved new departures in the selection, organization and use of sources.[8] In his Annual Report of 1933 Dean Smith referred to fourteen other sets of materials prepared in connection with the revised curriculum, but not published.[9] Thus Llewellyn was not working in isolation and some of the new ideas in his book were shared with several of his colleagues, three of whom were singled out in the introduction for special mention: 'Less obvious, but no less heavy, is the indebtedness to long-continued discussions with Underhill Moore, Herman Oliphant and Walter Wheeler Cook, especially on the side of analysis in terms of risk-allocation (Moore), of growing distrust of judicial rationalization (Cook), and of analysis in terms of significant type fact set-ups: overseas, documentary, etc. (Moore, Oliphant).'[10]

Although Llewellyn's is only one of a number of unorthodox works that were prepared at approximately the same time by a fairly closely integrated group of colleagues, it is deservedly the best known. Apart from its considerable scholarly merits, it was the first of the new style of course book to be published, it was in several respects the most revolutionary, it was based on the most articulate theory and it was probably the most influential on the subsequent development of works of this genre. In what respects did it differ from traditional casebooks on sales? The main differences can be dealt with under three heads which reflect three of the principal pre-occupations of Oliphant's *Summary* discussed above: (i) the range and use of source materials; (ii) the classification and arrangement of the subject-matter; and underlying these, (iii) educational objectives.

(i) *The range and use of source materials*

The typical casebook in the Langdell tradition consisted of little more than a collection of judgments. Llewellyn's book contains a substantial amount of text, which is concerned not only with analysis of doctrine and its historical development, but also discusses economic considerations, business practice and other factors which affect the expectations and behaviour of commercial buyers, sellers and middlemen. Such extensive use of 'extra-legal' sources was revolutionary for a book of this kind, but equally significant is the manner of presentation of these materials. One of its chief merits, as Brainerd Currie pointed out, is that it '.... did not offer social science materials in homeopathic doses. The author had himself assimilated and brought to bear the contributions of non-legal disciplines and had utilized them in preparing background materials which a lawyer or law student could appreciate without special conditioning.'[11]

Llewellyn's use of cases departed from tradition in several respects. The majority of 'cases' consisted of a summary of the facts together with the result, the reasoning of the court being omitted entirely. Behind this were two ideas, inherited from Corbin and Cook; first the idea that at least as much significance should be attached to what judges do (the result based on the facts as the judges saw them) as to what they say by way of justification.[12] Secondly, the idea that the facts of cases have a significance that transcends their significance as precedents and illustrations of doctrine: they are concrete illustrations of business situations, which give a flavour of practice beyond the particular legal issues involved; they are also excellent raw material for students to treat as problems, more closely related to 'real life' than artificial hypothetical fact-situations dreamed up by academic lawyers.[13] Thus the basis for selection of cases was not solely that of doctrinal significance.

The extensive use of digests of cases made it possible to include 801 cases for discussion, between two and four times the number to be found in the other leading sales casebooks of the time.[14] Forty-five per cent of the cases had been decided in the ten years prior to the publication of the book, which was admittedly a particularly active period in American sales law;[15] the 1919 edition of Williston's casebook offers a striking contrast: out of a total of nearly 400 cases there are only twelve from the period 1900–8 and twenty-two from the period 1909–19; thus cases from the eighteen years preceding publication represent less than ten per cent of the total. Llewellyn's emphasis on recent decisions was deliberate: in his view the fact-situations of recent cases were more likely to be indicative of typical recurrent problem-areas and typical modern business transactions than the old cases concerning sales of horses and other face-to-face transactions. Whereas Langdell and his descendants used cases primarily as examples of *the* relatively stable principles, Llewellyn's emphasis on recent cases reflects a sustained concern with contemporary problems.

Emphasis on recent cases did not in this instance involve a sacrifice of historical depth. Indeed one of the outstanding features of the book is the analysis of the growth of the law of sales, and notably of the shrift from *caveat emptor* to buyer's protection and the conceptual growth of 'warranty' in terms of the interaction of law and social and economic change. Some of the flavour of Llewellyn's style is distilled in the passage which introduces the analysis:

The law of seller's obligation as to quality ('warranty') presents the sweep of sales law in perhaps its most dramatic form. The picture begins in terms of a community whose trade is only one step removed from barter – your black horse, two stools, a jack-knife and thirty-four bushels of corn for my roan, an ox and two dozen eggs. Two vital presuppositions reign: first, that the goods in question are there to be seen; second, either that everybody knows everybody's goods, individually, in a face-to-face, closed, stable group; or that trade with strangers in a shop is an arm's length proposition, with wits matched against skill. In either event, only a fool believes anything he hears. In either event, the profits of talking a man into buying are fair and honorable. These are the days when an honest merchant's diary records: 'Bought 1,000 lbs. of sugar at so much; out of this, sold 1,300 lbs. at so much. The Lord blessed me with a fair profit.' Manufactured goods are handicraft articles, made by someone you know, and for the most local of markets.

Out of this we move gradually into a credit and industrial economy. Overseas trade in seaports introduces cargo-lot dealing, and dealing in goods at a distance, before they can be seen. Markets widen with improved transportation – internal waterways, railroads. This means reliance on distant sellers. Middlemen's dealings mean, sometimes, the postponement of inspection; always they mean some ignorance in the seller of the history of the goods. Industrialization grows out of and produces standardization, grading and sizing of lumber, grading and branding of flour or hardware, a certain predictability and reliability of goods. Contracts made by description, or by sample, which is a form of description, or by specification, which is an elaborate description, become the order of the day. Contracts come increasingly to precede production. Sellers begin to build for good will, in wide markets, to feel their standing behind goods to be no hardship, no outrage, no threat to their solvency from a thousand lurking claims, but the mark of business respectability and the road to future profit. The law of seller's obligation *must* change, to suit.

All of this is an uneven process. Men are trading whiskey for pork in Illinois long after blankets are handled in bale lots and on credit in New York City. England is until the 70's decades ahead of our country in the development. Our own law grows more rapidly in regard to quality than, e.g., in the corresponding rules on bills of lading. It grows unevenly by states. . . . Once seen, the drama of it makes one catch his breath.

And the conceptual growth is as striking as the shift from seller's to buyer's protection. 'Warranty,' in sales at first as a formulaic collateral contract; quality at first sharply distinguished from other phases of the deal; conditions and duties fused or confused; 'express' and 'implied' obligation beginning as different legal concepts, with different legal results; struggle and confusion in the court's dealings with the emergent normality of the executory contract.[16]

For all its originality, *Cases and Materials on the Law of Sales* marked no break from the library-bound tradition of legal writing. Llewellyn openly acknowledged this:

The picture is not complete. To fill it out would need a vast body of descriptive and statistical economic material which is as yet lacking. Partly the lack moves from the prohibitive amount of time required in turning out what seemed a worthwhile teaching tool. Partly it moves from the fact that the book is directed to law students, not to students of business; legal technique thus moves into the foreground, and an understanding of the business situation becomes not a primary object, but a means to making the legal job intelligible. Finally, there is the question of space and of technique. Sooner or later we must learn to bring to bear on our law curriculum an increased body of fact information; but the art is not easy, and we have to reckon, while it is being learned, with limitations of time and space. In the meantime, the descriptions of fact background inserted in the book must serve as best they can. Over-generalized and over-simplified as they are, they are nevertheless a first step, and a needed one.[17]

Llewellyn, then, perceived the *relevance* of empirical data to what he was doing, but in this case he was prepared to make do with what was readily available. As far as his own efforts were concerned, teaching and preparation for teaching took priority over fundamental research.

(ii) *Classification and arrangement*

Problems of classification of subject-matter need to be studied carefully by the proponents of a contextual approach to legal literature. During the Columbia curriculum discussions a great deal of attention had been devoted to these problems. Oliphant's *Summary* displays an awareness of the problems of devising any scheme of classification,[18] but goes rather further in dispensing with traditional legal concepts as a basis for classification than Llewellyn was prepared to go in his subsequent writing. In his longest discussion of the problem he dissociated himself from dogmatic functionalism:

The first truth, to be repeated for the benefit of 'functionalists,' is that the old concepts are not only with us still, but within their own areas are still fundamental.

I say 'within their own areas' because, increasingly, fields open which escape the older concepts. 'Fair Trade Acts' . . . or the concept of 'unfair labor practice,' or the impact of taxation on trust and business organization, or deposit insurance will serve to suggest what I mean.[19]

At the same time the shifting nature of these categories needs to be recognized:

The second truth is that any of these basic legal concepts (as a going factor in our law-work) changes not only its meaning, but its shape, and changes the direction of its 'drive,' as it is put to differing uses, among differing social and economic contexts.[20]

Llewellyn saw no simple solution to the problem of organization of teaching materials. There was a prospect of recurring strain between established legal categories and constantly changing social patterns and often a compromise had to be made between the claims of principles competing to be the basis of classification. The organization of *Cases and Materials on the Law of Sales* reflects such a compromise. Most, but not all, of the chapters are based on legal concepts.[21] The chapter headings represent a significant, but not a revolutionary, divergence from, for instance, their counterparts in Williston's casebook. So do the sub-headings. In diverging from the relatively neat traditional organization, Llewellyn was not able to substitute any simple alternative principle. The result is that the book is open to criticism on grounds of untidiness, a charge which the realist often has to bear in silence.

There were other departures from tradition. Most important was the shift of emphasis from the present sale to the contract for future delivery on the ground that the latter is far more important to the lawyer in practice and more typical of business transactions in a credit economy. This insight has been acted on by editors of later casebooks. Instead of starting with an historical introduction or examination of the contract of sale, distinguishing it from other contracts, Llewellyn plunged straight into the economics of business. The opening words of the first chapter set the tone : 'Price is the heart of the sales contract; and peculiarly so in sales to a dealer. Ours is a money economy, a price system; business centers on profit; profit centers on price.'[22]

In matters of detail the organization of the material is influenced by what the editor conceived to be recurring types of situation and typical problems presented to businessmen or to lawyers practising preventive law in commercial situations. Two of the most important chapters are organized around legal concepts—'warranty' and 'title' —but the treatment is functional. The chapter on warranty has as a central theme the changing meaning and use of the concept at different times and in different contexts; the main point of the chapter on title is to demonstrate that this concept has in fact very little functional significance in respect of allocation of risk, despite the central position given to it in traditional analyses of the law of sales.[23]

Two other features of the book are connected with Llewellyn's ideas about classification. First, there is a recurring theme of the need to be distrustful of broad generalizations and especially of 'lump concepts'. This theme reaches a crescendo in the analysis of 'title'. By 'lump concepts' Llewellyn meant abstract legal conceptions, such as 'right', 'possession', 'consideration', 'title to goods', and 'servant'. One of the 'common points of departure' of realists, he claimed was 'the belief in the worthwhileness of grouping cases and legal situations into narrower categories than has been the practice in the past.'[24] A general concept which 'lumped together' socially disparate situations (e.g. 'servant' in relation to vicarious liability in torts) or which was used in different contexts to perform different functions (e.g. 'servant' for determining for whose actions a 'master' is liable in torts, or for determining to whom a master owes a duty to provide a safe system of working or in relation to actions for enticement or non-tortious matters relating to insurance) was to be viewed with scepticism. He later added an important proviso: 'The quest for narrower, more significant categories is always a sound *first* approach to wide categories which are not giving satisfaction in use. But of course, once satisfactory narrow categories have been found and tested, the eternal quest recurs for wider synthesis—but one which will really stand up in use.'[25] In respect of 'narrow issue thinking', as he called it, Llewellyn was directly influenced by his former teacher, Hohfeld. The chapter on title is a good example of the application, and development, of Hohfeld's ideas. The weapons of analytical jurisprudence are here used as part of the armoury of legal realism.

Llewellyn was rather proud of another feature, the indexes. The 'topical' index was fairly conventional in form, but was exceptionally detailed. There was an index of cases by jurisdiction in addition to the usual table of cases. Most original was the index of commodities, which enables the reader to work through all the cases in the book dealing with agricultural raws and foodstuffs, or more narrowly with sugar or potatoes. These indexes are indicative of the great care that went into every aspect of the preparation of the book.

(iii) *Educational objectives: Llewellyn and Langdell*

Between the publication of Langdell's casebook in 1871 and the appearance of Llewellyn's in 1930, there had, of course, been experiments and modifications in respect of teaching materials. Not all of the unusual features of the sales book were entirely unprecedented. But by and large up to 1930 casebooks had followed a fairly standard pattern. Never before had this pattern been challenged in so many different respects in a single volume. Llewellyn's work marks a major step forward in the development of teaching tools in American law schools, and in significance it is of the same order as Langdell's work before it or the 'Yale casebooks' of the 1960s.[26]

At the root of the differences between Llewellyn's casebook and Langdell's is a difference in objectives. The materials were to be used for different purposes. It is true that both editors preached a vocational approach to legal education, but their respective images of the end product, the lawyer, were radically different. Langdell's image was tailored to fit his somewhat Germanic ideas of university education and was rather blurred:

Law, considered as a science, consists of principles or doctrines. To have such a mastery of these as to be able to apply them with constant facility and certainty to the ever-tangled skein of human affairs, is what constitutes a true lawyer; and hence to acquire that mastery should be the business of every earnest student of law.[17]

Langdell's articulation of the objectives of the case method did not do full justice to what he was doing. In claiming merely that he was trying to instil a mastery of doctrine, he did not make clear the value of the case method as a means of developing powers of reasoning and analysis. His disciple Keener made the point:

... the student is practically doing as a student what he will be doing as a lawyer. By this method the student's reasoning powers are constantly developed, and while he is gaining the power of legal analysis and synthesis, he is also gaining the other object of legal education, namely, knowledge of what the law actually is.[28]

In Langdell's image of the 'true lawyer' in this context no distinction is made between the main functions of lawyers as they are commonly expressed in the four crude personifications of 'the counsellor', 'the advocate', 'the judge', and 'the legislator'—the latter, even in American society, not being a role monopolized by lawyers. On the other hand, it is illuminating to see Llewellyn's casebook, in terms of the differences between these four standpoints.[29] Llewellyn's purpose is dominated by a view of his students as potential private practitioners.[30] Although he was aware of the different standpoints of the judge and the legislator, they are not in the centre of his focus. Indeed, his work at this stage reflects his experience of practice as an office lawyer for the National City Bank, only exceptionally concerned with litigious business, but very well placed to look at problems from the point of view of typical clients, who had in his case been large business concerns. In a footnote appended as an afterthought he acknowledged that he had taken too narrow a perspective when criticizing doctrine: 'The book errs, I think, in too happily assuming the needs of buyers and sellers to be the needs of the community, and in rarely reaching beyond business practice in evaluation of the legal rules.'[31] In time he developed a broader base for judgment.

Not only was Llewellyn's operative image of the 'lawyer' rather different from Langdell's, he also had a more comprehensive picture of what intending practitioners needed by way of legal education. His skills' analysis of lawyers' operations was not developed until later,[32] but already he saw legal education as having additional objectives to the mastery of legal principles and the development of facility in analysing doctrine. The Langdell tradition, in his view, was inadequate in two main respects : firstly, it did not take sufficient account of the wide variety of skills that lawyers were expected to exercise, some of which were teachable and were suitable for teaching in a university; secondly, 'the resulting technical skills, though sharp and well instilled, were narrow, and they remained so. The where-withal for vision was not given.'[33] Langdell's image of the lawyer was that of a narrow technician, Llewellyn's was of someone belonging to a profession that for its effective exercise required qualities of 'vision, range, depth, balance and rich humanity'.[34] His refusal to distinguish between the 'liberal' and 'vocational' study of law, the theme of a major address thirty years later,[35] is implicit in his justification for devoting so much space in the casebook to the history of warranty. The passage follows on directly from the one already quoted:

Because the struggles are not wholly over, because the confusion partly still persists, the study of this history has peculiar present value. It has *immediate* practical importance. But it has more. It has a deeper practical importance; a cultural value no professional man can safely do without. It is a study of how and why rules in the courts change, and concepts alter, and policies emerge. That process is the very bones and blood of law. The understanding of it is vital to a lawyer's dealings with the living law of his own case in court; it is no less vital to his placing of his work and his profession in the society both claim to serve.[36]

Conclusion

No apology is offered for this detailed analysis of a casebook. Its historical significance as a teaching tool has already been noted; several of the outstanding features of the sales article of the Uniform Commercial Code are anticipated in the book. For the jurist the important point is that the book is a concrete embodiment of realist jurisprudence, free for the most part from the exaggerations and loose generalizations that have blinded so many critics. Llewellyn's nine starting-points of realism[37] are all illustrated in a manner that is less likely to provoke needless controversy than their statement in the polemical context of the debate with Pound.[38] Nor could anyone studying the text with care come away with the impression that the author believed 'that talk of rules is a myth'[39] or that his cosmos was entirely judge-centred or that he had a shallow cynicism about the regularity or the rationality of official behaviour or that he thought of law as a 'series of erratic accidents' or that he identified natural science with legal science or that he was a positivist totally indifferent to questions of value or any of the other half-truths or naive distortions that have sometimes been attributed indiscriminately to realism.

Here a note of caution is necessary. The casebook is an early work, useful for understanding Llewellyn's thought but not a complete guide to his jurisprudence. Some of his ideas are there only in embryo; for some time yet his concrete work was to be ahead of his theoretical formulations. Fruitful use of his basic ideas anticipated their mature articulation. In particular there are a few statements, oversimplified or exaggerated, that are vulnerable to even quite elementary criticism. However, such criticism, it is suggested, is peripheral to the main concerns of the book. For the most part *Cases and Materials on The Law of Sales* is today largely of historical interest, marking a step forward in Llewellyn's development as a scholar and in the evolution of new forms of legal literature for students. However, the specialist in commercial law who is prepared to wrestle patiently with the detail will almost certainly find that this is a work which still repays careful study.

THE BRAMBLE BUSH[40]

The Bramble Bush is almost certainly the most widely read of Llewellyn's books. The 1951 edition has been something of a best-seller, judged by the standards of law publishing. The reasons for its popularity are obvious: it is short; it is written in a simple, direct, racy style; and it is a convenient Aunt Sally in the game of polemical jurisprudence, in which a jurist's least balanced statements are accorded the most attention. This is aptly symbolized, in this instance, by the fact that for some time it has been the only one of Llewellyn's works to have been used as a set text in the postgraduate Bachelor of Civil Law degree at Oxford.

The Bramble Bush was the outcome of an attempt to deal with a familiar problem. Every year in almost every law school one or more people are faced with the task of introducing first year students to the study of law. Typically the law student knows little about law and less about legal education; often he has misconceptions about both. Typically also law teachers have divergent opinions about the best way of effecting an introduction. There are enthusiasts and there are sceptics; there are preachers and Pyrrhonists; there are those who would induct the beginner slowly, by easy stages, and there are 'deep-enders', who would deliberately plunge him in out of his depth on the first day. Some would emphasize basic vocabulary, or elementary information, some broad perspectives, others basic techniques. Some believe that the student should be given a bird's eye view of the subject as a whole; others would cover the whole universe of knowledge, except, perhaps, law itself; yet others would embark immediately on the detailed study of particular fields. Some would spread the introduction over a whole year; some would dispose of it in a single hour. It is a matter which is likely to continue to offer law teachers perennial opportunities for disagreement.

In 1929 Llewellyn took on this task at Columbia. He showed himself to be an enthusiast, a committed deep-ender, and a fairly sophisticated evangelist. He took the assignment very seriously and went to unusual pains in preparing the series of eight scripted lectures which he delivered in 1929 and repeated in the following year. The medium suited him well: it enabled him to express in a relatively uninhibited manner some of his most deeply felt attitudes to his subject and his profession; there was also scope for some lively histrionics. The lectures were a resounding success, so much so that in 1930 he was persuaded to have them published as an introductory text. In the printed version, in addition to the eight lectures to first year students, he included one addressed to the same class at the start of their second year and a final one to the graduating class. The whole was given the title of *The Bramble Bush: On Our Law and Its Study*. The first edition was privately printed, but was quite widely circulated, so that it was soon well known, and, in some quarters, notorious.[41] A second edition was published by Oceana in 1951.

The title of the published version of the lectures is taken from a nursery rhyme:

> There was a man in our town
> and he was wondrous wise
> he jumped into a BRAMBLE BUSH
> and scratched out both his eyes –
> and when he saw that he was blind,
> with all his might and main
> he jumped into another one
> and scratched them in again.[42]

This symbolizes 'the total immersion theory' of legal studies. Llewellyn, like most of his colleagues, was a deep-ender: 'No cure for law, but more law. No vision save at the cost of plunging deeper.'[43] At first the student will feel confused, lost, blind. The remedy is the traditional American prescription: 'Rather must you immerse yourself for all your hours in the law. Eat law, talk law, think law, drink law, babble of law and judgments in your sleep. Pickle yourself in law—it is your only hope.'[44] For Coke's balanced diet of six hours a day spent in 'law's grave study' is substituted a fifty-hour week supplemented by other relevant activities outside working hours.[45] The symbol of the bramble bush refers to one of the principal messages of the lectures: law is very demanding; only if you give yourself to it wholeheartedly can you hope to succeed in law school and in legal practice; if you do give yourself in this way, then a legal career can be a means to fulfilment, or, as Holmes put it, 'a man may live greatly in the law'.[46] Thus total immersion is not merely the most effective way of inducting the beginner into the rigours of the American law school; it is also what will be demanded by most kinds of legal practice. To meet these demands—and to make them bearable, one must integrate one's approach to law and one's approach to life. Work in law must be seen as being an essentially humane activity, which will enrich one's personal life and which can itself benefit from outside reading and experience. The message is only fully articulated in the peroration of the eighth lecture:

Go then and read – in the law and out. By all means read. Work – at your art, your science, your philosophy – work even at your Mencken, if you must, or Heywood Broun. But bring the work home again, and merge it with your law. Read, too, from your own law out. This, in your law – in school and practice – is the one part of wisdom: trade, culture and profession all in one. . . .

Go, then, and read. Go then, and look, and *see*. I cannot say that that way fortune lies. I cannot tempt you with worlds to conquer, nor yet with worlds to save. Must you have the moon? I find this plain match enough, that flares for its tiny moment. Surely a nothing – tossed, it may be, for sport into the gutter. Yet a pitiful, brave flame. Some warmth, some light, some touch of burning courage. What have you more to ask – or to ask to be?[47]

Such rhetoric is not characteristic of *The Bramble Bush* as a whole. It is only towards the end that the underlying romanticism becomes apparent. The style of the first part is deliberately laconic. Indeed, parts of the first chapter, taken out of context, have sometimes been used to suggest that the author was an extreme radical or a cynical iconoclast.[48] Nothing could be further from the truth. The book is fundamentally idealistic and conservative. To understand this it is necessary to treat it as a whole and to see it in context; in particular, it is important to grasp its underlying assumptions about legal education and about the nature of the primary audience.

At the time Llewellyn was one of the most outspoken critics of American legal education. In a particularly virulent critique in 1935 he castigated law school practices as being 'blind, inept, factory-ridden, wasteful, defective and empty'.[49] In *The Bramble Bush*, too, he complained openly of 'the stupendous inadequacy, the lack of direction, the inefficiency in legal education'.[50] Taken by itself this extravagant language could be quite misleading, for it has to be set against his conclusion that legal education in the United States was probably better than most other types of education.[51] More important, *The Bramble Bush* accepts completely some of the basic tenets of the prevailing law school ethos: the principal function of the LL.B. is preparation for private practice; lawyers and law students are a class apart, members of a closed elite; undergraduate law students are initiates of the mysteries of the guild; they are expected to be professional, competitive, 'proud of their calling', conformist and, above all, hardworking. Individual opinions and initiatives are tolerated, even encouraged, within the limits of the professional ethic which does, after all, accept certain liberal and humane values. The world of the American law school from the time of Langdell's Harvard, for all its liveliness and willingness to experiment, was based on an underlying conformism, which was not seriously challenged until the upheavals of the late 1960s. *The Bramble Bush,* despite its unconventional style, contains one of the most forceful and articulate statements of the law school ethos. This may be one reason for its popularity among American law teachers.

The main purpose of the first eight lectures is evangelical, to promote certain attitudes to law and its study. Llewellyn was too sophisticated to think that this could be achieved merely by delivering a sermon:

> We have no great illusions, my brethren and I, as to how much good it will do you to be told these things in advance. We have learned by bitter experience that you will not take the things we tell you very seriously. You conceive this, I take it, to be somewhat in the nature of the pep meeting to which you were exposed when you first entered college. You expect me to tell you that you should be earnest about your work, and get your back into it for dear old Siwash, and that he who lets work slide will stumble by the way. You sit back with a cynical detachment, prepared in advance to let this anticipatory jawing slide comfortably off your neck and rump. Let him have his say. That is what he gets his pay for. But we, the sophisticated youth of this new century, we know that he means little of what he says, and what he does mean, as far as *he* is concerned, means nothing to us. The ungovernable hand of fate has put him in the chair; no help for that. The workings of society require us to let his mouthings fan our ears. Another of the conditions to admission to the bar.[52]

The structure and emphasis of *The Bramble Bush* is conditioned by Llewellyn's conception of his audience. As is apparent from the above passage, he assumes that they are all intending private practitioners of law.[53] This permits a single consistent standpoint and precludes any of the ambivalence about objectives that plagues English university law teachers.[54] They are beginners who need an introduction which is simple without being shallow. They need to be given not only a foothold, but also a sense of direction. Above all, they need to have communicated to them what it is that fascinates and engages those who love the law. Llewellyn also saw his audience as belonging to a disenchanted postwar generation, cynical about corruption in government and the pretensions of the captains of industry, lacking heroes: 'I meet in you also a homeless, forlorn idealism that is ill at ease among the disillusioned thoughts it lives among.'[55]

Why have they chosen law? Llewellyn picks on one possible motive that has been of concern to psychological researchers in the 1960s.[56] A very high percentage of American law students seem to come to law school seeking something fixed, authoritative, certain, a rock in a sea of exploded ideals:

> You come then to us. Whatever has gone, the law is left to you. Left to you as the fixed sure order of society. Left to you as that which controls the judges, which clothes the judge with a certain majesty even while and indeed because it does control him, which lifts him and his work to a level he could not attain alone.[57]

Llewellyn anticipates that his audience expect to devote their energies in law school mainly to learning established rules of law.[58] This comfortable belief, commonly held by laymen, is in the students' case fortified by their strong emotional vested interest in clinging on to it. At the same time this belief runs counter to the whole approach of the Columbia Law School of the time. Thus there is at the start a dangerous conflict between what the students expect and want and what the teachers are offering:

> And we? These fabrics we seize and tear as idle cobweb. These mirrors of old dear-held truth we shatter. The law dissolves itself before our acids. Right and justice come to figure as pretty names for very human acts done on often the less human of motivations. I have said before that this tendency of our teaching has caused me worry, in its aspect as developing the technician at the cost of the whole man. It gives me double pause in this connection – in its effect on young men already disillusioned beyond the portion of young men.[59]

This then is the central problem of *The Bramble Bush* as Llewellyn conceives it: to destroy a misapprehension about legal education, whilst persuading his audience that what is being attempted at Columbia is worthwhile. For the lost illusion a new faith must be substituted; after iconoclasm, a new idealism. *The Bramble Bush* is thus first and foremost a work of proselytization directed to a potentially sceptical and adverse audience. From this point of view the first eight chapters can be seen as a sustained and cleverly disguised piece of advocacy by an advocate who has studied his court with some care. The latent idealism is not bared until the audience's interest and enthusiasm have been aroused. Irony, self-deprecation, hard-headed analysis, down-to-earth advice on how to do it, all precede the full-blooded rhetoric of the eighth chapter.

Although the 'bramble bush' theme gives a basic unity to the first eight lectures, the early chapters deal with a variety of topics. The book is divided into two parts, 'the bramble bush' and 'the other one' (i.e. the second bush). The first part deals with the immediate needs of the beginner, the second concentrates on wide issues. In both parts general theory, practical advice and elementary introductory material are all intermingled. The first chapter, 'What Law is About', is largely directed to making the point that there is much more to the study of law than learning rules: it is argued that the main function of law is to settle and prevent disputes and disputes are a prime concern of practising lawyers, whether acting as advocates or counsellors; knowledge of rules is important, but is not enough for effective advocacy, still less for counselling. 'If rules were results there would be little need of lawyers'.[60] This, it might be thought, is both elementary and incontrovertible. Unfortunately Llewellyn dressed up the argument in general jurisprudential terms that have occasioned controversy, although it was not necessary for him to do so. This aspect will be considered in detail below.

After this relatively brief general introduction. Llewellyn turns directly to the immediate problems of the beginner. Law is studied by 'the case method'; what needs to be known about cases for maximum benefit to be derived from the method? The next three chapters set out to answer this question. They are the most detailed in the book, although they are for the most part elementary.[61] Llewellyn often criticized American law schools for overemphasizing the case method at the expense of other devices. Yet in *The Bramble Bush* he devoted almost a quarter of the space to problems of case study, as against, for instance, less than four pages to interpretation of statutes. In this he was not being inconsistent, as his advice was directed to ways of obtaining maximum benefit from Columbia Law School as it was, rather than from some ideal law school of his imagination. The case system dominated, so it required detailed attention.

Chapter 5, 'Ships and Shoes and Sealing Wax', deals, *inter alia*, with the place of logic in law, the relationship between rules and official behaviour, statutory interpretation, the Hohfeldian analysis of 'rights', and the bias of law school teaching towards appellate courts. Each of these topics is treated in less cursory fashion in works other than *The Bramble Bush*.[62]

The next three chapters form a unit. Starting in diminuendo with the short-range objectives of legal education, moving to a broader perspective in a brief treatment of Law and Civilization, they culminate in the crescendo of the eighth chapter. The final two

chapters are afterthoughts, for the most part elaborating on what
has gone before. Chapter 9, addressed to the same class at the start
of their second year, consists largely of advice on how to compen-
sate for the inadequacies of their legal education; the final chapter
takes as its main theme the unpopularity of the legal profession and
the ethical dilemmas of lawyers, anticipating his extensive writings
on the subject in later years and re-emphasizing the need for
idealism.

The key to the success of the original lectures lies in the fact that
they managed simultaneously to engage the interest and emotions of
the beginner whilst exposing him in a relatively simple way to some
basic insights into the common law and the world of the law school.
It has been suggested that much of *The Bramble Bush* is too difficult
for the beginner and that more profit would be derived from it by
second or third year students. Llewellyn himself admitted in the
foreword to the second edition that he had learned that 'their bite
for a beginning law student lies rather in November than in
September'.[63] But those who believe that a healthy attitude to the
study of law is best achieved by 'catching them young' and who
believe that *The Bramble Bush* attitude is healthy, would probably
agree that the potential gains from putting the book into a student's
hands at the outset of his studies outweigh any partial loss of understanding, a loss which can in any case be made good by re-reading
at a later stage. For the most part, then, one may conclude that *The
Bramble Bush* was outstandingly successful in fulfilling its main
objective.

The book, however, has also been treated as a serious contribution to general jurisprudence. Indeed, it gave Llewellyn an
unwelcome notoriety, which hurt and embarrassed him. Parts of
The Bramble Bush, taken with his articles on realism, stirred a
'tea-pot tempest', as he called it.[64] The scars are apparent in much
of his subsequent work.

Most of the jurisprudential ideas put forward in *The Bramble
Bush* are developed at greater length and in a more satisfactory
fashion in other writings which were not so obviously directed to a
particular audience. It is arguable that only in respect of the
chapters on case law is Llewellyn's most important discussion of a
topic to be found in *The Bramble Bush* – and it is not these chapters
that have been the source of the trouble. Readers of the book need to
remember that it represents a relatively young Llewellyn addressing

first year students rather than the older Llewellyn addressing experienced lawyers or fellow jurists. This is not to say that the first chapter is as vulnerable as some critics have suggested. For present purposes it will be adequate to show that two passages, read in context, do not bear the interpretation that they have been given and in any case are not representative of Llewellyn's mature views. Beyond this no attempt will be made to rake over the ashes of a controversy that is best forgotten.

Both offending passages occur in the early part of the first lecture:

This doing of something about disputes, this doing of it reasonably, is the business of law. And the people who have the doing in charge, whether they be judges or sheriffs or clerks or jailers or lawyers, are officials of the law. *What these officials do about disputes is, to my mind, the law itself.*[65]

And *rules*, through all of this, are important so far as they help you see or predict what judges will do or so far as they help you get judges to do something. That is their importance. *That is all their importance, except as pretty playthings.* But you will discover that you can no more afford to overlook them than you can afford to stop with having learned their words.[66]

These passages, and especially the two sentences in italics, are probably the most quoted statements of Llewellyn. In the foreword to the second edition, under the heading 'correcting an error', he admitted that he had used 'unhappy words' which were 'plainly at best a very partial statement of the whole truth'. The most depressing aspect of the behaviour of his critics is that on a number of occasions one or other of those passages has been cited since 1951, without any reference to the retraction and explanation in the second edition. It is difficult to understand how, quite apart from the context and from Llewellyn's other works, it is possible to continue to refer to the first passage as 'Llewellyn's definition of law' or the second passage as evidence for the view that Llewellyn (sometimes, by anonymous attribution, the realists) believed that 'talk of rules is a myth'.

Traditionally in jurisprudence a writer's definition of 'law', if he has one, is accorded close attention. In so far as such definitions can usefully be treated as the organizing concept of a whole theory, or as indicative of the boundaries of the theorist's focus of attention, it is a reasonable practice. In Llewellyn's case this practice proved to be most unfortunate. He normally explicitly refused to put forward a comprehensive definition of 'law',[67] but the words, 'What these officials do about disputes is, to my mind, the law itself' have regularly been cited as *Llewellyn's definition of law*; it is not unknown for his contribution to jurisprudence to have been evaluated solely in terms of these thirteen words.

Treated as the starting-point for a whole legal philosophy the statement was absurdly easy to criticize. One cannot but suspect that this is one of the reasons for its continued citation. Since Llewellyn retracted the statement and since it is not a particularly helpful clue to an understanding of his ideas, it is unnecessary to consider in detail the criticisms to which it has been subjected. However, it is worth looking briefly at two of the most common objections to the 'definition', for they do throw light on the scope of his theoretical interests at this stage of his thinking. First, it can be correctly pointed out that the concept 'official' presupposes a legal system from which 'officials' derive their authority and which provides criteria for identifying who is and who is not an official.[68] The same point can be made about 'judges', 'courts', and so on. Since such concepts presuppose the ideas of 'law', and 'legal system', 'law' cannot adequately be defined in terms of them. This is a valid point, but it could be an important one in relation to Llewellyn's thinking only if he had been led into serious error by a failure to realize this—if, for instance, this was indicative of the confusion of the concepts of 'authority' and 'power'. An examination of Llewellyn's writings of the period reveals that he made no such error. While it is true that, in some contexts, some such concept as authority or rule of recognition is merely presupposed, and some people might find his most detailed discussion of 'power' and 'authority' somewhat obscure, he quite clearly did distinguish between them.[69]

A second criticism made of the definition is that whereas the statement to some extent fits the perspective of a potential litigant or his lawyer, it is not so suitable from the standpoint of a law reformer or legislator and is totally inadequate from the standpoint of a judge.[70] Llewellyn acknowledged this latter point in his foreword to the second edition of *The Bramble Bush*:

They are, however, unhappy words when not more fully developed and they are plainly at best a very partial statement of the truth. For it is clear that one office of law is to control officials in some part and to guide them even in places where no thoroughgoing control is possible, or is desired.[71]

However, Llewellyn's 'error' is not so heinous in the context of the original statement. The object of the passage in question was to make forcefully and vividly to intending private practitioners of law the elementary point that rules are not everything in law, especially for practising lawyers, and that their focus of attention needed to be wider than that. The standpoint clearly was that of the private practitioner. This is hardly the context in which one would expect a general definition of 'law', intended as the starting-point for a comprehensive legal philosophy.

The claim that Llewellyn did not intend the sentence as a general definition of 'law' is also supported by the introductory passage to his first article on 'realism' which was also published in 1930. Here he specifically refused to define 'law' and he set out his reasons for so refusing.

The difficulty in framing any concept of 'law' is that there are so many things to be included, and the things to be included are so unbelievably different from each other. Perhaps it is possible to get them all under one verbal roof. But I do not see what you have accomplished if you do. For a concept, as I understand it, is built for a purpose. It is a thinking tool. It is to make your data more manageable in doing something, in getting somewhere with them. And I have not yet met the job, or heard of it, to which all the data that associate themselves with this loosest of suggestive symbols, 'law', are relevant at once. We do and have too many disparate things and thinkings to which we like to attach that name. [72]

The passage reveals a much more sophisticated understanding of the nature and functions of definitions than the critics of the famous sentence have allowed for. It also implies that at this stage Llewellyn was not attempting to expound a comprehensive theory of law. He was concerned with certain theoretical questions with wide implications, but not as yet with what he later referred to as 'a working whole view'. When he did start to develop this, his basic organizing concept was 'the institution of law-and-government', rather than 'law' *simpliciter*. [73]

The passage relating to rules as 'pretty playthings', if read in context, ought not to occasion difficulty. Limited to the standpoints of the advocate and the counsellor, it contains an important truth, perhaps a little overstated, about the uses of rules for such functionaries. It was clearly not intended, and it is ridiculous to treat it, as a rounded statement of Llewellyn's views on the place of rules in law. For this one should turn to his paper 'My Philosophy of Law' and, more important, to his unpublished book on *The Theory of Rules*.[74]

After the publication of *The Bramble Bush* in 1930, Llewellyn could hardly deliver the same lectures again to incoming classes at Columbia. However, he continued to be interested in the problem of inducting first year law students.[75] For over ten years he planned to produce *The New Bramble Bush*. In the late 1940s he got as far as writing first drafts of several new chapters, but in 1951 he gave up, concluding that '[T]he young fellow who wrote these lectures just isn't here any more'.[76] Instead he decided to restrict revision for the second edition to a minimum, a foreword, an afterword and a few minor textual amendments. The decision was probably wise; the original *Bramble Bush* lectures would have been buried in extensive theorizing about the nature of law and a very extended discussion of the legal profession. The draft chapters of the *New Bramble Bush* did not match the freshness and vitality of the original and its admirable compactness would have been sacrificed.[77]

When Llewellyn moved to Chicago he gave an introductory course to first year classes entitled 'Elements of Law'.[78] This was a required course, very much more substantial than *The Bramble Bush* lectures. It was something of a mixture, combining fairly extensive reading of Llewellyn's works (including *The Bramble Bush* and *The Cheyenne Way*) and intensive study of a series of cases concerning indefiniteness in contracts, products liability and foreign remittances. Although there were a number of Llewellynesque features, in many respects it resembled other 'legal method' courses, and it lacked the unique qualities of *The Bramble Bush*.

A single lecture from the course was published in 1953, under the title 'The Adventures of Rollo'. Both in emphasis and in the assumptions about the audience, there is a striking change from *The Bramble Bush*, as is evident from the opening paragraph:

And so little Rollo came to the University of Chicago Law School. His heart was high, and his eyes were filled with shining stars, because little Rollo knew that the world was waiting on his coming. A world to be shaped by little Rollo! Because, after all, little Rollo had read the great books; and he thought large thoughts. Easily and lightly he could balance a large thought and bounce it the way a trick sea lion bounces a ball upon his nose. And little Rollo had not yet waked up to the fact that there is no more inhumane thing among the humanities than a great idea unaccompanied by the experience on which it rests, devoid of the human meaning test by test, man by man, experience by experience, that made the great idea great. So that the formula of formulas is a bubble for a sea lion to play with, and the job, for anybody, of understanding becomes a job of getting down to the cases, of getting down to the people, and getting down to the happenings and events, the loves and the hates, the greeds and the fears, that went into making the great idea a great idea, and gave it bite.

Most of all, of course, is that true of the lawyer. A theologian perhaps may be able to take a great idea, work with it as such, as a shining goal; and a philosopher may be able to get towered away from all the world around him enough to contemplate his navel and a great idea simultaneously; and a poet can dream great beauty and put it into words that will convey something of the dream.
But none of these is the lawyer's function as a lawyer.[79]

The theme of the lecture is that 'the lawyer is ... the man of measures', the man who *par excellence* must master techniques of turning ideas into action. The principal theme is expressed in Llewellyn's favourite aphorism: 'Technique without ideals is a menace.... Ideals without technique are a mess.'[80] The change is more in style than in substance and if a new edition of *The Bramble Bush* were to be published, 'The Adventures of Rollo' might well be added to the original text.

To sum up: of all his published works *The Bramble Bush* conveys most clearly the flavour of its author's lecturing style—in other words one facet of Llewellyn as a teacher. It also contains one of the most eloquent statements of his personal credo about the rewards of legal work. It can be read as an introduction to his juristic ideas, but because it is addressed specifically to first year law students it should not be taken as representative of his work as a scholar nor as a jurist in 1930, still less of the more mature later work. To do so would be almost akin to judging the achievement of T. S. Eliot on the basis of *Old Possum's Book of Practical Cats*. Thus in approaching Llewellyn's first two legal books the modern reader will be well advised to pay as much attention to the nature of the medium as to the content of the message.

8

The Cheyenne Way

Most lawyers are more likely to associate the Cheyennes with high adventure than with juristic insight, and when informed that *The Cheyenne Way* deals with the dispute settlement processes of an American Indian tribe, they might well conclude that it is no concern of theirs. This would be unfortunate for the substance of the book is less exotic than its title suggests, although its setting and its form are certainly unusual. Indeed, it is a rare example of a book which is at once entertaining and profound and, for this reason, for many people it may be the most suitable introduction to the more general aspects of Llewellyn's thought.

Llewellyn's early acquaintance with the work of Sumner and Keller and his later reading of Max Weber stirred his interest in 'primitive law'. When he read Malinowski's path-breaking work, *Crime and Custom in Savage Society*[1] he found it stimulating, but he was irritated by the vagueness and high level of generality of much of the description. Certainly Malinowski's studies of the Trobriand Islanders represented an important advance. He was one of the first anthropologists who actually lived in the community he was studying; he saw more clearly than his predecessors how far the verbalized ideal norms of behaviour—how a people would state their 'customs'—could deviate from their actual behaviour, and by focusing on practices more than on norms he brought a breath of realism into anthropology. Moreover, he successfully challenged a then fashionable view by showing that the Trobrianders had mechanisms for the enforcement of reciprocal obligations that were comparable to the mechanisms found in advanced legal systems and that these were worthy to be called 'law'. But, complained Llewellyn, 'the author shows no sign of there being any adjudicating machinery, no sign even of open 'law' enforcement ... by the political chief, no sign of procedure save that which is the mobilization of opinion against the known guilty by open accusation—with the ceremonial suicide of the guilty as a counter-attack where the inevitable penalty is felt by the guilty to be excessive. It is regrettable that we have from Malinowski no clear and detailed statement as to whether and how far the political chief exercises legal functions.'[2] When he analysed his dissatisfaction further, Llewellyn came to the conclusion that Malinowski's most important omission was that he gave few details of what actually happened when disputes arose. Practice was described in very general terms, but in *Crime and Custom* only six actual cases were used.[3] From Malinowski's account it was difficult to tell what kinds of disputes were most common, who was involved in the process of settlement, or how settlement was achieved.

Llewellyn had barely started to develop this line of thinking when it was suggested to him, probably by Franz Boas, that he should get in touch with a promising graduate student in the Department of Anthropology at Columbia, E. Adamson Hoebel, who was interested in 'primitive law'.[4] Hoebel was faced with a problem. He wished to embark on a study of the legal life of the Comanche Indians, but more experienced anthropologists had expressed scepticism about the viability of the project, mainly on the ground that the Comanches had no 'law'. At that time the study of 'primitive law' was itself at a rudimentary stage of development. The predominating method was what Llewellyn and Hoebel later named 'the ideological approach'; the typical field technique consisted of interviewing informants and asking questions of the type: 'What is your rule about ... ?' 'What is the result when ... ?' or 'What would happen if ... ?' Quite apart from the general limitations and pitfalls of this technique, it is particularly ineffective in dealing with peoples who are inarticulate about their institutions, as the Comanches and other plains Indians tended to be. In 1949 Dr Ralph Linton, a leading authority on the Comanches was to remark:

Different cultures show a tremendous amount of difference in the degree to which their patterns are consciously formalized. My experiences with Polynesians and Comanches illustrate this: Polynesians can give you practically an Emily Post statement of what proper behavior should be on all occasions, whereas Comanches, when asked how they do anything immediately answer, 'Well, that depends.' They genuinely think of behavior as a range of unlimited, individual, freedom of choice, although when you take a series of examples of behavior ... you find actually quite a high degree of uniformity.[5]

Thus, apart from the definitional question whether 'primitive law' was 'law properly so called', there was a practical methodological problem of ascertaining what were the customary norms, if any, of a people like the Comanches.

Hoebel presented this problem to Llewellyn at their first meeting in June 1933; Llewellyn immediately outlined the methods he would use in investigating the legal processes of an American Indian tribe. As he talked he made notes. Hoebel left the interview with the notes which, he claims, provided the basis of his field method during the ensuing years. This method, an adaptation of the case method, will be considered in detail below. Llewellyn became Hoebel's supervisor for his doctoral thesis, which Hoebel successfully completed in 1934,[6] thereby confounding the sceptics. In 1935, after a less successful project among the Shoshones,[7] Hoebel suggested that the 'lawways' of the Cheyenne Indians might be a fruitful field for study. The Cheyennes had for more than a century led an adventurous nomadic existence on the Great Plains west of the Mississippi River; the main reason for choosing them was that they were known to have had developed institutions with coercive power vested in an organized body, which suggested that their ways of dispute-settlement and of preserving order might have been more institutionalized than was the case with the Shoshones. Hoebel started fieldwork among the Northern Cheyennes in the summer of 1935 and towards the end of the summer Llewellyn, accompanied by his economist wife, Emma Corstvet, joined him at Lame Deer in Montana for ten days. This was Llewellyn's first fieldwork among American Indians, and the only period he spent among the Cheyennes. This fact is indicative of the fairly clear division of the labour involved in the production of *The Cheyenne Way*. Hoebel did nearly all the fieldwork and collection of data and wrote the first draft of the middle section of the book, which is primarily descriptive. Llewellyn invented and subsequently developed the theory of investigation which guided in large part the collection and interpretation of data. He was also primarily responsible for the general theoretical and jurisprudential matrix.

Although his visit was short, it was in fact an extraordinarily fruitful ten days, in that Hoebel had saved up two most promising informants, Stump Horn and Calf Woman, and in addition to intensive and very productive sessions of interviewing, they attended a Peyote meeting and a number of informal social gatherings. Hoebel returned alone to the field in the summer of 1936.

A lengthy period of digesting, interpreting, drafting and rewriting preceded the publication of *The Cheyenne Way* in 1941. The finished product both in style and emphasis bears the unmistakable stamp of Llewellyn. The prose is more disciplined than usual, but the vigour and ebullience are still there. A vivid impression of the Cheyennes emerges from the book, but its essential significance is theoretical. A more straightforward and informative description of Cheyenne culture is to be found in Hoebel's admirable monograph *The Cheyennes, Indians of the Great Plains*, published nineteen years later.[8] Apart from the new light that it threw on a particularly interesting tribe, *The Cheyenne Way* is significant in several particular respects. First, it contains the first full statement and application of the 'case method' in a study of tribal law; second, it is an outstanding example of interdisciplinary cooperation. Third, the Cheyennes are presented as an example of a so-called 'primitive' people who had a genius for handling social conflict. Fourth, it marks an important stage in the development of Llewellyn's ideas; and finally, the book contains an important statement of Llewellyn's 'law-jobs' theory. The first four matters will be treated in this chapter, but consideration of the fifth will be postponed until later, when the 'law-jobs' will be considered in the context of Llewellyn's general sociology of law.

The authors' enthusiasm for Cheyenne culture is apparent throughout the book, culminating in a final chapter, which has not inappropriately been described as 'almost a prose poem in praise of Cheyenne juristic method'.[9] Their 'legal genius', the beauty of their methods, the 'juristic poetry' of the results are eulogized in terms that imply that it was almost an everyday matter for the Cheyennes to produce 'juristic work which in another culture would make the reputation of a Solomon or a Marshall or a Njal'.[10] It is not surprising that such lavish praise should have provoked some sceptical comments. However, any suggestion that the authors' enthusiasm seriously reduces the scholarly value of their work is to be discounted. It is possible to retain one's respect for the work while agreeing with Lowie[11] that it probably painted an over-romantic picture and exaggerated the extent to which the deftness of the Cheyennes in disposing of friction is unique or exceptional among tribal societies. The exuberant praise is a refreshing contrast to the patronizing style of some accounts of so-called 'primitive' tribes.

The Cheyennes were somewhat inarticulate, they lacked developed legal forms or a sophisticated system of concepts. What, then, constituted their 'legal genius'?

... we are referring to the classical Roman jurist's *ways of work*, the deftness and boldness of line with which the apt solution is marked in swift, sure strokes that fit at once justice, policy, and the given body of legal and social institutions – those ways of work which are the modern Romanist's delight and his despair.[12]

Most of the examples used as concrete illustrations of this admired 'Cheyenne Way' show shrewdness and ingenuity. Thus praise is given to a device used for detecting the mother of an aborted foetus,[13] to the invention of a solution of an unprecedented problem,[14] to the drawing of distinctions[15] and to the making of a carefully limited exception to a general rule.[16] Non-insistence on the literal performance of a promise which was performed in the spirit and other examples of a refusal to be tyrannized by forms are cited with approval.[17] More general indications of Cheyenne achievement are said to be the elimination of the feud, limited resort to appeals to the supernatural for assistance in fact-finding, and a frugal but effective use of legal fictions. Much of the authors' enthusiasm is directed to the results of particular cases, results which they consider to be apt, 'inevitable' and even 'beautiful'. These results are admired as *solutions* to *problems* and the crux of the claim put forward for Cheyenne 'legal genius' is that this was a tradition that fostered an instinct for creative problem-solving. The most persistent of all problems for the man of law is reconciling the conflicting demands of 'law' and 'justice'. This, it is claimed, the Cheyennes succeeded in doing:

Even if you wish to avoid subjective valuational judgments, you must concede, as was said earlier in regard to 'legalism', that such opposition produces a strain in the culture which is bothersome. 'Law' is, in function, a means to reach much the same ends which the feeling of 'justice' also reaches for. When the two grow distinct, the tool 'law' has ceased to be clean-shaped to its reason. And what the Cheyenne law-way shows here, for any man to see, is that a significantly high development of certainty and clarity, of prospective outcome, felt even by most litigants in the heat of controversy, can be achieved on a not unelaborate scale, without the growth of such 'law' and 'legal procedure' as rigidifies upon itself, and comes so into opposition with the felt justice of a newer generation. The Cheyenne law-way shows more. It shows that developed ritual, together with some quantum of very clear rule and imperative procedure, can be handled in favorable circumstances with flexibility, in terms of need, yet with no sacrifice at all of feeling for certainty and form.[18]

How much should the personal enthusiasms of the authors be discounted in this context? Undoubtedly there is room for differences of opinion about some of the solutions to the cases. Not every one would approve of an identification parade in which all the women of the tribe had to expose their breasts for public inspection for signs of lactation;[19] not all would accept that the soldiers acted 'soundly' in almost lynching Red Owl,[20] and so on. While we are rarely left in doubt as to the authors' reaction to these solutions, they are less informative about Cheyenne reactions. It may be argued that since there is room for disagreement about what constitutes 'justice' in some of these situations, not all the authors' claims that 'law' and 'justice' have been reconciled are substantiated. Similarly, some people may feel that the Cheyennes were somewhat cavalier in their treatment of accepted forms and that a more formalistic approach would be preferable, just as there will always be lawyers who prefer 'the formal style' to 'the grand style'. There is some force in such criticisms but fortunately they are not as damaging as may at first sight appear. The authors' data are distinguishable from their reactions to them. We may accept as accurate the account of the case of Chief Eagle's father but disagree with the opinion that this was a 'superb' solution.[21] The picture that we are given of Cheyenne juristic method is for the most part coherent and convincing and some of the claims for it are clearly substantiated. It seems reliable as a description to say that the Cheyennes had effective means of controlling friction within their society and that this effectiveness is due in large part to a problem-solving approach. Furthermore Llewellyn and Hoebel's admiration for this approach is not by any means idiosyncratic; many people on reading their account will agree that what is described, if it is accurate, is admirable. This appears to have been the reaction of most commentators; in so far as the authors' enthusiasm has not been infectious, criticism has been levelled at exaggerated praise rather than at the idea that the Cheyenne way was worthy of praise at all.

THE THEORY OF INVESTIGATION

The collection of data and the manner of presentation were guided by a carefully articulated theory, another good example of the self-consciousness of Llewellyn's realism. *The Cheyenne Way* has been particularly influential in respect of methodology and for this reason this aspect of the work deserves to be examined at length.

The authors begin the exposition of their 'theory of investigation' by outlining three main approaches open to them. The first, 'the ideological approach', concentrates almost exclusively on norms or rules which express notional patterns of conduct, 'ideal patterns', 'right ways', against which actual behaviour is to be measured. The ethnological work of Post and Kohler and the modern *Restatement of African Law* are examples of this approach.[22] The subject-matter of tribal law consists of rules which can be recorded in the form of a quasi-code or restatement, whether or not they are fully articulated by the people subject to them. In this approach the emphasis is almost exclusively on perspectives, i.e. on what people think.

There are a number of difficulties about this rule-centred approach. First, in some societies people do not think in terms of rules: 'A Comanche, or a Barama River Carib does not like to think that way. He finds trouble in reducing such general "norms" to expression or in stating a solution for an abstract or a hypothetical case.'[23] Secondly, neat collections of statements of rules may not by themselves adequately explain the results of decision-processes nor the part played by such rules in these processes. It is sometimes forgotten that rules do not perform identical functions in all contexts. Several anthropologists have observed that in some societies actual settlements of disputes frequently do not conform with what are held out to be the accepted norms of the society. For instance, Gulliver reports that among the Arusha of Northern Tanganyika (now Tanzania) there are commonly enunciated and accepted norms of behaviour and these norms are regularly quoted during the process of settling disputes between members of the tribe. Yet, says Gulliver, 'Whilst it would be incorrect to say that an agreed settlement of a dispute never wholly conforms with the relevant, socially accepted norm, it is true to say that such precise conformity is the exception.'[24]

The divergence between stated norms and actual results is not restricted to preliterate societies. Nor is the related phenomenon of 'normative ambiguity'—the coexistence of sets of norms which conflict or which at least have opposing tendencies.[25] Llewellyn himself convincingly illustrated the point with reference to the rules of interpretation of statutes by placing a collection of those rules, each backed by authority, into two parallel columns, with each rule in the left-hand column countered by an opposing rule in the right-hand column.[26] Another limitation of 'the ideological approach' is that it tends to ignore such phenomena.

Not all of Llewellyn and Hoebel's predecessors had been wedded to the ideological approach. In particular, Malinowski, Rattray and Barton had published outstanding studies which revealed a healthy scepticism about generalized statements of rules and which were based on sustained first-hand observations of actual behaviour. 'The norms are there, but they are buried in a rich lode of fact.'[27] The authors of *The Cheyenne Way* admired these works, but they found them deficient in two respects: first, the descriptions of behaviour were over-generalized, lacking in detail and failing to give a complete picture of how things actually worked. Secondly, they tended to concentrate on substantive law, neglecting the procedural aspects: 'If law, as the students of Anglo-American jurisprudence have long held, is secreted in the interstices of procedure, much is obviously missed in the substantive over-emphasis characteristic of the descriptive approach.'[28]

Llewellyn's main contribution to anthropology was to introduce a tool that corrected these two defects, i.e. the detailed analysis of actual disputes. This form of 'case method' is not to be confused with the Langdellian method of instruction nor with the standard use of cases by common law writers of treatises and articles. It is related to both, but it is distinct from them. Still less should it be confused with the use of hypothetical examples in questioning informants. The 'trouble case method' consists of examining in detail the processes involved in settling actual disputes. What happened, what each participant did in relation to the dispute, what steps were taken by what other persons, the final outcome, the reasoning of the deciders, the effects of the decision on the parties themselves, on future trouble cases and on the general life of the group are to be considered in depth. 'A case, a situation, was not to be let go until it had been wrung of its last possible implication for the whole.'[29] In *The Cheyenne Way* over three hundred pages of interpretation rest largely on this kind of treatment of only fifty-three cases.

The authors made a number of claims for the method : by studying actual cases the phenomenon of competing norms can be perceived and understood; it overcomes the problem of refusal or inability of informants to articulate norms; the extent of coincidence or divergence between articulated norms and the outcomes of dispute-settlement processes can be checked; trouble cases show how established forms are in fact used, which is more illuminating than a bare statement of the form; the relationship between the 'law' of the group and the 'sub-law stuff' of each sub-group may be brought out by the study of disputes; in a crisis one can actually see the culture at work; and finally, trouble-cases are in themselves important phenomena:

The case of trouble, again, is the case of doubt, or is that in which discipline has failed, or is that in which unruly personality is breaking through into new paths of action or of leadership, or is that in which an ancient institution is being tried against emergent forces. It is the case of trouble which makes, breaks, twists, or flatly establishes a rule, an institution, an authority. Not all such cases do so. There are also petty rows, the routine of law-stuff which exists among primitives as well as among moderns. For all that, if there be a portion of a society's life in which tensions of the culture come to expression, in which the play of variant urges can be felt and seen, in which emergent power-patterns, ancient security-drives, religion, politics, personality, and cross-purposed views of justice tangle in the open, that portion of the life will concentrate in the case of trouble or disturbance. Not only the making of new law and the effect of old, but the hold and the thrust of all other vital aspects of the culture, shine clear in the crucible of conflict.[30]

The authors might have stressed two other points. First, their method of presentation facilitates a relatively clearcut distinction between data and interpretation. One weakness of many of the works in the ideological tradition is that no such distinction is observed; often an element of interpretation is of necessity involved in the process of formulating a bare statement of rules.[31] Secondly, the illumination of the general by concentrated focus on the particular has close parallels with drama, in that the subject-matter is brought to life in a way that is not often achieved by a flat description. Although *The Cheyenne Way* contains comparatively little straightforward information about the Cheyennes, it offers profound insights into their culture, together with a vivid impression, coloured no doubt by Llewellyn's imagination, of its flavour and atmosphere and to use Malinowski's phrase, the other 'imponderabilia of native life'. Larger than life characters, the wise High Backed Wolf, the mean

Cries Yia Eya and the wilful Sticks Everything Under His Belt stalk the pages adding entertainment to illumination.

A possible criticism of the trouble case technique is that it is 'anecdotal', in the sense that crises are often not typical of ordinary life and that the cases selected for intensive analysis may well be untypical even of crises. By concentrating on the unusual a writer may give a distorted picture of the culture he is studying. This is especially likely if the epoch-making case is preferred to the 'petty rows, the routine of law-stuff' referred to above. Furthermore, if each case is to be analysed in detail and depth, only a relatively small sample is likely to be used, with a corresponding decrease in the chances of its being representative. These would be valid criticism of a work which relied on this method to the exclusion of all others, even if care was taken to obtain a spread of cases. However, Llewellyn and Hoebel insisted that the intensive analysis of cases was not the only technique that they recommended. The normal field techniques of the anthropologist were a necessary supplement to the study of cases. Their chapter on method was not intended as a substitute for a handbook on field-techniques.[32]

In *The Cheyenne Way* itself the potentialities of the technique could not be fully exploited. The book, written in the 'ethnographic present', relates to the period 1820–80. Hoebel's main field-work was done over fifty years later, and the cases reported are based almost entirely on hearsay and tradition. The 'trouble case method' is most effective and reliable when it is based on first-hand observation, and this was obviously not possible in the circumstances. The authors were fully aware of the dangers of relying on accounts by informants of events of long ago and they took great pains to cross-check different versions and to test reliability in other ways. They themselves were reasonably satisfied with the historical accuracy of most of their data; several reviewers of the book expressed admiration at the combination of caution and ingenuity that was displayed in dealing with such limited and tricky material. The authors were for the most part restricted to examining what their informants believed to have happened. It is, therefore, important to point out that even if the informants' accounts of cases were entirely fictitious they would still have been significant, for the stories were expressed in terms of Cheyenne concepts and are told against a background of actual institutions which are presupposed and taken for granted: 'war party', 'council of Forty-Four', 'Buffalo Chief', 'Dog Soldiers', a tribal hunt, and so on. An essential part of understanding the institutions of a society is to grasp the ways of thought of the people whose institutions they are. Myths and stories are as effective a way of getting at these 'perspectives' as are direct questioning or the recording of discussions that take place in dispute-settlement and other processes. In so far as stories and myths are considered to be significant by the informant, they are *primary sources* in respect of understanding the concepts, values, attitudes and thought patterns of the informants. The authors grasped this point, but they are open to the criticism that they did not press it far enough. As Hoebel himself has admitted, they could also have fruitfully subjected the Cheyenne language to much more intensive analysis. It was left to others, notably Gluckman and Bohannan, to wed the techniques of linguistic analysis to the gift of realism, the 'trouble case'.

Lawyers, especially English-trained lawyers, when they have devoted their attention to tribal law have rarely adopted the 'trouble case technique'. This can be seen by a glance at the fast-developing literature of 'African customary law', a literature which is remarkable for the disappointing lack of communication and interaction between lawyers and anthropologists.[33] The gap is partly to be explained in terms of different objectives, and different assumptions about the subject-matter, but above all in terms of differences in method. Even when lawyers have been modest enough to restrict themselves to a single tribe, they have normally been content to adopt the methodology of the English legal textbook writer, a methodology (if such a term can be appropriately applied to so unselfconscious a tradition) which, however well or ill-adapted it may be to the English context, often fits African customary law as comfortably as an Eton jacket would fit a surfbather. Generally speaking the lawyers have stayed close to the ideological approach; in respect of their use of cases they have tended to follow the example of English textbook writers rather than *The Cheyenne Way*. One result of this has been a tendency to consider substantive doctrines in isolation from the procedural contexts of their application and operation.

On the other hand, the leading anthropological works on customary law in Africa and elsewhere, although they do not conform to a single stereotype, have nearly all followed the example of *The Cheyenne Way* in rejecting 'the ideological approach' as being, at best, incomplete and in nearly every instance in making the detailed analysis of 'trouble cases' a crucial focus of attention. In so doing they have, *inter alia*, avoided the dangers of segregating 'doctrine' from 'process,' or 'substance' from 'procedure'; there is a certain irony in thus finding the anthropologists to be more direct inheritors of Maitland's teaching than his natural descendants, the common lawyers, when they have ventured outside their own culture. In sum, in recent studies of 'tribal' or 'customary' or 'primitive' law, whereas lawyers have rarely escaped from the clutches of a blinkered formalism, most anthropologists have been working in harmony with Llewellyn's brand of legal realism.

A proponent of the ideological approach might complain that in *The Cheyenne Way* the chapters on homicide, marriage, property and inheritance do not provide as systematic or as detailed information about these topics as might have been obtained if a different method had been adopted. From this he might be tempted to infer that 'the case method' may be appropriate to the study of *legal process* but not of *legal norms*. This argument is seductive, but the inference is unjustified. The main function of the chapters in question was to provide concrete illustrations of Cheyenne juristic method rather than to deal exhaustively with these topics for their own sake. The authors' prime concern was to analyse how the tribe handled the basic jobs of dispute prevention and dispute settlement and only incidentally to describe other aspects of their culture. It is wrong to infer from this that they denied that the Cheyennes had legal norms, or that the case method is not capable of being used in discovering what are the norms of a particular tribe. To argue thus involves confusing a plea for caution in formulating statements of norms with a claim that such formulations are impossible.

The Cheyenne Way itself contains a cautious statement of the law of killing expressed in normative form, prefaced by the *caveat* that this is 'a somewhat modernized and consciously articulate statement of the norms, as they appear in action, in the recorded cases and opinions'.[34] Scattered about the book are many other examples of statements of Cheyenne rules. Hoebel himself in a later work attempted to introduce an ideological element at a further remove. He sought to examine a number of cultures to determine their 'jural postulates', by which he meant the dominant values that guide and limit the devices actually made in any stable group. In his view 'every society, primitive or civilized, that has a law system has its jural postulates'. Thus, according to him, the postulates of the Cheyenne legal system could be expressed in the following form:

Postulate I. Man is subordinate to supernatural forces and spirit beings, *which are benevolent in nature.*
Corollary 1. Individual success and tribal well-being are abetted by the beneficent assistance of the supernaturals.
Postulate II. The killing of a Cheyenne by a fellow Cheyenne pollutes the tribal fetishes and also the murderer.
Corollary 1. Bad luck will dog the tribe until the fetishes are purified.
Corollary 2. The murderer must be temporarily separated from the social body.
Corollary 3. Violent behavior that may lead to homicide within the tribe must be avoided.
Corollary 4. Killing an enemy while in the presence of a tribal fetish is inimical to the supernaturals.
Postulate III. The authority of the tribal council is derived from the supernaturals and is supreme over all other elements in the society.
Postulate IV. The individual is important and shall be permitted and encouraged to express his potentialities with the greatest possible freedom compatible with group existence, but at the same time the individual is subordinate to the group, and all first obligations are to the maintenance of the well-being of the *tribe.*
Corollary 1. Rehabilitation of the recalcitrant individual after punishment is extremely important.[35]

It would be interesting to know what Llewellyn thought of this statement of Cheyenne jural postulates. One suspects that he may have felt uneasy about them and it is perhaps significant that, apart from the restatement of the law of killing, no such statement appears in *The Cheyenne Way.* However, Llewellyn was not dogmatic in his anti-dogmatism and he would have been more likely to have taken direct issue with Hoebel's belief that *every* system of law has jural postulates that can be articulated in so dogmatic a fashion, making no differentiation between the relative importance of the various postulates, indicating no exceptions and put forward in the form of a quasi-code.[36] The crux of the matter is that Hoebel's table can be safely regarded as a convenient summary of *some* particularly influential general ideas and assumptions, but there is a danger that it may be interpreted as something more pretentious, perhaps even as a purportedly complete logical system from which decisions were deduced; seen in this way, it would be both unsatisfactory from the point of view of a logician and misleading from the standpoint of a realist. It must be recalled that the ideological approach was not criticized because it was wrong, but was rather subject to certain *caveats*, viz: (i) bare statements of rules are not enough; (ii) bare statements of substantive rules divorced from any procedural context are apt to be misleading; (iii) confident dogmatic statements of rules should, in the first instance, be approached with caution, for they may oversimplify. Similar reservations are applicable to attempts to state 'the' basic postulates of a legal system. It is almost unnecessary to say that Hoebel respected these *caveats*.

REACTIONS

When *The Cheyenne Way* was published it was immediately recognized to be a work of major significance. Malinowski, Boas, Redfield, Lowie, Lévi-Strauss, Huntington Cairns, Timasheff and Pound were among those who praised it.[27] It is indicative of the breadth of the authors' frame of reference that different reviewers considered it from the point of view of its significance for anthropological method, sociological jurisprudence, legal practice in the United States, juristic method, the economics of primitive societies, comparative law, and interdisciplinary cooperation. Typically the irrepressible Llewellyn complained that the book had elicited no notice from psychologists.[28] More disappointing, however, was the fact that the book made a much greater impression upon anthropologists than upon jurists. By and large this has continued to be the case, as can clearly be seen by a brief survey of the subsequent literature of 'primitive law'. Few anthropological studies in this area have not been influenced, directly or indirectly, by *The Cheyenne Way*. Perhaps Max Gluckman, whose Barotse studies have added so much to the subject, may be made to speak for them:

Up to the year 1940 reports on the settlement of disputes among tribal peoples were relatively meager, and few of them worked out a detailed analysis of how mediating, arbitral, or judicial procedure and logic were applied to a series of cases. . . . [In the *Cheyenne Way* Llewellyn and Hoebel] raised new problems and set new standards in the analysis of tribal law.[29]

The Cheyenne Way acted as a general stimulus to anthropologists, not least because it convinced them that the law-ways of preliterate peoples were worthy of attention and were capable of study; it is not infrequently cited on points of substance; undoubtedly the most concrete indication of its influence is the extent to which the 'trouble case' method has become a standard tool of English-speaking anthropologists working in the field of tribal law.[40]

Interdisciplinary matchmakers might learn something about the conditions of successful collaboration from this unique example of a marriage between law and anthropology which lasted until the death of one of the partners.[41] The success was due in part to common, in part to complementary, characteristics. Both men were interested in jurisprudential questions and this provided an identity of objectives, the absence of which is the first obstacle to this type of collaboration. Both favoured the closer integration of the social sciences. Temperamentally they were well suited: each had a touch of the poet that enabled him to achieve almost instant rapport with informants and to appreciate the 'beauty' of Cheyenne techniques,[42] in other respects their characters were complementary, never more so than in the matter of obtaining a balance between imaginative insight and hard fact. Llewellyn's genius lay in devising new approaches, he was less fitted for applying them systematically. His inclination and aptitude for sustained fieldwork were limited. Hoebel on the other hand was both by training and temperament an excellent field worker; a man of notable intellectual humility, he was prepared to accept the role of disciple of Llewellyn's theories. He was, of course, predisposed to accept Llewellyn's ideas. Before they met they shared a common interest in the dynamics and functioning of institutions with human behaviour as the central focus. This was a meeting of realistic jurisprudence and functional anthropology. If Hoebel had been a rebel against Malinowski's functionalism, or if Llewellyn had been a more orthodox lawyer, collaboration would have been harder and much less fruitful. This basic harmony of approach was decisive in the success of this attempt to pool the skills and knowledge of scholars from two different disciplines. Both the relationship between Llewellyn and Hoebel and subsequent development in the study of tribal law are epitomized in Hoebel's striking dictum ' "Primitive Law" is the henchman of Legal Realism'.[43]

That *The Cheyenne Way* has been neglected by some students of Llewellyn's jurisprudence may also be due in part to a widespread scepticism about the relevance of the study of preliterate communities to the jurisprudence of modern industrial societies. Frank forcefully expressed the view that Llewellyn's time would have been better spent studying the law-ways of 'Tammany Hall Indians' in

New York;[44] some critics of *The Common Law Tradition* have doubted, in a somewhat dogmatic manner, the validity of the analogies that Llewellyn drew between the juristic techniques of the Cheyennes and of modern appellate courts;[45] rarely is *The Cheyenne Way* the subject of detailed attention in discussions of 'realism'.

His incursions into Indian law, and particularly his involvement with the Cheyennes, mark a crucial stage in the development of Llewellyn's thought. The inspiration for *The Cheyenne Way* comes from his early realism; some of the inspiration of his later ideas came from studying the Cheyennes. To the normal gain in self-understanding of any comparative work was added the particular value of studying a simple society, that is the opportunity to study a microcosm that can be seen in the round, relatively free from the refinements, distractions and confusions of complexity. It is never easy to see a modern industrial society as a whole in elemental terms. It is much easier to do so if one has first had the experience of a microcosm; Llewellyn's frequent use of examples from another kind of 'primitive society', the nursery, served much the same function.[46] There are, of course, many pitfalls in comparing the simple with the complex, but Llewellyn was not prone to underestimate the complexity of things, and he was careful not to push his analogies further than he felt was justified by repeated testing. Maitland once said: 'The traveller who has studied the uncorrupted savage can often tell the historian of medieval Europe what to look for, never what to find.'[47] Llewellyn would surely have agreed with this statement and its implications. What he derived from the Cheyennes was not a set of broad factual generalizations about law, but inspiration for some new tools for functional analysis. It is fair to say that *The Cheyenne Way* was a hypothesis-forming more than a hypothesis-testing book.

The Cheyenne study was the catalyst for a twofold advance in Llewellyn's thinking: first, it marks a definite shift to a more consistent and more general standpoint than previously. Llewellyn's early private practitioner orientation has already been remarked.[48] From now on, even when considering the detailed problems of specific participants, Llewellyn's perspective is consistently that of society as a whole. At the same time his ideas move more easily on to a general plane, with implications that are seen to transcend a particular society at a particular time. The 'law-jobs' theory is a theory about group-life that applies to almost any human group, complex or simple, large or small. It is the foundation for a general sociology of law that he continued to work towards for the rest of his life.[49]

The second advance is in respect of legal technology ('the job of juristic method'): it is at the time of the Cheyenne study that the associated ideas of 'craft', 'style', 'the job of juristic method', and 'legal aesthetics' are adopted as working concepts. In particular, Llewellyn specifically credited the Cheyennes with inspiration for one of the major themes of *The Common Law Tradition*: the idea of the Grand Style of appellate judging:

Then a few years later, the law of the Cheyenne Indians made clear to me what I had never before dreamed: to wit, that law and justice had no need at all to be in conflict or even in too much tension, but could instead represent a daily working harmony. For in common with most lawyers, and indeed with most jurisprudes, I had mostly taken for granted a sort of perpetual struggle between the needs of regularity and form and of the precedent – phase of justice on the one side and, on the other, any dynamic readjustment of a going system to what just needed to be done. Pound had rightly stressed shifting tides in the struggle, and that I had seen. But I had to get to the Cheyennes in order to wake up to the fact that tension between form, or precedent, or other tradition and perceived need requires, in nature, to be a tension *only for the single crisis*. It does not have to be a continuing tension in the legal system as a whole, because an adequately resilient legal system can on occasion, or even almost regularly, absorb the particular trouble and resolve it each time into a new, usefully guiding, forward-looking felt standard-for-action or even rule-of-law. To think of such steady readjustment – what Mentschikoff calls the legal artist's job of producing a new technical guiding form which can supply both needs at once – this was to get a further new pair of eyes. And it was on this foundation of experience with Cheyenne law that I became able to spot and understand the Grand Style as I met it in the early work of our own courts.[50]

9
Law in Our Society

Llewellyn's major published works have strong affinities with each other but they cannot be said to form a neat pattern. Each reveals aspects of his ideas and approach, but none brings them together into a single coherent statement of a general theory. At first sight Llewellyn's work appears to contrast sharply with that of system builders like Bentham and Lasswell. He felt constricted by collections of tightly drawn definitions;[1] he tended to use vague terms when working at a high level of generality; orderly presentation of his ideas did not come naturally to him and on the whole he was more concerned with 'theories of the middle range' than with 'ultimate questions'.[2]

However, he was fully in sympathy with systematic thinkers in believing in the value of seeing things in a broad perspective. He was also anxious to fit his ideas into a single, reasonably coherent framework. As early as 1927 he wrote a paper on 'Mechanisms of Group Control', which represents his first serious attempt to state a general sociological theory of law.[3] He was dissatisfied with it and withheld publication. Between 1927 and 1940 he made several further attempts, all of which were abandoned before completion.[4] The preparation of *The Cheyenne Way* stimulated him to try again. This time he was more successful and within a relatively short period, in 1940–1, he published three papers,[5] which taken together with *The Cheyenne Way* provide a fairly full and coherent picture of his general ideas at this stage.

Llewellyn saw these papers as only a beginning and at the time of his death he was just about to start on yet another attempt to make a general theoretical statement of his position. This was to have been his last major project. First at Harvard and Columbia in 1948–9 and thereafter at Chicago he gave a course entitled 'Law in Our Society', which became the main vehicle for developing his 'whole view', as he called it. The mimeographed materials for this course, together with his lectures, which he regularly recorded, were the materials from which he planned for a long time to work up a book on 'The Sociology of Law-Government'.[6] However, up to 1960 first the Uniform Commercial Code and then *The Common Law Tradition* had to be given priority. After the publication of *The Common Law Tradition* in 1960, he still had a number of commitments in connection with the code and he was also much in demand as a lecturer. He was due to retire in July 1962, and he had accepted an invitation to deliver a series of formal lectures in Germany in the following academic year. He had intended to make this the occasion of a final statement of his position and the text of the lectures was to be published as a book. As a preliminary to drafting the lectures, he brought together and edited a selection of his published articles and shorter pieces on jurisprudence and related subjects. On 5 February 1962 he wrote the preface to this book, but eight days later he died of a heart attack. The book was published posthumously with the title *Jurisprudence: Realism in Theory and Practice*.[7]

Thus Llewellyn died on the eve of starting on his last project. All there was to show for the proposed Freiburg lectures was a draft table of contents. This repeats almost exactly the chapter headings of the mimeographed materials on *Law in Our Society*.[8] Accordingly, this extraordinary document represents Llewellyn's last attempt to articulate a general theory: it is mostly in note-form, parts of it are rather cryptic, it is incomplete and Llewellyn did not intend it for publication. Some of it covers topics dealt with more fully in print. Yet it is without doubt the most important of the manuscripts left behind in the Llewellyn Papers for, despite its limitations, it embodies not only the latest, but also in some respects the fullest statement of a general theory. It is too condensed, too rich in detail and is generally too Llewellynesque for any attempted précis or restatement to be a satisfactory substitute for the original. Some short extracts are reproduced in appendix C in the hope that they will give an indication of the nature and style of the manuscript as well as making available some of the more important passages.[9] It requires someone who is both bolder and more patient than the author to undertake the challenging task of working the whole up into publishable form. Meanwhile this chapter can be treated as a critical introduction to the manuscript as well as an attempt to provide a coherent answer to the question: 'What was Llewellyn's theory of law?'

LLEWELLYN'S APPROACH TO JURISPRUDENCE

It was suggested in the first chapter that one of the main sources of misunderstanding about realism has been that 'the realists' have sometimes been treated as criticizing the articulate and relatively sophisticated theories of jurists of the Austinian school, when in fact the main target of their attacks on 'formalism' were largely inarticulate and unsophisticated working theories of academic lawyers like Langdell and Beale and, less directly, the assumptions underlying the approach of many American lawyers and judges.[10] At the root of such misunderstandings has been a tendency to treat all legal theories as comparables, because they fall within the sphere of 'jurisprudence'.[11] Before attempting to answer a question of the kind, 'What was X's theory of law', it is wise to face up to a preliminary question: 'What did X consider to be the nature and function of a "theory of law" '? It is particularly important to do this in the case of Llewellyn, who used the terms 'jurisprudence' and 'legal theory' interchangeably and not very precisely:

Jurisprudence means to me: any careful and sustained thinking about any phase of things legal, if the thinking seeks to reach beyond the practical solution of an immediate problem in hand. Jurisprudence thus includes any type at all of honest and thoughtful generalization in the field of the legal.[12]

Llewellyn sometimes roughly divided jurisprudence (or legal theory) into three branches, reflecting what he termed 'the what, the whither and the how of law': legal philosophy (concerned with 'ultimate' questions of ends and perhaps also with fundamental existential and epistemological questions), legal science (concerned with empirical description), and jurisprudence, or 'prudentia iuris' (the study of the machinery of law-and-government and the methods and techniques of participants in legal processes). In lectures he would illustrate the scheme by means of a chart:[13]

	Whither? Why?	What?	How?
Theory: Political	Philosophy	Science	Prudence
Legal	Philosophy	Science	Prudence

In *Law in our Society* Llewellyn's main purpose was to outline his own 'working whole view' and to encourage his students to develop their own. Although he recognized the need for specialization, he had little sympathy with what might be termed the Royal Tennis Tradition in jurisprudence,[14] in which it becomes a quaint, intricate, esoteric game, remote from contemporary life and understood by few beyond the handful of people who actually play it. Jurisprudence was too important in his view to be left to the experts. In particular, he believed that even the most humble practitioner could benefit both professionally and personally from having an articulate and coherent working theory. Every lawyer needs to understand his situation and his role, to clarify his aims and have a general conception of how to set about attaining them, and to be able to see all this in a broad perspective.[15] In his later work, especially in *Law in Our Society*, Llewellyn distinguished between 'jurisprudence for the hundred', 'jurisprudence for the hundred thousand', (for the bar and for the intelligent laymen), and 'jurisprudence for the hundred million'.[16] In a very high proportion of his teaching and writing he denied, not always convincingly, that he was concerned with 'jurisprudence for the hundred' and claimed to be operating at the level of 'jurisprudence for the hundred thousand'. In his teaching he consistently treated his students as intending private practitioners and a chief aim of his course on 'Law in Our Society' was to encourage each student to start to work out for himself a reasonably coherent and articulate working theory. In his writings, too, he regularly emphasized that jurisprudence had an important practical role to perform.[17]

In working at the level of 'jurisprudence for the hundred thousand', Llewellyn tended to make certain disclaimers about what he was doing. For instance, in *Law in Our Society* he explicitly excluded 'professional' philosophy; he maintained that his descriptive generalizations were 'pre-scientific'; the values he accepted were no more than 'fighting faiths', bolstered by 'the best reason we can muster'; his concepts were expressed in 'roughly workable, not "accurate" phrasing'; the basic approach was that of 'horse-sense'.[18] The title 'Law in Our Society' emphasized its American orientation. In short, Llewellyn claimed neither universality nor refinement for his ideas in this context. This was typical of most of his published writings.

Such disclaimers, and Llewellyn's personal preference for the 'low' philosophy of law could be misleading if taken out of context. It may be disconcerting to the specialist jurist to find Llewellyn adopting the persona of a folk-philosopher or sage. Does he really invite treatment as a latter-day Ben Franklin or an academic Mr Dooley? Or is he merely putting on a defensive mask to protect himself from judgment by scholarly standards? Is he being unduly modest or has he, by setting his sights too low, forfeited all claims to be treated seriously as a jurist? And is he espousing a crassly utilitarian view of theory?

A fairly confident negative can be returned to all those questions. It would be a mistake to see Llewellyn as a mere popularizer: he was a sophisticated jurist (sometimes too sophisticated even for the hundred, it seems), and he expected to be treated as a heavyweight. Some of his disclaimers may be ignored as being unnecessarily modest or self-protective. Moreover, as he well realized, the criteria by which the value and limitations of contributions to the 'high' and 'low' philosophies are to be assessed are not fundamentally different. When Llewellyn is vulnerable to criticism he is fair game, but for criticism to be fair account needs to be taken of his concerns and objectives. In the context of his time it was quite natural that Llewellyn should prefer the role of sage to that of pharisee. As a generalist he was aware of his limitations as a philosopher and sociologist. He was naturally attracted by the down-to-earth and the folksy. And the absence of a strong taught tradition of jurisprudence in America, together with the general climate of opinion, tended to make the role of sage an honoured one. Thus, for example, sages were sometimes made judges and judge-sages tended to become popular heroes—witness Holmes, Brandeis, Cardozo, Frankfurter and Learned Hand. A similar combination of a search for usable theory with a desire to communicate directly with non-experts is to be found in the work of Beard, Robinson and Dewey.[19] The conception of a working theory for participants underlies Llewellyn's approach to jurisprudence. The crux of the matter is that if the 'hundred thousand' are to benefit from the subject they need something simple, usable and useful; that simplicity is not to be confused with superficiality, nor utility with the banausic, and that jurisprudence as a subject has had to pay too heavy a price for the perfectionist tendencies of some of its high priests.

LAW-GOVERNMENT AS AN INSTITUTION:
THE LAW-JOBS THEORY

The starting-point for Llewellyn's 'working whole view' was 'the basic theory of the institution of law-government', commonly referred to as the 'law-jobs theory'.[20] The central proposition of this theory is that there are certain needs that must be met for a human group to survive as a group and for it to achieve the purposes for which it exists.[21] This applies equally to very small groups, such as a married couple or a partnership, and to the largest and most complex groups, such as a nation or state or even the world community. It is applicable to groups with a limited *raison d'être*, for instance a school debating team or a football club, as well as to groups that are related to many phases of the lives of their members, such as a family or tribe. It applies to groups which are ephemeral as well as to those which are enduring. The needs arise particularly from a facet of human nature, *viz.* that human beings have drives, desires and interests which tend to be incompatible. In so far as those 'divisive urges', as Llewellyn called them, are a source of actual or potential conflict and in so far as conflict is inimical to group-survival and to concerted effort to a common end, conflict-prevention and conflict-resolution are a necessary precondition of group-survival and group-effectiveness.

Llewellyn classified the main needs ('jobs') into six categories: (i) 'adjustment of the trouble case'; (ii) preventive channelling of conduct and expectations'; (iii) 'preventive rechannelling of conduct and expectations to adjust to change'; (iv) 'arranging for the say and the manner of its saying' (allocation of authority and procedures for authoritative decision-making); (v) provision of direction and incentive within the group ('the job of providing Net Positive Drive'); and (vi) 'the job of Juristic Method'.[22]

Groups which qualify to be called 'societies' have institutions, more or less developed and specialized, the peculiar function of which is to perform these 'law-jobs'. In Llewellyn's later usage 'law-and-government' (or 'law-government') is the term used to refer to such institutions. In society 'law-government' is the main but not the only institution for performing the six jobs listed above; conversely 'the law-jobs' are the main but not the only jobs of the institution of law-government.

In one of his summaries, Llewellyn continues:

In the doing of each of these law-jobs one can distinguish a bare-bones aspect which runs no further than the keeping of a society (or indeed of any group) together and alive; and, in addition, two ideal aspects. The one ideal aspect has to do with efficiency of operation. The other has to do with the realization of man's aspirations.

Around the law-jobs (which are inherent in the nature of any group, big or little) there develop (in any group) activities. When these activities become distinct enough to be recognizable as such, the stuff of law has thereby become observable as such. When men specialize in such activities, the men of law become recognizable. Both the men and the stuff show, as distinguishing marks, a more-or-less regularity of action, and show felt standards, more or less articulate, as to the manner and direction of such action. It is ill-advised to take either the practices or the standards, to take either the men or the practices-and-standards, as being alone somehow *the* substance of law. The going institution takes them in, all together. 'Precept' and 'principle,' e.g., to be part of a legal system, must be somehow actually at work in that system, and only in and through men and ideas *held* by men can they be at work.

Practice, again, is the bony structure of a legal system. Yet practice is no part of *law* except as it comes wrapped in and is measured constantly against the held norm or felt ideal. Men are the life blood of a legal system, yet men are not even of it, save as bedded in a context of tradition, both existent and becoming, which shapes the men even as it is being shaped by them.

Out of the conjunction of activities and men around the law-jobs there arise the crafts of law, and so the craftsmen. Advocacy, counseling, judging, law-making, administering – these are major groupings of the law-crafts. But mediation, organization, policing, teaching, scholarship, are others. At the present juncture, the fresh study of these crafts and of the manner of their best doing is one of the major needs of jurisprudence.[23]

Llewellyn considered 'institution' to be 'the central and most important concept of social science'.[24] When asked what he meant by the term, he used to refer his questioners to a well-known article by Walton Hamilton, which starts as follows:

Institution is a verbal symbol which for want of a better describes a cluster of social usages. It connotes a way of thought or action of some prevalence and permanence which is embedded in the habits of a group or the customs of a people. In ordinary speech it is another word for procedure, convention or arrangement.[25]

Hamilton maintained that it is impossible to try to give a detailed description of an institution in isolation from its social context, the edges are too blurred: 'Even if it is deliberately established an institution has neither a definite beginning nor an uncompromised identity . . . It cannot be shown in perspective or recognized in detail by the logical method of inclusion and exclusion.'[26]

The borderlands of 'institution' are accordingly rather vague. Hamilton also emphasized the imperfection of institutions and the part played by chance as well as intent in their development. Llewellyn's usage of 'institution' is slightly different:

An *institution* is in first instance organized activity built around the doing of a job or a cluster of jobs. A craft is a minor institution. A *major* institution differs in that its job-cluster is fundamental to the continuance of the society (or group) with typical resulting complexity.[27]

This is a more explicitly functional definition than Hamilton's. However, Llewellyn recognized that institutions could be 'crescive', in Sumner's terminology,[28] i.e. they could grow up as a result of instinctive response to need as well as by conscious invention, and he did not make the mistake of assuming that there cannot be 'functional' behaviour independently of rational, articulate purpose.[29]

Llewellyn's emphasis on the concept of 'institution' is understandable. By defining it in behavioural terms he was able to make human behaviour a central focus of his jurisprudence; by taking as his starting-point a sociological concept he hoped to facilitate communication between lawyers and social scientists; and he found positive virtues in its vagueness. He deliberately avoided precise stipulative definitions of abstract concepts because he could see little profit in them and a great danger that they would be used as arbitrary criteria of what is relevant and irrelevant to jurisprudence.[30] Finally, Llewellyn claimed that looking on law as an institution . . .

. . . provides two vitally serviceable points of orientation which freshen eyes and give a cross-check on what may be there to see. For, first, a going institution has jobs to do, and its function is to get them done effectively and well. This gives a pole of purpose and value to measure by. And, secondly, a going institution has results in life, and must be tested by them; and those results are capable of inquiry. The measure of the institution is, then, the measure of how its results check in fact, in regard to the actual doing of its jobs.[31]

Llewellyn's early approach to the problem of the definition of 'law' has already been considered in the chapter on *The Bramble Bush*.[32] It is now necessary to return to the topic. During the drafting of *The Cheyenne Way* Hoebel was anxious to include a general stipulative definition of 'law' in the text. Llewellyn disagreed. He set out his reasons informally in a letter:

The more I think about your universal definition of law, the less I am disposed to like it. I find it very difficult to frame any definition which covers the situation in a non-state, non-authority society, and also has adequate application to a modern society. My own approach has been to set up a Weberish 'ideal type' with a good many attributes, such as rules with verbal form, machinery for enforcement of a recognized claim, if needed, with exclusivity when applicable the force of the state behind action; a specialized enforcing, and litigation and counselling personnel, and the like. It will take quite a while to work out in detail every attribute necessary to present this ideal type. It will never find a complete counterpart in life, unless an arbitrary choice is made between the elements of certainty and of justice – a point over which I am still puzzling.

However, setting up some such type at one pole and unpredictable chaos at the other, we can, it seems to me, identify certain subject-matters or jobs which law stuff, in various degrees of primitivity or development of form or kind (procedure for adjustment, existing either apart from or in conjunction with, third-party personnel; supernatural sanctions existing either apart from or in conjunction with secular, and the like) is doing or accomplishing in any group or society. The only absolutely universal characteristics which I find, consist in the presence of these jobs which need doing, and in a *tendency* for any steps in the doing of them to take on, unless thwarted by governing causes, some aspects of regularity in regard to both pattern and personnel. I think this a sounder approach than any which rests upon a criterion of rule, of rightness, or of course of conduct, or of monopoly of force, or state command or of any other simple criterion that I have met.

The essence of an attack on the phenomena is the wherewithal to indicate *gradations*. Nothing in the matter of form is universal; and any definition built to fit primitive conditions falls down when the State steps in, not displacing the primitive forms, but running largely beside them, and only sometimes overlapping or conflicting.[33]

No general definition of 'law' appeared in *The Cheyenne Way*, but Hoebel, apparently unconvinced by Llewellyn's arguments, included one in *The Law of Primitive Man*: 'A social norm is legal if its neglect or infraction is regularly met, in threat or in fact, by the application of physical force by an individual or group possessing the socially recognized privilege of so acting.'[34]

The difference between Llewellyn and Hoebel on this issue was narrow. Llewellyn's refusal to commit himself to a general stipulative definition of 'law' did not preclude him from elucidating his usage of this and a number of related terms. Nor was his anlaysis very different from Hoebel's. By maintaining that law was only one of the institutions which perform the law-jobs in society, he was committed to accepting some distinction, albeit not a rigid one, between it and other institutions. In both 'The Normative, The Legal and the Law-Jobs' and in *Law in Our Society* he went very near to providing a definition by suggesting four characteristics which, when combined, serve to differentiate 'legal' from other institutions: specialized personnel or procedures recognized as carrying the stamp of authority of the whole, supremacy within the group, effectiveness and regularity.[35] This aspect of Llewellyn's elucidation of 'law' adds little that is new and it has been improved upon by other jurists, notably by Professor Hart.[36] In the 'Normative, the Legal and the Law-Jobs', Llewellyn also set out to elucidate a number of terms that he himself had coined: 'Law-ways', 'Law-stuff', 'jurid', 'skelegal', 'the Legal' (as contrasted with 'the legal'), and 'law-wavers'. With the exception of the first two, he fortunately made little use of these repulsive terms, consideration of which is best confined to the obscurity of a footnote.[37]

A number of points are worth making about Llewellyn's approach to the definition of 'law'. First, he was well aware that in ordinary usage 'law' is a word which is both vague and ambiguous. He did not make the elementary error of assuming that there is one 'true' or 'proper' meaning of the word and he realized that any general definition of 'law' must necessarily involve at least an element of personal recommendation or preference. In *Law in Our Society,* following the example of Pound,[38] he listed a number of different meanings that are to be found in common usage and commented: 'A "definition" which throws out any of those or similar aspects throws out something of significance to Jurisprudence.'[39]

As has already been mentioned, in the late 1940s Llewellyn adopted the concept 'law-government' in preference to 'law'. His justification for joining together 'law' and 'government' was that these two terms are often used to refer to institutions which are primarily concerned with the same basic function, 'the job that is fundamental to the existence of any society and of any social discipline at all; it is the job of producing and maintaining the groupness of a group.'[40] In trying to develop this idea he added:

The chart picture of the single institution would be a long ellipse, every point of circumference or area related, to some degree, to *each* of two imaginary foci. The one focus (never found alive) would be complete regularity utterly independent of judgment and person; the other (never found alive, either) would be non-recurrent action determined utterly by the particular acting official's idiosyncratic and also non-habitual choice. The 'law' phases of law-government are closer to the first focus; the more purely 'government' phases are closer to the second.[41]

At least the first four of the six 'jobs' listed above are normally done in a manner that approximates more nearly the 'law pole', they are characteristically 'law jobs', the others range widely between the poles. There are some other 'jobs', such as defence of the group, which come nearer to the governmental pole. By this slight adjustment of focus Llewellyn hoped to provide a common starting-point for jurisprudence, politics and sociology.

Finally, it should be noted that Llewellyn was trying to construct a theoretical model of 'law-government' as a tool of description in lieu of a dogmatic formulaic 'definition of law'. In this he was influenced by Weber's concept of 'ideal types'. For the traditional litmus paper tests of 'law' and 'not law' he was hoping to substitute a more flexible and generally more sophisticated tool of descriptive analysis.

It is not entirely clear whether Llewellyn looked on his 'law-jobs' theory as being more of an empirical than an *a priori* theory; that is to say, it is not clear whether he wished some of his general statements about the law-jobs to be treated as empirical generalizations capable of verification or to be treated as elucidating an armoury of related concepts of which 'group', 'divisive urges', 'law-government' and 'human behaviour' were the most important.[42] He used regularly to set students the exercise of 'testing' the theory against some group of which they had had first-hand experience. Over the years several hundred students did this exercise and some were stimulated to produce some very interesting papers.[43] There is no record, however, of any student having claimed 'to disprove' the theory. Indeed, it is not clear *how* it could be disproved. This suggests that the theory may be of a kind that is incapable of either proof or disproof in its major aspects, because it is essentially tauto-logical. Take, for instance, the proposition: 'The jobs, therefore, get themselves done after some fashion always—or the group simply is no more.'[44] On the face of it this looks like an important statement of fact. Let us test this by postulating a group in which the job of dispute settlement is not being done, yet the group seems to continue to exist. Is such a situation even conceivable? The answer to the latter question depends, in first instance, on how the terms 'group' and 'dispute settlement' are being used in this context. In ordinary usage it is meaningful to say: 'This group is riddled with conflict, but it continues to function'; but it is also meaningful to say: 'They are so riddled with conflict that they no longer deserve to be called a "group".' This is because in ordinary usage the idea of a 'group' implies harmony or cooperation, i.e. a non-conflict relationship.[45] It is possible for individuals to dispute about A, while being in harmony about B and C, but it is paradoxical to say that people are both in harmony and in conflict about the same matter at the same time. In ordinary usage 'group', 'conflict', 'dispute' and 'harmony' are vague terms. Llewellyn made no serious attempt to define them precisely in the context of the law-jobs theory. Accordingly he failed to give clear answers to such questions as: under what circumstances would it be true to say that a group no longer exists? When exactly can it be said that a dispute has arisen or has been settled? And so on. The result is that there is an unresolved doubt about such statements as 'the jobs get done after some fashion always —or the group simply is no more.' They can equally well be treated as tautologous or else as exceedingly vague statements of fact. Someone who wished to prove or disprove the law-jobs theory empirically would need first of all to restate it in precise, non-tautological terms.

How damaging is the conclusion that the law-jobs theory is both vague and contains an element of tautology? This depends on the purposes it is made to serve. When Llewellyn challenged his students to 'test' his theory, he may inadvertently have misled them as to its nature, but it is probable that many of them nonetheless found it illuminating to analyse groups of their acquaintance in terms of how the law-jobs were done. For this purpose the vagueness of such terms as 'group' and 'dispute' was not a grave handicap. Similarly the theory has been found to be useful in the initial stages of the Chicago Arbitration Project, which was explicitly concerned with the law-government of commercial groups and especially with the various modes of dispute-settlement resorted to by them.[46]

Llewellyn's terms are by no means useless because they are vague. 'Dispute settlement', for instance, is a most useful characterization. The study of judicial processes would have benefited a great deal if courts had been more regularly seen as just one type of dispute settlement mechanism, and if jurists had more readily tried to see courts from the broad perspective of the total picture of dispute settlement mechanisms in society. It is suggested that the law-jobs theory is best treated as providing a rough but useful tool for functional analysis. In this view, the list of six law-jobs can be treated as a crude check-list of questions to ask when examining the structure and operation of any human group: how are conflicts handled within the group? How is behaviour channelled so as to avoid conflict? How is authority to make decisions allocated? What procedures have to be followed in authoritative decision-making? And so on. By developing a set of concepts which could be applied to *any human group,* Llewellyn claimed to have provided a means of exploring the similarities and the differences between 'primitive' and modern industrialized societies, between the world community and smaller societies and between sub-groups within a major group ('the Entirety') or between the major group and some sub-group within it.[47] This claim surely deserves attention, for, if it is at all justified, it establishes Llewellyn's theory as one of major significance. In the form in which he left it, the theory was admittedly a crude one, in need of considerable refinement. It is particularly unfortunate that Llewellyn should have died when he was just about to redirect his attention to this subject.

It is not necessary at this point to comment in detail on each of the six principal law-jobs. Four of them receive extended treatment elsewhere in the present work.[48] Thus the first job, dispute-settlement, has been considered in connection with *The Cheyenne Way,*[49] and will be further explored in the chapter on *The Common Law Tradition*; the Theory of Rules is concerned with the uses and limitations of one of the most important devices for performing the second job of preventing disputes from arising,[50] the problem of adjustment to change constitutes one of the central themes of Llewellyn's work and the subject of juristic method is developed in the Theory of Crafts, which is considered below.[51] The remaining two jobs, the allocation of authority and the provision of incentives, were not topics on which Llewellyn had much to say.[52] However, it may be worth making a few general points here.

First, the list of six law-jobs was not meant to be exhaustive. In a supplement to *Law in Our Society* Llewellyn dealt rather perfunctorily with others, viz: defence, continuation of the law-government regime and a general residuary 'catch-all', which made allowance for the whole conspectus of differing opinions about the 'proper' role of government.[53] The six jobs selected for special attention were merely put forward as a rough characterization of what he considered to be the basic recurrent needs for the survival and operation of human groups.

Secondly, by emphasizing that the institution of law-government is not the only device for doing the law-jobs, Llewellyn provides a useful reminder that there are other devices which assist in performing the same functions. Writers on law sometimes seem to forget that courts are not the only, nor are they necessarily the most important, dispute-settlement mechanisms in society; similarly it is useful to be reminded from time to time that legal rules are only one of a number of types of device that can be used for channelling conduct and expectations. Whole areas of enquiry are suggested by this kind of approach. In what circumstances do disputants choose to resort to the courts rather than to some other type of mechanism? What percentage of accidents of type X ever reach the courts? To what extent are the results of disputes settled 'out of court' in conformity with established legal doctrine, in so far as this is clear? In respect of some particular example of 'law reform', to what extent did the legislators envisage a change in the legal rules as being in itself sufficient to produce a change in the relevant patterns of behaviour? To what extent did they explore the whole range of possible devices for channelling or rechannelling this type of conduct?

The law-jobs theory, by going back to fundamentals, forces one to see each specialized device or institution in the context of the total picture of the performance of certain basic functions. When this perspective is adopted an almost endless variety of questions is suggested.[54] Some of these questions may be familiar, but others will prove to be new or relatively neglected. One value of the law-jobs theory is that it makes such questions seem obvious and natural.

In summing up, Llewellyn gave credit to Max Weber for the basic insight:

The jobs to be done are jobs to be done; modern complexity of institution serves merely to highlight processes which require to be gone through, in some fashion, in any group. *The jobs, therefore, get themselves done after some fashion* always – or the group simply is no more. Hence if the officially announced imperatives fail to put themselves over, one must look elsewhere for the doing of the jobs. . . . Hence to see a Legal regulation which is not working is promptly to face a problem of further inquiry: what *is* working? and how?[55]

Finally, it is worth noting that Llewellyn saw the law-jobs theory as providing an intellectual framework sufficiently broad and flexible to accommodate most 'schools' of jurisprudence. In lecture nine of *Law in Our Society* he explicitly linked his consideration of the various 'traditional approaches' to the law-jobs theory:

If (i) an institution has jobs to do, and therefore needs a technical structure, and (ii) the technical structure is never in itself fully equal to the jobs, but can nevertheless get complex enough to raise a special set of problems in itself, and if, also, (iii) ways of the handling of the technical machinery are also things to worry over, then it follows that

(a) some thinkers will (and should) be concerned about what the jobs and ultimate goals are, and about how you can be sure about that;

(b) some thinkers will (and should) be worrying about finding or making orderly and meaningful shape in or with the technical structure;

(c) some thinkers will (and should) be attempting to judge measures against goals, in terms (i) of the factual results and (ii) of the particular values which are dear to those particular thinkers;

(d) some thinkers will (and should) be concentrating on the engineering aspects of the machinery, and their improvement simply as such.

(e) some thinkers will (and should) be worrying about general theory, or perfect theory, in the realm of 'testable' truth, with, conceivably, little or no direct interest in 'applied' or practical work.

The various traditional approaches in Jurisprudence vary primarily in regard to which of such lines each stresses, and in regard to how the one *or more* lines stressed are gone about. Each approach (i) offers solid values; (ii) needs help from others; and (iii) can (if corrective balancing is lacking) mislead into exaggeration, even into flat error. No jurisprude with a single dominant line of approach is to be trusted in his denials or his attacks. [56]

This passage provides a convenient framework for considering other aspects of Llewellyn's 'whole view'. The ensuing sections deal with his ideas on what he termed the Good (justice and natural law), the True (empiricism and 'the scientific analogy') and the Beautiful (legal aesthetics). Then two 'theories' are considered which relate directly to the law-jobs: 'The Theory of Crafts' is essentially an elaboration of the idea of juristic method. Rules are the most important instrument for performing the law-jobs and 'the Theory of Rules' brings together Llewellyn's ideas about their nature and function and related matters. These help to give a rounded picture of Llewellyn's general position, but for the most part they constitute some of the less developed aspects of his thought. Accordingly they will be dealt with rather more cursorily than the 'law-jobs theory'.

JUSTICE AND NATURAL LAW

The problem of justice is to the jurist what Mont Blanc is to the mountaineer: a challenge faced by many, but mastered by few. *Law in Our Society* contains Llewellyn's most sustained attempt to face the challenge.[57] The relevant section, although it is in note form, is at least as clear and is much more detailed than his longest published discussion of the subject. It is helpful for the light it throws on Llewellyn, but few are likely to regard it as a particularly remarkable contribution to a much discussed topic.

Llewellyn distinguished three 'levels of discussion' of justice: (i) 'ultimate justice', concerned with questions about fairness and the good life outside the context of any particular group; (ii) 'legislative social justice', concerned both with the furthering of the goals of a particular group and with questions of general distribution of objects of desire within the group; (iii) 'justice under existing law', concerned with the evaluation of results in particular cases of 'claim, grievance, dispute, [or] offense'.[58] In his view, an important first step in any disucssion of justice was to identify the appropriate level of discussion.

Llewellyn himself tended to deal rather cursorily with questions on the first level, as being in the realm of 'non-testable truth', not susceptible to proof.[59] They belonged to the realms of faith, characterized by Holmes as 'can't-helps'.[60] He concentrated on the second and third levels and, for the most part, his approach was empirical in that his main concern was to identify the principal stimuli that lead men within groups to react in terms of justice and injustice. This approach, although worked out independently, has close affinities with that of Edmond Cahn[61] and F. R. Bienenfeld.[62] Indeed, Bienenfeld's analysis of 'Justice in the Nursery' was taken as the starting-point for discussion of problems of justice in Llewellyn's course. Bienenfeld, building on the work of Piaget and Freud, begins by analysing typical demands made in the name of justice by young children in familiar nursery situations. He shows in simple terms that a number of values are regularly invoked in such situations—notably equality, desert, need, status and liberty—and that often a choice has to be made between competing values.[63] For instance, simple equality demands that the last remaining cake should go to child A, but child B is hungry and so his need is greater. Cahn, in *The Sense of Injustice*, uses a similar approach in his attempt to discover 'how

justice arises' and 'its biologic purpose' by treating the sense of injustice as an empirical phenomenon and analysing typical human
reactions to situations typically regarded as unjust.

It has been pointed out that empirical enquiries of the kind
envisaged by Bienenfeld and Cahn have so far yielded little beyond
vague generalities and that there are important unresolved methodological difficulties about investigating 'the bottomless pit' of
individual reactions to possible 'justice situations'.[64] It is arguable
that such difficulties are not insurmountable and that empirical
research along these lines, while unlikely to resolve all problems of
'justice', might be revealing; nevertheless it is fair to say that neither
Cahn nor Bienenfeld nor Llewellyn himself seems to have devoted
much attention to these difficulties. Moreover, none of them actually
pursued extensive research of the kind contemplated; rather they
used simple examples of a familiar kind to illustrate some of the
main values associated with the concept of 'justice'. My own experience has been that Bienenfeld's 'Justice in the Nursery' is a useful
teaching device for introducing some of the main themes to be explored in a discussion of justice, but that his analysis is of limited
value thereafter. Similarly, Llewellyn's treatment is quite helpful as
a preliminary exploration of the subject, but it is neither sufficiently
sustained nor sufficiently precise to add much to philosophers'
discussions of the topic.

As an ethical relativist Llewellyn maintained that 'every man of
conscience must hold his own perceptions of Justice to be the basic
ones'.[65] In analysing his own concept of social justice, he took as
his starting-point four attributes:

First, it is an aspect of the Good. Second, it has to do with conflict between
people and with removing or avoiding or regulating that conflict. Third, it
is heavily affected by the idea of fairness, and again by that phase of fairness
which we speak of as even-handedness. Fourth, it operates under the sad
fact of scarcity; in result, there will not be enough of it to go round, and
'solution' will be driven into preferring some to others, or into compromise.[66]

Llewellyn's personal values in this context were fairly straightforward, if not very precisely defined. Without committing himself
to a fixed hierarchy of values, he claimed to give a high priority to
four values: tolerance, basic minimum respect for human dignity,
'decent attention to need as well as merit', and 'a fair hearing
before a fair tribunal'. He was far from being a dogmatic egalitarian,

maintaining that equality was the residual value, which ought to operate unless inequality could be justified in terms of some other value such as merit or the needs of the whole group.[67]

Llewellyn's views on natural law may be considered briefly at this point. Lecture nine of *Law in Our Society* contains a lengthy discussion of natural law and reveals Llewellyn to be basically sympathetic, but cautious, in his approach to natural law philosophers.[68] Briefly, he sympathized with the concerns that motivated the quest for ideals, approved of the use of right reason, but rejected some of the claims commonly associated with theories of natural law. In particular he rejected three propositions: (a) that law as it is cannot be distinguished from law as it ought to be;[69] (b) that there are universal moral principles that are applicable to all people at all times and in all places;[70] and (c) that moral principles are susceptible of proof and do not rest ultimately on faith.[71]

Rather, Llewellyn believed (a) that it is both possible and desirable to talk of bad law and to distinguish law as it is from law as it ought to be;[72] (b) that clear guidance can only be obtained from moral principles that have been worked out in detail in the context of a particular society ('Guidance for a particular society must plant its feet in that society');[73] and (c) that ultimate values belong to the realm of faith and are not susceptible of proof.[74] The method of reason can, and should, be used to work out the implications of premises for particular situations, but 'first principles are in the realm of non-testable truth'.[75] Thus Llewellyn sought to reconcile his position as ethical relativist with his sympathy for natural law. It is pertinent in this regard to note that he selected out for particular praise in writings on natural law the detailed work of Gény and Jerome Michael,[76] rather than abstract philosophical discussions of natural law principles. What he particularly admired was the method of analysis they employed in attacking specific legal problems.

Llewellyn also insisted that there was no necessary incompatibility between natural law and legal realism:

Each sees the positive rules and concepts of here and now as present and potent. Each regards them as requiring re-examination in terms of their effective going value. Each sees one major guide to their evaluation in the service which they prove on examination either to render or not to render to the society which brought them forth. Each labors for the utilization of the greater leeways afforded by legislation, and the lesser leeways afforded by that case-law system which is built out of the rulings of a nation, to produce a finer and more effective set of guides for conduct and for judging And it is difficult for me to conceive of the ultimate legal ideals of any of the writers who have been called realists in terms which do not resemble amazingly the type and even the content of the principles of a philosopher's Natural Law.[77]

Finally, it is worth noting that although Llewellyn always remained sceptical of claims to universality in the sphere of morals, he was towards the end of his life essentially optimistic about finding common ground between seemingly irreconcilable ideologies and, over time, of broadening the scope of a worldwide ideological consensus.[78]

LLEWELLYN AND LEGAL SCIENCE

If jurisprudence of necessity includes a study of ideals for law, then realism is not [co-extensive with] jurisprudence. If, as I think, jurisprudence contains a dozen sub-disciplines, then realism deals with two out of the dozen: craft techniques and descriptive sociology. . . . Either and both are compatible with *any* philosophy about law's proper or immediate goals or about those of men in society. Realism in law is thus as ethically neutral as the science of mechanics or the art of bridge-building.[79]

Llewellyn's early association with Cook, Oliphant and Moore gave him some insight into the movement for an empirical science of law, but his strong professional orientation divided him from the more enthusiastic 'scientists' and he never felt at ease with quantitative methods. His own natural tendency was towards intuitive and common-sense 'realism' rather than to 'scientific' research, but he was clearly troubled by the problems of 'the scientific analogy' and he treated it at length in several substantial articles, as well as in numerous shorter published and unpublished writings.[80]

Unfortunately, as a group these cannot be said to be among the most orderly or the most rigorous of his works. In nearly every case he was responding to an outside stimulus, an invitation to address a conference, a book sent for review, or plans for some specific project. As a result, disconnected points and flat expressions of opinion outnumber closely reasoned argument. For the most part they define rather than justify a position. One paper entitled 'The Theory of Legal "Science" '[81] stands out. Initially a review of *Law and the Social Sciences* by Huntington Cairns, it contains one of the best discussions of the subject in print. It is notable not so much as an original philosophical contribution but rather for its basic sanity and balance. It is not well-known, no doubt because it was published in a rather obscure journal. From this particular article, supplemented by passages from other works, it is possible to extract a reasonably coherent, if not fully argued, collection of views on some of the major theoretical and practical issues surrounding the development of an empirical science of law.

(i) *The place of empirical description in legal theory:* Llewellyn, as we have seen, treated legal theory as covering a number of interdependent sub-disciplines which could be roughly divided into legal philosophy, legal science and legal prudence or into a larger number of subdivisions. Thus legal science is only part of legal theory. To assert the value and relevance of empirical description does not necessarily involve a denial of the value of any other activity, such as clarification of goals or analysis of legal concepts. Furthermore, a search for relative objectivity in description should not be confused with indifference to questions of value or with 'positivism' in the sense of a belief that value judgments are 'meaningless' or nonsensical. And, as is indicated by the passage quoted above, Llewellyn considered that realism was concerned with both 'science' and 'prudence', but not with all aspects of legal theory.

(ii) *The focus of attention:*

... it is *behavior* which must be the subject matter of an observational science, of objective character about things legal. Not rules of law, nor norms, nor yet imperatives, *save* as these flow from, or are reflected in, or operate upon, behavior, plus the checked urges, and the patterns of thought and of held ideal, which are properly included in that term.[82]

This statement too is susceptible to misinterpretation unless it is taken with the caveat that legal science, in this context, is only one of a number of possible approaches to law. It should not be taken to imply that expositions of doctrine or analytical jurisprudence, in which rules and concepts are the centre of attention, are in some sense invalid or wrong. Llewellyn did take the view that this form of inquiry had been given a disproportionate amount of attention relative to the amount accorded to legal science. Moreover, in his general theory, he emphasized the dangers of considering rules and concepts divorced from their purposes and the contexts of their operation. This is quite different from denigrating exposition and analysis of doctrine.

With human behaviour at the centre of attention, legal science can genuinely be claimed as one of the 'behavioural sciences' for 'the behavior side of matters legal is the *same* behavior which is susceptible of analysis also by a psychologist, an economist, or a sociologist'.[83] This provides a useful basis for linking law with other disciplines. If the principal functions of law are seen to concern the channelling of behaviour of officials and laymen, a basis for functional analysis is also provided. And Llewellyn agreed with Cairns in emphasizing that 'to make behavior in the legal aspects of life the subject-matter of a "science" is to overcome the obsession that *only the State* can have significance in this connection, and so to open up the closely comparable phenomena of primitive law in primitive society, and of sub-group "by-law" within our own society, for the revealing light they shed on legal phenomena in general.'[84]

It would be a mistake to seek for much precision in the concept of 'human behaviour' in this context. It is used to indicate a broad area of attention rather than to provide a precise demarcation of boundaries. A considerable variety of kinds of enquiry could be accommodated within Llewellyn's conception of legal science. Nor should the use of the term be taken as involving commitment to some particular 'school' or '-ism' — such as behaviourism in psychology or functionalism in sociology or anthropology.[85] Llewellyn had views on what kinds of research would be likely to be fruitful and on the values and limitations of various schools and trends in the social sciences; but these views were not simple deductions from a precisely defined set of theoretical concepts. On the whole his attitude was open minded and flexible on such issues.

(iii) *The analogy with the natural sciences: values and dangers:* Llewellyn took a similar common-sense position on the vexed question: Can there be any really 'scientific' knowledge about human behaviour? In his discussions of the work of Cairns and of Michael and Adler he was prepared, as a matter of faith, to accept the *possibility* that knowledge in the social sciences could satisfy the standards of reliability and generality set by the physical sciences.[86] But he was at pains to stress that the social sciences, and above all the science of law, were for the most part hundreds of years behind the physical sciences; in his words, they were at the 'pre-pre-science' stage.[87] In their impressive critique of criminology, *Crime, Law and Social Science*, Michael and Adler had concluded that while empirical scientific research in criminology was both possible and desirable there was as yet no scientific knowledge in the field.[88] Llewellyn took issue with them for their 'Himalayan' standards of what was workable in criminological research and for not making sufficient allowance for gradations in reliability.[89] In his discussion of Cairns' *Law and the Social Sciences* he reverted to the theme:

But when Michael and Adler divided knowledge into two essential categories: 'common sense' and 'scientific knowledge', they overlooked (and Cairns does not sufficiently stress) that the matter does not thus cleave neatly into *two* significant areas, but that it stretches out or sprawls instead between two poles. At the one pole is ignorance and *pure* guess. At the other pole is solid and thoroughly systematized scientific knowledge. 'Common sense' is, so to speak, in the South Temperate Zone. *Un*common sense, ordered, pondered on with care, and tested out once, and again, and yet again, in inconclusive but still illuminating corrective careful tests – that is so to speak, in the North Temperate Zone. Knowledge does not have to be scientific, in order to be on the way toward Science. Neither does it have to be scientific in order to be extremely useful. It is time that social 'scientists' should recognize this openly; it would save much confusion, and it would save more waste motion. What we need is knowledge moving carefully and cannily *toward* the scientific pole, accompanied by some rough indication of its present latitude. *That* is the scientific road *toward* Science. And progress on that road is valuable step by step.

Knowledge, I repeat, does not have to be scientific, in order to be useful and important.[90]

This passage provides some important clues to Llewellyn's reservations about 'the scientific analogy' and to some of his differences with dedicated 'Scientists' like Moore and Cook. Llewellyn saw several related dangers in stressing the analogy: it encouraged the hypercritical tendency that had been exhibited by Michael and Adler with their 'Himalayan' standards; the snobbery of 'scientism' might tempt some to select for study relatively trivial topics, merely because they are susceptible to quantification, which looks scientific. Even worse, matters not yet susceptible to reliable quantification might be dressed up 'in shoddy pseudo-quantitative form ... producing a type of garbage which has peculiarly affected the third-rate run of work in sociology'.[91]

Finally, a less harmful form of snobbery is the tendency to debase the coinage of the emotively respectable word 'science' by applying it to studies which fall far short of the high standards of rigour and generality set by natural sciences.[92]

Llewellyn's reservations about 'the scientific analogy' did not blind him to its virtues. Above all it set a standard to aim for in the long run:

> The minimum, as I see it, goes to the data being both objectively verifiable, without recourse to personal intuition or to revelation; and to those data being also verified; and to the range of the resulting inaccuracy being established with high probability, as a *part* of the 'data'; and, finally, to verifiable relations being established in communicable and freshly testable form. And if that is the minimum for Science in the field, then I repeat that I see no prospect of having much of it in my life-time.[93]

There were further virtues in the 'scientific analogy':

> The utter need of the clear hypothesis. Add: insistent attempt at objective observation; sustained objective recording of the data observed; cumulation and *comparison, consistent* cumulation and *ordered* comparison of observations, *with attention concentrated on any seeming discrepancies.* That is what leads to sharper and more critical hypothesis. Add: patience. If it took our friends in Physics these few hundred years to get to where their original rather simple (simple-minded, if you will) working premises – 'force', 'causation', and the like – needed to be refined; and, indeed to get to where an ordered grasp of ultimate bases of the whole began to seem even in the possible offing – then maybe our not so simple material may take us more than a minute or two, to master. Or again: we can learn from natural science that Big Things in the pursuit of science are not commonly achieved by going after Big Things. They come, vastly more, out of sustained, insistent, cumulative digging after smaller bits of testable and tested knowledge about small things; and out of concentrated study – including speculation – on matters little enough to be studied *closely*.
>
> And there is a final thing to learn, along with the value of the constantly sharpening hypothesis. That is, the additional need, from time to time, of some workers who just take a fresh look, and repose whole lines of work and interpretation.[94]

These two passages give some indication of Llewellyn's approach to possible strategies for developing an empirical science of law. On the whole he favoured an evolutionary, unprogrammatic approach. At base was a scepticism of the value of 'using seven-place logarithms to work out the rough carpentry of a building whose parts are being measured by thumb-joints—a different man's thumb-joint for each measurement'.[95] He favoured advance on a broad front, mainly through hundreds of modest projects.[96] He was inclined to be sceptical of ambitious and expensive macro-projects, but he recognized that some, like the Chicago Jury Project, might have a special value, particularly in respect of developing theory and basic techniques. A formidable obstacle to progress was shortage of man-power. He differed sharply from those lawyers who maintain that socio-legal work should be left entirely to the social scientists :

... the law men must in the main train themselves as social scientists; they cannot borrow enough help from outside; the methods from outside need reworking from legal data; the data from outside are not collected, and will not be, with an eye to legal needs; not enough social scientists can be lifted bodily into law; and only legal training can, in the main, provide the requisite background for weighing factor on the judgment-side, and for spotting things overlooked.[97]

To attract enough people into this kind of work, there were some difficult obstacles to be overcome. Not only would lawyers have to be made more sharply aware of the needs and of the relevance of this kind of work, but they would need training, not least to give them confidence. Further, they would need incentives in the form of a better market for their services and more recognition than they were accorded in American law schools even as late as the mid-1950s.[98]

(iv) *Llewellyn in the field:* In respect of socio-legal research Llewellyn was more of a staff officer than a foot soldier. Neither by temperament nor by training was he suited to the systematic collection of data. He knew that he was incurably innumerate and was mildly worried by the knowledge.[99] Typically he wrote almost entirely from his head; even the ordinary spadework of combing the law reports for relevant authorities did not come naturally to him although he often disciplined himself to do it; he was not methodical enough to be a good field worker, although his 'artistic' qualities sometimes produced spectacular results. He broke most of the rules of empirical method—not for him the carefully constructed research design, rigorous sampling techniques or the scrupulously tested questionnaire. He spent little or no time in the field for his principal works. He stayed only ten days among the Cheyennes; the rest of the collection of material for *The Cheyenne Way* was done by Hoebel. Both *Cases and Materials on the Law of Sales* and *Praejudizienrecht und Rechtsprechung in Amerika* were library based. The Uniform Commercial Code and *The Common Law Tradition* were planned and executed with little concern for social science techniques.[100] For only one major project, the study of the Pueblo Indians, did Llewellyn do a considerable amount of field work; instead of remaining a detached observer, he became emotionally and actively involved in Pueblo affairs; it is perhaps not a coincidence that this project was never completed.[101]

Llewellyn's first serious attempt at empirical research revealed some of his limitations as a field worker. Stimulated in part by the Columbia curriculum discussions on familial relations,[102] in part by the work of Jacobs and Angell which arose out of those discussions,[103] and in part, it has been suggested, by his own unhappy experiences surrounding the termination of his first marriage, Llewellyn set out to study divorce proceedings in New York.[104] His original concern was to explore the actual effects of rules of law in a particular area, as an example of the kind of work he had been advocating. However, instead of confining himself to testing rigorously and in detail some precisely formulated hypotheses, Llewellyn ended up with a general disquisition on marriage and divorce, a *pot-pourri* of general theory, statistical data and personal impressions. He spent some time 'observing' divorce proceedings and, with assistance, he attempted, rather half-heartedly it seems, a statistical analysis of some court records. But his speculative propensities spilled over, and in the end he made no orderly presentation of his findings. Under the heading of 'Method' he wrote in a footnote:

Nothing in the paper purports to have any guaranty more trustworthy than common sense and personal observation. Sample drillings into available data are offered in the footnotes. In one case only (the quantitative effects of the lawmen's work in non-support prosecutions . . .) did the available check-up seem to me to require modification of the views resting on personal observation and prior reading – i.e. on so-called insight. That of course affords no proof even of the views checked up, still less of the others. It does justify their submission.[105]

The outcome of this project was not a report of findings but a somewhat bizarre essay entitled 'Behind the Law of Divorce'. Two parts were published, a third part survives unfinished in manuscript. The article provoked some interesting reactions. Young B. Smith read it in draft. He was uncompromisingly damning of both substance and style and advised Llewellyn to suppress it.[106] On the other hand the sociologist Robert Angell was more polite, although he agreed with Smith's criticism of the style. He thought that Llewellyn's analysis of the functions of marriage was too vague, but that there was much that was novel and suggestive in what he had written.[107] Thurman Arnold wrote in a friendly letter that there were too many ideas and too much of the poet in the article, which reminded him of *Sartor Resartus*.[108] Other letters suggest a consensus: some suggestive ideas, but poorly ordered and too lyrically expressed. This seems to be a fair assessment. The divorce study was Llewellyn's sole attempt to imitate the 'scientists' during the years of the Columbia experiment. For the rest of the period he remained comfortably indoors, to the relief and benefit of nearly everyone.

If Llewellyn's own attempts at field work were not strikingly successful, the same could not be said of his interventions in other people's projects, particularly at the planning stage. Jerome Hall, E. Adamson Hoebel and Paul Tappan are among those who produced notable works as graduate students under his supervision.[109] His advice was sought by those responsible for some of the most successful socio-legal projects of the 1930s, including Charles Clark's studies of judicial administration in Connecticut and a number of bar surveys.[110] There are indications that he made a not insignificant contribution to those projects. But by and large the nature of this contribution remains constant: as a stimulator and as a sounding board he was unrivalled; for system and rigorous method even his acolytes had to look elsewhere.[111]

Conclusion. Four main factors interacted in Llewellyn's approach to legal science: his ideas about realism and about the social sciences generally; his recognition of some of the practical obstacles to the undertaking of systematic empirical research into law on a large scale; the personal qualities which he brought to such work himself; and the habits and attitude fostered by the case-law tradition in which he was nurtured. His general position may be briefly summarized as follows: he was willing to accept that ultimately it is conceivable that empirical research in the social sciences could satisfy similar criteria of objectivity to those of natural science, but that only the most elementary beginnings had been made in that direction; second, that 'objectivity' is a matter of degree and that even casual impressionistic observation is better than complete ignorance, provided that it is recognized for what it is; thirdly, that stress on the scientific analogy may be dangerous in that either the coinage of the term 'scientific' may be debased or, worse, that would-be scientists will consider as worthy of study only topics which are as yet susceptible to rigorous quantification, a narrow and often infertile area. In short, he favoured a common-sense strategy for research, based on a realistic appraisal of the obstacles in the way of quick advance, such as the cost, the lack of glamour in much of the work, and the shortage of personnel with appropriate training. Finally, one may infer from his behaviour, as well as from his articulated views, that he would have strenuously disagreed with any suggestion that in the search for understanding of the legal process there was no room for intuition and imagination. The half-way artist had as important a role to play as the fact-grubber.

We may conclude that for the most part Llewellyn showed both perception and balance in his general attitude to legal science, especially in view of the state of the social sciences at the time he formulated his position. He was not especially worried by the basic theoretical issues underlying discussions of an empirical legal science and to a philosopher his position may seem rather vague and simplistic. Rather, his was a pragmatic and sensible approach which could form the basis for a rounded strategy for developing the subject, giving due regard both to the importance of theory and to likely practical difficulties. Apart from the fact that Llewellyn hinted at rather than articulated such a strategy, one major corrective to his views is needed. He does not seem to have grasped fully, in terms of needs and priorities for money and manpower, the implications of the view that an empirical science of law could satisfy standards equivalent to those prevailing in the natural sciences, but that it was as yet at a pre-Newtonian stage of development. The strongly emotional tone of his critique of the 'scientists' in 1956 suggests that he was perhaps too close to events and had too big a personal stake in other activities to face up to some of the more uncomfortable issues of the relationship between professional training and socio-legal research and possible competing priorities in respect of them. In the outcome his plans for furthering legal science seem rather complacent and unambitious in relation to the possibilities and the needs.

LEGAL AESTHETICS[112]

According to the legal apocrypha Karl Llewellyn was originally seduced by the N.I.L., but once he had recognized the beauty of the letter of credit, this became his true love. It is not hard to pinpoint the source of this myth, for Llewellyn was well known for his propensity to use terms like 'lovely' and 'beautiful' in contexts where others would express their admiration more prosaically. However, his concern with beauty in law went beyond such rhapsodical use of language, for with apparent seriousness he expounded a theory of legal aesthetics.

By 'beauty' in this context Llewellyn meant fitness for purpose— the functional 'beauty of dam-race and turbine'.[113] The deftness of Cheyenne juristic techniques, 'the rule of the singing reason', the c.i.f. contract, the letter of credit and the Grand Style of judging are all satisfying for the same reason, that they are functionally apt. This kind of 'beauty' is to be contrasted with the ideal of 'structured beauty'—the *elegantia* of a neat, orderly, logically consistent system.[114]

The great monument to this esthetic ideal is the German Civil Code, read not as it stands on the page, merely, but read also against the rigorous, almost rigid German theories of construction and dogmatics which were in vogue for a decade after its adoption. It is a type of legal esthetics little practised among us.[115]

Llewellyn suggested that Langdell's analysis of consideration and unilateral contract was the best-known American example: 'Nothing could be more simply stated, more rigorously thought, more tightly integrated, more fascinatingly absurd to teach, more easy to "apply".'[116] He contrasted the attractions of Langdell's theory with those of the c.i.f. contract:

Another example is the law of the c.i.f. contract, which Lord Wright has recently held up to admiration as perhaps the most 'elegant' of our legal institutions. It is in my mind – though I may be unjust to Wright's shrewd juristic insight – that what stirs his praise is the logical clarity, the singleness, the sharpness of line, in the law governing this once standard contract for overseas commerce. The patterned succession of the seller's proper actions, as he arranges, as he ships, as he sends forward promptly the batch of documents; the neatly matched mortising of the due steps by the buyer, honoring the draft when the documents are presented, then paying the freight in cash before outturn of the merchandise, proceeding then, and again promptly, to inspection of the merchandise itself, until which all the built-up seeming rights stand subject to possible defeat; the courtly grace with which the steps and rights of one intervening banker, or two, or three, are laid out as in a minuet – this, I say, is what I suspect Wright to have primarily in mind when he speaks of 'elegance' in the law of this institution. What concerns me is that the aspects of that elegance are two; that but one of the two is basic to legal beauty; that that one is utterly basic, while the other is either an efflux or a tool, and, lacking the one, would be a simulacrum. It is not the structure, however sweet of logic and of line, that is the essence. Langdell's construct points that moral: magnificent in conception, impeccable in workmanship, it yet would not *function*; men do not, and courts will not, work according to that pattern. And that, in things of law, bars beauty. The history of the Langdell conception is one of a delighted welcome by law-teachers, which continues still, while piece after piece of the integrated whole continues to be junked; the holes consume the structure. The c.i.f. construct, on the other hand, has proved in test after test as surely, as cleanly, as smoothly gauged to the work it had to do as any legal engine man has yet designed. As a result, or as a means, a logical clarity is present, too. But the prime test of its legal beauty remains the functional test. Structural harmony, structural grandeur, are good to have, they add, they enrich; but they are subsidiary. So is ornament. Legal esthetics are in first essence functional esthetics.[117]

In this Theory of Legal Aesthetics Llewellyn appears to be trying to do little more than to re-fight the battle of functionalism versus formalism in terms of analogies drawn from the arts and especially from architecture. Much of his longest discussion of the Beautiful in law is taken up with exploring the concept of 'period-style' and the relative merits of the Grand Style and the Formal Style.[118] In this view the 'theory' is essentially a reassertion of the values underlying a functional approach: law should consistently be treated as a means to an end; solutions to legal problems, indeed to all problems arising from the law-jobs, should be judged as 'satisfying' to the extent that they fit 'sense', 'balance' and stated purpose. The values of *elegantia*—clarity, economy, logical consistency— are secondary values, but they are values none the less: 'The situation must be rightly grasped, the criterion rightly seen, the effect neatly devised to purpose, else neither clarity nor economy of language can serve true beauty.'[119] What constitutes 'rightness' in this context depends upon one's conception of the Good. Indeed the Theory of Justice (concerning the Good), the Theory of Science (concerning the True) and the Theory of aesthetics (concerning the Beautiful) are all part of a single quest:

There can be no test by effect, no working test, no test for functional Beauty, without inquiry into situation, process, and result in fact. Determination of the True becomes thus an inherent part of search for the Beautiful. But again, neither can there be test by effect, without inquiry into purpose against which to measure that effect, nor can there be such inquiry without search for the Good. It is a fortunate field to work in, this of law, in which the three great ultimates so clearly merge.[120]

Llewellyn gave credit for the inspiration of his lectures on 'the Good, the Beautiful and the True' to Diogenes Jonathan Swift Teufeldrockh, the fantastic German philosopher whose works seem anachronistically to parody Llewellyn's own writings.[121] Perhaps we should accept the hint and not take the theory of legal aesthetics too seriously. This need not stop us from concluding that if it is nonsense, it is quite sensible nonsense.

THE THEORY OF CRAFTS

Out of the conjunction of activities and men around the law-jobs there arise the crafts of law, and so the craftsmen. Advocacy, counseling, judging, law-making, administering – these are major groupings of the law-crafts. But mediation, organization, policing, teaching, scholarship, are others. At the present juncture, the fresh study of these crafts and of the manner of their best doing is one of the major needs of jurisprudence.[122]

Llewellyn's fullest statement of the 'Theory of Crafts' is reproduced in appendix C; it calls for only a brief comment here. The theory of the crafts of law is coextensive with the study of juristic method or legal technology. This includes but is wider than the study of lawyers' skills , for it encompasses all aspects of the means of getting the law-jobs done. Tradition, organization, professional ethics, job-analysis, specialization and training are among the topics that would need to be covered by a comprehensive theory of legal technology. Llewellyn felt that this was an important and neglected area and he devoted much of his attention to it in his later years. However, his main contributions were to specific phases and he did no more than sketch the rough outlines of a general theory in *Law in Our Society*.[123] The most important of his specific contributions in this area are considered in other chapters: the study of the Cheyenne techniques of dispute settlement,[124] his various activities in connection with the teaching of 'legal skills',[125] the course on legal argument,[126] and *The Common Law Tradition*,[127] which is for the most part a treatise on a number of related phases of juristic method.

The rudimentary nature of Llewellyn's theory of crafts should not be allowed to obscure its potential significance. It points to broad areas of neglected enquiry. It is not implausible to suggest that this neglect is attributable in large part to the dominance of rule-centred theories of law. Legal education provides a clear example. In the common law world, even in the United States, legal education has concentrated on the study of legal rules and principles. Even so-called 'practical' examinations have been strongly affected by the assumption that the principal characteristic of 'the good lawyer' is to know the law. The result has been that the techniques of such functions as advocacy, statutory interpretation, drafting, counselling and negotiation have rarely, at least until recently, been the subject of systematic study. Practitioners have had to learn in the school of 'experience' with the help of tradition, instinct and a few rules of thumb. Lack of systematic study has not only been at the back of haphazard training, but also helps to explain the slow progress of legal technology. The sociology of the legal profession as a subject also continues to hover around the edges of its subject-matter, without getting to the core, for lack of adequate tools of analysis and description of lawyers' operations.[128]

Some people may find Llewellyn's use of words like 'craft', 'craftsman', 'craftsmanship' somewhat quaint, carrying associations of a tradition-bound, individualistic, cottage industry. A Japanese critic has seized on this analogy to suggest that Llewellyn is the last prophet of the individualist era 'when justice depended on manual skill and when a law book could be a piece of romantic poetry'.[129] If he is right, then ironically the 'Theory of Crafts' points the way out of the cottage industry tradition towards a more systematic and up-to-date legal technology.

THE THEORY OF RULES

Rules are measures based on ideals, practices, standards or commands, measures cast into verbal form, authoritative verbal form, with sharp-edged consequences. They thus add a tremendous power at once of communication, of rigidification over time, and of flexibility. They are a well-nigh indispensable precondition to any degree of standardization of law-work across space and the generations. They stand with such relative conspicuousness to observation, they accumulate so easily, they can be gathered so conveniently, and they are so easy to substitute for either thought or investigation, that they have drawn the attention of jurisprudes too largely to themselves: to the rules – as if rules stood and could stand alone.[130]

Llewellyn discusses rules in various places in *Law in Our Society*, but he does not expound a discrete 'Theory of Rules' therein. This is a little surprising, for not only did he devote a section of *The Common Law Tradition* to just such a theory,[131] but, even more significant, during the 1930s he drafted a substantial part of a book, which he tentatively called *The Theory of Rules*.[132] This aspect of his thought deserves attention because it is one area where the interests of analytical and sociological jurists coincide. Moreover, Llewellyn's views on the subject have sometimes been misunderstood and misrepresented.[133]

The manuscript of *The Theory of Rules* consists of seven almost complete chapters and a few fragments. The original plan for the book envisaged a total of nine chapters. The manuscript is in a more advanced state than that of *Law in Our Society*, but it adds less to our understanding of Llewellyn's position because most of it relates to ideas that he also treated in his published works. Nevertheless it is of interest as being his most sustained discussion of legal rules and his only attempt to bring together all his thoughts on the subject in a single work (the 'theory of rules' in *The Common Law Tradition* is mainly concerned with rules in appellate courts). A summary of Llewellyn's 'Theory of Rules' is to be found in appendix B. This takes the form of a 'restatement' based not only on the manuscript book but also on a number of other published and unpublished works.

This restatement requires only a brief comment, for it does little more than reclassify ideas which are discussed elsewhere, especially in connection with *The Common Law Tradition*, the law-jobs theory, and legal science. The relationship of the 'Theory of Rules' to the 'whole view' is quite straightforward: rules are one of the main instruments (no more, no less) for performing the law-jobs and as such they deserve special attention. Improving the quality of legal rules is one of the most important tasks of juristic method; the Grand Style offers the preferred model for rules of law—'the rule with a singing reason' which at once provides guidance to judges, a reliable basis for prediction to practitioners and is, as far as is compatible with the other functions, capable of being understood by non-lawyers.[134]

Two other points are worth noting: first, it is important to distinguish between Llewellyn's statements about rules in general and his discussion of the functions of rules in appellate decision-making. Statements of the kind, 'Rules are not to control, but to guide decision',[135] are likely to occasion unnecessary controversy if they are considered outside the specific context of a discussion of appellate cases worth appealing. Finally, it is hoped that the restatement of Llewellyn's views will help to kill the misconception that he believed 'that talk of rules is a myth'[136] or that he denied the normative character of legal rules[137] or that he 'rejected rules as providing uniformity in law' (whatever that may mean).[138] Rather it should be apparent that his analysis of the nature and functions of legal rules is very much in line with some of the standard analyses current in Anglo-American jurisprudence, even if it does not add very much to them and is, in some respects, expressed rather loosely.[139]

CONCLUSION

If novelty is the touchstone of significance in jurisprudence, then Llewellyn's 'whole view' as set out in *Law in Our Society* and related works may not qualify as a legal theory of major significance. Perhaps he was being too modest about his potential contribution when in 1931 he suggested that none of the principal ideas associated with realism were new.[140] Only if the most stringent standards of originality were to be applied would this statement be true of the law-jobs theory, the theory of crafts, and some of the other ideas discussed in this chapter. But it is fair to say that in respect of his more general ideas Llewellyn did not make a sharp break from his intellectual ancestors. Indeed, in his efforts to develop a theory based on 'horse sense', originality was far from being his main concern. His primary objective was to bring jurisprudence down to earth and to provide a reasonably coherent framework of ideas for 'the hundred thousand'. It is in terms of this objective that this phase of his work is most fairly judged. It is perhaps more an indication of an aloofness in the Anglo-American tradition of jurisprudence than of Llewellyn's success in attaining his objectives that so far in the twentieth century he appears to have had few serious competitors in the enterprise.

10

The Common Law Tradition

INTRODUCTION

Of all Llewellyn's works *The Common Law Tradition* is the most fascinating and the most frustrating. It stands to *Bramble Bush* as a wise but eccentric elder statesmen to a brilliant young demagogue. As he reads and re-reads the pages the critic is beset by conflicting impressions: clear thinking and confused metaphor; candour and white-wash; erratically balanced; clear-eyed realism and tradition-struck romanticism; a thesis of classic simplicity elaborated in a Gothic structure; an impassioned plea for reason and common-sense; ideas worked over and polished for more than thirty years presented as a rude elementary analysis. The principal addressee is the ordinary practitioner, yet the Teutonic thoroughness of the documentation wearies all but the most patient scholar; empirical methods, idiosyncratically 'scientific', are used to verify hypotheses expressed in terms which look suspiciously metaphysical; a work of theory on the grand scale is advertised as a do-it-yourself manual for judges and advocates; the author preaches at greatest length where he has practised least—only ten pages specifically for the scholar, nearly one hundred and fifty for the judge. Richly specific in illustration, insipidly vague in general conclusion. A success and a disappointment.

Such paradoxes, those which are genuine and those which are only apparent, complicate the task of analysis and evaluation. They suggest ambivalence on the part of the author not only in respect of his conclusions, but also in respect of his aims, especially as to readership. An author's unresolved dilemma about his audience is inherited by his critics. If he has sought to please both the Hundred and the Hundred Thousand, as well as those in between, should his critics seek to do the same? *The Common Law Tradition* could easily be the subject of a book-length study. In fact, in addition to numerous reviews, it has already been the subject of at least one postgraduate thesis and of a substantial number of articles.[1] Here limitations of space would preclude any attempt at a 'definitive' treatment, if such were possible. The present chapter has more modest aims: first, to provide an introduction and a guide to the potential reader (nearer to the Thousand than the Hundred Thousand); secondly, to relate the book to Llewellyn's other work; and thirdly, to make a critical evaluation, with particular reference to its potential as a starting-point for further research.

The Common Law Tradition was over thirty years in the making. According to Llewellyn he began his researches into appellate judicial deciding in 1927.[2] For the next thirty years most of his academic work and some of his outside interests had some bearing, direct or indirect, on the end-product. Themes in *The Common Law Tradition* are anticipated in his juristic and commercial law writings of the 1930s, his course on legal argument, *The Cheyenne Way*, and several series of lectures. The concept of 'period style' can be related back directly to his interest in Romanesque and Gothic cathedrals, which he took up seriously as a hobby in 1931. *The Common Law Tradition* represents the last of several attempts to weave together many loosely related strands of thought about appellate judicial processes. A book on *The Theory of Rules* had been abandoned in the late 1930s; the plan to publish the Storrs lectures of 1941 on 'The Common Law Tradition' as a book was quietly dropped, partly because of their muted reception, partly because of the pressure of work on the code. His detailed work on specialized topics in commercial law and contract, on particular courts and individual judges, served as preliminary case studies. Yet in preparing for *The Common Law Tradition* itself, Llewellyn felt it necessary to embark on further extensive detailed studies of appellate courts in action before he felt ready to treat his researches as complete.

Thus the book is not only based on many years of thought and research but it also contains Llewellyn's final statements on a number of topics; discussion of some of these has been postponed until this chapter. The result is that some aspects of the book need to be examined at length. Parts of this chapter may prove to be unnecessarily detailed for the non-specialist, who may be well advised to do some judicious skipping. The arrangement is as

follows: first, the central argument is presented in outline; there
follows a detailed analysis of the main concepts used in the argument, including extensive consideration of Llewellyn's general ideas
on two topics which he treated in a number of works: the concept of
period style and the interpretation of cases and statutes. The descriptive thesis is next examined. In the following section, Llewellyn's
advice to judges, advocates and others (the prescriptive thesis) and
some other possible applications of the ideas in *The Common Law
Tradition* are discussed. The chapter concludes with a general
appraisal of the work.

THE CENTRAL ARGUMENT

For all the profusion of digressions, asides, appendixes and interstitial observations, the book is built around a discernible central
argument which is quite easily summarized:[3] Llewellyn begins with
a dogmatic assertion that there exists within the legal profession in
America a crisis of confidence in the appellate courts.[4] The bar
has ceased to believe that results are even moderately predictable,
or as he prefers to say, reckonable. The crisis was provoked by the
destructive effects of developments in logic and psychology on the
comfortable belief in 'legal certainty', a belief which rested partly
on a confusion between the process of deciding and the mode of
justifying a decision and partly on an exaggeration of the part
played by deductive logic in influencing and justifying practical
decisions. Juristic writings of the 1920s and 1930s were more successful in spreading disillusion than in aiding reconstruction. From a faith
in certainty there was a swing to a belief that appellate judicial
decisions are irrational and unpredictable. A faith in doctrine as
productive of certainty is misplaced, first because absolute certainty
is an unattainable ideal and secondly because no case merits an
appeal unless a technically good doctrinal argument can be put
forward by each side, and when this is done doctrine alone cannot
decide the matter. In nearly all such cases *at least* one lawyer is
shown to have been 'wrong' about 'the law'; yet it is not necessarily
discreditable to be counsel for the unsuccessful litigant. The main
purpose of the book is to show that contemporary appellate judicial
deciding in America is to a large extent rational, that law-making
by judges is not limited to the unusual or crucial or borderline or
queer case, but is part of everyday practice, and that such creativity

is quite compatible both with reasonable reckonability and with the demands of justice and the need for adjustment to social change.

For the purposes of analysis the core of *The Common Law Tradition* may be conveniently divided into two parts: (i) the descriptive thesis, concerning how appellate courts actually behave and the renaissance of the Grand Style; and (ii) the prescriptive thesis, which consists of Llewellyn's advice to the various categories of participant associated with appellate decisions. The argument can be broken down into a series of propositions as follows:

The descriptive thesis

(i) There was in the 1950s a serious crisis of confidence, in that many lawyers (and law students) believed the decisions of American state appellate courts to be arbitrary and unpredictable.

(ii) *The Common Law Tradition* demonstrates that the results of decisions of these courts are predictable ('reasonably reckonable'): (a) beyond what it is reasonable to expect of an institution settling disputes 'self-selected for their toughness';[5] (b) 'quite sufficiently for skilled craftsmen to make usable and valuable judgments about likelihoods',[6] and (c) 'quite sufficiently to render the handling of an appeal a fitting subject for effective and satisfying craftsmanship.'[7]

(iii) the decisions of American state appellate courts are reasonably reckonable *despite* the fact that: (a) the authoritative sources of law, especially precedents and statutes, are sufficiently malleable as to allow considerable leeway for differing interpretations by appellate courts; (b) American state appellate courts in fact use a wide range of different techniques in interpreting authoritative sources of law; and (c) most, but not all, of those techniques are accepted as legitimate.

(iv) The decisions of American state appellate courts are reasonably reckonable *because*: (a) there are a number of steadying factors which tend to promote stability and reckonability; in particular (b) there was in the 1950s a renaissance of the Grand Style of judging in American state appellate courts; and (c) the Grand Style of judging tends to promote reckonability.

(v) The Grand Style of judging is not arbitrary, because it involves overt response in a disciplined manner to situation sense, to reason and to considerations of justice.

(vi) *Conclusion:* since the decisions of American state appellate courts in the 1950s have been demonstrated to be reckonable and not to be arbitrary, it follows that the crisis of confidence was not justified.

The prescriptive thesis

(vii) Participants in appellate judicial processes should adopt the Grand Style.

From this restatement of the central argument of *The Common Law Tradition* it can be seen that it is built on an apparatus of concepts that are not in common use: crisis of confidence, reasonable reckonability, steadying factors, Grand Style, Formal Style, situation sense, leeways and techniques of interpretation, and legitimate precedent techniques. In the course of argument Llewellyn also resorts to hard worked notions, such as wisdom, justice and reason, which require elucidation. All of these concepts are examined in the next section, not only as a preliminary to understanding and evaluating Llewellyn's main contentions, but also because illumination is to be gained at least as much from the concepts themselves as from their particular application in the descriptive thesis.

THE CONCEPTUAL APPARATUS

Reasonable reckonability and the steadying factors

From Holmes' 'Path of the Law', through Frank's *Law and the Modern Mind* to modern jurimetric writings American 'realist' jurists have tended to give the impression that prediction of judicial decision-making (or its unpredictability) was their central concern. One of the themes of the present work is that Llewellyn's concerns were very much wider than this. However, at first sight the predictability of appellate decisions does appear to be the main focus of attention in *The Common Law Tradition*. In this view it would be correct to say that, whereas Frank's *Law and the Modern Mind* was directed to attacking the myth of certainty in law, Llewellyn's book was directed to attacking the myth of uncertainty underlying the alleged crisis of confidence. It will be argued below that Llewellyn sensed but did not clearly spell out the point that a lawyer's confidence in appellate courts is not solely a function of the predictability of judicial behaviour, but rests on a number of other factors. However, prediction provides the main theme of the overture of the book:

You cannot listen to the dirges of lawyers about the death of *stare decisis* (of the nature of which lovely institution the dirge-chanters have little inkling) without realizing that one great group at the bar are close to losing their faith. You cannot listen to the cynicism about the appellate courts that is stock conversation of the semi- or moderately successful lawyer in his middle years without realizing that his success transmutes into gall even as it comes to him. You cannot watch generations of law students assume, two thirds of them, as of course and despite all your effort, that *if* the outcome of an appeal is not foredoomed in logic it *therefore* is the product of un- controlled will which is as good as wayward, without realizing that our *machinery for communicating* the facts of life about the work of our central and vital symbol of The Law: the appellate courts, has become frighteningly deficient.

For the fact is that the work of our appellate courts all over the country is reckonable. It is reckonable first, and on a relative scale, far beyond what any sane man has any business expecting from a machinery devoted to settling disputes self-selected for their toughness. It is reckonable second, and on an absolute scale, quite sufficiently for skilled craftsmen to make usable and valuable judgments about likelihoods, and quite sufficiently to render the handling of an appeal a fitting subject for effective and satisfying craftsmanship.

It is in the contrast between these joyous facts and the therefore needless but truly perilous crisis in confidence that the book takes its start.[8]

In discussing prediction Llewellyn preferred the less elegant term 'reckonability' to the more conventional 'certainty' for two reasons: first, 'certainty' suggests an absolute, whereas the best that could be hoped for is a reasonable prospect of predicting correctly in about seven or eight cases out of ten.[9] Secondly, 'certainty' in law is commonly associated with the idea of 'certain rules', a phrase which is at best ambiguous in that it is not clear what exactly is being predicted—the outcome of a particular case, the justification for the outcome, or something else. Sometimes discussion of legal certainty is based on the assumption that if a general rule can be stated with confidence then the results of cases subsumed under that rule can be predicted with equal confidence. This assumption is in turn based on the deductive model of judicial decision-making, which was, of course, rejected by Llewellyn. Sometimes talk of certainty in law hides the kind of obscurity or confusion that is to be found in such statements as 'the rule is certain, but its application is doubtful'.

'Reasonable reckonability of result' avoids some of the pitfalls of the conventional terminology.[10]

Llewellyn considered that 'reckonability of result' was in large part a function of regularity of judicial behaviour. Without attempting an exhaustive analysis, he identified fourteen 'steadying' factors which, in his view, tend to promote such regularity:

(1) Law-conditioned Officials.
(2) Legal Doctrine.
(3) Known Doctrinal Techniques.
(4) Responsibility for Justice.
(5) The Tradition of One Single Right Answer.
(6) An Opinion of the Court.
(7) A Frozen Record from Below.
(8) Issues Limited, Sharpened, Phrased.
(9) Adversary Argument by Counsel.
(10) Group Decision.
(11) Judicial Security and Honesty.
(12) A Known Bench.
(13) The General Period-Style and Its Promise.
(14) Professional Judicial Office.[11]

With the exception of 'style', Llewellyn was content to deal with these factors on a common-sense basis, without defining his terms with precision or trying to establish by empirical means how and to what extent each factor affects judicial behaviour. It has been pointed out that he failed to consider, *inter alia*, the interrelationship between the various factors, the extent and nature of overlap and their relative importance.[12] Nevertheless the same critic acknowledges that the discussion 'is probably the most elaborate analysis of the nature of those discrete elements that substantially contribute to a constraint upon a judge (as contrasted with all other types of policy-makers) in arriving at a choice between alternatives.'[13]

Despite the limitations of this type of common-sense approach his treatment of the steadying factors is an example of Llewellyn at his best: a useful summary of years of the lessons of experience, balanced, perceptive and unpretentious. Its role in the argument is to remind readers of the presence of a number of factors which they would probably agree tend to some extent to promote regularity, and hence predictability, of judicial behaviour. The section purports

to do little more than provide a context for the detailed consideration of one of the factors—period style.

Style[14]

Llewellyn's importation of the concept of style into jurisprudential
analysis is a good example of his flair for drawing attention to 'the
neglected obvious'.[15] Judicial opinions can be extraordinarily
varied in respect of length, explicitness, individuality, the nature
and range of source materials relied on, the manner of handling such
materials, the modes of reasoning, and so on. 'Style' is a useful
generic term encompassing such characteristics of a series of opinions
as may be considered to be distinctive. It implies, albeit vaguely, a
degree of consistency in these characteristics. In Llewellyn's usage
the term refers to the manner of thought exhibited in judicial
opinions rather than to their literary style, in so far as these are
distinguishable.[16] One of the steadying factors in appellate courts
is the predominating style of a particular period. This is given
special prominence in *The Common Law Tradition*:

> It is the general and pervasive manner over the country at large, at any
> given time, of going about the job, the general outlook, the ways of profes-
> sional knowhow, the kind of thing the men of law are sensitive to and strive
> for, the tone and flavor of the working and of the results. It is well described
> as a 'period-style'; it corresponds to what we have long known as period-
> style in architecture or the graphic arts or furniture or music or drama. Its
> slowish movement but striking presence remind me also of shifting 'types' of
> economy ('agricultural', 'industrial', e.g.) and of the cycles or spirals many
> sociologists and historians discover in the history of political aggregations or
> of whole cultures.[17]

In *The Common Law Tradition* two types of style are postulated :
The Grand Style and the Formal Style. The Grand Style is epitomized in the work of the American courts in the 1840s and 1850s, and
by judges such as Mansfield, Marshall, Kent, Cowen, Cardozo and
Learned Hand.[18] It is 'the style of reason':

> . . . as overt marks of the Grand Style 'precedent' is carefully regarded, but
> if it does not make sense it is ordinarily re-explored; 'policy' is explicitly
> inquired into; alleged 'principle' must make for wisdom as well as for order
> if it is to qualify as such, but when so qualified it acquires peculiar status.
> On the side both of case-law and of statutes, where the reason stops there
> stops the rule; and in working with statutes it is the normal business of the

court not only to read the statute but also to implement that statute in accordance with purpose and reason.[19]

The Formal Style is authoritarian, formal, and 'logical'.

The rules of law are to decide the cases; policy is for the legislature, not for the courts, and so is change even in pure common law. Opinions run in deductive form with an air or expression of single-line inevitability. 'Principle' is a generalization producing order which can and should be used to prune away those 'anomalous' cases or rules which do not fit, such cases or rules having no function except, in places where the supposed 'principle' does not work well, to accomplish sense – but sense is no official concern of a formal-style court.[20]

The two styles differ in three major respects : first the Grand Style continually looks at the reason or 'principle' behind the rule, the Formal Style tends to emphasize bare precepts.[21] Secondly, the Grand Style is characterized by resort to 'situation sense', a concept which will require elucidation later; the Formal Style shuns overt consideration of social facts and takes refuge in the repetition of the terminology into which rules have been crystallized. Thirdly, the Grand Style is concerned with the sequence of rules and decisions and with providing guidance for the future far more than the Formal Style.[22] Different aesthetic urges are to be found behind each style; in the Grand Style the quest is for functional 'beauty' — fitness for purpose. In the Formal Style 'esthetics drove in the direction of cold clarity'.[23]

The differences between the two styles can be further illustrated in concrete terms: in the interpretation of a statute invocation of the literal rule of interpretation would be characteristic of the Formal Style; the mischief rule and the golden rule belong to the Grand Style.[24] In the handling of adverse precedents, distinguishing on the facts where the distinction cannot be justified in terms of sense or reason, simple citation of cases without discussing the facts, and use of precedent techniques branded by Llewellyn as 'illegitimate', would all tend to indicate the Formal Style.[25] Giving explicit consideration to the reputation of the judges in the prior case, the reinterpretation of a series of cases by classifying them on their facts into categories based on articulated principle; or when a 'principle theretofore unphrased is extracted from the decisions and applied'[26] or other 'fresh starts from old materials'[27] would seem to belong to the Grand Style. Other indicia of the Formal Style would include such statements as 'I must regretfully conclude...', or 'Policy is for the legislature, not the courts', or a reiteration of some version of the declaratory theory of the role of the judge. If this interpretation is correct the Grand Style and the Formal Style can be restated in the form of ideal types as in table 1 (opposite).

Llewellyn made no secret of his preference for the Grand Style. Indeed, 'formal' and 'grand' both have distinct emotive associations. Yet he intended that the two categories should be used descriptively. It is incorrect to reason: 'I do not like this opinion, therefore it belongs to the Formal Style.'[28] He was quite emphatic 'that the Grand Style, the Style of Reason, does not, as must always be insisted, guarantee an outcome or the use of a reason or the production of a rule of law which I like or agree with, nor yet one which you like or agree with.'[29] Nor is it paradoxical to talk of a poor Grand Style opinion: invocation of the mischief rule may be accompanied by an unacceptable diagnosis of the mischief;[30] formulation of a reason behind the rule may be open to criticism as being incomplete or too broad[31] or inconsistent with some other reason or otherwise defective; it is not inconceivable that a Grand Style opinion might involve the use of an 'illegitimate' precedent technique. Above all, the Grand Style does not necessarily accompany desirable results and the Formal Style undesirable results: 'style' refers to the mode of justifying the result rather than to the result itself.[32] Nevertheless, since the indicia of each type of style are not defined with precision, the reader may feel that in some passages in *The Common Law Tradition* Llewellyn's emotional reaction to an opinion may have been a factor in characterizing it as belonging to one style or the other.

In *The Common Law Tradition* the concepts of Grand Style and Formal Style are mainly used to depict general trends in broad terms. For such a purpose they are adequate as descriptive tools, just as there are contexts in which talk of styles in architecture or even 'schools' of thinkers may be adequate, even apt. However, in other contexts it may be as dangerous and misleading to pigeon-hole judges or courts into styles as it is to lump jurists into schools.[33]

The Common Law Tradition contains the seeds of a potentially fruitful approach to the comparative analysis of judicial opinions and of courts as working institutions. For example, to take a representative sample of the opinions of a court and compare and contrast it with a similar sample of the opinions of the same court at a different

RESTATEMENT OF GRAND STYLE AND FORMAL STYLE AS THEORETICAL MODELS

	Grand Style	*Formal Style*
Model of legal rule	To produce effects z or for reasons z or to remedy mischief z ⎱ if x, then y	If x, then y
Principle	A general proposition embodying a policy; its function is to guide, but not to control interpretation	A rule of a general kind which may be used as the basic premise of a syllogism
Diagnosis of a problem involving a question of law	The scope of x is doubtful	The scope of the rule is clear, but its application is doubtful
Court's conception of its role	(1) To resolve the doubt according to wisdom, justice and situation sense within the leeways accorded by the authoritative sources (2) To provide guidance for the future	To discover and declare the applicable rule and to apply it to the facts of this particular case
Sources which may be invoked in justification	(1) Authoritative sources such as statutes and cases (2) Principle (see above) (3) Policy, situation sense and 'reason'. (4) Social research findings (e.g. Brandeis brief)	(1) Authoritative sources such as statutes and cases (2) Principle (see above) (3) 'Logic'?
Typical techniques of interpretation	(1) Mischief rule (statutes) (2) Interpretation of cases in light of situation sense and policy rationales	(1) Literal rule (statutes) (2) 'Simple cites'; dogmatic assertion of ratio decidendi, heavy reliance on language of court in prior case
Aesthetics	Functional beauty (fitness for purpose)	Elegantia
Other indicia	(1) e.g. cessante ratione, cessat ipsa lex (2) Open acknowledgement of law-making function, albeit interstitial, etc.	e.g. (1) 'It is with great reluctance that I must conclude . . .' (2) 'This is a court of law, not of morals' (3) Declaratory theory of judicial function, etc.

time or of one or more different courts is potentially an illuminating
exercise[34] But opinions (and courts) are complex phenomena
about which it may be difficult to generalize. Concepts like Grand
Style and Formal Style are best treated as relatively simple theoretical models, more suited for painting a broad picture than for
detailed analysis.[35]

The speech of Lord Atkin in *Donoghue v. Stevenson* may be used
to illustrate this general point.[36] The case is generally regarded as
marking the liberation of the tort of negligence from the doctrine of
privity of contract, thereby enabling the modern law of negligence
to develop with increased sensitivity to changing social conditions.
Lord Atkin's speech exhibits some of the indicia of the Grand
Style: characterization of the situation in terms of modern manufacturer and consumer; overt reference to considerations of policy
and justice; careful re-analysis of the prior authorities; and a fresh
start given to the judicial development of the law of negligence.
This speech in *Donoghue v. Stevenson* performed much the same
function, and has much the same status in English literature and
myth, as has Cardozo's opinion in *McPherson v. Buick*.[37] At first
sight, therefore, it seems to be a clear example of the Grand Style.
However, an examination of Lord Atkin's handling of precedent
suggests an important reservation. Whereas Cardozo blandly sweeps
through 'precedents drawn from the days of travel by stagecoach',[38]
Atkin, faced with a series of long established contrary authorities,
employs a number of techniques for disposing of them which could
be described as 'formalistic'.[39] Since the bold innovating judge will
typically be innovating against the weight of authority, he is more
likely to be called on to employ techniques for avoiding or killing
earlier precedents. Some other techniques are 'formalistic' in that
they emphasize minute distinctions, or technicalities (e.g. distinguishing on the pleadings), although other techniques of dealing with
contrary precedents, such as overruling or not following or
distinguishing on the basis of some principle or policy, belong to
the Grand Style.[40] In England the strict *doctrine* of binding precedent combines with a strong tradition of deference to precedents of
English courts whether binding or not. Thus in *Donoghue v. Stevenson* Lord Atkin employed 'formalistic' techniques for disposing of
precedents decided in inferior courts when he had power, according to the general doctrine of precedent, to overrule or disapprove
or refuse to follow. Thus in the context of England, in order to

produce grand style principles a judge may be under pressure to employ formalistic means, just as, in *The Merchant of Venice*, 'justice' (in Shakespeare's view) was secured by invocation of a formalistic argument.[41] This is just one example of the way in which pressures may exist to make grand and formal style characteristics combine in certain types of context.

Such limitations on the utility of the broad categories of 'Grand style' and 'Formal style' should not be allowed to obscure the great potential of the systematic analysis and comparison of judicial opinions in terms of their stylistic properties.

'Justice' and 'the fireside equities'

Although, as Becht suggests, 'it takes good nerves' for a jurist to make 'justice' a working concept,[42] Llewellyn's use of the term need not occasion undue difficulty. Its principal use in *The Common Law Tradition* is in the context of the assertion that conceptions of 'justice' and 'fairness' in fact play an important part in judicial decision-making and justifying. Judges in fact regularly exhibit 'a felt duty to Justice, a felt duty to the law, and a third felt duty to satisfy both of the first two at once, if that be possible'.[43] In this context terms like 'fair', 'right' and 'decent', express adequately the feelings involved; similarly Edmond Cahn's concretized analysis of 'the sense of injustice' is closer to the judges' conceptions than either abstract philosophical theories of justice or the vague last resort of the man with a weak case.[44] Considerations of fairness, rightness and decency affect all courts, but in the Grand Style their influence is more open and regular. Then they operate not through 'the fireside equities' (factors peculiar to the particular case that may provoke sympathy) but at a more general level:

What is of interest . . . is that such words and the idea they carry can hardly reach and register unless they come all impregnated with a *relatively* concrete *going* life-situation seen as a *type*. The next aspect of the crux is that, in a *going* life-situation, fairness, rightness, minimum decency, injustice look not only back but forward as well, and so infuse themselves not only with past practice but with *good* practice, *right* practice, *right guidance* of practice: i.e., with felt net values in and for the type of situation, and with policy for legal rules. The crux is completed by the obviousness that this drives the whole 'justice' idea, inescapably in some part (I think, in prime part) forward, into prospect, not merely retrospect: into what one can perhaps call the quest for wisdom in the decision.[45]

Thus in the Grand Style, and hence in contemporary American practice, considerations of justice help evaluation of the situation seen as a type, but do not, and should not, have influence through the 'fireside equities'.[46] In the Formal Style the same considerations exert an influence, but less openly and evenly. For the purposes of *The Common Law Tradition* it was not necessary for Llewellyn to put forward a theory of justice of his own and he deliberately refrained from doing so. It is pertinent to note, however, that the materials for *Law in Our Society* contain the outline of such a theory.[47]

It has been pointed out that in some passages Llewellyn seemed to imply that the 'fireside equities' could be (sharply) distinguished from justice in the type-situation, or in other words that there are clear criteria for distinguishing between irrelevant and relevant facts.[48] In personal injuries litigation, for example, the 'facts' that the plaintiff is (a) poor, (b) beautiful and (c) a widow are normally treated as clearly irrelevant to the determination of liability. If these considerations in fact influence decisions, it is as 'fireside equities'. But there is a wide range of factors which fall within the no-man's land of the potentially or possibly relevant—for instance, such matters as the literacy and the bargaining strength of one of the parties to a standard form contract. There may be differences between systems of positive law (and differences of opinion as to the justice of the matter) in the treatment of such factors as relevant or irrelevant. Both in positive law and in prevailing conceptions of justice the criteria of relevance will often be vague; furthermore determination of relevance is not solely a matter of generality, of whether 'the facts' fit into a pattern. 'Beautiful widows', for example, are a type; but they belong to a category of 'facts' which for many purposes are treated as clearly irrelevant both by law and by accepted canons of justice. Llewellyn did not spell out this point, but it seems rather unlikely that he would have disagreed with it.

Situation sense

Llewellyn's use of 'justice' may be relatively clear, but some of his other concepts have occasioned difficulty. In particular, his use of 'situation sense' and 'reason' (occasionally 'right reason') have not only generated puzzlement but have also raised serious doubts about the consistency of his position in respect of values.[49] These terms are introduced immediately after the passage quoted in the last section:

Situation sense will serve well enough to indicate the type-facts in their context and at the same time in their pressure for a satisfying working result, coupled with whatever the judge or court brings and adds to the evidence, in the way of knowledge and experience and values to see with, and to judge with. *Wisdom* will serve well enough to indicate a goal of right decision weighted heavily with and for the future. *Reason* I use to lap over both of these, and to include as well the conscious use of the court's best powers to be articulate, especially about wisdom and guidance in the result.[50]

As it is the most important characteristic of the Grand Style, 'situation sense' is made a key concept in *The Common Law Tradition*; unfortunately it is also one of the most obscure. Llewellyn tried to explain himself by quoting the German legal scholar, Levin Goldschmidt:

Every fact-pattern of common life, so far as the legal order can take it in, carries within itself its appropriate, natural rules, its right law. This is a natural law which is real, not imaginary; it is not a creature of mere reason, but rests on the solid foundation of what reason can recognize in the nature of man and of the life conditions of the time and place: it is thus not eternal nor changeless nor everywhere the same, but is in-dwelling in the very circumstances of life. The highest task of law-giving consists in uncovering and implementing this immanent law.[51]

There is probably no other passage in Llewellyn's works more likely to breed puzzlement and misunderstanding than this one. Is this a headlong plunge into metaphysics?[52] Is there a soft centre to his hard-headed realism? Such suspicions seem to be confirmed by a passage, heavily italicized, which occurs a few pages further on:

Only as a judge or court knows the facts of life, *only as they truly understand* those facts of life, *only as they have it in them to rightly evaluate those facts and to fashion rightly a sound rule* and an apt remedy, *can they lift the burden* Goldschmidt lays upon them: to uncover and to implement the immanent law.[53]

'Situation sense' appears to involve 'true understanding' of the facts and 'right evaluation' of them. But how does one recognize 'true understanding' of the facts and 'right evaluation' of them. What are the criteria for determining 'right evaluation', 'right fashioning', 'a sound rule'?

That these passages are, at the very least, unclear is shown by the different interpretations that have already been given to them: in a thoughtful criticism of *The Common Law Tradition* Clark and

Trubeck asume that 'situation sense' must be each judge's personal intuitive feel for the facts, and they argue that the concept serves to disguise the important part played by subjectivity in judicial processes;[54] since Llewellyn's argument is that for the purposes of prediction the subjective elements can be largely ignored, this accusation could be rather damaging. On the other hand, Lasswell, in criticizing Llewellyn for not providing a systematic method of classifying fact-situations, seems to imply that 'situation sense' involves the ability to classify correctly any fact-situation into a set of established categories.[55] In this interpretation 'situation sense', far from being idiosyncratic and subjective, would involve a comprehensive system for classifying social facts, presumably on the model of Lasswell's own scheme.[56] The present writer, on the other hand, on first reading the Goldschmidt quotation jumped to the conclusion that it meant that there is a single perfectly just solution to every unique fact situation and that 'situation-sense' and 'reason' were the faculties which help judges in some undefined way to know or to discover this solution.[57] In this interpretation the passage implies a species of natural law theory that is intuitionist and metaphysical. A further examination of these passages suggests either that Llewellyn was inconsistent or that none of these interpretations was intended by him. In the first place he did not conceive of 'situation sense' as depending on personal idiosyncrasies or beliefs; he claimed that the standard of 'wisdom' to which he was appealing was not a personal one: 'it is rather a standard which aims to get idiosyncratic preferences largely hewn off until the standard becomes what the courts also are reaching for; something which can be hoped, on thought, to look reasonable to any thinking man; something that can even be hoped to look reasonable in the light of that *uncommon* sense, *horse* sense.'[58] In short, Llewellyn thought that the choosing of an appropriate fact-pattern was something other than a purely personal choice; the validity of Clark and Trubeck's criticism therefore depends on whether or not he managed to establish 'situation sense' as transcending such subjectivity. On the other hand, it is easy to infer from Llewellyn's other writings that he was not prepared to commit himself to a comprehensive value system of the kind advocated by Lasswell.[59]

It has already been shown that Llewellyn did not believe values to be in any way objectively verifiable and that he believed the social 'sciences' to have a long way to go before they could be appropriately termed 'scientific'.⁶⁰ It is also reasonable to infer that he would not have denied that choice of an 'appropriate type-situation' or 'to truly understand and rightly evaluate' necessarily involves making judgments of value.⁶¹ Llewellyn would concede that the 'sound' way in which Cardozo found a 'significant pattern' for the facts of *McPherson* v. *Buick* involved not only a realistic insight into social facts but also a value judgment as to the *needs* of persons injured by the product of a large-scale manufacturer.⁶² Thus reaching for 'situation sense' is claimed to be a matter neither solely of personal evaluation nor solely of reference to objectively verifiable categories.

Further Llewellyn often criticized the idea that there should necessarily be a single just solution or correct answer to every legal problem. He devoted a whole section of *The Common Law Tradition* to criticizing the idea of 'one single Right Answer'.⁶³ Just as in mathematics $\sqrt{1} = \pm 1$, both answers being equally correct, so in law several different solutions to one problem could in some circumstances all be more or less equally reasonable. By what criteria is this reasonableness to be judged, if not a personal one? The answer would appear to be 'something which can be hoped, on thought, to look reasonable to any thinking man'.⁶⁴ But, it may be asked, does this mean that thinking men will necessarily agree on whether a solution is reasonable or not? Llewellyn's answer would appear to be tentatively in the affirmative; people, he seems to suggest, who have knowledge of the social background and who have tried to work out a series of possible solutions are more likely to agree that certain solutions are worthy of approval than are people who make decisions in the dark. Or, to put it another way, people by the use of reason can at least narrow the range of their disagreements.⁶⁵

At least three different interpretations of 'situation sense' have been advanced that do not seem to accord with Llewellyn's general position. This should be sufficient to substantiate the charge of obscurity; it also raises a *prima facie* case of latent ambiguity. Two questions need to be asked in this respect: (i) did Llewellyn use 'sense' consistently? (ii) under what conditions can it be said that 'situation sense' is exhibited in a judicial opinion?

The meaning of sense: The Shorter Oxford Dictionary lists three primary meanings of the word 'sense': a faculty or capacity of perception or sensation, as in 'the five senses'; actual perception or feeling, as in 'his sense of the occasion'; and meaning or signification, as in 'he used the word in that sense'. Related words like 'sensible' and 'sensitive' have a similar but not coextensive range of meanings. In Llewellyn's usage of 'situation sense' is he referring to a faculty or to actual perception or to the signification or meaning of a situation or to something else? It is by no means certain that he was consistent. Sometimes he talks of 'use of situation sense',[66] 'bringing situation sense to bear'[67] and of 'judges' situation sense at work'.[68] This usage suggests that 'situation sense' is a faculty or capacity, like 'horse sense' or 'common sense'. This usage has associations with 'sensitive', as when he speaks of 'courts sensitive to decency'[69] or 'insensitive to the life-situation'.[70] It is also reasonable to infer an association in Llewellyn's mind with 'horse sense' and 'sensible' (the favourable associations of which are also to be remarked).[71] Thus a court is sensitive to a situation and sensible in using situation sense. In other contexts, however, 'sense' and 'situation sense' seem to be related to the situation rather than to the court or the judges. Thus Llewellyn talks of 'the quest for sense',[72] of 'problem-situation and its sense'[73] and 'what is seen as the vital situation sense';[74] in these contexts 'sense' cannot mean faculty, but it could mean either 'the meaning of the situation' or what would be sensible (i.e. judicious) in this situation.

Examination of Llewellyn's use of language suggests that he thought associationally about sense, sensible, horse sense, sensitive and situation sense and that he may at times have unconsciously switched meaning from passage to passage. Some such switches may be relatively harmless (although indicative of loose thinking), as when in ordinary usage the word 'sensible' is applied indiscriminately to a judge, to a decision and to a result. However, talk of 'the meaning of the situation' or of 'discovering sense'[75] in the facts has the same suggestion of a plunge into metaphysics as talk of 'recognizing', 'uncovering' or 'finding' 'immanent law'—the suggestion that somehow lurking within the situation is something which may be found, though not by any known empirical methods (but perhaps by a sixth or seventh 'sense'). If this analysis is correct it gives support to the view that Llewellyn was lured by his flirtation with natural law into a deviation from his normal stance as an empiricist and ethical relativist. However, the extent to which this detracts from the main thesis of *The Common Law Tradition* remains to be considered.

The indicia of 'situation sense': Even if 'sense' is confined to a faculty of making a sensible interpretation of a situation, the question remains: what are the indicia that this faculty has been exercised? It has been suggested that situation sense may be 'a Janus-faced concept' in that Llewellyn appears to give different types of reasons for concluding that it has been operative.[76] Rohan points out that sometimes it appears to involve familiarity with the general background of the facts—for instance, familiarity of an expert or near expert with the relevant trade practices in a commercial case.[77] In such instances 'familiarity' does not imply any explicit value judgment about 'needs' or other desiderata. In other instances, however, 'sense' is related overtly to some broad policy or principle, which clearly involves a judgment of value.[78] The point may be illustrated by comparing Llewellyn's treatment of the cases of *McPherson* v. *Buick* and *Legniti* v. *Mechanics and Metals National Bank.*[79] He finds situation sense in *McPherson* v. *Buick* in a principle based upon a judgment about 'the needs of life in a developing civilization', with its scope broadly indicated by such 'situational concepts' as manufacturer, modern consumer, and defective products.[80] Rohan contrasts Llewellyn's treatment of this case with his comments on some commercial cases which suggest 'that the essence of situation sense is a grasp of financial and banking practices',[81] one of the instances cited in his remarks on *Legniti* v. *Mechanics and Metals National Bank.* The principal issue in this case was whether an oral promise by a bank to cable a transfer of sterling (i.e. a foreign exchange transaction) was covered by the statute of frauds. The court upheld the contract in the light of commercial practice in respect of foreign remittances. Although the weight of authority plainly supported the view that this was a 'contract to sell' within the terms of the statute, Llewellyn was prepared to justify the result on the grounds that:

(1) Foreign exchange deals fall outside the statute's purpose and policy; oral deals not only work, but are necessary. (2) Foreign exchange is a significant unit-type of situation, whether the form by (sic) the bank's draft (not *sold*, but issued), or a payment (no *sale*, but a service), or a credit. Any distinction based on form would be arbitrary. Hence *for this purpose*, establishing a credit would also be treated as a service, and so outside the statute.[82]

Llewellyn elaborates on the matter as follows:

Surely the nub lies in the information from the briefs that word of mouth is the common method of closing such transactions and that an upset 'will be productive of much inconvenience'.... It is a good nub, and a wise decision; but there is nothing which suggests that the necessary understanding of situation and need was sitting, ready, on the bench; Cardozo's appreciation of banking, for instance, had no at-homeness at all in the hands-and-feet techniques of commercial bank operation. No, what we have is advocacy informing the court *at the appellate stage* about wise choice of concept and consequent rule, in view of the inherent needs of the type of situation; informing so persuasively that the court turns its back on the plain text of a statute to strong-arm an exception which the legislature has lacked the knowledge and prudence to provide.[83]

This statement is quoted by Rohan as an example of 'situation sense' referring to how things are done in commercial practice (i.e. a purely factual criterion) rather than to some policy or principle.[84] However, the passage does not support this interpretation; rather it suggests that 'situation sense' always involves both elements. Llewellyn's usage is, for the most part, consistent with this latter view. In the above passage the relevant policy is all but explicitly stated, *viz.* that the rules of the commercial law should suit the convenience and needs of bankers (*inter alios*). The fact that in very many commercial cases this policy (and others like it) is not in issue does not affect the point that in Llewellyn's use of 'situation sense' there is always at least one principle or policy involved. Sensitivity to the situation includes awareness of what policies or principles are relevant; in the Grand Style of judging they are typically made explicit. Where there is no conflict of principles, 'wise' decision is correspondingly easier. Where principles are in issue sensitivity to the situation will aid posing the issue in appropriate terms; but 'situation sense' offers no magic formula for choosing between competing principles. By 'Janus-faced' Rohan seems to mean that 'situation sense' is ambiguous in that it refers *either* to relevant policies or principles *or* to actualities of contemporary social life, such as existing commercial practice or usage.[85] Such an interpretation is probably unfair to Llewellyn, who seems generally to treat 'situation sense' as encompassing *both* elements. In some cases the main source of *difficulty* may be identifying relevant principles or choosing between competing ones; in others it may lie in classifying the facts appropriately; in yet others there may be difficulties about both phases. In all cases, however, exhibition of 'situation sense' involves both steps: the formulation of principles or policies *and* the classification of the facts into a general type-fact-situation. Indeed, it would be artificial and misleading to separate formulation of policy from classification of facts, because they are to a large extent interdependent.

If this interpretation is correct, further questions arise: what are acceptable principles? What are the criteria of 'appropriate' classification? Not surprisingly, Llewellyn did not allow himself to be drawn into giving dogmatic or precise answers to these questions. He was well aware that they are a fertile potential source of disagreement, even among 'reasonable' or 'thinking' men.[86] If this were not the case, judicial decision-making would not be so problematic. However, this is not to say that he provided no guidance or suppressed his personal views. There is a wealth of concrete illustrations in *The Common Law Tradition* of employment of 'situation sense' by judges. There are thus many examples of articulated principles and policies and of categorization of facts into general 'type-fact situations'. To *report* that a judge has articulated a principle or policy or has made such a categorization does not commit the reporter to approval of what he has reported. Thus to say 'Judge X exhibited situation sense' *can* be descriptive of Judge X's behaviour, without implying approval or disapproval. However, Llewellyn not only approved of situation sense, but also of many of the policies and categorizations that he found in the cases. Sometimes he kept separate his reporting of the result and of the style of the opinion from his evaluation of them. Sometimes, however, description and evaluation are not kept clearly distinct. Moreover, terms like 'Grand Style', 'sense' and even 'situation sense' carry clear suggestions of approval. Often this is excusable, because of the need to be succinct, but Llewellyn's analysis might have been more lucid if he had distinguished more clearly *reporting* on the use of situation sense from *approving* or *disapproving* of a judge's justification for his decision, which should in turn, be kept separate from *approving* or *disapproving* of the result in the case.[87]

The quotation from Goldschmidt revisited: The foregoing interpretation may provide the basis for a constant use of the term 'situation sense', but it does not explain Llewellyn's enthusiasm for the quotation from Goldschmidt concerning 'immanent law'.[88] It may be argued that that passage adds nothing to *The Common Law Tradition*, but the fact remains that Llewellyn clearly thought that it did. The term 'immanent law' carries with it the suggestion of something pre-existing, awaiting human discovery. This in turn has a metaphysical ring of the sort that arouses the suspicions of empirically minded jurists. Llewellyn, despite his late flirtation with Catholicism, remained firmly in the empirical tradition of jurisprudence. What then can account for this seeming deviation into metaphysics?

One possible explanation has already been suggested in chapter 6.[89] The Goldschmidt passage is remarkably similar to the final paragraph of Corbin's 'The Law and the Judges', a paper which anticipates to an extraordinary degree some of the main themes of *The Common Law Tradition* and which made a great impression on the young Llewellyn. The passage from Corbin reads as follows: 'That judge is just and wise who draws from the weltering mass the principle actually immanent therein and declares it as the law. This has always been the judicial function in all countries, and for its performance the judge must bear the responsibility.'[90] The 'weltering mass' in this context refers to the common consciousness of ordinary people rather than Goldschmidt's 'circumstances of life', but the idea of the wise judge uncovering immanent principles of law is strikingly similar. Llewellyn does not seem to have remembered 'The Law and the Judges' while writing this part of *The Common Law Tradition*, but his enthusiasm for the Goldschmidt passage might be explained in part by a feeling that he 'recognized' it without realizing why it seemed familiar. This must remain a matter of speculation and is probably only a partial explanation, even if correct. For a further clue we must look elsewhere.

'Situation sense' became a part of Llewellyn's vocabulary at a late stage and it is fair to say that his use of this term and some others in *The Common Law Tradition* would have benefited from some closer analysis; his belief in the wide range of agreement as to values among 'thinking men' also appears to be based more on faith than on evidence. It is significant that both Goldschmidt and Llewellyn were specialists in commercial law and that the context of the quotation from Goldschmidt is a discussion of commercial law.[91] It is also significant that Goldschmidt was a disciple of Savigny and in his work on the 'Universal History of Commercial Law' he made use of the concept of *'Volksgeist'* to describe the influence on the growth of the law of the ethos, the felt needs and the working expectations and usages of the mercantile community at different times in history. There are few branches of law which concern directly such a close-knit community with such a wide range of agreement as to what is 'right', 'fair' or 'reasonable'. It is possible to infer that, in Llewellyn's view, a 'sound' decision uncovering the 'immanent law' would be one in which the judge has sufficient experience and understanding of the usages and ethics of the particular trade and the way this kind of transaction would be conducted and how it fitted into the general pattern of commercial usage to be able to know what kind of solution would be likely to be deemed reasonable and acceptable by the mercantile community. A judge in a commercial case who can see the facts in the way businessmen would see them, as well as from the lawyer's point of view and from the point of view of the 'mores' of the community as a whole, has grasped the 'situation sense', and if he has a better than average understanding of the situation and the problem it presents, he has 'wisdom'. Lord Mansfield employed panels of merchants;[92] he also used to dine regularly with merchants from the city and cross-examined them closely about the practices of the more reputable of their number, thereby no doubt acquiring some of the essential background which made him adept at getting at 'situation sense'.

In the context of commercial law, 'situation sense' may be a meaningful, indeed an illuminating, term, although unrefined. But the law has to deal with communities among which values are by no means so widely shared and it also has to settle and prevent disputes between conflicting groups. If it were possible and proper for judges to commune regularly with trades union leaders and tycoons, with manufacturers and officials of consumer associations, they might well gain additional insights into the practices, expectations and predominating values of such groups, but whence would they derive 'appropriate' values for passing judgment on such conflicts of interest? Llewellyn does not appear to have faced this kind of question squarely, but one can infer from his writings part of the answer he might have given: first, a judge who consistently attempts to get 'a feel for' the situation as it occurred is more likely to see clearly what conflicts of value, if any, are involved in the dispute than a judge who looks at 'the facts' through the spectacles of formalism. As an obvious example, when judges feel themselves bound by doctrine to ignore the insurance element in dealing with motor accident claims in negligence, they will be ignoring situation sense. In individual cases the insurance factor may influence the decision under cover, as a fireside equity, with a consequent loss of reckonability of results. For the 'real' conflicts (in terms of the realities from the point of view of the parties and of non-lawyers generally) are not being faced up to explicitly but nevertheless may be exerting a pressure 'as disturbing or upsetting as an undertow'.[93] Secondly, it will also be found that in many disputes no serious conflict of values is involved and that once the facts are seen in a certain way the solution is self-evident, in the sense that as between the parties and/or in the eyes of the community as a whole no disagreement that may exist as to values is relevant to this particular dispute.

Thus one may conclude that Llewellyn's espousal of Goldschmidt's 'immanent law' did not necessarily commit him to some metaphysical theory. It is possible to explain his attachment to the passage and at the same time to put an interpretation upon it and upon the concept of 'situation sense' which is intelligible to the empiricist. The context of the Goldschmidt passage does suggest, however, that 'situation sense' is most appropriately used in respect of disputes which arise within groups or sub-groups which have an underlying consensus about relevant values. On this interpretation Llewellyn's advice to judges on the use of situation sense might be re-stated in some such terms as these:

Situation sense (summary)

Facts: (a) In interpreting a reported case, or in approaching a current case, start by studying the facts as a layman familiar with their general context might see them. Try to grasp what would have happened if things had been working smoothly and what it was that brought the dispute about. Analyse what interests are in conflict and formulate statements of policy that may be relevant.

(b) Try to fit the facts into some socially significant category or pattern, separating clearly irrelevant 'fireside equities' peculiar to this case from potentially relevant elements in the situation. In seeking for appropriate categories the following guidelines should be observed: (i) in categorizing the facts choose 'situational concepts' — i.e. categories which clearly refer to fact situations only and do not straddle facts and legal consequences; (ii) terms used and distinctions drawn by persons familiar with the context of the dispute (either as experts, observers or participants) may provide appropriate categories; (iii) the practices and expectations of such persons may also be of use;[94] (iv) one aspect of the problem is to characterize the facts at an appropriate level of generality. No general formula exists for this but: (a) the facts should be characterized as a type; (b) in first instance, the facts should be characterized fairly narrowly (e.g. hospital employing a doctor rather than employer-employee) and movement up the ladder of abstraction to broader categories should proceed with awareness of the dangers of lumping together disparate social situations under one head.[95]

Values: (a) Sometimes it will be found that after the facts have been categorized, there may be a consensus within the affected group or within society as a whole respecting applicable policies or principles. In such cases the selection of an appropriate situational concept may be sufficient to resolve the problem.

(b) in other instances, a conflict of principles or policies may be found. In such cases the process of categorization should have assisted in identification of the issues of policy, etc. but will not in itself resolve such conflict. However, even if reasonable men might disagree on the choice of conflicting policies, they might share common ground in limiting the range of choices.

Measures: (a) Determine what you consider to be the most appropriate line or direction of treatment and only then; (b) decide on what specific prescription is appropriate.[96]

This procedure provides no cure-all for finding 'appropriate' categories or choosing between competing values. 'No technique or method can ever be a cure-all'.[97] It will not assist in the disposition of marginal cases. Nevertheless it provides a broad framework which should maximize the role of reason in solving problems presented to appellate courts.

Reason and Candour

What is new in juristic thought today is chiefly the candor of its processes. (Cardozo)[98]

An institution we could not honor naked, we should not dare to strip. (Llewellyn)[99]

Llewellyn referred to the Grand Style as the style of reason;[100] indeed, situation sense and reason are the two principal indicia of the style. In his usage 'reason' was closely associated with candour and openness.[101] It is the converse of arbitrariness. A judge uses 'reason' when he makes articulate the premises of his reasoning, especially those premises which take the form of a value judgment or of a statement of purpose or policy. Thus the style of reason is the style of articulated reasons.

Llewellyn's emphasis on articulation was not restricted to justification of judicial decisions. He had no patience with the 'modern fetish of secrecy'[102] about judicial conferences, jury deliberations and other aspects of decision-making. An important objection to the Formal Style was that 'innovation also moved under cover, "like some Victorian virgin tubbing in her nightgown" '.[103] Central to his approach to law teaching was a rejection of the view that the crafts of law are a matter of ineffable art and that success in practice depends entirely on a combination of luck, innate ability and unanalysable 'experience'.

There is a strong vein of reticence within the common law tradition which runs counter to the candid rationalism espoused by Llewellyn. Suspicion of the realist movement has often gone deeper than the articulated criticisms of views attributed to realists. In some circles the realists have had an image of vulgar iconoclasts or muckrakers, characterized by a prurient interest in judicial psychology and digestion. The suggestion is that their concerns were in some way improper and their motives suspect. Another kind of attitude was revealed in a conversation between Llewellyn and a distinguished English judge, shortly before the former's death. The story goes that Llewellyn had expressed the opinion that it was desirable that judges should be quite open about the policy reasons that might influence their decisions and he had elaborated this view along the lines of his thesis in *The Common Law Tradition*. Llewellyn's argument was dismissed as naive and pernicious nonsense, at least in respect of the English context, on two principal grounds. First, that it was important to maintain at least the façade of the separation of powers; and, secondly, that a principal source of strength of the operation of the higher courts in England lay in the intimacy and trust that underlies the relationships of bar and bench, so that a great deal is communicated via tacit assumptions and subtle nuances which are just the opposite of the laborious and unglamorous approach that Llewellyn seemed to be advocating.

History does not relate how this conversation ended, but there is ample evidence that Llewellyn was far from being a juristic Gregers Werle,[104] concerned to shatter myths and illusions regardless of the consequences. He was quite explicit in justifying his emphasis on the value of articulation and candour. His principal reason was related to his concern for the improvement of 'juristic method'. First, 'covert tools, are not reliable tools';[105] the road to progress lies through conscious, rational and articulate method. Secondly, whereas some of the best practitioners may intuitively grasp the underlying principles of sound technique, the less talented may need to have even the obvious spelled out for them. Moreover, even the talented may find that systematic study of certain techniques may be quicker and more efficient than leaving them to be picked up by trial and error in practice. Hence Llewellyn's emphasis on the need for a 'theory of the legal crafts' and for the development of the teaching of skills as a part of formal legal education. Llewellyn was fond of recounting the fable of the centipede who became paralysed through wondering how he managed to coordinate his many legs.[106] The fable provides a salutary warning to the enthusiast for 'systematic' training in skills, both by reminding us that the most efficient way of learning some things is merely by doing them without thinking and by underlining the point that the skilful practitioner is not necessarily the person best suited to analyse and communicate the ingredients of his skill: 'The study of craft-work, the analysis thereof, the reduction of such matters to communicable working principles, is a separate art; there is a place for the side-lines man, if he can use his eyes.'[107]

To Llewellyn there was some value in the fable of the centipede, but, as he remarked in *The Common Law Tradition*, it was also important to remember that an appellate judge (or any other lawyer) is not a centipede.[108]

There was no essential conflict between Llewellyn's realism and his sometimes romantic love of tradition. Without succumbing to the Chinese argument that our ancestors were in all respects wiser than ourselves,[109] he tended to believe that much wisdom underlay most of the institutions of the common law and that they were, for the most part, functionally sound. This being so, detached observation and rigorous functional analysis should be welcomed rather than feared by the lover of tradition.

Reason and Motive
Fundamental to discussion of judicial processes is the distinction between the study of judicial reasoning (the logic of justification)

and the study of judicial decision-making (the process of decision.) The former type of enquiry requires the concepts and techniques of logicians and philosophers and is concerned with such questions as: to what extent do judges employ deduction, induction, reasoning by analogy and other types of reasoning in justifying their decisions? To what extent do judicial conclusions follow necessarily from their premises? Are there unique features of legal reasoning which differentiate it from other types of reasoning? What constitute good or valid reasons in legal justification? And so on. Such questions can be discussed without commitment to any particular conclusion about the causal connection between reasons articulated by judges in justifying their decisions and the decisions themselves.[110] On the other hand, enquiries of the second type are principally, though not exclusively, of a causal nature. The principal question here is: what factors actually influence judicial decision-making? This question concerns *motivation*; accordingly it requires an answer based on an acceptable psychological theory. It does not follow from this that psychologists are necessarily better equipped than lawyers to pursue this kind of enquiry, for it requires, *inter alia*, intimate knowledge of judicial procedures and ways of work, of the legal frame of reference, and of the kinds of phenomena that Llewellyn lists as major steadying factors in *The Common Law Tradition*. It may well be easier for a lawyer to acquire the necessary psychological equipment than for a psychologist to acquire an adequate foundation in law. Nevertheless the question is essentially a psychological one.

Sometimes in jurisprudential writings the distinction between study of the process of decision and study of the logic of justification is glossed over or ignored. Phrases like 'the nature of the judicial process' or 'judicial thought processes' or even 'decision-making' are used sometimes to refer to one type of enquiry, sometimes to the other, sometimes to both. The practice of glossing over the distinction is understandable, although it is not to be condoned. For there is a close connection between the two types of enquiry. The connecting link is the question: to what extent do the reasons advanced in justification reflect the actual motives for judicial decisions? (or, to put the matter more succinctly, but less precisely: how rational is judicial decision-making?) While it is possible to imagine someone studying judicial logic while believing that the reasons articulated by judges were 'mere rationalizations' bearing no relation to their actual motives, it is unlikely that the majority of serious students of legal reasoning proceed on such an assumption, if only because it would cast grave doubts on the value of their activity. It is reasonable to assume that most students of the subject believe that there is at least some correlation between judicial reasons and motives.[111]

Llewellyn did not fall into the elementary trap of confusing description of process with justification of results. He stated clearly that 'the opinion has no function of *describing* the process of deciding',[112] yet he was equally clear in his dissent from the view that judicial opinions are to be dismissed as 'mere rationalizations' which are valueless as tools for prediction.[113]

The Common Law Tradition treats of the prediction of results (decisions) through the study of opinions (justifications). Part of the argument is that Grand Style opinions provide a more reliable basis for predicting future decisions than Formal Style opinions, for two reasons: first, because more of the factors influencing a decision are brought out into the open; and secondly because the process of consciously treating these factors enhances the chance of their operating in a regular manner. In other words, conscious rational treatment of those factors is less erratic and arbitrary than pretending to ignore them. Llewellyn was not committed to the position that the reasons given in a Grand Style justification are the only factors influencing the decision,[114] but by and large there is a strong likelihood that they will be among the most important ones. Thus in the Grand Style there is more overlap between reason and motive than in the Formal Style. Accordingly a sequence of Grand Style opinions, taken with other known steadying factors, may provide an adequate working basis for the practitioner to make reasonably confident predictions. Whether Llewellyn satisfactorily established his claim that the Grand Style in fact promotes predictability will be considered in detail below.

Leeways for interpretation of authoritative sources

Legislative enactments (including constitutions, statutes and subordinate legislation) and decided cases are the two principal authoritative sources of law in Anglo-American jurisprudence. As such they contain the main raw material for fashioning legal doctrine and for providing answers to questions of law posed in appellate cases. Some of the most original aspects of *The Common*

Law Tradition are to be found in Llewellyn's discussion of the nature of the discretion that courts have in interpreting cases and legislation and of the range of techniques which are in fact used by American courts in the process of interpretation.[115] The general nature of case and statute law is only cursorily discussed in *The Common Law Tradition* itself; instead Llewellyn built on a number of ideas which he had elaborated in earlier works. To avoid repetition his various writings on interpretation are here considered together, first in respect of cases and then of statutes.

Case Law: There is a close connection between the emphasis placed by Llewellyn on disputes and dispute-settlement in his theory of law-government and his approach to precedent as a source of law. This is brought out by the opening paragraph of his article on 'Case Law' in *The Encyclopaedia of Social Sciences*:

Case law is law found in decided cases and created by judges in the process of solving particular disputes. Case law in some form and to some extent is found wherever there is law. A mere series of decisions of individual cases does not of course in itself constitute a system of law. But in any judicial system rules of law arise sooner or later out of such decisions of cases, as rules of action arise out of the solution of practical problems, whether or not such formulations are desired, intended or consciously recognized. These generalizations contained in, or built upon, past decisions, when taken as normative for future disputes, create a legal system of precedent. Precedent, however, is operative before it is recognized. Toward its operation drive all those phases of human make-up which build habit in the individual and institutions in the group: laziness as to the reworking of a problem once solved; the time and energy saved by routine, especially under any pressure of business; the values of routine as a curb on arbitrariness and as a prop of weakness, inexperience and instability; the social values of predictability; the power of whatever exists to produce expectations and the power of expectations to become normative. The force of precedent in the law is heightened by an additional factor: that curious, almost universal, sense of justice which urges that all men are properly to be treated alike in like circumstances. As the social system varies we meet infinite variations as to what men or treatments or circumstances are to be classed as 'like'; but the pressure to accept the views of the time and place remains.[116]

Llewellyn's most extensive published discussion of case law is to be found in chapters II to IV of *The Bramble Bush*. These forty-five pages remain one of the best introductions to the subject in print. They defy summary and there can be no substitute for reading the original. In the present context we are principally concerned with the malleability of judicial opinions, i.e. what it is about them that allows for differing interpretations to be put on them.

In interpreting a prior decided case a lawyer is concerned with four principal elements: the statement of facts, the issue or issues of law before the court, the result of the case, and the reasons given in justification of the result. Llewellyn considered the existence of leeways for interpretation of prior cases to be based on three interdependent factors: (i) the pliancy of the facts; (ii) the lack of fixed verbal form in the formulation of issues and of rules used in justification; and (iii) the range of legitimate techniques available to interpreters in handling prior cases.

(i) *The facts:* A famous passage from *The Bramble Bush* makes the main point:

Where are *the* facts? The plaintiff's name is Atkinson and the defendant's Walpole. The defendant, despite his name, is an Italian by extraction, but the plaintiff's ancestors came over with the Pilgrims. The defendant has a schmautzer-dog named Walter, red hair, and $30,000 worth of life insurance. All these are facts. The case, however, does not deal with life insurance. It is about an auto accident. The defendant's auto was a Buick painted pale magenta. He is married. His wife was in the back seat, an irritable somewhat faded blond. She was attempting back seat driving when the accident occurred. He had turned around to make objection. In the process the car swerved and hit the plaintiff. The sun was shining; there was a rather lovely dappled sky low to the West. The time was late October on a Tuesday. The road was smooth, concrete. It had been put in by the McCarthy Road Work Company. How many of these facts are important to the decision? How many of these facts are, as we say, legally relevant? Is it relevant that the road was in the country or the city; that it was concrete or tarmac or of dirt; that it was a private or a public way? Is it relevant that the defendant was driving a Buick, or a motor car, or a vehicle? Is it important that he looked around as the car swerved? Is it crucial? Would it have been the same if he had been drunk, or had swerved for fun, to see how close he could run by the plaintiff, but had missed his guess?

Is it not obvious that as soon as you pick up this statement of the facts to find its legal bearings you must discard some as of no interest whatsoever, discard others as dramatic but as legal nothings? And is it not clear, further, that when you pick up the facts which are left and which do seem relevant, you suddenly cease to deal with them in the concrete and deal with them instead in *categories* which you, for one reason or another, deem significant.

It is not the road between Pottsville and Arlington; it is 'a highway'. It is not a particular pale magenta Buick eight, by number 732507, but 'a motor car', and perhaps even 'a vehicle'. It is not a turning around to look at Adorée Walpole, but a lapse from the supposedly proper procedure of careful drivers, with which you are concerned. Each concrete fact of the case arranges itself, I say, as the *representative* of a much wider abstract *category* of facts, and it is not in itself but as a member of the category that you attribute significance to it. But what is to tell you whether to make your category 'Buicks' or 'motor cars' or 'vehicles'? What is to tell you to make your category 'road' or 'public highway'?[117]

Professor Julius Stone has refined this analysis in the context of the well-known controversy on determining the *ratio decidendi* of a case.[118] Taking the familiar example of *Donoghue* v. *Stevenson* he has pointed out that each of the elements in the case (such as the facts as to the agent of harm, the vehicle of harm, the defendant's identity, the nature of the injury to the plaintiff, etc.) can be stated at a number of levels of generality. For instance, the fact as to the agent of harm can be characterized as:

dead snails
or any snails
or any noxious physical foreign body
or any noxious foreign element, physical or not
or any noxious element.[119]

In criticizing Goodhart's 'material facts' theory of the *ratio decidendi*, Stone points out that the term 'the material facts' gives a misleading impression of some precise, fixed datum, whereas there can be an almost infinite variety of versions of the material facts, depending on the level of generality at which each 'fact element' is stated. To the contention that 'the material facts' are those which the deciding court explicitly or implicitly treated as material there are two objections. Firstly, the same judge in a single judgment may move at a number of different levels of generality. And, secondly, as Llewellyn put it:

. . . the court may tell you. But the precise point you have up for study is how far it is safe to trust what the court says. The precise issue which you are attempting to solve is whether the court's language can be taken as it stands, or must be amplified, or must be whittled down.[120]

(ii) *The Fluidity of Judicial Opinions:* A critical difference between statutes and cases, according to Llewellyn, is that whereas in the case of statutes there are 'frozen words',[121] the same is not the case in judicial opinions:

Our judge states his facts, he argues his position, he announces his rule. And lo, he seems but to have begun. Once clean across the plate. But he begins again, winds up again and again he delivers his ratio – this time, to our puzzlement, the words are not the same. At this point it is broader than it was before, there it is narrower. And like as not he will warm up another time, and do the same job over – differently again. I have never made out quite why this happens. A little, it may be due to a lawyer's tendency to clinch an argument by summarizing its course, when he is through. A little, it may be due to mere sloppiness of composition, to the lack, typical of our law and all its work, of a developed sense for form, juristic or esthetic, for what the Romans knew as *elegantia*. . . . But whatever the reason, recurrent almost-repetition faces us: also the worry that the repetition seldom is exact.[122]

Once again *Donoghue v. Stevenson* provides a good illustration. Lord Atkin begins his speech by posing the issue in two different ways:

. . . the sole question for determination in this case is legal: Do the averments made by the pursuer in her pleading, if true, disclose a cause of action? I need not restate the particular facts. The question is whether the manufacturer of an article of drink sold by him to a distributor, in circumstances which prevent the distributor or the ultimate purchaser or consumer from discovering by inspection any defect, is under any legal duty to the ultimate purchaser or consumer to take reasonable care that the article is free from defect likely to cause injury to health.[123]

The averments of facts in the pleading were more specific than their characterization in Lord Atkin's formulation of the issue. Thus in this passage alone Lord Atkin has moved at more than one level of generality. However, the more general statement is in turn a little less general in some respects than the formulation of the governing proposition in the closing paragraph of the speech :

My Lords, if your Lordships accept the view that this pleading discloses a relevant cause of action you will be affirming the proposition that by Scots and English law alike a manufacturer of products, which he sells in such a form as to show that he intends them to reach the ultimate consumer in the form in which they left him, with no reasonable possibility of intermediate examination, and with the knowledge that the absence of reasonable care in the preparation or putting up of the products will result in an injury to the consumer's life or property, owes a duty to the consumer to take that reasonable care.[124]

In this passage the agent of harm, for instance, has changed from 'an article of drink' to 'products' (in another passage it is 'articles of common household use')[125] and the nature of the injury has moved from 'injury to health' to 'injury to the consumer's life or property'. This by no means exhausts the range of Lord Atkin's movement up and down ladders of abstraction. His speech also contains the famous 'neighbour principle':

The rule that you are to love your neighbour becomes in law, you must not injure your neighbour; and the lawyer's question, Who is my neighbour? receives a restricted reply. You must take reasonable care to avoid acts or omissions which you can reasonably foresee would be likely to injure your neighbour. Who, then, in law is my neighbour? The answer seems to be – persons who are so closely and directly affected by my act that I ought reasonably to have them in contemplation as being so affected when I am directing my mind to the acts or omissions which are called in question.[126]

Here, of course, Lord Atkin has moved up to a very high plane of generality and he has been frequently criticized for this. In this formulation, then, the nature of the agent of harm and the nature of the injury have become immaterial. The defendant is 'a neighbour' rather than a 'manufacturer of an article of drink', and he is liable for either acts *or omissions*. Judged by the neighbour principle the material facts of *Donoghue* v. *Stevenson* can be simply stated to be that there were two neighbours, one of whom injured the other by negligent conduct.

Subsequent English decisions, moving within the leeways set by *Donoghue* v. *Stevenson*, have not accepted any of Lord Atkin's formulations as *the* governing one.[127] The duty of care exists in situations not covered by the narrower characterizations, but it is also settled that the neighbour principle is too wide.[128]

These extracts from Lord Atkin's speech also illustrate the interdependence of statements of the facts, posings of the issue and formulations of potential *rationes decidendi*. In the first passage Lord Atkin incorporated a statement of the facts by reference to the pleadings, posed the issue first by reference to the pleadings and then in his own words; in the other two passages quoted he stated propositions of law. In each of them he is *characterizing the facts* at particular levels of generality. This is simply explained by reference to the standard propositional form of any legal rule. In posing an issue of law, the form is: if X, then Y? (or then What?). A statement of the facts is 'The facts are X'; a statement of the governing rule: 'if X, then Y'. In talking of 'levels of generality' or 'materiality' of facts we are concerned with the mode of characterizing X.[129] Llewellyn's emphasis on 'situation sense', his advice to advocates that 'the statement of the facts is the heart', such ideas as 'narrow-issue thinking' and his general concern with the facts of cases are all directly related to the idea that the categorization of facts into a type-fact-pattern is a crucial stage in legal thinking. In case law the lack of fixed verbal form allows some leeway in categorization of facts and thus is the principal but not the only source of discretion in interpretation of prior cases.

(iii) *The range of legitimate techniques of interpretation:* Every common lawyer knows that there are a number of ways of dealing with a precedent, such as following, distinguishing on the facts, distinguishing on the pleadings, overruling, or not following. One of the most valuable parts of *The Common Law Tradition* is the discussion of such precedent techniques.[130] Although many jurists before Llewellyn had commented on the flexibility inherent in a system of precedent, never before had this phenomenon been documented in such convincing detail; never before had its complexity been so clearly revealed. From his samples of cases he collected a 'selection' of sixty-four distinguishable techniques.[131] There are, for instance, four ways of 'killing the precedent':

45. Must be confined to its exact facts.
46. Can no longer be regarded as authority, since *Younger* v. *Older* (Means *Younger* v. *Older* itself was illegitimate, if consciously silent about its effect on prior authority).
47. Involves a misapplication of the true principle (or rule).
48. Is (explicitly) overruled.[132]

One of the indicia of the Grand Style is awareness and exploitation of the variety of available techniques. Llewellyn's samples clearly show that a wide variety of precedent techniques was *regularly* employed by the state appellate courts. This provides some evidence of a renaissance of the Grand Style and supports the conclusion that:

. . . the little case, the ordinary case, is a constant occasion and vehicle for creative choice and creative activity, for the shaping and on-going re-shaping of our case law.[133]

The section on precedents is one of the best parts of *The Common Law Tradition*; its value has been well put by Becht:

This imposing gathering of methods for dealing with precedent gains by the fact that the author appends footnote references to illustrate each one, but the persuasive effect comes chiefly from the fact that the reader recognizes all as familiar, though he could not readily produce an illustration of many of them. The author himself appeals finally to this ultimate as his best evidence. [134] While no item in the list is unknown to a lawyer ('the neglected beauty of the obvious') the cumulative impact of the *collection*, its implications about the amount of freedom that exists inside the doctrine of precedent, may be quite new and may require a re-examination of his fundamental attitude toward both courts and law, with further implications for his own practice. [135]

Llewellyn admitted that his selection of sixty-four precedent techniques was incomplete and crude.[136] He made no attempt to set up a precise taxonomy; some of his categories overlap, others are by no means clear. He achieved his object of showing that there is a wide range of techniques in regular use, but his work could be carried much farther; indeed it seems that this is a topic which could be fruitfully developed by more systematic analysis, now that Llewellyn has pointed the way.

An important question to be considered is the relationship between *techniques* of interpreting cases and the *doctrine* of precedent. Strictly speaking the doctrine of precedent consists of rules (and, perhaps, conventions) which prescribe what an interpreter must, may, or can do with previously decided cases. Thus in England the Court of Appeal *must* follow decisions of the House of Lords; it *may* follow decisions of inferior courts, but it *can* instead overrule them.[137] Thus the *doctrine* prescribes in what circumstances particular techniques must, may or may not be employed. Doctrine regulates, but does not describe, practice. In the United States the doctrine of precedent is both permissive and vague: permissive in that there are frustrations in which a court is strictly *bound* to follow the decision of another court; vague in that the border line between 'legitimate' and 'illegitimate' precedent techniques is not precisely defined. England, on the other hand, is famous for its allegedly strict doctrine of precedent and much scholarly attention has been paid to it. It is true that there are a number of rules that prescribe that certain classes of precedent are binding: for instance, the rule that decisions of the House of Lords are binding on all inferior courts, or the rule, modified in 1966, that the House of Lords was bound by its own decisions.[138] However, there is a high degree of permissiveness and vagueness in the English system too: all legitimate precedent techniques are open to the House of Lords today and many are open to inferior courts; for instance, any court *may* distinguish any decision. The English rules on precedent are vague both on the border line between legitimacy and illegitimacy of techniques and on the question: what constitutes the binding part of a case?—one aspect of the much discussed problem of the *ratio decidendi*. Where a doctrine of precedent is permissive or vague or both, there is ample scope for a wide range of differences in the *practice* of courts in handling prior precedents.

The jurisprudential literature on precedent has concentrated very largely on the doctrine of binding precedent. Very little has been said in print about the practice of precedent, even where the distinction between doctrine and practice has been observed. Since doctrine does not describe practice such discussions tend to be lacking in realism and, at times, even present a misleading picture. Once again, Lord Atkin's speech in *Donoghue v. Stevenson* can be used to illustrate the point. Lord Atkin was faced with a situation in which 'the weight of precedent' was clearly against him. Yet examination shows that almost all the precedents discussed by him were decisions of courts inferior to the House of Lords.[189] Thus, according to the doctrine of precedent, it was permissible to overrule or not follow almost all the opposing authorities. In fact Lord Atkin did nothing of the sort. Instead he used a variety of techniques, some of dubious legitimacy, to distinguish, explain away or kill the other authorities; these techniques would have been available to him even if *all* the cases in question had been decisions of the House of Lords. Whether, if they had been, Lord Atkin (or the appellant) would have behaved in the same way is quite a different matter. This obvious feature of *Donoghue v. Stevenson* has been ignored in nearly all discussions of the case.

Llewellyn, by concentrating on the practice of precedent, revealed a much more complex phenomenon than most theoretical discussions would suggest; at the same time, he opened up a whole field of potential research, as yet largely unexploited, some of which might be susceptible to quantitative techniques.

Leeways in interpretation of statutes: In his first year teaching Llewellyn used to place great emphasis on the theme: 'You cannot read a statute like a case'.[140] Sometimes he would get the whole

class to chant in unison: 'Never paraphrase a statute'[141] to implant
'the lesson of the frozen word'. He even expressed the idea in verse:

> A statute is a piece of prose
> for study most meticulous
> and any *solid* lawyer knows
> that to read 'they's' for 'these' and 'those'
> is utterly ridiculous.
>
> A statute, in both thought and word,
> is semi-architectural;
> and it is bad, it is absurd,
> when any phrase or Act is blurred
> by 'reading' that's conjectural.
>
> The text lays out, the *text you see,*
> unyielding, all perimeters;
> though slight penumbra there must be
> you'll find in force and quantity
> sharp, given verbal limiters.
>
> A *'purpose,'* (on the other hand)
> diffuse or categorical,
> announced, implied, or radar-scanned,
> is what you need, to understand
> the statutory oracle.
>
> 'Purpose' was always, and remains
> what lends to *words* all guiding spirit.
> New statutes bind by their intent
> old statutes by what might be meant
> what else is sense or half-way near it?[142]

There were, moreover, other differences between cases and statutes:

Now the essential differences between statutes and the law of case decisions
are these. A judge makes his rule in and around a specific case, and looking
backward. The case shapes the rule; the judge's feet are firmly on the
particular instance; his rule is commonly good sense, and very narrow. And
any innovation is confined regularly within rather narrow limits – partly by
the practice of trying hard to square the new decision with old law; it is
hard to keep daring innovations even verbally consistent with old rules. And
partly innovation is confined through conscious policy: case law rules
(though new) are applied *as if* they had always been the law; this derives
from our convention that 'judges only declare and do not make the law'.

Knowing that the effect of their ruling will be retroactive, and unable to foresee how many men's calculations a new ruling may upset, the judges move very cautiously into new ground. Then, when a case had been decided, it enters into the sea of common law – available to any court within the Anglo-American world, and peculiarly, within this country. Finally, and important here, case law is flexible around the edges; the rules are commonly somewhat uncertain in their wording, and not too easy to make definite. Else why your study?

But statutes are made relatively in the large, to cover wider sweeps, and looking forward. They apply only to events and transactions occurring *after* they have come into force; that element of caution disappears. They are, moreover, a recognized machinery for re-adjustment of the law. They represent not single disputes, but whole classes of disputes. They are political, not judicial in their nature, represent re-adjustments along the lines of balance of power, decide not single cases by a tiny shift of rule, but the re-arrangement of a great mass of clashing interests. Statute-making, too, is confined within what in relation to society at large is a straitened margin of free movement; but in comparison to courts the legislature is a horse without a halter. Finally, statutes have a wording fixed and firm. And their effect is local for the single state. You cannot reason from a statute to the common law. The statute of one state affords no ground for urging a like conclusion in another with no similar statute. If anything, the contrary. The presence of a statute argues rather that the common law was otherwise in the state of the statute – and hence everywhere.[143]

Despite this stress on the differences between cases and statutes, Llewellyn was emphatic in *The Common Law Tradition* that 'the *range* of techniques correctly available in dealing with statutes is roughly equivalent to the range correctly available in dealing with case law materials'.[144]

What are the sources of this leeway? Most are familiar: the language of a statute may be vague or ambiguous; unforeseen contingencies may arise; there may be gaps or inconsistencies in the text; the policy of the statute may be vague, or outdated, or one which the court feels is unacceptable (e.g. 'a plain political grab'[145]); doubt may be occasioned by difficulty in reconciling the statute with the main body of the law; above all, the problem remains of classifying particular fact situations — 'do they or do they not fit into the statutory boxes?'[146]

Law, like other dogmatic systems,[147] has recognized authoritative methods for handling authoritative materials, for instance, the rules of statutory interpretation. Ostensibly the function of these rules is to reduce or eliminate doubt by prescribing 'correct' techniques of interpretation. However, it is well known that the common law rules of statutory interpretation provide a particularly striking example of 'normative ambiguity'—i.e. the phenomenon of 'the tendency of doctrines of the common law to travel in pairs of opposites'.[148] With the help of two research assistants Llewellyn provided detailed documentation of this phenomenon in an exceptionally vivid way. A collection of over seventy purported canons of construction, each backed by authority, was placed into two parallel columns, with each entry in the left-hand column countered in the right-hand column by an entry which either contradicted or emasculated it. For instance:

THRUST AND COUNTERTHRUST

1 'If extreme hardship will result from a literal application of the words, this may be taken as evidence that the legislature did not use them literally.' Ballon v. Kemp, 92 F.2d 556, 558 (D.C. Cir. 1937).

'It is not enough merely that hard and objectionable or absurd consequences, which probably were not within the contemplation of the framers, are produced by an act of legislation. . . . (I)n such case the remedy lies with the law-making authority, and not with the courts.' Crooks v. Harrelson, 282 U.S. 55, 60 (1930).

2 'The two [statutes] are in pari materia and must be construed together.' Sanford's Estate v. Commissioner, 308 U.S. 39, 44 (1939).

'(T)he rule of in pari materia is resorted to only in cases where the meaning of a statute is ambiguous or doubtful.' Northern Pac. Ry. Co. v. United States, 156 F.2d 346, 350 (7th Cir. 1946).

3 'The meaning of a word may be ascertained by reference to the meaning of words associated with it.' International Rice Milling Co. v. NLRB, 183 F.2d 21, 25 (5th Cir. 1950).

A 'word may have a character of its own not to be submerged by its association'. Russell Motor Car Co. v. United States, 261 U.S. 514, 519 (1923).

4 'Where words of a particular or specific meaning are followed by general words, the general words are construed to apply only to persons or conditions of the same general kind as those specifically mentioned . . .'. Lyman v. Commissioner, 83 F.2d 811 (1st Cir. 1936).

'[The rule] gives no warrant for narrowing alternative provisions which the Legislature has adopted with the purpose of affording added safeguards.' United States v. Gilliland, 312 U.S. 86, 93 (1941).[149]

Thus, according to Llewellyn, although cases and statutes are different in nature and require different techniques of interpretation, the extent of the leeway for interpretation is broadly similar; moreover, the role of the interpreting court is much the same whether it is interpreting a case or a statute:

And everything said above about the temper of the court, the temper of the court's tradition, the sense of the type-situation, and the sense of the particular case applies here as well.

Thus in the period of the Grand Style of case law statutes were construed 'freely' to implement their purpose, the court commonly accepting the legislature's choice of policy and setting to work to implement it. (Criminal statutes and, to some extent, statutes on procedure were exceptions.) Whereas in the Formal period statutes tended to be limited or even eviscerated by wooden and literal reading, in a sort of long-drawn battle between a balky, stiff-necked, wrongheaded court and a legislature which had only words with which to drive that court. Today the courts have regained, in the main, a cheerful acceptance of legislative choice of policy, but in carrying such policies forward they are still hampered to some extent by the Formal period's insistence on precise language.[150]

Although Llewellyn assented to the proposition that American law schools had traditionally over-emphasized cases at the expense of statutes, in both *The Bramble Bush* and *The Common Law Tradition* he concentrated principally on case law. His discussions of statute law are briefer and less carefully documented. This is particularly noticeable in respect of his treatment of the range of techniques of interpretation: his selection of precedent techniques was based on intensive study of a series of consecutive opinions of particular courts; the exercise on canons of statutory construction was not based on the study of random samples of judicial opinions nor was it confined to specific jurisdictions. Llewellyn did take one sample of statutory material from a single jurisdiction, Ohio 1937, but this represents a much less thorough basis for his findings on statutory techniques than for precedent techniques, as he acknowledged.[151]

The limits of the leeways:

The last thirty-five years of Jurisprudence have made clear the quantum of leeway to too many lawyers who will become Judges. The last thirty-five years have not, in Law School, made clear the narrow limits of the leeway.[152]

Llewellyn in his later writings was at pains to emphasize that discretion, or, as he put it, 'leeways', are not an all-or-nothing matter. Discretion to interpret prior cases may be limited in practice by a number of factors. First, and most important in this context, is the point that typically the interpreter is faced not with an isolated precedent but with a cluster or a series of related cases. The problem then is to work the group of cases into a single pattern. Llewellyn stated, perhaps overstated, the matter in *The Bramble Bush*:

For the truth of the matter is a truth so obvious and trite that it is somewhat regularly overlooked by students. *That no case can have a meaning by itself!* Standing alone it gives you no guidance. It can give you no guidance as to how far it carries, as to how much of its language will hold water later. What counts, what gives you leads, what gives you sureness, *that is the background of the other cases* in relation to which you must read the one. They color the language, the technical terms, used in the opinion. But above all they give you the wherewithal to find which of the facts are significant, and in what aspect they are significant, and how far the rules laid down are to be trusted.[153]

There are other factors which in practice may limit the exercise of discretion in selection of precedent techniques:

True, the selection is frequently almost automatic. The type of distinction or expansion which is always *technically* available may be psychologically or sociologically unavailable. This may be because of (a) the current tradition of the court or because of (b) the current temper of the court or because of (c) the sense of the situation as the court sees that sense. (There are other possible reasons a-plenty, but these three are the most frequent and commonly the most weighty.)[154]

One final factor in limiting discretion, possibly subsumed under the 'tradition' or the 'temper' of the court, is the not very clearly defined sense of what is decent or legitimate and what is unfair or illegitimate. This was again, for Llewellyn, a matter of *limited* discretion:

It is silly ... to think of use of this leeway as involving 'twisting' of precedent. . . . The phrase presupposes that there was in the precedent under consideration some one and single meaning. The whole experience of our case-law shows that that assumption is false. It is, instead, the business of the courts to use the precedents constantly to make the law always a *little* better, to correct old mistakes, to recorrect mistaken or ill-advised attempts at correction – but always within limits severely set not only by the precedents, but equally by the traditions of right conduct in judicial office.[155]

The nature of judicial discretion in interpreting cases and statutes is such, according to Llewellyn, that judicial advancement of the law is more by almost daily cumulative adjustment than by sudden dramatic leaps forward. This is one of the key conclusions of the book:

... For the long haul, for the large-scale reshaping and growth of doctrine and of our legal institutions, I hold the almost unnoticed changes to be more significant than the historic key cases, the cumulations of the one rivaling and then outweighing the crisis–character of the other.[156]

THE DESCRIPTIVE THESIS

The bulk of the *Common Law Tradition* is taken up with three matters: elaboration of the conceptual apparatus, analysis of reported cases as evidence and illustrations of the descriptive thesis, and varying kinds of advice to participants in appellate judicial processes and to others (the prescriptive thesis). In so far as the book can be said to have a discernible structure, it is built around the descriptive thesis. The present section is concerned with the question: by what means and how satisfactorily did Llewellyn seek to establish his conclusions? For this purpose the core of the descriptive thesis may be restated as follows: (i) There was a crisis of confidence in American state appellate courts in the 1950s. This crisis was not justified because (ii) despite the leeways open to appellate courts in interpreting cases and statutes, (iii) there are a number of factors which promote regularity, and hence predictability, in the behaviour of these courts, and (iv) (a) there was in this period a renaissance of the Grand Style, and (b) the Grand Style promotes predictability and reduces arbitrariness.

Of these propositions (i) was simply asserted without much analysis or evidence to support it. Llewellyn amply illustrated (ii), but he made no serious attempt to go beyond common sense in his discussion of (iii); however, in respect of (iv) he went to immense pains to support his thesis with evidence and argument.

Between one-quarter and one-third of the book is taken up with detailed examination of approximately six hundred reported cases, nearly all of them decisions of state appellate courts.[157] These constituted almost the only evidence adduced to support the descriptive thesis. Four questions about Llewellyn's method need to be considered. First, why did he rely so heavily on reported cases?

Secondly, did the opinions selected for analysis constitute a suffic-iently representative sample? Thirdly, to what extent are reported cases representative of the work of state appellate courts? And, fourthly, was Llewellyn's mode of analysis of judicial opinions adequate for his purposes?

Why did Llewellyn rely so heavily on reported cases?

In the first place, there is *the threat of the available.* This is the lesson from the almost inevitable tendency in any thinking, or in any study, first to turn to the most available material and to study that – to study it exclusively – at the outset; second, having once begun the study of the available, to lose all pers-pective and come shortly to mistake the merely available, the easily seen, for all there is to see.[158]

In law the law reports and the statutes are the most readily available primary sources. Langdell sanctified the submission of the academic lawyer to dominance by these sources through his frequently quoted dictum to the effect that law is a science and that 'all the available materials of that science are contained in printed books'.[159]

As a young man Llewellyn reacted against the intellectual tradi-tion symbolized by Langdell's statement. Yet in *The Common Law Tradition* he deliberately restricted himself to the study of reported opinions. Does this represent a *volte-face*?

Llewellyn justified his self-denying ordinance on two grounds. First, the law reports obviously have great advantages just *because* of their availability.[160] Other sources of evidence are peculiarly inaccessible: the conscious and unconscious thought processes of judges, except as exhibited in their opinions, are likely for the fore-seeable future to remain at least as sequestered as the deliberations of jurors. Such matters as extra-judicial pronouncements and bio-graphical details may be valuable as supplementary sources but their potential is limited in comparison with the rich profusion of the law reports. In the 1930s Llewellyn had tried to get some newly appointed judges, who were former colleagues, to keep notes of their methods of decision-making; his attempt was a failure.[161] He was thus well aware of the practical difficulties of relying heavily on other sources.

Llewellyn's second reason was that the law reports have great unexploited potentialities. Lawyers, jurists and other social scien-tists have been blind to them 'as a curiously valuable, accessible and time-cheap fountain of instruction about life'.[162] Lawyers have tended to treat them 'primarily as repositories of doctrine'.[163] In *The Common Law Tradition* Llewellyn advocated a different approach:

What is needed, and all that is needed, is first to read the reports for what they are: human histories about situations which have arisen in our society And, second, to group together for instruction – in a way which other literature rarely, in equivalent time, permits – six or a dozen or forty significantly comparable histories, to be thought about together: whether in terms of situation, or in terms of process, or along any other line.[164]

This way of reading cases was not only of general educational value, but also, Llewellyn claimed, it was the easiest way for a busy practitioner to study a particular court, especially if it were working in the Grand Style. In his last public appearance, in a lecture on appellate advocacy, Llewellyn urged that in preparing an argument an advocate should start by studying the tribunal.[165] Whereas some passages in *The Common Law Tradition* may seem to suggest that reading the law reports 'properly' would be enough, in this lecture Llewellyn made it clear that he looked on the law reports as only one of the sources available to the practitioner for this purpose.

The point that the potential of the law reports has not been fully exploited in the past, is not itself a good reason for using *only* the law reports as source material in *The Common Law Tradition*. Nor is it an answer to his own argument that concentration on the most accessible sources is likely to produce a distorted perspective. This point will be elaborated in connection with the next two questions.

Was Llewellyn's sample of reported cases representative? In contrast with the selective use of cases by most writers on jurisprudence, Llewellyn claimed that the majority of cases analysed in the text were chosen at random.[166] For his principal sample he selected three states from each of the following regions: the east coast, the west coast, the middle west and the centre and southwest. In respect of each he read a sequence of cases from the most recent available reports; all the cases in the main sample were decided within the period 1957-9. In order to test typicality he prescribed the following procedure for himself:

For a first approach, then, opinions should as heretofore be read in sequence. A promising first lead would be to read until four of them were found which overtly used situation-sense in the testing or shaping of the rule applied, and check how many cases one had to cover in order to turn up the four. That would sample typicality. If, however, those four did not reasonably sample the court's personnel, as well, further reading would be called for. In any event, every opinion examined in the process would have to be accounted for, so that those which proved 'positive' for our hypotheses would fall into due perspective with reference to their frequency and typicality.[167]

The contemporary samples from twelve states were supplemented by a number of others, chosen in a different manner. There were runs of cases from earlier periods in New York in 1842 and 1939, Ohio in 1844 and 1953, and Pennsylvania in 1944. The dates and the sequences were again picked at random (except to ensure that opinions by Cowen were included), but the jurisdictions were selected on subjective criteria. Examples of the work of Mansfield and Cardozo are also considered in detail, without any suggestion that they are representative.

Although Llewellyn's sampling technique might seem idiosyncratic to a purist, it is reasonable to assume that he eliminated 'bias' in his selection of cases adequately for his purposes and that he avoided falling into elementary sampling errors. He made no attempt to quantify his findings. If anything, it might be argued that his samples are unnecessarily extensive for the purpose of establishing such vague conclusions as the findings that courts are frequently resorting to situation sense or that a wide range of precedent techniques is in daily use or that there is a widespread renaissance of the Grand Style. On the basis of his samples more precise hypotheses might have yielded 'harder' and more detailed conclusions.

To what extent are reported opinions representative of the work of the state appellate courts? In concentrating on reported cases, Llewellyn was almost exclusively concerned with decisions on questions of law or mixed law and fact; he was not concerned with other types of judicial decision-making, including the equally difficult, relatively neglected, areas of fact-finding and sentencing. His awareness sharpened by Frank's criticism, he was careful to stress the distinction between trial and appellate courts; he refused to talk of 'the judicial process', recognizing as he once put it, that judicial processes 'come in Heinz varieties';[168] he noted, but did not stress the point, that cases taken on appeal are by their very

THE COMMON LAW TRADITION 249

nature not representative of the bulk of cases coming before trial courts[169] He also noted that a majority of appellate decisions are affirmed without opinion. He quoted Cardozo's statement that a majority of cases in his court 'are predestined, so to speak, to affirmance without opinion'[170] and that 'nine-tenths, perhaps more, of the cases that come before a court are predetermined'.[171] Llewellyn's research for *Praejudizienrecht* had revealed that in 155 N.E. (1927) 64 per cent of appeals to the New York Court of Appeals were affirmed and 6 per cent were reversed without opinion,[172] and he quoted the view of Justice Loughran of the same court to the effect that 'the outcome was pretty certain about eight times out of ten, as soon as the court got their minds around the case, but that there was no such certainty about the ground of the decision'.[173]

It is perhaps a little surprising that in *The Common Law Tradition* Llewellyn should have glossed over the implications of the estimate that between 70 and 90 per cent of appeals to American state appellate courts are foredoomed, and so, in his usage, not worth appealing.[174] One of the claims for the book is that it is a realistic study of a particular type of institution as it operates in fact. A rounded study of the daily work of state appellate courts would have required a detailed examination and explanation of such estimates. In his manuscript on *The Theory of Rules* Llewellyn had suggested that Cardozo's estimate supported his views about the inadequacy of the guidance to judges and practitioners provided by the existing rules of law, taken by themselves:

If (Cardozo's) suggestion held true ... then one would have to settle down to an inquiry *into how a bar came to be appealing that ninety per cent of cases*. One could account for some as desperate chance appeals where the stake was high; for some as bitter-ender appeals where the grudge bit deep; for some as boob-appeals because some lawyers are incompetent; for some as booby-trap appeals because the clients were being taken for extra fees; for some as vexation appeals by a defendant to gain delay or by a plaintiff to work a settlement on nuisance value. Stretching all the cynicism I can muster, I still find it hopelessly insufficient to make such groupings over nine appeals out of ten foredoomed as assumed. I see no choice but to turn for an explanation to some unclarity in the rules as effectively showing the heterogeneous mortals who wear black robes upon the bench just what, irrespective of their personality, they are supposed to do with cases as cases arise.[175]

This theme is not pursued in *The Common Law Tradition*. Nor is there extended discussion of the relationship of the work of state appellate courts to the work of all courts and to the total picture of dispute settlement in general. It is taken for granted that state appellate courts occupy a key position in this total picture. It would not have been a work of supererogation to have tried to place this specialized case study of the juristic method of a particular type of tribunal in a broad context; at the very least setting the study in perspective would have allayed any lingering suspicion that Llewellyn himself had become a victim of the danger which he had characterized as the threat of the available. It would also have helped to make clear the relation of this specialized study to his general theory of law-and-government. Furthermore, it will be suggested later, it would have disposed more satisfactorily of the alleged crisis of confidence than his attempts to show that the Grand Style promotes reckonability.

Was Llewellyn's mode of analysis of judicial opinions adequate for his purposes? Llewellyn claimed that he read his samples of opinions in much the same way as historical documents are read by historians.[176] He reported at considerable length on his findings. Although the pages are enlivened by frequent incidental observations, he concentrated for the most part on indicia of the Grand Style and the Formal Style and on the precedent techniques that were being used by the courts. In fact in analysing the cases he was concerned with a rather limited range of variables; he did not, for instance, consistently have regard to factors relating to the socio-economic status of the judges or the parties, or some of the other factors that have been given prominence in jurimetric analysis. He made no attempt to quantify his findings and only spasmodically doffed his cap to systematic social science techniques. Nor did he always distinguish very closely between data and interpretation. A first condition of objective analysis is the establishment of precise categories with criteria of identification which eliminate personal judgment except in border-line cases. The limitations of 'Grand Style', 'situation sense' and other central concepts in Llewellyn's analysis have already been explored. When Llewellyn reads through twelve cases from Massachusetts and reports that he finds clear use of situation sense in at least six of them, an element of trust on the part of the reader is still demanded even though Llewellyn gives a brief paragraph to each case.[177] A student who goes off to read the same run of cases before he reads Llewellyn's interpretation may well arrive at the same conclusion, but it is by no means certain that he will. Indeed, the reader is sometimes left with a nagging suspicion that the vagueness of the indicia of the Grand Style and Formal Style allowed Llewellyn's subjective preferences to creep into his analysis.

Thus despite the enormous labour put into his treatment of his samples of cases, Llewellyn's method seems somewhat casual and impressionistic. He is more at ease, indeed more illuminating, when he starts 'to wander with you for a bit in a more leisurely fashion ... and smoke a pipe or two among phases of our Style of Reason at Work'.[178] Llewellyn's principal hypotheses—that there is a renaissance of the Grand Style and that there is a wide range of precedent techniques—are so vague that a systematic method of analysis was not necessary to support them.[179]

The renaissance of the Grand Style: Llewellyn claimed only to have found the Grand Style predominating in four contexts: in Roman law of the classical period, among the Cheyennes, in the United States in the early nineteenth century and again in the United States from about 1940.[180] The Formal Style, on the other hand, was particularly marked in the period from 1870 until 1940. Thus in this interpretation American state appellate courts between 1800 and 1950 went through a cycle of Grand Style dominance followed, after a gap, by the Formal Style which was replaced again by a gradual resurgence of the Grand Style. In respect of the first period Llewellyn's interpretation accords with Pound's account of 'the formative era' of American law.[181] There also seems to be a widely held view that the state courts generally seemed formalistic and slow to respond to the changes associated with the industrial and technological revolution that swept America at the turn of the century.[182] However, Llewellyn's periods are so broad, and the concept of a predominating period style is so vague, that it is impossible to evaluate this sweeping interpretation of American judicial history. Detailed historical research might well reveal a more complex picture.

Llewellyn, of course, adduced extensive evidence of a widespread renaissance of the Grand Style. *Prima facie* this evidence is convincing. However, the extent of the spread is not precisely assessed; moreover, a number of individuals have expressed scepticism about the matter. Wetter, for instance, found evidence of judicial decadence;[183] Mermin has doubts about the applicability of the thesis to Wisconsin;[184] MacNeil suggests that the Grand Style may have been more marked in some fields (like labour law and constitutional law) than in others: 'If you drove your weary way through the opinions of the New York Court of Appeals on contract cases, or almost any court on cases involving the parole evidence rule, you would find that the formal style flourishes like ragweed.'[185] Breitel and others have voiced similar doubts which could only be resolved by careful testing of hypotheses more detailed and precise than Llewellyn's.[186]

A seemingly important part of Llewellyn's thesis is the proposition that when the Grand Style predominates prediction is easier. However, this claim is carefully circumscribed. The Grand Style is listed as only one of fourteen *major* steadying factors which combine to promote reckonability. The standard is the reckonability of 'a reasonable, sometimes a very good, business risk',[187] well short of complete 'certainty'. It is the outcome of the case which is being predicted, not the grounds for the decision.[188] The base line for prediction is when the trial is over, pending appeal; by this time the facts are settled, the appellate court, the issues, the opposition, etc. are known.[189] In short, the claim is little more than that the Grand Style is one of the factors which offer guidance to the counsellor as to the advisability of pressing an appeal.

Llewellyn did not try to test the claim empirically, but he did give some reasons in support of it:

... first, the Grand Style is the best device ever invented by man for drying up that free-flowing spring of uncertainty, conflict between the seeming commands of the authorities and the felt demands of justice. Second, when a frozen text happens to be the crux, to insist that an acceptable answer shall satisfy the reason *as well as* the language is not only to escape much occasion for divergence, but to radically reduce the degree thereof. ...[190] Third, the future-directed quest for ever better formulations for guidance, which is inherent in the Grand Style, means the on-going production and improvement of rules which make sense on their face, and which can be understood and reasonably well applied even by mediocre men. *Such* rules have a fair chance to get the same results out of very different judges, and so in truth to hit close to the ancient target of 'laws and not men'.[191]

Such assertions apart, Llewellyn based the claim on two arguments, which may be termed respectively the *a priori* argument and the *ex post facto* argument. The *a priori* argument can be restated as follows: a case is not worth appealing (or contesting on appeal) unless there is a doubt about the law. A doubt about what the law is cannot be resolved by the authorities alone.[192] Accordingly it can only be resolved by resort to other considerations, such as justice, policy, and situation sense. In a Grand Style justification such other factors are openly discussed; in a Formal Style justification they are not; instead there is merely a pretence that the doubt is resolved by the authorities. Accordingly the Grand Style provides a more reliable basis for prediction because it gives a more complete account of the factors actually influencing decision than does the Formal Style. Furthermore, when such factors are treated openly they are likely to influence decisions in a more regular manner ('covert tools are unreliable tools').[193]

Except, perhaps, for the last sentence, which is speculative, the reasoning seems valid, subject to two important caveats. First, the argument assumes that the existence of a legal doubt is a constant. This is a questionable assumption, for people can disagree as to whether or not there is a doubt. For instance, it is not uncommon to find one party maintaining that the meaning of a statute is clear, while his opponent contends the opposite. Such disagreements are difficult to resolve as there is no clear consensus about the answer to the question: 'Under what circumstances is it true to say that a legal doubt exists?' One possible answer is that a legal doubt exists when lawyers in fact disagree as to what the applicable law is, but this is not very helpful since it is typically part of the job of lawyers to disagree when they are representing opposing parties. Alternatively one can say that a legal doubt exists when a technically good case can be advanced by each side. This would seem to be Llewellyn's meaning, for it relates directly to his thesis concerning the leeways available in interpreting cases and statutes. But 'a technically good case' is a relative term, for clearly some arguments based on authority are stronger than others. For instance, in *Donoghue* v. *Stevenson* the weight of precedent clearly favoured the original defendants (the manufacturers); in justifying their decision in favour of the original plaintiff Lord Atkin and his colleagues concentrated a major part of their efforts on establishing a legal doubt by explaining away authorities and showing that they did not *necessarily* support the defence. The persuasiveness of their justification in its positive aspects derives mainly from arguments appealing to situation sense and justice, rather tenuously backed by authority. In short *Donoghue* v. *Stevenson* can be seen as the victory of a possible but weak technical case, backed by 'non-legal' factors, over a relatively strong technical case.

Once it is recognized that the existence of a legal doubt can itself be a matter of controversy, the scope of the *a priori* argument is reduced. For the difference between the Grand Style and the Formal Style is no longer seen to be solely as a difference in the manner of justification of decisions in which all are agreed that there was a legal doubt. A Grand Style judge, because he is more responsive to non-legal factors, may be more likely to argue that there is a legal doubt than a Formal Style judge. Thus a major part of Lord Atkin's achievement in *Donoghue* v. *Stevenson* was that he was prepared to respond to a challenge to what had previously been regarded as well-settled law by the great majority of the legal profession. The achievement of the plaintiff's lawyers was to *establish* the doubt as much as to resolve it. The *a priori* argument does not apply to such cases; indeed, one may ask whether it can seriously be contended that Lord Atkin's conclusion in *Donoghue* v. *Stevenson* was more predictable than Lord Buckmaster's or, in general terms, whether the behaviour of judges known to be bold is more or less predictable than those who are known to be timorous souls.[194] The *a priori* argument begs such questions.

The second caveat to the *a priori* argument may be even more important. The argument, as stated above, only relates to the conclusion that the Grand Style promotes reckonability in respect of *cases worth appealing*.[195] Indeed, in at least one passage Llewellyn seems to admit that in less puzzling cases a Formal Style court may, 'by giving the more familiar an edge up on the wise', possibly behave more predictably than a Grand Style court.[196] Since Llewellyn took the view that probably only between 10 per cent and 30 per cent of cases in fact appealed were worth appealing, the *a priori* argument refers to a minority of cases coming before appellate courts, and these by their nature the least predictable. Presumably in respect of cases clearly not worth appealing the style of the court would make little or no difference to the predictability of the outcome. In cases marginally worth appealing, Llewellyn conceded that the Formal Style might promote predictability at the expense of wisdom.[197]

This caveat is important when considered in relation to the crisis of confidence. To show that it was unjustified, Llewellyn's strongest point (though unproven and understressed) should have been that the great majority of appeals are doomed *irrespective of whether the court employs the Grand Style or the Formal Style.* If the two caveats are taken together it appears that the argument that the Grand Style promotes reckonability (itself less than certainty) only applies to a small minority of cases taken on appeal and so is of marginal relevance to the crisis of confidence in so far as that is based on a feeling that the behaviour of appellate courts is unpredictable.

These caveats are of particular significance in relation to one of the standard criticisms of legal realism, *viz.* that the rule sceptics exaggerated the ambiguity of legal rules and the range of creative choice open to judges, because they failed to stress that most rules have 'a central core of habitually established content surrounded by a penumbra of doubtful cases'.[198] Such criticism, echoed by Hart, Cardozo and others, does not apply to Llewellyn, because he was not talking about rules in all contexts but about rules in the context of appellate cases worth appealing.[199] There is a certain irony in the fact that Llewellyn, along with other realists, was regularly accused of laying too much stress on uncertainty in law, whereas the thrust of his argument in *The Common Law Tradition* was that even in the most doubtful cases reasonable reckonability is attainable.

The *ex post facto* argument: Llewellyn did not claim that his samples of cases provided direct evidence of the proposition that the Grand Style promotes reckonability. But he did maintain that Grand Style decisions tend to generate after the event recognition of the rightness, sometimes even of the inevitability, of the result.[200] Talk of 'recognition' in such circumstances and of the 'wisdom of hindsight' stirs a responsive chord in many people. Such talk is not nonsensical, for it is rooted in experience; but the psychological state may be more complex than the language suggests. Llewellyn argued that the orthodox demand for certainty in law was often a disguised demand for this kind of *ex post facto* recognition:

What is then needed is men – a bench – right-minded, learned, careful, wise, to find and voice from among the still fluid materials of the legal sun the answer which will satisfy, and which will render semisolid one more point, as a basis for a further growth. And the *certainty* in question is that certainty *after the event* which makes ordinary men and lawyers *recognize as soon as they see the result* that however hard it has been to reach, it is the right result. Then men feel that it has *therefore* really been close to inevitable.[201]

A *feeling* after the event that a decision was 'inevitable' because it is felt to be right has no necessary connection in logic or in fact with the claim that the decision was predictable in advance. Accordingly it is by no means clear that Llewellyn convincingly proved his optimistic contention that 'satisfying' decisions are more predictable than others. Julius Cohen makes the point:

And what of Llewellyn's claims of predictability? His hypothesis that such 'sense' is a predictable judicial phenomenon in leeway situations seemingly would have had greater weight had he posed the problem of 'sense' to lawmen *before* the judicial decisions, and tested the accuracy of their reactions later against the finished decisional product. How many lawmen, for example, would have sensed the 'good sense' of *Palsgraf* before the case was decided, and could have predicted its outcome at that time? Llewellyn's experiment in intersubjective reactions was not structured to account for this time variable. Instead, it attempts to assess *now* on the basis of the bias and conditioning of *hindsight*. Better than this for a testing of this hypothesis would have been an insistence on the freshness of *foresight*.[102]

The crux of the matter is that the *ex post facto* argument is best treated as not being an argument about prediction at all. It essentially involves the assertion that the Grand Style is more likely to satisfy people's feelings as to what is just and appropriate than the Formal Style, both in respect of results and of their justification.[203] Interpreted thus, it has a direct bearing on the crisis of confidence, in that confidence in the courts rests at least as much on their keeping reasonably in step with public and professional opinion as on the predictability of their behaviour. Moreover, it is reasonable to infer from many passages that Llewellyn's enthusiasm for the Grand Style was only marginally related to the proposition that it might increase reckonability. This was, as it were, a bonus. Thus a close examination of *The Common Law Tradition* suggests that it has rather less to say about prediction than at first sight appears.

The descriptive thesis: conclusion

The descriptive thesis may have provided a convenient peg on which to hang a number of general ideas about judicial processes, but the thesis itself does not carry conviction. The crisis of confidence is merely asserted to exist and is not very carefully diagnosed; the discussion of the steadying factors is not confined to American state appellate courts in the 1950s, and is based on common sense impressions rather than evidence; neither the renaissance of the Grand

Style nor the propensity of the Grand Style to promote predictability is established beyond reasonable doubt. Moreover, even if the descriptive thesis is accepted as proven, its conclusions are too vague to be of much value. Fortunately, the significance of *The Common Law Tradition* is only marginally dependent on the validity of the descriptive thesis. The detailed analysis of hundreds of cases may be of limited value as evidence, but it does provide some admirably concrete illustration and explanation of some rather elusive ideas. It is in these ideas rather than in the historical conclusions that the chief value of the book lies, and concreteness of illustration is one of its cardinal virtues.

THE PRESCRIPTIVE THESIS

The prescriptive thesis is concerned essentially with method and consists largely of advice to all those connected with appellate court work on how to approach their respective tasks. The basic prescription is 'adopt the Grand Style'. Llewellyn spells out the implications of this for the judge, the advocate, the counsellor and the scholar in the form of advice of varying length, concreteness and style. The scholar is only directly addressed in one section of nine pages and in a few asides;[204] the counsellor is accorded little more than three pages:[205] the advice to appellate advocates is summed up in twelve precepts, a twenty page nutshell of 'The ABC's of appellate argument',[206] the judiciary is counselled less peremptorily in nearly one hundred and fifty pages of 'conclusions for courts', a discursive review of more than twenty loosely related topics.[207]

To some extent these differences reflect the relative importance of the various participants in achieving the goals of right decision and wise law-making; moreover the roles of these various functionaries overlap without being co-extensive. Their viewpoints may be different, but they are involved in a single process. Although Llewellyn did not spell it out in a systematic manner, it is not difficult to piece together his conceptions of the various roles and their interrelationships. The appellate judge has a dual duty: the duty to decide the particular dispute in accordance with law and justice and the duty to contribute to the development of the law.[208] This latter duty is done principally through his reasoned *justification* for his decision. The advocate also has a dual duty: to advance his client's case, but only in so far as this is consistent with his duty to

truth and justice and the ethics of his profession. His main task is
persuasion.[209] The roles of judge and advocate overlap in so far as
what constitute good reasons for the purpose of persuasion should
also constitute good reasons for the purpose of justification. A good
brief should be almost identical in substance with a good opinion,
although certain practical exigencies may demand some differences
in style of presentation. Llewellyn even advises advocates to include
in their written brief a carefully phrased passage which may be
adopted by the court as its own:

If a brief has made the case for what is right, and has made clear the reason
of the rightness, and has found and tailored and displayed the garment of
law to clothe the right decision fittingly, then it is not only unwise but
indecent not to furnish also in that brief a page or two of text which gathers
this all together, which clears up its relation to the law to date, which puts
into clean words the soundly guiding rule to serve the future, and which
shows that rule's happy application to the case in hand. What is wanted is a
passage which can be quoted verbatim by the court, a passage which so
clearly and rightly states and crystallizes the background and the result that
it is *recognized* on sight as doing the needed work and as practically demanding to be lifted into the opinion.[210]

Just as the roles of advocate and judge coincide without being co-
extensive, so too do the roles of advocate and counsellor. One such
overlap concerns prediction. It is necessary here to distinguish
between prediction of outcome and prediction of other matters.
Typically an appellate judge is not concerned with prediction of
outcome: it borders on the ridiculous to talk of predicting one's own
decisions; and the judge is only marginally concerned with predicting the decisions of other tribunals, except perhaps in respect of the
possibility of reversal on appeal. It may be that appellate judges
should be concerned with possible consequences of their decisions
on the behaviour of people concerned, and even of possible consequences of advancing a particular justification,[211] but it is fair to
say that prediction is not central to the role of judging. Similarly
an advocate, acting as advocate, is not primarily concerned with
predicting the outcome of the case he is arguing. His principal function is persuasion.[212] However, as Llewellyn continually emphasized, the advocate is trying to persuade a particular tribunal. Accordingly he has to predict the likely response of each of its members to
any particular line of argument. Where the facts and the issues are
settled and the composition of the court is known, he has a much

more concrete basis for making predictions than the counsellor advising at an earlier stage in litigation or in the rather different situation of drafting a document or giving 'preventive' advice of some other kind.

Prediction is central to the role of the counsellor, but his circumstances are different from those of the advocate:

He is not like the person pressing for legislation, who must often push out to the limit of the feasible and risk pushing beyond; in that area you get what you can get while the legislative getting is good. In sharp contrast, office-counsel can in all but rare circumstances play well inside any penumbra of doubt; he can work, like an engineer, with a substantial margin of safety; he can chart a course which leaves to others the shoal waters and the treacherous channels. For unlike the ordinary advocate, the counselor need not take the situation as it comes, but can shape and shore it in advance; he can draft documents and set up lasting records against the accidents of memory, death, or disappearance of witnesses, even to some extent against the hazard of bad faith – doubly so if he keeps his protective drafting within those bounds of reason which make a court want to give effect to manifest intent; trebly so if he sets a picture of situation and purpose which can appeal even to an outsider as sensible, reasonable, and inherently probable – and it is comforting how much of this last can be gotten by careful counsel into documentary form. Besides (or perhaps first), office-counsel are in peculiarly good position to study and discriminate among rules and rulings with reference to how strong and solid any of them is, how much weight it will carry, how far the relevant type-situation is already at home in judicial understanding or is of a character to find a ready welcome. After such discrimination, it is on the rocklike law-stuff that the sane counselor does his building. Finally, wherever advising counsel can rely on being able to control any relevant litigation, another vital contingency is set to dwindling.[213]

Llewellyn dealt rather cursorily with the role of the scholar.[214] In respect of appellate courts he saw his distinctive role as that of systematization. He is 'today's appointed apostle of order in legal doctrine'.[215] As such he is the natural ally of the judge in his role of improving and bringing order and clarity to the law.[216] In this capacity both are concerned with a broader perspective than the advocate or the counsellor, tied to the immediate interests of individual clients. Thus the judge has a focal position, as he alone is regularly concerned with the particular and the general simultaneously.

This in outline is Llewellyn's picture of the interrelated roles of the main functionaries concerned with the appellate judicial process.

Although in general his ideas reflect the relative importance of the various parties, his treatment of them is uneven and less than systematic. The advice to counsellors and scholars is cursory and some relevant parties, notably the legislator, are given no direct guidance. Nearly all of the detailed advice is directed to advocates and judges.

Appellate advocacy—'The art of making prophecy come true'
Llewellyn summarized the implications for advocates of the theory of the Grand Style under twelve heads. These represented a distillation of years of thought, matured principally through his courses on legal argument.[217] In *The Common Law Tradition* he confined himself to what he considered to be basic—'the ABC's of appellate argument'. What follows is an epitome of an epitome. The starting-point is to study the relevant court: 'The target is the particular tribunal'.[218] If the court or its composition is unknown an appeal is more risky, which should influence the decision whether or not to appeal.[219] A technically good case 'in law' is not enough to win a case worth appealing, but a technically good case is necessary.[220] Any technically good case presupposes some classification of the facts; the manner of presentation of the facts is crucial as a vehicle for catching interest, posing the issue favourably, and for laying the basis for a coherent, concentrated argument: 'the statement of facts is the heart':

> It is trite, among good advocates, that the statement of the facts can, and should, in the very process of statement, frame the legal issue, and can, and should, simultaneously produce the conviction that there is only one sound outcome.[221]

The facts should be presented as an example of a type, as a simple pattern, with the sense of the type-situation taking priority over 'fire-side equities'.[222]

The crux of the matter, according to Llewellyn, is to make arguments from sense, justice and the law combine to support the same conclusion:

> The real and vital central job is to satisfy the court that sense and decency and justice require (a) the rule which you contend for in this *type* of situation; and (b) the result that you contend for, as between these parties. *You* must make your whole case, on law and facts, make *sense*, appeal as being *obvious* sense, inescapable sense, sense in simple terms of life and justice. If that is done, the technically sound case on the law then gets rid of all further

difficulty: it shows the court that its duty to the Law not only does not conflict with its duty to Justice but urges to decision along the exact same line.[228]

One concern, only touched on casually in *The Common Law Tradition* but frequently discussed by Llewellyn in other contexts, was what he termed 'the ethics of argument'.[224] Lawyers are familiar with the potential conflict between an advocate's duty to his client and his duty to truth and justice, epitomized by his status as 'an officer of the court'. In the United States canons of professional ethics and conventions of etiquette tend to be either silent or vague on the limits of decency in argument, to use Llewellyn's term. He had definite personal views which often went beyond and sometimes conflicted with the A.B.A. Canons of Ethics.[225] He summarized his overall position as follows :

(1) all law and all the works of law and of lawyers have a single dominant function: the pursuit of Justice; and

(2) that in view of the fact that law is administered by men, who must be *persuaded*, if they are to further Justice by their administering, it becomes legitimate, proper, necessary, laudable, *in a proper cause*, for the advocate to resort to sophistry gross or insidious, and to evocation of emotion or prejudice, to get the result; but

(3) that he will indulge either dishonest thinking, or the building of a case on passion, at risk of his own soul.[226]

Although Llewellyn concluded that the matter was primarily one for the conscience of the individual advocate, he was quite specific in his approval or disapproval of certain practices. To an English lawyer he would appear to push the limits of decency rather far and to be prepared to condone rather too readily the uninhibited pressing of a client's cause, if the cause is considered to be just:

It is, for instance, indecent (to my mind) to miscite a case to the court. I have little ethical quarrel, *in a good cause*, with omitting citations. . . . Again, it is to my mind indecent to distract a jury's attention from the argument being made by one's opponent, when that argument is fair. It is indecent to misquote the record. It is indecent to offer testimony known to be perjured.[227]

Even on this latter point he was prepared to enter some controversial caveats.

Llewellyn's treatment of the ethics of advocacy may help to clarify one minor puzzlement about *The Common Law Tradition*. This is the distinction between legitimate and illegitimate precedent tech-

niques.[228] It will be recalled that in discussing the leeways of
precedent Llewellyn listed a selection of sixty-four different techniques he had collected from actual cases. Most of these he stated to
be 'legitimate' or 'impeccable', a few he branded as 'illegitimate'. Just
as the Canons of Ethics tend to be vague on questions of the limits
of decency in argument, so the doctrine of precedent provides very
little precise guidance on the legitimacy of particular precedent
techniques. Llewellyn points out that the use of techniques is
controlled by the prevailing craft tradition,[229] but his own demonstration of the variety and flexibility of actual practice supports the
view that there is scope for differing opinions about the 'legitimacy'
of this or that technique. Whereas Llewellyn emphasized that his
judgments on the decency or otherwise of particular tactics in
advocacy represented merely his own personal opinion, he was less
explicit about his confident labelling of particular precedent techniques as legitimate or illegitimate. Yet it would seem that the latter
is just as much a matter of personal opinion, no more, no less, than
the former. To have made this clear would not have invalidated
Llewellyn's thesis and might have eliminated a source of potential
misunderstanding.

In *The Common Law Tradition* Llewellyn outlined a working
theory for appellate advocacy. He was not attempting to write a
how-to-do-it manual. His advice differs from that to be found in
such manuals not so much in its conclusions as in its foundations.[230]
In lieu of an anthology of unrelated do's and don'ts garnered
principally from 'experience', he makes suggestions for an integrated
approach based on his conception of the Grand Style. Llewellyn's
advice is quite specific, but it is also clearly related to a general
theory and this makes for both consistency and simplicity. Thus
'situation sense' provides a theoretical base for the precept that 'the
statement of facts is the heart,[231] similarly the 'principle of concentration of fire' is directly related to the idea of harmonizing law and
justice in the Grand Manner;[232] so too with other specific, mundane
precepts.

Llewellyn's treatment of legal argument thus provides a suitable
testing ground for the general claim that his approach fostered the
integration of theory and practice. In this context the claim rests on
two principal ideas: first, that command of a skill presupposes
understanding of the context of the exercise of the skill—in the
case of advocacy this would include understanding of the nature of

the arena and the process involved, and of the raw materials, (such as the sources of law), on which the skill is to be exercised. Secondly, that what constitutes good advocacy is to some extent susceptible of analysis and articulation; it is not solely a matter of intuition, innate flair and art picked up or developed ineffably through experience. In other words skill presupposes understanding and is teachable beyond the point of a few rules of thumb.

It is suggested that the value of Llewellyn's working theory of appellate advocacy depends on the answers to three questions: is the advice sound? Is it usable? Is it likely to lead to better advocacy (does it add anything?)? The author is neither a practising advocate nor an American and is not in a position to attempt to give a full answer to these questions. However, some preliminary observations may be advanced. As to soundness: Llewellyn purported to derive his ideas in part from analysis of the practice of advocates he particularly admired.[233] What constitutes excellence in advocacy is to some extent a matter of opinion, but Llewellyn's selection of 'great advocates' represents a widely shared view. A theory based on analysis of admired practice is less likely to be 'unsound' than an *a priori* theory, provided the analysis is valid. Secondly, in content Llewellyn's advice does not differ fundamentally from that to be found in leading American handbooks on advocacy, such as Wiener's *Effective Appellate Advocacy*.[234] Thirdly, experienced practitioners who reviewed *The Common Law Tradition* appear for the most part to have approved Llewellyn's ideas, some with marked enthusiasm.[235] These points suggest that a *prima facie* case can be made for the soundness of Llewellyn's advice.

The next questions cannot be answered so confidently. Llewellyn's claims are modest. He emphasized that his advice was elementary and incomplete. His concern was to communicate, to 'a wide variety of lesser men', what the leaders of the profession already know, even if they have failed to articulate it.[236] On the whole, the advice, although general, is quite capable of application. It is not vulnerable to a common charge of men of affairs against theory, *viz.* that it is too vague to be useful. Without research of a rather difficult kind one can only conjecture about the claim that formal teaching of advocacy or provision of an articulate working theory is likely to make a significant difference to standards of advocacy. Like most other contemporary teaching it remains largely a matter of faith.[237]

At the very least it can be argued that this claim is as plausible as most other claims made for law teaching.

Conclusions for courts

Whereas his advice to advocates is reduced to a few elementary propositions, Llewellyn's 'conclusions for courts' are discursive and defy summary. A general injunction to the judiciary to be wise, upright, balanced and sensible sounds vapid when divorced from the mass of detailed illustration that accompanies it.[238] In *The Common Law Tradition* this advice is concretized in a variety of ways: through exploration of the concept of the Grand Style; through analysis of the methods of individual judges who are held up as models, such as Mansfield, Cardozo, Rutledge, Cowen and Hough;[239] and through consideration of a variety of specific topics, from prospective overruling to the uses of law clerks and amicus briefs. The gist of Llewellyn's general advice to judges has already been considered in the sections on 'style' and 'situation sense'. His opinions on the various topics he deals with are interesting, but they are for the most part less directly connected with his general theory than is his advice to advocates; they do not need a commentary and there is no substitute for reading them in the original.

Comparative analysis of judicial opinions

Although not explicitly part of the prescriptive thesis, another application of *The Common Law Tradition* deserves attention.

Llewellyn used to set exercises in elementary analysis of style as part of his jurisprudence course in Chicago. Typically each student had to select at random three volumes of law reports from one jurisdiction (normally the student's home state) representing three different periods in the previous 150 years. He was required to read in each volume the first 100–150 pages of judgments of the same court and to ask himself to what extent a distinctive style was discernible for the period. I remember this as one of the most illuminating exercises I was ever set to do as a student, despite the vagueness of our instructions. Certain differences between the phenomena to be compared were so obvious and so striking that no refined apparatus of analysis was necessary for the principal lesson to be learned. This lesson was that there is more than one way of reading the law reports, and that if one approaches them in the manner of a historian reading historical documents (and this clearly allows for a variety of approaches), one can learn a great deal about the courts as institutions and about the enormous variety that is discernible in respect of numerous variables. Even in the course of this elementary exercise a whole range of lines of enquiry suddenly became apparent; for instance: questions about the nature and value of the cases coming to that court; questions about the characteristics of the parties and their representatives; questions about the education, careers, attitudes, and role conceptions of the judges; questions about the extent and nature of the authoritative source material thought to be relevant;[240] questions about the techniques employed in handling the material; and questions about more elusive matters, such as one's impressions of the fairness and impartiality and soundness of the personnel of the court. Much of this is elementary and obvious. Yet, and this was the crux of the matter, such questions were touched on interstitially and unsystematically, if at all, in the standard discussions of 'precedent', 'case law' and 'the judicial process'. If they were obvious, they had often been neglected.

The first attempt to develop this kind of stylistic analysis in a systematic manner was undertaken at Chicago by a Swedish doctoral student, J. Gillis Wetter, with Llewellyn and Rheinstein as his supervisors. Wetter's research culminated in a book, *The Styles of Appellate Judicial Opinions, A Case Study in Comparative Law*, published in 1960.[241] Wetter expounded a general theory of styles, largely based on the intensive analysis of just under forty cases, selected from Sweden, Germany, Arkansas, California, England, Canada and France. The opinions are quoted in full in their original language, except that those from Sweden have been translated into English. Thus, independently of the exposition and commentary, the book serves as a convenient anthology of opinions from six jurisdictions. Although the sample cannot be claimed as representative, it provides a striking illustration of the variety of judicial styles. The style of Wetter's own contribution is also unusual—not least in its attempt to work Llewellyn's inspiration into a formalized general theory in the continental manner.[242]

Wetter's book, as he himself emphasizes, only marks a modest start.[243] The possible field of enquiry is extensive, at least encompassing all courts from which reportable opinions emanate. Comparison may be made between different courts within a single jurisdiction and between courts in different jurisdictions; where there is a practice of signed opinions,[244] comparison may be made

between the styles of individual judges. Similarities and differences
may be explored in relation to a wide range of characteristics. The
search for explanations of similarities and differences may be a route
to profound insights about the nature of judicial processes and of
courts as institutions.

APPRAISAL

When *The Common Law Tradition* was first published in America
it attracted what was probably unprecedented attention for a work
of jurisprudence; yet not one review appeared in a British legal
periodical. The American reviewers were almost unanimous in their
enthusiasm. Some of the praise can be discounted as loyal and
gracious eulogy, substituting for a *festschrift*; some detractors may
have remained tactfully silent. However, most of the praise seems to
have been genuine. There were only three weighty dissents: Philip
Kurland, a colleague of Llewellyn's at Chicago, published a mock-
ing review that was witty, hurtful and unspecific.[245] Mark de Wolfe
Howe penned a scathing attack, stemming largely from aesthetic
disdain for the prose style; this was to have appeared in a
symposium, but Howe withdrew it on learning of Lewellyn's death
in February 1962.[246] The most fully argued critique came from a
close friend, Charles E. Clark, who in collaboration with David
Trubeck maintained that Llewellyn had betrayed the cause of
legal scepticism by under-emphasizing the part played by personal
or subjective factors in judicial decision-making.[247] The great
majority of reviewers confined themselves to relatively minor doubts
and criticisms, while hailing the book as a major contribution to
jurisprudence.

Nevertheless, reading between the lines of the reviews, one can
sense an undercurrent of disappointment. This is confirmed by
numerous informal discussions with American law teachers and by
the modified rapture of discussions of *The Common Law Tradition*
which were published after the first rush of enthusiastic reviews.[248]
Ten years after its first publication one gains the impression of a
fairly widespread consensus among Karlophiles: a major work,
but by no means the masterpiece that Llewellyn had hoped it would
be.

If this judgment is sound, it verges on the tragic. Of all Llewellyn's
books *The Common Law Tradition* involved the greatest investment

of time, effort and emotion. It became a focal point for many of his ambitions at the end of his life. Some of its faults are probably attributable to this. *The Common Law Tradition* was to be his *magnum opus*; in it lay his best hopes for overdue appreciation of his contributions as a jurist; it was to be an epitome of his ideas on judicial processes, with little left out. It was to be both scholarly and useful, novel and sound. The hurtful stigma of the irresponsible iconoclast must be erased, so the work must be balanced and respectable; yet the essential validity of his early 'realism' must be affirmed.[249]

Llewellyn's anxiety is also apparent in his indecision about his readership. The principal addresses are ostensibly the bar, who need to have their faith restored in the appellate courts.[250] He protests, too often to carry conviction, that he is only concerned to articulate 'the neglected obvious', elementary and unrefined, so that what is intuitively grasped and acted on by the best lawyers may be made available to the second rate and to the beginner. The manner of presentation belies the claim. It is absurd to maintain that *The Common Law Tradition* is either elementary or easy. Few readers have found it so, despite the relative simplicity of the central thesis. How many practitioners can be expected to take seriously the contention that five hundred and sixty-five pages of jurisprudence is meant for them? Llewellyn's repeated disclaimers of refinement indicate that he was all too conscious of the critic looking over his shoulder; the specialist jurist on the look out for imprecision and for further realist 'howlers'; the sceptical fellow-scholar, requiring to be satisfied by the evidence; and the social scientist, suspicious of 'common sense' and of non-quantitative techniques.

The Common Law Tradition represents an enormous investment of work as well as of emotion. The variable effects of the investment are apparent in the structure and in the prose. Both are over-wrought, the prose has some redeeming features, the arrangement has few, if any. Discussion of method appears in the middle of presentation of evidence; that evidence is not collected together in one place, nor is analysis of the conceptual apparatus; at times the book looks more like an anthology of ideas and opinions than a single coherent whole. There is some unnecessary repetition. There is a marked unevenness in the treatment of similar topics.[251] In short, in respect of structure the book is undisciplined. This lack of discipline may be in part a function of over-anxiety to leave nothing unsaid and to provide copious documentation of the main argument. Between one-quarter and one-third of the book is taken up with 'evidence' and illustrative material. This gives an admirable concreteness, but it does not make for easy reading.

The book is further complicated by being made to revolve around the alleged crisis of confidence on the part of the bar; Llewellyn neither documents nor analyses this phenomenon. It has little bearing on the main thesis, except perhaps as a rhetorical device for catching interest by pinpointing a sharp contrast between the main conclusions (viz. there is a renaissance of the Grand Style) and a supposedly widely held belief. The principal themes of the book are not dependent on the beliefs or the morale of the bar at a particular moment of time. The purpose of making the book appear to pivot on the crisis was to catch the attention of practitioners and judges. Llewellyn's concern to identify with practitioners and judges may help to explain, if not to justify, this apparently perverse arrangement. One effect was to create a serious imbalance by making a transitory and ill-defined phenomenon the focal point of a work that was meant to be of lasting value and wide significance.

Another weakness of *The Common Law Tradition* is the eccentric methodology; judged by basic social science criteria it falls short of accepted standards: the principal categories are elusive, the hypotheses are vague and are not clearly expressed in verifiable form, data are not consistently separated from interpretation, the sampling is idiosyncratic, and the findings are not presented in orderly fashion. While some of the principal conclusions about predictability are asserted rather than proved, the methods used to establish the renaissance of the Grand Style and the variety of precedent techniques may have been unnecessarily elaborate. It is not so much that failure to adopt suitable methods invalidates the most important conclusions as that those conclusions might easily have been much more precise and sophisticated if the conceptual apparatus had been more refined.

Llewellyn missed another important opportunity in that he failed to put this highly specialized study in its proper perspective. Although he emphasized that he was confining his attention to *American state appellate* courts, he did not make sufficiently clear that he was concentrating on a small proportion of the work of those courts, that is on *appellate cases worth appealing*. This may have misled some readers into exaggerating such matters as the range of the leeways or the importance of differences in judicial style or the significance of the saying that 'rules are not to control, but to guide decision'.[252] More fundamental is the point that by failing to put American state appellate decisions in the context of the total picture of dispute-settlement in American society, Llewellyn left unanswered the question: How socially significant is this type of institution? This is a strange lapse, for few juristic theories are better suited than the law-jobs theory for providing just this kind of perspective.

The Common Law Tradition is a warty giant, but it is a giant nonetheless. For many books it would mean consignment to oblivion if the judgment were accepted that its faults included bad organization, deficient methods, indecision concerning readership, and lack of perspective. *The Common Law Tradition* will survive such a judgment. It would do so even if it were to be shown that there was no crisis of confidence among the bar in the 1950s, nor any renaissance of the Grand Style, or that there is more to the view than Llewellyn allowed that the Formal Style promotes 'certainty'. The reason is simple. The basic perceptions and analysis of the book are sound and show ways to a more profound understanding of appellate judicial decision-making than any prior analysis. It contrasts sharply with the graceful simplicities of Cardozo on the one hand and the facile and shallow scientism of much jurimetric analysis on the other. The chief weaknesses are remediable: the terminology can be refined; more orderly techniques for analysing and comparing judicial opinions may be evolved; better methods for testing predictability have begun to be devised, and so on. The crux of the matter is that *The Common Law Tradition* is founded on a number of *aperçus*, some original, others neglected, which are of fundamental importance and which provide a starting-point for a wide range of potentially fruitful investigations: the steadying factors; the styles of judicial opinions; the range of techniques for interpreting cases and statutes; techniques of appellate advocacy and of other specialized roles; even the elusive 'situation sense' are among the ideas that could inspire valuable research. These are the more obvious ones related to the general argument; there are many other suggestive *obiter dicta* buried in the detailed analysis. Despite its faults, *The Common Law Tradition* promises to be a rich source of insight into judicial processes for many years to come.

The Genesis of the Uniform Commercial Code[1]

INTRODUCTION

The Uniform Commercial Code is the product of one of the most ambitious legislative ventures of modern times. *The 1962 Official Text with comments* fills a substantial volume of 731 pages. The Code contains over four hundred sections, divided into ten articles, and covers most, but not all, of the extensive field of commercial law.[2] Between July 1953 and July 1966 the Code was enacted in fifty-one jurisdictions. By the end of 1969 only one American State, Louisiana, had held back.

In its brief life the Code has generated a vast literature. There is a quarterly journal devoted entirely to it. A bibliography published in 1966 ran to 176 pages and listed over fourteen hundred items;[3] the compiler of the 1969 edition of the same bibliography noted that 'the past two years have produced over 500 law review articles as well as over 100 books and pamphlets devoted exclusively to the Code'.[4] This flood of literature shows no signs of abating.

Where so many experts have rushed in, an outsider is tempted to emulate the angels. However, in a study of Llewellyn the Uniform Commercial Code cannot be ignored: over a period of fifteen years (1937–52) he devoted a major part of his energies to it and his contribution represents one of his greatest achievements. The full story of his participation could well be the subject of a book in itself. The present study is concerned with Llewellyn's contributions to commercial law only in so far as they have a direct bearing on his juristic ideas. The reader must look elsewhere for a systematic examination of the Uniform Commercial Code as a commercial law

document[5] or for a blow-by-blow account of the conflicts that had to be resolved during the long process from original concep-
THE GENESIS OF THE UNIFORM COMMERCIAL CODE 271 sed on two related questions: first, what part did Llewellyn play in the code project? Second, what is the nature of the relationship between the finished product and Llewellyn's jurisprudential ideas?

Neither of these questions is susceptible of a simple, clearcut answer. The Uniform Commercial Code has been referred to as 'Llewellyn's Code',[7] 'Code Llewellyn',[8] 'Lex Llewellyn'[9] and, by one learned writer, as 'Karl's Kode'.[10] There is even rumour of references to a 'Llex Llewellyn'. Yet one of the claims most commonly advanced in favour of its adoption was that rarely, if ever, in legal history can so many lawyers and other interested parties have been actively involved in the preparation of a single legal instrument.[11] Soia Mentschikoff entitled an article: 'The Uniform Commercial Code: An Experiment in Democracy in Drafting';[12] as early as 1950 it was claimed that over a thousand lawyers and businessmen had participated in the project and thereafter the numbers continued to grow;[13] Llewellyn was always emphatic that even the preliminary drafts were products of teamwork and it will be seen that the idea of consensus was an important element in his approach. While there is no doubt that Llewellyn was easily the most important single figure, there were others whose contributions must be recognized, not least in the exertions of individual reporters such as Prosser, Bunn, Gilmore, Dunham and Mentschikoff. William A. Schnader, the President of the NCC and a former Attorney-General of Pennsylvania is sometimes referred to as 'the father of the Uniform Commercial Code' in recognition of the fact that the original idea was his and that he played a crucial role, especially in respect of promotion and enactment. Llewellyn's personal contribution cannot be assessed in isolation from the efforts of these and many other persons.

Since the Code was in large part a product of teamwork, it is not possible to delineate with precision the exact role of Llewellyn or any other leading participant. But it is possible to outline his share in general terms and to point to certain specific features of the Code which can fairly be attributed to him. At least in respect of such features it is also possible to examine the relationship between the Code and Llewellyn's general ideas. Here, too, there is a need for caution. The Code does not provide a simple example of the application of a general theory to a concrete problem. It is clear that the traditions of the sponsoring bodies, limitations of time and money, considerations of political expediency, the personalities of individual participants and, above all, the pragmatic tendencies of Llewellyn himself, are among the factors which complicate the picture and preclude any possibility of analysis solely in terms of the ideas of the Chief Reporter. But it is equally clear that these ideas were operative to a high degree and that some of the most striking features of the Code are to be explained in terms of them.

I propose to consider Llewellyn's relationship to the Code in two stages, first historically and then analytically. The remainder of the present chapter, then, is devoted to a brief historical account of the preparation of the Code and of Llewellyn's part in it. This provides a basis for answering in general terms the question : to what extent was this really Llewellyn's Code? In the next chapter some detail is added to this general overview, by considering analytically the relationship between a number of Llewellyn's general ideas and selected aspects of the Code.

THE NATIONAL CONFERENCE OF COMMISSIONERS ON UNIFORM STATE LAWS AND THE AMERICAN LAW INSTITUTE

The story of the Uniform Commercial Code has its roots in the history of two national institutions, the National Conference of Commissioners on Uniform State Laws and the American Law Institute.[14] Both of these came into being in response to the need for unification, simplification and betterment of law in the United States. The NCC was founded, largely on the initiative of the American Bar Association, in 1892. From the outset the conference consisted of unpaid commissioners appointed by the governors of the states: up to 1940 it had rarely met more than once a year and for the most part it had restricted its activities to preparing and promulgating acts which it recommended for adoption to the legislatures of the various states.[15] Over a long period of time it was conspicuously successful in securing the wide adoption of uniform statutes relating to commercial law, as is shown by the following table :[16]

Uniform Act	Promulgated	Number of States in 1958
Negotiable Instruments Law	1896	48
Uniform Sales Act	1906	34
Uniform Warehouse Receipts Act	1906	48
Uniform Stock Transfer Act	1909	48
Uniform Bills of Lading Act	1909	31
Uniform Conditional Sales Act	1918	10
Uniform Trust Receipts Act	1933	32

Although the widespread adoption of these statutes represents an impressive record of achievement by the National Conference, the table also provides evidence of some of the limitations of that body. Their successes were limited almost entirely to the commercial law field, and pioneering ventures such as the Uniform Act on Contribution Among Tortfeasors met with little support. Although by 1940 seven major uniform acts had over time been adopted by a substantial majority of American jurisdictions, in some cases by all of them, the process had been extremely slow and laborious. For instance, it had never taken less than ten years between the date of promulgation of an act and its adoption by a majority of the states; it took forty-seven years to secure the enactment in every jurisdiction of the Uniform Stock Transfer Act, promulgated in 1909; after fifty years only thirty-four states had enacted the Uniform Sales Act. Further difficulties arose when the conference proposed amendments. For example, although all jurisdictions enacted the Uniform Warehouse Receipts Act, even as late as 1958 only sixteen had adopted the amendments proposed by the conference in 1922.[17] Thus up to 1940 the conference had not satisfactorily resolved the problem of reconciling the need for uniformity with the need for continuous improvement and adaptation to changing conditions.

The American Law Institute has its origins in a project for a 'juristic centre for the betterment of the law' that was proposed by members of the Association of American Law Schools in 1921. An extremely distinguished committee of forty, under the chairmanship of Elihu Root, was established in 1921 and reported in 1922.[18] The report of the committee is over one hundred pages long and it contains what is still one of the best orthodox analyses of the major contending forces at work in promoting and fighting uncertainty, complexity and lack of uniformity in American law. The main recommendations of the committee were that the American

Law Institute should be set up and that its first major undertaking should be to prepare a 'Restatement of the Law'.

The *Restatement* is a curious hybrid, reflecting a mixture of influences. As the committee saw it, there were two chief defects in American law, uncertainty and complexity. The main sources of 'uncertainty' were seen to be lack of agreement on fundamental principles, lack of precision in the use of legal terms (an echo of Hohfeld),[19] conflicting and badly drawn statutory provisions, over-subtle distinguishing between precedents, the great volume of recorded decisions, the low standards of legal education of judges and lawyers, and the number of novel legal questions occasioned by social and economic development. The committee saw complexity as being partly inevitable, reflecting modern conditions, but partly due to the lack of systematic development of the law, to the un-necessary multiplication of administrative provisions and to the factors promoting lack of uniformity of law between jurisdictions. While paying tribute to the achievements of the National Confer-ence and expressing admiration for their methods, the committee sought a device which would enable them to bypass the multiplicity of state legislatures which had been the great stumbling-block as far as the NCC was concerned.

The committee considered that the first priority should be the reduction of uncertainty and complexity. Their preferred solution was a series of 'Restatements', which would set forth in clear and simple terms a statement of principles where the law was clear and offer a recommended solution where the law was unclear or lacking in uniformity. In order to achieve this aim the work would have to be the product of meticulous scholarship, tested by prolonged scrutiny and criticism by members of the bench and bar, for it would need to carry more weight as a persuasive authority than ordinary textbooks and encyclopaedias.

The *Restatement* form is a theoretical hybrid, glossing over the distinction between neutral exposition (description) of what the law is and statements of preference or recommendations as to what the law ought to be (prescription). One of the fundamental themes of realist jurisprudence is, of course, that the nature of authoritative legal materials is such that they do not always yield one correct answer as to what the law is, with the result that equating exposition of the law with a simple model of descriptions of the empirical world is misleading.[20] The *Restatement*, while based on meticulous analysis of the authorities, recommends solutions with relatively few inhibitions when the authorities do not speak with a single tongue. The method is that of interstitial development of the law by simplification and by expressing choices between competing alternatives.[21] Its value for practical purposes lies in its accessibility, its relative simplicity and its decisiveness. The two latter qualities reduce its value for the historian or for the theorist who is looking for a reliable contemporary 'description' of the state of the law at a particular moment of time, a quest which some would consider to be misconceived in any case.

The *Restatements* have also come under fire from other quarters. To the radical reformer they are over-cautious as instruments of legal development since they only attempt to change in the absence of a consensus, and restrict themselves to choosing between alternatives that have already been adopted somewhere. Although reasons are regularly given for preferring a particular solution, they are rarely of the kind that would satisfy the sociologically minded jurist or the advocate of systematic law reform. In short, the *Restatements* have been instruments of slow evolution rather than of a reformist approach.

A study of the first volume of *The Proceedings of the American Law Institute* makes it clear that the *Restatements* were always conceived as instruments for the betterment of the form, and to a lesser extent, the substance, of the law, a practical solution for a practical problem. It is hardly less clear why this particular instrument was invented for the purpose. Three main factors in combination virtually dictated the choice of some such solution: the first and overriding consideration was that the legislatures must be by-passed. The committee in its Report were circumspect in dealing with this matter and provided some comforting traditional reasons for not making statutes or codes their chosen instrument.[22] John W. Davis at the First Meeting of the Institute was more blunt: 'None of us here, I fancy, certainly none of those who are familiar with Congress or the forty-eight legislatures of our states, anticipate that this labor shall be committed to their charge.'[23] Secondly, the nature of the instrument was to some extent dictated by the class of men who would primarily be responsible for doing the work. The need was occasioned by failure of both the courts and the legislatures to act as instruments of unification and simplification. There had not been a single hierarchy of superior courts to act as a unifying agency for the common law and to provide a limited number of bodies on which to drape a doctrine of precedent. The result was that there was a multiplicity of courts of roughly cognate authority handing down literally thousands of decisions annually, so that by the end of the nineteenth century American lawyers were already drowning in a sea of decisions. It is a plausible hypothesis that in common law countries the opportunity for academic lawyers to have themselves accepted as authoritative 'sources' of law is greatest when there are either too few or too many precedents for the courts to rely on conveniently. In a developing legal system there may be so few that even an elementary local textbook which conjures doctrine out of the most variegated sources stands a good chance of being used for want of anything better; in the United States the courts must have thirsted for some simple escape from the labours of handling thousands of precedents. Where the legislatures are too many and the courts are overproductive, the bar, as always, being too busy, the academic lawyer gets his chance.

A third factor, it is suggested, was that the *Restatements* would have to generate their own authority and influence. They would be authoritative only to the extent that they would in fact be used by the legal profession and the courts. To this end any suggestion of utopian or radical reforms would need to be discounted. The acceptability of the *Restatement* would be enhanced by being primarily expository in form and style. Meticulous scholarship, bearing the stamp of approval of an institution with which the leaders of all branches of the profession would be associated, and with the element of reform minimized, would be its source of strength.[24] Prestige plus easiness to use form the basis of the *Restatement's* influence. Its semi-official character inevitably restricts the *Restatement's* effectiveness as an authoritative source of law. Where legislative enactment is feasible, it is still preferable. Although for a period the *Restatements* made more headway than the projects of the NCC, in recent years the difference has not been so marked and several important uniform laws have gained widespread acceptance. The most substantial of these, and the first in time, was the Uniform Commercial Code.

THE FEDERAL SALES BILL AND THE REVISED UNIFORM SALES ACT[25]

The creation of the Uniform Commercial Code represents one

phase in the history of the struggles of various national organizations with the intractable problems of unification, simplification and modernization of law in the United States. The project has its immediate roots in a number of attempts to remedy deficiencies in the Uniform Sales Act. This Act, for which Samuel Williston had been chiefly responsible, was modelled on Chalmers' Sale of Goods Act, 1893. It was adopted by the NCC in 1906 and by 1937 had been enacted in over thirty jurisdictions.[26] The first important impetus for revision came from the movement to introduce a federal sales act, applicable to inter-state and foreign transactions. In 1922 a committee of the American Bar Association produced a draft Federal Sales Bill which contained modifications of and additions to the Uniform Sales Act. Williston himself assisted in the preparation of this draft. This particular bill made little headway in Congress. In January 1937, Congressman Walter Chandler of Tennessee introduced a new bill,[27] in the House of Representatives. This bill followed the Uniform Sales Act very closely. Widespread interest was stimulated. The most significant response came from the Merchants' Association of New York, which set up a committee under the chairmanship of Hiram Thomas to study the bill. Their report, which was published in February 1937,[28] supported the introduction of a Federal Sales Act as an instrument of unification, but suggested some amendments which would lead to significant departures from the Uniform Sales Act. The bill was re-drafted in the light of this report. This embodied nearly all of the proposals of the Merchants Association and was introduced in Congress by Chandler in July 1937.[29] It was referred to the Committee on Interstate and Foreign Commerce, where it died. However, it was resuscitated two years later by Representative Herron Pearson of Tennessee.[30] In the interim there had been considerable activity. In 1937 the ABA had adopted a resolution urging the enactment of such a bill; in 1939 the AALS devoted a round table to the bill and this formed the basis of a symposium published in the March 1940 issue of the *Virginia Law Review*, to which Llewellyn contributed a paper.[31] There was a broad consensus in favour of the bill before Congress, but a number of detailed criticisms were voiced. Concurrently the Rome Institute for Unification of Private Law had been actively concerned with preparation of a Uniform Law on International Sale of Goods with which Llewellyn has been briefly associated in 1931–2. A second draft of this was published in 1939.

Naturally all of these activities were followed closely by Llewellyn. For nearly twenty years he had specialized in this area and he had for a long time been highly critical of the Uniform Sales Act. Chandler's first bill spurred him to action. He contacted Chandler and Thomas and a number of other individuals interested in reforming the law of sales. He found himself in substantial agreement with Thomas, except that he favoured rather more sweeping changes than they had proposed. He persuaded Thomas to try to work through the NCC, but when he first tried to stimulate the NCC into activity he ran into difficulties, for he found himself in a minority on the question of priorities between uniformity and reform. Llewellyn saw a Federal Sales Act as a means of promoting general reform of the law of sales. If Congress acted, it would be difficult for the states not to fall into line.[32] On the other hand, a majority of the Executive Committee of the NCC, including the President, William A. Schnader,[33] saw a Federal Sales Act which diverged from the Uniform Sales Act as a serious threat to uniformity. Furthermore, Schnader himself was a supporter of decentralized government and was suspicious of moves which might increase the influence of Congress over commercial law. In October 1937 the Conference on Uniform State Laws in its meeting in Kansas rejected a motion by Llewellyn that a committee should be set up to follow and co-operate with the preparation of a Federal Sales Bill. Instead, it resolved that the Federal Sales Act should conform as nearly as possible with the Uniform Sales Act. However, there was a good deal of sympathy with Llewellyn's ideas. At the same meeting it was decided to invite him to take over the chairmanship of the Commercial Acts section and Schnader indicated[34] that it was still open to him to pursue plans for reform of the Uniform Sales Act and that the defeat of his motion should not be treated as a matter of consequence.

THE CODE PROJECT: PLANNING AND PRELIMINARIES

In the long term the delay in the enactment of the Federal Sales Bill and the initial caution of the NCC were a blessing for Llewellyn. For after 1939 the initiative for pursuing the matter passed to the NCC and during the next stage, the preparation of a Revised Uniform Sales Act came to be treated as a pilot project for a much more ambitious matter, a comprehensive commercial code. It was

Schnader who was responsible for the transition. He had become President of the NCC after a period of relative inactivity by that body. He was one of a reform-minded group in the organization who were anxious to make it more effectual. The record of the NCC up to that time showed that the one area in which there had been a relatively consistent demand for uniformity had been commercial law. In September 1940, at the 50th Annual Meeting of the NCC in Philadelphia, Schnader in his Presidential Address took the opportunity to review generally the work of the conference and to put forward some ideas for its future activities. The first public suggestion for a comprehensive code was introduced briefly, almost casually, in this speech:

Our splendid commercial acts were prepared and adopted by this Conference many years ago. Many changes in methods of transacting business have taken place in the meanwhile.

In addition, they were adopted and recommended piecemeal. In a number of respects, there is overlapping and duplication, and in some instances, inconsistency, in dealing with negotiable instruments, bills of lading, warehouse receipts, stock transfers, sales and trust receipts.

Could not a great uniform commercial code be prepared, which would bring the commercial law up to date, and which could become the uniform law of our fifty-three jurisdictions, by the passage of only fifty-three acts, instead of many times that number?[35]

This statement marks the beginning of the public campaign for a code, but it had been anticipated by a great deal of preparatory work. Three memoranda by Llewellyn on plans for the code survive in his papers, all dated 1940 and preceding Schnader's speech to the conference.[36] They do not tell the whole story, but they clearly indicate that Llewellyn and Schnader were working closely together and were the two people most active in developing the idea at this stage. The original idea may have been Schnader's, but nearly all of the first detailed planning was done by Llewellyn. By the time of the first official announcement the general strategy in respect of objectives, scope and method had been worked out. Although this strategy changed over time, the basic conceptions survived for the most part and they represent some of the most important and visible aspects of Llewellyn's contribution.

In September 1940 a First Draft and Report on a Revised Uniform Sales Act was presented to the conference by the Commercial Acts section. This was principally the work of Llewellyn, who had worked intensively for five weeks on the draft during the summer. He had taken as his starting-point the second Federal Sales Bill and he had also found useful a study of this bill by a committee of the Association of the Bar of the City of New York;[37] but Llewellyn's draft constituted a complete re-working and contained a number of new proposals. After consideration of this draft by a Committee of the Whole, the Conference set up a reconstituted committee on a Revised Uniform Sales Act, with instructions to produce a Second Draft based on the first 'to be planned as a chapter in the projected Uniform Commercial Code'.[38]

During the next academic year George Bogert of the University of Chicago and Llewellyn both used the First Draft and Report in their courses on sales. The flood of literature on sales in the law journals swelled and numerous comments and suggestions poured in. Then, in the summer of 1941, Llewellyn worked intensively on the draft for two months and by the end of August had produced a report, which was circulated in the form of a printed book of 288 pages,[39] containing a very detailed critique of the Uniform Sales Act and the case-law surrounding it, an analysis of the problems of producing a semi-permanent code and a complete new draft, backed by extensive annotations and comments. This was immediately recognized as a remarkable feat and earned high praise in several quarters.[40] Corbin reports that a leading trustee of Columbia, who had been incensed by some public pronouncements of Llewellyn's to the point that he formally demanded his discharge, read the report and was so favourably impressed that he immediately went to Dean Smith and confessed that he had made a serious error of judgment about Llewellyn.[41] The draft also served to convince the NCC that a complete code was a desirable project and that Llewellyn was the person best qualified to direct it.[42]

At the 1941 meeting of the Conference Schnader announced that he had held tentative discussions with the American Law Institute about the possibility of making the code a joint project.[43] This approach to the American Law Institute came at a time when the first phase of their work on the ambitious Restatement project was nearing completion. There were in fact some members who felt that on the completion of this project the ALI should be dissolved, but a majority of the executive were in favour of continuing and saw in the proposed code an undertaking desirable in itself, which fitted

in very well with the objectives of the Institute.[44] Schnader and
Llewellyn saw clear advantages in cooperation. The NCC had an
unwieldly structure and the quality of its membership was rather
variable. Membership of the ALI was a professional honour restricted mainly to leaders of the bench, the bar and the law schools;
it offered the promise of influential backing in raising funds, in
obtaining cooperation, and in gaining acceptance of the finished
code, and it provided a means of associating many more leading
lawyers with the project. As it was put in the application for a grant
to the Falk Foundation: 'Study of the code by 950 leading lawyers
of the country is incomparably more advantageous than study by a
mere 150.'[45] The procedures used in preparing the Restatements
could be adapted quite easily for the Code project.[46] Finally, there
was already in existence a contract of cooperation between the
two bodies under which a Joint Tortfeasors Act and a Property Act
had been produced. There was no serious obstacle to making a
further arrangement. It was agreed to start with a cooperative
project restricted in the first instance to sales and this was arranged
in 1942. The ALI nominated Llewellyn as their Chief Reporter. The
following November Soia Mentschikoff became Assistant Chief
Reporter. Thus the sponsorship was obtained of the two most
influential bodies concerned with unification and improvement of
the law.

Between 1942 and 1944 plans for the Code were developed
slowly and various efforts to raise funds were made, principally by
Schnader and William Draper Lewis, the director of the American
Law Institute. By May 1944 the financing of the code project was
assured by a grant of $150,000 from the Falk Foundation, backed
by approximately $100,000 subscribed by various individuals and
business concerns. During this period Llewellyn wrote a series of
memoranda about the Code, and helped to draft applications for
funds, but his main efforts were directed to the Revised Uniform
Sales Act. The principal activities were summarized by Llewellyn
in 1943 as follows:

The year 1942–3, moving under an adaptation of the Institute's procedures
presented a complete revision and rearrangement of the draft, a first canvass
of the whole and substantial completion of a second canvass by the advisers
in an unparalleled series of meetings at five week intervals. In addition, the
Conference Committee spent eight days reviewing the results. The Conference itself (the Committee sitting between sessions) devoted some two-

thirds of its entire 1943 meeting to the Act, and approved it subject to changes which may be found needed by the Joint Revising Committee, and subject to similar action by the Institute.[47]

This draft was considered at the ALI Conference in Philadelphia in May 1944.[48] By then both organizations were convinced of the desirability and feasibility of the code project and, after further discussion at the NCC meeting in September, a formal agreement was drawn up between the two organizations and signed on 1 December 1944.[49]

This document, which was generally referred to as 'the Treaty', is important, for it established the constitutional framework of the code project. The key provisions read as follows:

II. Organization Diagram

The cooperative organization shall consist of the following:

1. A Chief Reporter
2. An Assistant Chief Reporter
3. An Editorial Board composed of two representatives of the Institute, two representatives of the Conference and the Chief Reporter.[50]
4. Reporters for appropriate parts of the Code.[51]
5. Advisers for each Reporter, the Advisers to be six in number, three selected by the Conference and three by the Institute.
6. Reportorial groups, each group consisting of the Director of the Institute as chairman, a Reporter, his Advisers, and ex officio the Chief Reporter, the Assistant Chief Reporter, and the Assistant Director of the Institute, who shall preside in the absence of the Director.
7. Special committees, if and when the Editorial Board deems that their appointment would be helpful. If and when appointed such committees may be committees of the Conference, Committees of the Institute, or joint committees of the Conference and the Institute, as the Editorial Board determines.

Duties of the various units
1 and 2. Chief Reporter and Assistant Chief Reporter

The Chief Reporter shall have general supervision over the work of all other Reporters and their assistants.

Subject to approval by the Editorial Board, he shall give instructions to the Reporters as to the theory on which drafts shall be prepared, style, and the general scope of comments.

All drafts shall be presented to the Chief Reporter for editing and shall be by him presented to the Editorial Board for approval as to general scope and content before submission to the Commercial Law Acts section of the Conference, the Council of the Institute, the Conference, or the Institute.

As ex officio members of the several Reportorial Groups, the Chief Reporter and Assistant Chief Reporter shall have the right at their pleasure to attend any meeting of any Reportorial Group and participate in its deliberations.

Also, the Chief Reporter and Assistant Chief Reporter shall co-operate with each Reporter and participate with him in the presentation of drafts to the section, the council, the Conference or the Institute.[52]

This agreement clearly established that although the ultimate responsibility was vested in the Editorial Board, the Chief Reporter was to be the lynch-pin of the whole enterprise; each article was initially the responsibility of a separate group of people (the Reporter and his advisers), and each draft had to be presented to the Council of the ALI and the Commercial Acts section or the Property Acts section of the NCC. As the one person who could appear in every arena in which matters pertaining to the Code were discussed, the Chief Reporter had a key role in ensuring that the unity in substance and in style of the Code was maintained. Perhaps most important of all was the responsibility vested in the Chief Reporter for the general theory and style of each article, and by implication for the Code as a whole. Even before the 'treaty' was concluded, the main lines had been established by Llewellyn and he provided the first guidelines for reporters in respect of scope, approach and style.

The strategic constitutional position of the Chief Reporter was strengthened in fact by his role in the selection of key personnel and by the actual composition of the Editorial Committee and the advisory committees. Perhaps his most important choice was Soia Mentschikoff as Assistant Chief Reporter, a choice which initially occasioned some raised eyebrows, but which soon was recognized as a brilliant appointment. As his former pupil and research assistant, as his devoted disciple, with an unrivalled understanding of his approach, and, from 1946 as his wife, she could be relied on to be both loyal and consistent in promoting Llewellyn's views. Once again, Llewellyn had as his partner someone who not only shared his ideas, but complemented his personality almost ideally in every phase of the work: suspicions that the project was a theorist's dream-castle would be further allayed by the participation of Mentschikoff, who until 1948 was a Wall Street lawyer and very much a practitioner's lawyer; her practice had been mainly in Labour Law and, as Llewellyn was never tired of repeating, she brought the 'fresh eye of the non-expert' to most areas of commercial law. She was shrewd and formidable in handling people; she had extraordinary technical ability and facility in drafting and her capacity for calm, lucid presentation in committee or on a public platform has become legendary. In presenting drafts Llewellyn and Mentschikoff would alternate, providing a contrast in styles that facinated and perhaps sometimes bemused the audience. As a performer on the floor of the ALI or the NCC Llewellyn was capable of assuming any of a number of guises, but with Mentschikoff the range was greatly increased.

Between them Llewellyn and Mentschikoff were Reporters for over half the Articles of the Code and there were no sections which were not at some stage revised or completely redrafted by one or both of them. Normally the responsibility for presenting drafts for consideration by the Editorial Board, the ALI and the NCC lay with Reporters of individual articles, but almost invariably either the Chief Reporter or the Assistant Chief Reporter, usually both, were present, ready to intervene when necessary, and sometimes taking over the main task of presentation. The appointment of Soia Mentschikoff as Llewellyn's assistant immeasurably increased the extent of Llewellyn's influence, notably in the preliminary stages, but also after he himself was devoting less time to the project, and even after his death in 1962.

Llewellyn had a free hand in the choice of Reporters; selection was done after informal consultation with the inner establishment of whom Schnader, Lewis and later, Judge Herbert Goodrich were the most important members. In some instances non-experts were deliberately chosen as Reporters, for reasons which will be discussed later. This policy, coupled with the fact that several of those chosen, notably Dunham, Gilmore and Leary, were promising young men near the start of their careers, further entrenched Llewellyn's influence. Llewellyn could also be confident of commanding a majority on the Editorial Board of five nearly all of the time. He was himself a member, Schnader trusted his judgment and Harrison Tweed, the other ALI representative, was a devoted admirer. It has been said that if Llewellyn found these two opposing him on some issue connected with drafting, he realized that he was probably mistaken. Thus, Llewellyn nearly always had the support of the Editorial Board, which had official responsibility for the project; furthermore the Treaty was so drafted that the Chief Reporter and the Assistant Chief Reporter were not subject to dismissal by the board; if the question had arisen, probably they could only have been ousted by joint action of the executives of the two sponsoring bodies. In fact this question never arose.[53]

Finally, Llewellyn also had a say in the composition of the advisory committees, which formed the teams to work with each Reporter. In selection, trouble was taken to bring together people who could be expected to work together as a team. For example, of the six members of the advisory committee on the crucial second Article, Arthur Corbin, Tom Swan (a former dean of Yale Law School) and Willard Luther had previously been closely associated; as had Sterry Waterman (now a federal judge) and Charles Hardin. The only 'outsider' was Hiram Thomas, who had been the key figure in the Merchants' Association moves for a Federal Sales Act; he had worked closely with Llewellyn at that time and fitted in with no difficulty at all. This group complemented each other very well: Llewellyn, Thomas and Hardin between them were a rich source of information about commercial practices; Corbin was an unrivalled repository of case-law learning; Swan was said to provide a sense of structure; Waterman and Mentschikoff were used as uninhibited non-experts, providing the 'fresh look' and the commonsense of the outsider; Luther's capacity for succinct expression gave birth to the expression—'Now, let's Lutherize the draft.'[54] This team provided the model for selection of other advisory groups.

PREPARATION OF THE FIRST COMPLETE DRAFT (1944–9)

A detailed description of the process involved in preparing the first complete draft would be tedious and is, in this context, unnecessary. For the present purpose it is enough to describe the procedure in general terms. Each article was first assigned to one or two reporters, or associate reporters,[55] and an advisory group of six, most of whom were practitioners or judges. The initial drafts were first revised with Llewellyn and Mentschikoff before submission to the advisers for comment and criticism. After an article had undergone at least three such cycles, a draft was presented to the Council of the ALI and the Commercial Acts Section or Property Acts Section of the Conference. Further revisions would be made in the light of the comments of these bodies before drafts were forwarded to the full meetings of the ALI and NCC, which met jointly after 1948. Yet more revisions would then be made and the process repeated until each draft article was approved by the members of the two sponsoring organizations. Meanwhile a draftsman usually had informal contact with interest groups concerned with the article for which he was responsible and with specialists in the field. By late 1948 Llewellyn was reasonably satisfied with all the articles except Articles 4 and 9. By May 1949 a complete draft together with comments was printed and published.

Thus after 1944 the Code project became a genuine team effort. Between 1944 and 1949 Llewellyn played a very active part, but the Code was by no means his only interest. During the period he continued to carry a full teaching load, as indeed he did throughout his association with the project; he maintained a steady, though diminished, output of articles in fields other than commercial law; he did fieldwork among the Pueblos in New Mexico during several of the summers; he was chairman of a number of committees, and in 1948–9 he was a visiting professor at Harvard, while still doing some teaching at Columbia, so that he had to commute between Cambridge and New York during term-time. Thus the Code was at no stage a full-time job for him and from 1948 onwards he devoted increasing time to academic work. At this point he began to turn back to jurisprudence. By now most of his work on the Code was done. He continued, however, to act as Chief Reporter until his death, but from 1949 an increasing share of the burden of work was assumed by Soia Mentschikoff, who up to that point had been in full-time employment, first as a member of a New York law firm and from 1948–50 as a visiting professor at Harvard Law School, their first woman law professor. From 1949–51 she did not have a full-time post and during this time she was able to spend a great deal of time on Code activities. Thereafter she continued to relieve her husband of much arduous promotional work, especially after 1955, when for medical reasons he had to work at a more leisurely pace.

CONSULTATION AND CRITICISM (1949–53)

After the publication of the first complete draft in May 1949, comments were invited from a wide variety of sources and a number of organizations were encouraged to undertake special studies of the Code. Between 1949 and 1952 memoranda and reports were received from Bar Associations, law firms, official committees set up in various states, and commercial and business concerns such as the Association of American Railroads (1950), The American Bankers' Association (1951), the National Canners Association (1951), and the American Warehousemen's Association (1951). Literally thousands of suggestions were received from every part of the country. After requests from the ABA and others that they should be allowed more time to study the Code, it was agreed to postpone submission to the Legislatures until at least 1952. However, from 1950 a publicity campaign was launched by means of pamphlets, articles, addresses and special institutes or conferences.

Naturally much of the comment, published and unpublished, was critical. But there was surprisingly little concerted opposition to the Code at this stage. The most important reasoned attack took the form of an article by Samuel Williston in *The Harvard Law Review* for February 1950.[56] His main target was Article 2, but he also condemned the Code in general for being unnecessarily radical. Apart from some detailed criticisms of the Sales Article, Williston's objections add up to a typical example of a conservative defence of the *status quo*. The arguments directed against the Code as a whole and generally against the Sales Article can be briefly summarized: the project is iconoclastic and unwise and will be a retrograde step. There will be a difficult transition period, during which a great deal of uniformity of law will be sacrificed. In so far as there is need for change, this would be best done by piece-meal amendment. There is, however, no need for radical change. The Uniform Sales Act deliberately followed the Sale of Goods Act very closely even in its phraseology and this has permitted uniformity between American and Commonwealth jurisdictions, especially England and Canada.[57] The novel phraseology of the Code is particularly to be deplored because not only does it create unnecessary differences from legislation prevailing in other common law jurisdictions, but also there will be a considerable amount of uncertainty until a body of case law has grown up around the Code. 'Lawyers are well aware that the words of a long statute, comprehending a large branch of law, never clearly give the answers to all possible problems. Years of judicial decisions are necessary to resolve the problems.'[58] Williston also listed a number of particular criticisms of the draft, including a strong attack on the down-grading of 'title' as a central concept.

Williston's arguments about the danger that the Code would reduce rather than promote uniformity have some force, at least at the international level. They underline the basic dilemma facing those who wish to promote both uniformity and modernity in law. His arguments could be used against any attempt to change any uniform law. Williston's assumptions and what he did not say are in some ways more revealing than his explicit arguments. Above all he was silent about the defects in the existing situation that had stimulated the urge for reform. He made no attempt to answer the claims of the proponents of the Code that the Uniform Sales Act was in many respects out of touch with business practice or unclear or unnecessarily complicated or inconsistent with other commercial acts. In his argument against a fresh terminology, he did not try to evaluate Llewellyn's claim that the terminology of the Code reflected more closely the language of business and would be more easily understood by people most closely affected by it.[59] Williston appears to have assumed that it was sufficient that the Uniform Sales Act was comprehensible to lawyers. Llewellyn doubted whether even that was so. The draftsmen of the Code were more concerned with 'the ease with which it can be understood and applied by merchants without resort to litigation'.[60]

Another difference appears to be that Williston's approach was based on certain simple ideas which he took for granted as contrasted with one which was more self-conscious about objectives and methods. Williston assumed that a precisely worded statute backed up by a corpus of decided cases was *the* way of obtaining certainty in the law. Llewellyn saw this as just one of a number of means of attaining 'reasonable reckonability'. Williston does not seem to have adequately faced the problem of devising an instrument which must cope with different social and economic conditions, varying from trade to trade, from place to place and from time to time. Llewellyn saw this as a primary problem of uniform legislation in the commercial field. Although by no means totally insensitive to business practice, as draftsman of the Uniform Sales Act and other uniform laws, Williston was prepared merely to make a few concessions to business usage, rather than relatively systematically to analyse the problem of providing a body of commercial law which fitted the expectations and needs of businessmen in a free enterprise economy. It is significant that in attacking Llewellyn's discarding of title as a central concept, he made no attempt to meet Llewellyn's criticisms, viz. that 'title talk' merely gave a facade of certainty and that, as far as the behaviour of the courts was concerned, title had for a long time been only spasmodically an operative concept.[61] There is little sign, in this article at least, that Williston had grasped this point at all.

The clash between Williston and the proponents of the Code must have been painful for both sides. Williston, whatever his limitations, was admired and liked by those who disagreed with him. Corbin, in an article published shortly after Williston's, denied that he was replying to the earlier article or that it was thinkable that he would enter into a controversy with his 'beloved friend and revered teacher'.[62] Llewellyn also had ambivalent feelings towards Williston. He genuinely admired him as a scholar and frequently praised his contributions at the turn of the century. *Cases and Materials on the Law of Sales*, it will be recalled, was dedicated to Scrutton and to Williston, 'the master and the builder of our law of Sales'. However, Williston's approach was just not acceptable. His faith in the value of sustaining the *status quo* was matched by Llewellyn's faith in the promise of reform. Llewellyn was at pains in his writings on the Code to praise the Uniform Sales Act in quite lavish terms and to emphasize that the Sales Article was a development in a direction that had already been charted by Chalmers and Williston.[63] Corbin commented as follows:

I was not in touch with Williston when he opposed enactment of the Revised Sales Act. He certainly trusted Tom Swan and me. But he was the *author* of the old Sales Act; and the new one was sprung on him as a *complete* overhauling in the framing of which he had no part. There was more of the old Act embodied in the new one than he knew. He was 80; and the wording was strange. Williston's limitations grew out of the fact that he was the product of the leading Harvard Faculty of 1870–1895, a Faculty that convinced its students that it had arrived at final principles.[64]

Perhaps Williston should be given the last word. In a private letter to Llewellyn, dated 19 May 1949, he wrote:

Of course my fundamental objection, which I retain with all humility, is restating the law, even where no substantial change is desired, in new words (even if better) when the old words have been interpreted in the United States for more than forty years, and are in many cases identical with the words in the English statute in force there and in her colonies, and not likely to be changed there.
You will pardon an old hunker like me citing as authority Lord Thurlow's

reply to a leader of a band of dissenters who sought for amelioration of their political disabilities: 'I'm against you, by God, sir, I'm in favor of the established church; and if you'll get your damn religion established I'll be in favor of that too.'

I recognize that what happened to Lord Thurlow's wishes may well happen to mine, and if so, like him, 'I'll be in favor of that too'.[65]

Discussions of legislative reform tend to have a ritual quality. Whatever the subject and the context one may expect that both sides will claim that their solution will promote certainty, will satisfy the consumer and will be more wise. This controversy is no exception. The sponsors of the Code were not impressed by Williston's criticism and it appears to have had no noticeable effect.

In 1952, Emmet F. Smith, house counsel of the Chase National Bank, started what was the nearest thing to an organized campaign against enactment. He produced two substantial mimeographed statements criticizing the Code both in general terms and in detail and these were widely circulated throughout the United States. Smith's arguments were generally neither well conceived nor well presented and the most remarkable feature of his campaign is that it was virtually unique in this period.[66] Smith tried, unsuccessfully, to persuade prominent bankers to organize opposition to the Code in Pennsylvania, but he and his banking colleagues were more successful in New York and were instrumental in having the Code referred to the New York Law Revision Commission.

Why was there so little organized opposition to the Code? Apart from the widespread recognition that reform was badly needed, several reasons may be advanced in explanation. First, in determining the scope of the Code, most of the fields which could be expected to be the subject of political controversy were excluded or treated as severable.[67] Ironically, Article 9, which dealt with some of the most contentious subject matter, eventually won some crucial support for the enactment of the Code.[68] A second factor was the skilful diplomacy and political management of Schnader. Another reason for the relative lack of organized opposition was the manner in which criticism was handled. The desire to find as much common ground as possible between those affected was genuine and was seen to be so. The widespread consultation, the invitation of criticism and suggestions for improvement, and the courteous and patient manner in which critics were heard, must have drawn the sting of many potential opponents. Issues were frequently re-opened.

From the records it appears that repeatedly the Code staff waived the opportunity to silence criticism as they might have done by pointing out that the matter had been settled by a vote of the sponsoring bodies.[69] Llewellyn's lack of 'pride of opinion' was often remarked and undoubtedly the open-minded and good-humoured manner in which he usually reacted to criticism was of crucial importance.[70] In this respect the complex procedure of presenting and debating successive drafts favoured the Reporters, for it meant that they nearly always had more than one opportunity for getting something accepted. Some of Llewellyn's favourite ideas—for instance, the unconscionability provisions and the inclusion of letters of credit—were only accepted at the second or third attempt after initial opposition had been worn down or circumnavigated. On more than one occasion, it is said, the Code draftsmen were able to get their way by re-wording sections that had been voted down, without changing their substance.

Finally, it may be pointed out that the 'democracy' of the process was a qualified democracy. Despite extensive consultation and public discussion the project was inevitably under the control of a tightly knit group. Moreover, the membership of the NCC and ALI was composed very largely of judges, leading private practitioners, whose main clientele would tend to be capitalist enterprises, and a sprinkling of established academic lawyers. Lawyers of all kinds tend to have a vested interest in the *status quo*; a reasonably high proportion of the members of both organizations, especially the ALI, could be expected to be moderately 'liberal', but without seriously challenging established institutions and ways of doing things. The overwhelming majority of those consulted could also be expected to share similar values: bar associations, large law firms, banks, commercial interest groups, and individual lawyers. The voices of organized labour, small consumers and opponents of the capitalist system were muted or inaudible. Two classes of people who might have been advocates of a different viewpoint, the ordinary politician and radical-minded academic lawyers, had limited scope. The politicians were told, with some justification, that this was a technical reform, a matter best left to the judgment of lawyers and businessmen. Academic lawyers, by virtue of their calling, might be expected to be more open-minded in contemplating innovations, more willing to experiment, more sympathetic to the consumer and generally more attracted to sweeping reforms than either practitioners or businessmen. In fact the relatively few academic lawyers who played a significant part in the preparation or discussion of the various drafts,[71] 'were not radicals', as Kripke says, 'not communists, or anarchists, or revolutionaries of any kind'.[72] Indeed, one might ask how many American academic lawyers of that time, particularly those who specialized in commercial law, could be so described. Llewellyn himself was sympathetic to the consumer and 'the little man', but he gave the impression of being less consistently consumer-oriented than some of his fellow academics. He was as interested as anyone in achieving a fair allocation of risk, but he was also particularly concerned with the relatively uncontroversial objectives of unification, simplification and modernization. It is worth noting that the most articulate outside critic of the Code, Beutel, was a law professor;[73] so was Grant Gilmore who was the one member of the Code team who felt strongly that too many concessions had been made to powerful pressure groups, notably to bankers, in respect of Article 4.[74] What has not been generally recognized is the extent to which the Code contains provisions which are basically protective of consumers, although not labelled as such, for instance the provisions concerning warranties and limitations on remedies for breach, unconscionability, good faith and commercial reasonableness in disposition of defaulting collateral and, perhaps, revocation of acceptance. The full potential of these provisions may have been obscured by the propaganda for enactment of the Code which was directed almost solely at financing institutions with their powerful state lobbies. Had the Code project been started twenty years later, after the national conscience of America had been stirred by the wider recognition of poverty and social injustice, the propaganda about the Code might have been different, but the substance would not necessarily have changed significantly. As it turned out, the problems of poor consumers, described graphically in Caplowitz *The Poor Pay More*,[75] did not agitate the NCC until the late 1960s when a start was made on uniform consumer protection legislation.[76] It is arguable that at that time equally effective protection for the consumer could have been achieved through judicial development of key sections of the Code.[77]

THE NEW YORK LAW REVISION COMMISSION STUDY AND AFTER

The original strategy for obtaining adoption of the Code was to concentrate first on some of the principal commercial states, especially California, Illinois, New Jersey, New York, Ohio and Pennsylvania. Of these New York was the most important. It was here that the Code sponsors experienced their first major setback. In 1952 Governor Dewey had included the Code in his legislative programme. But opposition, initiated in the first place by members of the Chase National Bank and the law firm of Milbank Tweed, made itself felt late in 1952, with Emmet Smith as the mouthpiece. In January 1953 a joint report was issued by committees of the Association of the Bar of the City of New York and the New York State Bar Association. The report contained a recommendation that there should be a full-scale official study of the Code. On 8 February 1953 Governor Dewey, after taking private advice, directed the New York Law Revision Commission to undertake such a study and a generous allocation of $300,000 was made for this purpose.[78]

In 1954 the commission held hearings in a number of centres in New York State at which supporters and opponents submitted written and oral evidence. Concurrently a number of consultants were engaged to consider the Code from a variety of points of view. Besides very detailed studies of each article, and some other technical studies, there was one of particular jurisprudential interest, published under the title 'Problems of Codification of Commercial Law'. This was the product of the joint efforts of Edwin W. Patterson of Columbia and Rudolf B. Schlesinger of Cornell. The former was mainly responsible for the section on codification of commercial law in the light of jurisprudence and the latter for an analysis of the Uniform Commercial Code in the light of comparative law. This ninety-six page study was one of the most interesting features of the reports of the NYLRC which eventually filled six substantial volumes.

The final report of the commission was issued on 29 February 1956, almost exactly three years after the study was instituted. The exercise had cost nearly one-third of a million dollars, not very much less than the original Code project up to 1950. During this period a moratorium was called on attempts to have the Code enacted elsewhere, but consultation and promotional activities continued. From the early days of the New York study it was obvious that there would be a lot of criticisms to be met. Rather than wait for the commission to report, the sponsors decided to reactivate the Editorial Board in the summer of 1954. Sub-committees were appointed for each article. Every criticism made to the commission was studied by the appropriate subcommittee and a number of amendments referred to the Editorial Board were approved by it and published as: 'Supplement No. 1 to the Uniform Commercial Code' in January 1955.[79] The final report of the commission dealt with the Code, as amended by this supplement. By this device a lot of criticism which might have been included in the final report was anticipated and dealt with. Meanwhile members of the Code staff maintained a dialogue with the commission, who were willing to cooperate. When its subcommittees made tentative recommendations to the commission, these were often referred to subcommittees of the Editorial Board, which sometimes made tentative comments on them. Naturally the Code's Reporters had an opportunity to present evidence at the commission's hearings. Llewellyn made brief introductory and closing statements in respect of most articles, and he and Mentschikoff jointly presented Article 2. Towards the end, feeling that at no time had the general case for the Code been adequately put to the commission, they petitioned for an opportunity to be heard orally. On 16 August 1954 Llewellyn appeared before the commission and made a somewhat emotional statement on behalf of the Code. The text, read outside the context of that occasion, gives the impression of being one of his most interesting essays in advocacy.[80] It also contains the most coherent statement of his ideas on the Code (it is reproduced in Appendix E). Coming, as it did, after the main oral hearings had been completed, it performed the function of a closing speech for the defence. For the rather hard-boiled 'court' his performance may have been too laden with emotion to be completely appropriate and it is, in any case, difficult to say what impression, if any, it made on the commission.

On 29 February 1956 the commission reported. Their main report was a typewritten document of a little over one hundred pages which did not attempt to go into great detail. When it was eventually published it was supported by appendices in a volume of just under five hundred pages, much of which represented a condensation of other material. So comprehensive was the New York study that it virtually pre-empted the field. During the period of the study a number of other bodies also examined the Code and subsequently several states set up commissions to study the Code before enactment. However, their reports were dwarfed by the New York study, and most of them made no attempt to duplicate it. Thus the intensity of this study, coupled with the commercial importance of New York state, combined to make the commission's report the most important single outside influence on the next version of the Code, the important 1957 edition.

The commission's report represented a partial victory for the sponsors of the Code, but a victory for which a price had to be paid. The most important conclusion was that a 'careful and foresighted codification of all or major parts of commercial law'[81] was desirable and that 'such a code is attainable with a reasonable amount of effort and within a reasonable time'.[82] They recommended, however, 'that the Uniform Commercial Code is not satisfactory in its present form and cannot be made satisfactory without comprehensive re-examination and revision in the light of all critical comment obtainable'.[83]

According to Schnader's estimate, the commission gave 'about an 80 per cent approval of the Code',[84] while Walter Malcolm painted a more optimistic picture, by pointing out that the bulk of the commission's criticisms were on minor points of drafting and that only on two major issues of policy were there disagreements of substance, viz. whether letters of credit should be included in the Code at all and on the conflicts of laws rules adopted in the 1952 draft.[85] Certainly some of the most important features were approved by the commission: the idea of having an integrated code, the presence of comments (although there was criticism of some of the drafting and disagreement about their status as aids to interpretation), the principal innovations in the Sales Article, most of the policies of seven of the nine articles, and the radical, and potentially controversial, treatment of secured transactions in Article 9. Although the drafting of many sections or subsections was criticized, many of these criticisms were concerned with minutiae. The aggregate of changes recommended by the commission was substantial, but the number could well have been greater but for the close liaison between the Code subcommittees and the staff of the commission before the final report was prepared. There are also grounds for believing that some proposals for change were not made in the report because it was known that these would be unacceptable to the sponsors of the Code.

The reactivation of the Editorial Board and its cooperation with the New York Commission minimized delay in producing a revised version, and, after intensive effort by the board and a series of subcommittees,[86] a new version of the Code was produced in November 1956, only nine months after the commission's report Llewellyn played a less prominent part in this phase and then principally in the role of defender of some parts of the 1952 draft which had been subject to criticism. The recommendations of the Editorial Board were published in a form which made clear the exact nature of the changes made in response to the suggestions of the New York Commission and those of a number of other bodies. The recommendations were accepted by the sponsoring organizations. Reporting to the NCC in 1957, Schnader said:

> I think, although I have not counted it up, it is fair to say that we adopted fully ninety per cent of the recommendations of the New York Law Revision Commission in one form or another. When I say we adopted them, I mean we did not always adopt them in exactly the same language. We didn't take all the recommendations. For example, they said: 'Drop Article V entirely. . . .'
>
> The Editorial Board felt that in states other than New York Article V would be a very useful article and therefore instead of dropping it, we thoroughly revised it, and it is still part of the Commercial Code.[87]

How much of Llewellyn's approach was sacrificed in the process? To obtain an exact answer to this question it would first be necessary to establish a more precise set of categories than we have at present for differentiating between different styles and techniques of drafting. Then the successive drafts of each article, and especially the *1956 Recommendations of the Editorial Board*, would have to be submitted to minute analysis; these would have to be compared with formulations made by Llewellyn elsewhere. Even then there would be some intractable methodological problems. This has not been done. Until someone undertakes this arduous task, we must rest content with a more impressionistic treatment.

It is generally believed that the 1952 version of the Code was more influenced by Llewellyn than that of 1957. However, just as between 1937 and 1952 he had genuinely accepted many suggestions of others as desirable, so he agreed that the 1957 text represented, in some respects, an improvement on the earlier one. On certain matters on which he felt strongly, such as the retention of Article 5, the New York proposals were rejected.[88] Some other matters of disagreement relate to points of detail which bear no clear relation to his jurisprudential ideas or his general approach. The main general issue relevant to our present concern was over the style of drafting. And this issue is blurred. The commission took a pragmatic attitude to drafting techniques and their report, in any case, represents a compromise. Commenting on the widespread use of flexible standards like 'reasonableness' and 'good faith', they recognized that this involved a deliberate abstention from detailed regulation and took the position that 'the wisdom of this approach must be decided separately for each instance in which it is used'. They accordingly judged each example separately and criticized, as being too loosely drawn, a number of sections in which such terms appeared. Similarly, many of their criticisms of specific sections seem to have stemmed from a desire for greater precision, which led them to prefer 'lawyerlike' concepts to the vaguer terms of ordinary business parlance. As one of their consultants, Professor Robert Pasley, put it:

In fact, generally speaking, the commission was a little dubious about the widespread use of business terminology throughout the Code. Not that it has anything against business terminology as such – it's often very convenient – but it often lacks precision. It often means something in one part of the country, something else in another part, or as between different industries or lines of business. Throughout, the commission was anxious to see a statute that would have an ascertained or ascertainable meaning.[89]

Just as Llewellyn was not dogmatic in insisting always on an 'open-ended' approach to drafting, so the commission was pragmatic on this matter, and, indeed, criticized some parts of the Code for adopting rigid rules which would not permit of a desired flexibility in their application.[90] Nonetheless it is clear that the commission's preference tended to be for tighter and more detailed drafting.[91] The acceptance of the commission's suggestions led to a more tightly drafted instrument, at least in respect of Articles 3, 4 and 9, but it must be remembered that the Code is still held out to be a rare example of open-ended drafting, judged by the standards of modern Anglo-American lawyers.

Grant Gilmore's conclusion on the matter, although it simplifies a little, appears to sum up the position correctly :

It was, I believe, Karl's non-systematic, particularizing cast of mind and his case-law orientation which gave to the statutes he drafted, and particularly to the Code, their profound originality. He was a remarkable draftsman and took a never-failing interest in even the minutiae of the trade. His instinct appeared to be to draft in a loose, open-ended style; his preferred solutions turned on questions of fact (reasonableness, good faith, usage of trade) rather than on rules of law. He had clearly in mind the idea of a case-law Code: one that would furnish guide-lines for a fresh start, would accommodate itself to changing circumstances, would not so much contain the law as free it for a new growth. The tastes of the practising lawyers, who advised the draftsmen, were, in most cases, opposed to the flexible ideas of the Chief Reporter: they preferred, they insisted on, a tightly-drawn statute, precise, detailed, and rigid. Among the many drafts of the Code which appeared, beginning in 1946, the early drafts were in many ways closer to Karl's conception of the Code than were the final drafts. In the concluding phase of the drafting, concessions were inevitably made to what might be called political pressures; I do not mean to suggest that those pressures were in any sense evil or malevolent. I have come to feel that Karl saw more clearly than his critics and that the Code as he initially conceived it might better have served the purposes of the next fifty years.[92]

THE CODE AFTER 1956

Between the publication of the 1957 official text and the end of 1966, forty-eight jurisdictions including Hawaii and the Virgin Islands, enacted the Code. Llewellyn's role at this stage was peripheral. He was widely regarded as being less effective in promoting than in preparing the Code. He was now hard at work on *The Common Law Tradition* and his health was such that he had to proceed with care. It has been suggested that the efforts he expended on the Code in the 1940s affected his health. During the last five years of his life he wrote one article on the Code and gave a number of addresses as part of the campaign to make it better known. However, the main activity at this stage was planned and supervised by Schnader and executed by local groups and individuals in each state. By the time of Llewellyn's death twelve jurisdictions had adopted the Code; the great breakthrough came in September 1962 when New York at long last followed suit. Thereafter the compliance of the remaining jurisdictions was virtually assured. The speed with which the next thirty jurisdictions acted in the period 1962–6 broke all records in the history of the NCC.

To complete the story to date, one final development must be mentioned briefly. After the publication of the 1958 Official Text, which diverged only slightly from the 1957 Official Text, the Editorial Board considered that it was *functus officio*. However, a new problem arose, as state after state adopted local variations, thereby threatening to undermine uniformity.[93] In 1965 Schnader estimated that of the first thirty states to enact the Code, only Pennsylvania had not departed from the official text and that up to 1 January 1965 a total of 522 amendments were introduced by adopting jurisdictions, California and Wisconsin being the worst offenders with 125 and 47 respectively. The significance of this figure can easily be exaggerated, for a high proportion of those divergencies are in respect of filing arrangements in Article 9, and other matters in which uniformity is not of paramount importance. Nevertheless, there was cause for concern. In an effort to regain control of the situation a further grant was sought and procured from the Falk Foundation to finance the establishment of a Permanent Editorial Board, under the joint sponsorship of the ALI and the NCC : 'to assist in attaining and maintaining uniformity in state statutes governing commercial transactions and to this end to approve a minimum number of amendments to the Code'. In 1962 a new Official Text was promulgated incorporating twenty-six amendments, but the board then took a strong line and, in its second report (October 1964), it rejected all subsequent non-uniform amendments. An interesting battle was beginning to develop, the Permanent Editorial Board holding as its key card the possibility of the enactment of a Federal Commercial Code 'governing commercial transactions to the limit of the jurisdiction of Congress over interstate commerce'.[94]

However, by 1966 it had become clear that something would have to be done about Article 9. In its third report the board said:

By the time the November meeting was held, 337 non-uniform, non-official amendments had been made to the various sections of Article 9. Some sections had been amended by as many as 30 jurisdictions, each jurisdiction writing its own amendment without regard to the amendments made by other jurisdictions and, of course, without regard to the Official Text. 47 of the 54 Sections of Article 9 had been non-uniformly amended.

In view of this distressing situation and in view also of the fact that various practicing lawyers and law teachers have written articles or textbooks pointing out certain respects in which Article 9 might be improved, the Board decided that the time had arrived for a restudy in depth of Article 9 on Secured Transactions.[95]

Accordingly a review committee was set up under the chairmanship of Professor Herbert Wechsler to conduct a 'restudy in depth' of Article 9 and to report to the Permanent Editorial Board. The Review Committee circulated preliminary drafts in 1968 and 1970 and their final report was approved by the Permanent Editorial Board, with some amendments, in February 1971. The proposed revision of Article 9 will provide an interesting test of the willingness and ability of the state legislatures to cooperate in maintaining uniformity of the Code while allowing its sponsors to be responsive to criticisms and to changing conditions.

'LLEWELLYN'S CODE'?

I have not attempted in this brief historical outline to dig far below the surface of recorded events. Even in this limited exercise a degree of speculation and value judgment has been unavoidable where there have been gaps and conflicts in the evidence or where the very nature of the enquiry makes precise delineation impossible. There does, however, seem to be widespread agreement on the following points:

(i) The original idea for a complete commercial code was probably Schnader's.

(ii) Almost all of the initial planning in respect of scope, objectives, method and style was Llewellyn's and even the later editions of the Code are remarkably close to his original conception.

(iii) In so far as drafting can be isolated from critique of drafts, on a very crude estimate rather more than half of the initial drafting was done by Llewellyn and Mentschikoff, Llewellyn being primarily responsible for the general sections in Article 1 (excluding definitions), Article 2 and Article 5. Even in respect of the other articles his role as Chief Reporter involved him in extensive re-working of every provision.

(iv) Llewellyn's official position under 'the Treaty' between the ALI and the NCC, his key role in selection of personnel, coupled with Schnader's confidence in him, and Mentschikoff's loyalty and acceptance of his ideas, gave him an unassailably strategic position for influencing events up to the point of promulgation of each draft.

(v) The Code was the product of teamwork. Llewellyn only exceptionally used his key position to push through pet ideas of his own in the face of opposition; rather he regularly exhibited a rare openness to suggestion and this was a key factor in allowing the ideas and suggestions of a very large number of people to have a part in the drafting process. Most of these suggestions tested his factual assumptions or related to matters of expression. 'Democracy' within the institutional context of the Code project was one of Llewellyn's operative ideas, but inevitably much of the effective power was vested in a small group.

(vi) Although concessions were made to placate opponents, there were few, if any, matters on which Llewellyn made sacrifices of principle or substance to save the Code. Some commentators may have exaggerated the significance of the changes made after the NYLRC study, but there is little doubt that the imprimatur of the commission was of great political significance in getting the Code adopted.

(vii) Llewellyn's principal contributions were made in the period 1937 to 1953, and most importantly in the first phases of planning and drafting between 1940 and 1949. He played a relatively minor role in respect of publicizing and securing enactment of the Code. After 1955 his health was such that he had in any case to slow his pace. Before then he considered that his main contribution had been made. His ideas, however, continued to have influence through the activities of Soia Mentschikoff, who continued to play an active part after his semi-retirement from the project and even after his death in 1962.

12

The Jurisprudence of the Uniform Commercial Code

This brief study of the history and institutional setting of the Code shows that the relationship between its basic theory and the finished product was not simply one of conception and execution. The project was neither conceived nor planned *a priori*. Schnader's idea was stimulated by his concern, as President of the NCC, that the institution was not achieving its aims. Commercial law appeared to be the one area in which there was a consistent demand for uniformity. The ALI and the NCC consisted of leading lawyers who could be expected to be suspicious of innovation. The existing Uniform Commercial Acts and the working procedures adopted for the Restatement project were the obvious starting-points for discussion of scope, substance and working procedures. From the outset it was clear that if a code was to have a good chance of being enacted it would have to satisfy three principal groups of people: the lawyers in the sponsoring organizations, the more organized pressure groups outside the legislatures, and the legislators themselves. An *a priori* conception of an ideal commercial code would have needed considerable modification to survive the processes which culminated in enactment in a multiplicity of legislatures. Llewellyn never articulated such a conception. In short, the desirable and the feasible were not sharply distinguished.

This, then, was the context of Llewellyn's activities. What he considered desirable was set in a framework of assumptions largely fixed by a particular situation. There had to be a promotional aspect about much of what he wrote or said in public about the Code. He had to adopt a persona, play a part, in which the theorist and the radical in him were played down, if not entirely suppressed. There was scope for the colourful personality and for the flashing insight, but within leeways set by the need to convince practical men that this was an able lawyer, with a real feel for and knowledge of business practice, concerned with practical problems in a practical manner. With the ALI in particular it was important for him to avoid projecting the image of the wild-eyed radical; in its place he had to substitute Genius in the service of Men of Affairs. There can be little doubt that Llewellyn thoroughly enjoyed the role; but such was his empathy with the majority of the other participants that to see this solely in terms of role-playing would be misleading.

Given the situation and the man it would be unwise to seek for a tight logical theory underlying the Code. Nevertheless, Llewellyn's approach was governed in large part by a number of operative ideas which are closely related to his general theoretical position. This chapter is devoted to the exploration of this relationship in connection with a number of selected topics.

OBJECTIVES AND UNDERLYING VALUES

The Code is to be judged by the usefulness and convenience of its own organization, by the ease with which it can be understood and applied by the merchants without litigation, by the aid that it gives to the courts in reaching just decisions in accord with the mores and usages of honest dealers and by the flexibility and effectiveness of its suggested remedies.[1]

The official purposes and policies of the Code were articulated in s. 1–102(2) of the 1952 text:

(a) to simplify and modernize and develop greater precision and certainty in the rules of law governing commercial transactions;
(b) to preserve flexibility in commercial transactions and to encourage continued expansion of commercial practices and mechanisms through custom, usage and agreement of the parties;
(c) to make uniform the law among the various jurisdictions.[2]

This is a fair statement of the principal general objectives that Llewellyn pursued, but it requires amplification in the light of his more detailed and less formal pronouncements of his aims. Normally his starting-point was dissatisfaction with the existing state of the law.[3] The objectives listed in section 1–102 are for the most part remedial, referring by implication to alleged defects in the pre-existing situation: simplification implies that the prior law was both

unnecessarily complex and was not easily understood by businessmen; 'modernization' implies that the prior law had not kept abreast
with changes in technology, in business practice, in methods of
financing and, to a lesser extent, with changes in the climate of
opinion in respect of values; mention of a need 'to develop greater
precision and certainty in the rules of law' implies that insufficient
guidance was given by the prior law to counsellors and others who
wished to make predictions about legal consequences; in Llewellyn's
view, a simple-looking formula, however precise, was unlikely to
provide a reliable basis for prediction if it did 'not fit the situation
and the situation's set of problems'.[4]

One aspect of the aim of simplification was of particular concern
to Llewellyn. Since the early 1920s, when he lectured to bank clerks,
he had been impressed by the need to make laws more accessible and
intelligible to those most closely affected by them.[5] This was one of
the main points in his first important general memorandum on the
Code. In it he pointed out that there had in the past been a tendency
for Uniform Commercial Acts and the Restatements to be addressed
to lawyers, whereas 'commercial law requires to be for commercial
men, as well as lawyers'.[6] While Llewellyn conceded that it was
not practicable to hope for 'business law made plain to every layman',[7] he felt that much of the technicality of the previous
Commercial Acts was unnecessary and had no positive value. He
was emphatic that in a democracy:

> The legal profession needs to have the men of commerce think of law and
> legal work, not as a baffling intricacy of unununderstandable technicality, but as
> a helpful device which can be seen, directly, to be helpful though safety
> requires the use of a lawyer's skills in developing its help. The fact that the
> automobile is a friendly device has not reduced the need for mechanics; it
> has, on the other hand, increased the service rendered by mechanics. But
> that has depended on ready availability of the automobile to the public, on
> the public's understanding enough about it to use it – and so to learn when
> to consult the mechanic. So with commercial law.[8]

As far as possible the draftsmen treated businessmen, as well as
lawyers and judges, as the principal addressees of the Code. An
attempt was made to use concepts familiar to businessmen; technical
legal terms and complex clauses were avoided where possible, and
in general 'the conveyancing approach to drafting by means of all-
inclusive detailed statement [was] rejected . . .'.[9] Where appropriate,
too, sections dealing with transactions were organized with the needs

of lay participants in mind. For example, s. 2–502(2) presents the seller's duties in the form of a catalogue of acts which the seller must perform, unless otherwise agreed, and this can be read as a set of instructions addressed directly to sellers.[10] The policy of simplification was not implemented in a crude or doctrinaire fashion, but it is generally accepted that, whatever its limitations, the Code represents a considerable advance in this direction when compared to its predecessors.

Llewellyn saw very clearly that the policy of simplification involved giving over some discretion to the courts:

Technical language and complex statement cannot be wholly avoided. But they can be reduced to a minimum. *The essential presupposition of so reducing them is faith in the courts to give reasonable effect to reasonable intention of the language.*[11]

Llewellyn did not see the granting of such discretion to the judiciary merely as the inevitable price of simplification, for he also maintained that 'semi-permanent Acts must envisage and encourage development by the courts'.[12] And not only by the courts, as s. 1–102(2)(b) makes clear. In that section the aims of preserving flexibility and of encouraging continued expansion of commercial practices envisages a law-creating role for the business community: the Code was conceived as an instrument which would provide the starting-point for a new phase of development, unfettered by too heavy a legacy of past authority and allowing, within broad limits, for adaptation to varying conditions.[13] As the adoptive child of many legislatures the Code was drafted in the expectation that it would probably have to last without major alterations for a substantial period, at least thirty years, perhaps fifty, perhaps even longer, with the prospect of an increasing momentum in the rate of technological and other change. As Schlesinger pointed out in his submission to the NYLRC, some of the nineteenth-century continental codes started out as instruments of drastic social reform, but because of the obstacles to regular revision of a code even in a unitary state they eventually became in many respects obstacles to progress.[14] Not only did the Uniform Commercial Code start out as less of a reforming instrument than its continental cousins, but its position as a Uniform Act, the creature of many legislators, makes uniform revision and amendment very much harder. The machinery set up to keep the Code constantly in review, the Permanent Editorial Board, has so far been principally concerned to maintain uniformity by discouraging divergences from the official text. In short, its main function has been to discourage change. When it seeks to introduce amendments to the Code, its position is such that it will be very difficult for it to be effectual, and the prospects of success in the face of determined opposition are likely to be limited.

The final purpose explicitly stated in the text of the Code was uniformity. Undesirable diversity in commercial laws was in part attributable to defects in the old Uniform Acts which had resulted in diversity in interpretation, and in confusion in areas where there were overlaps or gaps or malfunctioning; it was also due to the almost inevitable process of growing apart over time to which the new Code would also be susceptible in the long run.

Most of the articulated objectives, taken singly, are relatively conventional and uncontroversial. Few people would seriously question the desirability of seeking modernity, uniformity, 'certainty', clarity, consistency, and the avoidance of unnecessary complexity in a commercial statute or code. If 'simplification' includes making law comprehensible to laymen, there will be cavillers; when 'flexibility' leads to open-ended drafting, there is room for differences of opinion.[15] The extent to which 'adaptability' and 'certainty' or 'flexibility' and 'uniformity' are compatible goals has long been a matter of juristic controversy. At various points in the preparation of the Code these matters were the subject of disagreement, but, as was noted above, the issues were not posed sharply and disagreements were resolved pragmatically and by compromise, in a manner which makes analysis difficult.

From some points of view the finished Code might be said to be a relatively conservative document. Such departures as have been categorized as radical relate mainly to technical matters: the integration of a major part of commercial law into a relative unity, the downgrading of 'title' in sales; the simplification of secured transactions, and the departures in terminology and the general style of drafting, are some of the most commonly cited examples. None of these raise in a direct fashion policy issues of a kind likely to excite laymen. Neither in policy nor in substance nor technique does the Code represent a drastic break with the traditions of the common law. Llewellyn characterized the Revised Uniform Sales Act as 'a return to the Mansfield approach', but even some of his Mansfieldian ideas did not survive, such as the provisions for the use of merchant experts in the determination of mercantile facts, an idea modelled explicitly on Mansfield's merchant's jury.[16] It can be pointed out that the project operated within a framework of assumptions about a free-enterprise economy, a respect for private property and for the existing structure of business, and the desirability of free competition within broadly framed leeways; these assumptions were never seriously questioned. It is also true that some matters commonly associated with 'consumer protection' were left to local regulation and that when objection was made to the draft s. 1–102(3),[17] on grounds that it tended to limit freedom of contract, a revision was made in order that the Code should be seen to state 'affirmatively at the outset that freedom of contract is a principle of the Code'.[18] If these are indicia of 'conservatism' then the Code was a conservative document. *Per contra*, in addition to the matters mentioned above, it can be pointed out that the general requirements of good faith, reasonableness and unconscionability, together with certain express provisions from which there could be no contracting out, set new limits to the principle of freedom of contract, for the most part in ways likely to mitigate inequalities of bargaining power, so that the Code is potentially more of a 'consumers' charter' than some have imagined.[19]

In any event, to label the Code 'conservative' would not necessarily be to condemn it. Its defenders can point out that there was little evidence of widespread demand for more sweeping reform at any time during the process of its preparation. The political and institutional context of this process was such as to discourage overt response to such demands. Llewellyn himself saw commercial law primarily as an instrument for facilitating certain kinds of economic activity and he had no political or ideological hobby-horses to ride in this area, unless his concern with fair distribution of risk can be so described. Throughout, his overriding objective was to achieve certain limited goals and these did not include the introduction of fundamental changes in the structure and patterns of business nor in drastic re-ordering of values in commercial life.

LLEWELLYN'S IDEAS ON CODIFICATION AND HIS APPROACH TO THE CODE

The word 'code' has no settled usage in the common law world. Patterson, in his submission to the New York Law Revision Commission, suggested that a partial definition would ascribe five principal characteristics: 'Orderly, authoritative (i.e. enacted by legislation), selective (i.e., only the *leading* rules), comprehensive (i.e. all of the leading rules) and unified (i.e. on a single subject matter).'[20] The Code, with a few relatively minor exceptions, was adjudged to satisfy this standard. Llewellyn would probably have accepted this analysis, but would have placed more stress on its being an integrated unit, consistent in form, in substance, in terminology, and in directive principles and to be treated as a whole by its interpreters.[21]

In his discussions of the Code Llewellyn rarely made explicit reference to the famous controversies about codification. Nor in his advocacy for its adoption did he actually cast his arguments in such general terms. Almost invariably he emphasized that the Code was a particular instrument specially designed for solving a particular set of problems. Nevertheless, implicit in his approach were certain attitudes towards and ideas about codification, and in other contexts, notably in teaching jurisprudence, he often discussed the ideas of Savigny, Carter, Field, and other leading participants in debates about codification. Since the approach he in fact adopted in practice appears to be consistent with his general teaching, it is useful to start by examining his theoretical position on this topic.

Characteristically this position was a deliberately flexible stance between two extremes; just as characteristically he depicted these extremes in colourful and somewhat exaggerated terms. On the one hand was hopelessly naif optimism, symbolized by the approach of Frederick the Great: 'This is the concept of a book of rules that [covers] all cases that are going to arise, decides them in advance and makes it possible, therefore, for true certainty to exist and for the complete elimination of the . . . troubling element of the person in dealing with the law.'[22] Frederick is said to have hoped that his code would be so simple and so comprehensive that 'the whole body of modern advocates would be rendered useless';[23] at first he forbade interpretation and ordered that in case of doubt recourse should be had to legislative authority. The significance of this 'signal failure',[24] in Llewellyn's view, was all the greater because at that time Prussia was a compact, relatively simple, pre-industrial society. Llewellyn was also inclined to treat Bentham as an extremist in respect of codification; he was more sympathetic to the efforts of David Dudley Field in New York, but he nevertheless considered his projects to be 'ill-conceived'[25] and over-ambitious.

Thus Llewellyn dissociated himself from the attitudes of those who saw codification as *per se* producing a high degree of 'certainty' in law or as eliminating the discretion of the courts.

Llewellyn was rather more gentle, even affectionate, with the opponents of codification. If the fault of the enthusiasts was a naif optimism about the possibility or the value of crossing bridges before one reaches them, contrasting faults were to be found in the absence of orderly planning in much of the common law, at which he poked gentle fun in his informal lectures:

Our own architecture is extremely crude, as you will appreciate if you ever study the system of any well-codified body of law, such as the German Civil Code, the Swiss Civil Code, the Code Civil; you compare that kind of architecture with ours and [ours looks] like a kind of Topsy with neither head nor tail nor plan, that just growed. It looks like one of these old New England farm houses . . . a house that had another piece stuck on when the first son got married and another piece stuck on when the second son got married, and a third piece stuck onto the second piece when the first grandchild got married, and the barns around here, along with the red carriage house and various other things placed in some kind of queer fashion, none of them having any particular initial plan, none of them having any particular relation to anything – each one nice enough, as far as it goes, rather nice lines, too. Rather solidly built, close to the earth and homely and satisfactory. . . . Where was the plan? . . . Nevertheless . . . it houses its people and its work quite satisfactorily; I think ours does, though at some cost in inconvenience. You keep, if I may stay with the figure for a moment, you keep tripping as you move from one level to another, from one part of the house. . . . [Have] you ever been through one of those old houses? . . . and suddenly dropped, bang, down an extra step and landed on your face? Well, our architecture is somewhat like that.[26]

These two images are relevant to Llewellyn's approach to the Uniform Commercial Code. It is impossible to cover all contingencies; it is foolish and dangerous to try to do so: foolish because it involves underestimating the range and complexity of possible contingencies; dangerous because, in the architectural analogy, the codifier is both the architect and the builder of the structure; it is left to those who have to live with it to furnish, to decorate and, where necessary, to make alterations and additions. Underlying Llewellyn's approach, then, are certain basic conceptions about the relationship of the codifiers to two groups of people—those affected by the Code (the law consumers) and those charged with deciding cases under it. The relationship with both groups must be based on two ideas: the codifier needs to recognize his own limitations of understanding and foresight and he must trust the law consumer and the decision-maker to act with good faith and good sense in normal circumstances. Thus the image of the codifier of the Uniform Commercial Code is not the dictatorial legislator, pretending to omniscience, to prescience and to a capacity to make wise provision for all difficult cases in advance of their occurrence. Nor is the image of the typical law consumer the shark or the trickster, but rather the respectable merchant who can be expected to act with good faith, decency and commercial reasonableness. Similarly, the image of the decision-maker is not the shyster, twisting the instrument to suit his own ends, nor the literal-minded formalist, but the grand style judge or arbitrator responding to the guidance provided by authoritative legal materials, and by common sense and justice. For Holmes' 'bad man' is substituted the respectable man of business,[27] for the slot-machine or the shyster is substituted the conscientious craftsman.

Llewellyn's criticisms of Savigny and Carter are also relatively mild. Although he considered Carter to be even more extreme than Savigny in his opposition to codification, Llewellyn treated him sympathetically, praising in particular *The Ideal and the Actual in the Law*.[28] In a perceptive article in the *Encyclopaedia of the Social Sciences* he gives a succinct summary of what, in his view, were the strengths and weaknesses of Carter's ideas. It also contains in a nutshell most of Llewellyn's own general ideas on codification :

The chief virtue of Carter's position is his insistence on the huge scope of extra-official controls in law and on the limitations set thereby to official action. The chief vice of the positive analysis is oversimplification. Carter deliberately disregards, for example, the whole law of governmental organization and of legal procedure; he overlooks modern administrative regulation. The multiformity and conflict of subgroup 'customs' is hopelessly scanted. The realm of flux in which there is no custom and in which officials really create; even more the realm of tolerance in which official determinations, though they counter existing custom, are carried through; and finally the practical effects of judicial 'tyranny' – these are too detailed for the vague vastness of Carter's picture. Negatively, his argument attacks not codification as it is – a fresh and fertile start for case law, which at its best already incorporates existing tendencies – but the utopian ideal of the blinder advocates of codification: a closed system, 'certain' – and dead.[29]

That Llewellyn, while actively involved in a codification project, was able nonetheless to deal with codification controversies with some detachment was due in part to the fact that his approach to codification was essentially pragmatic. Abstract discussions of the advantages and disadvantages of codification did not appeal to him. Nor did discussions about the 'proper' meaning of the word 'code'. Still less did he accept the idea that there was one model form of 'code' by which all codes should be judged—an idea which seems to underly some criticisms of the Uniform Commercial Code made by civil law trained commentators. His plans for the Uniform Commercial Code were formulated with reference to a particular problem which arose in a specific context at a particular moment in history.

It has been pointed out that the Uniform Commercial Code is not a 'Commercial Code' in the continental sense. Certainly if one contrasts it with, for example, the French Commercial Code, there are certain important differences. First, the latter presupposes a more general civil code, which is applicable both to fill in gaps and to assist in interpretation. It has been said authoritatively that a 'civil code must remain the general private code, the code of commerce being limited to applications and derogations'.[30] The Uniform Commercial Code on the other hand, while presupposing much of the general body of common law doctrines of contract, and explicitly providing for supplementation from principles of common law and equity,[31] purports to be the governing instrument over a wide area of law. In certain cases it explicitly diverges from common law contract rules and no attempt has been made deliberately to frame the Code in traditional contract terms. Indeed it has been suggested that the Code undermines some long-established contract principles and that it is stimulating American lawyers to reformulate traditional conceptions of contract to fit the Code rather than vice versa.[32] Thus the Uniform Commercial Code to a large extent is an independent piece of legislation in contrast with the French Commercial Code which is just a part of an integrated system of codes. Secondly, the French Commercial Code is 'commercial', in the sense that it governs merchants (commerçants), that is to say persons who are principally engaged in 'acts of commerce'. French commercial law provides for different procedures from civil law for special tribunaux de commerce and makes special provisions with relation to such matters as proof, rates of interest, and bankruptcy.[33] The Uniform Commercial Code, on the other hand, makes no provision for such a court nor is its application restricted to contracts between merchants, although in some circumstances more arduous standards are imposed upon merchants and there are some special provisions relating to them. But it does little to undermine the long established integration of the common law and the law merchant. Thirdly, and most important of all, the Code was drafted in the expectation that it would be interpreted by common law trained lawyers and judges and in the hope that they would adopt 'the Grand Style' in their approach to it.[34] Although it is notoriously dangerous to generalize about differences between 'common law' and 'civil law' techniques, one can state with confidence that there would have been important differences both in style and arrangement if the image of the typical prospective interpreter in the mind's eye of the draftsman had been a civilian rather than, for example, a judge of the New York Court of Appeals.

This leads on to the final point. There are some features of the Code, such as the emphasis on 'good faith' (*bonne foi*) and unconscionability, which will be familiar to a continental jurist; Llewellyn's attitude to commercial usage has echoes in Ehrlich, and, in general, the Sales Article is closer to the 1939 draft of the Uniform Law on International Sale of Goods than was the Uniform Sales Act and there are other general indications of Llewellyn's familiarity with civil law. The Code is, however, generally recognized to be a 'common law code' and for this it has been criticized on two main grounds: first, it has been suggested that not enough systematic comparative study was undertaken in respect of the continental experience of codification of commercial law;[35] and secondly, an opportunity was missed in preparing the Code to bring about a simultaneous unification at international as well as at national levels. During the drafting of the Revised Uniform Sales Act, Ernst Rabel, who was officially connected with the Rome Institute's project for the unification of the International Law of Sales, wrote to Llewellyn and to Lewis urging that this opportunity should be taken. His plea appears to have fallen on deaf ears.[36] It is particularly interesting that Rabel was one of the few critics to argue that the draftsmen of the Code were not being radical enough. While praising the Revised Uniform Sales Act (Draft No. 1) as 'an outstanding work' and noting that it approached the views of the Rome Institute in a number of important particulars,[37] he regretted that no serious attempt had been made to marry the two drafts:

In the points in which the Draft and the Project differ, the preferable solution is probably sometimes to be found in the one sometimes in the other text. They do not differ because of national peculiarities, but because of lack of co-operation.[38]

Rabel argued that the project differed from the RUSA draft in having 'very consciously worked out a method to reach the nearest possible legal equivalent to the commercial conceptions'.[39] In short, his argument was that the main remaining differences between the two drafts was that the Rome Project had been more systematic in its attempt to achieve an identical goal with that of the Code, the marrying of commercial law and commercial practice.

'IF I WERE A CHEQUE' – THE EMPIRICAL BASIS OF THE UNIFORM COMMERCIAL CODE

If a statute or code is viewed primarily as an instrument for encouraging, discouraging or facilitating certain kinds of behaviour, that is to say as a means of achieving certain effects, it can be argued that a first step in evaluating it should be to try to find out what effects the law has in fact had, desired or otherwise. Similarly, in drafting such legislation a natural starting-point, in this view, would be to obtain as comprehensive and reliable a picture as possible of the range of behaviour to be covered, of its social context and of relevant trends and conditions, and to make projections as to what measures are most likely to maximize the desired result with the least risk of producing undesired side effects. The study of conditions, trends and effects is a form of empirical inquiry. Such legislative 'fact research' has not yet become a regular feature of law-making or legal research either in the United Kingdom or the United States, although there has been some movement in this direction in recent times. The reasons for the neglect of empirical research may include failure to perceive the relevance of factual data to the making and evaluation of laws, the expense in time and money involved in collecting data, the alleged tedium or lack of glamour of much of this kind of research, and a tendency on the part of participants in law-making processes to dismiss such work as not being feasible without bothering first to define what might be desirable.[40] This latter tendency is associated with a general willingness to accept as an adequate substitute the undifferentiated opinion-evidence of experts, interest groups and others.

It is sometimes suggested that the Uniform Commercial Code sits too comfortably within the Anglo-American tradition of 'unscientific' law making. In so far as 'realism' involves some commitment to relatively systematic collection of data, this suggestion raises an important doubt about the relationship between Llewellyn's practice in respect of the Code and the jurisprudential ideas that he preached in other contexts. It also raises some interesting questions about the relevance and utility of empirical research as a basis for law-making.

It may help to clarify some of the issues if we start by postulating two crude theoretical models of recommended procedures for the preliminary phases of law-making and law reform. On the one hand there could be 'the committee room model': a committee or commission, consisting mainly of 'experts', all or most of whom are lawyers, considers an area of law which is thought to be in need of reform and makes recommendations which may or may not be embodied in the form of a draft bill. Typically, 'evidence' is invited from interested parties, from experts and, sometimes, from the public at large. Such evidence may be mainly factual, but may well be a mixture of fact, opinion and prescription, based on the experience of the witnesses, their conception of their own or the public interest, and judgments by lawyers about what would be technically feasible and desirable. Typically, little or no systematic research is undertaken by the committee itself and, if research is undertaken, it is nearly always armchair or library research, which rarely goes further than an inquiry into the existing state of the law. Typically, systematically gathered empirical data are not considered as a necessary basis for making recommendations and there is generally a faith in the adequacy of experience and common sense to provide sufficient relevant information which is sufficiently reliable. Rigorous empirical research involving accepted social science techniques is not considered necessary or even relevant.

This model can be contrasted with the 'scientific model', which is implicit in the idea of a 'Science of Legislation'. Leaving aside for the moment questions of feasibility and cost, we can state the ideal to be scientifically validated data concerning all matters which are relevant to the subject of reform and which are susceptible to empirical investigation. Although common sense would indicate the exploitation of available sources of information, special research would typically need to be undertaken, involving careful planning and rigorous procedures. Research and prescription would be clearly differentiated, and the 'information' provided by interested parties would be treated with especial caution. Even where practical obstacles would prevent the collection of all the desired data, the delineation of what information might be relevant and useful involves a more arduous intellectual procedure than is characteristic of the committee-room model.

If these are fair constructs, then it is also fair to say that more often than not the Anglo-American tradition has approximated more closely to the committee-room model than to the other.[41]

A possible charge against Llewellyn would appear to be that whereas his theoretical ideas committed him to looking towards the 'scientific model', in respect of the Code he made no serious attempt to break away from the committee-room pattern. One critic concedes that he brought to bear 'a rich but unrigorous' experience of business life,[42] but implies that the Code is just one example of the failure of realists, such as Corbin and Llewellyn, to break free from the library-bound, case-oriented tradition of the common law.

As a preliminary to examining possible defences against this charge, it is relevant to recall Llewellyn's attitude to the scientific analogy in legal research. This can be summarized in three propositions: the empirical study of law as a branch of behavioural science is still only a 'pre-pre-science';[43] 'knowledge does not have to be scientific to be useful and important';[44] and the 'scientific analogy' can tempt people to try to run before they can walk; in some legal contexts this 'is like using seven-place logarithms to work out the rough carpentry of a building whose parts are being measured by thumb-joints—a different man's thumb-joint for each measurement'.[45] At this stage of the development of legal sociology, it is unreasonable to ask of law-makers that they should do more than produce rough carpentry. The scientific model might provide an ultimate goal, but it may be inappropriately seductive at this early stage, especially in relation to practical activities.

Thus, questions of feasibility apart, Llewellyn was not necessarily predisposed to a 'scientific' approach to the Code. But this in itself does not constitute a complete defence to charges that his actions were inconsistent with his theories and that the Code did not have an adequate empirical base. Llewellyn does not seem to have anticipated this kind of criticism and so he is not his own advocate in the case that is presented here.

The first line of defence would be that some research was in fact undertaken. However, it must be conceded that there was virtually no systematic project research of the kind postulated by the scientific model. There were no orderly research designs, disciplined sampling or carefully tested questionnaires.[46] Such fieldwork as was done tended to be *ad hoc*; Llewellyn revisited the National City Bank to observe how bank collections were transacted; Mentschikoff investigated brokerage practices for Article 8; Gilmore, Dunham and Leary all made forays to various institutions to find out how particular transactions were carried out in practice. But fieldwork was the exception. Where, then, did the draftsmen purport to obtain information about business practice and other relevant matters? It is generally conceded that Llewellyn's own knowledge and understanding of many phases of business were truly extraordinary.[47] His two years with the National City Bank had laid the foundation: not only had he been involved in numerous transactions, but he had also made a point of visiting every part of the bank to see each phase of its activities for himself. Subsequently, for over thirty years he had specialized in the field of commercial law and—and this is perhaps the crux of the matter—he was fascinated by the subject and his interest in the minutest detail of even the most mundane type of transaction was quite insatiable. In reading cases, in visiting institutions, in talking to bankers, in thinking about problems, his preoccupation was always with patterns of practice, both in their daily operation and as illuminated by crises. After meetings of Code committees he could be seen in the bar cross-examining distinguished bankers or businessmen tenaciously and with a sensitive ear always for the nonfunctional or the improbable or 'the beautiful'. His questioning tended to be specific, guided principally by a concern with function and process. 'If I were a cheque and I arrived in your bank where would I go? ... What would be done to me first? Why? ...'. If Llewellyn's methods were unrigorous, his knowledge of business practice was reputedly rich in insight, 'feel' and in detailed information.

A second source of information was reported cases. A social scientist may be sceptical about, but cannot dismiss entirely, Llewellyn's claim that he learned a great deal about commercial life from reading the law reports. Again it must be remembered that his approach to the reading of cases was unusual, especially as regards concentration on the facts: who were the parties? What did they do when? What happened? How typical was this situation? Why was there a dispute? As with the related methods employed in *The Cheyenne Way*, his technique of reading cases could not on its own be a satisfactory source of empirical information. But as a starting point for investigation or as a means of supplementing and refreshing already compendious knowledge the law reports are rich, digestible and, above all, easily accessible.

A third source of information was the 'floor' of the NCC, which brought together an extraordinarily wide range of practical experience, from small-town lawyers from Montana to a variety of types of practitioners from the large cities. One of the main functions of holding full meetings of the NCC and ALI to discuss drafts was to test the factual assumptions on which each section was based. The standard model for presentation was said to be: this is the factual situation as we see it; these are the policies involved; this is our proposed solution.[48] Thus the main factual assumptions of the draftsmen were made explicit, and everyone present had an opportunity to test these assumptions against his own knowledge and experience and feel for the situation, and to point out discrepancies. There is no evidence to suggest that members of the NCC suffered from noticeable inhibitions about doing this, for they frequently raised points concerning local practice and problems. It is also significant that during the period of preparation of the Code the prevailing ethos of the NCC demanded that members should participate *pro bono publico* and not as representatives of special interests.[49] This is an important departure from the committee room model in which a great deal of evidence comes from interested parties acting in a representative capacity.

Although the device of using the 'floor' of the NCC and ALI to check the factual assumptions of the various drafts might not be as systematic as project research, it had certain obvious advantages: it was relatively quick and cheap; the factual assumptions being tested were directly related to specific draft sections; and, as participants in the law-making process, the informants were likely to be more serious and generally more cooperative than they could have expected to be if they had been plied with questionnaires or interviewed by research workers.

A second line of defence is that only in certain limited respects is detailed factual information relevant to law-making in the field of commercial law.[50] Although Llewellyn did not talk explicitly in these terms, he had relatively clear assumptions about the range and nature of the main data that would be relevant to his purposes. In contemplating the vast panorama of commercial activity in the United States he assumed that the first need was to establish working categories which reflected the most significant differentiations and which would provide the main lenses for perceiving and classifying situations. Within the framework of perception the most important need for detailed information concerned how transactions were performed. Here the search was not for precise quantitative data but rather for a reasonably accurate picture of standard practices and of the kinds of problems that tended to recur. Precise information about the number of cheques handled by banks, or the frequency of a particular type of transaction, would in many instances be of little or no use to the law-maker.

An anecdote pin-points one of the practical objections that can be made against the 'scientific model'. Grant Gilmore tells of an occasion when he was sent to visit a New York firm of brokers to find out how a particular transaction was carried out on the floor of the New York Stock Exchange. One of the partners explained to him in great detail how it was done; then, since he had not witnessed the transaction personally during the previous three months, he called in one of his juniors and asked him to describe, without prompting, how the same transaction was carried out. His description was quite different from that of his superior. On further investigation it turned out that shortly before Gilmore's visit there had been a strike and during this period some corners had been cut. This simplified procedure had proved to be more satisfactory than the old one and so it had been adopted as part of the regular practice.[51] The intended moral of this story is that many areas of business practice change so rapidly that research into what happens, however rigorous and expensive, could be useless or worse. When it is remembered that the Code was being designed to cover an enormous variety of commercial situations, in a large number of jurisdictions, and would also have to stand the test of time, it became obvious that empirical research into all relevant aspects of the situation would have had to be on a gigantic scale and in any case could still only deal with the past and the present.

It has been suggested that these points support the paradoxical conclusion that the longer a Code is built to last, or the wider its scope, the less is the research that needs to be done.[52] While this is not based on impeccable logic, it contains a core of truth, *viz.* that a legislative instrument that is intended to last a long time or to cover a variety of situations needs to be built in such a way that it is not dependent on precise and constant factual underpinnings. In commercial law the 'realism' that is needed is that of a balanced and reasonably accurate picture of the whole scene in terms of patterns of practice, of recurrent problems and of projected future trends. The precision and elegance of 'scientific' research is more appropriate where the focus is narrower and something more specific than a broad framework is called for. It may also be useful where opinions and attitudes need to be investigated.

Of course, scepticism of the 'scientific model' could be carried too far. There may have been some instances where rigorous research procedures would have been appropriate. For example, analysis of the comments might reveal a number of factual assumptions that were both capable of verification and would be more appropriately tested by systematic empirical research than by the methods that were in fact used. It is interesting to note, however, that critics who have been suspicious of Llewellyn's alleged 'unscientific', 'impressionistic' or 'anecdotal' approach to facts have yet to point to any major factual assumptions of the Code that were misleading or inaccurate. Nor have suggestions been forthcoming as to specific empirical research that might have been worth doing. Without such concrete suggestions criticisms of the empirical base of the Code and of Llewellyn's approach are rather hard to evaluate.

Finally, there is the question of feasibility. Even if it could be shown that in some areas the information available to the sponsors was neither sufficiently comprehensive nor sufficiently 'hard', it is arguable that there were severe practical limitations on what they could have done to remedy the situation. Here it is important to recall the institutional context of the Code project. Before Llewellyn had started to make plans for the Code, the NCC had become the main sponsor. The 'treaty' with the American Law Institute was also concluded before the working procedures had been fully worked out. The traditional procedures of the two sponsoring institutions, although not identical with the committee-room model, were far removed from the scientific model. While tradition did not rigidly dictate any particular procedure for the Code, it would have been difficult to depart significantly from the past practices of the sponsors. Llewellyn himself, far from being dissatisfied with those practices, felt very much at home at meetings of the NCC and neither he nor his colleagues seem to have been unduly worried by the problem of obtaining the information they needed. Thus the institutional context, reinforced by the predispositions of the Code personnel, the pressure of time and the relative modesty of the financing, made it virtually inevitable that empirical research on a large scale could not have been undertaken, even if it had been needed.

To conclude, in order to substantiate the contention that the sponsors of the Code were at fault in not undertaking or promoting systematic empirical research, it is submitted that the critic needs to establish the following points : (1) that there were certain specific questions which were capable of being answered by acceptable methods of empirical research and to which the framers did not have sufficiently reliable answers; (2) that such information was necessary or important as a basis for making rational decisions in connection with the preparation of the Code; in particular that this kind of information would have sufficient general significance to be of value in respect of a Code, destined to cover a wide sphere of economic life over an extensive geographical area for a considerable period of time; and (3) that it would have been feasible for the sponsors of the Code to undertake or promote such research and that the costs in time and money would have been justified by its importance.

The defence of Llewellyn offered here is admittedly tentative and incomplete. It is not inconceivable that a specialist in commercial law, familiar with the Code and with social science techniques, might be able to suggest one or more projects which would satisfy these criteria. However, I know of no evidence to suggest that the main factual assumptions of the codifiers were seriously inaccurate or incomplete.[53] To date, the criticism of the Code on this count has been insufficiently specific to raise a case to answer. It seems that the importance of disciplined empirical research to law-making (at least in fields such as commercial law) can easily be exaggerated by those who accept a simple *a priori* model of 'scientific' law reform. In particular, where the search is for understanding the functions of transactions, quantitative data are likely to be of marginal utility.

It is to be hoped that a careful attempt will be made to ascertain and evaluate the practical consequences of the Code project. Such an investigation could contribute to the better understanding of law-making generally. Moreover, there is, it seems, a body of opinion which is sceptical to a greater or lesser extent about the social and economic importance of the Code. For instance, I have heard the view expressed informally that the Code is 'a gigantic irrelevance'. It is rather difficult to pin down exactly what is implied by such a judgment, but it may suggest such propositions as (1) that the Code has had little or no effect on the practices of businessmen and has had no significant economic consequences; (2) that it has not ·made the learning or handling of commercial law significantly easier or more efficient for law students and legal practitioners; and (3) that the Code contributed little or nothing to the solution of any major social or economic problem of the day in the United States, and that in this sense it is 'irrelevant'. Indeed, it has been hinted that the Code may have been counterproductive by diverting attention, energy and resources into the production of an elephantine and largely trivial literature and away from more 'worthwhile' pursuits. These charges represent an extreme and no doubt crude version of an opinion that may be held in some quarters in American law schools. Not unnaturally there will be many who disagree profoundly with such views. It may be that a disciplined approach to this issue would involve, *inter alia*, a rather complicated and elusive form of cost-benefit analysis. It is beyond my competence even to suggest how such an analysis might be undertaken. The purpose of this section has been merely to draw attention to the issue rather than to attempt to resolve it.

PURPOSE AND REASON IN THE UNIFORM COMMERCIAL CODE

Llewellyn's teleological view of laws as instruments of policy found clear expression in the Uniform Commercial Code. If a legislative provision is a means to certain ends, good social engineering requires that as far as possible the means selected should be co-extensive with the ends; the draftsman should endeavour to give clear expression to the ends as well as the means and the interpreter must be given every encouragement to interpret the instrument in accordance with its objectives. Llewellyn put the matter as follows:

Drafting Techniques and Policies.
1. The principle of the *patent reason*: Every provision should show its reason

on its face. Every body of provisions should display on their face their organizing principle.

The rationale of this is that construction and application are intellectually impossible except with reference to *some* reason and theory of purpose and organization. Borderline, doubtful, or uncontemplated cases are inevitable. Reasonably uniform interpretation by judges of different schooling, learning and skill is tremendously furthered if the reason which guides application of the same language is the *same* reason in all cases. A patent reason, moreover, tremendously decreases the leeway open to the skilful advocate for persuasive distortion or misapplication of the language; it requires that any contention, to be successfully persuasive, must make some kind of sense *in terms of the* reason; it provides a real stimulus toward, though not an assurance of, corrective growth rather than straitjacketing of the Code by way of case-law.[54]

Three main devices for implementing this approach were employed in the Code: explicit rules of construction are included in Article 1, requiring interpretation of the Code in accordance with its purposes;[55] secondly, the general objects of the Code and, in a few instances, the specific objects of particular rules, are made explicit in the text of the Code itself; thirdly, the Code is supplemented by extensive Comments prepared by the draftsmen as an important aid to interpretation. Each of these devices will be considered in turn.

Liberal interpretation made mandatory
The history of judicial interpretation of statutes in the common law world is sometimes seen as a battle between 'literal' and 'liberal' approaches to interpretation. These different approaches have found expression at a general level in the apparently conflicting principles of the Literal Rule and the Mischief Rule or the Rule in *Heydon's Case*.[56] A third principle, 'the Golden Rule', prescribes that when a literal interpretation would lead to an absurdity, then the courts may depart from the literal meaning of the words. The Code is most unusual in that it *requires* the adoption of a 'liberal' aproach. Section 1–102(1) reads :

This Act shall be liberally construed and applied to promote its underlying purposes and policies.[57]

This instruction is amplified in the accompanying comment:

This Act is drawn to provide flexibility so that, since it is intended to be a semi-permanent piece of legislation, it will provide its own machinery for expansion of commercial practices. It is intended to make it possible for the law embodied in this Act to be developed by the courts in the light of unforeseen and new circumstances and practices. However, the proper construction of the Act requires that its interpretation and application be limited to its reason.... The Act should be construed in accordance with its underlying purposes and policies. The text of each section should be read in the light of the purpose and policy of the rule or principle in question, as also of the Act as a whole, and the application of the language should be construed narrowly or broadly, as the case may be, in conformity with the purposes and policies involved.[58]

A similar explicit provision is made in respect of remedies by Section 1–106:

The remedies provided by this Act shall be liberally administered to the end that the aggrieved party may be put in as good a position as if the other party had fully performed but neither consequential nor special nor penal damages may be had except as specifically provided in this Act or by other rules of law.[59]

None of the provisions requiring liberal interpretation of the Code had any counterparts in prior Uniform Acts; indeed they must be almost unique in Anglo-American legal history.

Explicit statements of policy incorporated in the Code
Having required that the Code be interpreted in accordance with its policies, the draftsmen proceeded to make these policies explicit. The general objects are stated in s.1–102(2) which was quoted above. Where appropriate, 'purpose' was articulated in specific rules. A good example of a provision which provides for discretion to be exercised by commercial institutions within the limits of a general and clearly stated purpose is s.4–107(1), dealing with bank deposits and collections:

(1) For the purpose of allowing time to process items, prove balances and make the necessary entries on its books to determine its position for the day, a bank may fix an afternoon hour of two P.M. or later as a cut-off hour for the handling of money and items and the making of entries on its books.[60]

In fact, only sparing use was made of the device of incorporating specific statements of purpose in the rules themselves. There are several good reasons for this. One disadvantage of detailed statements of purpose is that they tend to lengthen and complicate the text of the instrument; one of Llewellyn's objectives was to produce a text that would be simple, succinct and easy to read. Often, purpose can be easily inferred from the provision, and spelling it out would be otiose. Furthermore, as Patterson pointed out in his submission to the New York Law Revision Commission, articulation of purpose can create difficulties, where otherwise none would have existed. He cited as an example his experience with the Tentative Draft of the New York Insurance Law Revision in 1937:

> The Comments, intended to explain simply why some changes were being made, aroused nearly as much opposition as the statute itself. In the numerous subsequent published drafts no comments were given. The revision was enacted in 1939.[61]

Patterson's remarks were directed particularly against 'official' comments. He preferred reasons to be indicated in the text, if possible. But his arguments apply with even greater force to incorporating explicit statements of reasons as part of the text. The danger is not only that reasons may arouse controversy during the course of enactment, but also that they may sometimes hinder rather than aid interpretation. The basic reason for this is simple. The ends are not necessarily co-extensive with the means. Statements of purpose are at least as susceptible as are statements of 'substantive' rules to vagueness, ambiguity, obscurity, difficulty of reconciliation with other statements, and so on. The task of the interpreter is first and foremost to interpret the instrument of the policy rather than the policy itself. Llewellyn, as a protagonist of a liberal approach, went no further than advocating that statements of purpose should be *aids* to interpreting the instrument.[62]

Purpose to be inferred from choice of language and articulation of situation sense

Despite the sparing use made of explicit statements of purpose, it is clear that the 'rule with a singing reason' was the basic model for the draftsmen.[63] An alternative technique to explicit statements of purpose 'consists in making the purpose of a provision appear on its face by the choice of language and by the organization of the thought in the light of the situation'.[64]

This can be illustrated by reference to the special provisions concerning merchants in Article 2. In respect of a number of matters, for example the statute of frauds, firm offers and warranty of merchantability, 'merchants' are put in a special position. The

reason for this is that those who hold themselves out as having knowledge or skills peculiar to practices involved in a transaction, on the
one hand need less protection from formalities and on the other
hand should not be allowed to take advantage of the ignorance or
lack of skill of others. Whereas the Sales Article requires honesty in
fact of everybody in respect of performance and enforcement of
sales contracts, a higher standard is demanded of merchants, viz.
observance of reasonable commercial standards of fair dealing for
the trade concerned.[65]

The basic reason for differentiating professionals from others is
incorporated in the definitions of 'merchant' and transactions
'between merchants' (2–104(1) and (3)), so that the reason for the
differentiation and the criterion of differentiation are made co-
extensive. The reason is thus apparent on the face; it is further
emphasized by the Comment on section 2–104, which begins:

This Article assumes that transactions between professionals in a given field
require special and clear rules which may not apply to a casual or inexperienced seller or buyer. It thus adopts a policy of expressly stating rules
applicable 'between merchants' and 'as against a merchant' wherever they
are needed instead of making them depend upon the circumstances of each
case as in [the Uniform Sales Act and The Uniform Bills of Lading Act].[66]

'Merchant' is defined in terms of skills and knowledge in a very
general manner; the Comments make it clear that for different purposes, different classes of people would be counted as 'merchants'.
Thus the warranty of merchantability (s.2–314) is only implied 'if
the seller is a merchant with respect to goods of that kind'; but for
the purposes of the sections[67] which are based on acquaintance
with normal business practice, no such limitation is placed on
'merchant', so that a bank or even a university might be included in
the category for the purposes of a mercantile transaction in which
they are regularly involved. However, 'a lawyer or bank president
buying fishing tackle for his own use is not a merchant'.[68]

The treatment of 'merchants' in the Sales Article is different from
their treatment in other articles. 'This reflects a functional difference in situation. In sales the professional can be either a buyer or a
seller, and so the linking of honesty and commercial reasonableness
is made general.'[69] But, for example, in respect of secured transactions the professional is typically the lender, and in respect of
letters of credit and bank collections 'the professional' tends recur-

rently to be at the same end of the transaction. In these articles special provisions concerning standards of behaviour for professionals are spelled out in detail. Thus the provisions in the Sales Article in respect of 'merchants', read with the Comments, illustrate Llewellyn's ideas about good rules: purpose is articulated, scope is as far as possible made coextensive with purpose and is related to typical recurrent situations (situation-types), and the boundaries of application are drawn in broad general terms, 'using a zone rather than a surveyor's line to border the rule'.[70] The courts are given clear and articulate guidelines, but are left discretion in respect of application to particular situations, and flexibility is provided by incorporating criteria which will have different content in different types of situations, for example the standards of a particular trade and 'knowledge or skill peculiar to the practices or goods involved in the transaction'.[71]

The Comments

The very full commentary which accompanies the official text is the main device for articulating and explaining the policies of the Code provisions. The correct designation is 'comments of the National Conference of Commissioners on Uniform State Laws and the American Law Institute'.[72] The term 'official comments' is sometimes used, but this may be misleading in that they have been formally adopted neither by the floors of the sponsoring bodies nor by legislatures which have enacted the Code and in some cases were not even made available to the legislators. For the sake of brevity they will be referred to here as 'The Comments'. Although not entirely unprecedented, they are sufficiently unusual to deserve detailed consideration.

A variety of devices for clarifying 'the intention of the legislature' in respect of statutes has grown up in different jurisdictions. The Preamble in English statutes up to the end of the nineteenth century, *travaux preparatoires* in France and some other continental systems, explanatory memoranda which accompany bills in Denmark and the Republic of Ireland, are important examples.[73] In the United States, as might be expected, various devices have been employed from time to time. Prior to the Uniform Commercial Code it had been the practice of the NCC to publish relatively brief 'commissioners' notes' to accompany any uniform acts that they promulgated. These have been given a similar status to reports

of commissions as aids to interpretation.[74] The history of the first
Uniform Sales Act was very much in the minds of the draftsmen of
the Code.[75] Williston's treatise, first published in 1909, three years
after the Uniform Sales Act was first promulgated, had in practice
exerted such an enormous influence over the interpretation of the
act that it had amounted to 'the delegation to private persons of
essentially legislative power'.[76] This was the main reason for the
decision to have 'official' comments accompanying the Code.
Llewellyn's ideas on the subject are to be found in a draft comment
on section 1 of the Revised Sales Act:

Under Subsection (2) the courts are expressly authorized to consult the
Comments in interpreting and applying the principles of the Act. The
Comments thereby acquire a status more than equivalent to that of a
Committee Report on the basis of which a proposed bill has been enacted
by the legislature. Sustained effort has been made to make the reasons and
purposes of the Act apparent on the face of the text wherever possible. The
Comments are further designed to state with clarity and precision the intent
of each section and to integrate the Act as a whole by pointing out the
relationship between one section and another.

The purpose of the Act as to uniformity is restated in order to continue
the policy of the Original Act, Section 74, and to emphasize the special
recognition long accorded by the courts to decisions under the Uniform
Commercial Acts which have been handed down by tribunals of coordinate jurisdiction. The use of the Comments as a yardstick of legislative
intent should further promote the uniformity of interpretation of the Act.[77]

In an 'Informal Appendix' to the Third Draft of the Revised
Uniform Sales Act, Llewellyn says of some sample draft comments:

The Official Comments put no queries and canvass no doubts. They aim at
straight exposition of purpose and effect of the section and of its relation to
the prior law and the other portions of the Act. The problem of bulk relates
only to how far the Comments shall go into specific illustration and specific
case-material.[78]

After an ambitious start, a gradual whittling down of the scope
and status of the Comments took place. In 1951, at the suggestion
of the ABA section, two provisions were added to make clear that
'if text and comment conflict, text controls' and that 'prior drafts
of text and comments may not be used to ascertain legislative
intent'.[79] Early drafts included a section which read as follows:

The Comments of the National Conference of Commissioners on Uniform
State Laws and the American Law Institute may be consulted in the

construction and application of this Act but if text and comment conflict, text controls. . . .[80]

These three provisions were dropped in 1956, after criticism by the New York Commission, who objected to deviation from established practice in respect of legislative history and considered that the provision allowing the reference to Comments gave them undue weight, despite the fact of its being only permissive.[81]

The style of the final Comments represents a compromise worked out over a long period of drafting and redrafting, especially in respect of the Sales Article. Llewellyn's first attempts tended to be lengthy and not to follow a set pattern. Llewellyn and Mentschikoff expended an enormous amount of time on the first drafts of the Sales Comments during the period 1943–5. As was acknowledged later, a great deal of effort could have been saved had the drafting of text and Comments been done concurrently.[82] This procedure was sometimes followed in respect of other articles. The final drafts of the Sales Comments are much more compressed than the first ones.

In their final form the Comments have a standard format. The starting point is a reference to 'Prior Uniform Statutory Provision'; where there is none this is indicated. The nature and purposes of any change from the prior law are then analysed or the purposes of the provision are discussed. There follow, where appropriate, 'Cross References' and 'Definitional Cross References', which considerably facilitate the use of the Code, even though the former cannot be relied on to be exhaustive. The Comments vary considerably in length; they tend to be more detailed than comparable devices used elsewhere, but generalization on this point is dangerous.[83] It is difficult to make any general remarks about style, except perhaps to reiterate that the language is deliberately simple and articulation of purpose is the outstanding characteristic. In the 1962 edition of the Code, it has been estimated that the Comments stand to the text in a ratio of four to one. To supplement the extracts already quoted, it may help to quote one of the shorter comments *in toto*:

Section 9–111. Applicability of Bulk Transfer Laws.
The creation of a security interest is not a bulk transfer under Article 6 (see Section 6–103).

Comment

Prior Uniform Statutory Provision: None
Purposes:

The bulk transfer laws, which have been almost everywhere enacted, were designed to prevent a once prevalent type of fraud which seems to have flourished particularly in the retail field: the owner of a debt-burdened enterprise would sell it to an unwary purchaser and then remove himself, with the purchase price and his other assets, beyond the reach of process. The creditors would find themselves with no recourse unless they could establish that the purchaser assumed existing debts. The bulk transfer laws, which require advance notice of sale to all known creditors, seem to have been successful in preventing such frauds.

There has been disagreement whether the bulk transfer laws should be applied to security as well as to sale transactions. In most states security transactions have not been covered; in a few states the opposite result has been reached either by judicial construction or by express statutory provision. Whatever the reasons may be, it seems to be true that the bulk transfer type of fraud has not often made its appearance in the security field: it may be that lenders of money are more inclined to investigate a potential borrower than are purchasers of retail stores to determine the true state of their vendor's affairs. Since compliance with the bulk transfer laws is onerous and expensive, legitimate financing transactions should not be required to comply when there is no reason to believe that other creditors will be prejudiced.

This section merely reiterates the provisions of Article 6 on Bulk Transfers which provides in Section 6–103(1) that transfers 'made to give security for the performance of an obligation' are not subject to that Article.
Cross Reference:
Section 6–103(1).
Definitional Cross Reference:
'Security interest'. Section 1–201

The main function of the Comments is as an aid to interpretation, which avoids some of the rigidities of a tight style of drafting. Some doubts have been expressed about their juridical status. 'How high', asks Honnold 'can the comments lift themselves by their own bootstraps?'[84] It is relatively easy to give a common sense answer at a general level. The Comments have three great advantages: they bear the imprimatur of those responsible for the Code and so they have strong claims to be authoritative; they were prepared concurrently with the drafting of the Code, and so are not vulnerable to any suggestion of hindsight or second thoughts; they are, above all, accessible and easy to use. Beyond that they stand on their merits. No rule prescribes that they must be followed; the courts may use them, but how much weight they attach to them is at their discretion. In practice, as was to be expected, judges have referred to them extensively, have usually followed them, and have only occasionally deviated from them[85] As decisions interpreting the Code and secondary commentaries proliferate the comments may decline in importance to some extent, but they may confidently be expected to continue to hold their own as a prime aid to interpretation of the Code.

In addition to narrowing the range of doubt and furthering uniformity of interpretation, the Comments serve a number of other functions. They help to integrate the Code; they provide an introduction which makes it more intelligible to the lawyer, the law student and the layman; the cross-references make for speedy and efficient use; the references to the prior uniform acts assist in the tracing of legislative history. Their value is widely acknowledged. Such criticism as has been levelled at them has mainly concerned detail, or omissions, or execution, or blames them for failing to resolve all doubts, rather than the idea of having comments at all. In his fair and balanced critique, Skilton, whilst complaining of 'qualitative and stylistic unevenness',[86] concluded that they represent a net gain, indeed, that 'study of the Comments is indispensable to a knowledge of the Code'.[87]

CATEGORIES[88]

The main organizing concept: 'movement of goods'
It is commonly said that the Code is 'functionally organized'. Presumably this means that its principle social and economic function is to provide a legal framework for 'the movement of goods, the payment therefor, and the financing thereof'.[89] As can be seen from the memorandum quoted above, this was the principal criterion for determining the ground to be covered. Sales were taken to be the key transaction in the flow of goods from manufacturer to consumer and the Sales Article was treated as the central pillar of the Code. Secured transactions, commercial paper, bank deposits and collections and letters of credit are all functionally important for paying for and financing the flow of goods. But, as Schlesinger remarked, '.... the draftsmen, for good practical reasons, did not ride the functional horse through thick and thin'.[90] Insurance was not included, mainly because some of it was politically controversial. Similarly, commercial codes in civil law countries

treat of 'commercial agency', but agency is not limited to commercial situations and the civilians have had many difficulties in fitting commercial law into the framework of the general law;[91] in the Code this problem is avoided by leaving agency to the general law.[92] Conversely, not everything included in the Code is functionally limited to the movement of goods. As was often pointed out in discussion, letters of credit, cheques and other forms of commercial paper are used for a wide variety of purposes other than financing 'commercial' transactions. It was also argued that investment securities have a rather thin functional justification for inclusion in the Code, but their inclusion was justified on the ground that they had been dealt with in the earlier uniform legislation which was being repealed. Thus it is clear that while the Code is for the most part organized round the movement of goods, by no means all branches of law relevant to this function are included, and there are areas covered by the Code which related to other spheres of economic activity. It is clear from the records that the coverage of the prior uniform acts and political expediency played an important part in the determination of the scope of the Code, which can accordingly be said to have been governed by pragmatic rather than by dogmatic functionalism.

Replacing an over-broad category by a number of narrower categories

The de-emphasis of 'title' in the Sales Article is, of course, the principal illustration. The first Comment on Article 2 states:

> The arrangement of the present Article is in terms of contract for sale and the various steps of its performance. The legal consequences are stated as following directly from the contract and action taken under it without resorting to the idea of when property or title passed or was to pass as being the determining factor. The purpose is to avoid making practical issues between practical men turn upon the location of an intangible something, the passing of which no man can prove by evidence and to substitute for such abstractions proof of words and actions of a tangible character.[93]

Under the 'title theory' the procedure was to start by asking when title passed from seller to buyer and upon this single issue to purport to determine questions relating to such matters as risk of loss, insurability, the right to recovery of the price, the rights of creditors and liability to tax. In face-to-face transactions, for example, a sale of a horse by Farmer A to Farmer B, fixing the moment of time that 'title' passed was not necessarily difficult; but in the modern commercial context there are typically a number of stages in the journey from manufacturer or producer to ultimate consumer. Thus, to use Malcolm's examples, consider the difficulty of determining when title passes in the case of wool in the movement 'from grower to commission agent to commodity credit corporation, to mill, to wholesaler, to retailer. Or consider passage of title to natural gas moving by pipeline from producer, to gas company to New England distributor, to householder.'[94]

In the Uniform Commercial Code the allocation of risk, the availability of remedies, and a number of other matters which traditionally turned on passing of 'title', are made the subject of a series of specific rules which purport to reflect widespread practices and expectations of businessmen. For instance, risk of loss is governed by detailed rules which make no mention of 'title'. Section 2–509 deals with risk of loss in the absence of breach:

(1) Where the contract requires or authorizes the seller to ship the goods by carrier

  (a) if it does not require him to deliver them at a particular destination, the risk of loss passes to the buyer when the goods are duly delivered to the carrier even though the shipment is under reservation (Section 2–505); but

  (b) if it does require him to deliver them at a particular destination and the goods are there duly tendered while in the possession of the carrier, the risk of loss passes to the buyer when the goods are there duly so tendered as to enable the buyer to take delivery.

(2) Where the goods are held by a bailee to be delivered without being moved, the risk of loss passes to the buyer

  (a) on his receipt of a negotiable document of title covering the goods; or

  (b) on acknowledgement by the bailee of the buyer's right to possession of the goods; or

  (c) after his receipt of a non-negotiable document of title or other written direction to deliver, as provided in subsection (4)(b) of Section 2–503.

(3) In any case not within subsection (1) or (2), the risk of loss passes to the buyer on his receipt of the goods if the seller is a merchant; otherwise the risk passes to the buyer on tender of delivery.

(4) The provisions of this section are subject to contrary agreement of the parties and to the provisions of this Article on sale on approval (section 2–327) and on effect of breach on risk of loss (section 2–510).[95]

In the Uniform Commercial Code 'title' is reduced in importance, but is not eliminated (s.2–401). Llewellyn realized that it still had a general residuary function and that there would continue to be rules outside the Code, such as public regulations which might make particular consequences turn on the passing of title (Comment on 2-401). In Section 2-401 an attempt is made to make it easier to determine when title has passed in situations where this becomes a material issue. In the first instance this is a matter for explicit agreement between the parties, but in the absence of such agreement the section makes detailed provisions which as far as possible are related to some specific action of one or other of the parties. For example, where delivery is to be made without moving the goods and if the seller is to deliver a document of title, title passes at the time and place of delivery of such document, unless otherwise explicitly agreed (2-401(3)).[96]

Replacing a series of narrow categories by a single broad category— Article 9

In his theoretical writings, especially in his younger days, Llewellyn was so concerned to emphasize the value of narrow-issue thinking as a weapon against *over*-generalization that he risked creating the impression that he discounted the value of soundly based generalization. Any doubts on this score may be resolved by a brief look at Article 9, which deals with secured transactions. The old law governing secured transactions was notoriously complicated and technical. A series of different devices had grown up independently of each other at different times in an uncoordinated fashion : pledges, warehouse receipts, field warehousing, chattel mortgages, conditional sales, trust receipts, factors' liens, assignment of accounts receivable, and leases with or without option to buy. Each of these had its own formalities, its own requirements for recording or filing, and to a large extent, its own rules; yet all of them were related to a single broad function, *viz.* the facilitation of credit and the securing of payment or performance of an obligation.

The main defects have been well summarized by Malcolm:

Consequently today, within a single state, the means of obtaining security is simply a patchwork of odd devices that are replete with variations with little logical sense; gaps that are hard to fill; unnecessary duplications; and traps for the unwary. When there is added to this confusion within a single state a very great variation in rules in almost every one of the forty-eight states you have confusion worse confounded. The result simply means great inefficiency in the giving and taking of security, which inefficiency is paid for by the business community and the public as a whole.[97]

The solution adopted by the draftsmen is based on the perception that, despite the wide variety of situations covered, at the basis of nearly all transactions involving security in personal property there are two principal objectives: first, protecting a creditor or secured party against the risk of insolvency or bankruptcy or dishonesty of the debtor (this is achieved in the Code by putting the secured party in a priority position as against other creditors); secondly, providing simple means of notifying competing creditors of the security interest. Subsidiary policies adopted in the article are prevention of monopoly of a debtor by a single lender, and preventing overreaching of a debtor by a secured lender.[98] By keeping these objectives clearly in mind, the draftsmen were able to achieve a major simplification of the law within the framework of a policy of expanding the availability of secured credit.

Article 9 substitutes a set of new categories for those of the old law of secured transactions. The artificial distinctions between forms of device are made unimportant and the article applies 'to any transaction (regardless of its form) which is intended to create a security interest in personal property'. Thus, for several series of detailed rules based on artificial forms of device is substituted a single body of general principles centering around a concept ('security interest in personal property') which is directly related to the basic function of all these devices. The old devices are not abolished but are all treated as security interests and the main distinctions are made to turn on the function of the financing and the nature of the collateral. The broad effect is to provide for a single type of security interest, created by contract, involving a uniform filing procedure (where appropriate) and giving uniform protection to debtors, roughly equivalent to that afforded to a mortgagor.

A completely uniform set of rules was not possible. But such distinctions as are made in the article are, for the most part, also 'functionally' based. For old distinctions based on the form of the device are substituted others which reflect operative differences in the kind of property involved or the use to which it is put. The first distinction is between 'goods' and rights embodied in various types of paper, such as negotiable instruments and documents of title. Then there are contract rights, accounts and a residuary category of general 'intangibles'. The main classification of goods is between those which are in the process of distribution ('farm products' and 'inventory') and those which have come to rest ('consumer goods' and 'equipment'). These four categories are mutually exclusive and the comments advise that in borderline cases 'the principal use to which the property is put should be determinative'.[99] Thus a private car counts as 'consumer goods', but a company car held by a car dealer for sale would be 'inventory', as would a fleet of cars owned by a car rental agency. 'Farm products' would be different again. Actual differences in the nature or in the use of these goods require some different provisions to be made in respect of such matters as protection of buyers of collateral which is subject to a security interest[100] (9–307), in certain questions of priority,[101] and in determining the place of filing.[102] Thus as far as possible distinctions have been drawn only where practical considerations dictated and they were based along lines suggested by those very considerations. Thus Article 9 seeks both to clarify and to simplify the law and this is done by the adoption of a set of categories which are broader and more 'functional' than their predecessors.[103]

The use of flexible standards

The deliberate use of flexible standards such as 'reasonableness' is a familiar feature of legal systems everywhere. In his classic analysis of the Barotse, Gluckman states:

Thus the law lives and develops because its key concepts, 'reasonable' and 'customary', define general standards which are applicable to social positions and actions which are themselves only definable in similarly general terms. The concepts are, in the usual jurisprudential terms, *flexible*: more specifically they are *elastic* in that they can be stretched to cover new types of behaviour, new institutions, new customs, new ranges of leeway.[104]

Extensive use of flexible standards (such as 'reasonable', 'seasonable', 'usage of the trade') is made in the Code. This is the main device for allowing the Code to adapt to varied circumstances and to changed conditions. The Code differs from prior legislation more in the extent than in the manner of use of such devices.

The deliberate adoption of an 'open-ended' style of drafting, which is sometimes contrasted with a 'conveyancing approach',[105] has occasioned rather less adverse comment than might have been expected. Nevertheless it has been argued, by commentators who equate 'precision' with 'certainty', that the extensive use of vague concepts in the Code will inevitably lead to uncertainty and lack of

336 KARL LLEWELLYN AND THE REALIST MOVEMENT

uniformity.[106] Such criticism was unacceptable to Llewellyn. In the commercial field 'reasonable reckonability' of outcome was most soundly based on the premise that in the market commercial necessity generates to a large extent its own uniformities of values and patterns of behaviour; commercial self-interest spurs most businessmen to act within widely recognized leeways of decency and honesty: gross abuses tend to be self-defeating and can be checked in any case by making 'honesty', 'good faith' and 'reasonableness' the principal baselines for adjudication. Implicit in this view is a belief that legal rules have a more marginal role to play in generating business expectations than some critics of the Code allow and that tight drafting will often be at least as likely to defeat commercial expectations as to provide a basis for them. The Code is founded not only on faith in the capacity of the business community for satisfactory self-regulation within a framework of very broadly drafted rules, but also on a faith in judges to make honest, sensible, commercially well-informed decisions once they have been given some base-lines for judgment.[107] Thus 'reckonability' can be hoped for if judges can be expected to act in accordance with business expectations; uniformity within the leeway of broad rules will be promoted by uniformities of expectations, values and practices within the commercial world. Llewellyn's ideas in this area received their fullest exposition in *The Common Law Tradition*. In law ambiguity (in the sense of two distinct meanings) is rarely deliberately employed; vagueness (as contrasted with precision) is, however, recognized as having its uses. The draftsmen of the Code, while occasionally deliberately employing vague general concepts, made a deliberate attempt to cut down imprecision, ambiguity and inconsistencies of usage, where these were not considered to have positive value. The main instrument employed for this purpose is the stipulative definition. Section 1–201 contains no less than forty-six general definitions applying throughout the Code. Great pains were taken to ensure that the terms so defined were used consistently and in accordance with their definitions.

Furthermore, all the other articles, except one (Article 6—Bulk Transfers), contain substantial sections devoted to definitions, in many cases incorporating by cross-references definitions set out in other parts of the Code. These vary in precision, in detail and in form. Some purport to give a comprehensive definition, others merely clarify some particular point (e.g. 'Branch' includes a separately incorporated foreign branch of a bank).[108] There is not much that is particularly remarkable about the definitions, many of which were framed after the substantive provisions had been drafted.[109]

LLEWELLYN'S WRITINGS ON COMMERCIAL LAW AND CONTRACT AND THEIR IMPLICATIONS FOR THE CODE

In addition to the casebook on Sales and the Uniform Commercial Code, Llewellyn published a substantial number of articles on contract and commercial law.[110] Some of these have been highly regarded by experts in the field. No attempt will be made here to do justice to them as contributions to the study of substantive law, but a brief note on the relationship of the more important of them to Llewellyn's other work is called for.

Outstanding is a series of four articles on sales which were published in quick succession in the period 1937–9.[111] These represent Llewellyn at his best: they are models for the treatment of commercial law in its economic and social context; they are excellent case studies of judicial technique; and they are at the same time valuable contributions to legal history. Perhaps in no other of his published writings was Llewellyn so obviously in command of his subject matter. These four articles develop in detail themes already adumbrated in the casebook, but with significantly increased range and depth.

From the juristic point of view other papers can be seen as illustrations of Llewellyn's general ideas. A substantial part of 'On the Rule of Law in our case Law of Contract' is devoted to the problems of extracting doctrine from judicial decisions in a particular field of substantive law.[112] 'Through Title to Contract and a bit beyond', Llewellyn's most detailed discussion of 'title' in sales, is a concrete example of the search for narrow categories.[113] 'Meet Negotiable Instruments', an admirable functional introduction to the subject, involves the conscious application of some of Llewellyn's educational ideas:

The approach and material here presented are an attempt to carry forward the lines of teaching 'private' law suggested in (1941) 54 Harv. L. Rev. 775. This holds of the effort to both give and simplify background; to make the types of instrument visualizable; to focus on process; to reduce the number of cases intensively discussed while integrating the background of these cases sufficiently to build a readily understandable whole; to build from the simple but persisting situation toward to the more complex one; to play the whole in terms of classroom practice in lawyer's doing: here the practical handling of a well-built statute. With effort thereby to save classroom time, even while indulging a wider perspective. The initial course of two semester-hours is to be followed at students' option by another on 'Practice of Banking', also two units, in which banking material is conceived merely as an exercise ground for training in simple counselling and simple advocacy.[114]

These ideas are again apparent in 'Commercial Transactions', a paper prepared as part of a refresher course for lawyers returning after the war. This was republished under the title of 'The Modern Approach to Counselling and Advocacy Especially in Commercial Transactions'.[115]

Llewellyn taught contract for many years, but he published relatively little on the subject. Here he was very much the disciple of Corbin in most matters except style.[116] In his contract writings he was particularly ebullient:

... it is not safe to reason about business cases from cases in which an uncle became interested in having his nephew see Europe, go to Yale, abstain from nicotine, or christen his infant heir 'Alvardus Torrington, III.' And it may even be urged that safe conclusions as to business cases of the more ordinary variety cannot be derived from what courts or scholars rule about the idiosyncratic desires of one *A* to see one *B* climb a fifty-foot greased flag-pole or push a peanut across the Brooklyn Bridge.[117]

Llewellyn was a consistent critic of the theory associated with Langdell, Williston and the first Restatement of Contracts. This has been restated by one critic as follows:

We learned that there are certain expressions of mutual assent to which the law appends an obligation arising from the express or plainly implied 'promises' of the parties. The legal obligation is strictly limited to the promises. These promises are discovered in *the* unvarying method by which human beings contract with each other, namely, by means of 'offers' embodying 'promises' directed by 'offerors' to particular 'offerees' who 'accept' by manifesting assent either by tendering a promise or an act. The agreement thus made is enforcible at law or in equity if and only if the promises involved 'detriment to the promisor.' Otherwise the agreement was not supported by 'consideration' and was a bare nudum pactum. Case variations were hung on the construct like ornaments on a Christmas tree, glittering but essentially useless.[118]

Llewellyn had a number of fundamental objections to this

theory: first, it was over-generalized; second, it was a product of pre-industrial face-to-face transactions and of *laissez-faire* ideology, which fitted neither commercial need nor the way modern courts were behaving in fact, partly out of sensitivity to commercial need; and third, it encouraged an artificial and obnoxious kind of formalism:

The rules of Offer and Acceptance have been worked over; they have been written over; they have been shaped and rubbed smooth with pumice, they wear the rich deep polish of a thousand class rooms; they have a grip on the vision and indeed on the affections held by no other rules 'of law', real or pseudo. For it was Offer and Acceptance which first led each of us out of laydom into The Law. Puzzled, befogged, adrift in the strange words and technique of cases, with only our sane feeling of what was decent for a compass, we felt the warm sun suddenly, we knew that we were arriving, we knew we too could 'think like a lawyer': That was when we learned to down seasickness as *A* revoked when *B* was almost up the flag-pole. Within the first October, we had achieved a technical glee in justifying judgment then for *A*; and succulent memory lingers, of the way our dumber brethren were pilloried as Laymen still.[119]

It has been suggested, in an important article by Eugene F. Mooney, that the Uniform Commercial Code has quietly but effectively subverted the orthodox theory of contract. The Code, it is argued, covers most commercial transactions and 'commercial transactions account for an overwhelming number of contracts in any industrial nation'.[120] The Code (especially Article 2) is based on Llewellyn's ideas on contract, in particular on the substitution of 'agreement-in-fact' for 'promise' as the basis of contractual obligation. The effect has been that contract doctrine in the United States is being made to adjust to the Code rather than vice versa, and that this is reflected in the Second Restatement of Contract in which the dichotomy between unilateral and bilateral contract has been dropped, and changes have been made, which appear to accord with Llewellyn's ideas, in respect of 'mutual assent, option contracts, revocability, indefiniteness and acceptance'.[121] 'All in all', Mooney concludes, 'Llewellyn nearly swept the board clean.'[122]

If this thesis is valid, and that is best left for the experts to dispute, it is probably fair to say that Llewellyn was just one among a number of teachers of contract who were persistent critics of the orthodox theory.[123] If anyone was the key figure, it was Corbin. However, in so far as the Uniform Commercial Code is directly influencing the growth of contract doctrine in the United States today, Llewellyn's writings on contract gain an added significance.

CONCLUSION

The foregoing analysis, although elementary, should be sufficient to confirm the judgment that 'despite the numbers of persons involved in the drafting of the Code, the extent to which it reflects Llewellyn's philosophy of law and his sense of commercial wisdom and need is startling.'[124] The most striking aspect is the extent to which ideas associated with 'the Grand Style' were operative in the drafting process: the search for commercially significant type-fact patterns; articulation of purpose and policy; 'where the reason stops there stops the rule';[125] provision for the development of new commercial usages and for adjustment of the law to changing conditions and values; and 'faith in the court's ability to judge wisely whenever it understands the base lines for judgment'.[126] For the jurist, perhaps the most important single lesson to be learned from the Uniform Commercial Code is that the Grand Style is not merely a style of judging, but provides a model for law-makers and, indeed, for lawyers of all kinds.

13
Miscellaneous Writings

The complete bibliography of Llewellyn's published works contains two hundred and forty-six items. The number is almost doubled when the unpublished manuscripts are added. In writing about Llewellyn selection is inevitable, and a strong element of subjectivity is necessary in such selection. This is particularly so when we are confronted with Llewellyn's shorter works and his unfinished projects. The writings discussed in this chapter concern the Sacco-Vanzetti case, the legal profession and legal education, and the unfinished project on Pueblo Indian law. If there is any connecting thread running through these diverse topics it is that they illustrate three phases of Llewellyn as a liberal intellectual. They have been chosen for the additional light they may throw on a variety of themes that have been explored in earlier chapters.

THE SACCO-VANZETTI CASE[1]

The Sacco-Vanzetti case has a special place in history and legend. It is one of the best documented criminal cases in American legal history; no other American trial has stimulated such a literary outpouring of novels, plays and poems. The basic facts can be briefly summarized : on 15 August 1920, in South Braintree, Massachusetts, two men were murdered during the course of an armed robbery of a shoe factory payroll. The attackers got away in a car. Twenty days later Nicola Sacco and Bartolomeo Vanzetti, two Italian working-class immigrants, were arrested; in May 1921, Vanzetti was tried and convicted for offences committed in another hold-up; in July, 1921, both men were convicted on indictment for the South Braintree murders. There followed a lengthy legal campaign to save their lives : between July 1921 and October 1924 eight motions for a new trial were denied by Judge Thayer, the original trial judge whose fairness raised the main doubt about the case; between October 1924 and April 1927 conviction was upheld on appeal to the Supreme Court of Massachusetts, several further motions for a new trial were denied, and on 9 April 1927 Judge Thayer finally sentenced the accused to death. In response to public pressure Governor Fuller referred the petition for executive clemency to a special advisory committee under the chairmanship of the President of Harvard, A. Lawrence Lowell. The Governor accepted the Lowell committee's advice and refused clemency. Further desperate attempts to raise the matter again in the courts failed. Then, on 23 August 1927, almost exactly seven years after the murders, Sacco and Vanzetti were executed by electrocution.

The case has sometimes been called the American *Dreyfus case*. Internationally as well as nationally it provoked a long and furious campaign of protest and counter-protest.[2] Led initially by left-wing political organizations, the majority of protesters saw the conviction of Sacco and Vanzetti as a monstrous example of judicial murder of innocent men, who had been persecuted because they were radicals; public opinion in Massachusetts was hostile to the accused and some reactionaries interpreted the protest movement as a subversive attack on the institutions and structure of American society. The polarization of views is brought out by Llewellyn:

Who are the two men whose names recur, whose lives and honor are the immediate stake in all this story.

Niccola Sacco, an Italian, resident in Massachusetts from his eighteenth year. A solid workman, who learned his trade outside of hours, a shoe-worker, a 'good cobbler', and 'edger.' A simple-hearted devoted husband and father. A lover of nature – who in prison found difficulty writing to his friends unless blue sky heartened and cheered him through the bars. An idealist, bent on improving the lot of working-men, so strong, so unafraid in his convictions that on trial for his life, before a jury whom he knew to be prejudiced against such views, he preached his beliefs, prepared to be a martyr to his faith.

Niccola Sacco, (the same Niccola Sacco?), a foreigner discontented with our institutions, yet content to abide among them. One who forsook all decent views for Socialism, even for Anarchism. Living and earning here, yet fleeing to Mexico in fear of being drafted to defend the country. The user of a false name. A man who would lie lightly to his employer to cover up a morning on leave which he had spent in talk and not on business. A gun-toter. An agitator. A man too indifferent to American ways to seek during twelve years of freedom to learn English decently, too stupid to learn

English decently during seven years in jail. An associate of that Vanzetti whom we know to have been convicted of an attempted holdup in Bridgewater.

Bartolomeo Vanzetti, a man who had forsaken his home in Italy and a good living with a farmer-family whom he loved, because his conscience would not let him be a party to exploiting men. A man who, though without wife and children, astonished his neighbors by his steadiness and effort at his work. A man who, ready to throw himself into the place of danger in defense of his fellows, was chosen to go up to New York to discuss the further defense of Salsedo, a radical held incommunicado by the Federal authorities in their wild deportation drive of 1920; that Salsedo whose 'questioning' is suspected of having driven him to seek relief in suicide. Vanzetti, a man whom person after person, of judgment, insight and sensibility, learned to know after the time of his imprisonment; and whom each of those who learned to know him came to honor, respect, admire, even love. A man framed up before the present trial, on a charge made against Sacco, too, until for Sacco an unshakable alibi was proved, in order to make easy the conviction in the case in hand.

Bartolomeo Vanzetti (the same Bartolomeo Vanzetti?), a radical leader, a speechmaker, an anarchistic agitator; closely concerned with that Salsedo, who was dangerous enough to induce the Federal authorities to hold him incommunicado till, seemingly, he confessed his guilt by suicide. A gun-toter, Vanzetti, as well. A man convicted previously of another desperate crime of violence. A man the more dangerous because of his brains and gift of leadership. A draft-dodger. A liar, who lied copiously and confessedly on his arrest. A believer in violence. An associate, a sympathizer, a 'comrade' of those radicals who threatened and even exercised outrageous violence in efforts to terrify the authorities into giving him up without punishment.

Opinions differ, you may observe, about these two. Two things are certain: they were Italians and radicals; they were accused of murder.[3]

In itself the case was not especially remarkable: the crime was a rather sordid example of crude amateurish gangsterism; the innocence or guilt of Sacco and Vanzetti is still a matter for argument; so too is the question of the fairness of their trial—certainly it would not have been difficult to find clearer and more spectacular examples of unfair judicial proceedings in the United States at that time; although Vanzetti, in particular, proved to be a remarkable man, this did not become apparent until after public controversy had gained its own momentum. One of the most notable facets of the case was the unanimity of the decision-makers: 'The trial judge, the trial jury, the Supreme Judicial court, and the Advisory Committee each and all, decided every vital issue against [the accused].'[4]

Yet a significant sector of informed opinion felt that the proceedings were unfair.

The affair became important as a focus for protest and as a symbol. Public outcry was slow in coming. It was not until four years after the trial at Dedham in 1921 that the conscience of American intellectuals was really aroused. There had been communist-inspired demonstrations in Europe in 1921, the American Civil Liberties Union (with which Llewellyn was involved) had taken up the case, as had a few individuals, but it was only later in 1925, after further agitation by left-wing organizations in the United States and Europe, that public attention was caught. However, when they did become engaged the intellectuals, according to Felix, made it 'the only significant intellectual occurrence in the United States between the first World War and the Depression'.[5] Heywood Broun, John Dewey, Felix Frankfurter, Walter Lippman, Samuel Eliot Morison and Dorothy Parker in the United States, and Albert Einstein, H. G. Wells, John Galsworthy, and Romain Rolland from outside were among the many prominent people who spoke out for Sacco and Vanzetti. After their execution their story inspired a voluminous literature; it provides the central theme of Maxwell Anderson's *Winterset,* Upton Sinclair's *Boston,* and John Dos Passos' *The Big Money* (part of *U.S.A.*); it also features prominently in works by authors as diverse as S. N. Behrman, H. G. Wells, James Thurber and James T. Farrell. By 1948 a total of one hundred and forty-four poems about Sacco and Vanzetti had been found,[6] and two scholarly works have been devoted to analysing the impact of the affair on the American intelligentsia.[7]

Llewellyn's association with the Sacco-Vanzetti case falls into two parts. Prior to their execution he campaigned actively on their behalf; according to his account his interest was first caught in the spring of 1926 by some disturbing passages in the opinion of the Supreme Court of Massachusetts in rejecting the appeal of the accused in *Commonwealth* v. *Sacco and Vanzetti,* 'of which I had vaguely heard'.[8] Soon he was seeking to stir up support among law teachers for a review of the case *de novo*.[9] Nothing came of it. At this stage the campaign of protest became more virulent. Llewellyn's principal contribution was to organize a petition by law teachers to Governor Fuller, asking that a special commission of enquiry be set up to look into the case and to advise on executive clemency. The letter was moderate in tone and emphasised the need for public confidence to be retained in judicial institutions.[10] On 1 June, in response to numerous demands of this sort, Governor Fuller set up the Lowell Committee which, after holding hearings, advised against clemency. Fuller, after further consultation, accepted the advice and the execution was rescheduled for 23 August. Llewellyn was among those who were thoroughly dissatisfied with the report of the Lowell Committee, but his public criticism was restrained. Three days before the execution he made an appeal over the radio, urging listeners to petition Governor Fuller for a last minute commutation.[11] This was one of his most impressive pieces of advocacy, eloquent yet restrained, appealing simultaneously to emotion and to reason, and setting the case in broad perspective. The address ended as follows:

With Sacco and Vanzetti the jury system of this country is on trial. Daily in every city you are permitting lawyers to win – or lose – cases by playing on the passions of the jury – murder cases, accident cases – every jury case. Is the plaintiff a pretty woman? Play it up. Has the defendant a widowed mother? Play it up. Prejudice of class and caste and race and nationality. Jury men grin, and enjoy the lawyers' show. Lawyers grin, and pocket the fees. *You* sit and let it happen: the open invitation to the unfair trial. This is the crime against justice men fear to have been committed in the case of Sacco and Vanzetti. We must appeal to Fuller that they may be saved. But we must awake to our responsibilities, awake, and stay awake, if a hundred and a thousand of such cases are not to go on occurring without notice. We must awake, or no change happens. We must stay awake because the process of legal and constitutional change is slow. Make no mistake: cases as dubious as this one are occurring now, occurring everywhere, occurring daily. Make no mistake: they will continue as long as citizens are content to sit in comfort – ignorant, happy, quiet, ineffective. And once again make no mistake: the first step toward change is commutation for these two. Their lives have become a symbol for the demand that trials in court be fair. Without your help the symbol may change form: and become their deaths.[12]

This passage helps to explain the continuance of the Sacco-Vanzetti campaign after their execution in 1927. The case was symbolic of wider discontents. Like other *causes célèbres* it was to some extent an ambiguous symbol. Common to most interpretations was a feeling, ranging among individuals from suspicion to certainty, that the accused were convicted not because of what they did but because of what they were. Beyond that there was scope for a variety of views: to the working-class it could represent capitalist oppression; to immigrants, the non-acceptance of the alien in American society;

to liberal intellectuals, the persecution of radicals and reds; to anarchists the corruption of the whole social system; to Llewellyn it represented the failure of its judicial institutions to live up to the ideals of the American polity. This became the main theme of the second phase of his Sacco-Vanzetti activities.

In 1928 he accepted an invitation to join the council of the recently formed Sacco-Vanzetti National League. Their programme included the publication of the official record of the case, the Lowell Committee Report, and the letters of the accused; to work for reforms indicated by the case, and to establish the innocence of Sacco and Vanzetti.[18] In the same year Llewellyn undertook on behalf of the league to edit a collection of critical analyses of the Lowell Committee Report. As the project progressed, the conception changed, and the last plan was to make it a book about the case as a whole, tentatively entitled *Sacco and Vanzetti v. The Commonwealth: An Indictment of the workings of our Judicial Institutions.* This was never completed, although as late as 1935, when the league was dissolved, Llewellyn expressed the hope that it would one day be published.[14] However, an advanced draft of approximately half of the intended chapters has survived in typescript and this is sufficient to give a fairly clear picture of Llewellyn's approach to the case.[15]

The book was to take the form of an anthology of essays linked together by a commentary by its editor. It was to be concerned equally with the primary issue of the fairness of the trial in this particular case and with the adequacy of judicial fact-finding procedures as illustrated by the record. The guilt or innocence of the accused was to be treated as secondary to the question whether the trial and post-conviction procedures had been fair; the whole was to be treated as a case study of the working of American judicial institutions.

Most of the completed manuscript relates to the original trial: it includes a lengthy analysis of the evidence by Edmund Morgan, leading to the conclusion that at the very least the guilt of the accused was not established beyond reasonable doubt and that the trial was a travesty of justice: 'Against a masterful prosecution was opposed a hopelessly mismanaged defence before a stupid trial judge.'[16] This is set against an analysis of the proceedings by a Canadian judge, Mr Justice Riddell, who concluded that: 'On our Canadian principles, these two men had a fair trial as far as any one can judge by the printed record.' Riddell's analysis had previously been published;[17] parts of Morgan's contribution were subsequently incorporated in revised form, into Joughin and Morgan's *The Legacy of Sacco and Vanzetti*. Also planned for inclusion were an analysis of the procedure of the Lowell Committee, and a review of Vanzetti's trial for robbery at Bridgwater, prior to the South Braintree murders.

The underlying theme of the passages written by Llewellyn was that the Sacco-Vanzetti case was important, not because it was unique, but because it was typical.[18] In particular, it revealed the fact-finding machinery of the courts as being seriously defective. A primary purpose of the book was to press the argument

that all the public can do about it is to kick the civil bar; that the problem of improvement is a technical one, and that only technicians are equipped to handle it. And finally, that until the civil bar gets kicked into a sense of its duty as the public watchdog over criminal procedure, we get no reforms on the legal side, as distinguished from the administrative side.[19]

Unfortunately Llewellyn never got round to writing the final section in which he could have been expected to go into detail about his views on criminal process. Most of the sections he did write were introductory, either concerned with particularities of the case or too general to be of much value. There are some good passages, but the introduction tends to be rather repetitive and Llewellyn seems in places to be over-eager to appear judicious. However, some aspects of the manuscript as it stands deserve comment.

First, it is worth noting that this study confutes the suggestion that Llewellyn was not interested in courts of first instance and was blind to the problems of judicial fact-finding.[20] As he often pointed out, one reason for the tendency of academic lawyers to concentrate on the work of appeal courts was that the relevant materials were more readily available.[21] A subsidiary reason for Llewellyn's interest in the Sacco-Vanzetti case was that it was exceptionally well documented and so provided an unusual opportunity for a thorough case study of judicial fact-finding. It must be conceded, however, that Llewellyn seems to have been more at home with appellate opinions than with trial records. This is hardly surprising, for the fact-sceptic's path is not easy and Llewellyn was relatively inexperienced in this art.

Secondly, the manuscript contains one of Llewellyn's best discussions of the rule of law. He was emphatic that the crucial question for the public was not whether the accused were guilty, but whether they had received a fair trial.[22] At the time, he professed to have an open mind on the question of their guilt; at a later date he is reported as saying that he believed that Vanzetti at least was probably guilty. The crux of the matter was that a community which allows prejudice or passion to enter into its judgments is harming itself:

If, then, we are faithful to the form of government we have inherited, and to the spirit which breathes through that form of government, we cannot allow a radical, however much we despise his views, and though those views attack our government itself, to be more quickly believed guilty of any specific offence than would a man whose views on government we most approved. If we are faithful to our form of government we must set out, with gritted teeth, to judge the evidence for its own value, although the defendant be the rankest revolutionary. *That we owe, if not to him, then to ourselves.*[23]

Llewellyn considered at some length the difference between the 'specific act' and 'whole man' conceptions of criminal justice, and concluded that the former, along with the ideal of a fair trial, were 'of the essence of American institutions'.[24] The cause for concern in the Sacco-Vanzetti case was that practice had not measured up to ideal. He made the point in terms which link it to his juristic writings:

There are two American traditions. They war, each with the other. Each is American.
American politics reaches beyond the patter of Fourth of July speeches. It covers what *happens*. American law is not exhausted with paper rules on books. It extends to *what goes on, to what officials do* about disputes, about suspects, about criminals with influence, about trial and pardon – and the third degree. The American Constitution is not limited to a venerable document prepared a century and a half ago, with nineteen passages on paper added since; the American Constitution is the actual framework of our government as we are governed. And when Fourth of July patter does not square with the influence of the machine, when the rules on the books do not square with the third degree or the biassed judge, when the paper Constitution says freedom of speech and assembly, but the governing officials deport, or break up meetings – then we have *two* lines of phenomena and not one. And anybody who likes either one of them can point to it as American. I see no clarity to be gained by denying that bigotry, intolerance, manipulation and even corruption of the police and of the judicial machinery to protect men dear to those in power and to attack or frame their enemies – or their victims – I see no clarity to be gained by denying that these are an

established American tradition. If years and repetition make dignity, they are an 'honorable' one.

There is, thank God, another and opposite American tradition.[25]

Llewellyn's approach to the *Sacco-Vanzetti* case is rather different from that of the popular protest: whilst the majority were convinced that the accused were innocent, he thought this was doubtful, but irrelevant to the main issue; where others saw the case either in terms of class (the Massachusetts establishment versus the alien worker) or in terms of personalities (with Vanzetti as martyred hero, and Judge Thayer as the principal villain), Llewellyn saw it largely in institutional terms, the constructive question being: how can we improve our institutions to limit the influence of human weakness and passion? It has been suggested that the case stirred American intellectuals because the apparent victimization of two Italian immigrants became a symbol for the intellectuals' own sense of alienation and rejection from American society.[26] In so far as this is true of the intellectual contribution to the protest, it is not applicable to Llewellyn. The case was important to him because he felt, as an American, that his own institutions, for which he was ultimately responsible, were failing to live up to his society's ideals.

THE LEGAL PROFESSION

Let this be written large, for senior partners in law factories to ponder on: Law does not exist for corporation executives alone. It is not, even, for stockholders alone, or those whose income tax, can, under proper counselling, be cut. The courts, especially, are for *all* citizens who have, or believe they have, rights of which their own efforts fail to induce fulfillment.[27]

One of Llewellyn's main interests during the 1930s was the legal profession. An examination of the leading American bibliography on judicial administration and the legal profession shows that with one or two notable exceptions lawyers and their work had not been a subject of systematic study prior to 1931.[28] In the post-Depression years a widespread concern about the economic position of the bar stimulated a series of bar surveys, which represent the first attempts at systematic empirical research into the profession. During these years there was also a good deal of self-analysis and criticism centering around the organization of the profession, legal ethics, and such matters as 'over-crowding' and 'unauthorized practice'.

Llewellyn played a leading part in this movement. In addition to writing a number of papers,[29] he was a member of an advisory committee of the Association of American Law Schools in cooperation with bench and bar which in 1933-5 sought funds for an ambitious national survey of the bar.[30] Their attempts were unsuccessful but eventually such a survey was undertaken just after the second world war.[31] He was consulted in connection with bar surveys in New York, Connecticut and New Jersey,[32] he was a member of the Board of Directors of the New York Legal Aid Society, and from 1937-9 Chairman of a special ABA committee on Legal Service Bureaus.[33] It was at his prompting that a crippled New York lawyer, Bill Weiss, started a legal clinic at which he gave advice and help, often free, and never for more than $10.[34] This clinic, in turn, helped to stimulate interest in plans for a nationwide chain of legal service bureaus. Later, during the 1940s, Llewellyn was supervisor of the Columbia Legal Aid programme, thereby bringing together his interests in legal services for the underprivileged and legal education.[35] The most important of Llewellyn's activities consisted in his campaign, carried on vigorously in public speeches and in articles, for providing a wider range of legal services for the members of the lower and lower-middle income groups.[36] Writing in 1947, Reginald Heber Smith, author of the classic work *Justice and the Poor*, wrote in a letter: 'You and Lloyd Garrison are the men who woke the Bar up to its duty and opportunity in connection with persons of moderate means.'[37] It is rather difficult, in fact, to isolate Llewellyn's contribution from that of a number of people who were concerned with the same problems at that time, notably Lloyd Garrison, Charles Clark, Isidor Lazarus, John Bradway and Reginald Heber Smith himself. All of these men have a place in the related histories of the development of legal aid services and of the systematic study of the legal profession.

Typically, Llewellyn's contribution consisted less of undertaking systematic research as of producing a flow of stimulating suggestions for research projects and for new types of organization to meet the problems of the bar. Most of his ideas are to be found in two important papers 'The Bar Specializes—With What Results?' and 'The Bar's Troubles and Poultices—and Cures?'[38] These papers defy summary. They contain, in compressed form, ideas which have subsequently formed the basis of whole books and research projects. Thus the suggestion that specialization and standardization of certain kinds of legal work could lead to much cheaper and more efficient service became one of the central themes of Johnstone and Hopson, *Lawyers and Their Work* (1967).[39] In 1933 Llewellyn wrote, 'the old ethics of individualism in practice simply do not fit metropolitan conditions.'[40] Nearly thirty years later Jerome Carlin, a pupil of Llewellyn's, took this idea as the basis for his notable studies of the solo practitioner in Chicago and of lawyers' ethics in New York, concluding *inter alia* that the most common offender against canons of ethics is the individual practitioner, 'Abraham Lincoln turned urban'.[41] Llewellyn was one of the first to agitate for a national bar survey; and yet he foresaw the difficulties of attaining objectivity and clear-sightedness in this area, difficulties which were not entirely overcome by the famous ABA Survey of the Legal Profession.[42] Anyone who has had occasion to think about the problems of teaching legal ethics will recognize how much insight is packed into the following passage:

The members of the law factory are, however, concerned for the ethics of their lesser brethren, whose security in livelihood the obsolete ethic on non-solicitation of business chokes off like a tourniquet. And one of the remedies they who mourn the wane of ancient ways have been prescribing is the introduction of compulsory courses on legal ethics in the schools.

The *naiveté* of the assumptions underlying this prescription should not prevent perception of its lasting value. Social advance is here again a product less of intention than of fortunate guess. A notion that lectures on legal ethics conjure ethics into the listener is childish, in almost the exact measure in which the listener is he whom it is wished to cure. None the less, to spread instances before the future lawyer will inform him of some of the problems he must face, and give him some idea of the risks he runs by any unconventional solution. If he needs not ethical *raising*, but ethical *preparation*, it may do good. Yet to instructors trained in case-method teaching, and reacting as experienced teachers to the difficulty of inculcating ethics by a preachment, this seemed too little return for the outlay in time. Especially, and understandably, they rebelled at the implicit assumption that lectures would mean results – in the 'unfit'.

The first move – taken long before the American Bar Association had officially pronounced – was the collection of a casebook on legal ethics. This fitted the already traditional teaching technique. It provided concrete cases, with authoritative rulings. But so far as ethical training is concerned, the study of authoritative rulings tends rather to a training in unethics, being a careful delineation of precisely how far the lawyer can go *without* disbarment, with copious suggestion as to how to do most of the things lawyers ought not to be doing.

An instructor of vision, alive to the reasons that make one rule rather than another useful for the ends law is to serve, can use the concrete instances to get somewhere; but such an instructor is driven forthwith not to authority, but to the facts of law practice, in order to inform his judgment. Hence the almost simultaneous development these last years, all over the country, of courses and collections of materials on The Legal Profession – to see it as it is.[43]

There was one idea which Llewellyn particularly stressed. Unlike Bentham, he did not consider that the interest of lawyers is in 'direct and constant opposition to the interest of the community'.[44] Rather he saw that at the root of complaints about overcrowding was an unexploited identity of interest between lawyers and the public. There was too little work to support the whole profession, yet lawyers' services were in practice available to only a relatively small proportion of the population. Llewellyn argued that lawyers' services should be organized in such a way that they could be provided at a cost which would be within the reach of members of the middle and lower income groups.[45] His most common prescription was that bar associations should organize clearing houses based on four points:

(1) to discover (as the legal departments of business houses do) what the recurring transactions are which can be largely routinized; (2) to make both the routine and the limits of its value available to every lawyer, and especially to the lawyers on the list; (3) to fix maximum fees for services which on this basis can be performed for such fees; and (4), last and not least important to bring home to the public what service it needs, and where that service can be had, at a reasonable figure. The legal aid societies would not be backward in cooperating. And much of the necessary work they have already done.[46]

Although Llewellyn favoured one particular institution, the legal service bureau, his writings were based on a deeper analysis of the problems of the bar and hint at many ideas which have subsequently become familiar—collective professional responsibility, preventive practice ('legal hygiene' was Llewellyn's phrase), stratification within the profession, the need to think in terms of standardization and economies of scale and the need to find a collective substitute for advertising by individuals. These are ideas which anticipate the growth of lawyer reference programmes and neighbourhood law offices and even of a compensation fund for victims of lawyers' incompetence and dishonesty, such as was introduced in England by the Law Society in 1941.[47]

Llewellyn's writings of this period are focused on certain problems of the time. They are full of ideas which are suggestive, but most of these he did not attempt to develop systematically. Even by the late 1960s the compressed insights of some of his papers of the 1930s had not all been fully exploited by specialists in the sociology of the legal profession, although the subject had by that time grown into a recognized area of specialization.[48] At a later phase Llewellyn did start to develop at a theoretical level his ideas on one phase of the subject—his theory of the crafts of law, which has already been considered.[49]

LLEWELLYN AND LEGAL EDUCATION

In recent years there has been growing realization of the relevance of the sociology of the legal profession to the development of legal education. Llewellyn sensed this, without fully articulating it.[50] As was pointed out by Max Weber, who lawyers are, what they do, what is their function in society, how they conceive their roles, and their approach and perspectives are conditioned largely by their training and by the nature of the legal tradition to which they were first exposed.[51] Conversely any formal system of legal training, in so far as it is purposive, is necessarily based on assumptions, whether implicit, explicit, or only half-articulated, about the nature and functions of the legal profession.

It might be thought that the avowed vocationalism of American law schools would have simplified for them the problem of formulating their educational objectives. While most law schools and law teachers assumed that their main aim was to produce 'good lawyers', what constitutes a 'good lawyer' in this context was rarely the subject of serious analysis. For instance, the image of the legal practitioner underlying Langdell's approach to legal education could easily be shown to be over-simple and unrealistic even in his own day. But it was extraordinarily influential. Similarly the counter-images of Langdell's opponents such as Holmes, Frank and Lasswell and McDougal,[52] while they provided a useful corrective were hardly less crude.

Some of the reasons for this are not hard to find. During Llewellyn's lifetime an extensive literature on legal education accumulated.[53] Its quality did not match its bulk. Although over the years there was some improvement, by and large 'legal educa-

tion' was not thought to deserve the same criteria of rigour, detachment and accuracy that are applied to 'respectable' scholarship.
Little serious research was done, and there was a lack of an adequate
general theory and a refined terminology; the complexity of the
subject tended to be under-estimated and such intellectual tools as
had been developed by serious students of education were largely
ignored by legal educators. In short, the literature of legal education
was more the work of worried amateurs than of professional
specialists.

Llewellyn was a teacher for over forty years, he cared deeply
about education, and there were few aspects of his work which
were unaffected by pedagogical concerns. Yet he belonged to the
amateur tradition of legal education : while he made some valuable
contributions as a pioneer, witness the Casebook on Sales, the
Bramble Bush, the course on Legal Argument, and his teaching of
jurisprudence, his writings *about* legal education are uneven and
disorganized; and, for all his flair, his classroom performance lacked
the consistency of the true professional.

There are, however, two specific contributions made by Llewellyn
in the direction of a more systematic approach to legal education.
In the early 1940s he was appointed chairman of an AALS committee on curriculum. This committee was one of a number set up
to consider the immediate post-war problems of American law
schools. The committee appears to have been dominated by two of
its members, Llewellyn and Professor David Cavers of the Harvard
Law School.[54] Both of them were interested in the idea of systematic training in legal skills, and this was made the basis of the well-
known report of the committee which was published in 1944. The
nature and authorship of the report is indicated by the fact that in
1945 the text was republished as an article under Llewellyn's name
under the title 'The Place of Skills in Legal Education'.[55]

The report took the case method of instruction as a starting-
point. It acknowledged that Langdell had been responsible for a
major advance by switching the emphasis in legal education from
acquisition of knowledge to training in skill.[56] However, for a
number of reasons, notably the increased complexity of law, the
case method was no longer an efficient way of developing the skills
that it had induced in Langdell's time. Moreover, there were other
skills—interpretation of statutes, appellate advocacy, simple drafting, counselling, and certain not very clearly defined 'public law

skills'—which could be taught more directly and efficiently by other means. The report was emphatic that what they were recommending, far from being mere training in the tricks of the trade, would be more compatible with the accepted ideals of university education than the mere acquisition of knowledge (by inefficient means) to which much legal education had descended. At the time it was published the report was notable for three ideas: first, that law school methods, however stimulating for the better students, were failing to produce minimum technical competence in all students. Second, that systematic and direct teaching of certain professional skills is both possible and desirable; and third, that the teaching of selected skills is not necessarily illiberal.

In the light of subsequent developments, on certain key points the report seems rather vague—for instance, there was no comprehensive analysis of lawyers' operations; and the exact nature of some of the particular skills considered was not probed and their 'teachability' was mainly a matter of optimistic assertion. However, it directed attention to a neglected subject and it struck another blow against the strongly entrenched assumption that the curriculum could only be classified according to fields of law.

It is difficult to assess the influence of the report, because it was only one of a number of contributions to the rethinking of legal education that were made about that time. However, it is clear that since 1944 there has been considerable interest in 'skills teaching', and an extensive literature on the subject has developed.[57] However, there is as yet no reliable basis for assessing the effectiveness and economy of most skills' courses. Some specific developments concerning teaching of skills subsequent to 1944 deserve brief mention. First, Llewellyn was personally involved in trying to further the teaching of appellate advocacy and drafting.[58] In collaboration with David Cavers and Ralph Fuchs he formulated plans for a project on legal drafting.[59] Although this particular project proved abortive, all three of the orginal protagonists were subsequently involved in promoting this kind of training. More significant is the fact that two important contributions to the development in training in legal skills were subsequently made by former pupils of Llewellyn. At the University of Cincinatti Professor Irvin C. Rutter in conjunction with a series of particular courses developed the best theoretical analysis of lawyers' operations that has yet appeared in print.[60] Rutter received a considerable amount of encouragement from Llewellyn, who stage-managed and chaired a round table discussion of Rutter's work at the AALS convention in 1960. Another disciple of Llewellyn, Charles D. Kelso, was responsible for the first major application of programmed learning to the study of law to be published. It is not a coincidence that this was devoted to 'case skills', and that Llewellyn's ideas on case law are explicitly made the basis of Kelso's programme.[61] What is significant about the work of Rutter and Kelso is the systematic nature of their approach, which marks the introduction of some educational professionalism into law teaching.

PUEBLO INDIAN LAW-GOVERNMENT[62]

The Pueblos of New Mexico consist of a number of separate communities, divided into three distinct language groups: Tanoan, Keresan and Zunian. In 1961 there were nineteen surviving Pueblos, ranging in size from under a hundred inhabitants to over four thousand. Few, if any, surviving tribal societies can have such an extensive and rich record of their history. Few other cultures have proved so resistant to the assaults and enticements of western civilization. Since the sixteenth century the Pueblos have been subject to almost continuous Christian influence, but Christianity did not drive out the tribal religion and many facets of tribal life are essentially the same as they were before the time of Columbus.[63] To archaeologists and anthropologists what was fascinating was their history and culture; to Llewellyn the absorbing problem was how to preserve what he called the 'tribal core' of these 'communist' societies within the framework of American society.

The Pueblos, despite their reticence, are one of the most studied of Indian groups. Their religiosity, the power of their priests, and the cohesiveness of their culture led some early investigators to ignore or to underemphasise the significance of the secular leaders as agents of social control. In particular, Ruth Benedict in her well-known work *Patterns of Culture*[64] painted an idealized picture of the Pueblo of Zuni in which the secular authority was dismissed in a single paragraph as being of little importance and largely unnecessary. Zuni would appear from her account to be little short of an earthly paradise in which there was hardly any job for law. However, as Hoebel was to conclude, 'it appears to be an absence of investigation (in the case of organic theorists [like Benedict] a selective bias) rather than an absence of formal control that has left the legal undiscovered'.[65]

In 1945 Llewellyn and Hoebel obtained a grant from the Columbia University Social Science Research Council to study the law-government of some of the eastern, Keresan-speaking Pueblos. In some ways the project was a natural successor to *The Cheyenne Way*: the reputed communalism of the Pueblos promised a sharp contrast to the more individualistic Comanches and Cheyennes, while the suggestion that they had no real 'law' provoked the same scepticism that had underlain Hoebel's first approach to the Indians of the Plains. Because the Pueblos consisted of a number of discrete communities they offered unusual opportunities for comparative study. However, it was as much chance as design on their part that led Llewellyn and Hoebel to embark on the project.

Shortly after the publication of *The Cheyenne Way*, while Llewellyn was visiting Boulder, Colorado, he casually expressed an interest in seeing some of the Indian communities in New Mexico. News of this interest reached William A. Brophy, a lawyer who was Special Attorney for the United Pueblos Agency at Albuquerque, New Mexico, and who happened also to be an admirer of *The Bramble Bush*. He contacted Llewellyn.[66] Twenty years later Brophy described their first meeting as follows :

He put me at ease and we talked on a porch. And we went out to see some Pueblos. I remember well that I had just had some rough case out at Zia and I asked Karl to go there so he could get the basic material and give me advice. But once having the case he launched into the System. We sat on a rock in the shade with (as I remember) Juanito Medina, Lorenzo Medina and (I think) old man Andres. 'What do you do when you have heard everything?' 'We decide.' 'What do you do then?' 'We ask the man: Are you satisfied?' 'Suppose he says he is not satisfied with your decision what do you do?' 'We dig deeper!' Then Karl jumped and shook and got excited like a Shaker, and continued his probing.[67]

Writing of Llewellyn's later achievement, Brophy continued:

He gave those Indians confidence that they had a system of justice that was not to be laughed at as some of the B.I.A. [Bureau of Indian Affairs] people did. He gave them dignity by his very interest. For no man of his eminence would be interested in learning about foolish things. And this recognition that the Pueblo Systems were real systems of justice radiated out among all the Pueblos. He gave me an understanding which I no more than sensed before or perhaps never even had the sense to recognize before. And he made me more effective.[68]

In introducing Llewellyn to Zia, Brophy had not been entirely disinterested. The Pueblos were largely self-governing, with civil and criminal jurisdiction over all matters occurring on their land except a few serious offences.[69] Their leaders were at this time under pressure on two fronts: on the one hand, members of the younger generation were restive and the prospect of the return of Pueblo tribesmen who had served in the American forces posed a threat to authority and tradition; on the other hand, their autonomy was in danger of being seriously eroded by the federal and state courts. On several occasions Pueblo officials had been gaoled for applying harsh punishments in execution of Pueblo law, and their confidence was being undermined through uncertainty about their legal position vis-à-vis the United States Government. The New Mexico courts, too, had in respect of divorce and *habeas corpus* begun to exercise jurisdiction which the Pueblo leaders considered clashed with their traditional prerogatives.[70]

Brophy, who admired many facets of the Pueblo system, felt that their autonomy could be more effectively defended if Pueblo law and procedure were recorded. It would then be better understood both by federal and state courts, as well as by individual tribesmen. He felt, too, that Pueblo officials might benefit from advice on handling some of their administrative and legal problems. He saw in Llewellyn's visit a possible opportunity, but he could hardly have anticipated the enthusiasm with which Llewellyn reacted. It was virtually a case of love at first sight. Thereafter Llewellyn felt an emotional and mystical bond with the Pueblos which coloured his relationship with them, especially with the older generation.

Brophy secured the agreement of leaders of several Pueblos that an invitation should be sent to Llewellyn and Hoebel to come to investigate their legal processes and to act as unofficial consultants. He also secured official government support for the project.[71] Thus, from the start, the relationship with the Pueblos involved a combination of research and practical assistance. In contrast with the Cheyenne project, Llewellyn did a substantial amount of field work on this occasion. He visited New Mexico for substantial periods during five consecutive summers from 1945–9 and again in 1951. However, much of the actual collection of data was done by Hoebel, Mentschikoff and a variety of assistants.[72] For not only did Llewellyn have few pretensions to be an efficient fact-gatherer, but he also became increasingly involved as a participant in Pueblo affairs. Besides acting as an unofficial adviser on a variety of matters, he drafted law and order codes for the Pueblos of Santa Anna, Santa Domingo and Zia and he assisted their officials in a number of specific cases and helped to formulate general policies on such matters as membership of the Pueblo, divorce, and religious tolera-tion.[73] He and Hoebel helped the Pueblo of Zia to obtain a facsimile of an important ceremonial snake pot that had been removed by an anthropologist many years before and presented to the United States National Museum in Washington. In all these activities Llewellyn exhibited extraordinary sensitivity to and respect for the Pueblo point of view, and in the process of working for them gained a great deal of insight into their problems and the ways they handled them.

Unfortunately, he did not manage to capitalize on this experi-ence. His practical assistance to the Pueblos seems to have been of real value, but the research project yielded little in the way of concrete results. This is regrettable, for it had considerable potential. It is to be hoped that something may yet be salvaged from the extensive field notes that survive;[74] however, Llewellyn's legacy contains only three matters that are likely to be of any general significance: the draft codes of law and order; a proposal for a comparative study of Pueblo and Soviet law; and the concept of 'the parental' model of law-government. Each of these deserves a brief comment.

The Codes

The principal way in which Llewellyn sought to help the Pueblos was by drafting a series of codes of law and order.[75] These had three main aims. First, to increase the chances of non-interference by the federal and state courts by establishing that there were clear rules of law and order and that the procedures for decision satisfied national standards of due process. Secondly, to ensure that the basic rules of the Pueblo were known and understood and accepted by those to whom they applied. And thirdly, to provide guidance to Pueblo officials in the exercise of their authority.

Extracts from one of the codes and related documents are re-produced in Appendix F. The codes were concerned with the position of officials, with procedure, and with the extent and limita-tions of authority within the Pueblo. They were deliberately simple and short and did not purport to cover all of substantive law.

Rather, they were envisaged as a sort of social contract, a combination of a rationale for exercise of authority within the Pueblo concerned and a statement of the basic rules relating thereto. They represent a straight forward application of some of Llewellyn's favourite ideas: articulation of purpose alongside prescription; open-ended drafting with extensive use made of standards of reasonableness, good faith and fairness; a bill of duties accompanying a bill of rights; and a simple style which aimed above all at communicating the substance and the rationale of their law to the people who were subject to it. Llewellyn saw very clearly that the way to preserve 'the tribal core', as he called it, was to make membership of the Pueblo ultimately dependent upon the acceptance of a clearly articulated set of principles. Dissenters were free to leave, but if they stayed they had to accept the conditions of membership. The ultimate sanction was expulsion.[76]

The codes are so simple that at first sight they may not seem to be remarkable. However, informed opinion suggests that they successfully harmonize Pueblo rules with American concepts of due process and individual rights, and that they catch the spirit as well as the substance of the traditional mode of administering justice, whilst mitigating some of its harshness.[77] They compare favourably with other attempts to record or restate the laws of pre-literate societies, especially in not isolating substantive rules of law from their procedural context.[78] Of the preamble to one of the codes, D'Arcy McNickle, an American Indian writer, has said: 'It is a simple statement, aimed at the guidance of a few score men, women and children. Yet one wonders when at this moment a more profound document on human government might be written.'[79]

Pueblo-Soviet Parallels

The original plan for their research envisaged a study not very different from *The Cheyenne Way*. However, it was not long before the project underwent a decided shift in emphasis. Whereas in *The Cheyenne Way* they had been particularly interested in juristic method, among the Pueblos it was the communalistic regime and ideology which attracted their attention. Here Llewellyn was caught off-balance by the difficulty of reconciling his bourgeois liberal views with his admiration for a regime that seemed at once totalitarian, communalistic and theocratic:

The small but almost 'complete' Pueblo governments and systems of law-and-administration force inquiry into a large number of bedrock problems in political philosophy. For example, the relation of religious freedom to a Church-State Unity and the problems of toleration, tolerance, and repression of dissenting views in terms of the kinds of dissent: passive, active, aggressive, obstreperous. Or, the problem of combining a high degree of collective control of economic life with a very material degree of individual or family independence and even economic initiative amid changing economic conditions. Or the problem of maintaining or adjusting an ingrained ideology without disruption of its values, with a younger generation affected by a wider and utterly diverse ideology; and of producing peaceful relations with an utterly diverse neighboring, and to some extent, predatory, culture. Or, the manner and degree in which officially unrecognized changes creep in under maintenance of the older ideology and forms.[80]

At an early stage Llewellyn began to see striking similarities between Pueblo and Soviet society, and in 1946-7 he prepared detailed proposals for a project on Soviet law which would run in parallel to their research in New Mexico. Unfortunately, for reasons unconnected with its merits, this project never materialized. It is worth quoting at length Llewellyn's tentative formulation of projected lines of comparison, both because of their intrinsic interest and because they throw some light on his views on the vexed question of the validity of comparisons between primitive and advanced systems of law government:[81]

Being aware that the proposed comparison of one of the hugest States in history with a 'State' of 250-2,000 persons has a surface appearance of the silly, I append a series of significant comparisons and possible cross-illuminations which seem to me evident as soon as noted. I proceed on my fundamental hypothesis that the basic problems of government and the law-jobs, of the development of the human being in relation to his culture, and of the integration of a culture, are essentially identical regardless of the size of the group concerned and can attain sufficient complexity in a small group to shed significant light on even the more intricate problems of a large one. In the Pueblo this degree of complexity has been attained. Compare, for instance:

(1) The paternalistic, patient, but unyieldingly absolute approach to criminal 'justice', with the accompanying phenomenon of what may be sloganized as 'joyous confession'.

What comes back from Nuremberg in regard to the views of the Soviet participants on just methods of trial might almost have been dictated by a Pueblo leader. When applied to a *member* of the We-group, you have the otherwise baffling phenomenon of personal internal release of any ordinary recalcitrant as, under the relentless psychological pressure, he finally re-identifies himself with his own, sees and confesses what is in psychological essence sin as well as guilt, and joins in his own condemnation. Neither a Soviet court nor a Pueblo court is happy when a culprit out of the recognized We-group cannot be brought to *approve* his penalty.

This must be studied in more than a single culture to make clear that it is a process and method of great human significance, not a possibility merely in a primitive or face-to-face grouping. Note the bearings on discipline in the family, and those on discipline in the medieval Church.

(2) The problem of the unyielding official ideology, in regard to any of the liberties: its bearing on the political structure (tight central control, passive general assent); on the selection of leaders and policies (co-option of young Tories, elimination of young radicals, schism among rival ortho-doxies with policy-differences operating only under cover – but operating); on the training of the young; on – seemingly among the Soviets also – the development of three strikingly diverse types of human being: the rounded leader (who among the Pueblos has a wisdom and shrewdness utterly amazing); the 'good soldier' type, loyal, effective and unthinking, who is the backbone of administration; the great ruck, quiescent, undeveloped, vaguely baffled.

Prior descriptions of the Pueblos have concentrated on the last; but both of the other types are strikingly present. Current reports suggest something closely similar among the Soviets.

(3) Closely related, when one adds centralized communal economic management plus communal 'ownership' of all basic utilities and resources, is the drive of ambition toward power rather than wealth, and the question of what lines of outlet are found for family-feeling.

On the economic side the Pueblos are in the main holders-back rather than five-year Planners, land-minded rather than industry-minded. For that very reason, parallels in process and result offer deeper light.

(4) A rationalization machinery whereby basic economic or political change is worked into the orthodoxy is at constant work in both systems.

(5) A significant further parallel, though I do not think we can reach it in the Soviet system, lies in the processes of formation of attitude and opinion in a 'public' which has no effective means of inter-communication. The slowness of gossip, rumor or news to spread, within a Pueblo, almost passes belief. And for myself, I incline to believe that a solid belief in and fear of witchcraft produces social and personal effects closely resembling the results of fear of informers and secret police.

(6) The problem of adjusting to an outside world based on different, competing, and 'dangerous' ideology and institutions shows fascinating parallels. Pueblo 'secrecy' has been interpreted as defensive and religious. What of Soviet 'secrecy?' Both cultures indoctrinate at high power and seek to avoid contamination. Each seeks to borrow and absorb differentially.

Each takes productive technology but seeks to rule out the liberty-ideology which gave rise to the technology, the distribution system which might accompany the technology, the consumption-ideas and ideals which are the counterpart of the production-ways in the neighboring system. That the Pueblos are tiny and subject, the Soviets mighty and huge, again only reinforces the value of process-study.

(7) The processes of federation are at work in both cultures. Though here I think political conditions to be so different that there is little cross-light to be had, only light on the general federation problem from its two extreme ends. I would point out, however, that this aspect of the Soviet system has peculiar interest.[82]

These ideas were put forward merely as possible starting-points for enquiry. Llewellyn was well aware that some of his suggested parallels might prove to be misconceived and that complexity itself was a factor to be taken into account. Thus, if it transpired that rumour in fact travels fast in the Soviet Union or that the selection of leaders is a much more complicated matter than is suggested by Llewellyn' s second paragraph, this would not necessarily mean that a comparison between aspects of Soviet and Pueblo cultures might not be illuminating. The value of comparative study is thought to lie in the heightening of awareness that can be occasioned by identifying similarities and differences between two phenomena that have sufficient characteristics in common to afford a basis for comparison.[83] Llewellyn's hope was that Americans, in particular, might find it easier to understand Soviet culture by approaching it through the study of Pueblo societies which were at once American, simple, and relatively free from the strongly emotive ideological associations of communism.[84] The basis for comparison, in his view, was to be found in the idea that the social organization of both groups approximated to a single theoretical model of law-government, which he characterized as 'parental'. This theoretical model is examined in the next section.

The 'Parental'

Commentators have remarked on the 'paternalistic' or 'protective-educative'[85] aspects of Soviet law as evidenced by such matters as their reputed concern for 'the whole man' rather than the particular act, their emphasis on confession and reintegration into society, and the use of judicial proceedings to dramatize and propagate civic virtues. Llewellyn saw such matters as belonging to a wider configuration of factors which tended to coincide and which he characterized as 'parental'. His 'parental' model (ideal type) applied both to total systems of law-government and to dispute-settlement mechanisms. In respect of the latter, the 'parental' was contrasted with 'the adversary'; the 'parental pole of law-government' did not have a single opposite pole, as he explained in his most complete discussion of the concept:

The 'parental' pole for charting a profile of the law-and-government institutions of a society or other group would represent a centering of the absolute at one end of a series of axes: (1) on the axis of Power, it would represent absolute power in a single hand, both inwardly toward the group-members and outwardly in foreign relations; I suppose the other pole would be pure anarchy in either form: power in none, or equal power in each. (2) on the axis of Personnel of law-and-government, the pole is the single person, with one-man's effective choosing, directing, supervising, disciplining and removing a very high latitude situation; any constitutional regime with wide suffrage and a good chance for rise by merit will serve as partial contrast. (3) on the axis of Penal Purpose, the parental pole represents confession, repentance, purification and reintegration of the offender, precisely as in the perfectly run family; any other goal is in contrast, with protective extirpation close-up to the pure-parental. (4) along the axis of Procedure (in cases of dispute or grievance or offense), at the pole the judge-king knows the facts before 'trial', has all the initiative, and runs essentially a solemn ceremony, on the criminal side, of confession and cure, on the civil side, of confession, atonement and complete reconciliation. Any admixture of adversary-type procedure, litigants' initiative, etc., moves far away along this axis. (5) along what might perhaps be better seen as seven different axes, but which I shall call Planning – organization and guidance of the polity – the parental pole is where Papa knows best and in simple consequence says what shall be done and how. One starts moving away from the pole when papa is limited to some manner or time, or by his own prior official action (as in Daniel's case.) (6) on the axis of Participation, the pole is unquestioning acceptance with rejoicing; I suppose the utter other pole would be out far beyond any 'democratic' regime: a unanimous spontaneous revolution. I feel rather clear the need for dealing with some such other axis as the Knowledge-Regime, with the parental pole representing simple omniscience and considerable emphasis, as one moves away from that pole on the openness of channels of communication and of opportunities for inquiry.[86]

This passage was probably written shortly before Llewellyn's death; it may be one of a number of manuscript fragments that he drafted in conjunction with an article on juvenile courts on which he was working when he died.[87] Although he never fully developed his theoretical model, he used the term 'parental' for a considerable time.[88] Indeed, he claimed to have started to become aware of a difference between 'parental' and less authoritarian modes of organization during his work in boys' camps when he was a young man,[89] but it was not until his early encounters with the Pueblos, twenty years later, that he became aware of a configuration of factors which he felt to be significant. Subsequently he came to see similar patterns in the prototype of the American nuclear family, the medieval inquisition, certain phases of Church government, and in the Soviet system.[90] But he did not carry through his analysis in respect of law-government systems.

In *Law in Our Society* Llewellyn elaborated his analysis of 'parental' in connection with dispute-settlement mechanisms.[91] In this context the contrast between the 'parental' and 'the adversary' will be seen to be very close to the familiar contrast between 'inquisitorial' and 'adversary' models of judicial proceedings. Here Llewellyn may be deemed to have made an original contribution by widening the focus of attention to include all types of dispute-settlement mechanism, while suggesting that there may be some connection between inquisitorial types of judicial proceeding and parental modes of government on a larger scale. However, the value of the 'parental' concept is difficult to assess, for Llewellyn's analysis was rudimentary and he did not himself have occasion to use it in a sustained piece of analysis. It would seem that, not uncharacteristically, he produced the nucleus of an important idea, but left it to others to refine and develop it.[92]

14

The Significance of Llewellyn: an Assessment

When Llewellyn first embarked on the study of law in 1915, the American law school world was at the beginning of a new phase. The broad pattern of its development for the next fifty years had already been anticipated in several important respects: Langdell's educational reforms had by then captured the leading law schools: Holmes and Pound had already charted the path for a more socially oriented approach to law; the revolt against formalism was well under way; and organizations such as the NCC had already begun their efforts to unify and modernize some branches of the private law of the various states; papers by Corbin, Hohfeld and Bingham had recently appeared, foreshadowing the growth of the Realist Movement and a rich, but confused period of juristic activity. The last years of Llewellyn's life and the period immediately after his death saw a series of events which suggested that the law school world was again entering a new era: for example, the implications of the computer were being explored; there was a marked increase of political and social consciousness in the law schools; there were signs of a corresponding decline in enthusiasm for the life of the law, and, perhaps, for the jealous mistress herself. The idea of love of the law, so eloquently expressed in *The Bramble Bush* and Holmes' speeches, seemed quaint to many law students of the sixties. There had also been significant academic developments: in particular the revitalization of analytical jurisprudence, and new interests in system building and mathematical models and jurimetrics were symptomatic of a trend in some quarters away from the revolt against formalism. In the social sciences generally there was a greater maturity and self-confidence which was reflected in such fields as criminology and the study of the legal profession. This in turn generated a new optimism about attempts to develop law as a social science.

In this perspective, it is worth asking: what is the significance, historical and contemporary, of Llewellyn's work? In certain particular respects Llewellyn's contributions are now mainly of historical interest. His casebook on sales was the first, and most notable, of a series of similar works that introduced important modifications into the Langdellian prototype, without destroying it. Since 1930 American legal literature for students has slowly increased in variety but has continued to be dominated by this modified prototype. Secondly, in the 1930s Llewellyn played a modest but nonetheless significant role in stimulating the development of the systematic study of the legal profession and the extension of legal services for the underprivileged. Since the second world war both subjects have made considerable progress in the United States, so that today the sociology of the legal profession is one of the more developed areas of the sociology of law and 'Poverty Law' is one of the more fashionable 'new' subjects. Thirdly, the 'case method' of *The Cheyenne Way* has been assimilated into the conventional armoury of anthropological field techniques and has been used in most subsequent anthropological studies of tribal law. The potential of the approach of *The Cheyenne Way* has not yet been realized in lawyers' treatments of this kind of subject matter. Fourthly, Llewellyn shares with others, Jerome Frank in particular, credit for fostering a greater consciousness of the possibilities of systematic training in 'legal skills'. Although there has been much talk about this, and some individuals have tried to develop the subject, realization of its promise probably must await the arrival of a greater degree of educational professionalism in universities. Fifthly, Llewellyn has a place in history as the principal architect of the Uniform Commercial Code. By virtue of its widespread adoption the Code is important in itself and has attracted considerable attention. It was both a product of, and itself further stimulated, re-examination of a wide range of long-accepted common law doctrines in commercial law and contract.

Finally, Llewellyn was a member of the realist movement, its most sophisticated jurist, and a central figure in its most important controversy. As its leading interpreter, however, he may inadvertently have obscured as much as he illuminated the nature of the movement.

These were not the achievements of a solitary individual working in isolation. As an innovator Llewellyn was swimming with the tide: up to 1930 he was more acolyte than pioneer of legal realism; his contributions to legal education and to the study of the legal profession, and still more so to the Uniform Commercial Code were as much the products of joint enterprise as of individual effort; although *The Cheyenne Way* broke new ground in anthropology, no common lawyer could claim to have invented the idea of approaching law through actual cases. It must also be remembered that by the time he rose to eminence his world was too large and too complicated to be dominated by a few individuals. In paying tribute to Llewellyn's achievements we do him no dis-service by putting them in a proper prospective.

'So much for his contributions as a pioneer, but what of his significance for the future?' a sceptic may ask. 'From now on why should anyone read Llewellyn? In particular, why should those who are offended or puzzled by his style of writing go to the trouble of studying his works?' These are fair questions: opinions will differ on the answers. In my personal judgment several specific works will continue to repay study for many years to come. *The Cheyenne Way* is a pleasure to read, is rich in aperçus and contains the best introduction to the 'law-jobs' theory; this is further developed in 'The Normative, the Legal and the Law-Jobs', which is Llewellyn's most substantial theoretical paper; *The Bramble Bush* is still capable of firing the enthusiasm of beginners and, at the very least, makes good bed-time reading for the convinced Karlo-phile. It should not, however, be treated on its own as a scholarly contribution to juristic thought. The paper on 'The Theory of Legal Science' contains one of the sanest discussions of this topic in print; no student of appellate judicial processes can afford to ignore *The Common Law Tradition*, despite its defects; it is not easy to read and the gist of its argument is best obtained from secondary sources, but it is too rich in suggestive insights to be ignored. A number of essays on specific topics are still of value, and this is particularly the case with most of the articles on contract and commercial law of the middle period. The same is true to a lesser degree of his writings on the legal profession, although these have to some extent been overtaken by events. Llewellyn's comments on other jurists are often penetrating. The indexes to *Jurisprudence* and *The Common Law Tradition* are useful in this respect, but the richest source is *Law in Our Society*. Otherwise the unpublished writings, of which *Law in Our Society* and *The Theory of Rules* are the most substantial, are mainly of interest to specialists. So too is *Cases and Materials on the Law of Sales*, which still contains some rich ore for the sales scholar. Among the less demanding works, two pieces of advocacy are my personal favourites: Llewellyn's broadcast on behalf of Sacco and Vanzetti and the edited version of his general statement to the New York Law Revision Commission about the Uniform Commercial Code.

So much for particular works: to answer the sceptic's questions at a more general level it is advisable to revert once more to Llewellyn's basic concerns. Four preoccupations underlie much of his thought. Two are shared to some extent by most other jurists, two are relatively unusual. The first is how to reconcile the need to generalize and to simplify with the need to take account of the uniqueness and the complexity of each individual situation. This applies equally to normative and to empirical contexts. Llewellyn's concern with this problem is reflected in his suspicion of all forms of very broad generalization, including purported universal principles of natural law and many accepted formulations of legal rules; but it is also to be seen in his recognition of the need to work towards 'scientific' generalizations of fact and broad, simply stated, principles to guide action. The concept of 'situation sense', his advocacy of resort to narrow categories and the flexible concepts of the Uniform Commercial Code all represent attempts to resolve this dilemma. So, too, in a rather different way, was the case method of *The Cheyenne Way* in its emphasis on the search for general illumination from the study of unique events. The central precept of Llewellyn's realism, 'see it fresh', was a reminder of the need to stay close to the actual and the particular and thus to avoid the chief pitfall of formalism, that of oversimplification through remoteness from day-to-day reality; whereas the other precept of realism, 'see it whole', emphasised the need for a coherent frame of reference. Cautious striving towards the establishment of significant patterns, as embodied in the concept of 'situation sense', was Llewellyn's main formula for resolving the basic dilemma.

Another concern, also shared by many jurists, is how to reconcile the need for stability and the need for adaptation on the part of human institutions. Llewellyn's espousal of the Grand Style represents his general attitude. The idea of *recapturing* a method of evolutionary change satisfied at once his love of the traditions of the common law with his recognition of the need for continuous movement in a world of change.

Llewellyn's next concern reflects the strains in his make-up that have been roughly characterized as 'the poet' and 'the lawyer'. How to reconcile the values of 'vision' and 'imagination' with the more austere values of intellectual discipline is a theme familiar to physical scientists. It seems less common in jurisprudence. To an unusual urge to find outlets for imaginative self-expression in legal scholarship, add a lack of stylistic inhibition and a few minor idiosyncrasies and we have at least gone some way towards accounting for the strangeness of the Llewellynesque.

Fourthly, while it is not uncommon for theorists to seek a *rapprochement* between 'theory' and 'practice', Llewellyn's persistent urge to operate at the level of participant working theory is rare in jurisprudence, if not unique. Many of those who have revolted against the Royal Tennis Tradition, have rejected all jurisprudence as being esoteric and useless; few, if any, have rivalled Llewellyn's consistency in seeking to provide for participants usable theory, drawing on the best modern thought available in a variety of disciplines, whilst maintaining a broad perspective and liberal values. Llewellyn's emphasis on 'Juristic Method' is linked to this concern: for participants law involves the practice of a set of crafts, in which the attainment of excellence depends on skill, on know-how at least as much as on know-what. Thus a working theory for participants must deal adequately with legal technology. With some justification Llewellyn considered this line of thinking to be his most original contribution to jurisprudence.

The 'significance' of a theorist depends largely on the extent to which his main concerns are considered important ('Was he asking worthwhile questions?') and the relative quality of his response to them ('How helpful is he in providing satisfactory answers?'). Some of Llewellyn's concerns belong to the mainstream of juristic thought, some have the value of rarity. All four that have been mentioned are sufficiently fundamental to transcend the limits of a particular time or place. This supports the judgment that although Llewellyn was very much a man of his time, and very much an

American, the solid core of his work is neither ephemeral nor parochial.

There remains the question of quality. On this each must judge for himself: to analytical jurists Llewellyn's use of language will often appear loose and unnecessarily metaphorical; some social scientists will find his approach to fact too anecdotal and impressionistic, falling short of their standards for objective description; his impatience with much of 'professional philosophy' is not likely to win many friends among professional philosophers; some lawyers will find him too fancy-free. Conversely others will find virtues corresponding to these limitations. Despite his faults Llewellyn is, in my view, the jurist who has the most to offer to anyone who is concerned to adopt or to develop an approach to law which is both solidly grounded and undoctrinaire and which escapes the constrictions of formalism. He may have been less original as a thinker than Holmes, less erudite than Pound, less systematic than Lasswell, but he has more to say than any of these on *how* to get to grips with the problems of implementing this kind of approach in a variety of contexts: in legal literature, in legal education, in advocacy, in writing judicial opinions, in the study of tribal law or the law-government of sub-groups, and in law reform. He was not a systematic thinker and he rarely said the last word on a subject. But his capacity to fertilize, to stimulate and to put familiar things in a fresh perspective is perhaps unsurpassed in the common law world. At his best, he succeeded in his ambition to emulate the 'childlike vision' of John Dewey, who was his ideal of the 'realist'. This is why, of the many eulogies accorded to him during his lifetime and after his death, that of his former colleague and friend Elliott Cheatham was perhaps the most apt:

He might have written the lines, 'the world is so full of a number of things', and he is one of the few men at law who will be remembered as persons a century from now. He had vision and insight and the willingness to put things as he saw and felt them – something of the freshness of outlook of the boy, who saw and so said the King had no clothes on.

This is a tribute to genius, and it is deserved.

PART THREE

Conclusion

15
The Significance of Realism

The indeterminacy of 'realism' and the dangers of generalizing about 'the realists' have been a recurrent theme of this book. Yet the label has stuck and the modern reader, confronted with an apparent morass of literature by 'realists' or about 'realism', may quite reasonably ask for some general guidance. How much of this literature deserves to survive? What is a good way to approach it if one is to avoid both unwarranted generalization and barren controversy? In particular, what should law students in North America, the British Isles or elsewhere be encouraged to learn from the study of American legal realism? A partial answer to these questions is implicit in what has been said earlier. The purpose of the present chapter is to deal with them in a more direct fashion.

Some of the more obvious pitfalls of interpretation are quite easily avoided if the realist movement is approached on three different levels, which may be roughly characterized as the historical, the analytical and the applied. The realist movement should be viewed, in first instance, not as a school of jurisprudence but as an historical phenomenon. The starting point should be to identify the concerns of particular individuals at particular moments in time. In Part One some of the concerns of some key figures were sketched. From this preliminary account, which should not be treated as a substitute for a detailed history, it is apparent that the intellectual roots of the realist movement were rather complex. From the many strands that became entangled with each other, perhaps four sets of questions can be singled out as having been of particular concern to leading figures at Harvard, Yale and Columbia law schools during the period of the rise of the realist movement: (1) What should law schools be teaching, by what methods? (2) What should be the scope and methods of legal research? Is an empirical science of law possible and, if so, how can it be developed? (3) How far are

legal institutions, concepts, principles, and rules adequately performing their proper role in a rapidly changing American society?
In particular, what is the actual and potential role of courts,
especially appellate courts, as agencies of legal change? (4) What is
the relationship between law as a discipline and other social sciences
such as economics, sociology, psychology and anthropology? How
can communication and cooperation between law and the social
sciences be extended?

These were, of course, not the only questions that were ot concern
during this period, individuals differed in the priority they attached
to them and the issues were not always posed so starkly or in
identical terms. However, such questions did represent a dominant
focus of attention, and certain general points can be made about
them. First, these are not, in first instance, 'ultimate' or 'philosophical' questions. One of the safer generalizations that can be made
about realists from Corbin (or Gray) to Llewellyn or Douglas or
Moore is that they did not look on themselves as philosophers. It is
to their credit that they perceived that there was some connection
between legal philosophy and the problems of legal education,
legal research and legal literature, but their primary concern was
more with the latter than with the former. Yet much of the secondary literature, especially that which has emanated from England,
pictures 'the realists' as legal philosophers who gave imperfect
answers to philosophical questions about the nature of law rather
than as scholar-teachers who made valuable contributions to the
discussion of a medley of less fundamental issues. While it may be a
valid exercise to subject the views of any writer to philosophical
scrutiny, such an exercise may have a distorting effect unless it is
made clear that philosophical questions were tangential to his concerns. A second point is that the realist movement grew up in the
atmosphere of the 'revolt against formalism'. For many American
jurists, from Holmes to McDougal, the major irritant was an
approach and attitude to law of which Langdell and his followers
became the chief symbol. A shared enemy provided a unifying
element, but there was divergence both in the grounds for attack
and even more so in the remedies proposed by way of alternative.
Thus Holmes, Gray and Frank all in different ways provided
rationalizations for the practising lawyer's scepticism of the cloistered, library-bound academic. But in so far as they had any constructive alternative to offer, their solutions tended to be rather

different. At Yale in the period immediately after 1913, Corbin, Hohfeld and Cook while sharing with their opponents a tendency to concentrate on appellate court judgments, used the weapons of analytical jurisprudence to show that the 'over-logical' adherents of the deductive model of judicial reasoning (whoever they might be) had been indulging in 'pseudo-logic'. Their 'constructive' contributions, of which Corbin's work on contracts is the outstanding example, tended to be at a less general level. The Scientists and the Prudents at Columbia followed in the footsteps of Pound and Holmes in maintaining that law should not be treated as an autonomous, self-contained discipline, but should be set clearly and consistently in its social and economic context. But while the Scientists took their first faltering steps outside the library and, in the view of many, fell flat on their faces, the Prudents combined a traditional interest in vocational training with a more complacent view than the Scientists of the problems of integrating law and the social sciences. Thus a united front was not maintained against the common enemy, and after the Columbia crisis the realist movement became too fragmented for generalization to be fruitful. That realism began to be treated as a single phenomenon *after* the crucial split is best seen as one of the ironies of history. It may be another that the lawyers wooed the social scientists before the latter were ready for them.

Analytical treatment of the ideas of leading realists presents some problems. Much of their work, including some of the best, was not intended as a contribution to general jurisprudence and it is not easy to isolate passages which are potentially of general significance or lasting value from those which were mainly directed to ephemeral or parochial concerns. In the literature of legal realism are to be found intelligent discussions of such topics as the nature and function of law, classification, the relationship between law and the physical and social sciences, the nature and functions of legal concepts, legal reasoning, interpretation of statutes and cases, corporate personality, the role of fictions, symbols, ritual and myths in law, the nature of judicial processes, as well as of topics which are not commonly associated with 'Jurisprudence'. One lesson to be learned from viewing the realist movement in its historical context is that analytical treatment of ideas and theories associated with 'realism' must start with particular writings of named individuals.

Without attempting to provide a comprehensive guide to the literature of legal realism, it may be useful if I give my personal evaluation of the work of those individuals, apart from Llewellyn, whom I have treated as the leading pioneers of the movement— i.e. Corbin, Hohfeld, Cook, Moore, Oliphant and Frank. I have already ventured the opinion that Llewellyn is much the most important theorist among the realists. What of the others? How much of their work is still worthy of attention? It is probably fair to say that of the remaining six, Hohfeld has the strongest claim to be treated as a theorist of the first rank. His work on *Fundamental Legal Conceptions* is still often taken as the starting point for discussion of 'rights' and related concepts; although his analysis has been carried further by others, and there are grounds for believing that he was anticipated by Bentham in most important respects, the work deserves to rank as a classic. Hohfeld's less well-known paper, 'A Vital School of Jurisprudence and Law', also repays study.

Corbin will continue to be read for a long time as one of the great contract scholars, and, more generally, his work in that field provides a possible model for those who are seeking a non-formalistic method of analysis and exposition of substantive law without wishing to make a radical break with tradition; but his more general writings are now of little more than historical interest. Herman Oliphant, too, is more likely to be remembered for his contribution to events at Columbia and Johns Hopkins than as an original or distinguished thinker. As for Walter Wheeler Cook, his writings on conflicts continue to serve as a useful irritant to specialists in the field; his views on 'the scientific analogy', especially as set out in the paper 'Scientific Method and the Law', represent his most important theoretical contribution; this aspect of his work deserves to be reassessed in the light of recent developments in the philosophy of science. The time is also ripe for a reappraisal of the work of Underhill Moore. While there may be force in the criticism that his parking studies were based on too simplistic an interpretation of behavioural psychology, it has yet to be established whether, and if so in what respects, the theoretical basis of Moore's attempts to develop an empirical science of law was misconceived. It would not be entirely surprising if Moore were eventually to be recognized as one of the more original thinkers among the realists, perhaps even as an unfulfilled genius.

There remains Jerome Frank. The fact that his work is eminently readable will no doubt ensure that he will continue to be read. It is to be hoped that in future law students and academic commentators will pay more attention to *Courts on Trial* than to *Law and the Modern Mind*. There can be little doubt that he performed an important service by showing up the distorting influence of 'appellate court-itis'. Clever rather than wise, a dilettante intellectual rather than a scholar, a brilliant controversialist, but somewhat erratic in his judgments, in his juristic writings Frank exhibited the strengths and weaknesses of a first-class journalist.[1] His essential contribution was to complement Holmes in the role of spokesman for the bar against the Ivory Tower tendencies of academic lawyers. The American legal profession has been fortunate in having had in this role two men, who in different ways were both eloquent and immune from accusations of anti-intellectualism.

There is much more to the literature of realism than the writings of a few individuals. There is first of all a mass of detailed studies which could be considered to be to a greater or lesser extent applications of 'a realist approach'. There is also a great deal of writing about realism, or provoked by it. Even their most severe critics have acknowledged that many realists were stimulating and provocative. Professor Hart has suggested that some of the American literature on realism can be illuminatingly read as a debate.[2] The suggestion is a good one, but it may be more appropriate to see the position in terms of a series of debates on a variety of issues. Unfortunately the standards of debate in modern jurisprudence have tended to fall short of those of the mediaeval disputation. Llewellyn, who felt strongly that he had been regularly misrepresented and misunderstood, had some scathing things to say about polemical jurisprudence:

Though
 (a) jurisprudes are mostly lawyers, so trained in the rhetoric of controversy, with
    (i) its selective, favorable posing of issues, and
    (ii) its selection, coloring, argumentative arrangement of facts, and
    (iii) its use of epithet and innuendo, and
    (iv) its typical complete distortion of the advocate's vision, once he has taken a case, so that he ceases to even take in any possibility which would work against him (as especially in the prevalent 'romantic' type of advocacy), that
 (b) it has proved necessary to police their work as advocates by
    (i) forcing them to define issues by a careful system of phrased pleading, served back and forth with opportunity for answer, under the supervision of a responsible and authoritative tribunal, and

    (ii) limiting their arguments to the issues so drawn, and

    (iii) confining the 'facts' to which they can resort to a record, and

    (iv) barring guilt by association, or by imputation, or without proof of particular offense, etc., yet

  (c) in Jurisprudence every man

    (i) states his own issue, misstates the other man's issue, beclouds the or-any issue, evades the or-any issue, etc., uncontrolled by procedure or by answer, or by authority (and cases where a jurisprude has stated an issue fairly are museum-pieces), and

    (ii) uses his rhetoric also without control, and

    (iii) is free to dream up 'facts' even by anonymous imputation, and

    (iv) consequently always rides his strawman down.

  (d) Whereas in law one party always loses, or each must yield something, in Jurisprudence there is thus Triumphant Victory for All. This makes for comfort, if not for light.[3]

Anyone approaching the polemical literature on realism would be wise to heed this warning and to be selective in what he chooses to read. The cruder misrepresentations are best ignored, as are some of the wilder statements of some people who have been labelled as 'realists'. Thus it is best to discount as misleading allegations that 'the' realists favoured totalitarianism or unfettered official discretion or that they denied the very existence of rules or that they espoused extreme versions of economic determinism, moral nihilism or psychological behaviourism. It should be abundantly clear that Karl Llewellyn never espoused such views; if passages supporting such interpretations are to be found in the writings of one or more individuals who might reasonably be identified as 'realists', it would not be difficult to show that they were untypical or peripheral to the main concerns of the core members of the realist movement. 'Debate' at this level tends quickly to deteriorate into a sterile form of witch-hunt.

While individual realists have often been the victims of misrepresentation, even this kind of misunderstanding has had some positive aspects. The process of exposing errors has stimulated critics to clarify their own ideas. Fuller and Kennedy, for example, in discussing realism have made interesting contributions to the perennial debate between Natural Law and Positivism.[4] John Dickinson, Karl Olivecrona and H. L. A. Hart are among those who have done work of lasting value in the process of showing why it is inadequate to define law in terms of predictions, or what is wrong with the belief that 'talk of rules is a myth' or why the notion of 'legal right' cannot be elucidated simply in terms of brute fact.[5] It is of relatively minor importance that it is not always easy to identify passages in which these ideas were clearly expounded, for exposure of error can be illuminating irrespective of whether it has in fact been prevalent or has not even been subscribed to by a single prominent person. Jurisprudence seems to need its Aunt Sallies.

Those who have a taste for disputation can find some illuminating material on some issues which might still be considered to be 'live'. As already indicated, the scepticism of practitioners about the systematizing inclinations of some academic lawyers is dramatized by Holmes's attacks on Langdell and his colleagues; Frank articulated other aspects of the practitioner's dissatisfaction in his attack on 'appellate court-itis'. Dickinson, Wechsler and Dworkin are among those who, in different ways, have subtly defended the need for principled decision-making and the Rule of Law in face of the view that judicial creativity is both inevitable and desirable.[6] Llewellyn's typology of the Grand Style and the Formal Style pinpoints a recurrent strain which is not confined to the work of judges. While the case for the Grand Style has been made with force and eloquence, the defenders of the Formal Style have tended to be less articulate. Partial defences have been made in terms of 'judicial restraint' and 'neutral principles'; students of the English scene in particular have had in recent years to face the question whether emphasis on judicial law-making may not sometimes be a form of conservative politics masquerading as radical jurisprudence.[7] But a fully argued case, perhaps in terms of the functions of formalism, has yet to be made in the modern context.

In respect of empirical investigation of the law in action, realists have had to face attacks on more than one front. On the one hand, many lawyers take the view that such enquiries should be left to social scientists, thereby raising questions as to whether, and, if so, when, it is desirable or feasible to treat law as an autonomous discipline rather than as part of the behavioural sciences; on the other hand, charges of 'barefoot empiricism' and 'naive realism' have been levelled against some realists who, like Llewellyn and Frank, were sometimes prepared to rely on common sense, experience and intuition as sources of information and insight. Related to this is the fact that the espousal by Cook, Moore and others of various versions of 'the scientific analogy' produced a variety of sceptical reactions from within the realist movement as well as from without. Realists were largely pioneers in the development of an empirical science of law and the 'debate' in this area even now remains at a relatively unsophisticated level.

Debate and disputation no doubt have a useful role to perform in the development of juristic thought. But as one hacks one's way through the tangled undergrowth of confused and confusing jurisprudential controversy one is left with a strong impression that a great deal of it has been artificial and unnecessary, as well as repetitive. A puzzling question is why has realism been so controversial? Granted the dangers of generalizing about 'the realists', if there is one thread that runs consistently through the work of American jurists from Holmes through Pound and the pioneers of the realist movement to Lasswell and McDougal and beyond it is this: that there is more to the study of law than the study of a system of rules; that for most purposes legal doctrine should be seen in the context of legal processes and legal processes should be seen in the context of the totality of social processes. This surely deserves to be a truism; it is demonstrably part of 'the neglected obvious', but it is hardly the stuff of persistent controversy. Few jurists, few practising lawyers, and few academic lawyers have consciously and openly opposed the proposition that it is desirable to adopt a broad perspective and consider the law in its social context. The uncontroversial nature of the core of realism is illustrated by the current ambivalence towards the realist movement of many American law teachers, who sometimes speak of 'realism' as a passing phase while acknowledging its continued vitality. Their attitude can best be expressed by adapting a well-known incantation: 'Realism is dead; we are all realists now'.

While there may be pockets of resistance to the development of a 'contextual approach', for most law teachers in the United States and elsewhere in the common law world the crucial question is not Whether? but How? Here Karl Llewellyn's evaluations of the realist movement come into their own. For he maintained that its main contribution was not to be found in the more general ideas, but rather in their determination to apply in a 'sustained and programmatic' way ideas which had been made almost commonplace by Holmes and Pound at the level of abstract theory, but the practical implications of which had not been fully realized.[8] In 1931 he wrote:

What is as novel as it is vital is for a goodly number of men to pick up ideas which have been expressed and dropped, used for an hour and dropped – to pick up such ideas and set about *consistently, persistently, insistently to carry them through.*[9]

Llewellyn's final evaluation of the achievements of the realist movement would appear to have been that there was relatively little new or controversial about the beliefs shared by most of its members, that their occasional overstatements at a theoretical level were of minor significance, and that the chief characteristic of the movement was that its members wished to try to act on their beliefs, especially in research and teaching, in a more sustained and systematic way than the great majority of their predecessors had done. Thus his argument appears to be that the realist movement should be judged primarily by its fruits, especially by the extent, the quality and the value of the research and writing it inspired, rather than by the worthwhileness or originality of its contributions to legal theory. Thus the Columbia casebooks, empirical research projects, reforms in legal education, changes in the style and orientation of contributions to law reviews, the Uniform Commercial Code, and the resurgence of the Grand Style were better indicia of the achievements, and failures, of the realist movement than its contributions to jurisprudence for the hundred. In short, the suggestion is that the main achievement of the movement was to concretize sociological jurisprudence.

Llewellyn's suggestion is attractive. It should be obvious that the realist movement and the work of individual realists would of necessity feature prominently in a balanced general appraisal of developments in the United States in legal education, legal research and legal literature during the period 1920 to 1970.

If it is fair to say that the main achievement of the realist movement was to concretize sociological jurisprudence, then no study of their work should be confined to discussions of very general topics. Perhaps the most important lesson to be learned from a study of realism is a partial answer to the question: What difference can it make in practice to adopt a sociological (or realist or contextual) approach to law? One simple way to set about obtaining an elementary answer is to compare and contrast examples of legal 'products' in the making of which formalist and contextual ideas have been operative. Of course, any attempt to chart the 'influence' of the movement with precision could easily lure the unwary into crude or subtle pitfalls of the 'post hoc, propter hoc' variety. The chapters

384 KARL LLEWELLYN AND THE REALIST MOVEMENT

on the Uniform Commercial Code illustrate some of the difficulties of relating general ideas to particular legal artifacts. This kind of enquiry is elusive, but it is not impossible, at least at a common-sense level. Thus it is both feasible and useful even for undergraduates to undertake elementary analysis along these lines. For instance, judicial opinions can be compared and analysed in terms of the Grand Style and the Formal Style or similar, more refined, models; it is illuminating to compare and contrast the Sale of Goods Act, 1893 with Article 2 of the Uniform Commercial Code, the approaches of Corbin and Williston and Pollock to, e.g., the Statute of Frauds, or Salmond on *Torts* with Atiyah's *Accidents, Compensation and the Law*. Casebooks based on Langdell's prototype can be compared and contrasted with compilations of 'Cases and Materials' such as those prepared at Columbia in the 1930s or at Yale in the early 1960s. It is interesting to consider the work of Willard Hurst in juxtaposition to that of writers who have narrower conceptions of legal history. Further examples can easily be culled from the literature of international or comparative law or, indeed, from almost any other field of legal endeavour. Even in quite elementary exercises of this kind it is, of course, important to keep asking to what extent differences between 'approaches' or particular pieces of work can be explained in terms of operative ideas which could be categorized as 'jurisprudential'. The answers will not always be obvious. And this, too, may help to drive home the lesson that jurisprudence need not be a subject apart.

If law students are able to do such elementary exercises in comparative analysis, it should not be beyond the capacity of legal scholars to undertake this type of enquiry in a more sustained manner on a broader front. Here, as elsewhere, substantial progress will be unlikely without adequate support from theory. In this respect there are limitations on the value of the literature of realism. In so far as it is a fair verdict that the most worthwhile achievements of the realist movement were at the 'applied' level, this involves an admission that it made a relatively insignificant theoretical contribution to the development of a systematic sociology of law. This is the main complaint of Lasswell and McDougal. Whereas most critics have tended to find the 'realists' interesting only in so far as they were seen as 'extremists' who went too far, Lasswell and McDougal have argued that they were moving in the right direction, but that they did not go far enough.[10]

Myres McDougal himself in his early days at Yale was an enthusiastic disciple of realism; but after a time he sensed that there was something lacking in the ideas of his mentors. His need was satisfied by the systematizing tendencies of Harold Lasswell who had already made a profound impact on American political science. For thirty years Lasswell and McDougal have collaborated and crusaded under the banner of 'Law, Science and Policy'. LSP, as it is popularly known, has close affinities with the ideas and perspective of Jeremy Bentham. It is a combination of utilitarianism and Freudian psychology, supplemented by some of the insights of American social science, and encased in an elaborate terminology which has been relentlessly expanded and defined by Lasswell and his associates. LSP has been applied extensively to the field of international law, especially by McDougal himself, and in a number of other fields by a rather variegated group of disciples.[11]

In a simplified account of the history of Anglo-American jurisprudence LSP can be seen as almost completing a cycle which began with Bentham. His comprehensive theory was succeeded by the narrower but no less rigorous gymnastics of English analytical jurisprudence. Through Pound American jurisprudence regained a breadth of perspective but lost much of the conceptual rigour of Bentham's approach; nor did Pound's theories prove to be very effective as tools of detailed analysis. Holmes too produced penetrating insights without providing usable tools for exploiting their potential. For a brief period before his death Hohfeld promised to reunite exact analysis with a broad vision, but the promise was not fulfilled. The realist movement inspired a series of attempts to work out in detail the implications of sociological jurisprudence in the context of the special concerns of a group of jurists most of whom were law teachers. A major stimulus to LSP was a feeling that the ideas and methods of the realists were not sufficiently systematic and that in particular they had failed to adopt an adequate framework of concepts and explicitly stated values. One outcome was the return of Jeremy Bentham in modern dress.

This particular cycle is not quite complete. For LSP has not gained widespread acceptance. Too often its disciples appear to stagger and groan under the weight of its elaborate paraphenalia of definitions and check-lists. *Parturiunt montes....* Those who have not accepted LSP have tended either to ignore it entirely or to dismiss it not so much on the basis of detailed criticism as on grounds of taste—that it seems to be wearisome, or too pretentious, or unpalatable in some other way. The theory deserves better of its critics, but to date the literature does suggest that so far LSP has been viewed as a somewhat cumbersome tool-kit and it has failed to be used as a weapon in the way that Bentham's ideas were used by the philosophical radicals.[12] One reason for this may be that LSP has been seduced by the scientific analogy too far away from informed common sense. The current revival of interest in Bentham, combined with a more sympathetic understanding of the realist movement, may hold out hope for the achievement of a *rapprochement* in a form which will be more widely accepted.

A general framework for enquiry of this kind is badly needed, if jurisprudence is to make significant progress in the coming years. Such a framework could be of particular value in the formulation of middle order theories—a task which, in my view, should be accorded a high priority in the immediate future. For example, there is a need for coherent working theories to guide the development of legal education, literature for law students, and the work of law reform bodies, such as the English and Scottish Law Commissions. In developing countries there is too little useful theory to guide change in the legal sector or to assist clear thinking about the potential contribution of law-trained personnel to strategies of economic development and other aspects of nation-building. At the level of description there is a dearth of usable hypotheses to act as catalysts to the advancement of such promising fields as the comparative sociology of the legal professions. In fashionable growth subjects such as environmental control and poverty law, the evolution of useful concepts and the formulation of testable hypotheses must also command a high priority. These are just some examples of areas in which we can still echo Holmes: 'We have too little theory in the law rather than too much.'[13]

In the next phase of Anglo-American jurisprudence lawyers will continue to look to the social scientists and to others for assistance. There are indications that social science has more to offer us today than it had in the twenties and thirties; similarly philosophers have in recent years provided jurists with some usable techniques of conceptual analysis. But it is important to guard against the tendency to allow vague calls for interdisciplinary co-operation to perform the role of a ritual incantation—a hopelessly optimistic prayer for a *deus ex machina*. One of the main lessons to be drawn from the story of the realist movement is that it is easy to ignore or to underestimate the difficulties, theoretical and practical, of sustained interdisciplinary work. It is easy for inflated optimism to be replaced by sour disillusion; it is difficult to strike a balance between professional self-confidence and willingness to seek help from outside. Anglo-American legal culture has its share of chauvinists and masochists —those who would go it alone and those who would reject most of the rich intellectual heritage of the law. Such extreme views could easily provoke some futile polemics, but they represent in exaggerated form two broad alternative strategies for developing a contextual approach to law: the one approach emphasises broadening the study of law from within, building on a long tradition of humanistic scholarship by lawyers and jurists. The other emphasises the value of looking at law from without, through the spectacles of one or more other disciplines. Jurisprudence is broad enough to accommodate both strategies and many variations on them.

In the interpretation presented in this book, the leading American realists by and large chose the strategy of broadening the study of law from within. Law was their primary discipline and they were proud of it. As sociologists or psychologists or anthropologists or economists or philosophers they were, at best, intelligent amateurs. They have most to teach those who wish to treat law as their primary discipline, while keeping it steadfastly in its place as one of the great humane studies. From this point of view a primary function of Jurisprudence, and of jurists, is to serve as a conduit, to channel into the intellectual milieu of the law, concepts, techniques, insights and information from neighbouring fields. Seen thus, 'traditional' Jurisprudence still has an important role to perform.

In developing working theories and usable hypotheses there will be some of us who will feel attracted simultaneously by thinkers as seemingly diverse as, for example, Bentham and Llewellyn. Both are products of the intellectual milieu of the common law and they have more in common than may at first appear. In so far as there are differences, one of the problems is to strike a balance between the systematic generalizing tendencies of a Bentham or a Lasswell and the sensitivity to the nuances of the particular of a Karl Llewellyn. Where a healthy balance can be struck, perhaps there lies the best hope for the preservation and exploitation of what is worthwhile in the common law tradition.

AFTERWORD

Framing Llewellyn[1]

Introduction

The original objective of *Karl Llewellyn and the Realist Movement* (hereafter *KLRM*) was to provide a stimulus and a guide rather than a substitute for reading Llewellyn's writings. When I was invited to write an afterword to this edition of the book, I was concerned not to undermine this aim. The decision not to try to revise or update the original text forty years on was easy; to provide systematic updates through the footnotes would have been distracting; to attempt a comprehensive critical survey of the literature since 1971 on Llewellyn, the Realist Movement, and the Uniform Commercial Code would have required much more space and would have been a further distraction from Llewellyn's own writings. What follows is divided into two parts: Part A is a personal memoir which provides some background to my connection with Llewellyn, how I came to put his papers in order and write this book, the aftermath of its publication, and my relations with Soia Mentschikoff Llewellyn and Herbert Hart. Part B, intended more for specialist readers, reflects on selected developments since 1971 that bear on the book, on Llewellyn's continuing significance, and on some unfinished agenda. It also provides links to the literature of the past forty years. Rather than rely solely on fading memories, Part A draws heavily on contemporaneous documents and prior accounts written closer in time.[2]

---

[1] I am grateful to Terry Anderson, Clayton Gillette, Andrew Halpin, Nicola Lacey, Fred Schauer, and Penelope Twining for helpful comments and suggestions.

[2] In particular, W. Twining, *The Karl Llewellyn Papers* (Chicago: University of Chicago Law School, 1968) (hereafter KLP); *Law in Context: Enlarging a Discipline*

Part A. KLRM: a personal memoir

I am sometimes asked if I was predisposed to be attracted to Realism. Two incidents that took place shortly after I first graduated from Oxford in 1955 provide one clue. At Oxford the only legal subject that had caught my interest had been jurisprudence – but this was in tension with my parents' relentless emphasis on practicality. So I set out to learn about the realities of qualifying as a barrister. My first stop was the office of Gibson and Weldon, a private crammers, who efficiently prepared people for the Bar examinations. I was interviewed by a cynical man who urged me to be realistic. The examiners want the facts as set out in the textbooks and nutshells, not independent thought, speculation, personal opinions, or other academic waffle. What were needed were facts, facts, facts, and only facts. This was sound, practical advice from a hard-headed Gradgrind, but not what I wanted to hear.

Shortly afterwards I visited a solicitor's office in order to learn about the realities of legal practice. He specialized in personal injuries cases. I told him that *Salmond on Torts* had been my favorite textbook. He said in effect: 'You don't want to believe what you read in the books. They are quite misleading. We usually represent insurance companies and we always settle. Anyway, the whole personal injuries system needs a radical overhaul.' I experienced culture shock. I felt that I had been *betrayed* by Salmond – how could you *understand* the law relating to personal injuries or the tort of negligence if you know nothing about insurance, settlement, and alternatives to the common law action for negligence?[3]

(Oxford: Oxford University Press, 1997) (hereafter LiC); *The Great Juristic Bazaar: Jurists' Texts and Lawyers' Stories* (Aldershot: Ashgate, 2002) (hereafter, GJB); and *Globalisation and Legal Theory* (Evanston: Northwestern University Press, 2000) (hereafter (GLT). See also *General Jurisprudence: Understanding Law from a Global Perspective* (Cambridge: Cambridge University Press, 2009) (hereafter GJP).

[3] I still hold that the edition of *Salmond* I encountered was deeply misleading. Later editions made a few concessions to the point. Patrick Atiyah's *Accidents, Compensation and the Law* (1st edition, 1970, 7th edition, by Peter Cane, Cambridge: Cambridge University Press, 2006) is the classic prototype for an alternative perspective. Recently, when I told this story about *Salmond*, a distinguished legal philosopher said that one learns about such matters in courses on civil procedure. That is not true when the courses and books belong to the same intellectual tradition as *Salmond* – you just learn the rules. In my view, doctrinal texts like *Salmond* complement contextual works, like Atiyah's, not vice versa. On the working precept "context first" and rules as responses to problems, see William Twining and David Miers, *How To Do Things With Rules* (Cambridge: Cambridge University Press, 5th edition, 2011) ch. 2.

An interest in theory in tension with insistent demands for practicality; then two sharp doses of realism: you must learn up the law in books, but don't believe a word that they say. There are many ways to be realistic and many different kinds of things to be realistic about. The relationship between the law in books and the law in action, and more subtle ways of articulating such tensions, has always been central to my academic concerns. So, yes, I was probably predisposed towards American Legal Realism. But my interpretation of "R/realism" has had an English bias: I have never thought that it was only or even mainly about adjudication; I have never read Llewellyn or other Realists as saying that rules were radically indeterminate, or illusory, or unimportant; and I have never thought that concern about being "realistic" about law was peculiarly American. As a result I have been quite critical of commentators who treat Realism as an American exclusive, or equate "realism" with a form of "rule-skepticism", or restrict the idea of "R/realism" to adjudication generally or even to adjudication about questions of law in American appellate courts. I treat Realism with a capital R as an historical phenomenon – a peculiarly American intellectual movement that rose and faded between the two World Wars – and "realism" with a small "r" as a concept at the centre of questions about what is involved in understanding law. The history of the Realist Movement sets a context for Llewellyn's writings, but I could have been more emphatic in KLRM that Llewellyn's continuing interest depends more on the extent to which he illuminates relations between theory and practice and what it means to be realistic about law.

How I came to Chicago and Llewellyn

It was partly by chance that I came to work with Llewellyn. By 1956 I had decided that I wanted eventually to pursue an academic career in law, but in Africa rather than the United Kingdom. I also wanted to learn more about jurisprudence and to see something of the United States. I heard that Professor F. H. Lawson, the professor of comparative law at Oxford, was responsible for placing promising Oxford graduates in leading American law schools. When I told Lawson of my interest in the United States and jurisprudence, he asked

AFTERWORD 391

me which living American jurists I most admired. I needed notice of that question, for apart from adulatory references to Holmes and Pound and denigratory references to madcap Realists – jazz jurisprudence for a jazz age[4] – American jurists had not featured in the Oxford curriculum. I went away and read Fuller's *The Law in Quest of Itself*, which I found enthralling, and Llewellyn's *The Bramble Bush*, which I thought intriguing, but mystifying. I returned to Lawson and told him that my first choice was Fuller and my second Llewellyn. So I wrote to Harvard saying that I would like to come and sit at Professor Fuller's feet; I was not interested in obtaining a degree, but I needed funding. Harvard responded kindly that they only had scholarships for degree courses, that I was a bit young, and I had anyway missed the application date for the coming academic year. Having learned my first lesson about American law schools, I applied to the University of Chicago in a more conventional way and was awarded a Commonwealth Fellowship to start in September 1957.

In KLRM, I have quoted my first impressions of Llewellyn and my experience of him as a teacher, as I remembered them in 1963–4.[5] I have nothing to add to these, except to correct a possible impression that I spent the whole academic year under his tutelage. The terms of my fellowship required that I follow an intensive program, which would justify the award of a JD degree after only one year of study. I took courses given by Nicholas de Belleville Katzenbach, Edward Shils and Edward Levi, Malcolm Sharp, J. B. Schneewind, William Winslow Crosskey, Alison Dunham, and Max Rheinstein, as well as a course on international commercial transactions taught by the formidable team of Katzenbach, Llewellyn, Mentschikoff, and Steffen.[6] The University of Chicago Law School had a star-studded faculty. I now regret not having seized the opportunity to take

---

[4] C. K. Allen, *Law in the Making* (Oxford: Clarendon Press, 4th edition, 1946), p. 45.

[5] KLRM at pp. 114–16.

[6] The text also omits to mention that I nearly left Chicago after about two weeks because I categorically refused to take Aaron Director's "General Theory of Price" – the basic introduction to law and economics – on the ground that my fellow students told me that, if you disagreed with the teacher, you failed. This was the year of Sputnik. I stormed into the office of my director of studies – Roger Cramton, in his first quarter of teaching – and told him that I thought that I had come to the University of Chicago, not the University of Moscow, and that I refused to be brainwashed by someone whose ideology was diametrically opposed

courses by Harry Kalven, Walter Blum, Philip Kurland, or Kenneth Culp Davis.[7]

So my contact with Llewellyn was in fact quite limited: I took his course on "Law in Our Society", I audited parts of his seminar on appellate advocacy, and he supervised one paper. We established an immediate rapport and I quickly became fascinated by him both personally and intellectually. But it was not until later – especially when putting his papers in order – that I began to get a grounded sense of what he was about. Unfortunately, I did not take Llewellyn's course on Elements (I was an Oxford graduate!) and in KLRM I underestimated its significance, an omission that I shall rectify in this afterword.

After graduating from Chicago in 1958, I took up a teaching post in Khartoum for three years and moved on to Dar-es-Salaam in 1961. Almost my only direct contact with Llewellyn was that he sent me a copy of *The Common Law Tradition*, with a characteristically generous inscription. I was generally preoccupied with the excitement of institution building in newly independent countries, adjusting common law ways of doing things to local conditions, and keeping a few pages ahead of the class – in my first year I was required to teach five different courses. However, by then Llewellyn was profoundly influencing my approach, not only to teaching jurisprudence, but also more generally to thinking about law in its social, political, and economic context.[8] A single episode illustrates

to mine. Fortunately, he caved in, because I was serious about leaving. Elsewhere, I have recounted some subsequent clashes with Aaron Director, which are not relevant here except that they illustrate differences between the worlds of Oxford and the University of Chicago at the time, not least in respect of the prevailing ideology and the arrogant sense of superiority of Oxonians. It took me several months to appreciate the strength and sophistication of the culture of elite American law schools. (Manuel Atienza and Raymundo Gama, "Entrevista con William Twining", DOXA: Cuadernos de Filosofia del Derecho 32, 713–28, 2009).

[7] The atmosphere and ethos of the University of Chicago Law School at the time is captured well by George W. Liebmann, *The Common Law Tradition: A Collective Portrait of Five Scholars* (New Brunswick: Transaction Publishers, 2005). See also Edward Shils (ed.) *Remembering the University of Chicago: Teachers, Scientists and Scholars* (Chicago: The University of Chicago Press, 1991), especially the foreword and chapters on Milton Friedman, Harry Kalven, Frank H. Knight, Edward Levi, Richard McKeon, Max Rheinstein, and George Stigler.

[8] I have tried to capture some of this in "The Camel in the Zoo" in Issa Shivji (ed.) *Limits of Legal Radicalism* (University of Dar-es-Salaam, 1986), reprinted in LiC, ch. 2.

this influence. At Oxford, Professor Herbert Hart had first aroused my interest in jurisprudence and had introduced me to the then prevailing methods of analytical philosophy. A year in Chicago had modified, but not weakened my attachment to Hart's approach. When Hart's *The Concept of Law* came out in 1961, I recognized this as an important book, but unlike many others I was not overwhelmed by it. I read it as a prolegomenon. I remember spending an evening in Dar in December 1961 in heated discussion with a visitor from Oxford who maintained that it was self-evident that Hart's book would from now on be the starting point for all serious jurisprudential discussion. I do not remember exactly what I argued, but in retrospect it is clear that it must have been Llewellynesque. Unfortunately, he proved to be right and what Hart later called "that wretched book" became an obsession that continues after fifty years.[9] Whether or not this was an epiphanic moment, it revealed an underlying tension in my attitude to my two jusrisprudential mentors, which needs to be probed in depth. Is it possible to be a loyal disciple of both Hart and Llewellyn?

Karl Llewellyn died suddenly on 13 February 1962. I heard the news quite soon afterwards in Dar-es-Salaam. In 1984 I recounted the next stage as follows:

It may have been on a beach in Dar-es-Salaam that I heard the news of the death of Karl Llewellyn. It was quite possibly the same beach on which we later played Frisbee with the late Wolfgang Friedman, who had come out to teach about Law and Economic Development . . . the same Wolfgang Friedman who in an earlier era had been a forerunner of the English Realist Revolution . . . if indeed England has undergone something that can be so described.

It was February, 1962. Academic news travelled fast in those days, for this was the peak period of American, indeed Western, interest in Africa . . . the brief era of the neocolonial honeymoon. This was the period in which a Scottish philosopher could justify his transfer to the Sudan on the ground that Khartoum was more central

[9] Hart to Twining, cited by Nicola Lacey in *A Life of H. L. A. Hart: The Nightmare and the Noble Dream* (Oxford: Oxford University Press, 2004), p. 233. The context was an invitation to visit Belfast to give some classes in 1967, when he indicated that he was willing to talk about anything "except that wretched book". In May 2011 the fiftieth anniversary of the publication of *The Concept of Law* was celebrated in Oxford by a series of high-level seminars involving more than fourteen discussants and commentators. The quality of commentary was high, the speakers were all intimately familiar with the text, but I felt that Herbert Hart himself would have been dismayed with this fixation on what he had intended as a prolegomenon and he might well have suggested that it was time to move on.

*than Aberdeen. Almost every week we entertained at least one visiting fireman from
the United States who was clocking up mileage, buying local carvings, selling American legal education, and passing gossip along the circuit.*

*I was upset by the news about Karl. I had found him an inspiring teacher; I was
fond of him and I knew that his premature death meant that his final statement of
his most general theory would never be completed. At the time I saw him as only one
of a number of teachers from whom I had learned much. But Llewellyn's impact on
me was growing as I reflected on the implications of his ideas for academic law in
East Africa. They had more resonance than most other juristic ideas for young expa-
triates who were trying to make sense of the bizarre unrealities of the common law in
a social context, nay a climate, that was not hospitable to Carbolic Smoke Balls.*

*As an expatriate Englishman I naturally subscribed to the airmail edition of
the* [London] *Times. When it became apparent that the Times had not noticed
Llewellyn's death, I quickly drafted an obituary and sent it off. In due course I received
a curt rejection, which implied that readers of the Times were not interested in obscure
American jurists. I was already well aware of the caricatures and sneering critiques
of American Realism in English textbooks of the time. Incensed, I decided to convert
the British public to Llewellyn by writing an article about him. Wishing to quote from
his marvelously rich, if cryptic, course materials on Law in our Society, but retaining a gentlemanly concern for the niceties of copyright, I wrote to Soia Mentschikoff,
Llewellyn's widow, for permission to quote from them. With a promptness never to be
repeated, she replied almost by return, suggesting that I should come to Chicago to
consult "one or two unpublished manuscripts." She would fix it. So in 1963 I set out
from Dar-es-Salaam to Chicago, earning my fare by delivering a series of lectures on
customary law in East Africa, a late example of armchair legal anthropology.*[10]

This account from 1984 is essentially accurate. The slightly sar-
donic tone was intended to signal the unreliability of memory and
the elusiveness of "realism", with a nod towards "postmodernism",
just coming into fashion in law at the time.

Excursus: Soia Mentschikoff Llewellyn[11]

At this point I need to introduce Llewellyn's third wife and widow,
Soia Mentschikoff Llewellyn, who hardly features in KLRM and

---

[10] Reproduced from "Talk about Realism" (Dewey Lecture, October 23, 1984) 60
New York University Law School 329, reprinted in W. Twining, *The Great Juristic
Bazaar* (Aldershot: Ashgate, 2002) at pp. 93–5, (original italics).

[11] Soia was known professionally as Soia Mentschikoff, but socially she liked to be
called Mrs Karl Llewellyn. The main sources for this excursus, apart from firsthand
knowledge and numerous obituaries, are Connie Bruck, "Soia Mentschikoff, The
First Woman Everything" (The American Lawyer, 36, October 1982); Symposium

then mainly in relation to the UCC. That was probably appropriate for the book. But Soia was both an extraordinary person and a central actor in the present story: she invited me to come to Chicago to look at Karl's papers; she lured me into putting them in order; she was an essential source of information and reference point in writing about Karl; she did much to keep his memory alive after his death, not least when she was dean of the University of Miami Law School (1974–82) and as co-author of the book based on his materials for "Elements". My wife became her intimate friend. Soia treated me like a somewhat wayward son – bright-eyed and bushy-tailed, but with some quirky ideas of my own.

Soia Mentschikoff deserves at least one full-scale biography and it is sad that none has yet been completed. First, the basic facts: born Moscow 1915; settled in New York, 1918; Hunter College, AB 1934; Columbia Law School, LLB 1937; private practice in New York 1937–47 (partner, Spence, Hotchkiss, Parker and Duyree from 1944); Associate Chief Reporter, UCC; married Karl Llewellyn, 1947; visiting professor, Harvard Law School 1947–9; University of Chicago 1951–74 (professorial lecturer, then professor, 1962);[12] dean, University of Miami Law School 1974–82; (visiting professor from 1967); died 1984.

Her public image is replete with hyperboles. Franklin Zimring called her the "first woman everything":[13] inter alia, she was the first woman to teach at Harvard Law School; the first woman partner of a major U.S. law firm; the first woman president of AALS; and the first woman listed as a possible U.S. Supreme Court nominee.[14] In Miami

in Honor of Dean Soia Mentschikoff, 37 U. Miami L. Rev. (May–September, 1983); Zipporah Wiseman, "Soia Mentschikoff" in R. M. Sakolar and M. L. Volcansek (eds.) *Women in Law* (Westport, CT: Greenwood Press, 1996) and in *American National Biography* (New York: Oxford University Press, 1998). See also Robert Whitman, "Soia Mentschikoff and Karl Llewellyn: Moving Together to the University of Chicago Law School", 24 Connecticut L. Rev 1119 (1992). For a bibliography of her main published writings see Wiseman (1996). The bulk of her professional papers are in the Special Collections of the University of Chicago Library. In April 2012 most of her remaining papers, other than those to do with her deanship and the Arbitration Project were transferred from Miami to Chicago.

[12] The University of Chicago forbade joint appointments of spouses (a nepotism rule), so Soia did not become a tenured professor until Karl died. This did not faze her.

[13] Cited by Bruck (1982) *op. cit.* n.11.

[14] She was twice nominated by her former colleague, Nicholas de Belleville Katzenbach.

she was known as "the Czarina" and as Snow White, who brought in seven dwarfs, mainly young graduates of the University of Chicago Law School, to transform the University of Miami according to her own lights – or Karl Llewellyn's. She was persuasive, inspiring, autocratic, tough-minded, funny. She was a brilliant practical lawyer and a superb fixer. She was repeatedly called "an artist in the law", but she wrote little.[15] In 1971 she was judged by *McCall's* magazine to be one of the fifty women who had made the greatest contribution to American society. She refused to be labeled a feminist.

She was a formidable personality. She was shrewd, she read people well, and she could be very effective – some called it forceful or cogent, others manipulative or domineering. One of her favorite precepts was reputedly: 'In any transaction, when you push the button, you'd better know who's gonna die over there – because if you *don't*, it might be you.'[16] Karl, who adored her, is reported as introducing her as a speaker with the words: 'but you shall hear Soia, my gal can sail ships'. One Miami colleague is reported as saying: 'She always sets the terms of discussion, and in such a way that she cannot lose. . . . You have to watch her all the time. She can smile and eat you alive.'[17]

Of course, I had a different angle on Soia. As a student, my first impression was of a large, imposing, grey-haired woman, soft-spoken, with a no-nonsense style. I had difficulty following her teaching, both because her voice was very low and what she said assumed a commercial background that I lacked. The Llewellyns threw good parties and in 1957–8 we went to their house several times. My wife said that she had no dress sense. I did not see her as a dominant character in the law school and I had little idea of her legendary reputation.

Later, especially after the completion of the book, we became part of the family. We saw her in the roles of dutiful daughter,

---

[15] Her personal style is evident in "Reflections of a Drafter" 43 Ohio State L. Jo. 537 (1982) in which the term "horsing around" is used more than once to describe the behavior of members of a legal elite during the preparation of the UCC. See also the posthumous lectures (reconstructed by Irwin Stotzky) "The Last Universal Discipline", 54 University of Cincinnati L. Rev 695 (1986) and I. Stotzky, "Soia's Way: Toiling in the Common Law Tradition", 38 U. Miami L. Rev. 373 (1984).

[16] Cited by Bruck (1982), *op. cit.*

[17] Ibid.

relaxed hostess, and intimate friend. Many viewed her as a Russian Earth Mother. She and her mother attended the Russian Ortho- dox Church regularly and on one memorable Easter we went with them. "Mama Toi" made her daughter speak to her in Russian. We went walking with her in Ireland, except we were more behind than with. Soia longed to return to Russia – she had not been back since she left and Karl worried that she would be held to ransom by the Soviets. So one year at her house in Coral Gables we planned a grand tour, sitting on the floor round a map of Russia. Soia had very grand ideas about the itinerary, including going from Lenin- grad to Tashkent by train. When I pointed out that there was no railway connection, she took a pencil and drew a line on the map: 'There is now', she said. Somehow, that epitomised Soia. She did visit Russia once before she died, but to our great regret we were unable to go with her.

I loved and respected Soia. But there was one difficulty: I had to cope with the biographer's problem of a living widow – to maintain professional detachment while ensuring her cooperation. She was one of the two most formidable women I have ever had to deal with – the other being my mother. How did I manage? First, she liked and trusted me and left me to get on with it. Second, she did not take archives (or history or biography) very seriously. If I had not become involved, she would probably have dumped most of Karl's papers. She looked on them as relics and was amused by my fascina- tion with them. Third, she genuinely respected my independence. She realized that I was sympathetic to Karl, but that I needed to be free to criticize, and that it was important that the book should not be mere hagiography. And, fourth, she seemed apathetic or indif- ferent. She would answer my questions face to face, almost never by correspondence; she made some suggestions about people to con- tact, but she was quite reluctant to look at drafts; I suspect that she never read the completed book – certainly she never commented on it and I did not ask her. I felt that in an important sense she did not want to know. For some time she was devastated by Karl's death, and later she did not seem to want to dwell on the past. All this might have counted for little, but for the fact of distance. In Chicago I put the papers in order and collected material, but my research also took me to New York, New Haven, Philadelphia, Min- neapolis, New Mexico, and California. Nearly all of the writing was done away from Chicago and Coral Gables, first in New Haven in

1965, later in Northern Ireland in the period 1965–71. During that time I only saw Soia on brief visits once or twice a year. Moreover, I was under pressure to produce a work of serious scholarship: I had been appointed to a chair in Belfast largely on promise and the book was to be the means of proving myself.

Accordingly, dealing with Soia turned out to be less of a problem than I had feared. Insofar as I am perceived as being too loyal a disciple, one need not blame Soia's influence.[18] There is, however, one exception to this – the story of the Uniform Commercial Code.[19] I am not a commercial lawyer and have very little business sense – Soia once told me that I would never understand the credit economy. She was as anxious as I was to get the UCC chapters right. One day, after I had asked some questions that showed I was struggling with the Code records, she shook her head and in effect said: 'I don't see why you are bothering with all those papers; all of the important decisions affecting the Code were taken on the phone – I was at one end of the line, and the person at the other end is DEAD.'[20] I knew that the making of the Code had been controversial, both within the team and in getting it approved and enacted. I was anxious to hear all sides of the stories, but I was regularly frustrated. Soia was correct in suggesting that the papers were not very informative about disagreements and that some of the main players were

[18]   E.g., Manfred Weis, review of KLRM, Archiv für civilistische Praxis , 174, (1974) 90 ff; cp. Colin Tapper "remarkably detached", (review, 1973 JSPTL (NS) 168–9. (book review).

[19]   She also made a significant contribution to the biographical chapter (ch 6). Here the initiative was mine. I plied her with questions about Karl's childhood and family (there was little in the papers) and quirks, and I used her as a sounding board to check that my facts were accurate and my judgements were on the right track. Towards the end I consulted Ernie Haggard, a psychologist who had worked closely with both Karl and Soia, as to whether my take on Karl's personality was plausible. Without any hint of a Freudian interpretation, he made some helpful suggestions. I did not meet Betty, Llewellyn's first wife, and had only one perfunctory interview with his second wife, Emma Corstvet, who understandably did not give me access to her papers. So I did not get a balanced picture of Karl's marital relations – but this did not matter much, because I was not trying to write a rounded biography. Later Schlegel learned a lot from interviews with Corstvet (John Henry Schlegel, *American Realism and Empirical Social Science* (Chapel Hill: University of North Carolina Press, 1995), index under Corstvet). On Robert Whitman et al. and the Corstvet papers, see below pp. 427–30.

[20]   Of course, I cannot recall her exact words, but I am confident about the punchline.

dead. Other key figures, such as Bill Schnader, Homer Kripke, and Walter D. Malcolm, died before I could meet them or were otherwise unavailable. When I interviewed two others, Grant Gilmore and Alison Dunham, they seemed very reticent about disagreements. By 1970–1 I had failed to get any detailed material of significance on the internal disagreements in the Code process, so I made two decisions: first, that I would candidly present the Llewellyn-Mentschikoff version of events and, second, I would try to stimulate an oral history project on the making and enactment of the Code whilst memories were fresh and the survivors still survived. I attempted to make the first point clear in the footnotes to chapters 9 and 10. With the help of Professor Robert Summers I tried to stir some interest in the history and politics of the UCC and in a footnote I urged surviving participants to record their memories of the project.[21] As far as I can tell, these efforts failed.[22] Commercial lawyers showed little interest in the topic and even to this day I am told there is no adequately researched general history of the making of the Code.[23]

The Karl Llewellyn Papers

I arrived in Chicago in April 1963. Karl had died suddenly and unexpectedly on the night of 13 February 1962. It was term time and he was due to teach a class the next morning. His death came as a shock to many. Fourteen months later, when I was given the key to his office, I was told that no one had been inside it since his death, not even a cleaner. It was indeed exactly as he had left it, except that a thin layer of black Chicago grime covered everything on the desk. If it was like a shrine, I behaved more like a grave robber than an archeologist or a scene of crime officer. I made no attempt to leave things in their place until a record was made of their location. I did, however, notice that the very top piece of paper (on a

[21]   KLRM, p. 458, n. 6.
[22]   See, however, Symposium: *Origins and Evolution: Drafters Reflect Upon the Uniform Commercial Code* 43 Ohio State L. Jo. 535 (1982). Also, Homer Kripke, "The Importance of the Code", 21 U. Toledo L. Rev. 591 (1990) and "ALI audiovisual history. No. 2, Homer Kripke" (American Law Institute, 1991).
[23]   See, however, n.139 below. In my view chapter 9 is incomplete, especially in respect of internal disagreements, but it can claim to be an authentic, if thin, account of Soia's version of events. See further her "Reflections of a Drafter" (1982), *op. cit.* above n.15.

yellow pad) was a handwritten poem in both English and German.[24] I rummaged through the papers on the desk and in the drawers and a filing cabinet, until I found what I was looking for – two or three drafts of unpublished pieces and some transcripts of lectures that had been recorded. I took these to Soia, implying that my mission was accomplished. She pointed out that Karl had a study at their home, 4920 Kimbark Avenue, and I should also inspect that. There was more there including some sets of teaching materials. When I reported that I had finished, she said that she thought there was also a cupboard with more paper in it. There was. At this stage, I realized that Soia was leading me on. I responded by moving in. I planned that when I was alone in the house I would case the joint from basement to attic. Sure enough the basement held more boxes, including at least one unopened tea chest indicating transport by rail from New Haven to New York. Karl had moved from Yale to Columbia in 1924. I worked my way up through the house, searching methodically and relatively free from inhibition, acting like a professional burglar. I found a few more enclaves of material. As I reached the attic, a door opened and out popped the head of a little old lady. We were both shocked. She looked afraid. I did not know that anyone was there, but I realized that this was probably Soia's mother. She had arrived from Russia in 1916 and knew (or claimed to know) no English. I know no Russian. All I could do was repeat "Szoia, Szoia, Szoia". She did not shoot me.

I am an archivist manqué. I had no training, but I had been involved in projects for preserving legal records in both Sudan and Tanzania. So it did not take much to persuade me to try to put Karl's papers in order. The law school financed the project in exchange for the return of Karl's office.[25] Intermittently over the next two years (1963–5) I supervised the exercise, assisted by Edmund Kitch Raymond Ellinwood (former pupils), Dori Dressander (a former secretary), and my wife, Penelope. We did not consult the university librarian or those responsible for archives. They might not have approved of the idea of the project, let alone our rough and ready methods. But at least the job got done.

[24] I included it in KLP despite Gerhard Casper's advice that it was embarrassingly bad and unpublishable. Whitman treats it as significant (see below n.104(iii)).

[25] In 1964 I also had grants from the Ford and Rockefeller Foundations to visit institutions and work-study programs in the United States in connection with my job in Dar-es-Salaam.

Rootling through a person's papers, especially those of an untidy magpie, is one of the best ways of getting to know them. I learned more about Karl from this exercise than I did from my direct contact with him in 1957–8, or from interviews, or even from casual reading of his works. Of course, it was not a substitute for careful reading, but it was a marvelously illuminating way of getting inside his mind. This is how I tried to evoke the experience in 1965, shortly after completion of the project:

'The amount of material was daunting. Seven large filing cabinets, tightly packed, have not sufficed to house the collection in its ordered state, even after the removal of irrelevancies, duplicates, and "such lumber as was not literary".[26] Originally three or four times as much space had been taken up. The disorder was magnificent. Little pockets of order, occurring in periods like geological strata, remained as evidence of the efforts of valiant secretaries to introduce a system, but more often than not even these had been subverted by a poltergeist whose capacity for subtle misplacement amounted at times to genius.

It is impossible to work with the papers without being made acutely conscious of Llewellyn's personality, always vivid, sometimes dominating, easily tempting one from the path of conventional legal scholarship. I confess to having indulged myself so that sometimes my quest for Llewellyn the jurist has become a quest for Llewellyn the man. In the early stages this was almost inevitable. The disorder was in itself revealing and produced juxtapositions that accentuated certain aspects of his personality. Lying cheek by jowl with an unpublished manuscript in German or a comment on a section of "the Code" would be a newspaper clipping about a lecture to a Bar association on its failure to meet the public's needs or an unfinished poem or the draft of a letter, probably never sent, lambasting a well-known jurist about some unwarranted idiocy.

Such juxtapositions give color to one of the more popular images of Llewellyn: Renaissance man, full-blooded, rumbustious, "universal", a sort of Benvenuto Cellini of the law schools. Mercurial of temperament, he generated anecdotes almost as fast as he generated ideas. There are stories of heated clashes with his superiors; of a rhapsody over the magnolias in bloom interfering with the drafting of the Uniform Commercial Code;

---

[26] An allusion to Thomas Carlyle, *Sartor Resartus* (Everyman edition, 1964), p. 17.

of flights of oratory that his audience never forgot. The best known is the story of his adventures in the German army from which he emerged with the Iron Cross. Several contradictory versions exist, and the task of piecing together an authentic account has not been made easier by the fact that Llewellyn, normally reticent about the episode, gave currency to two versions – one of which reads like a military romance, the other tending to the mock heroic.'[27]

Once enmeshed in the project of dealing with the papers, it was perhaps inevitable that I should write a book about him. I was determined that this should be a serious work of scholarship about his ideas. It was to be an intellectual biography, focusing on particular works and setting them in the context of his life and intellectual milieu.

The Llewellyn papers project was completed in 1965. I compiled a short book on the collection and we prepared a catalogue.[28] I also completed an article introducing Llewellyn to a British audience, as I had originally planned.[29] My aim was to arouse interest in his ideas and bury the image of him as a rule-skeptic who believed "that talk of rules is a myth".[30] My method was Collingwoodian: identify the author's concerns in the context of his place and time; pinpoint the questions arising from these concerns and summarize the answers he gives and the reasons for these answers; then assess the implications and applications of his answers for today's reader.[31] Rather than focusing on the general debates about Realism, or *The Bramble Bush*, or *The Common Law Tradition*, I chose instead two books that illustrated what was involved in a different, more "realistic" approach to studying law than the current British "blackletter" orthodoxy. *Cases and Materials on the Law of Sales* illustrated in a very concrete way Llewellyn's alternative approach to a mainstream legal subject. *The Cheyenne*

[27]   KLP pp. 11–13.

[28]   W. Twining, *The Karl Llewellyn Papers* (Chicago: University of Chicago Law School, 1968); R. Ellinwood, Jr. and W. Twining. *The Karl Llewellyn Papers: A Guide to the Collection* (Chicago: University of Chicago Press, 1967, revised edition, 1970; supplemented and updated by Sheri H. Lewis, 1994).

[29]   William Twining, "Two Works of Karl Llewellyn", 30 Modern Law Review 514 (1967) and 31 id. 165 (1968).

[30]   See below pp. 406–7.

[31]   On R. G. Collingwood see GJB, ch.2.

Way included the first statement of the law jobs theory, his introduction of the case method to anthropology, and a striking example of what later came to be known as "the legal imagination".
Both books were evidence of Llewellyn's sophisticated approach
to rules and revealed English treatments of the Realists to be
unscholarly caricatures. The article made almost no impact on
English textbooks on jurisprudence.

This preliminary work set the pattern for other chapters in the
first draft of the book as I conceived it. Over several years, when I
could make time from other commitments, I ploughed through
each of Llewellyn's other main works, including *The Bramble Bush*,
the writings on Realism, the Uniform Commercial Code, the commercial law writings, *The Common Law Tradition*, and the unpublished, incomplete manuscripts of *Law in our Society* and *The Theory
of Rules*. It was solid, careful work, as Karl and Soia would have
wanted; it produced accurate introductions to each text. But it was
dull, and I knew it. After one half-hearted attempt to obtain a contract before the book was completed, I turned for advice to Arthur
Leff, a friend at Yale, who sadly died in 1981. He wrote back saying that he had a small reading group at Yale that semester and
he could give it to them to read. So I sent him the manuscript.
Some months later, I received a letter which was fairly polite, but
confirmed that they thought it rather pedestrian. In addition to
a few detailed comments they made two suggestions: first that I
should drop the biographical detail as being irrelevant to a jurist's
ideas and, second, that I should set Llewellyn's work in the much
broader political, social, and educational context of the time.[32] I
rejected the first piece of advice – I am a committed contextualist.
I accepted the second with alacrity and in a relatively short period –
mainly in a cottage in the Mourne Mountains – I dashed off the
first draft of what are now the first five chapters of KLRM. I was on
top of the material and wrote a coherent narrative mainly from my
head. Several commentators have said that they are the best chapters in the book.[33]

[32] In addition to a joint letter from the group signed by Leff, I met two of the three
students in the group, Duncan Kennedy and Richard Danzig. They were friendly
and polite, but confirmed that it was dull. This was the start of a long, but fragmented, friendship with Duncan Kennedy.

[33] Others have suggested that as an overall interpretation of American Legal Realism, it puts Karl Llewellyn too much at the centre – he was rather marginal to

After the criticisms from Leff's reading group, I added the first five chapters, tried to enliven the others, but retained and developed the biographical chapter. In 1971, I delivered the manuscript to Weidenfeld and Nicolson, with a great sense of relief.[34] It was another eighteen months before it finally appeared in print. The book was widely reviewed, but – perhaps unfortunately – it did not stir up much controversy. There were a few criticisms, but nothing that requires a substantial defense.[35]

Excursus B: Llewellyn and Hart

By the age of twenty-four I was indebted to two luminaries who sometimes seemed irreconcilably different. Much of my early theoretical work involved attempts to resolve this tension.

At a personal level, Llewellyn was curious about my attachment to Hart – whom he had heard of but had not read – indeed in 1957 there was not much by Hart to read. He questioned me about Oxford analytical philosophy and how it differed from the general semantics of Korzybski or Hayakawa or the more populist Stuart Chase.[36] I had no idea. Llewellyn was not enthusiastic about

the groups at Columbia and Yale and my interpretation downplays the concerns about law as social science. (see Schlegel and Hull, below n.108) My response is that, first, what I then wrote about Realism was setting a context for a book on Llewellyn and, more important, part of my argument has consistently been that as self-appointed spokesman for the Realists he obscured as much as he illuminated, not least the diversity of the scholars who were loosely lumped under that label. Most generalizations about Realism are false or trivial or both, as I argued in my Dewey lecture in 1984 (see below n.77). However, I fully agree that Schlegel, Kalman, and others have added a great deal to our understanding of relations between law and the social sciences in the period 1920–50. (see below n.101).

34 Weidenfeld's were publishers of the Law in Context series, of which I was co-editor. There was a distribution agreement with Oceana, the publisher of *The Bramble Bush.*

35 I shall not repeat here responses and mea culpas already published in TAR and JJM. See further notes 77 and 88 below.

36 Llewellyn owned a copy of Alfred Korzybski's *Science and Sanity* (1st edition, 1933, Lancaster, PA: The International Non-Aristotelian Library Publishing Co.) and some books by Stuart Chase, but how carefully he studied them is unclear. He may also have been familiar with the work of S. I. Hayakawa. In an interesting review of the translation of *Praejuzienrecht und Rechtsprechung in Amerika*, Dennis Patterson has suggested that in his Leipzig lectures of 1929 Llewellyn

abstract philosophical analysis; if he had known of Oxford's snob-bish distain for sociology, he would have disapproved.

When I first met him, Llewellyn rescued me from what was known as "Korzybskian paralysis" – a state of being stuck in an end-less regress about the meaning of words, following any answer to the question: What do you mean by that? by repeating the same question.[37] Karl used the analogy of a craftsman discovering a new tool – for example, the advent of the adze in Gothic archi-tecture – and then fixating on it as the only tool and overusing it. This was an effective way of liberating me from an obsession and putting "linguistic analysis" in its place as a useful, but limited technique masquerading as a philosophy. Llewellyn – and more broadly the law school – also opened my eyes to some deficien-cies in my English legal education. Three in particular: an almost exclusive focus on legal doctrine; an overconcern with private law; and an almost complete divorce from both legal practice (what law-yers do) and the law in action (how law works). Chicago provided some key missing ingredients: linking law with the social sciences; a dialectical approach to every issue; a very intellectualized, but nevertheless down-to-earth approach to legal practice and the law

"prefigured much of what Wittgenstein would ultimately be credited with having achieved" (Dennis Patterson "Law's Practice" 90 Columbia Law Rev. 575 (1990), at 576), viz the idea that practice rather than rules is the ultimate source of legal meaning. See also D. Patterson, *Law and Truth* (New York: Oxford University Press, 1996). I am not qualified to analyze the affinities or otherwise between Llewellyn's view of language with Korzybski, Hayakawa, or the later Wittgenstein. Patterson's general interpretation of Llewellyn shares with my own an emphasis on the significance of "juristic method". However, his broader argument points in a direction of postmodern, perhaps Rortyan, epistemology, convincingly crit-icized by Brian Leiter in *Naturalizing Jurisprudence* (Oxford: Oxford University Press, 2007), ch. 5, "Why Quine is not a Postmodernist". This involves issues too complex to pursue here; suffice to say that there is scope for a thorough philosophical exploration of Llewellyn's views on language and his epistemol-ogy, which in the past I have associated with Deweyian (as opposed to Rortyan) pragmatism (see GJB, pp. 131–2, n. 126).

37 KLP, p. 6. I have recently found a paper I wrote for Llewellyn's jurisprudence course that has on the front the following comment by KNL: 'I think it was very good for you to do this. I don't know exactly why I think so. There is a feeling that you have been under some kind of intellectual pressure, maybe because a confident framework proved to be a horse that wouldn't run. This is a shock. A good man, however, bubbles. I take this as bubbling. The only thing it has, for anybody except you, is life'. This fairly typical comment ends with an equally typical note of encouragement.

in action; a demonstration of the interdependence of theory and practice; and a concern for justice.

As the account of my early encounters with the realities of qualifying for the bar and personal injuries practice show, I sensed that there were some gaps in my legal education. In 1957–8 Chicago helped me to identify and to start to fill these gaps. In addition, when I read *The Cheyenne Way* and learned about the law jobs theory, it fitted well with my earlier readings in legal anthropology and African law (Gluckman, Fallers, Bohannan, Elias, Gulliver) and my own impressions of law in East Africa. So it is hardly surprising that I was "converted" to Llewellyn and some aspects of the American law school.

Hart was a relatively new phenomenon in 1957–8 (*The Concept of Law* was published in 1961) and Llewellyn was not very interested. Hart, on the other hand, was quite genuinely puzzled by my enthusiasm for Llewellyn. He gave me the impression that I had suffered a lapse of judgement and of taste and, although he did not say so, implied that I was being disloyal. In *The Karl Llewellyn Papers* I made a good deal of play with Llewellyn's enthusiasm for Thomas Carlyle and his use as a pseudonym Carlyle's mythical figure Diogenes Jonathan Swift Teufelsdrockh, the Philosopher of the Clothes.[38] I sent Hart a copy of the book. He responded with a friendly postcard which reads:

17/7/68

Thank you very much for the K.L. papers. Many congratulations on your account of him. Excellent and most sympathy-provoking. The analogy with Carlyle always has struck me as very strong (Needless to say I dislike Carlyle (most of all what he stood for) while recognizing his genius. Yours HLAH

'The sound and the thunder of the Odyssey'.[39]

So far as I can tell, Hart had not read far beyond *The Bramble Bush* before he published *The Concept of Law*. He has been rightly criticized for attributing to Llewellyn the view "That talk of rules

---

[38] See KLP, pp. 11–12, 17–18; see further KLRM, pp. 120, 421. I interpreted Llewellyn's Teufelsdrokh papers as at best "semi-serious". Natalie Hull treats them as more significant. See especially "The Romantic Realist: Art, Literature and the Enduring Legacy of Karl Llewellyn's 'Jurisprudence'", 40 The American Jo. of Legal History 115 (1996).

[39] A reference to Andrew Lang's *As One Who for a Weary Space has Lain* – in fact it is the "surge and thunder", but the sense is clear enough.

is a myth".[40] He did once in conversation grudgingly acknowledge that Llewellyn's account of the law jobs was "a useful categorization" – perhaps meaning that it was a helpful, but secondary, way of classifying the functions of law. Later Hart acknowledged that he had erred in accusing Llewellyn of being a "rule skeptic", as he interpreted it, but he still used the idea of rule skepticism as a point of reference.[41]

The fact is that neither of my teachers had read the other or was much interested. And at first sight they were very far apart in style, in provenance, and in disciplinary expertise: Hart, an Oxford philosopher, had had a busy Chancery practice for seven years and disliked it.[42] Llewellyn had loved his shorter period of commercial practice; his nonlegal background was in ethnography, sociology, and to a lesser extent economics. Hart's main interest was elucidation of concepts, Llewellyn's how law works in practice.

I did not think that I was being disloyal to Hart. In particular, I continued to admire and use his methods of conceptual elucidation – but no longer so obsessively. I was attracted by his modified utilitarianism and his John Stuart Mill liberalism as exemplified by his writings on prostitution, homosexuality, and punishment. Perhaps more important, I stayed with Hart's positivist position, which was much more robust than Llewellyn's.[43] Critics of positivism miss the mark when they attribute a belief that "might is right" or an

---

[40] See next note.

[41] H. L. A. Hart, *The Concept of Law* (1961) at pp. 132–7 (citing the famous passage in *The Bramble Bush* about rules as "pretty playthings" that Llewellyn had already retracted). Hart later half-retracted this attribution to Llewellyn in "American Jurisprudence Through English eyes: The Nightmare and the Noble Dream" (1977, reprinted in *Essays in Jurisprudence and Philosophy* (1983), ch.4 at p. 128) in which he interprets some of Llewellyn's ideas a bit more sympathetically (citing *Jurisprudence: Realism in Theory* and *Practice* and *The Common Law Tradition*) while complaining of his obscurity (at p. 137). There Hart interprets Llewellyn as a moderate subscriber to "the Noble Dream" view of adjudication. Hart's criticism of the view that "talk of rules is a myth" is quite cogent; the difficulty is finding anyone who subscribed to it. This is not to say that there is a consensus on the answer to the question: Under what conditions is it true to say that a rule exists? on which see Twining and Miers (2010), *op. cit.*, at pp. 102–7.

[42] Lacey, *op. cit.*, at pp. 47–8, 112–13.

[43] In respect of Llewellyn I agree with Leiter's view that Realism, which is not a theory of law, typically presupposes a version of Legal Positivism. (Leiter (2007, *op. cit.*, at pp. 55–7, 104–6).

indifference to justice and morality or a kind of scientistic attachment to brute fact to legal positivists like Bentham and Hart. Bentham distinguished the is and the ought for the sake of the ought; although in *The Concept of Law* Hart claimed to be advancing a descriptive theory of law – and so was more concerned with the is – he was also quite clear that he considered that distinguishing is and ought was necessary for clarity of thought in evaluating, criticizing, and reforming law – and he was quite active in public debate on such issues. His positivism was moral rather than amoral.[44]

Perhaps more significant in this context is a matter of attitude or affect. I was quite surprised by Llewellyn's claims that he *loved* the common law, by his *pride* in being a good lawyer, and his fascination in details of how things work (craft, technique, technology).[45] I had from early on taken an instinctive dislike to the culture of the Inns of Court and I sensed that Hart was at best ambivalent about his life at the Bar. The ideas of loving the law and being proud of being a lawyer were new to me. Although I learned to share Llewellyn's fascination with the crafts of law – for example, his nuanced differentiation of sixty-four different precedent techniques[46] – I have stayed with something like Hart's tough positivism: there is nothing inherently good or attractive or lovable about positive law from an external point of view. The scholar needs to look on power and authority with relative detachment: law is very often a product of other people's power – whether it is in a foreign legal system or an ancient one or, for the most part, in one's own country or society or broader milieu, such as Europe.[47] Of course, if one is participating in a particular legal system that one feels to be legitimate it may often be

---

[44] See Neil MacCormick, "A Moralistic Case for A-Moralistic Law" 20 Valparaiso L. Rev. 1–41 (1985).

[45] His collaborator, Hoebel, was regularly impressed by Llewellyn's skills of analysis: 'In awe one day [I] queried, "Karl, how do you do it?" "Why, Ad", he replied, with more pride in his profession than in himself, "I am a case-trained lawyer – and what is more, I am one of the three best in the country".' (E. Adamson Hoebel, 'Karl Llewellyn: Anthropological Jurisprude', 18 Rutgers L. Rev. 735–44 (1964) at p. 743).

[46] KLRM, pp. 237–9.

[47] W. Twining, "Other People's Power: The Bad Man and Legal Positivism 1897–1997" 63 Brooklyn 189 (1997) (reprinted in GLT, ch. 5) and "Institutions of Law from a Global Perspective: Standpoint, Pluralism and Non-state Law", in M. Del Mar and Z. Bankowski (eds.) *Law as Institutional Normative Order* (Farnham: Ashgate, 2009), ch. 2.

appropriate, sometimes even obligatory, to try to help it to become "the best it can be"; but that is one kind of participant standpoint, not that of a scholar whose main concern is understanding the phenomenon. Hart captures this attitude well when he says:

[T]he identification of the central meaning of law with what is morally legitimate, because orientated towards the common good, seems to me in view of the hideous record of the evil use of law for oppression to be an unbalanced perspective, and as great a distortion as the opposite Marxist identification of the central case of law with the pursuit of interests of the dominant class.[48]

Concepts are thinking tools. For clarity of thought one needs tools for description as well as tools for evaluation, critique, and advocacy. So maybe for me Hart and Llewellyn mainly complemented each other, Hart providing methods of conceptual elucidation, a model for describing and analyzing modern municipal legal systems with relative detachment, and an exemplar of English-style democratic liberalism. Hart tells us what (state) law is; Llewellyn provides a lens on what law (more broadly conceived) does, and a way of conceiving of nonstate law, legal pluralism, and the how of the actual operations of laws, lawyers, and legal orders.

On this interpretation they are *different*, without *disagreeing*. To the extent that they focused on different questions that is plausible. But their concerns overlapped, and at first sight they provide dissimilar perspectives on similar, if not identical, questions. So we will need to look more closely at where they may be difficult to reconcile. This, I believe, is one reason why Llewellyn's vision of law is of continuing significance – a matter to which I shall return at the end.[49]

Part B KLRM 1971–2011

KLRM was completed in 1971. It is a product of its time and it would be foolish to try to update the text. Even extensive annotations would distract attention from Llewellyn's own writings, to which this book is intended as a guide. Here I shall merely try to plug a few gaps in KLRM, comment selectively on developments relevant to considering Llewellyn today, and provide some signposts

[48] Hart (1983) *op. cit.*, at p. 12.
[49] See below pp. 441–3. On other attempts to reconcile analytical and empirically-oriented perspectives in jurisprudence, see GJP, pp. 54–60.

towards significant recent literature. This section deals briefly with
(a) writings by Llewellyn published since 1971; (b) writings about
Llewellyn and Realism generally; (c) developments in jurisprudence since 1971; (d) developments relating to the UCC and commercial law generally; and (e) unfinished agenda.

(a) Llewellyn's works made accessible
Three books by Llewellyn have been published since 1973: *Rechts,
Rechtsleben und Gessellschaft* (1977);[50] a translation of the main text
of *Praejudizienrecht und Rechtsprechung in Amerika* (1933) as *The Case
Law System in America* (1989);[51] and *The Theory of Rules* (2011).[52] In
addition there has been a reissue of *The Bramble Bush*.[53] All of these
have been well edited, with helpful introductions. I had access to
the originals before I wrote KLRM, but their publication makes
some of Llewellyn's most important works available and is evidence
of a continuing interest in him in the United States.[54]

---

[50] *Rechts, Rechtsleben und Gessellschaft*, edited and introduced by Manfred Rehbinder
(Berlin: Duncker und Humblot, 1977). Useful discussions of Llewellyn's Ger-
man works include Michael Ansaldi, "The German Llewellyn", 58 Brooklyn L.
Rev. 705 (1992) and James Q Whitman, "Commercial Law and the American
Volk: A Note on Llewellyn's German Sources for the Uniform Commercial
Code", 97 Yale L. Jo. 156 (1987). See also Dennis Paterson (1990) on the sig-
nificance of *Praejudizienrecht*, discussed above n.36.

[51] *The Case Law System in America*, edited with an introduction by Paul Gewirtz,
translated by Michael Ansaldi (Chicago: University of Chicago Press, 1989).

[52] Karl Llewellyn, *The Theory of Rules* (edited and introduced by Frederick Schauer)
(Chicago: University of Chicago Press, 2011).

[53] Karl Llewellyn, *The Bramble Bush*, with an introduction and notes by Sam
Sheppard (New York: Oxford University Press, 2008).

[54] A great deal of primary material relating to the drafting and enactment of
the UCC has also been published, a number of Llewellyn's articles have been
anthologized, and an unpublished manuscript entitled "A Required Course
in Jurisprudence" was included in W. Twining (ed.) *Legal Theory and Common
Law* 1986 Oxford: Blackwell, ch. 14 (a longer version of this was printed in
Llewellyn's *Jurisprudence: Realism in Theory and Practice* (Chicago: University of
Chicago Press, 1962). On Robert Whitman's (and his co-authors') use of the
Emma Corstvet papers, see below pp. 427–30. Francis J. Mootz, Jr. (ed.) *On Philosophy in American Law* (New York: Cambridge University Press, 2009) reprints
Llewellyn's 1934 paper of that title and uses it as a jumping-off point for over
thirty short essays on "the role that philosophy might play at this juncture in
the history of American legal thought". The essays are varied and variable in
quality, but taken together they provide an interesting commentary on some,

Of the remaining unpublished works by Llewellyn, the unfinished text of *Law in Our Society* is clearly the most important. I shall deal with that in the last section. One other work deserves comment here: Soia Mentschikoff and Irwin Stotzky, *The Theory and Craft of American Law – Elements.*[55] This and cognate works build on Llewellyn's Elements course in Chicago, the full significance of which I did not realize when I wrote KLRM. So this deserves another Excursus.

Excursus C "Elements"

> He that hath a Gospel
> For all earth to own –
> Though he etch it on the steel
> Or carve it on the stone –
> Not to be misdoubted
> Through the after-days
> It is his Disciple
> Shall read it many ways.[56]

I did not take Llewellyn's course on "Elements". If I had done so, I might have been less critical of *The Common Law Tradition*, for I would have seen more clearly the point of studying a sequence of cases from a single jurisdiction, to trace not only the development of a single thread of doctrine case by case, but also to view the court as "a working institution", its style(s) of reasoning, and the operation of contextual factors. In KLRM, I wrote: 'Although there were a number of Llewellynesque features, in many respects "Elements" resembled other "legal method" courses, and it lacked the unique qualities of *The Bramble Bush.*'[57] In retrospect, this does an injustice to the course and the materials, both in terms of its conception and its influence.

---

but by no means all, aspects of contemporary American legal theory. They also include a number of comments on and interpretations of Llewellyn that claim to be "fresh looks".

[55] S. Mentschikoff and I. Stotzky, *The Theory and Craft of American Law – Elements* (New York: M. Bender, 1981).

[56] "The Disciple", *Rudyard Kipling's Verse, 1885-1926* (definitive edition) (London: Hodder and Stoughton, 1940), at p. 774.

[57] KLRM, p. 151.

Dennis Hutchinson has written an interesting history of the course, which was begun by Edward Levi and Roscoe Steffen in Chicago in 1937.[58] Levi handed it over to Llewellyn when he joined the Chicago faculty in 1951. Llewellyn produced a set of materials that, in Hutchinson's words, "could not have been more different from the Levi-Steffen approach".[59] Llewellyn continued to require students to read Levi's short classic, *An Introduction to Legal Reasoning*, but he dropped all of the philosophical texts and substituted his own materials, mainly sequences of cases from New York. Both Levi and Llewellyn were concerned to teach case law reasoning, but Levi emphasized conceptual development and relied quite heavily on secondary materials; Llewellyn focused on intensive reading of judicial opinions in full, unadorned by any notes or other extraneous material.[60]

At Chicago from 1951 until Soia Mentschikoff moved to Miami, "Elements" was taught almost exclusively by Llewellyn himself or jointly with Mentschikoff and, after his death by Mentschikoff alone. The course is still taught under the deliberately open-ended rubric of "Elements" in at least three law schools – Chicago, Miami, and Cardozo.[61] For a number of years, the Llewellyn tradition was carried on by former students who had taken one of the three Chicago versions.[62] Generally, these teachers stuck very closely

[58]   Dennis J. Hutchinson, "Elements of the Law", 70 The University of Chicago Law Review 141 (2003).

[59]   Ibid. at p. 152.

[60]   Llewellyn did assign some outside reading, but deliberately did not supplement the cases. An inventory of the various editions of "Elements" materials can be found in the *Guide to the Karl Llewellyn Papers* at pp. 73–4 and the 1994 supplement.

[61]   Up to 1962 "Elements" was taught in Chicago by Llewellyn, sometimes with Mentschikoff, who continued to teach it after his death until she moved to Miami. When she became dean she made "Elements" the foundation course at the University of Miami Law School. In the early days it was taught exclusively by graduates of the University of Chicago who had been taught by Llewellyn or Mentschikoff or both. It has survived, though not without controversy.

[62]   For example, until quite recently the main teachers in Miami were Terry Anderson, who took Llewellyn's course; Alan Swan, who had Llewellyn and Mentschikoff; and John Gaubatz and Irwin Stotzky, who had Mentschikoff alone. In 2010–11 Anderson and Stotzky were still teaching "Elements" at Miami. In the 1980s I participated in teaching "Elements" in some years, usually co-teaching with Anderson, but I had not taken the Chicago course, and deviated somewhat in conception and method. Leslie Gerwin, who (along with Paul Shupak,

to the Llewellyn-Mentschikoff conception of the course, though sometimes substituting different sequences of cases and using different classroom methods. However, as the Llewellyn-Mentschikoff alumni were replaced, the course naturally changed in conception and scope as well as methods. Even in Miami some versions of "Elements" now owe little or nothing to Llewellyn.[63]

Three questions arise: What was Llewellyn's conception of the course? What was distinctive about it? Is something of value being lost as it fades away? Here, I can only give brief answers to these questions.

Llewellyn saw "Elements" as one crucial part of a liberal legal education.[64] Law as a liberal art has three basic components: (i) basic technical competence; (ii) a clear vision of the ethos and meaning of legal practice and of the role of law in society and in the world as a whole; and (iii) the spiritual or aspirational aspect of life in the law – including the quest for "the Good, the True and the Beautiful in Law".[65] Llewellyn's version of "Elements" focused primarily on (i) and aspects of (ii), without greatly emphasizing it, and hinted at (iii) largely through osmosis.[66] As an introductory course

another Chicago graduate) introduced the course at Cardozo, had been taught by both Anderson and Mentschikoff at Antioch Law School, but that is another story (see below n.70).

[63] It seems highly likely that the original title "Elements of Law" was deliberately open-ended to give individual teachers a wide discretion about objectives, methods, and scope. There are many ways of introducing students to the discipline of law. (KLRM, p. 141). Some of the differences within the Llewellyn-Mentschikoff tradition can be seen by comparing the Mentschikoff-Stotzky book with Eva H. Hanks, Michael E. Herz, and Steven S. Nemerson, *Elements of Law* (Cincinnati: Anderson Publishing, 2004), a book that emerged out of the Cardozo course.

[64] K. N. Llewellyn, "The Study of Law as a Liberal Art", Address at the Dedicatory Celebrations, University of Chicago Law School, April 30, 1960, reprinted in Llewellyn, *Jurisprudence* (1962) *op. cit.*, as ch. 17. Extracts are included in Mentschikoff and Stotzky, *op. cit.*, at pp. 272–92. The quoted passage is at p. 276.

[65] Llewellyn, "On the Good, the True and the Beautiful in Law" 9 University of Chicago L. Rev. 224 (1942) reprinted (in part) in *Jurisprudence* (1962) *op. cit.*, ch. 8. See KLRM, pp 197–9.

[66] This is Terry Anderson's interpretation. The 1951 edition of *The Bramble Bush* captures some of components (ii) and (iii). The course description for Anderson's course in Miami, which he claims is the closest to the original Llewellyn version, reads: 'Elements introduces students to the theory and craft of the common law. It is a skills course in which the materials studied are simply exercise materials for the developments of three skills: (1) how to read and analyze appellate decisions with the skill necessary to use them in constructing persuasive arguments and in

it could do no more than lay a foundation. Llewellyn believed that a sound liberal legal education involved a range of skills, but "Elements" was focused very largely on one skill set, reading and using reported cases.[67] Reading included fast and slow reading, reading single cases and sequences from a single court, looking at what judges were doing as well as what they were saying, how they were reasoning in a specific institutional setting, not only justifying their individual decisions, but also persuading their brethren to move in the same direction. For example, the sequence of indefiniteness cases from New York[68] were used to show, inter alia, how a great Grand Style judge (Cardozo) can lead a court to make a significant development in legal doctrine while working within the constraints imposed by the institution and tradition.[69]

"Elements" has been taught for over seventy years, mainly in three law schools, sometimes more. It is one of the most tangible markers of Llewellyn's influence. Naturally, different teachers have interpreted it differently, in respect of objectives, methods, and materials – sometimes merely substituting different materials, sometimes doing radically different things. In some instances, little more than the name survives. Those who follow in the Llewellyn tradition of "Elements" read his ideas in many ways.

counseling clients how to take advantage (or avoid the adverse consequences of) the law as established through the date of the particular case; (2) how to read a sequence of cases from a single jurisdiction to see the roles that the lawyers and judges played in applying and developing the law; and (3) how to develop persuasive arguments using a sequence of cases that a lawyer could use to persuade the court to decide a hypothetical case in favor of her client. The intensive in-class discussions and exercises are supplemented by a series of extensive readings that introduce students to the writings of legal theorists during the periods in which the cases arose. The course concludes with a final examination.' Compare the Mentschikoff-Stotzky longer formulation in *The Theory and Craft of American Law: Elements, op. cit.*, introductory note (pp. xv–xxxv).

[67] Llewellyn considered that reading and using statutory material was also important, but he did not place much emphasis on this in "Elements", perhaps because he felt that these skills should be developed in other courses and that some of the basic case law skills of reading and reasoning were transferable to statutes.

[68] Included in Mentschikoff and Stotzky, *op. cit.*, at pp. 297–554.

[69] Interestingly, in this course Llewellyn did not set exercises in constructing legal arguments or applying case law skills, whereas some of his former students have done so. For example, Anderson and Gaubatz have regularly used exercises as a preparation for mooting and appellate argument. In some years Llewellyn taught appellate advocacy/legal argument as an upper-level skills course.

Three books on legal method by acknowledged disciples illustrate some of the variations. Soia Mentschikoff and Irwin Stotzky's
The Theory and Craft of American Law (1981) is based closely on
Llewellyn's "Elements" materials. It includes the sequences of cases,
nearly all from New York, that Llewellyn used, but adds questions
and annotations that include many references to doctrinal developments in the law. Llewellyn's *The Bramble Bush* and Levi's *Introduction to Legal Reasoning* (but significant, not *The Cheyenne Way*),
are prescribed as supplementary reading, together with six essays
that "add background and theory to the case materials" (xix). The
introduction deals cursorily with the functions of law and "mechanisms that precede court intervention", meaning negotiated settlement, mediation, arbitration, administrative decision making, and
legislation. But the focus is relentlessly on upper court litigation
dealing with questions of law in relation to techniques of judging
and advocacy in handling cases and to a lesser extent legislation.
The introduction of the book contains a more elaborate introduction to the basic skill of briefing a case than Llewellyn may have
done, but the meat of the book consists of very detailed study of the
craft of judging and appellate advocacy in the American common
law tradition.[70]

Kelso's *A Programmed Introduction to the Study of Law: Part I Case
Skills* attempted to transform Llewellyn's ideas on the subject into a
self-instructional programmed learning text.[71] This is mainly interesting as an early attempt at introducing programmed learning
into law. The medium inevitably involved a rather formalized interpretation of Llewellyn's ideas.

---

[70]   In a thoughtful review of *The Theory and Craft of American Law* (33 Jo. Legal Education 64 [1983]) Leslie Gerwin and Paul Shupak, professors at Cardozo, compare Llewellyn's original materials, this book, and other American books on legal
method at the time. They acknowledge that Mentschikoff and Stotzky are largely
true to Llewellyn, not least in their emphasis on skills, and crafts, and courts as
working institutions, but criticize them for adding supplementary materials that
may divert students onto focusing on substantive law rather than skills, on rules
rather than legal crafts. They interestingly point out that most introductions to
legal method aim to teach the skills of a law student, whereas Llewellyn and Mentschikoff consistently focus on how leading lawyers and judges actually handle cases.

[71]   Charles D. Kelso, *A Programmed Introduction to the Study of Law: Part I Case Skills*
(Indianapolis: Bobbs-Merrill, 1965), reviewed in Katherine O'Donovan, William
Twining and Rex Mitchell, "Legal Eagles or Battery Hens?" 10 Jo. Soc. Public
Teachers Law (NS) (1968) 6.

William Twining and David Miers, *How To Do Things with Rules*[72] might be interpreted as an application and extension of the ideas of Llewellyn, Hart, and others in a mainly British context. The educational conception is quite different from the original "Elements" course in that there is a greater emphasis on theory, the skills involved centre on rule handling in general, not just in legal contexts, and in the later editions on skills of systematic and self-conscious reading and using a much wider range of kinds of texts as materials of law study. It also devotes much more attention to legislation. Llewellyn's direct influence can be found in the treatment of rule handling in the context of the law-jobs theory, and in some particular ideas such as precedent techniques, Grand Style judging, and the ABCs of appellate advocacy. More important, the central thesis of the book is that problems that give rise to the interpretation and use of legal rules and other "law stuff" are by no means unique to legal contexts and that law is *au fond* a very human affair and the study of law can itself be a liberal art. In short, the book is influenced by Llewellyn's ideas, but not by his "Elements" course.

Other courses on legal method *claim* to teach basic case law skills. Many do not live up to this claim, but some do. So, apart from the emphasis on sequences of cases from a single court, and some of Llewellyn's ideas, what was distinctive about Llewellyn's version of "Elements"? Of course, when Llewellyn or Menschikoff were teaching the course, it was special because of the teachers. But, in the hands of their disciples, however loyal, I would say: beyond that, not much. The main claim relates to the intensity of the focus on reading a small number of cases. In short, depth is given priority over coverage. This is admirable, but how far it is unique is difficult to say.

Is there something in Llewellyn's original conception of "Elements" worth preserving or rescuing? In KRLM I argued that *The Bramble Bush* has survived and been influential not because its message was radical or iconoclastic, but rather because it expressed in a unique style the central ethos of the American law school.[73] I still

---

[72] William Twining and David Miers, *How To Do Things With Rules: A Primer of Interpretation* (London: Weidenfeld and Nicolson, 1973; 5th edition, 2010, Cambridge: Cambridge University Press).

[73] See KLRM, pp. 140–52, esp. p. 143. Cf. William C. Jones, review of *The Theory and Craft of American Law*, 37 U. Miami L. Rev. 867 (1983).

think that this is right, although I would today express this view differently. Of course, American law schools and their environment have changed in many ways since 1930, but there has also been considerable continuity in the basic ethos and the underlying tensions between liberal and vocational objectives that concerned Llewellyn.

For a long time I have felt uneasy about some aspects of American law school culture in its various manifestations and some of that is reflected in unease about the Llewellyn-Mentschikoff conception of "Elements", which after all is based on a particular vision of legal education. The fault does not lie in Llewellyn's brave attempt to reconcile liberal and vocational objectives, knowledge, skills, and ideals (know what, know how, know why), and to bridge theory and practice. On that I am still a quite loyal disciple. But pedagogically I am worried that three sets of ideas get conflated and make the "Elements" plus *Bramble Bush* approach too conservative. In short, there are important differences between learning about Hercules, trying to emulate him, and mastering basic intellectual skills needed by a beginning law student.[74]

This is too complex a matter to pursue in depth here.[75] The basic point is this: Llewellyn's main concern in teaching first year students was first, to counter the expectation that legal education consists solely in learning doctrine and, second, to provide an alternative to the Langdell case method, which was too narrow both in respect of the range of skills inculcated and in respect of perspective – "the wherewithal for vision was not given".[76] Llewellyn is generally judged to have been largely successful in respect of communicating the central realist message viz. that for most purposes the study of rules alone is not enough. But "Elements" did not mark a sharp break from Langdell in respect of the materials to be studied, the skills to be developed, and the goal of setting a broad context and framework for an undergraduate legal education. Furthermore, his fascination with the workings of appellate courts in action conflated studying *about* (knowledge/understanding) and studying

---

[74] See LiC passim. On the distinction between professional skills and the basic skills needed by a first year law student, see Gerwin and Shupak, above n.70.

[75] I intend to develop this argument elsewhere. Some indications can be found in "Reading Law" (Seegers Lectures), 24 Valparaiso L. Rev. 1 (1989) and "Taking Facts Seriously" (34. Jo. Leg. Ed 22 [1989]), both of which are reproduced in LiC (1997).

[76] *Jurisprudence, op. cit,* pp. 375, 377.

how (skills) in a way, which in my experience has left some teachers and many students unclear about the main learning objectives of the course.

(b) Writings about Llewellyn and Realism since 1971

(i) Two supplements to KLRM In 1985 Weidenfeld and Nicolson and Oklahoma University Press agreed to reissue KLRM. I decided not to revise the text for reasons stated in the postscript. Since then, rather than revise it, I have supplemented it with two substantial essays.[77] As both are easily accessible and rather long, they have not been appended to this edition.

Timed to coincide with the reissue of KLRM, I devoted the 1984 Dewey Lecture at NYU Law School to "Talk About Realism". In the period between 1971 and 1984 there had been an explosion of interest in jurisprudence and modern legal history. I summed up the major developments as follows:

[In 1971] Jurisprudence in the United States was muted, and, at least in England, Realism was thought to be discredited. Neither Marxism nor economic analysis of law had many adherents in law schools in either country. Terms such as 'critical legal studies', 'sociolegal', 'contextual', 'structuralism' and 'phenomenology' have all gained currency in the law school world since then. The same period has seen major contributions to Legal Theory, broadly conceived, from Dworkin, Finnis, Fuller, MacCormick, Nozick, Rawls, Raz, Summers, Unger and many others. It has been a particularly rich period in the history and theory of contracts. Legal history has blossomed and diversified, and there have been interesting developments in legal anthropology. Particularly pleasing has been the revival of a contextual approach to the history of political thought by Skinner and others. The effect of these and other developments is to create a different intellectual climate for interpreting and assessing the continuing significance of the Realist legacy.[78]

---

[77] W. Twining, "Talk about Realism" 60 NYU L. Rev. 329 (1985) reprinted in GJB, ch. 5 (hereafter TAR) and W. Twining, "Karl Llewellyn's Unfinished agenda: Law in Society and he Job of Juristic Method" (1993) (hereafter JJM) first published in *Chicago Papers in Legal History*; reprinted in GJB, ch. 6. Shorter versions were published in 48 U of Miami Law Review 119–58 (1993) and U. Drobnig and M. Rehbinder (eds.) *Rechtsrealismus, multikulturelle Gesellschaft und Handelsrecht: Karl N. Llewellyn und seine Bedeutung heute* (Berlin, Dunker and Humblot, 1994), pp 71–112.

[78] TAR at pp. 332/96.

"Talk About Realism" focused on some of the implications of these developments for understanding R/realism. Distinguishing between historical accounts of the American Realist Movement and elucidation of realism as a juristic concept, I welcomed the increased interest in legal biography and the detailed historical work by Schlegel and others that had begun to emerge,[79] but I was sharply critical of loose generalizations about "Realism" and "the Realists", whom I continued to interpret as a variegated bunch of scholars and thinkers. These generalizations not only distorted history, but also tended to marginalize the most original ideas of individuals – for example, Frank on fact finding, Llewellyn on the law jobs, Moore's conception of "science", and Willard Hurst's historiography. In particular, I criticized five tendencies: to treat Realism as a full-blown theory of law; to assume that Realism was mainly or entirely about adjudication – sometimes even only appellate adjudication of questions of law; the claim that the Realists had been essentially negative or nihilistic; the implication that they had contributed nothing constructive or original; and suggestions that most Realist writings were politically or ideologically motivated, linked closely to the progressive movement and the New Deal (some were; others, including Llewellyn's, were not). I concluded that most historical generalizations about the Realists were false or trivial or both. Furthermore, there was a tendency to criticize Realism or individual Realists for their alleged answers to questions remote from their concerns. My criticisms mainly restated and extended points I had made more mutedly in KLRM.

The concept of "realism" remains elusive – after all, what is reality? In "Talk About Realism" I extended my analysis in relation to Llewellyn's use of the term and to the development of "law in context" and "socio-legal studies" in the United Kingdom.[80] This

---

[79] See below n.101.

[80] Since 2004 a new Legal Realist movement has emerged, spearheaded by Stewart Macaulay and colleagues at Wisconsin and the American Bar Foundation. It acknowledges the ancestry of old American Legal Realism, but claims to be less court-centred and to place more emphasis on a rigorous approach to the methodological problems of interdisciplinarity and on bottom-up perspectives and the role of law in the lives of ordinary people and other norm users. This is a welcome development. One hopes that the label will not attract futile controversy about its meaning and scope.

underlined the question-begging tendency of the concept, and I concluded that it should not be used to bear much weight.[81]

"Talk About Realism" can be read as an update and gloss on KLRM twelve years after its first publication. My second supplementary essay was rather different. In 1993, the centenary of Llewellyn's birth was celebrated in Leipzig and Chicago in strikingly different ways. "Karl Llewellyn's Unfinished Agenda: Law in Society and the Job of Juristic Method" was delivered in different versions to the two audiences.[82] The seminar in Leipzig, four years after the fall of the Berlin Wall, resulted in a useful scholarly collection that focused mainly on Llewellyn's sociology of law and the UCC. It showed that interest in his work was still alive in Germany.[83] The event in Chicago was sparsely attended and, I believe, my paper was the only publication resulting from it. In Chicago, it appeared that Llewellyn had been sidelined, perhaps because of the rise of economic analysis of law.[84]

The main function of my 1993 lecture was to assess Llewellyn's continuing significance a century after his birth, slightly more than thirty years after his death, and twenty years after the first publication of KLRM. Re-reading this assessment a further twenty years on, my overall judgement has not changed much. I also took the opportunity to say some more about the law-jobs theory and the course materials on *Law in Our Society*. This deserves a brief comment.

The lengthy discussion of "the job of juristic method" was in part stimulated by a puzzle: there seems to be a lacuna between

---

[81] "Talk about Realism" (TAR) includes extensive comments on a number of topics, which I shall not discuss here: (i) the relationship between American Legal Realism and critical legal studies (especially notes 21, 87); see now Wouter de Been, *Legal Realism Regained: Saving Realism from Critical Acclaim* (Stanford: Stanford University Press, 2008) (ii) Bruce Ackerman on "Legal Constructivism" (n. 55); (iii) Llewellyn's attitude to John Dewey (n. 126; see now Paul Maharg (2007), *op. cit.*, below n.101, on the relations between Dewey and the Columbia Law School in the 1920s); (iv) the relationship between realism and (a) "law in context" and (b) socio-legal studies in Britain (at pp. 136–44); (v) further thoughts on the concepts of "realism", "common sense", and "horse sense" (notes 129 and 30).

[82] JJM, *op. cit.*, n.77. See also Twining, "The Law in Context Movement" (2008), *op. cit.*, n.100 below.

[83] Drobnig and Rehbinder (eds.) (1994), *op. cit.*, n.101.

[84] See below pp. 434–5.

Llewellyn's treatment of American appellate adjudication, especially in state courts, as developed in *The Common Law Tradition*, and his law-jobs theory, as outlined in *The Cheyenne Way* and developed in several articles, especially "The Normative, the Legal and the Law-Jobs: The Problem of Juristic Method".[85] In KLRM I had criticized Llewellyn for not setting his particular study of one kind of American court in the broader context of litigation and dispute processing in American society, in much the same way as Arthur Leff's group criticized my first draft.[86] Apart from two incidental references to the Cheyennes, there is no mention of the law-jobs theory. Yet as I commented in KLRM: 'This is a strange lapse, for few juristic theories are better suited than the law-jobs theory for providing just this kind of perspective.'[87] In my 1993 paper I argued that the "the job of juristic method" provides the link between these two aspects of Llewellyn's work – his general sociological theory of law and his specialized study of one kind of American institution at a particular period of history. This term embraces all the ways in which the law jobs get done – by institutional structures, legal devices, handed-down skills, individual inventiveness, and so on. "The theory of crafts" dealt with one aspect of juristic method and, along with other sub-theories, was never fully developed in Llewellyn's teaching materials for *Law in Our Society*, although there are some suggestive pointers.[88]

---

[85] 49 Yale L. Jo. 1355 (1940). Although it is difficult to read, I still consider this Llewellyn's most important published paper on the sociology of law. This view was shared by Roscoe Pound, who called it "much the best outline of a sociology of law and the way of going about it which has appeared," (II *Jurisprudence* St Paul: West, 1959 at p. 196) and by Neil MacCormick (conversations with the author). The article now needs to be read with the manuscript of *Law in our Society* (see below pp. 439–43).

[86] Below p. 439.

[87] KLRM, at pp. 268–9.

[88] JJM also includes comments on a number of topics, which I shall not discuss here: (i) functionalism (notes 50 and 51, see now GJP 102–12); (ii) Skills and legal education (pp. 171–6/GJB, pp. 22–8); (iii) Llewellyn and Weber (n. 82), a topic that needs further exploration; and (iv) Morton Horwitz's thesis that Llewellyn was a radical in his youth who retreated into a much more conservative position on adjudication in his later writings, especially *The Common Law Tradition*. (Horwitz, *op. cit.*, n.101, supported, among others, by William C. Heffernan, "Two Stages of Karl Llewellyn's Thought", 11 Int'l Jo. Soc. L 134 [1983]). My view, that there is much more continuity in Llewellyn's thought

It is worth underlining why this failure to link a specialized study of appellate adjudication with its broader context is important. First, not only have commentators wrongly suggested that Realism's focus is solely on adjudication, some have further compounded this by restricting it to appeals on questions of law, omitting or downplaying Frank's concern with fact finding, which is also surely an aspect of adjudicative decisions.[89] In my view, treating the contested trial as paradigmatic – especially the contested jury trial – also distorts perceptions of the place of adjudication in the total process of litigation, which in turn can be set in some broader context, for example as one kind of dispute processing.[90] Thus even some Realists can be criticized from the point of view of the law-jobs theory for having had rather narrow, decontextualized conceptions of adjudication and litigation.

As significant, from the point of view of contemporary jurisprudence, is the fact that one of the most powerfully argued contemporary theories of law is based on an even narrower conception of adjudication. Ronald Dworkin's central theses (whether we characterize them as a theory of law, a theory of adjudication, or a theory of legal argumentation) are premised on a conception of adjudication that is bizarre from any realistic perspective: legal reasoning

than this thesis suggests, is supported by Paul Gewirtz and Michael Ansaldi (1993, *op. cit.*, n.51) and Frederick Schauer (2011) *op. cit.*, n.52 on the basis of their close study of Llewellyn's earlier writings. See also Neil MacCormick and Zipporah Wiseman, "Llewellyn Revisited" (review of *The Case Law System in America*, 70 Texas L. Rev. 771 [1992]). The difference is partly one of emphasis, but Llewellyn was never a radical about indeterminacy in adjudication.

[89] Critics of Frank, e.g., Leiter, focus on Frank's more polemical *Law and the Modern Mind* (New York: Brentano's) while ignoring his more important *Courts on Trial* (Princeton: Princeton University Press, 1949), which was the starting point for my own work on evidence. Llewellyn's copy of the first edition of *Law and the Modern Mind*, heavily annotated, has recently resurfaced and will be deposited in the Llewellyn collection in Chicago.

[90] On over-concentration on contested jury trials and appellate courts and the significance of a total process model of litigation, see William Twining, *Rethinking Evidence* (Cambridge: Cambridge University Press, 2nd edition, 2006) at pp. 169, 220–1, 249–52, and 314. A total process model is adopted in T. Anderson, D. Schum, and W. Twining, *Analysis of Evidence* (Cambridge: Cambridge University Press, 2nd edition, 2005), which is mainly concerned with construction of arguments about questions of fact. Reasoning about questions of law and questions of fact is involved in many legal practice contexts and at many stages of litigation, not just in courts.

is equated with reasoning about disputed questions of law in hard cases and all other kinds of reasoning that occur in legal contexts are ignored. The actual job of judging includes fact finding, ruling on admissibility, case management, controlling proceedings, sentencing, other post-trial decisions, and various kinds of judicial administration, not all of which are trivial or secondary or parasitic or intellectually uninteresting. Dworkin is rightly concerned with the truth conditions of propositions of law and justifications for interpretation and application of such propositions. These are important topics, but on their own they hardly constitute a theory of law. Dworkin places great emphasis on the "practicality" of his theory, but he only focuses on one aspect of the practices of judges, let alone of other participants in legal processes. Llewellyn's emphasis on the study of particular courts as working institutions provides a sharp contrast to Dworkin's narrow conception of adjudication even in respect of hard cases. Where their interests overlap, for instance in regard to appellate judicial discretion, their conclusions could be interpreted as being not very far apart, though they are arrived at by different routes and expressed in different language.[91] From the point of view of jurisprudence, the most significant divide is their very different visions of what is involved in a practical understanding of law. Dworkin dismisses Llewellyn's kind of jurisprudence as "sociological" (a term of disdain) and "philosophically uninteresting".[92] But for the purpose of understanding

[91] Although Llewellyn and Dworkin both emphasize the limits of "strong discretion", it is to a large extent for different reasons. The extent and significance of the practical implications of their differences are contestable. For example, they appear to disagree about whether hard cases "have one right answer", but that depends on how Dworkin's thesis is interpreted; see Neil MacCormick, *Rhetoric and the Rule of Law* (Oxford: Oxford University Press, 2005), pp. 276–80. An illuminating way to explore their similarities and differences on discretion in such cases is to ask: How far does Dworkin's Hercules fit Llewellyn's conception of a Grand Style judge? In light of Dworkin's latest work, it is clear that they differ significantly on issues of meta-ethics. Ronald Dworkin, *Justice for Hedgehogs* (Cambridge, MA: Belknap Press, 2011) is a powerful argument for objectivity in ethics. Llewellyn's position on these issues wavered from time to time, but he is usually interpreted as a moderate subjectivist (see KLRM, pp. 185–7, which may too readily label him an "ethical relativist"). Of course, Llewellyn made no claims to be a moral philosopher. Comparison of Llewellyn and Dworkin's views on adjudication in hard cases/appellate cases worth appealing raises complex issues that require further exploration.

[92] E.g., "The sociological question has neither of much practical nor much philosophical interest. The doctrinal question, on the contrary, is a question both

law, the question should surely be: "What questions are jurisprudentially interesting?"[93]

A third work in which I build on and interpret Llewellyn needs a brief mention. My book, *General Jurisprudence: Understanding Law from a Global Perspective* (2009) (GJP), explores the implications of so-called globalization for the discipline of law and for jurisprudence as its theoretical, or more abstract, part. Globalization only became part of the agenda of our discipline in the 1990s, more than thirty years after Llewellyn's death. However, I have found the law-jobs theory and his conception of realism meet some of the challenges of globalization better than the great bulk of our heritage of legal theorizing, which to an extraordinary extent has been rooted in the sovereign state and municipal law and societies as closed units.[94] In chapter 4 of *General Jurisprudence* I try to refine the law-jobs theory as the basis for constructing a plausible total picture of law as institutionalized normative ordering in the world as a whole.[95] This requires further elucidation of some concepts – such as group, institution, social practice, system, and function – and a defense of Llewellyn's basic ideas against standard criticisms of "functionalism".[96] The aim is to construct a conceptual framework that can accommodate nonstate law, legal pluralism, and various levels of ordering transnational, supranational, international, and sub-national relations, and that is reasonably inclusive without extending to all social institutions. My thesis involves a "thin functionalist" interpretation of the law-jobs theory. I have also formulated a flexible definition of "legal" for the limited purpose of indicating how one might construct a map or total picture of legal phenomena from a global perspective.

---

of enormous practical and considerable philosophical significance." Dworkin (2006) at pp. 97–8. See further GJP, pp. 25–30 and F. Schauer, "Institutions and the Concept of Law: A Reply to Ronald Dworkin (with some help from Neil MacCormick)" in Macksymilian Del Mar and Zenon Bankowski (eds.) *Law as Institutional Normative Order* (Farnham: Ashgate, 2009), ch.3.

[93] See further below, at pp. 442–3.

[94] On Neil MacCormick as an important exception see below p. 442.

[95] On "total pictures" and contextual thinking ("see it whole") see GJB, pp. 140–2, LIC, pp. 298–9, and GLT, pp. 136–45.

[96] GJP, ch. 4. See also ch. 15 ("Surface law") on "the gap" between "law in books" and "law in action".

The original stimulus for the law-jobs theory was the challenge of finding out about "the law-ways" of the Plains Indians, perceived to be reluctant or unable to articulate their ideas in terms of general rules or norms.[97] The solution was to enquire how the law jobs got done in any group through the study of particular cases. I have normally interpreted the main value of the law-jobs theory as heuristic in that it provides a set of questions that one can ask about the social practices of any group through analyzing actual cases.[98] Most commentators have ignored this heuristic aspect and have dismissed the theory as an example of outdated functionalism.[99] Chapter 4 of *General Jurisprudence* sets out a defense in terms of "thin functionalism", whilst following Llewellyn in refusing to provide a general definition of law outside a specific context. I hope that my approach in this chapter is one of which Llewellyn would have approved.[100]

(ii) Interpretations of KNL and of Realism generally since 1971   The most significant development in our understanding of Realism

---

[97]   KLRM, pp. 154–5.

[98]   For examples of the heuristic use of the law-jobs theory see GJB, pp. 164–7, 193.

[99]   See below pp. 433–4.

[100]   Others of my publications which go beyond KLRM in interpreting Llewellyn and R/realism include (a) *General Jurisprudence* (GJP, *op. cit.*) ch. 4 (law jobs and defining law) and ch 10 (surface law).) (b) "The Law in Context Movement" in P. Cane and J. Conaghan (eds) *The New Oxford Companion to Law* (Oxford: Oxford University Press, 2008) 680–2; (c) Review of Natalie Hull, *Roscoe Pound and Karl Llewellyn*, 115 LQR 152–60 (1999); (d) Review of *The Case Law System in America*, 100 *Yale Law Jo* 1093-1102 (1991); (e) "Alternative to what? Theories of Litigation and Dispute-Settlement in Anglo-American Jurisprudence: Some Neglected Classics", 56 M.L.R. 381 (1993); (f) "Law and Social Science: The Method of Detail", *New Society*, June 27, 1974; (g) "Law and Anthropology: A case-study in Interdisciplinary collaboration", 7 *Law & Society Rev*, 561 (1973), reprinted in R. Luckham (ed.) *Law and Social Enquiry: Case studies of Research* (Scandinavian Institute of African Studies ICLD [1981]); (h) "Alan Swan: The Chicago Connection" 64 University of Miami Law Review 9–14 (2009); (i) Entries on C K Allen (6–7); W. W. Cook (125); John Dickinson (149–50); Jerome Frank (190–3); Karl Llewellyn (319–22); J. H. Wigmore (531–5); Samuel Williston (543–4) and Hessel Yntema (554–5) in *Biographical Dictionary of the Common Law*, ed. A. W. B. Simpson (London, Butterworth 1983); (j) "Normative and Legal Pluralism" (Bernstein Lecture, 2009) 20 Duke Jo of Comparative and International Law Journal pp.473–517. (2011).

since 1971 has been the growth of interest in legal biography and intellectual history.[101] In particular, research by Purcell, Schlegel, Kalman, Hull, Duxbury, Horwitz, and others has broadened and deepened our understanding of American legal history in the first half of the twentieth century. The nearest approach to a full biography of Llewellyn is Natalie Hull's excellent book, *Roscoe Pound and Karl Llewellyn*.[102] This draws on a wide range of archival sources and produces some new information about Llewellyn, including the fact that he was the subject of a full-fledged security

[101] More than a dozen books published since 1973 deal extensively with American Realism and to a lesser extent with Karl Llewellyn. These include, in chronological order: Edward A. Purcell (1973) *The Crisis of Democratic Theory: Scientific Naturalism and the Problem of Value* (Lexington: University of Kentucky Press); G Edward White, *Patterns of American Legal Thought* (Indianapolis: Bobbs-Merrill, 1978); Robert S. Summers (1982) *Instrumentalism and American Legal Theory* (Ithaca: Cornell University Press,); Laura Kalman, (1986) *Legal Realism at Yale 1927–1960* (Chapel Hill: University of North Carolina Press); Morton J. Horwitz (1992) *The Transformation of American Law 1870-1960: The Crisis of Legal Orthodoxy* (New York: Oxford University Press); Ulrich Drobnig and Manfred Rehbinder (eds.) (1994) *Rechtsrealismus, multikultirelle Gesellschaft und Handelsrecht: Karl Llewellyn und seine Bedeutung heute* (Berlin: Duncker and Humblot); John Henry Schlegel (1995) *American Legal Realism and Empirical Social Science* (Chapel Hill: University of North Carolina Press); Neil Duxbury (1995) *Patterns of American Jurisprudence* (Oxford: Clarendon Press); N. E. H. Hull (1997) *Roscoe Pound and Karl Llewellyn: Searching for an American Jurisprudence* (Chicago: University of Chicago Press); George W. Leibman (2005) *The Common Law Tradition: A Collective Portrait of Five Legal Scholars* (New Brunswick: Transaction Publishers); Paul Maharg (2007) *Transforming Legal Education: Learning and Teaching the Law in the Early Twenty-first Century* (Farnham: Ashgate); Wouter De Been (2008) *Legal Realism Regained: Saving Realism from Critical Acclaim* (Stanford: Stanford University Press); Brian Z. Tamanaha (2010) *Beyond the Formalist-Realist Divide: The Role of Politics in Judging* (Princeton: Princeton University Press). Most of these have good bibliographies through which the extensive periodical literature can be traced. The postscript to the 1985 reissue of KLRM lists the main periodical literature between 1971 and 1985. In addition there have been brief entries in biographical dictionaries (e.g., Roger K. Newman (ed.) (2009) *The Yale Biographical Dictionary of American Law* (New Haven: Yale University Press); and A. W. Brian Simpson (1984) *Biographical Dictionary of the Common Law* (London: Butterworth); and the growing number of legal encyclopedias and companions, to say nothing of house histories of particular law schools. There have also been doctoral theses by scholars in Continental Europe, including Francois Michaut, Wouter de Been, and Felix Sanchez Dias.

[102] N. E. H. Hull, *Roscoe Pound and Karl Llewellyn: Searching for an American Jurisprudence* (Chicago: University of Chicago Press, 1997), reviewed by the author in 115 LQR 152 (1998).

investigation by the FBI in the early 1950s. Hull places more emphasis than I do on Karl's "poetic side"[103] and suggests that he was politically more active, more courageous, and less ambivalent than I may have suggested in KLRM. She treats both Pound and Llewellyn as "bricoleurs" who drew eclectically on a variety of intellectual streams in order to construct a form of jurisprudence that was quintessentially American. I think that both Pound and Llewellyn were more cosmopolitan and their ideas are of wider geographical significance than she suggests. Whether Llewellyn's "whole view" can be interpreted as being more coherent than an eclectic patchwork quilt is an issue that I consider later. However, we agree that he is at least as interesting for particular insights as for any general theory that can be attributed to him. Hull's book is well worth reading, but it does not claim to be a rounded biography. Rather it focuses on the relationship and underlying similarities between Pound and Llewellyn, despite their apparent disagreements.

More recently, Robert Whitman has published a series of interesting, mainly co-authored, papers that deal with particular aspects of Llewellyn's life and concerns.[104] The five papers supplement KLRM

---

[103] Hull charges me with underestimating the significance of Llewellyn's poetry: she acknowledges that I emphasize Llewellyn's poetic side and agrees about the quality of his verse, but suggests that Llewellyn took himself more seriously as a poet than I allowed. The question of quality is a matter of opinion, but if I were to revisit his whole ouevre, I doubt that I would change my view that "no great talents await discovery" (KLRM, p. 119). I would quibble about characterizing as "poems" the UCC or some of his introspective musings, but if her main point is that Llewellyn sometimes used poetry as a medium to express his inner concerns and feelings in language that ordinary prose could not capture, I do not disagree. How far his poems throw otherwise inaccessible light on his juristic ideas is more debatable. (cf. Murray, Whitman, and P. Schirrer [1997] *op. cit.*).

[104] (i) Robert Whitman, "Soia Mentschikoff and Karl Llewellyn: Moving Together to the University of Chicago Law School", 24 Connecticut L. Rev. 1119 (1992); (ii) Dom Calabrese, Peggy Pschirrer, and Robert Whitman, "Karl Llewellyn's Letters to Emma Corstvet Llewellyn from the Fall meeting of the National Conference of Commissioners on Uniform State Laws", 27 Connecticut L. Rev. 523 (1995); (iii) Henry F. Murray, Peggy M. Pschirrer, and Robert Whitman, "The Poetic Imagination of Karl Llewellyn", 29 U. Toledo L. Rev. 27 (1997); (iv) James J. Connolly, Peggy Pschirrer, and Robert Whitman, "Alchoholism and Angst in the Life and Work of Karl Llewellyn", 24 Ohio N. U. L.Rev. 43 (1998); (v) Peter Dinunzio, Elinor Kim, and Robert Whitman, "Karl N. Llewellyn: How Icelandic Saga Literature Influenced the Scholarship and Life of an American Legal Realist", 39 Connecticut L. Rev. 1923 (2007).

in a number of ways. The first in time deals with Karl's letters to his wife, Emma Corstvet, during a meeting of the National Conference of Commissioners on Uniform State Laws in 1941. As an informal snapshot of Llewellyn's view of the process and the atmosphere of the meetings it adds color to the more staid accounts of the drafting process. The second gives details of the circumstances of the Llewellyns' move to Chicago and confirms the judgement that this change rejuvenated him after a period of turmoil and crisis in the last years at Columbia. The third explores in depth Llewellyn's "poetic" side and follows Hull in suggesting that I was too dismissive of his poetry. I find little to disagree with here about Llewellyn's personality, but I stick by my assessment of his talent as a poet. The fourth, and the most substantial, deals in great detail with Llewellyn's alcoholism and other personal problems, largely on the basis of letters from Karl to Emma in the last years of their fraught marriage. The fifth is a detailed analysis of Llewellyn's fascination with Icelandic sagas. I did not take this very seriously and barely touched on it in KLRM. I can recommend the article and leave the readers to form their own opinions as to whether Whitman's emphasis on this aspect of Llewellyn's thought is well judged.

Some of these articles are based on the papers of Emma Corstvet Llewellyn to which I did not have access. In addition to producing many new facts, Whitman has probed intimate details of Llewellyn's private life in order better 'to understand Llewellyn and his times, but more importantly to understand the progression of his thought'.[105] This raises issues about the relationship between intimate biography, academic life and juristic ideas that have been debated in relation to Nicola Lacey's brilliant biography of Herbert Hart.[106] It is strange to find my two most influential teachers the objects of this kind of treatment. Juxtaposed, the two accounts reveal unexpected similarities between Hart and Llewellyn: both suffered from inner turmoil, self-doubt, depression, and concerns about their sexuality (though of different kinds); both characterized themselves as "outsiders"; both were skeptical about objectivity in morals, but had doubts about their skepticism; there is even some

---

[105]   Whitman et al. (1998), at p. 113.

[106]   Lacey (2004), *op. cit.*, n.9, discussed in Twining, "Schauer on Hart", 119 Harvard Law Review Forum 105–12 (2006).

similarity in their being subjected to gruesome forms of "therapy" for their problems; both authors suggest that inner turmoil contributed to creativity. But, of course, Hart and Llewellyn had very different backgrounds, intellectual milieux, styles, and conceptions of jurisprudence. Whitman justifies his use of intimate personal detail to illuminate "the progression of [Llewellyn's] thought" and different phases of his career. Lacey is a feminist who rejects the private/public distinction and "who treats jurisprudence as a form of social practice in which the personal and the professional are seamlessly linked".[107] Some commentators have objected to such revelations as being an unseemly invasion of privacy, demeaning to the subjects, and largely irrelevant to their ideas. I have found reading Lacey and Whitman's revelations about people with whom I have had close, but not intimate, relations both distressing and illuminating. Neither author can be accused of unseemly prurience, but the same cannot be said of all readers and commentators. In Lacey's case I think that these details help to explain Hart's career and trajectory (his obsession with Dworkin, for example). They explain some aspects of his thought, such as his disdain for sociology and his deference to Oxford philosophers as a reference group, but it throws less light on the rule of recognition, the internal point of view, and the distinction between primary and secondary rules. In respect of Llewellyn, Whitman's account provides a plausible explanation of why Llewellyn devoted so much time to the Cheyennes and the Pueblos; it suggests that some of his most important theoretical writings were produced at times of personal crisis, and explains some of his career decisions, including the move to Chicago. The issues are too complex to pursue here and, since Whitman plans to turn these articles into a book, this is work in progress and it would be premature to comment on it in detail.

Whitman's articles and interpretations supplement KLRM. On many points we agree, but where we differ, the question whether they substantially challenge my interpretations of forty years ago is less clear. What is clear is that they add significantly to the literature, but they will not be to everyone's taste. It is also clear that, like Hull's, Whitman's contribution falls short of a rounded biography that sets Llewellyn's writings and other contributions in the con-

---

[107] Samantha Besson, "Deconstructing Hart" (review of Lacey) 6 German L. Jo. 1093 (2005) citing Lacey (25).

text of a fuller account of his life and times than KLRM attempted. There is still room for such a work.

Interpretations of Realism in general and Llewellyn continue to appear.[108] Here I shall comment on two attempts to construct a solid philosophical underpinning for American Legal Realism, whose main proponents did not claim to be philosophers. Some commentators have criticized KLRM for not setting out Llewellyn's system or general theory as a coherent whole. In the past, my standard answer has been that Llewellyn was not a systematic thinker – one should read him more for particular insights and arguments – and that my aim in KLRM was to present each of his works in the context of his immediate concerns and general intellectual development. As a guide to specific works, this approach was, I think, justified. But Llewellyn himself had planned a final work which promised to be a synthesis of his whole view. So it is reasonable to ask: Can we not reconstruct what he had in mind?

Here it is important to distinguish between biography, intellectual history, interpreting actual texts, and "rational reconstruction" of a thinker's ideas in terms of what he or she could, might, or should have said – that is moving beyond charitable reading to making a thinker's theory or text "the best it can be".[109] This distinction is illustrated by two interesting attempts at rational reconstruction of Legal Realism as a coherent and defensible position or theory. First, Robert Summers' *Instrumentalism and American Legal Theory* aims to reconstruct "a meaningful and distinctive theory of law and its use" from general tendencies in American legal thought between 1890 and 1940.[110] The author focused on texts from Hol-

---

[108]   Of the extensive shorter literature I would single out Hanoch Dagan's "The Realist Conception of Law" 57 University of Toronto L. Jo. 607 (2007) and Frederick Schauer's Introduction to Llewellyn's *Theory of Rules* (2011, *op. cit.*) as being of particular interest.

[109]   Paraphrasing Ronald Dworkin, *Law's Empire* (London: Fontana, 1986), ch. 2. cf. 'By "rational reconstruction" is meant the activity of explaining fragmentary and potentially conflicting data by reference to theoretical objects in the light of which the data is seen as relatively coherent, because presented as part of a complex, well-ordered whole.' Neil MacCormick and Robert Summers (eds.) *Interpreting Statutes – A Comparative Study* (Aldershot: Ashgate, 1991) at p. 19.

[110]   Robert S. Summers, *Instrumentalism and American Legal Theory* (Ithaca, NY: Cornell University Press, 1982). There are excellent, generally favorable, reviews by Willard Hurst (82 Michigan L. Rev. 852 (1984), and Roger Brownsword (48 Modern L. Rev. 116 (1985)).

mes, Dewey, and Pound as well as leading Realists and presented a model of "pragmatic instrumentalism" as a distinct fourth (American) tradition that sits alongside analytical positivism, natural law, and historical jurisprudence. Rather than defend it as a fully worked out view, he suggested that it had yet to fulfill its promise – there is "important unfinished business".[111] Summers was quite fair to the texts, but openly went beyond them. I have some difficulty understanding what is the precise relationship between his ideal type and the original texts and their authors. This is not history, but neither is it Summers' own theory. So it is unclear what status this reconstruction has. Summers' book contains much interesting material, but in respect of the Realists he falls into the trap of looking for shared ideas and leaving out the most interesting contributions of individuals, such as Frank on fact finding and Llewellyn's law jobs.[112]

A different kind of philosophical reconstruction is offered by Brian Leiter in *Naturalizing Jurisprudence*.[113] One of Leiter's critics, Michael Moore, describes the project as follows:

Utilizing his considerable sophistication, Leiter would reconstruct the Realist programme in light of the contemporary philosophical movements known as naturalism and pragmatism. On Leiter's reconstruction, the Legal Realists had good naturalist and pragmatist grounds for turning jurisprudence into a social science of judicial behavior.[114]

Moore's main objection is historical. As philosophers, "the Realists were simply confused".[115] Leiter's response is:

My interpretation is, after all, a reconstruction 'it puts back together' in philosophical terms the largely unphilosophical arguments and positions of the American Legal Realists. The philosophy is mine, the basic arguments and ideas are theirs.[116]

[111] Summers (1982) at pp. 61, 223, 256–8, *et passim.*
[112] For a longer analysis of Summers' book see TAR, n.24 (GJB, pp. 103–4).
[113] Brian Leiter, *Naturalizing Jurisprudence: Essays on American Legal Realism and Naturalism in Legal Philosophy* (New York: Oxford University Press, 2007).
[114] Michael Moore, *Educating Oneself in Public: Critical Essays in Jurisprudence* (Oxford: Oxford University Press, 2000) at pp. 32–3, cited by Leiter at p. 103. See further Michael Steven Green, "Leiter on the Legal Realists", William and Mary Research Paper No 09-98 (Law and Philosophy forthcoming).
[115] *Ibid.,* p. 33.
[116] Leiter at p. 104.

Leiter's work is a welcome attempt to bridge the divide, which has grown to a chasm, between recent analytical legal philosophy concerned with a priori analysis of abstract concepts and empirical legal studies. I share with Leiter the view that there is continuity between analytical and empirical enquiries and it is refreshing to find a philosopher taking the idea of legal realism seriously.[117] I also broadly sympathize with his critique of some tendencies in analytical legal philosophy.[118] However, I do take issue with one aspect of Leiter's approach. He continues the practice of making misleading generalizations about the Realists and of focusing on alleged *shared* ideas, with hardly any reference to the distinctive contributions of individuals.[119] Since Realism "naturalized" is Leiter's theory, he is of course free to restrict it to adjudication on questions of law. But if he had focused on one thinker, for example Llewellyn or Frank or Pound, and attempted a rational reconstruction of their ideas as a whole, he might have articulated a richer, more interesting, and less narrow theoretical position in each case.[120]

---

[117]   The "Naturalist Turn" in philosophy is a morass, involving a wide spectrum of views that cannot be pursued here. I have some doubts about the need for a sophisticated philosophical justification for the proposition that there is and should be an intimate relationship between conceptual elucidation and empirical legal studies. If one looks on concepts pragmatically as thinking tools, as Bentham, Dewey, and Llewellyn all did, it is clear that empirical legal studies need appropriate and usable conceptual tools for interpretation, description, and explanation of legal phenomena. One task for analytical jurisprudence is developing such tools (see GJP, pp. 21–5, 54–6, 445).

[118]   Leiter (2007), ch 6. Leiter sums up the increasingly widespread feeling that aspects of analytical legal philosophy have gotten bogged down in repetitious, unworldly, and possibly trivial debates: 'Now it is curious that this kind of methodology debate is found nowhere else in philosophy, not even in the domains of practical philosophy, of which Perry insists jurisprudence is properly a branch. It is an interesting question – at least sociologically, perhaps philosophically too – why jurisprudence should have been afflicted with this debate, while moral and political philosophers go about their business only bothered – if bothered at all – by the skeptics about intuitions and concepts' (at pp. 164–5). Cf. Andrew Halpin, "The Methodology of Jurisprudence: Thirty Years Off the Point" (2006) 19 Canadian Jo. Law and Jurisprudence 67, and Schauer (2009), *op. cit.*, n.92.

[119]   p. 61.

[120]   A striking example is Leiter's criticism of the seemingly widespread acceptance of "the Frankification" of Realism, meaning Frank's extreme interpretation of "the Core Claim" of Realism (ibid. at pp. 61–3). This refers to the unpredictability of decisions on questions of law; yet no mention is made of Frank's

As noted previously, a great deal has happened in legal theory since Llewellyn's death, especially in the 1960s and 1970s. Hart's *The Concept of Law* (1961) was published only a few months before Llewellyn died. Some movements became salient after 1962. We can only speculate about how he would have reacted to critical legal studies, feminist jurisprudence, critical race theory, poststructuralism, autopoiesis, various forms of postmodernism, Continental European "critical theory", and recent long-running debates between positivists and anti-positivists. Conversely, although there have been some comments on aspects of Llewellyn's work from these perspectives,[121] on the whole he has been ignored or treated as marginal by devotees of these trends or movements.

There are two major exceptions to this pattern: sociology of law and law and economics. First, Llewellyn has been seen as a significant pioneer in sociology and anthropology of law. However, the anthropologists generally treat *The Cheyenne Way* as being merely of historical significance.[122] Sociologists and social theorists have tended to dismiss Llewellyn as a follower of discredited 1930s functionalism.[123] The former judgement seems reasonable, but I have defended Llewellyn's law-jobs theory as being more Mertonian than Parsonian and thus immune from most of the standard criticisms

argument that the main source of uncertainty in litigation relates to fact finding. I used Frank's one interesting idea – that academics should take fact finding seriously – as the jumping-off point for my work on evidence. However, I treat Frank as a thinly disguised idealist and reformer, rather than as a skeptic in any strong sense of the term: see my *Rethinking Evidence* (Cambridge: Cambridge University Press, 2nd edition, 2006), ch. 4. On a possible richer reconstruction of Llewellyn's "Whole view", see below 439–42.

[121] On Horwitz and critical legal studies, see above n.88(iv).

[122] A conference at Bellagio in 1985 marked a watershed in legal anthropology. Several leading scholars acknowledged that in treating small-scale societies as self-contained, timeless units they had neglected broader historical and geographical contexts. (See June Starr and Jane Collier, *History and Power in the Study of Law* (Ithaca: Cornell University Press, 1989). While echoing this criticism, Laura Nader's introduction to a reissue of *The Cheyenne Way* in the *Legal Classics Library* (Delman, NJ: Gryphon, 1992) is generally very sympathetic. See also L. Nader, *Life of the Law: Anthropological Projects* (Berkeley, CA: University of California Press, 2005).

[123] E.g., Alan Hunt, *The Sociological Movement in Law* (London: MacMillan, 1978) 46–53; cf. Roger Cotterrell, *The Sociology of Law: an Introduction* (London: Butterworth, 1992).

of functionalism.[124] There is room for a re-appraisal of Llewellyn's continuing significance in the sociology law (not least in relation to his criticisms of Ehrlich and Weber),[125] his ideas on legal technology or juristic method, and in comparison to the contributions of Neil MacCormick and Philip Selznick.[126] Frederick Schauer's edition of *The Theory of Rules* (2011) also opens up possibilities of reappraisal of Llewellyn's contribution to the general theory of norms.

With respect to law and economics the situation is less clear. From an early stage Llewellyn took an interest in the relationship between law and economics.[127] His first wife was an economist and he was familiar with the work of Commons, Veblen, Robert Hale, and Berle and Means, for example. His work on commercial law and business practice had an important economic dimension. Edward Levi, in an obituary, credited him with having done pioneering work in the relationship between law and economics.[128] However, economic analysis was never a central concern.

Although law and economics as a discernible movement did not come into prominence until later, the foundations had already been laid at the University of Chicago by the time Llewellyn arrived in 1951. The Chicago School of Economics, spearheaded by Milton Friedman, was in full flow; Aaron Director, strongly supported by Dean Edward Levi, had begun teaching in the law school and is reputed to have converted Levi to his narrow, technocratic version of economic analysis of law – a pure form of classical free market theory. By the time I joined as a student in 1957, Director's "General The-

---

[124]   The fullest defense is in GJP, ch 4.

[125]   Llewellyn made some sharp criticisms of Ehrlich in *Recht, Rechtsleben und Gesellschaft, op. cit.*, n.50, in respect of the concepts of "custom" and living law"; he was generally more sympathetic to Weber (some of whose work he began to translate in the 1930s [K. L. P. B. II. 44]). A review copy of Max Rheinstein's edition (with Edward Shils) of *Law in Economy and Society* (Cambridge, MA: Harvard University Press, 1954) was found among Soia Mentschikoff's papers. The first part contained extensive marginalia by Llewellyn, some seemingly critical. The book is now deposited with the Llewellyn papers in Chicago. There is scope for a detailed exploration of the differences and affinities between Llewellyn and Weber.

[126]   See Martin Krygier, *Ideals in the World: The Thought of Philip Selznick* (Stanford University Press, forthcoming). On MacCormick see below p. 442.

[127]   See especially Llewellyn, "The Effect of Legal Institutions Upon Economics" 15 American Economic Review 665–83 (1925).

[128]   11 U. Chi. L. School Record 29 (1962), cited KLRM, p. 113.

ory of Price" was a prerequisite for antitrust and cognate courses.[129] Llewellyn seems to have been ambivalent, perhaps even unenthusiastic, about this development.[130] It was a very different kind of economics from that of his youth and, strikingly, the leading Chicago pioneers are not cited in his later writings: for example, the indexes of *The Common Law Tradition* and *Jurisprudence: Realism in Theory and Practice* contain no entry for Director, Friedman, Coase, or Stigler. Conversely, many of the leaders of law and economics seem not to have been very interested in Llewellyn.[131] Posner and Duxbury are surely correct that law and economics did not grow out of Realism.[132] I have not tried to canvass the literature, but it would hardly be surprising if Llewellyn is largely marginal to today's concerns, except where commercial law and economic analysis clearly overlap.[133]

Developments in the UCC and commercial law

I am not a specialist in commercial law. I have not tried to follow the many developments in the story of the UCC over the last forty

[129] See above n.6.

[130] Neil Duxbury, in his useful account of the beginnings of the movement in Chicago, suggests that Llewellyn "disapproved" of this type of legal-economic analysis. This may well have been the case, but I have no evidence of it. Neil Duxbury, *Patterns of American Jurisprudence* (Oxford: Oxford University Press, 1995), ch 5 at p. 343. Later Soia Mentschikoff and Henry Manne, a powerful leader in the movement, failed to get on in Miami and Manne removed his institute to George Mason University – but that could have been due more to a clash of personalities or faculty politics than an ideological falling out.

[131] See however, Douglas Baird, "Llewellyn's Heirs" 62 Louisiana L. Rev. 1287 (2002): 'Our own generation's giants of commercial law – scholars such as Lisa Bernstein, Robert Scott, and Alan Schwarz – are at once Llewellyn's critics and his true heirs. In finding fault with Llewellyn, they too often fail to understand that they stand on his shoulders'. at p. 1288. Cf. Kipling: *'And His Own Disciple Shall wound him worst of all.'* Kipling, *op. cit.*, n.56, last stanza (original italics). Some economic analysis of the UCC can be interpreted as involving implicit criticism of Llewellyn's ideas on the Code.

[132] See above n.101.

[133] See the works cited in the next section. A continuing link between legal anthropology and economic analysis is the work of Robert Ellickson, see for example his *Order Without Law: How Neighbours Settle Disputes* (Cambridge MA: Harvard University Press) and "Law and Economics Discovers Social Norms", 27 Jo. Legal Studies 531 (1998).

years. This section only suggests a way into the literature. For the non-specialist a good starting-point is Douglas Litowitz, *Perspectives on the Uniform Commercial Code.*[134] This is a helpful anthology of short readings covering many topics, including the drafting, enactment, methodology, and interpretation of the UCC, Llewellyn's contribution, the politics of amendment and federalization, recent scholarship, and assessments of the Code. This is useful and reasonably up to date as general background. There are collections of more substantial essays edited by Clayton P. Gillette and Jody S. Kraus and Steven Walt.[135] For reference, there are some substantial treatises,[136] numerous hornbooks and course books, practitioner services, and websites.[137]

Apart from specialized journals,[138] there is a massive, scattered, proliferating periodical literature. Highlights of the academic commentaries are indicated in the anthologies mentioned earlier. My impression, as a non-expert, is that theoretical, historical, and empirical writings on the UCC are rather fragmented.[139] There is

[134] Douglas E. Litowitz, *Perspectives on the Uniform Commercial Code* (Durham, NC: Carolina Academic Press, 2nd edition, 2007)

[135] Clayton P. Gillette (ed.) *The Creation and Interpretation of Commercial Law* (Aldershot: Ashgate, 2003); Jody S. Kraus and Steven D. Walt (eds.), *The Jurisprudential Foundations of Corporate and Commercial Law* (New York: Cambridge University Press, 2000); see also the excellent Symposium, *Essays in Honor of William D. Hawkland: Unifying Commercial Law in the 20th Century: Understanding the Impulses and Assessing the Effort* 62 Louisiana L. Rev. No. 4 (2002).

[136] E.g., Robert S. Summers and James J. White, *Uniform Commercial Code* (St. Paul, MN: West, 6th edition, v. 4, 2010) and William D. Hawkland, *Uniform Commercial Code Series* (looseleaf) Eilmette, IL: Callaghan (regularly updated).

[137] The National Conference of Commissioners on Uniform State Laws has two websites that contain a mass of both current and historical material (http://www.nccusl.org/ and http://www.law.upenn.edu/bll/ulc/ulc/htm).

[138] E.g., *Journal of Law and Commerce* and *the Uniform Commercial Code Law Journal.*

[139] See, however, Zipporah Wiseman, "The Limits of Vision: Karl Llewellyn and the Merchant Rules 100 Harvard L. rev. 465 (1987); Robert Whitman, "Karl Llewellyn's Letters to Emma Corstvet Llewellyn from the Fall 1941 Meeting of the National Conference of Commissioners on Uniform State Laws", 27 Connecticut L. Rev 523 (1995); Allen R. Kamp, "Uptown Act: A History of the Uniform Commercial Code: 1940–49", S.M.U.L.Rev. 275 (1998) and "Downtown Code Code: A History of the Uniform Commercial Code 1949–54" 49 Buffalo L. Rev. 359 (2001); and *Symposium, Origins and Evolution: Drafters Reflect Upon the Uniform Commercial Code*, 43 Ohio State L.Jo. 535 (1982). See also, R. Speidel, "The New Spirit of Contract", 2 Jo. L. and Commerce 193 (1982).

some discussion of the relationship between Llewellyn's jurisprudence and the Code (especially article 2),[140] the extent to which he compromised during the drafting process,[141] and whether his influence survives.[142] Based mainly on her detailed empirical research in several industries Lisa Bernstein published a series of forceful articles criticizing Llewellyn's assumptions about the desirability and feasibility of making the Code responsive to merchant practices and expectations[143] and describing how diamond merchants in New York and other merchant groups and trade associations have developed their own sets of rules and institutions that they consider superior to the state legal system.[144] Without necessarily mentioning Llewellyn, economic analysis of law has been used to explore whether open-ended standards or "bright line rules" are preferable.[145] Robert Scott and others have shown convincingly

[140]   See Wiseman (1987) and Allen R. Kamp (1998) and 2001, *op. cit.*, n.139, the extracts in Litowitz, *op. cit*; John D. Wladis, "UCC section 2-207: The Drafting History", 49 Business Lawyer 1029 (1994) (drawing extensively on several archives); and Alan Schwartz, "Karl Llewellyn and the Origins of Contract Theory", in Kraus and Walt, *op. cit.* (2000). Much discussed is Richard Danzig, "A Comment on the Jurisprudence of the Uniform Commercial Code" 27 Stanford L. Rev. 621 (1975) (arguing that the UCC gives too much power to judges), opposed briefly but forcefully by Grant Gilmore, in *The Ages of American Law* (New Haven: Yale University Press, 1977). See further Litowitz, *op. cit.*, ch.4.

[141]   E.g., Wiseman (1987) *op. cit.*

[142]   Gregory E. Maggs, "Karl Llewellyn's Fading Imprint on the Jurisprudence of the Uniform Commercial Code", 71 U. Colorado L. Rev. 541 (2000).

[143]   Lisa Bernstein, "Opting out of the Legal System: Extralegal Contractual Relations in the Diamond Industry", 21 Jo. Legal Studies (1992); "Merchant Law in a Merchant Court: Rethinking the Code's Search for Immanent Business Norms"' 144 U. Pa L. Rev 1765 (1996); "The Questionable Empirical Basis of Article 2's Incorporation Strategy: A Preliminary Study" 66 U. Chicago L. Rev. 710 (1999); "Private Commercial Law in the Cotton Industry: Creating Co-operation Through Rules, Norms and Institutions", 99 Michigan L. Rev. 1724 (2001). Bernstein's work seems to me to be very interesting, but I do not have the expertise to assess to what extent, and in what respects, her findings undermine the working assumptions of the UCC. Commercial lawyers are split on whether we are better off with the UCC, for all its faults, than without it, See Litowitz, *op. cit.*, ch. 10.

[144]   Bernstein, *op. cit.*, last note.

[145]   E.g., Robert E. Scott, "The Case for Formalism in Relational Contract", 94 Northwestern L. Rev. 847 (2000); cf. Geoffrey P. Miller, "Bargaining on the Red-Eye: New Light on Contract Theory" (May 6, 2008). NYU Law and Economics Research Paper No. 08-21. Available at SSRN: http://ssrn.com/abstract=1129805.

that the key to Llewellyn's basic ideas about sales is to be found
in his writings on sales in the 1930s rather than his later jurisprudence.[146] In retrospect, I regret that I did not do justice to the sales
articles in KLRM.

There have been many criticisms of Llewellyn's impressionistic and anecdotal approach to facts. Empirical research has challenged some working assumptions of the UCC, but I have not
found any convincing suggestions about how future commercial
legislation can as a practical matter be based on systematic and rigorous empirical research or the extent to which there is a middle
ground of trying to rely on the best available data and experience,
when more rigorous research is not feasible.[147] We have not got very
far in determining what empirical information is relevant, desirable, and feasible in law making. There is still a tendency to assume
an all-or-nothing view – criticizing intuition, horse sense, practical experience, and expert opinion. In the era of evidence-based
medicine and evidence-based policy – which sometimes exhibit
tendencies to inappropriate scientism – perhaps the time is ripe
to re-examine Llewellyn's ideas of "horse sense" and his dictum
"knowledge does not have to be scientific to be useful and important"[148] – especially in the context of law making and assessing the
impact of legislation.

Part C Unfinished agenda
We have seen that since Llewellyn's death almost fifty years ago several of his works have been made more accessible, including some
published for the first time. Commentaries on Llewellyn in particular and on Legal Realism continue and there is a steady stream of
writing about the Uniform Commercial Code. All of these suggest
that interest in Llewellyn is still alive.

We have also seen that there is some unfinished business. Karl
Llewellyn and Soia Mentschikoff both merit a substantial personal
biography. There is a need for more detailed history of the drafting, politics, and subsequent life of the Uniform Commercial Code

---

[146]   Robert E. Scott, "The Rise and Fall of Article 2", 62 Louisiana L. Rev. 1009
(2002) esp. at 1014–29.

[147]   KLRM, pp. 313–21.

[148]   Llewellyn, "The Theory of Legal 'Science'", 20 N. Carolina L. Rev 1 (1941) at
p. 22. This article is still well worth reading.

and, more broadly, of commercial law in America in the twentieth century. Fifty years on there is still plenty of scope for fresh interpretations of and perspectives on Llewellyn and Realism.

However, it is not surprising that many people may think that as a thinker and a person, Karl Llewellyn is mainly or merely of historical interest. His influence on commercial law is probably waning. He does seem to have faded from many jurisprudence courses and he has not been in the centre of the most salient Anglo-American debates. How significant or relevant he is today is a largely a matter of individual judgement, depending on one's concerns and interests. However, I shall conclude by making the case for treating Llewellyn's unfinished work as of particular contemporary importance.

In KLRM, I reported that at the time of his unexpected death Llewellyn was planning a series of lectures in Germany which would be a vehicle for a restatement and summation of his "Whole View". I devoted chapter 9 to his course materials on *Law in our Society* and included some extracts in an appendix. I expressed the hope that someone else would take up the challenge of producing a complete edition of this work.[149] It is undoubtedly the most important of Llewellyn's surviving unpublished manuscripts and, if well edited, it might come to be seen as his most important work. Rescuing and constructing an authentic text of this work presents a formidable challenge. There are several versions of the course materials. They are cryptic, allusive, and incomplete, requiring extensive annotation. There are also transcripts of recordings of numerous classes given in this and related courses; some untranscribed tapes may be rescuable; and there are student essays and notes which bear on the manuscript.[150] Of course, Llewellyn's published writings also contain clues to what he might have meant, and they can be used to complement and supplement the core text in various ways. Reconstructing this as a definitive text will be as difficult as doing the same for some of Bentham's unpublished works.

---

[149] KLRM, pp. 171–2.

[150] The *Guide* to the Karl Llewellyn Papers lists over 100 transcripts headed "Jurisprudence" (starting at Harvard in 1948–9) and a number of other potentially relevant items. I have retained my student notes on Llewellyn's course, the essays I wrote for him (with his extensive comments), and some preliminary material relating to editing *Law in Our Society*.

Producing an accurate, well-furnished text of *Law in our Society* would be an invaluable contribution. There is a further challenge. There is a different job of reconstruction that might be done. Earlier I raised the question whether Llewellyn's "Whole view" rather than just his "realism" could be subject to rational reconstruction in the mode of Summers or Leiter.[151] My criticism of Leiter was not intended as a rejection of rational reconstruction. For a well-qualified philosopher to construct a sound philosophical foundation and justification for a position that has been previously expressed in less abstract terms can be a valuable exercise. Leiter's reconstruction of a philosophical basis of "the Core Claim" of Realism is quite plausible, if controversial: 'The Core Claim of Legal Realism consists of the following descriptive thesis about judicial decision-making: *judges respond primarily to the stimulus of facts.* Put less formally – but also somewhat less accurately – the Core Claim of Realism is that judges reach decisions based on what they think would be fair on the facts of the case, rather than on the applicable rules of law.'[152]

This only thinly describes what individual Realists in fact said; rather it gives an interpretation of what they should have said in order to ground their shared views in a tenable philosophical position. My objection is that Leiter's interpretation of "the Core Claim" fails to capture what is most interesting, original, or significant about Llewellyn's contributions to understanding law. Even in respect of American appellate adjudication the formulation "that judges respond primarily to the stimulus of facts" reduces a complex way of looking at things to a single proposition. Leiter's interpretation of the "Core Claim" fits Llewellyn, but in a simplified way. More important is the point that Llewellyn's views on American appellate adjudication are only one aspect of Llewellyn's idea of realism. This in turn is only one component of his whole view, which contains many other interesting theories, sub-theories and ideas.[153] A philosophical reconstruction of this whole view would cover all or nearly all of it in a coherent fashion,[154] spell out the connections

---

[151] Above pp. 430–2.

[152] Leiter (2007), *op. cit.*, pp. 21–2.

[153] KLRM, ch. 9.

[154] On the scope of "the whole view" see KLRM, p 171. On whether Llewellyn was merely an eclectic "bricoleur" see above 427.

between the parts, identify internal tensions and inconsistencies, and link the underlying assumptions to recognizable philosophical position or positions. The task, in short, would be to articulate a philosophically defensible interpretation of Llewellyn's main ideas. Llewellyn was not a philosopher; he worked at lower levels of abstraction and often expressed a personal dislike for abstract philosophizing. There is room for this kind of philosophical reconstruction within jurisprudence, so long as it does not claim imperialistically to be the only route into understanding law and provided it is based on careful reading of the texts. I did not attempt this in KLRM, so there is still a job to be done.

But if Llewellyn is today mainly of historical interest, why bother? Let us pause for a moment to consider our heritage of Anglo-American jurisprudential thought. Nearly all canonical Anglo-American jurists of the twentieth century – Hart, Raz, Dworkin, Rawls, Finnis – and most Europeans have focused on municipal legal systems as the central, in some cases, the only example of real law. Furthermore, their assumptions fit the doctrinal tradition of Western academic law – a focus on what the official or state law says and reasoning about this and not much else.[155] The heritage is unempirical, even for those who treat law as a species of social institution. One way of expressing this gets to the root of Hart's limitations as a jurist: he conceptualized law in terms of social fact, but refused to take social facts seriously. He did not explore in depth the institutional nature of law nor adequately acknowledge that institutions are formed by their political, social, and economic contexts. Rather he focused attention on law as a system of rules (later developed by his successors as "law as reasons for action") and missed an opportunity to build a bridge between analytical jurisprudence and empirical legal studies.[156] In the last twenty years or so the models of legal systems of Hart, his followers, and his main critics are widely perceived to sit uneasily with forms of law or law-like phenomena with which legal scholars and practitioners are increasingly concerned: public international law, regional law, transnational commercial law, religious law, customary law, and various forms of "soft law". The main late

[155] GJP, pp 5–7.
[156] See GJP, pp. 56–60; Nicola Lacey, "Analytical Jurisprudence versus Descriptive Sociology Revisited" 88 Texas L. Rev. 945 (2006); Frederick Schauer, "(Re)taking Hart" 119 Harvard L. Rev. 852 (2006) (Review of Lacey (2004)); William Twining, "Schauer on Hart" 119 Harvard L. Rev. Forum 122 (2006).

twentieth century jurists who provide an alternative model of legal ordering, which is both broader and more empirically sensitive, are Karl Llewellyn and Neil MacCormick.[157] It is not possible here to compare MacCormick and Llewellyn in detail, but both of them conceive of law in terms of institutionalized ordering, and accept ideas of nonstate law and legal pluralism; thus they provide some theoretical framework for viewing and studying legal phenomena in an era of globalization.[158] So far from being of mainly historical interest, Karl Llewellyn's central ideas, especially as incompletely articulated in *Law in our Society*, are more relevant than ever at the start of the twenty-first century.

The mission of an institutionalized discipline is advancing and disseminating knowledge and understanding of its subject matters. The mission of the discipline of law is advancing and communicating knowledge and understanding of legal phenomena. What is at stake here is not the scope and range of these phenomena, but different conceptions of what is involved in understanding them. There are clearly many routes to understanding law. Here, the question is not which is the best, but whether Karl Llewellyn still

[157]   Neil MacCormick's final quartet of books, *Law, State and Practical Reason*, goes beyond rational reconstruction to a synthesis and development of his own "whole view" bringing together his philosophical positions (epistemology, ethics, political morality, and logic) and his more specific contributions (e.g., on sovereignty, nationalism, the rule of law, reasoning and rhetoric, precedent and statutory interpretation) as a coherent whole. MacCormick is the main modern legal philosopher to attempt to bridge the divide between analytical legal philosophy and empirical legal studies. He was familiar with Llewellyn's main writings and, although not uncritical, admired his work, especially the law jobs theory. (see above n.85). Unlike leading sociologists of law, such as Selznick and Cotterell, but like Llewellyn, MacCormick treated law as his primary discipline and a broad, critical understanding of law as his central concern. Above n.47. See further W. Twining, "Neil MacCormick", Procs. of the British Academy (forthcoming, 2012).

[158]   This is not to downplay the significance of other thinkers, including Glenn, Tamanaha, Santos, Sen, and others who have also contributed a great deal to the broadening of our understandings of law. In *Law in our Society* Llewellyn began to develop his own theory of justice, inspired in part by Edmond Cahn and F. R. Bienenfeld (KLRM 186–5). This is much closer in spirit to Amartya Sen's *The Idea of Justice* (Cambridge, MA: Harvard University Press, 2009) than to Rawls' "transcendental idealism". Sen is, of course, a much more sophisticated moral philosopher than Llewellyn. The interesting question here is whether this aspect of Llewellyn's whole view is compatible with the core of Sen's theory.

has a distinctive contribution to make to the enterprise. In order to avoid unnecessary polemics, let me start with might be considered a balanced or middle of the road view of what is involved in understanding law. In an excellent introductory book, John Adams and Roger Brownsword state that in the context of English legal education 'An "understanding" of law is provided primarily by an ability to conceptualize legal phenomena . . . to account for the way in which law operates, and to evaluate its operation.'[159] The key point is that understanding law involves all of these and is incomplete – indeed, potentially misleading – if the focus excludes any of these three ingredients: concepts, values, and social facts. On this simplified view, the central message of realism is that understanding law involves studying both the law in books and the law in action. Llewellyn's whole view, of which realism is just one part, is one example of a rounded conception of understanding law that accommodates multiple perspectives, ethical, analytical, and empirical concerns and specialized enquiries rooted in a flexible conception of law as a social institution.

[159] John H. Adams and Roger Brownsword, *Understanding Law* (London: Fontana Press, 1992). This is an excellent book, which provides a very different model from "Elements" and *The Bramble Bush*. Although written by two committed Kantians, the authors introduce conceptions of law drawn from Hart, Weber, Llewellyn, and neo-Kantianism as alternative conceptions that are all part of "understanding law". As part of this, they distinguish between questions of law and questions about law, between first-order questions (raising matters of description, explanation, evaluation, and conceptualization) and second-order questions "concerning the status of our first-order understanding of law", p. 26.

Notes

INTRODUCTION

1 Max Rheinstein, obituary of Karl Llewellyn in 27 *Rabels Zeitschrift für Auslandisches und Internationales Privatrecht*, 601–5 (1962); cf. Hurst, *The Growth of American Law, passim*, esp. ch. 1 (1950).

  Professor Rheinstein's account has been adopted largely because it represents the perspective of a distinguished legal scholar who was a contemporary of most of the leading realists. It is an interpretation of American legal history from the standpoint of a particular insider, and it reflects, in a general way, the perspectives of the main protagonists in our story. A student of economic development, a political scientist interested in state legislatures, or a black militant could be expected to select quite different matters for emphasis.

2 *Ibid.*

3 Cf. Llewellyn on 'the threat of the available,' *Jurisprudence*, 82–3, discussed below, pp. 246–7.

4 The Litchfield Law School was a famous private law school which was established in 1784 and which for many years, until its demise in 1833, attracted students from all over America. Many successful lawyers and public figures were alumni of the school.

5 On the American Law Institute and the National Conference of Commissioners for Uniform State Laws see, ch. 11.

6 Rheinstein, *op. cit.* (n.1). See generally A. Sutherland, *The Law at Harvard* (1967). The treatises of Williston on Contract and Wigmore on Evidence were particularly influential.

7 Morton G. White, *Social Thought in America: the Revolt Against Formalism* (2nd ed.), Beacon (1957). See also B. Crick, *The American Science of Politics* (1959); Perry Miller, *The Life of the Mind in America* (1965); V. L. Parrington, *Main Currents in American Thought* (1927–30). For further references see J. Stone, *Social Dimensions of Law and Justice*, ch. 1 (1966). Regretfully in this study I have not been able to draw on G. Tarello, *Il Realismo Giuridico Americano* (1962).

8 White, *op. cit.*, 13.

9 *Ibid.*, 14; but Holmes, for example, found much to admire in Bentham and Mill.

10 *Ibid.*, 237.

1 LANGDELL'S HARVARD

1 On Langdell, see especially *The Centennial History of the Harvard Law School* (1918); Sutherland, *The Law at Harvard* (1967); Llewellyn, *Jurisprudence*, 376–9 (1962); Fessenden, 'The Rebirth of the Harvard Law School', 33 *Harv. L. Rev.*, 493 (1920).

2 On American legal education, see especially A. Harno, *Legal Education in the United States* (1953); R. B. Stevens, *Two Cheers for 1870: The American Law School 5 Perspectives in American History*, 405 (1971).

3 On Holmes see below, pp. 15ff; Frank, *Courts on Trial*, ch. xvi (1963 ed.). Frank's first butt was Langdell's colleague Joseph Beale, *Law and the Modern Mind*, ch. VI *et passim* (1930).

4 *A Selection of Cases on the Law of Contracts*, preface, p. viii (1871).

5 *Record of the Commemoration . . . on the Two Hundred and Fiftieth Anniversary of the Founding of Harvard College* (1887).

6 Sutherland, *op. cit.*, 175.

7 *Op. cit.* (n.4 above).

8 That this idea became a firm part of the Harvard tradition is illustrated by an incident involving two of Langdell's followers, Beale and Ames. In 1902 President Harper of the University of Chicago invited the Harvard faculty to assist in the establishment of a law school, *inter alia* by seconding Beale to act as the first dean. As a condition of cooperation Beale and Ames insisted that 'only strictly legal subjects' should be taught by 'a faculty consisting *only* of lawyers'. This went quite contrary to proposals made by Professor Ernst Freund, the great pioneer of administrative law, who was then a professor of political science at Chicago. Eventually a compromise was achieved, and Beale went as dean from 1902–4. Comment, 'Ernst Freund, Pioneer of Administrative Law', 29 *U.Chi.L.Rev.*, 755, 763–70 (1961–2), discussed by Stevens, *op. cit.* (n.2 above).

9 Llewellyn, *op. cit.*, at 377.

10 Cited above, p. 12.

11 Above, p. 11.

12 See below, p. 354.

13 Rheinstein, *op. cit.*, 602.

14 14 *Am.L.Sch.Rev.*, 233 (1880). Cf. Holmes' comment to Pollock on Langdell's casebook: 'A more misspent piece of marvellous ingenuity I never read, yet it is most suggestive and instructive . . . to my mind he represents the powers of darkness. . . . He is all for logic and hates any reference to anything outside of it and his explanations and reconciliations of the cases would have astonished the judges who decided them. But he is a noble old swell, whose knowledge, ability and idealist devotion to his work I revere and love.' as in *Holmes–Pollock Letters*, 17 (1941 ed. Howe). See also Howe, 11, *Justice Oliver Wendell Holmes: The*

Proving Years, 155–9 (1963). Holmes was both an alumnus of Harvard law school in the pre-Langdell era and taught there during the first period of Langdell's deanship (1871–83). He was elevated to the bench of the Massachusetts Supreme Court in 1883, but continued to maintain a close interest in the Harvard Law School.

15 Llewellyn, for instance, published several eulogies of Holmes in which he scarcely mentioned any of his ideas.

16 *The Common Law,* 1 (1881); also 14 *Am.L. Rev.,* 233.

17 One may infer from the context of the quotation that Holmes did not intend to deny any place to logic in the law.

18 *Collected Legal Papers,* 172–3 (1920).

19 *Ibid.,* 194–5.

20 *Ibid.,* 198.

21 *Ibid.,* 197.

22 *Ibid.,* 187.

23 *Ibid.,* 180.

24 *Ibid.,* 171.

25 E.g. H. L. A. Hart, *The Concept of Law,* 55–6 (1961).

26 E.g. *ibid.,* 143.

27 'The Path of the Law', 167.

28 *Ibid.,* 202.

29 E.g. Hart, *op. cit.,* 134–44. Holmes' biographer suggests that 'Holmes in the beginning, at least, was led toward the prediction theory of law by an impulse more critical than philosophical'. When he first emphasised the predictive element in law, in lectures at Harvard in 1872, he was mainly concerned to criticize Austin's command theory, by showing that law looked different from the standpoint of a practitioner advising his clients. Howe, 11, *Justice Oliver Wendell Holmes: The Proving Years,* 75 (1963).

30 This is not to deny a connection between legal philosophy and legal education; indeed, their interaction is too often overlooked: a coherent theory of legal education presupposes some general conceptions about law and some legal theories have been stimulated, at least in part, by puzzlements about problems of legal education. It is doubtful whether a consistent and rounded philosophy of law can be extracted from Holmes' various pronouncements; it seems that the importance Holmes attached to the conception of 'the bad man' and prediction of judicial decisions was closely connected with his desire to persuade law students to identify with private practitioners. As Howe suggests, *op. cit.,* 75–6, he may have been gratified to find that talking of law in terms of prediction had led him to a position compatible with the prevailing philosophy of science, but it is unlikely that philosophical concerns led him to this position.

31 Much of Holmes' attitude to legal education is summed up in a much

quoted dictum: 'I say the business of a law school is not sufficiently described when you merely say that it is to teach law or to make lawyers. It is to teach law in the grand manner, and to make great lawyers.' 'Use of Law Schools', *Speeches*, 30 (1913).

32 For discussions of Gray, see *The Centennial History of the Harvard Law School 1817–1917* (1918); *John Chipman Gray* (1917); L. Fuller, *The Law in Quest of Itself*, 48–55 (1940, Beacon ed. 1966); Cross, *Precedent in English Law*, 152–5 (2nd ed. 1968); Hart, *The Concept of Law*, 137–44 (1961).

33 An impression of Gray's reputation and standing with the legal profession can be gained from a passage in *The Centennial History of the Harvard Law School*. 'Gray eventually became a convert to the case system at the time when Langdell's method was meeting with much opposition among practitioners. He was most valuable in convincing the bar of Boston that there must be something in the new fangled way of doing things or Gray would not have believed in it. The fact that a practical man, not only interested in scholarly things, not only interested in what the law had been or was going to be or ought to be, but also interested in what it was and now happened to be – that such a man believed in methods of teaching and administration that were being adopted, counted for much'. *Op cit.*, 211. For a typically lucid discussion by Gray of case teaching, see 1, *Yale L. J.*, 159–61 (1892). Gray's conceptions of treatise writing can be gleaned from the Preface to *The Rule Against Perpetuities*: 'Such a book should deal with the whole of its subject, its history, its relation to other parts of the law, its present condition, the general principles which have been evolved and the errors which have been eliminated in its development, and the defects which still mar its logical symmetry, or what is of vastly greater moment, lessen its value as a guide to conduct.'

34 Gray to President Eliot, 8 January 1883, quoted in Howe, II, *Justice Oliver Wendell Holmes: The Proving Years*, 158 (1963).

35 First published Boston 1886.

36 First published Cambridge 1888–92, 6 vols.

37 First published New York 1909 (Carpentier Lectures, Columbia University, 1908). Citations below are from the Beacon Press edition (ed. Roland Gray) (1963).

38 Holmes to Laski, 4 January 1925, 1, *Holmes-Laski Letters* (ed. Howe), 693 (1953).

39 Ch. IV *et passim*. Gray repeatedly quotes in support of his position a passage from a sermon by Bishop Hoadly: 'Nay, whoever hath an absolute authority to interpret any written or spoken laws, it is he who is the law giver to all intents and purposes, and not the person who first wrote them.' Benjamin Hoadly, Bishop of Bangor, *Sermon preached before the King*, 12 (1717). As Patterson points out, Gray's argument leads him

'to the curious position that the rules laid down by a court in deciding a case are "the law" for that case but are only sources of the law for "the next case".' *Jurisprudence*, 210 (1953).

40 p. 84. This is not very different from Salmond's phrase 'the rules recognised and acted on in courts of justice'. However, Gray was anxious to deny that law pre-existed judicial decisions. Curiously, for one who is sometimes categorised as a 'realist', Gray concentrated on explicit judicial statements ('rules *laid down* by the courts'–cf., however, p. 1, where he uses the phrase 'the general rules which are *followed*') rather than on actual judicial behaviour ('what the courts do in fact'). This seems to have led him to gloss over possible discrepancies between what judges say and what they do and, more surprisingly, to ignore in his long discussion of precedent the difficulties of determining the *ratio decidendi* of a case.

41 For critical discussions see, e.g., Cross, Fuller, Hart, *op. cit. supra*, n.32.

42 Gray liked to test theories in 'the hard pan of fact' and this may be one reason why he is often called a 'realist'. Moreover, apart from his general sturdy common sense, there are some specific aspects of *The Nature and Sources of Law* that may have led people to link him to the realist movement. For example, his emphasis on judicial law-making; his argument that on many points the legislature had 'no real intention' (172); and his dismissal of the theories he attributed to Austin, Savigny, and Carter on the grounds that they did not 'fit the facts'. He appears to have thought that he had sufficiently disposed of Austin's theory of sovereignty by pointing out that in practice '[t]he real rulers of a political society are undiscoverable' (79); he dismissed Savigny's proposition that law has its existence in the common consciousness of the people (the *Volksgeist*) on the ground that a major part of the law is unknown to the people and that the opinions of jurisconsults, to whom Savigny assigned the role of interpreters of the *Volksgeist* on matters of detail, do not in practice represent the *Volksgeist*. *Per contra*, it is arguable that Gray emphasised only two of Llewellyn's nine 'starting-points' of realism (see p. 79), that his ideas on legal education and legal research were closer to those of Langdell than to those of Corbin, Cook, Llewellyn or Frank, and that his theoretical ideas were in several respects more orthodox than those of Holmes (e.g. he discounted the prediction element). It is not important whether or not Gray is classified as a 'realist', but for present purposes it is worth emphasising that *historically* he seems to have contributed less to the rise of the realist movement than is commonly supposed.

43 (1917), 3 *A.B.A.J.*, 55; also in 27 *Int. Jo. Ethics*, 150 (1917), 22 *Pa.B.A Rep.*, 221 (1916).

44 8 *Col. L. Rev.*, 605 (1908).

45 57 *H.L.R.*, 1 (1943).

46 44 *Am. L. Rev.*, 12 (1910).

47 19 *Green Bag*, 607 (1907).

48 'Liberty of Contract', 18 *Yale L. J.*, 464 (1909).

49 *Jurisprudence*, 496 (1960); cf. *ibid.*, 7–8n (1930). There is a good discussion of Pound and legal realism in Rumble, *American Legal Realism*, ch. I (1968).

50 Pound's phrase: e.g. 'The Need for a Sociological Jurisprudence', 19 *Green Bag*, 607, 611 (1907).

51 A number of people have commented on Pound's failure to inspire. Holmes confided to Laski in 1924: 'I always blow Pound's horn. I admire and am overwhelmed by his learning, but I rarely find that unexpectedness which as you say is the most attractive thing. It worries me to think that perhaps or probably I don't do him justice, but few of his own thoughts about the law seem to me important contributions' (Howe (ed), 1, *Holmes-Laski Letters*, 651); Laski replied in similar vein (*ibid.*, p. 655). Llewellyn noted that there was little sign of direct influence by Pound on contemporary jurists, except on Felix Frankfurter, and possibly to a lesser extent on Cook: 'Cook, Corbin, Moore, Oliphant and Clark . . . all derive heavily from Holmes. None, save for the early association of Cook already mentioned, draws in any important measure on Pound. Rather, already set in their views, did they go back over Pound's work critically, accepting here, rejecting there, in the light of their own thinking. Obvious, although not conclusive, evidence is the almost total absence in the writings of any of them of Pound's vocabulary' (Llewellyn MS; unused footnote for 'Some Realism about Realism', 1930).

52 Sutherland, *The Law at Harvard*, 250 (1967). For a revealing defence of Pound's cautious approach to 'new devices' in terms that suggest that Harvard had no need to innovate, see Sayre, *The Life of Roscoe Pound*, 231–3 (1948).

53 Llewellyn, *Jurisprudence*, 378. One of the striking features of Sutherland's substantial history of Harvard (*op. cit.*, n.52) is that the teaching of jurisprudence is only mentioned incidentally in a very few places.

54 Pound, 'Classification of Law' reprinted 37 *Harv. L. Rev.* 933 (1924).

55 Pound's thesis for a doctorate in botany of the University of Nebraska, published in revised form as Pound and Clements, *Phytogeography of Nebraska* (1898). Sutherland, writing of Pound's *Outlines of Jurisprudence* (1st ed. 1903), comments: 'One interested in Pound's intellectual tendencies does well to consider the nature of this book. It suggests his *Phytogeography of Nebraska;* it is a book of scientific ordering, of minutely detailed nomenclatural terms. Here is a botanist, explaining the taxonomy and nomenclature of justice' (*op. cit.*, 237).

56 *Op. cit.*, n. 54.

57 See below, p. 70 *et seq.*

58 E.g. Llewellyn, *Jurisprudence*, 7–8n, 496; Oliphant, 'Parallels in the Development of Legal and Medical Education', 167 *Annals*, 162 (1933). Frank, in a lengthy discussion of Pound's views on certainty in law, concludes that Pound is either inconsistent or else too readily takes refuge in vague generalities to break free from 'the myth of certainty' and other prejudices of the legal profession. In short, he viewed him as a conservative lawyer masquerading as a radical jurist (*Law and the Modern Mind*, part II, ch. 1, appendix XIV *et passim*). One of Llewellyn's more generous assessments is to be found in *Law in our Society* (MS):

> Unique: Roscoe Pound, attempting to gather, to winnow, and to somewhat organize the wheat. A sort of incarnation of our case-law system at its best: *not* tied down to any theory beyond where it proves useful; an earthy willingness to pick up a good idea wherever one turns up; a hesitancy about pressing any theory over-far; a flat unwillingness to even try to get it all into a single logico-systematic scheme – working, instead, by areas. The weakness has been a drawing back from wrestling with the details of the daily work; I think, because Pound did not have the 'craft' concept to work with.

59 Arnold, *Fair Fights and Foul* (1965). This should not be read as suggesting that Arnold was dissatisfied with Harvard Law School when he was a student. His 'revolt' came later (ex. rel., Professor Clarence Morris).

2 CORBIN'S YALE

1 'Some Realism about Realism', Llewellyn, *Jurisprudence*, 42, 46–8 (1931), discussed below, ch. 5.

2 29, *Yale L. J.*, 83–4 (1919); on the Yale Law School, see F. C. Hicks, *The Yale Law School* (4 pamphlets, 1935–8).

3 The principal sources for this account of Corbin are (i) Corbin, 'Sixty-Eight Years at Law', 11, *Yale Law Report*, no. 3, 20 (1965); (ii) Corbin, 'A Creative Process', 6, *Yale Law Report*, no. 1, 17 (1959); (iii) personal interviews and correspondence with Corbin 1963–5.

4 On the 'Yale system', see F. C. Hicks, *Yale Law School: 1895–1915 The Years of Hendrie Hall*, 43 *et seq* (1938).

5 1, *Yale Law Report*, no. 4, 5 (1955).

6 *Ibid.*, 6.

7 Corbin to Llewellyn, 1 December 1960; elsewhere Corbin added: 'Fortunately, most of my legal opponents were equally incompetent' ('Sixty-Eight Years at Law').

8 E.g. 'Karl [Llewellyn] started with Sumner; Hohfeld started with Austin; Corbin started with neither. To me, Austin was merely a *name*' (Corbin to Twining, October 1965).

9 *Ibid.*

10 *Yale Review*, 234–50 (1914).

11 *Op. cit.* above (n.3). See also, 'What is the Common Law?', *Am. L. Sch. Rev.*, 73 (1912); 'Jural Relations and their Classification', 30 *Yale L. J.*, 226 (1921); 'Legal Analysis and Terminology' 29 *Yale L. J.*, 163 (1919), 'The Restatement of the Common Law by the American Law Institute'; 15 *Iowa L. Rev.*, 19 (1929); review of Allen, *Law in the Making*, 38 *Yale L. J.*, 270 (1928).

12 In 1963 the author visited Corbin at his home in Hamden in order to interview him about Llewellyn. By then Corbin was nearly 90; his hearing was impaired and he could only read with considerable effort. He had just completed work on a supplement for his monumental treatise on contracts. Beside his chair was a box of manilla cards on which each new decision affecting contracts was noted with care in longhand as the advance sheets came in. In the previous six months, Corbin said, he had noted approximately two thousand cases in this fashion. Long after most scholars would have handed over such 'mechanical' work (Corbin would have rejected this description of it) to younger men, he had ploughed on relentlessly and only stopped when it became a physical impossibility to continue. This patient, careful, relentlessness was Corbin's cardinal virtue.

13 '[T]he rules of action customarily followed in the community, lately referred to by Lord Chancellor Haldane as *Sittlichkeit*' (240). Cf. 'A man who knows the *Sittlichkeit*, the justice, of his time, and who knows also that his own interest and the interest of all that he holds near and dear require him to decide in exact accordance therewith. . . . Such a judge is independent. . . . It is, indeed, a high and arduous task to acquire the knowledge necessary to such independence; for to know the *Sittlichkeit* requires that one must know in advance the amount of criticism his decision will provoke, the number and the character of the threats that will be made and carried out, the volume of the clamor.' *Ibid.*, 249–50. The term 'mores' was made fashionable by William Graham Sumner, who was prominent at Yale during Corbin's early years there – see below, p. 92.

14 P. 250. See below pp. 223–6.

15 To take two examples. 'What is the test of right and wrong, of truth and error, of sound law and bad law? The final test is survival in conflict. The fittest survive' (247). Or the following overstatement of the scope of judicial discretion: 'The fact is that the judge is a *lawmaker*. He acts under no compulsion different from that under which anyone else acts when making any kind of a decision. . . . The judge's will is as free as the banker's will or the will of the homicide' (235). Cp. Llewellyn on leeways of discretion and their limits in *The Common Law Tradition*, 19ff.

16 P. 249.

17 'Sixty-Eight Years at Law', 20. Corbin's method of testing 'tentative working rules' did not correspond with the simple model of induction

in which a generalization is based on consideration of all known instances. For Corbin pointed out that, as conditions and values changed . . . 'precedents have been forgotten, have been disregarded and evaded, have been flatly disapproved and overruled ('The Law and the Judges', 242). It should be noted that Corbin talks in terms of rules as 'generalizations' which can be 'induced'. By so doing he does not necessarily commit himself to equating normative propositions (such as rules) with descriptive propositions, for it is widely accepted that it is meaningful to talk of 'inducing' rules from a series of cases. Considerations of space preclude a full analysis here. A simple answer is that it is the fact element in the legal rule (the protasis) which is the subject of 'generalization'. On Llewellyn's distinction between 'real rules' and 'paper rules', see below Appendix B.

18 Corbin to Llewellyn, 1 December 1960.
19 See below, p. 408.
20 See below, ch. 10 and pp. 316–7.
21 P. 246. To the modern sociologically minded jurist this view may seem rather naive. Cf., for example, Kahn-Freund, writing on the experience of the Royal Commission on Trades Unions and Employers' Associations: 'Once more (as so often) those of us who are lawyers were taught the elementary lesson that the law reports are the worst possible mirror of society. They convey to the beholder a distorted image in which that which is marginal appears as typical, and this may be one of the reasons why sometimes the judgments of lawyers on social policy are so surprisingly warped and ill-founded'. 33 *M.L.R.*, 241, 242 (1970).
22 P. 245, quoting a letter from Kent to a correspondent (1828). Llewellyn, in developing this idea, rejected the crude version that judges first make up their minds on a hunch and then seek for an *ex post facto* rationalization for it. This to him was as naive an oversimplification of a complex process as the view that judicial decisions simply involve the application of rules to facts (see generally, *The Common Law Tradition, passim*).
23 Professor Simeon Baldwin (1840–1927), a leading figure in the Yale Law School for over fifty years, and the staunchest defender of the 'old Yale system' of instruction; see Hicks, *Yale Law School 1895–1915*, 63–85.
24 Corbin, interview, 1963.
25 Langdell, cited above, p. 11.
26 In 1917, at the end of the first year of Swan's deanship, several members of the faculty resigned because they felt that 'the ideal of the new administration was actually to convert and transform the Yale Law School into a sort of replica of the Harvard Law School'. C. P. Sherman, *Academic Adventures*, 193 (1947).
27 W. N. Hohfeld (1879–1917); his most important papers were collected

in *Fundamental Legal Conceptions as Applied in Judicial Reasoning* (ed. W. W. Cook, 1923; shorter ed. with a foreword by A. L. Corbin, 1964). On Hohfeld's ideas, see Stone, *Legal System and Lawyers Reasonings*, ch. 4 (1964), and references to the extensive literature cited there. On Hohfeld as a teacher, see Llewellyn *Jurisprudence*, ch. 26 – an appreciation written while Llewellyn was still a student at Yale. This was originally published in 28 *Yale L. J.*, 795 (1919). See also lecture dated 26 April 1955, K.L.P.C. Series M. 10.

28 *Op. cit.* (n.27), foreword.

29 *Ibid.*, 64.

30 See Stone, *op. cit.*, 161.

31 Corbin's account is of interest:

> When, in 1923, Williston was made *Reporter* on Contracts by the American Law Institute, he chose me as his chief adviser (not so named) and eventually as a 'Co-Reporter'. As such adviser, I worked over every Section of the Restatement, submitting alternative drafts of Sections, Comments and Illustrations. Williston chose *Oliphant* also as an adviser; and he expressly told us two that he accepted Hohfeld's classification of *concepts*, though not every one of Hohfeld's *terms* (especially 'liability') and that he wished every part of the Restatement to be *consistent* with Hohfeld. He singled out Oliphant and me, as being more expert in Hohfeld's analysis than himself, to keep out a constant eye for any inconsistency. Oliphant, without raising any controversy, tired of the job and resigned within two years. I saw it through to the end. Williston welcomed *every* criticism and suggestion, adopting the forms and suggestions if they withstood full discussion. I regarded my function as supplementing Williston in two ways: (1) Analysis of facts and terminology; (2) The modernization of doctrine to accord with the evolutionary process.
>
> Corbin to Twining, October 1965. Bigelow also adopted Hohfeld's analysis in his preliminary work on the *Restatement of the Law of Property*, Corbin, foreword to Hohfeld, *op. cit.* (n.27).

32 See below, pp. 137 and 331.

33 According to Corbin, Hohfeld acquired a copy of Austin when he was a college student in the University of California (Corbin to Twining, 1965). This copy, heavily annotated, is in the library of the Yale Law School.

34 This is not to say that Austin was the prime target of Corbin, Cook and Llewellyn (see above, p. 29).

35 Llewellyn, lecture, 26 April 1955, K.L.P.C. Series M. 10.

36 Hohfeld, *Fundamental Legal Conceptions 357 et seq.* (1923).

37 *Ibid.*

38 W. W. Cook (1873–1943), after graduation from Columbia in 1894, was first an assistant in mathematics at Columbia (1894–5), then a John Tindall Fellow in physics at Jena, Leipzig and Berlin (1895–7); on his return to the United States he continued as an assistant in mathematics

until 1900. However, in 1901 he earned a master's degree in law and immediately took up law teaching. Goebel *et al.*, *A History of the School of Law, Columbia University*, 262–3 (1955). See also Llewellyn lecture, 9 May 1955, 16–8, K.L.P.C. Series M. Cook's writings include *The Logical and Legal Bases of the Conflict of Laws* (1942), 'Scientific Method and the Law', 13 *A.B.A.J.*, 303 (1927), *Johns Hopkins Alumni Magazine*, vol. 25, 213–36 (1927), 'Hohfeld's Contributions to the Science of Law', 28 *Yale L. J.*, 721 (1919), and an essay in Kocoureck (ed.), *My Philosophy of Law* (1941), at 49–66.

39 Goebel, *op. cit.*, 263. A warmer assessment of Cook's character is to be found in obituary notices by Homer F. Carey and Hessel Yntema in 38 *Ill. L. Rev.*, 347 *et seq.* (1944).

40 *Ibid.*

41 See especially 'Scientific Method and the Law'.

42 'My Philosophy of Law', 52–3.

43 'Scientific Method and the Law', 232.

44 *Ibid.*, 229–30, supported by a quotation from Beale.

45 *Ibid.*

46 In discussing critics of 'mechanical jurisprudence' Dworkin points out: '. . . they are right in ridiculing its practitioners. Their difficulty, how-ever, lies in finding practitioners to ridicule. So far they have had little luck in caging and exhibiting mechanical jurisprudents (all specimens captured – even Blackstone and Joseph Beale – have had to be released after careful reading of their texts).' 'Is Law a System of Rules?', in Summers (ed.), *Essays in Legal Philosophy*, 27 (1968).

47 W. W. Cook, *The Logical and Legal Bases of the Conflict of Laws, passim* (1942).

48 Corbin saw this as Cook's Achilles heel: '[H]e planned to start at Johns Hopkins a legal research institute, quite separate from law practice, one that would parallel the great Medical School at J.H. . . . Apparently Cook failed to realize that the great Medical School at J.H. was closely connected with and dependent upon medical *practice*, and that the great medical leaders there had been active practitioners. Cook had *never practised law*.' Corbin to Twining, October 1965.

49 Yntema, *op. cit.* (n.39); Cheshire, *Private International Law*, 34–5 (6th ed. 1961).

50 See below, p. 81.

51 Austin Scott (1925), 3 *Proc. Am. Law Inst.*, 230; denied by Cook in *The Logical and Legal Bases of the Conflict of Laws*, 47.

52 *Ibid.*, and 'My Philosophy of Law'.

53 Unlike Moore (see below), Cook did not consider that his early analytical work was based on 'false hypotheses'. Rather he considered that his analysis of legal decisions and his statistical enquiries into judicial administration were both examples of 'scientific empiricism' applied

to the study of 'legal phenomena'. See e.g. *The Logical and Legal Bases of the Conflict of Laws*, 46–7. While he did not commit himself to the view that identical methods were appropriate to both types of enquiry, by failing to differentiate clearly between different types of 'legal phenomena', Cook failed to give an adequate account of the difficulties of treating judicial decisions simply as empirical phenomena. See, further, below (n.56). Cook accepted Dewey's somewhat controversial 'empirical theory of evaluation' (see 'My Philosophy of Law', 60–4).

54 20 *Col. L. Rev.*, 716 (1920); 21 *Col. L. Rev.*, 395 (1921).

55 33 *Ill. L. Rev.*, 497 (1939).

56 A critique of Cook's theory of an empirical science of law could be developed along three main lines: first, his dismissal of 'mechanical jurisprudence' was far too facile (see above (n.46)). By choosing a simplistic target for attack, he failed to come to grips with less naive versions of 'formalism'. The alternative theory that he proposed was hardly less simplistic. Secondly, following Holmes, he accepted uncritically the idea that statements of the kind 'X has a duty' are simply predictions; accordingly he glossed over some of the problems of developing an empirical science in a field in which normative propositions (e.g. rules) have a central place. See Hart, 'Definition and Theory in Jurisprudence', 70 *L.Q.R.*, 37 (1954) and *The Concept of Law*, ch. VI. Thirdly, as suggested above (n.53), he failed to give an adequate account of what he considered to be valid methods of investigating various types of 'legal phenomena'.

57 Corbin to Twining, October 1965. Goebel, *op. cit.*, 263, says that Cook's salary of $10,000 a year was 'higher than the salary paid at that time to any other law teacher anywhere'. However, Dean Stone's salary was probably higher in 1919. Mason, *Harlan Fiske Stone* (1956).

3 COLUMBIA IN THE 1920's

1 The principal sources for this section are: (i) J. Goebel *et al.*, *A History of the School of Law, Columbia University* (1955); (ii) *Reports of the Dean of the Law School, Columbia University* (annual, 1925–38); (iii) unpublished memoranda etc. in the Treasure Room of the University of Columbia Law School (permission was refused to consult faculty minutes and other Columbia records); (iv) H. Oliphant (ed.), *Summary of Studies in Legal Education by the Faculty of Law of Columbia University* (1928); (v) B. Currie, 'The Materials of Law Study,' I and II, 3 *Jo. Leg. Ed.*, 331 (1951), III, 8 *Jo. Leg. Ed.*, 1 (1955); (vi) A. T. Mason, *Harlan Fiske Stone*, ch. 9 (1956); (vii) The Karl Llewellyn Papers which, however, contain relatively little material relating to the principal events dealt with in this chapter.

2 See generally Goebel, *op. cit.*, 11–25.

3 The best account of Moore's career up to 1929 is to be found in Goebel, *op. cit.*, 249–52, which is the main source of this passage. See also Columbia University, School of Law, Alumni Association *Bulletin* of May 22 1929, and obituaries by William O. Douglas, 59 *Yale L. J.*, 188 (1950) and Charles E. Clark, *ibid.*, 191. Moore's most important writings are to be found in Kocourceck (ed), *My Philosophy of Law*, 203–25 (1941), 23 *Col. L. Rev.*, 609 (1923), 38 *Yale L. J.*, 703 (1929), various articles in the *Yale Law Journal*, 1929–33, and the famous article on 'Law and Learning Theory' with Callahan in 53 *Yale L. J.*, 1 (1943). Moore's papers are deposited in the university library at Yale. See also Northrop, *The Complexity of Ethical and Legal Experience*, 29–34 (1959).

4 Columbia Alumni Association, *Bulletin, op. cit.*, p. 4 (n.1).

5 Especially J. Watson, *Psychology from the Standpoint of a Behaviorist* (1919).

6 Goebel, *op. cit.*, 251. Currie reports Llewellyn as telling a similar story. No date is given for the event in these accounts, but it is unlikely to have been before 1922 when the second edition of his *Cases on the Law of Bills and Notes* (with Howard L. Smith) appeared. In fact Moore continued to publish occasional relatively 'conventional' writings in the area, e.g. his introductory book on *The Law of Commercial Paper* (1929).

7 'At the summit of his teaching career he turned his back upon classroom success for research of the most extensive and persistent character and of the most novel kind for any law teacher of our age. His further teaching – and, of course, it was still extensive – was geared entirely to his conception of law as determined by facts and as being itself an "artifact", and to his fiery crusade to follow what he believed to be the scientific approach to the ascertainment of the institutional background that shapes and indeed was our law. Hence he set himself, with a staff, to the most detailed and laborious investigation of limited areas of social or business activity to determine the precise impact of actual happenings upon the course of law. Nor would he allow anything to deter him from his dedicated task, not even the almost universal doubts and questionings, not to speak of more ribald comments, of his compeers in the legal world'. Clark, 59 *Yale L. J.*, 191 (1950).

8 See below, pp. 47–8.

9 See below, pp. 136–7. The 'narrow categories' idea was in part inspired by Hohfeld's analysis.

10 See below, pp. 216ff.

11 See Goebel, *op. cit.*, 265–7, Reuschlein, *Jurisprudence: Its American Prophets*, 280–7 (1951).

12 6 *AALS Handbook*, 52–3 (1928).

13 14 *A.B.A.J.*, 71 (1928) criticized by Llewellyn on a number of occasions, e.g. *The Common Law Tradition*, 14n, 18. Perhaps Oliphant's most

important work, apart from his *Cases on Trade Regulation* (1923), was his research at Johns Hopkins, cited below, p. 404.

14 Mason, *op. cit.*, 128.

15 *Ibid.*, 131ff.

16 Goebel, *op. cit.*, 299, 493.

17 *Ibid.*

18 Currie, III, 5.

19 Smith to Stone, 3 May 1921, quoted by Mason, *op. cit.*, 128.

20 Currie, I, 333-4.

21 *Goebel, op. cit.*, 300.

22 See generally Oliphant's *Summary*, chs. 8 and 9. Twining, O'Donovan and Paliwala, 'Ernie and the Centipede', in J. A. Jolowicz (ed.), *Division and Classification of the Law*, 10-29 (1970).

23 Oliphant, *Summary, the*, 71.

24 *Ibid.*, 75.

25 Currie, III, 74.

26 'Legal Education for Public Policy', 52 *Yale L. J.*, 255 (1943).

27 Oliphant's *Summary* is nearly two hundred pages in length. It was published in 1928 and circulated to all member schools of the A.A.L.S. In form it represents an attempt to produce a reasonably coherent statement out of the written and oral contributions of his colleagues. This was a virtually impossible task, for the contributions varied greatly in quality, several important phases of legal education were ignored or only touched on lightly, and there were fundamental differences of opinion in respect of objectives. Furthermore, the document reflects Oliphant's personal biases and interests: for example jurisprudence, comparative law and international law are only mentioned cursorily, a disproportionate emphasis is placed on business studies, and there is an almost complete lack of historical perspective. Moreover, some important disagreements were never resolved. The result is that the document fails to fulfil its promise to be a coherent statement of a comprehensive theory of legal education, comparable to Lasswell and McDougal's *Legal Education for Public Policy*, published fifteen years later. Nevertheless it contains a rich brew of ideas; in particular the discussion of classification, the critique of the case method from the standpoint of a social scientist, and some of the chapters on individual subjects still repay study.

28 Currie, I, 334-5.

29 Goebel, *op. cit.*, 297-303.

30 Oliphant, *Summary*, 20.

31 *Ibid.*, 21.

32 *Ibid.*, 22-3.

33 The most authoritative source on the deanship crisis is the *Columbia*

History, 303–5. The reader is left in no doubt about the sympathies of the editors.

34 At 304–5.

35 At 23.

36 Generalizations about either of these groups should be read subject to a number of caveats. First, these were by no means two close-knit and constant factions regularly opposed to each other over a whole series of issues. The record of the positions taken by each individual is in any case by no means complete, but it is clear that the extent and degree of commitment to any position varied from person to person and from time to time. Second, this categorisation would be a serious oversimplification if it were taken to suggest that the scientists were opposed in general to the idea of professional training or that the prudents did not appreciate the relevance of empirical research or that all or any were indifferent to questions concerning the ends of law. At best one or other of these suggestions might be a half-truth if applied to a particular individual. To take but one example: Michael and Adler were later to accuse some Scientists of 'raw empiricism' (*Crime, Law and Social Science*, 422–3 (1933)), and were accused in their turn, by Llewellyn, of moving towards a 'crude rationalism' (34 *Col. L. Rev.*, 277, at 284, 291 (1934)) in their emphasis on the need for a 'rational science' of criminal law based upon the principles of ethics and politics (*op. cit.*, preface, p. xiii). It requires only a nodding acquaintance with the work of, e.g., Jerome Michael, to realize that any such accusations in each case would need to be qualified considerably and that neither could be neatly categorised as Philosopher, Scientist, or Prudent. The same would apply in varying degrees to each of their colleagues in 1928. Highly intelligent and individualistic men such as these cannot be so simply pigeon-holed. No one better illustrates the complexity of the actual situation than Llewellyn himself, who probably learned most from the Scientists, and sympathised with many of their ideas, but as will be seen ended up firmly in the camp of the Prudents.

37 Columbia University Law School, Dean's *Reports*, 1928ff.; Goebel, *op. cit.*, ch. XIII–XIV.

4   AFTERMATH OF THE SPLIT

1 See especially Reports of Dean, Columbia Law School, particularly for 1933 and 1937; Goebel, *op. cit.*, and Currie, *op. cit.*

2 Goebel, *op. cit.*, 311.

3 *Ibid.*, 331, citing Dean's Report for 1937.

4 See Currie, *passim*, for a very full discussion. On Llewellyn's casebook see below, ch. 7.

5 Goebel, *op. cit.*, 336–7.

6 Dean's Report, 1933.

7 Generally see A. Schlesinger, *The Age of Roosevelt: The Coming of the New Deal* (1959); Thurman Arnold, *Fair Fights and Foul* (1965); Rumble, *American Legal Realism*, 76–7 (1968).

8 See below, p. 194.

9 See Llewellyn, 8 *Jo. Leg. Ed.*, 399, 401–2 (1956); Goebel, *op. cit.*, 333–4.

10 *Op. cit.*, III, 4.

11 *Ibid.* I, 337.

12 *Ibid.* I, 338.

13 No student of American legal education, or of realism, can afford to ignore Currie's masterly articles. They provide the balance and the historical perspective lacking in Oliphant's *Summary*. Only on three related points does the present interpretation diverge significantly from his, and these are on matters of emphasis. First, Currie somewhat underplays the depth of the split that developed between the two chief factions at Columbia. Secondly, and related to this, he may have accepted too readily the judgment of their contemporaries that the efforts of those who left Columbia for Johns Hopkins and Yale were inevitably doomed to failure. Thirdly, as an American law teacher, Currie is less inclined than an outsider to question the assumption that the casebook or 'course book' was the best vehicle for furthering the integration movement.

14 On Johns Hopkins Institute, see (i) Johns Hopkins University *Bulletins*, 1928–33; (ii) Johns Hopkins Institute of Law *Bulletins;* (iii) Albert Shaw, 'Research in Law and Justice', *Review of Reviews*, 1931; (iv) Cook, 'Scientific Method and the Law', *Johns Hopkins Alumni Magazine*, March 1927 (reprinted 13 *A.B.A.J.*, 303 (1927)); (v) H. Yntema, 'Walter Wheeler Cook', 38 *Ill. L. Rev.*, 352 (1944); (vi) Johns Hopkins Institute of Law, *Monographs in the Study of Judicial Administration in Ohio*, 1931–6 (13 monographs).

15 Johns Hopkins University *Report*, 1928–9 at 423.

16 *Ibid.*, 424.

17 *Ibid.*, 425–7.

18 Johns Hopkins Institute of Law, *General Statement* (1928).

19 W. W. Cook, *The Logical and Legal Bases of the Conflict of Laws* (1942).

20 Publications of the Institute of Law of The Johns Hopkins University included: *Monographs in the Study of Judicial Administration in Ohio* (1932); *Bulletins of the Study of Judicial Administration in Ohio* (1932); *Monographs in the Study of the Judicial System of Maryland* (1931–2); *Bulletins of the Study of the Judicial System of Maryland* (1931–2); *Monographs of Survey of Litigation in New York* (1931–2); *Bulletins of Survey of Litigation in New York* (1931–2); Yntema, *Analysis of Ohio Municipal Court Acts* (1933); Marshall, *Unlocking the Treasuries of the Trial Courts* (1933); *Comparative Judicial Criminal Statistics: Six States, 1931* (1932); *Comparative Judicial*

Criminal Statistics: Ohio and Maryland (1932). For a full bibliography of the Johns Hopkins studies see unpublished dissertation by Wilfrid E. Rumble Jr., 'The Foundations of American Legal Realism' (Dept of Political Science, Johns Hopkins University).

11 Oliphant, *A Study of Day Calendars* (Baltimore, 1932); J. H. I., *Statistical Studies in Judicial Administration* (Baltimore, 1932).

12 Yntema gave the following explanation:

> There was indecision in the University counsels, inspired by malice abroad as well as by doubts within, and the decision by the faculty of the Institute to concentrate in the field of judicial statistics, a necessarily expensive form of research, though it appeared at the time essential in view of the increasingly stringent situation, appears in retrospect to have fallen short of the more basic objectives in view. But those were merely incidental to the prime difficulty – the circumstance that the venture took place on the eve of the depression. (38 *Ill. L. R.*, 352 (1944)).

> See also A. Conard (ed.), *Report of Conference on Aims and Methods of Legal Research* (1955) for comments of Llewellyn (10–4) Yntema (72–3) and Cavers (22).

13 Goebel, *op. cit.*, 305.

14 *Yale Law School: Annual Report of the Dean*, 33 (1930–31). See further (below, pp. 188ff).

15 See especially Clark, Douglas and Thomas, 'The Business Failures Project – A Problem in Methodology', 39 *Yale L. J.*, 1013 (1930).

16 See Clark and Shulman, *A Study of Law Administration in Connecticut* (1937).

17 Hutchins and Slesinger, 'Some Observations on the Law of Evidence – the Competency of Witnesses', 37 *Yale L. J.*, 1017 (1927); cf. 16 *Yale Rev.*, 678 (1927); 28 *Col. L. Rev.*, 432; 38 *Yale L. J.*, 283 (1928), 41 *Harv. L. Rev.*, 860 (1928). For other references see Yale Law School, Dean's Reports, 1929–35.

18 Moore and Sussman, 'Legal and Institutional Methods Applied to the Debiting of Direct Discounts', 40 *Yale L. J.*, 381, 555, 752, 928, 1055, 1219 (1930–31). Moore, Sussman and Brand, 'Legal and Institutional Methods Applied to Stop Payments of Checks', 42 *Yale L. J.*, 817, 1198 (1933).

19 Moore and Callahan, 'Law and Learning Theory', 53 *Yale L. J.*, 1 (1943), discussed by Northrop, 59 *Yale L. J.*, 196 (1949) and Yntema, 53 *Yale L. J.*, p. 338 (1943–4).

20 One of the more balanced discussions is G. Schubert, 'The Future of Public Law', 34 *Geo. Wash. L. Rev.*, 593 (1966).

21 8 *Jo. Leg. Ed.*, 399, 400 (1956); also in Conard, *op. cit.*, n.22.

22 *Ibid.*, 403.

23 *Ibid.*

24 *Ibid.*, 401.

35 Llewellyn mitigated his remarks with some complimentary references to Cook, Moore and Oliphant in the footnotes, but his tone contrasts sharply with his earlier, more sympathetic discussions, e.g. in 6 *Am. L. Sch. Rev.*, 670 (1930), and *Jurisprudence*, 77 (1931). Llewellyn's speech in 1956 might be interpreted as an indirect attack on what he considered to be the over-reliance on quantitative methods of some of his colleagues at Chicago.

36 E.g. Zeisel, Kalven and Bucholz, *Delay in Court* (1959) does not even mention Oliphant's studies on the subject.

37 See, however, Rumble, *op. cit.*, above, n.20, and F. Northrop, 'Underhill Moore's Legal Science', 59 *Yale L. J.*, 196 (1950).

38 Arnold, *Fair Fights and Foul*, 67–8 (1965).

39 The semi-success of realism and the accompanying sense of frustration continue to be a theme in more recent discussions of realism, for example:

> At least in the better law schools 'functionalists' and 'realists' are no longer lonely aliens in a hostile world. In truth they probably outweigh in influence, if not in number, the Langdellians. Holmes, Pound, Jerome Frank, Llewellyn, Lasswell and McDougal have fought and won the battle for recognition. Now the problem is simply one of fulfillment. The door is open, and the way is clear to those who wish to make law an instrument of social policy. All they have to do is to do it.
>
> In other words, the problem that frustrates so many students and professors today is a deep dissatisfaction with the prevailing system of legal education, coupled with an inability even to envision the improvements they all sense are necessary. The fact that Langdell and his disciples are no longer realistic targets of abuse only adds to their frustration.

C. Woodard, 'The Limits of Legal Realism: an Historical Perspective', 54 *Virginia L. Rev.*, 689, 732 (1968).

40 Allen, *Law in the Making*, p. 45 (4th ed., 1946).

5   THE REALIST CONTROVERSY 1930–1

1 30 *Col. L. Rev.*, 431 (1930), reprinted *Jurisprudence*, 3–41.

2 Jerome Frank (1889–1957) is usually treated as one of the two leading 'realists', Llewellyn being the other. In the present interpretation, however, Frank is something of an outsider. Whereas Hohfeld, Corbin, Cook, Oliphant, Moore and Llewellyn were all law teachers associated with either Yale or Columbia Law School or both, Frank was a practioner and an alumnus of the University of Chicago, whose connection with Yale started after the publication of *Law and the Modern Mind* and some of his most influential papers. More important, Frank's main target of attack was the intellectual orientation of almost all American academic lawyers, who focused undue attention on appellate courts, with consequent distortions in their vision of legal processes and in their

programmes of legal training. From his point of view, the perspectives of Corbin, Llewellyn and Hohfeld were hardly less 'unrealistic' than those of Beale and Langdell. Although he said little directly about the issues that divided the scientists and the prudents at Columbia, it is apparent that he had little sympathy for the ambitions of the scientists to do 'objective' empirical research (see Frank, *If Men were Angels*, 294 (1942), and Reuschlein, *Jurisprudence: Its American Prophets*, 215), and that the Columbia reforms of legal education did not go nearly far enough in the direction of clinical legal training to satisfy him (on which see *Courts on Trial*, ch. 16).

Of course, Frank's ideas were developed in much the same intellectual milieu as those of the Yale and Columbia realists. On the one hand the Harvard of Langdell and Beale symbolised a common enemy (see below, n.4); on the other, the leaders of the revolt against formalism, in particular Holmes, provided some common intellectual ancestors. However, Frank's special interest in psychoanalysis and psychiatry was not shared by the other six 'core members'. On Frank, see especially Julius Paul, *The Legal Realism of Jerome N. Frank* (1959); E. Cahn, *Confronting Injustice* (1966); W. Rumble, *American Legal Realism* (1968); J. Mitchell Rosenberg, *Jerome Frank: Jurist and Philosopher* (1970).

3 See especially, *Courts on Trial* (1949). While there are hints of Frank's 'fact-scepticism' in *Law and the Modern Mind*, this aspect of his thought was developed at much greater length in his later writings.

4 Especially ch. 4. Three Harvard jurists, Langdell, Beale and Williston, are the most clearly identified targets of attacks on formalism by 'core' realists, especially Frank, Cook and Llewellyn. For Frank on Langdell, see *Courts on Trial* ch. 16; for Cook on Beale, see *The Logical and Legal Bases of the Conflict of Laws* (1942). For Cook on Williston, see pp. 39-40.

Llewellyn had little to say about Beale. While he was critical of both Langdell and Williston, he also recognised their achievements. For instance, Llewellyn dedicated *Cases and Materials on the Law of Sales* to Williston and Scrutton.

5 Frank, *op. cit.*, part II, ch. 7.

6 *Ibid.*, part II, ch. 6.

7 See especially part III, ch. 2: 'Mr Justice Oliver Wendell Holmes, the Completely Adult Jurist'.

8 44 *Harv. L. Rev.*, 697 (1931).

9 Pound to Llewellyn, 21 March 1931. Pound played a prominent part in the work of the Wickersham Commission, which reported in 1931: *Enforcement of Prohibition Laws: Report of the National Commission on Law Observance and Enforcement*, Washington, 1931.

10 '1. A functional attitude, *i.e.*, study not only of what legal precepts and doctrines and institutions are, and how they have come to be, but of how they work. Thus far the sociological jurists have been going. But our new

realist in jurisprudence will urge particularly study of concrete instances of rules or doctrines or institutions in action, in such number and by such methods as to be able to reach valid general conclusions.

2. Recognition of the existence of an alogical, unrational, subjective element in judicial action, and attempt by study of concrete instances of its operation to reach valid general conclusions as to the kinds of cases in which it operates most frequently, and where it operates most effectively or most unhappily for the ends of the legal order.

3. Recognition of the significance of the individual case, as contrasted with the absolute universalism of the last century, without losing sight of the significance of generalizations and conceptions as instruments towards the ends of the legal order. At this point they have been anticipated by Stammler, but they will approach the subject in a different way through psychology.

4. Giving up of the idea of a necessary sequence from a single cause in a straight line to a single effect, and hence of the one sovereign legal remedy for every difficulty and one necessary solution of every problem. There will be recognition of a plurality of elements in all situations and of the possibility of dealing with human relations in more than one way. . . .

5. A theory of interests and of the ends of the legal order based on or consistent with modern psychology, without being tied absolutely to any particular dogmatic brand of psychology of the moment.

6. A theory of values, for the valuing of interests, consistent with modern psychology and philosophy, without being tied fast to any particular body of psychological or philosophical dogma of the moment.

7. A recognition that there are many approaches to juristic truth and that each is significant with respect to particular problems of the legal order; hence a valuing of these approaches, not absolutely or with reference to some one assumed necessary psychological or philosophical basis of jurisprudence, but with reference to how far they aid lawmaker, or judge, or jurist in making law and the science of law effective, the one toward the maintaining, furthering, and transmitting of civilization, the other toward organizing the materials and laying out the course of the legal order' (Pound, 'The Call for a Realist Jurisprudence', 44 *Harv. L. Rev.* pp. 710–11 (1930)).

11 44 *Harv. L. Rev.*, 709 (1931).
12 Pound to Llewellyn, 21 March 1931.
13 The best analysis is in Llewellyn *op. cit.*, n.1.
14 Memo, 1931, K.L.P.A., II, 65.
15 MS, K.L.P.A., II, 65.
16 Pound to Llewellyn.
17 Cf. Hart, in 71 *Harv. L. Rev.*, 601–2 (1958).
18 See below (n.38).

19 Rumble, *op. cit.*, 45; Yntema, Frank, Dickinson and Fuller are among those who expressed reservations about the appropriateness of the term 'realism' to characterise the ideas associated with jurists such as Llewellyn and Frank. The name has stuck nonetheless.

20 Cf. Pound, 'By "realism" [the realists] mean fidelity to nature, accurate recording of things as they are, as contrasted with things as they are imagined to be, or wished to be, or as one feels they ought to be.' 44 *Harv. L. Rev.*, 697 (1931). Cf. Frank, *Courts on Trial*, 401–2, *Law and the Modern Mind*, preface to sixth printing (1949). Yntema considered the term 'philosophically inapposite': 14 *Vanderbilt L. Rev.*, 317 (1960).

21 See below (n.23).

22 See especially *The Common Law Tradition*, 509–10, *Jurisprudence* 54, 57. This is a point of some importance. While several prominent members of the realist movement, including Llewellyn and Frank, had specialized interests in the nature of judicial processes, it is quite misleading to suggest that the significance of the realist movement is limited to its contributions to this topic. Moore's parking studies, Llewellyn's work on tribal law and the Uniform Commercial Code, and the Columbia curriculum discussions, all provide examples of work in which judicial behaviour was not the exclusive or even the primary focus of attention. Much of the thrust of realism was to react against an intellectual tradition which encouraged over-concentration on courts, especially appellate courts. The association of realism with the study of judicial processes has been a source of two related errors: (i) the idea that some realists were particularly interested in the topic has been confused with the idea that all realists *defined* law in terms of decisions by judges. This may have been true of Gray and of anyone who can fairly be said to have *defined* law in terms of predictions of what the courts will do in fact. But Llewellyn, for example, saw judicial processes as only one phase of legal processes in general (see below, pp. 175ff and ch. 10); he did not include a general definition of law as one of the shared starting-points of realism; (ii) the fact that some realists, e.g. Frank, were sceptical of the predictability of judicial decisions has been confused with the idea that a realist is one who by definition *concludes* that such decisions are unpredictable. Llewellyn was on safer ground in using 'realism' to refer to a way of looking and not to what is found by the observer – he himself, in *The Common Law Tradition*, concluded that there was a surprisingly high degree of predictability in the decisions of American state appellate courts that he had studied (which might not be true of other jurisdictions). Indeed the term 'scepticism' begs some questions: were all the hypotheses of those who advanced descriptive or explanatory theories of judicial behaviour 'sceptical'? Were, e.g., Frank and Corbin, sceptical about the same things? Is the term 'sceptic' approp-

riate to so optimistic and romantic a person as Llewellyn? See further, above p. 32.

Two major studies which suffer by virtue of treating realism as being primarily concerned with judicial processes are Rumble, *American Legal Realism* (1968), and Moskowitz, *Some Aspects of American Legal Realism* (1963), D.Phil.Thesis, Oxford. Cp. G. Tarello *Il Realismo Giuridico Americano* (1962).

23 It can be argued that there is a difference between those who merely acknowledge the validity of a belief, those who *stress* it, and those who act on it. Thus, for example, a realist could be defined as someone who actually observes the 'law in action . . .', etc. The objection to this is that Llewellyn did not use the term in this sense – and in polemical contexts he stressed the point that most jurists believe in realism. If the test of a 'realistic' approach is actually undertaking regular *first-hand* observation, how many of the actual individuals associated with the realist movement would satisfy such a test?

Perhaps the most common source of misunderstanding of Llewellyn has been that his stress on the value of making actual behaviour a focus of attention was sometimes interpreted as involving the denial of the value or validity of other types of enquiry. But, as he pointed out, to assert that one body of material is worth study, does not involve the assertion that another should be ignored.

'Legal realism' is sometimes used in a rather different way to mean 'What X, a realist, believed', or 'What the realists believed' or 'Those beliefs that were held in common by the realists'. Here 'realism' is not a *criterion of identification* of 'realists', but a shorthand way of referring to the ideas of one or more actual people. Thus, for example, 'Llewellyn's legal realism' may be a shorthand way of referring to Llewellyn's legal ideas (or to one part of them). The usage is understandable, but is fraught with pitfalls when applied to 'realists' in that it may tempt people to think (a) that the membership of the realist movement is clearly established; (b) (i) that all members of the realist movement had identical ideas or (ii) that the common ground between members of the realist movement is established. These assumptions are, at the very least, questionable.

24 Rumble, *op. cit.*, at p. 2, agrees that 'there is no infallible method to determine who is a legal realist'. He adopts Llewellyn's list of twenty and accepts Patterson's suggestion (*Jurisprudence*, 539 (n.7)) that Arnold and Felix Cohen should be added; he completes his list with Rodell. This selection, it is submitted, is unnecessarily arbitrary. Frank (preface to sixth printing of *Law and the Modern Mind*) mentions Green, Radin, Arnold, Douglas, and perhaps E. M. Morgan as fact-sceptics and seemingly considers Cook, Yntema, Oliphant, Hutcheson, Llewellyn and himself as 'constructive sceptics' of one sort or another (see above, n.22).

Garlan, *Legal Realism and Justice* (1941), while making no attempt
at a definitive list of 'realists', avoids most of the dangers of generalizing
about realism. Salmond, *Jurisprudence* (12 ed., Fitzgerald) (1966)
seemingly treats Holmes, Llewellyn, Frank and Gray as 'American
realists' who 'share the view that the law consists of the pronouncement
of the courts' (p.4, n.). *The Bramble Bush* is the only work of Llewellyn's
that is cited. Reuschlein, in *Jurisprudence – Its American Prophets* (1951),
treats the following as realists (or 'neo-realists'). Bingham, Arnold,
Llewellyn, Green, Frank, Radin, Yntema, Douglas, F. Cohen, Lerner,
Nelles, T. R. Powell, Rodell, Laski and Garlan. Cook and Oliphant
are treated under the separate heading of 'The scientific method'.
Reuschlein attaches no special significance to this classification.

25 The image of 'the realists' as a group of *young* men needs to be taken
with a pinch of salt. The youngest person in Llewellyn's list (Tulin) was
thirty in 1931 and the average age of the twenty was over forty at that
time.

26 *Jurisprudence*, 44.

27 *Ibid.*

28 *Ibid.*, 47n.

29 Especially Patterson, Lorenzen, Powell and Radin.

30 Moreover, he had been at Columbia until 1925.

31 In fact, Bingham had been a visiting professor in Columbia in 1926–7;
Frank was later to teach part-time at Yale (1946–57), having been a
research associate at an earlier date.

32 E.g., A. A. Berle, T. Arnold, W. Hamilton. In fact the last two were
in Frank's original list of suggestions. Frank to Llewellyn, 17 March 1931
(K.L.P.A., II, 65, b).

33 Especially at Yale: G. Dession, R. M. Hutchins, Walter Nelles, Fred
Rodell. Later Yale became the headquarters of Harold Lasswell and
Myres S. McDougal, whose 'Law, Science and Policy' built on, but
went beyond, the ideas of some realists. At Columbia, A. A. Berle,
R. L. Hale, J. Hanna, A. Jacobs and Jerome Michael were among
those whose names have sometimes been associated with 'realism'. It
would be of little value to debate the appropriateness of the label in
the case of each of these individuals, but it is reasonably clear that their
inclusion would be no more out of place than the inclusion in Llewellyn's
list of, e.g., E. W. Patterson or F. Lorenzen or M. Radin.

34 Most of this correspondence survives in K.L.P.A., II, 65. It provides
valuable evidence of the then views of many of the jurists included in
Llewellyn's 'sample'.

35 *Jurisprudence*, 42n.

36 *Ibid.*

37 *Ibid.*, 52.

38 *Ibid.*, 53, 74. See also *The Common Law Tradition*, appendix B.

39 'Some Realism About Realism', 68.

40 *Jurisprudence*, 55–7.

41 Dias, *Jurisprudence* (2nd ed.), 471 (1964) (modified in 3rd edition (1970)).

42 *Ibid.*, 475. For evidence *contra* see especially *The Common Law Tradition*, *passim; Cases and Materials on the Law of Sales*, introduction, p. xi (where Llewellyn makes it clear that he is concerned both with what courts say *and* what they do, in so far as these can be distinguished); *Jurisprudence*, pp. 56–8. See below, pp. 229–31.

43 Salmond, *Jurisprudence* (12 ed., Fitzgerald) 35n. (1966).

44 Cross, *Precedent in English Law* (1st ed.) p. 49, n. (1961). This is a strange statement in the light of *The Common Law Tradition*, which is ignored even in the second edition (1968).

45 Pound, *Jurisprudence I*, 271 (1959). Cf. Allen, *Law in the Making* (5th ed.), 42 (deleted in the latest edition), Mechem, 21 *Iowa L. Rev.*, 669, 670–71 (1936). Llewellyn, *per contra*, had much to say about regularity of official behaviour; see e.g., *Jurisprudence*, 29–30 (1931), and *Law in Our Society*.

46 Friedrich, *The Philosophy of Law in Historical Perspective*, 176 (1958). This is so wide of the mark that almost any of Llewellyn's major writings can be used to refute it. See especially below, ch. 9 and appendix B. For a good general discussion of charges that the realists were indifferent to normative questions, see Rumble, *American Legal Realism*, ch. 5 (1968).

47 Goodhart, introduction to Kantorowicz, *The Definition of Law*, xviii–xix (1958). This statement might have some basis in the tendency of 'Scientists' like Cook and Oliphant. For Llewellyn's position see especially *The Common Law Tradition* 56, 131ff (discussed below at pp. 229–31).

48 Hart, *The Concept of Law*, 133, 232, 250 (1961).

49 Pound, 44 *Harv. L. Rev.*, 698, as interpreted by Llewellyn in *Jurisprudence*, 50. Not applicable to Llewellyn, see below, ch. 10.

50 Hall, 44 *Va. L. Rev.*, 323 (1958). Hall seems here to confuse the significance of the contribution of realists to discussion of a rational system of evaluation with acknowledgement that such a discussion is relevant to jurisprudence. See Rumble, *op. cit.*, 222ff. For further examples of this type of misunderstanding see Llewellyn, 'Through Title to Contract and a Bit Beyond', 15 *N.Y.U. Law Rev.*, 163 (n.5).

6 THE MAN

1 The main sources of this section are (i) first-hand acquaintance with Llewellyn 1957–8 (see further 'The Quest for Llewellyn', in Twining, *The Karl Llewellyn Papers* (1968)); (ii) interviews with Professor Soia Mentschikoff (widow), the late Professor Kenneth Latourette (cousin), Dr Emma Corstvet Llewellyn (second wife), Professor E. Adamson Hoebel, the late Professor A. L. Corbin, Professor Ernest Haggard,

and numerous friends and colleagues; (iii) various published memoirs of Llewellyn especially by Edward H. Levi: (11 *U. Chi. L.S. Record*, 29 (1962)), Grant Gilmore (71 *Yale L. J.*, 813 (1962)), A. L. Corbin (*ibid.*, 805, 8 *Yale Law Report*, no. 2, 9 (1962)), William O. Douglas (29 *U. Chi. L. Rev.*, 611 (1962)), Charles E. Clark (*ibid.*, 614), William A. Schnader (*ibid.*, 617), Harry W. Jones, 'Pelagius' (*ibid.*, 619), Takeo Hayakawa (18 *Rutgers L. Rev.*, 717 (1964)), E. Adamson Hoebel (*ibid.*, 735), Charles D. Breitel (*ibid.*, 745), J. Beem (7 *U. Chi. L. S. Rec.*, no. 2, 18 (1958)), Max Rheinstein (27 *Rabels Zeitschift fur Auslandisches und Internationales Privatrecht*, 601 (1962)); (iv) autobiographical fragments and reminiscences by Llewellyn scattered throughout his writings; the most sustained attempt at autobiography appears in a series of lectures given in the course on 'Law in our Society' in 1955 in which he traced a large part of his own intellectual development, K.L.P.C. Series M.

2 Ex rel. Soia Mentschikoff Llewellyn.

3 'Behind the Law of Divorce', 33 *Col. L. Rev.*, 251(n) (1933).

4 Ex rel. Soia Mentschikoff Llewellyn, confirmed by Kenneth S. Latourette.

5 MS. 'A Non-Conformist Puzzles over Education', K.L.P. B.V. 4.C., 3 (1924).

6 K.L.P. B.V.7. Llewellyn was the camp's 'disciplinary counsellor'. This experience, he claimed, taught him a great deal about 'adjudication and justice, criminal law and the general nature of the decisional process' (Lecture, 10 May 1955). Sumner had made the point that an excellent mode of understanding social phenomena was to visit the frontier or some relatively simple primitive community. Llewellyn found that a boys' camp was an equally good example of a simple face-to-face group which each year went through the phases of formation, development and the breaking-in of new recruits; it had the further advantage that he could be a participant-observer of the processes of law-government within the group. He never tried to exploit his experiences systematically, but he quite frequently used examples from boys' camps to illustrate general jurisprudential points, for example:

'[I]t was in boys' camp that I discovered that there was nothing inherently unjust about a retroactive decision, if the decision could be adequately fore-felt by the people concerned. There was never any difficulty in getting a boy to accept a penalty on the basis of something that there was no rule against, if he became convinced that the spirit of the camp was against the activity he had indulged in. And that is very useful for a man who otherwise worries how to reconcile, for example, an emergent case with the concepts of justice ... you discover that it works. We leave it out of the criminal field for very different reasons, political in nature and not having to do with the inherent qualities of justice at all' (*ibid*).

The principal lesson that Llewellyn claimed to have learned from working as a camp counsellor was that the fundamental problems with which law is concerned are common to nearly all human groups and that these problems are apprehended most easily by observing simple face-to-face groups, especially those which are in a state of flux (see the law-jobs theory, below, p. 175).

7 See further, below pp. 123ff.

8 The following account of Llewellyn's German schooling is based on an unpublished paper entitled 'Llewellyn and Germany" by Dr Ulrich Drobnig, who interviewed several of Llewellyn's contemporaries and examined some publications of the Realgymnasium. Dr Drobnig's chief informant about this period was Hans Lachmund (see below, note 11).

9 Bibliography, nos. 17, 22, 33, 34, 39, 147, 180. The most important of these is the book *Präjudizenrecht und Rechtsprechung in Amerika* (1933), on which see Radin, 33 *Col. L. Rev.*, 199 (1933).

10 Kocoureck to Llewellyn (1934); Ehrenzweig, interview (1964).

11 Drobnig, *op. cit.*, 3 (n.8). Llewellyn made many German friends. Much the closest of these was Hans Lachmund, the son of his English teacher. Lachmund remained in touch with him until his death. Both followed legal careers, Lachmund becoming a judge in Mecklenburg. When Llewellyn returned to Germany in 1928 and again in 1931 the two saw a great deal of each other and they even started to collaborate on an article on procedure.
Another close friend was Liesel Spencker, a young Schwerin girl, who was also admired by Lachmund. Her name recurs in Llewellyn's letters to Lachmund and in 1927 he wrote: 'And Liesel was for ten years the model to which every girl who wanted to please me had to adapt herself. Even my wife has much in common with Liesel' (Llewellyn to Lachmund, August 1927). Ultimately Liesel married Wilhelm Frels of Leipzig; Llewellyn was a frequent visitor to their house when he was a visiting professor there in 1932, and that summer Liesel accompanied him on his tour of French cathedrals. However, it was another girl, Else Hagen, also a friend from his Schwerin days, to whom Llewellyn became engaged in 1915 after he had been wounded in the field. The relationship did not last, for Else's parents insisted that Llewellyn should live in Germany, which he was unwilling to do. The engagement was officially broken off after the United States' entry into the war, two years later.

12 Quoted by Drobnig, *op. cit.*, 3.

13 *Ibid.*

14 *Ibid.*, 4.

15 K.L.P. T., II, 6.

16 Mrs Margarethe Lachmund to Mrs Arthur Schiller, March 1962.

This corrects an error in Twining, *The Karl Llewellyn Papers* at p. 42, which suggests that Llewellyn's efforts were abortive.

17 On Yale, see G. Pierson, *Yale: College and University 1871–1937* (1955); F. C. Hicks, *Yale Law School* (4 pamphlets, 1935–8). The atmosphere of Yale College of the period is evoked in Owen Johnson's story, *Stover at Yale* (1912, reprinted 1968 with an introduction by President Kingman Brewster).

18 K.L.P., S., I.

19 *History of the Class of Nineteen-Fifteen*, 226.

20 Corbin, 8 *Yale Law Report*, no. 2, 9 (1962). He maintained that his main reason for taking up boxing was to teach himself to control his temper (ex rel. Soia Mentschikoff Llewellyn).

21 *Ibid.*

22 Drobnig, *op. cit.*, 5.

23 E. P. Morris (1853–1938), Dunham Professor of the Latin Language and Literature, Yale 1909–19. See MS fragment K.L.P. B. V. 4a.

24 William Graham Sumner (1840–1910), economist and sociologist. See especially the account by A. G. Keller, *Reminiscences (Mainly Personal) of William Graham Sumner* (1933). James G. Leyburn, 15 *Int. Enc. Soc. Sci.*, 406 (1968). Also Llewellyn MS, 'Sumner's Essays', K.L.P. B. V. Sumner's shift to sociology seems to have followed swiftly on the publication of Spencer's *The Study of Sociology* (1875), Leyburn, *op. cit.*

25 It is not clear from the records whether Llewellyn was actually taught by Keller but it is highly likely that he was; there is definite evidence that he had some personal contact with him. K.L.P. S.I. (diary, 1916). Llewellyn claimed that reading Sumner had been the most exciting experience of his undergraduate days. Lecture, 1955, K.L.P. C. series M.

26 W. G. Sumner, *Folkways – A Study of the Sociological Importance of Usages, Manners, Customs, Mores and Morals* (1906, reprinted Mentor Books, 1960, ed. W. L. Phelps – from which the page references are taken).

27 *Op. cit.*, 32.

28 *Op. cit.*, 33.

29 *Op. cit.*, 42–3.

30 Sumner placed great emphasis on the unplanned nature of the folkways; he was also well known for his advocacy of *laissez-faire* ideas; in view of this it is not surprising that certain dicta gave currency to the notion that he had a fatalistic attitude towards social change and thought that legislation and reform could only follow and could never bring about such change. This has rightly been shown to be an incorrect interpretation of Sumner's views (H. Ball, G. E. Simpson, K. Ikeda, 'A Re-examination of William Graham Sumner on Law and Social Change', 14 *Jo. Leg. Ed.*, 299 (1962)). The problem of reform was in fact a central concern of his. Although inclined towards pes-

simism, and contemptuous of those who underestimated the toughness of folkways and mores, he was not a fatalist. Reform and correction were difficult, but far from hopeless; indeed one of his main hopes for the science of society was that it might 'lead up to an art of societal management which should be intelligent, effective and scientific' (*Folkways*, 114).

31 G. P. Murdock, 9 *Enc. Soc. Sci.* (1933).

32 *The Cheyenne Way*, 275.

33 See below, p. 176.

34 See Phelps preface to *Folkways*; for Llewellyn's attitude to philosophers see below, pp. 172–4.

35 'Non-Conformist Puzzles over Education', MS K.L.P. B. V. 4.c. (1924). Llewellyn sometimes distinguished between eccentrics (cool non-conformists who 'moved the world') and rebels (emotional and often ineffectual). He liked to think of himself as an eccentric rather than as a rebel and was willing to conform in unimportant matters, if this was necessary to further a cause: 'To sell radical ideas you need to wear tails' (ex rel. Soia Mentschikoff Llewellyn).

36 Lecture, 26 April 1955, K.L.P. C. series M.10.

37 *History of the Class of 1915*, 246–7.

38 See generally F. C. Hicks, *Yale Law School, op. cit.*; A. L. Corbin, 'A Creative Process', 6 *Yale Law Report*, no. 1 (1959); 'Sixty-Eight Years at Law', 11 *ibid.*, no. 3 (1965).

39 Letter to Arthur Hermann, 28 September 1918.

40 Ex rel. A. L. Corbin. It seems likely that Llewellyn also had contact during the same summer with Professor Ernst Freund of the University of Chicago Law School, who seems to have made a great impression on him; see 'The Adventures of Rollo', 2 *U. Chi. L. S. Record* (1953).

41 There is a substantial amount of material on the relationship between Corbin and Llewellyn, notably (i) Corbin MS., 'An Account by A. L. Corbin of his association with Karl N. Llewellyn', 26 September 1965; (ii) Twining, correspondence with Corbin 1963–5; (iii) Corbin, 'A Tribute to Karl Llewellyn', 71 *Yale L. J.*, 805 (1962); (iv) Corbin, 'Sixty Eight Years at Law', 11 *Yale Law Report*, no. 3, 20 (1965); (v) for Llewellyn on Corbin, see K.L.P. B. II, 11, and 33 *Col. L. Rev.*, 1085 (1933).

42 Corbin to Llewellyn 1 December 1960; this is a long and very enthusiastic letter on *The Common Law Tradition*.

43 See below, ch. 10.

44 Llewellyn's approach to legal analysis often contrasted quite sharply with his speculative work. In the former he strove to be the meticulous craftsman – in the view of some he was inclined to be over-meticulous; in writing and talking jurisprudence he was quite often slapdash.

Cases and Materials on the Law of Sales and *The Bramble Bush* exemplify this duality.

45 Corbin, foreword to Hohfeld, *Fundamental Legal Conceptions*, X (1964 ed.).

46 28 *Yale L. J.*, 795 (1919), reprinted, *Jurisprudence*, ch. 26.

47 See below, note 55.

48 'There – still unwritten – was his greatest single contribution; still unwritten but given to students', *Jurisprudence*, 492.

49 Lecture, 26 April 1955, K.L.P.C. Series M.10. See also *The Bramble Bush*, 84–9.

50 *Ibid.*

51 See below, p. 137.

52 Lecture, 26 April 1955.

53 Count A. Korzbyski, *Science and Sanity* (1933), which much impressed Llewellyn when it was published.

54 E.g., *Cases and Materials on the Law of Sales*, introduction, xxiii. 8 *Jo. Leg. Ed.*, 399–403 (1956), discussed above, p. 63.

55 One incident related by Llewellyn gives some indication of the strength of his feelings for Hohfeld and of the nature of his relationship with Cook at that time. Shortly after Hohfeld's death, Cook accepted a post at Columbia. A rumour spread among the students at Yale that Cook was planning to 'steal' Hohfeld's ideas on conflicts of laws and publish the work as his own. Llewellyn got hold of the key of Hohfeld's office and took his notes and a heavily annotated edition of Story on *Conflicts* with the intention of writing an article on 'Hohfeld's Logical and Legal Basis of the Conflicts of Laws' to anticipate Cook. He abandoned the project only because he could not understand the notes. Subsequently Cook published an influential work entitled *The Logical and Legal Bases of the Conflict of Laws*, without any significant acknowledgement of Hohfeld. The story was told by Llewellyn in a lecture (26 April 1955, K.L.P. C. Series M. 10). Corbin expressed surprise and scepticism on hearing this story in 1965. He pointed out that Cook and Hohfeld had worked closely together. Cook became Hohfeld's literary executor and edited a selection of his writings. Both men were interested in conflicts and they had been thinking along parallel lines before they met; both, for instance, had long had a contempt for the work of Joseph Beale. Cook frequently acknowledged his general intellectual debt to Hohfeld. Even if Cook had been guilty of 'stealing' Hohfeld's ideas on conflicts – a charge that would be difficult to substantiate – Llewellyn was prepared to concede that this was probably a case of inadvertent plagiarism.

56 Henry Wade Rogers (1853–1926) was Dean of the Yale Law School from 1903 to 1916. See F. Hicks, *op. cit.*, 58–63. Llewellyn's views on Rogers were forcibly expressed in a lecture on 10 May 1955. K.L.P.

Series M. 15. Corbin, too, was not enthusiastic about Rogers: 4 *Yale Law Report*, no. 2, 2–4 (1958).
57 Llewellyn lecture, *op. cit.*, 1.
58 William Howard Taft was President of the United States from 1909 to 1913 and Chief Justice of the United States from 1921 to 1930. On his time at Yale (1913–21), see F. C. Hicks, *Taft and New Haven* (1945).
59 See especially *The Common Law Tradition*, 21–2; lecture, 9 May 1955, K.L.P. Series M. 14.
60 See below, 68n.
61 Lecture, 9 May 1955.
62 On 'beauty' in law, see *Jurisprudence*, 171–96, and ch. 9.
63 See below, p. 168.
64 Lecture, 10 May 1955.
65 *Ibid.* See also K.L.P. C. Series A and B (1923 and 1924).
66 See Walter K. Earle, *Mr. Shearman and Mr. Sterling and How They Grew* (1963), especially 218–24. A substantial number of Llewellyn's working papers survive from this period, K.L.P. E.
67 On Lancaster, see Earle, *op. cit.*, 229–30; Llewellyn, 16 *Albany L. Rev.*, 1 (1952), and lecture, 10 May 1955.
68 *Op. cit.* n.37, at p. 247.
69 Memo., 'Biography', K.L.P. S. I.
70 *Ibid.*
71 Corbin to Twining, 1965.
72 A bound collection of *Documents of Marshall Conferences* is preserved in the Treasure Room of Columbia University Law School library.
73 *Ibid.*, especially Memo no. 3 by Llewellyn.
74 Yntema to Twining, 11 October 1965.
75 Interview, Hamden 1965.
76 See also Corbin, 'A Tribute to Karl Llewellyn', 8 *Yale Law Report*, 9–10 (1962).
77 Ex. rel. Grant Gilmore, 1968.
78 E.g., the minutes of the Yale Law School faculty show that an invitation was extended to Llewellyn at a later date, but are silent on the matter during this period.
79 Some of Llewellyn's working papers on the Uniform Trusts Receipts Act survive in K.L.P. F.II. These contain some interesting evidence on the historical relationship between this Act and Article 9 of the Uniform Commercial Code.
80 Memo on 'Possible Uniform Commercial Code', K.L.P. J. II.1.b. (1940); quoted below, appendix E.
81 A seemingly small change marks the start of a breakthrough. In 1925 the Columbia Law School catalogue listed courses on mortgages and suretyship, with casebooks by Kirchwey and Ames prescribed by the instructor, K. N. Llewellyn. In 1926, however, Llewellyn and Magill

jointly offered 'Security I' and 'Security II' and used their own materials. Thus a single 'functional' category (securing of credit) was substituted for two legal devices (mortgages and suretyship) as the basis of organisation; the ground covered in the new courses was rather more extensive, without any increase in the time prescribed for study. The class hours for the various courses are of interest: 1925: mortgages (3 hours), suretyship (3 hours); 1926: security I (3 hours), security II (2 hours); 1927: security I (3 hours), security II (3 hours). See Currie, II, 72–3, on the disappointments of the Columbia experiment in respect of saving time by reorienting the subject-matter. Llewellyn remained optimistic: 35 *Col. L. Rev.*, 671 (1935). The shift to security as an organising concept anticipated the basis for the major simplification of this area of the law in Article 9 of the Uniform Commercial Code. Llewellyn was not the first to suggest that security would be a good organizing concept; Dean Stone, for instance, had made a similar suggestion in 1924, 10 *A.B.A.J.*, 233, 235 (1924), Currie, II, 12. John Hanna took over the courses on security from Llewellyn and Douglas and eventually produced two highly regarded casebooks: *Cases and Other Materials on Security* (1932); *Cases and Materials on the Law of Creditors' Rights* (1931).

82 35 *Col. L. Rev.*, 651, 652 (1935).
83 Leipzig (1933); see Radin, 'Case Law and Stare Decisis', 33 *Col. L. Rev.*, 199 (1933), a review article of the book.
84 *The Common Law Tradition*, 339.
85 Drobnig, 'Llewellyn and Germany', MS., 26. The ensuing account draws heavily on this paper.
86 MS., 'Llewellyn's Inquiry into Judicial Deciding' (1956–7) (attached to later editions of *Law in Our Society*).
87 K.L.P. D. VII.
88 Llewellyn to Nussbaum, 17 December 1931.
89 K.L.P. citation mislaid.
90 Rheinstein, *op. cit.* Llewellyn began to translate some of Max Weber into English about 1935 (K.L.P. B. II. 44). He did not complete the project but thereafter he regularly acknowledged Weber as a major influence, the exact nature of which is not entirely clear.
91 Especially lectures, 1955. K.L.P. C. Series M.
92 Drobnig, *op. cit.*, 26.
93 See below, ch. 13.
94 *Ex. rel.* A. L. Corbin (unconfirmed).
95 A collection of press cuttings and some correspondence relating to this incident are to be found in K.L.P. S.I. See especially *New York World Telegram*, 14 August 1934. A leader in the *New York Herald Tribune* on the same day commented:

A PROFESSOR IN PRACTICAL POLITICS

It is announced that the Knickerbocker Democrats are going to back Karl Nickerson Llewellyn, Betts professor of jurisprudence at Columbia University for member of the Democratic State Committee in place of the redoubtable James J. Hines, than whom there is no more hard-boiled or practical politician in Tammany Hall.

It suggests a Daniel entering the lions' den. We sympathize strongly with Mr. Llewellyn in the grief that will be his before the Hines crowd gets through with him, but we strongly applaud his courage and approve the spirit that moves him to get into active politics. After the primary campaign he will know a great deal more than he does now as to how Tammany leaders operate and as to the difficulties involved in dislodging them. And, if his spirit is not broken and his zeal for reform continues, he will be in a better position to be effective in future fights to rescue the Democratic organization of the 11th Assembly District from the clutches of Mr. Hines.

Professor Llewellyn has a record of service in working to improve the administration of the law – making it more vital – and in raising the standards of the legal profession. It is an encouraging sign when educators are willing to desert their theories and engage in the active rough and tumble of political combat. Too seldom have some of our other educators now in public life bothered to test their theories in the clinics of actual experience.

96 Llewellyn's position is set out in 'Should Congress Enact a Federal Sedition Law?', 14 *Congressional Digest*, 251 (1935). Llewellyn campaigned actively during 1935 to oppose a Bill on Incitement to Disobedience of Military and Armed Forces. K.L.P. T. II.3.

The question is sometimes asked: why did Llewellyn not join other radical jurists from Columbia and Yale who went to Washington as New Dealers? The answer appears to be that, first, he was not basically in sympathy with the welfare orientation of most New Dealers, and secondly, his experience in New York politics had made him realise that he was vulnerable to blackmail because of his German connection and this made him reluctant to enter public life.

97 One reason for Llewellyn's less active involvement in such activities after 1942–3 was fear of doing anything to jeopardise the Uniform Commercial Code Project. His campaigning for legal aid was not affected.

98 See below, pp. 349ff.

99 See below, ch. 8.

100 See below, ch. 11.

101 See below, p. 337.

102 A series on the same topic was given as the North Lectures at Franklin and Marshall College, also in 1941.

103 See below, ch. 10.

104 See below, p. 354.

105 On the Pueblos, see below, ch. 13. On the Commission on the Rights etc. of the American Indian, see K.L.P. I. IV.

106 See below, ch. 9. Transcripts of thirty-three lectures given in this course are to be found in K.L.P. C. Series H. (1948–49). Llewellyn had taught jurisprudence jointly with Patterson at Columbia and some of his lectures in 1947–8 anticipated the new course at Harvard.

107 See *Handbook of A.A.L.S.* (1949).

108 See below, pp. 283–4.

109 As early as 1930 Llewellyn wrote the following inscription in his presentation copy of *The Bramble Bush* for Harry Bigelow of the University of Chicago Law School: 'To Harry Bigelow whose school I hope shortly to see crowd these seaboard institutions to the wall. 11/1/30 Karl' (Information of Professor Sheldon Tefft).

110 Levi, *op. cit.*, n.1.

110A From Twining *The Karl Llewellyn Papers*, pp. 7–10 (1968).

111 Holmes, 'Profession of the Law' (1886). *Speeches*, 22 (1913). The phrase 'the half-way artist' as applied to Llewellyn is to be found in *The Bramble Bush*, 126.

112 See generally K.L.P. B.V. and VI. On his 'war essays' see below, p. 482.

113 Printed in Twining, *The Karl Llewellyn Papers*, 113 (1968).

114 See *The Common Law Tradition*, 398–9 (Air: Pelagius; Arrangement: Jerry Green and Christopher Moore).

115 *Put in His Thumb*, preface, v (1931); reviewed by W. Nelles, 41 *Yale L. J.* 646 (1932).

116 *Ibid.*, 12.

117 MS. K.L.P. B.VI. As Llewellyn admitted in the preface to *Put in His Thumb*, his serious poems contain 'echoes of John McClure, or James Stephens, or Sandburg, or Masefield'. He might have added Ogden Nash:

> 'When a girl gets a man by the testickles
> The rest tickles' (MS fragment).

There is a limerick on the same theme in an MS entitled 'Somewhat Lewd Loud Limericks': K.L.P.B. VI.

118 Much of Llewellyn's writing is characterised by deliberate informality: '. . . I care little for propriety, and less for manner, if – as I believe – occasional lapses from the accepted taste and dignity of print give more hope of making vivid to the students who are a teacher's life some of the more passionately held convictions which motivate his living' (*The Bramble Bush*, Preface (p. 8 of 2nd ed.)). Perhaps because of its informality, perhaps because it is often casually allusive, perhaps because of its rhythm, Llewellyn's prose may deceive by its apparent simplicity: the style invites skimming, the substance often requires slow perusal. This is particularly the case in those passages where the

author seems to be proceeding by free association, running together in a single compact passage whole groups of ideas that need to be slowly and cautiously unpacked by the analytical thinker. Thus the obstacles to understanding Llewellyn are not solely a matter of taste.

119 E.g., Thurman Arnold to Llewellyn, June 1933; interview with Professor Stanley Kaplan. There were also some curious parallels between Carlyle's fictitious account of his experiences with the Philosopher of [the] Clothes and my own research on Llewellyn. In *Sartor Resartus* 'a young enthusiastic Englishman, however unworthy' (Everyman ed., 14 (1964)) becomes an admirer of a foreign savant who is unknown 'or what is worse misknown' in England (*ibid.*, 11). So the question arises:

How could the Philosophy . . . and the Author of such Philosophy be brought home in any measure to the business and bosoms of our own English Nation? (*ibid.*, 6). Not the least of the obstacles is that of style:

Occasionally, as above hinted, we find consummate vigour, a true inspiration; his burning thoughts step forth in fit burning words, like so many full-formed Minervas, issuing amid flame and splendour from Jove's head; a rich, idiomatic diction, picturesque allusions, fiery poetic emphasis, or quaint tricksy turns; all the graces and terrors of a wild Imagination, wedded to the clearest Intellect, alternate in beautiful vicissitude. Were it not that . . . circumlocutions, repetitions, touches even of pure doting jargon, so often intervene (*ibid.*, 22).

His mode of thought is also unfashionable:

Our Professor's method is not, in any case, that of common school Logic, where the truths all stand in a row, each holding by the skirts of the other; but at best that of practical Reason, proceeding by large Intuition over whole systematic groups and kingdoms; whereby, we might say, a noble complexity, almost like that of Nature, reigns in his Philosophy . . . a mighty maze, yet, as faith whispers, not without a plan (*ibid.*, 38).

For such reasons it is obvious that 'a paramount popularity in England we cannot promise him' (*ibid.*, 20). Some of the contemporary reviewers of *Sartor Resartus* made themselves ridiculous by trying to prove that Carlyle *was* Teufelsdrockh. Their fault was not only lack of humour, but also oversimplification. Similarly the rich potential of *Sartor Resartus* for apt quotations offers a strong temptation to press this analogy too far. There is little evidence of a close affinity between their political or philosophical views. Llewellyn was not Carlyle, nor was he Teufelsdrockh.

120 Woodward, *The Age of Reform*, 524 (1938).
121 K.L.P. C.P. II, 4 (1959).
122 See especially 'On the Good, The True and The Beautiful in Law' (1942), *Jurisprudence*, 167, and bibliography, items 245, 246. Unpublished MSS. K.L.P. Z. I-IV. On the Teufelsdrockh Papers, see Twining, *The Karl Llewellyn Papers*, 43-4 (1968).

123 E.g., 'The Normative, the Legal and the Law-Jobs', 49 *Yale L. J.*, 1355 (1940), and some passages in *The Common Law Tradition*.

124 MS, 'Drama, Dramatics and Kids', K.L.P. B.V. 8.a.

125 While Llewellyn's penchant for the folksy and the unsophisticated was quite marked it only represented one side of him. His taste in music, the graphic arts and architecture was catholic and reasonably well-informed – he was, for instance, a lover of classical music, especially Bach and Beethoven, as well as jazz and folk songs; and while he may not have been enthusiastic about Kant and Hegel, his discussions of Aquinas, Aristotle and Weber do not suggest a general lack of sophistication.

126 H. Cairns, review of *The Cheyenne Way* (1942), 55 *Harv. L. Rev.*, 707, 710.

127 See further, appendix A.

128 One story in circulation dramatizes this quality in a different context. Llewellyn had persuaded a rather reluctant Cardozo to sit for the exiled Russian sculptor, Sergei Konenkov. Llewellyn attended one of the sittings and found Konenkov almost despairing of being able to 'capture' Cardozo. At his first attempt, Konenkov had depicted Cardozo as hard and ruthless, without catching any of his warmth or idealism. So Llewellyn bought some clay and on the following day he came back with a small head which he had produced himself. When Konenkov saw it he was delighted, claiming that he now realised what was wrong with his first efforts; he then proceeded to produce a new bust which satisfied Llewellyn. (Ex rel. Soia Mentschikoff Llewellyn and Professor E. Haggard – there is some doubt about the exact details of the story.) Castings of the work are housed in the law schools of Columbia, Harvard and the University of Chicago. Such stories, for this one is not unique, may not convince the sceptical, but they helped to confirm Llewellyn's reputation for 'genius'. Llewellyn, who was on close terms with Konenkov, obtained commissions for him to do busts of Holmes, Cardozo and Boas. He also did one of Llewellyn. Konenkov eventually returned to Russia.

129 See, for instance, Corbin's judgment:

It was a constant joy, both personally and intellectually, to work with him. I was aware that he had highly poetic and emotional tendencies; and I sometimes advised keeping one's 'feet on the ground'; but whenever Karl's mind was concentrated on a juristic problem, I have never known anyone who did clearer thinking or who reached sounder results ('An Account by A. L. Corbin of his Association with Karl N. Llewellyn', September 1965, (MS)).

130 It is significant that Llewellyn greatly admired John Dewey. They were colleagues at Columbia for several years and Llewellyn sometimes attended meetings of a seminar on legal philosophy given in the law school jointly by Dewey and Edwin Patterson. Llewellyn was sympa-

thetic with many of Dewey's ideas, but he did not look on himself as a 'Deweyian' in logic and philosophy and he deplored some of the excesses of Dewey's disciples in the field of education. As with Holmes, Llewellyn's admiration for Dewey was as much personal as intellectual: 'Since Thomas Jefferson or Benjamin Franklin there has been nobody with the sweet, childlike, open eye to see things fresh that Dewey had' (lecture, 31 March 1959, K.L.P.C., series P, 29). Dewey's method corresponded exactly with Llewellyn's conception of realism: 'His method of dealing with problems is still and will always be the great and needed method: Take a fresh look, look to see what is there, and what it is about, and re-pose your issues in those terms' (MS, 'John Dewey and our Law', 4. K.L.P.B., III, 14 (1949)).

Unfortunately Dewey failed to approach law in the same way as he had approached politics, art and education. Llewellyn blamed Patterson for this, in that he had treated Dewey first and foremost as a logician and had diverted his attention too much in the direction of abstract theorising and away from taking a 'fresh look' at actual legal processes. He had written one or two important articles, but his potential had not been exploited. Llewellyn's private ambition, as he once confessed in a lecture, was to perform the role of a Dewey in jurisprudence, trying to do for law what the great man had done for other subjects. The most pleasing compliment that could be paid to Llewellyn was to compare him to John Dewey.

131 The main sources for this section are (i) interviews with Soia Mentschikoff Llewellyn and E. Adamson Hoebel; (ii) miscellaneous Llewellyn MSS especially 'Position Re Religion, 1943', K.L.P.B.V.4.d.

132 Memo, 'Llewellyn to Members of Commission on the Rights etc. of the American Indians' (undated), K.L.P. I. IV.

133 'Position re Religion, 1943'. This is a particularly revealing document in which Llewellyn repeatedly draws analogies between his approach to jurisprudence and the code and his approach to religion; for example,

... What Paul did was to put *structure, carrying-power*, under Jesus' teachings. I find I feel about Paul the same way I feel about great lawyers whom I think to have gone sometimes off track. He over-intellectualized, so far as he *wrote*. ... Let me then stay as close as I may to Jesus' and to Paul's living rather than – or better, together with – his writing.
With this, 'rebel' and 'non-rebel' begin to line up. I observe with amusement that I am duplicating in religion a twenty-year road in legal work' (*ibid.*).

134 According to Soia Mentschikoff Llewellyn this letter was drafted about ten days before Llewellyn's death, when he claimed that he had at last understood the idea of salvation through Jesus Christ. Up till then he had not really accepted the Divinity of Christ; his own religious ideas had rather been in the style of Old Testament Puritanism,

emphasising the idea of a harsh God sitting in judgment on the individual, tempering justice with mercy (symbolised for Llewellyn by the Virgin Mary), but not giving much scope to the idea of forgiveness of sins and the possibility of a fresh start during one's lifetime. Thus only at the very end of his life did Llewellyn show signs of being relieved of the burden of a harsh Puritan conscience.

135 See below, Appendix A.

136 Jerome Michael of Columbia Law School, a close friend of Llewellyn's, was trying to get his support for an Anti-Discrimination Manifesto within the AALS. A draft letter to Michael, justifying his reasons for not supporting the move survives in K.L.P. R.J. Michael (undated).

137 See below, p. 292.

138 See below, ch. 13.

139 As indicated in the text there are differing opinions about Llewellyn's 'liberalism' among those who knew him, including some of his intimates. The interpretation adopted here is essentially that of Soia Mentschikoff Llewellyn. It must be conceded, however, that this is not the only tenable view.

140 '[Characteristically, natural lawyers] use human reason (Right Reason – the best they have, tested as best they can test it, with results conceived as Right) to explore for and ascertain the Right goals of a legal system, and they then propound their results explicitly as *the* Right Goals. (Contrast Ihering, whose emphasis is on process – the part played by purpose; the horse-sense inadequacy of over-abstract self-centred conceptualism in actual legal work; men's interests as driving factors, etc. – with his ultimate values largely unstressed or implicit; or Holmes, to whom ultimate goals were 'can't-helps', and 'fighting faiths', not subject to the test of reason – *though to be lived by and fought for*; or Dewey, whose Ultimates – e.g. ongoing ever-unfolding of the perfectability of average human nature in self-disciplined freedom; and ever-widening tolerance and growth – are largely implicit, only his *methods* and more immediate goals (democracy; education for growth and responsibility) being really proclaimed; or Pound, again proclaiming a method, but preaching mainly as goals some *interstitial* goals such as due process, judicial review, effective court organization and procedure, balance in approach' (*Law in Our Society*, MS, 60 (1950 ed.)).

141 *Op. cit.* (n.136).

142 See below, p. 367.

143 A crucial point of disagreement between Llewellyn and Hoebel was whether the traditional 'parental' dispute-settlement mechanisms of the Pueblos were consistent with the ideals of American democracy as reflected in the adversary process.

144 See below, p. 187.

145 To Llewellyn 'due process' connoted principally the idea of a fair hearing and adequate representation, where necessary. The concept has been broadened by judicial decisions in recent years.

146 'Technique without ideals is a menace; . . . ideals without technique
are a mess': 'The Adventures of Rollo', 2 *U. Chi. L. Sch. Record*, 3, 23
(1952). See also, 'What Law Cannot Do for Inter-Racial Peace',
Jurisprudence, 480 (1957).

147 Llewellyn left behind him a very substantial collection of papers,
including some important unpublished manuscripts. In 1964 I undertook to supervise the sorting and arrangement of this collection prior
to their presentation to the University of Chicago. The project was
completed in 1965 and the Karl Llewellyn Collection is housed in the
library of the University of Chicago Law School. Two publications
were associated with the project: a detailed mimeographed inventory
of the collection (Ellinwood and Twining: *The Karl Llewellyn Papers:
A Guide to the Collection* (revised ed. 1970)) and a short book entitled
The Karl Llewellyn Papers (1968). The latter contains a personal memoir
of Llewellyn, a description and evaluation of the collection, bibliographies of Llewellyn's published and unpublished works, and a
selection of shorter manuscripts which had not previously been
published. While there is inevitably some overlap between *The Karl
Llewellyn Papers* and Part Two of the present work, they are intended
to complement each other.

7   TWO EARLY WORKS

[Parts of chs. 7–9 are based on an article originally published in 30
M.L.R. 514 (1967), 31 *M.L.R.* 165 (1968).]

1 The review of Campbell was published in 40 *Harv. L. Rev.*, 142 (1926).
The other reviews were published in 32 *Yale Law Jo.*, 299 (1923), *ibid.*,
633 (1923), 33 *Yale Law Jo.*, 226 (1923), *ibid.*, 894 (1924), 34 *Yale Law
Jo.*, 454 (1925), 25 *Col. L. Rev.*, 980 (1925), *ibid.*, 1101 (1925).

2 40 *Harv. L. Rev.*, 143, 144–5 (1926).

3 *Ibid.*, 145.

4 *Op. cit.*, ix.

5 C. C. Langdell, *A Selection of Cases on the Law of Contracts* (1871). Further
notable examples are McDougal and Haber, *Property, Wealth, Land*
(1948); Mueller, *Contract in Context* (1951); Dession, *Criminal Law,
Administration and Public Order* (1948) and nearly all of Corbin's works.

6 Most striking, perhaps, is the change made in the third edition of
Woodward's *Cases on the Law of Sales* (1933) by the editor, Lawrence Vold.
To quote the preface:

One distinctly new feature not found in the earlier editions has been added.
An attempt has been made to relate the legal material definitely to the business
facts of current marketing transactions. To this end occasional extracts from
certain business literature, or briefer references thereto, have been from time

to time included in the footnotes. To this end there is also now included in the appendix, not only a group of typical business documents frequently encountered in current sales transactions, but also a few samples of illustrative practical cases and comments taken from the business side of marketing.

Specific credit for this is given by Vold to Llewellyn.

7 See Ehrenzweig, 'The American Casebook: "Cases and Materials" ' (1944), 32 *Georgetown Law Journal*, 224; Currie, 'The Materials of Law Study III' (1955), 8 *J. Leg. Ed.*, 1 *et seq.*

8 See above, ch. 4.

9 Report of Dean Young B. Smith, Columbia, 12–3 (1933).

10 At p. xxiii.

11 8 *Jo. Leg. Ed.*, 50 (n.224) (1955).

12 At this time Llewellyn accepted the then fashionable psychological theory of rationalisation with fewer reservations than he did subsequently (see especially *The Common Law Tradition*, 11 *et seq.*); but it should be noted that even at this stage he by no means ignored completely the reasoning of the judges, and a fair number of judgements are reproduced *in toto*, representing approximately one-third of the material. Subsequently he was to distinguish more clearly the psychology of decision-making from the logic of justification. If the book had been revised twenty years later the editor might also have been more inhibited about making his own digests of the facts of cases.

13 On the handling and distortion of facts in judicial processes, see introduction, x, and 6 *Am. L. Sch. Rev.*, 670, 675 (1930).

14 The 1919 edition of Williston's *Cases on Sales* has 1,196 pages and just under 400 cases; Woodward (1913) has approximately 250 cases in 791 pages; Falconbridge, a Canadian book, has 680 pages and about 175 cases.

15 Introduction, xxii.

16 *Op. cit.*, 204.

17 P.XI. cp. MS, 'Babel versus Teamwork: Jurisprudence since 1900', at 5. K.L.P. B III 36(d) (1942–3).

18 H. Oliphant, *Summary of Studies in Legal Education*, ch. ix (1928). See also, J. A. Jolowicz (ed.), *Classification and Division of the Law* (1970).

19 'On the Problems of Teaching "Private" Law', 54 *Harv. L. Rev.*, 775, 787 (1941).

20 *Op. cit.*, 788.

21 The chapter headings read as follows: Book I. *The Contract for Sale:* Chap. 1: 'The Price Term of the Contract'; Chap. II: 'Place and Manner of Delivery'; Chap. III: 'Seller's Obligation as to Quality: "Warranty" '; Chap. IV: 'The Buyer's Remedies: Further Technical Aspects'; and Chap. V: 'Quantity and Time of Delivery'. Book II. *Property in Goods*: Chap. VI: 'Title'; Chap. VII: 'The Unpaid Seller and the Goods'; Chap. VIII: 'Conditional Sales: Instalment Contracts';

NOTES TO CHAPTER 7 483

Chapter IX: 'Intervention of a Financing Agency in Sales Transactions';
Chapter X: 'Certain Policies Overriding Intent'; Chapter XI: 'Statute
of Frauds'; Appendix A: 'Uniform Acts'; Appendix B: 'Typical Forms'.

22 *Op. cit.*, 1.

23 'Study of the actual use of the title concept by the courts in contract
for future sale results in the conclusion that the allocation of title is in
fact determined repeatedly by features of the contract which serve
equally well to solve the problem without recourse to the title concept
itself' (introduction, xiv.)

In a letter to Soia Mentschikoff, dated 23 February 1962, Professor
Milton Handler wrote:

> I was one of the rare professors who had the sagacity to master and employ
> with, I hope, some effectiveness, his monumental but difficult casebook. I
> vividly remember our joint appearance before the Seminar on Legal Education
> in which both of us reviewed Llewellyn's Cases and Materials on Sales. I was
> supposed to be the critic and he the defender. As it turned out, the roles were
> reversed. He was very pleased when I said that his Warranty chapter – which I
> think is one of his many great contributions – was Brahmsian in organization.
> There he applied the classical symphonic form to the presentation of legal
> doctrine. He had two themes: the substantive and procedural. There was first
> the enunciation of both themes; then the further development of each separ-
> ately; and finally a recapitulation or coda in which the two were interrelated
> and then combined. The lesson that he was trying to put over was that pro-
> cedural atavism frequently nullified substantive advances. He was very pleased
> and I very proud that I had unlocked the secret which had eluded most of his
> professorial colleagues.

24 Above, p. 79.

25 *Jurisprudence*, 56n.

26 E.g., Donnelly, Goldstein and Schwartz, *Criminal Law* (1962), Goldstein
and Katz, *The Family and the Law* (1965), Katz, Goldstein and
Dershowitz, *Psychoanalysis Psychiatry and the Law* (1967).

27 *Op. cit., ibid.* On Langdell's educational ideas, see above, p. 11.

28 Preface to *Cases on the Law of Quasi-Contracts* (1888), cited by Redlich,
The Common Law and The Case Method, 24 (Carnegie Foundation,
Bulletin no. 8, 1914).

29 Cf. Pound, *Jurisprudence II*, 129. On standpoint, see Twining 'The Bad
Man Re-visited' *Cornell L. Rev.*, (forthcoming).

30 This is apparent from the introduction and from the much criticised
chapter I of *The Bramble Bush*. Llewellyn's dictum: 'What these officials
do about disputes is, to my mind, the law itself' (2nd ed. 12, modified in
the foreword) and Holmes' parallel statement in 'The Path of the Law'
were each made in the context of an address to intending private practitioners – with the image of 'the counsellor' very much in the forefront
of the mind of the speaker. See below, p. 148.

31 *Op. cit.*, xv (n. 3).

32 See especially 'The Place of Skills in Legal Education' (Report of Committee on Curriculum, drafted by Llewellyn), *Handbook of Association of American Law Schools*, 159–201 (1944); 75 *Col. L. Rev.*, 345 (1945). Cf. Rutter, 'A Jurisprudence of Lawyers' Operations', 13 *J. Leg. Ed.*, 301 (1961). See further, below, p. 354.

33 'The Study of Law as a Liberal Art', *Jurisprudence: Realism in Theory and Practice*, 375, 377 (1960).

34 *Ibid.*, 376.

35 *Ibid.*

36 *Ibid.*, 204–5.

37 Above, p. 79.

38 See above, ch. 5.

39 For citations, see above, pp. 80–1, 411.

40 The main sources used in this section were: (i) Llewellyn, *The Bramble Bush*, 1st ed. (1930), 2nd ed. (1951); miscellaneous drafts for *The New Bramble Bush*, K.L.P. B. III. 4, B. IV. 13; transcripts of 5 Bramble Bush lectures (1931), K.L.P. C. Series C. (ii) Reviews by Gilmore, 60 *Yale Law J.*, 1251 (1951), and Frank 40 *Yale L. J.*, 1120 (1931). Frank, although enthusiastic, considered Llewellyn's moderation 'exaggerated', *ibid.*, 1122. A Llewellyn MS., 'Reviews of The Bramble Bush', K.L.P. B. II. 7. contains five satirical reviews by Llewellyn in the vein of an outraged practitioner, a bolshevik revolutionary, conventional 'Yalumbia' and 'Harmchigan' reviewers, and a layman who berates its essential conservatism.

References to *The Bramble Bush* in this chapter are to the second edition, because this is more generally available.

41 See especially foreword to 2nd ed., 10.

42 At 4.

43 *Ibid.*, 106, Cf. 119.

44 *Ibid.*, 96.

45 See G. Williams, *Learning the Law*, 2 (6th ed. 1957).

46 Holmes, 'The Profession of the Law' (1886); *Speeches* 22 (1913). Cf. the peroration of 'The Path of the Law'.

47 At 128–9.

48 See below, p. 148.

49 'On What is Wrong With So-Called Legal Education', 35. *Col. L. Rev.*, 651, 653 (1935).

50 At 139.

51 At 139–40.

52 At 11.

53 See also introduction to *Cases and Materials on The Law of Sales*.

54 On this, see Twining 'Pericles and the Plumber', 83 *L.Q.R.*, 396 *passim* (1967).

55 At 123-4. Cf. 11.

56 E.g., L. Eron and R. Redmount, 9 *Jo. Leg. Ed.*, 431, 437-8 (1957).

57 At 124.

58 Especially 11-6, 92-5.

59 At 124.

60 At 18.

61 This aspect of *The Bramble Bush* is discussed below, pp. 231ff.

62 On rules, see above, p. 18, below, ch. 9, and Appendix B; on statutory interpretation, see below, ch. 10; on Hohfeld, see above, ch. 2.

63 At 7.

64 At 9.

65 At 12. Cf. 20, 'Thus far I have told you that what law was about was the dealing with disputes. That it was made up *largely* of what officials do about disputes' (italics added). See further passage cited below at p. 348.

66 At 14-5. The private practitioner orientation of the paragraph from which this comes is very clear.

67 See below, pp. 177-80.

68 E.g. Hart, *The Concept of Law*, 133 (1961). See generally D. Moskowitz *Some Aspects of American Legal Realism* D. Phil. Thesis, Oxford (1963).

69 See generally 49 *Yale L. J.*, 1355 *et seq.* (1940).

70 E.g., Dickinson, 79 *U. Pa. L. Rev.*, 833, 838 (1931). Cf. Pound, *Jurisprudence*, II, 129-32 (1959).

71 At 9. After the publication of *The Bramble Bush*, F. Beutel wrote a critical but friendly letter in which he said, *inter alia*: 'Your definition of law in the first chapter states what, to me, is only a half truth.' Llewellyn's marginal comment is: 'Right.' 15 November, 1930. K.L.P. R. II. 6.

72 *Jurisprudence*, 3 (1930).

73 Moskowitz, *op. cit.*, 396-99, points out correctly that Llewellyn returned to the theme of 'what officials do about disputes' in other parts of *The Bramble Bush* (13, 20, 21, 75, 83, and 85) and in some of his other writings in the period 1928-31. Moskowitz continues: 'Contrary to Llewellyn's claim, this definition does not appear on one page only to be disregarded throughout the rest of the book. It is employed consistently throughout the book and the purpose of the critics in quoting the sentence is not to take the sentence out of context but to use that sentence as a summary of the theory expounded in the book' (396). This misses the point of Llewellyn's objection to the continued citation of the sentence, for the following reasons: (i) this was not Llewellyn's 'definition of law'; (ii) the context of *The Bramble Bush*, as outlined in the present chapter, is consistently ignored by critics; (iii) it seems odd that critics should persist in paying attention to an early statement which has been retracted, while almost totally neglecting Llewellyn's more sophisticated

and scholarly discussion of the concept of law in 'The Normative,
The Legal and the Law-Jobs' (see below). Moskowitz justifies his
observance of this extremely dubious practice on the lame excuse that
Llewellyn's later writings 'are not generally considered to be typical of
realism' (402). See also Friedrich, *The Philosophy of Law in Historical
Perspective* (2nd ed.), appendix.

74 See below, p. 200.

75 In 1931 he delivered a series of five introductory lectures which purported to supplement *The Bramble Bush*. Transcripts are to be found in
K.L.P. C. Series C. (1931).

76 At 7.

77 K.L.P. B. III. 4 (1947–51). Four complete chapters and a number of
draft fragments survive.

78 Sets of materials for this course are in K.L.P. M. There are also the
transcripts of a limited number of Elements' lectures in K.L.P. C.
Series N and O.

79 2 *U. of Chi. L. Sch. Record*, no. 1 (1953).

80 *Ibid.*

8   THE CHEYENNE WAY

1 B. Malinowski, *Crime and Custom in Savage Society* (1926). According to
Llewellyn:

I hit the law-jobs first under the star of Keller and Sumner (in that order), and
then of Hohfeld (the atomizer) Cook (the logician), Corbin (the combiner of
Hohfeld and Cook with Sumner-like thinking). I got worried.... And I had
been studying boys in boys' camps, and men in faculties, and written records.
And then I had found Ehrlich, and had been somewhat crushed in spirit, because he had seen so much; and after that I had found Max Weber....

Ms, 'Llewellyn's Appendix on Allocation of Responsibility' (for *The
Cheyenne Way*), K.L.P. I. 1. During the late 1920s and early 1930s
Llewellyn had relatively close personal contact with Franz Boas, the
doyen of Columbia anthropologists. Llewellyn described Hoebel as 'a
Boas-schooled anthropologist' (*ibid.*).

2 *Ibid.* An anthropologist has commented:

In Malinowski's earlier work, *Argonauts of the Western Pacific* (1922), the Trobriand 'chief' emerged more as a ceremonial leader than a political one. It is
not surprising, then, that Malinowski would have difficulty fixing the chief's
judicial capacity in *Crime and Custom* (1926). More important, Malinowski was
primarily concerned with mechanisms maintaining order and equilibrium in
Trobriand culture as a whole; to him, reciprocity inherent in social structure
fulfilled this function. In this view, precise analysis of cases which would reveal
the legal role of particular individuals or agencies would not be needed. (Miss
M. Johnston, communication to the author.)

NOTES TO CHAPTER 8   487

3 Hoebel, *The Law of Primitive Man*, 34 (1954).

4 The following account of the genesis of *The Cheyenne Way* is based partly on material in K.L.P. I, partly on an interview with Professor Hoebel, and partly on Hoebel's article 'Karl Llewellyn – Anthropological Jurisprude', 18 *Rutgers L. Rev.*, 735 (1964).

5 Cited by Hoebel, *The Law of Primitive Man*, 40 (1954).

6 Ultimately published *sub nom. The Political Organization and Law-Ways of the Comanche Indians*, Memoirs of the American Anthropological Association, no. 54 (1940).

7 See Hoebel in *American Anthropologist* 37, 320–51 (1935); *ibid.*, 41, 440–57 (1935); and *op. cit.*, appendix A, 135–42.

8 *The Cheyennes, Indians of the Great Plains* (1960). Readers of *The Cheyenne Way* were referred to George Bird Grinnell's *The Cheyenne Indians* (1923) for a general account. See also Grinnell *The Fighting Cheyennes* (1915).

9 Cairns, 55 *Harv. L. Rev.*, 707, 710 (1942).

10 *Op. cit.*, 329.

11 44 *American Anthropologist*, 478–9 (1942); doubts were also expressed by Redfield and Levi-Strauss, *op. cit.* (below, n.37). However, in 1967 Hoebel was prepared to say 'Lowie notwithstanding, I have yet to see any people whose legal culture is described in the anthropological literature who come close to the Cheyennes in juristic skill, except Max Gluckman's Lozi. It could be, as Lowie suggests, if other tribes were studied with the same detailed attention to process and solution, that other good examples would turn up.' Hoebel to Twining, September, 1967.

12 At 313.

13 At 118–9.

14 At 314.

15 *Ibid.*

16 At 316–7.

17 At 318–9.

18 At 333.

19 At 119.

20 At 160.

21 At 315.

22 For a critique of the early phases of *The Restatement of African Law*, see Twining, *The Place of Customary Law in the National Legal Systems of East Africa* (1964); for a reply, see Cotran, 'The Place and Future of Customary Law in East Africa', in *East African Law Today* (I.C.L.Q. Supplement no. 12, 1966), 85–9. Cotran maintains, *inter alia*, that while working on the *Restatement* in Kenya he did analyse 'trouble cases', but his description of his method suggests that it was quite different from that of Llewellyn and Hoebel.

23 *The Cheyenne Way*, 22. A common response to the refusal of informants to talk in terms of rules has been to conclude that 'these people do not really have "law".' This was the reaction of the anthropologists who were sceptical about Hoebel's Comanche project. Another response has been to seek for norms implicit in the behaviour or talk of informants, especially those who are participants in decision-making. Thus Fallers, on finding that the elders among the Basoga of Uganda were unable or unwilling to talk in terms of general rules, attempted to find general principles of law implicit in their questions and comments during judicial proceedings (Fallers, 'Customary Law in the New African States' (1962), 27 *Law and Contemporary Problems*, 605), see further Fallers' valuable work, *Law Without Precedent* (1969).

24 Gulliver, *Social Control in an African Society*, 241 (1963) (*cf.* Pospisil, *Kapauku Papuans and Their Law, passim*, but especially 286–88 (1958)). Gulliver's theoretical models of the 'judicial' and the 'political' types of dispute-settlement processes (296 *et seq.*) need to be considered in the light of modern jurisprudential writings on 'the nature of the judicial process'.

25 Proverbs provide a simple illustration: *e.g.* 'Too many cooks spoil the broth', but 'Many hands make light work'. The writer has been told of an instance, which he has been unable to substantiate, of a tribe on the east coast of Africa which was exposed to Islamic influence. At conclaves in which disputes about succession were settled, it would regularly occur that one party would advance an argument based on tribal custom, to be met by an opposing argument based on Islamic notions. When asked by an anthropologist why they did not resolve this kind of doubt once and for all, by agreeing on a single consistent body of rules, his informants reacted with incredulity that anyone should make so naive a proposal. How, he was asked, could disputes be satisfactorily settled, if there was only one set of rules to fall back on?

26 'Remarks on the Theory of Appellate Decision', 3 *Vanderbilt Law Rev.*, 395 (1950), reprinted in part in *The Common Law Tradition* at appendix C (1960). Several other writers have commented on the general tendency in the common law for 'doctrines to travel in pairs of opposites' (*e.g.* Lasswell & McDougal, discussed Bodenheimer: *Jurisprudence* (1962), pp. 140–3). Julius Stone goes so far as to say that 'competing versions of a legal category are a normal feature of the authoritative materials in the common law', *Legal System and Lawyers' Reasonings* 254 (1964).

27 Hoebel, *op. cit.*, 35.

28 *Ibid.*, 34.

29 *Ibid.*, 748 (n.4).

30 At 29.

31 See Twining, *op. cit.*, 47–9 (n.22).

32 At 21–2.

33 Notable recent exceptions include L. Fallers, *Law Without Precedent*, M. Gluckman (ed.), *Ideas and Procedures in African Customary Law* (1969), and the work of Richard Abel on the customary law of wrongs in Kenya (see especially 17 *Am. J. Comp. L.*, 573 (1969)).

34 At 165.

35 Hoebel, *The Law of Primitive Man*, 142–3.

36 For a balanced general discussion of the notion of jural postulates, see G. Sawer, *Law in Society*, 147 ff. (1965). An anthropologist has commented:

> In Hoebel's particular usage, jural postulates are selected to be consistent with principles set in a culture's basic postulates. Like Morris Opler's themes or Ruth Benedict's culture patterns, the basic postulates regulate the selection of all traits in a culture from a range of possibilities; conflicting or ambiguous norms find their place only as a negative measure of a culture's integration.
>
> Listing jural postulates allows for certainty and predictability in judicial behavior. However it is hard to reconcile this view of culture with that which perceived the dynamic role of the trouble case, as suggested in the original formulation of the case method. (Miss M. Johnston, communication to the author.)

37 Malinowski, 2 *Lawyers Guild Review*, 1 (1942), a review article believed to be Malinowski's last completed work; Redfield, 9 *U. Chi. L. Rev.*, 366 (1942); Lowie, 44 *American Anthropologist* (*N.S.*), 478 (1942); Levi-Strauss, 1 *Jo. Legal and Political Sociology*, 155 (1942); Cairns, 55 *Harv. L. Rev.*, 707 (1942); Timasheff, 7 *Am. Sociological Rev.*, 130 (1942); Hamilton, 10 *U. Chi. L. Rev.*, 231 (1942); Pound, 5 *University of Toronto L. Rev.*, 1 (1943).

38 Final Report on *The Cheyenne Way* to Columbia Social Science Research Council, K.L.P. I. 1. 4, (1943).

39 M. Gluckman, *The Ideas of Barotse Jurisprudence*, 1 (1965).

40 E.g. Richardson (Kiowa, 1949), Lips (Naskapi, 1947), Smith and Roberts (Zuni, 1954), Gluckman (Barotse, 1955 and 1965), Holleman (Shona, 1952), Bohannan (Tiv, 1957), Pospisil (Kapauku, 1958), Colson (Plateau Tonga, 1952), and Gulliver (Arusha, 1963), Fallers (Soga, 1969). This list is by no means exhaustive. Of the few works on tribal law by anthropologists in which the method was not extensively used, four of the best known were intended primarily as handbooks for courts – Cory and Hartnoll (Haya, 1945), Cory (Sukuma, 1953), Schapera (Tswana, 1938), Howell (Nuer, 1954), *cf.*, Epstein (ed.), *The Craft of Social Anthropology* (1967). In a general account of the development of anthropological studies of primitive law, the contribution of others, *e.g.* Hobhouse and Radcliffe-Brown, would have to be considered.

41 In the mid-1940s Llewellyn and Hoebel embarked on a study of the

Pueblo Indians of New Mexico (see below, ch. 13). Llewellyn died before this project was completed.

42 On 'beauty' in law, see below, pp. 197-9.

43 Hoebel, *op. cit.*, 48 (n.6). See further, Twining 'Law and Anthropology' (forthcoming in *Law and Society Review*).

44 J. Frank, *Courts on Trial*, 77 (1963 ed.).

45 E.g. *Social Meaning of Legal Concepts* (ed. Cahn), 112 (1950). Cf. the general scepticism of Hayakawa, 18 *Rutgers L. Rev.*, 717, 722-33 (1964). See also Stone, *Social Dimensions of Law and Justice*, 102, 764 (1966). Redfield, in justifying his scepticism about the 'beauty' of Cheyenne juristic method, also gives the best reason for being cautious about analogies between 'primitive' and 'modern' societies; 'Law has an easier time of it in primitive society than it has in a modern society, for in the former there is a strong consensus, a common moral order, and consistency of custom and institution'; 9 *U. Chi. L. Rev.*, 366, 369. On Llewellyn's optimism about the prospects of consensus in the United States see below, p. 436.

46 E.g. Ms, 'Law in the Family', K.L.P. B. II. 19 (193-).

47 F. W. Maitland, *Collected Papers*, vol. III, 300.

48 Above, p. 138.

49 Below, p. 175.

50 *The Common Law Tradition*, 513 (n.12). Llewellyn continued:

This is the kind of contribution by anthropology to Jurisprudence for which I have always hoped. You suddenly hit upon beauty and vision in a strange culture, and you may be the person in whom a seed takes root, so that light is shed at home. The values of comparative law and comparative politics are not different, except that the chances of deep illumination may be less.

9 LAW IN OUR SOCIETY

1 E.g. Lasswell and Kaplan, *Power and Society* (1950).

2 See Merton, *Social Theory and Social Structure*, part 1 (1967 ed.).

3 K.L.P. B. II, 22.

4 The most important are K.L.P.B.I., 2, 6; K.L.P.B.II, 17, 21, 36, 42; K.L.P. D. D, VII (in German).

5 I.e. (i) 'The Normative, the Legal and the Law-Jobs', 49 *Yale Law Jo.*, 1355-1400 (1940); (ii) 'My Philosophy of Law', in Kocoureck, (ed.), *My Philosophy of Law*, 181-97 (1941); (iii) 'The Theory of Legal "Science",' 20 *N. Carolina L. Rev.*, 1-21 (1941). (i), which is the most important, was published just before *The Cheyenne Way*. Roscoe Pound paid tribute to it as 'much the best outline of the task of a sociology of law and the way of going about the performance of it which has appeared'. II *Jurisprudence*, 196 (1959).

6 *Law in Our Society: A Horse-Sense Theory of the Institution of Law*: Topical Syllabus (1948-1958) (hereafter cited as *Law in Our Society*). For an

inventory of the various editions of *Law in Our Society* see Ellinwood and Twining, *The Karl Llewellyn Papers: A Guide to the Collection*, section L, 70–2 (revised ed. 1970).

7 What exactly Llewellyn intended to be the relationship between *Jurisprudence: Realism in Theory and Practice* and the successor to *Law in Our Society* is not entirely clear. The preface to the former makes no reference to the proposed book; the papers collected are not meant to be representative of Llewellyn's writings as a whole, for not only are none of his commercial law papers included, but also three of his most important papers on jurisprudence are omitted: 'The Normative, the Legal and the Law-Jobs', 'The Theory of Legal "Science" ', and 'My Philosophy of Law' (see note 5 above); a possible explanation of the omission of these from *Jurisprudence* is that Llewellyn was keeping them in reserve for use in connection with the next book. Llewellyn claimed that the papers included in *Jurisprudence* were organized around the single theme of 'realism': this does not in itself explain either some of the omissions or some of the inclusions. Indeed, the selection seems somewhat idiosyncratic, so that although it is useful in that it brings together in convenient form a number of Llewellyn's writings, it fails to convey adequately the underlying unity of his thought.

8 See below, Appendix C.

9 See below, p. 497ff.

10 See above, p. 35.

11 On the term 'jurisprudence', see Patterson, *Jurisprudence*, 7–10 (1953); Dias, *Jurisprudence* (2nd ed.), 1–3 (1964).

12 *Law in Our Society*, 11. See, further, appendix C.

13 This is a reconstruction from a number of sources, especially (i) author's notes on 'Law in Society' lectures, 1958; (ii) *Jurisprudence*, 86; (iii) 'Theory of Legal Science', 2. Llewellyn attributed the distinction between 'science' and 'prudence' to C. Merriam, *New Aspects of Politics* (2nd ed. 1931). Llewellyn did not attach much significance to the scheme, and in *Law in Our Society* he divided the material up into a number of 'theories', viz. (i) the basic theory of the institution of law-government (the law-jobs theory); (2) theory of the crafts of law; (3) theory of theories and of truth (which overlaps with theory of legal science); (4) theory of justice; (5) theory of American appellate judicial decision. There were also rudimentary sketches for a 'theory of dogmatics' and a 'theory of problem solution'. Elsewhere he also developed a 'theory of legal rules' (see below, p. 200) and a 'theory of legal aesthetics' (below, p. 197). 'Theory' in this contest means little more than a fairly coherent collection of ideas on a topic.

14 See C. P. Harvey, 27 *M.L.R.*, 365 (1964). Purists refer to the game as (real) Tennis.

15 Llewellyn's most eloquent statement of the utility of this kind of working

theory is to be found in a memorandum in which he argued the case for making jurisprudence a compulsory subject at Columbia. The memorandum ends as follows:

In sum, then, a compulsory third-year special course in Jurisprudence seems to be an obligation we owe to every man who is to be a lawyer. That he may try, on his own, to see Law, whole. That he may try, on his own, to make what he has been doing, and what he is to do, take on a meaning, as a Whole. That he may enter into recognition that his profession is not apart from life, a thing of drudgery, but part of life, a thing of eternal service. That law may regain for him, for each of him, its rightful status as a liberal art, as a humanity, as the very focus and balance-wheel of men's lives together. K.L.P. A., II, 30 (1940).

16 *Law in our Society*, 6–8 (see below, p. 499). Llewellyn sometimes distinguished between the 'high philosophy of law', most of which 'gets not only beyond law but beyond most of us' and the 'low philosophy of law' which is simple and accessible:

It deals with how things human go round, with how men go about their business, it roots in daily life and yields horse-sense and sometimes better-than-horse-sense for any lawyer's daily dealing with his daily problems. It aims to be 'philosophy' not in the sense of a discipline with a high name and chairs in universities, but in the old sense of 'philosophy' as working human wisdom – 'philosophy' like that of Will Rogers, Mr. Dooley and Mr. Tutt. When it comes to law, the low 'philosophy' is not content to be *about* law in the large and remote and vague; it wants to get down to cases, down to lawyers' or judges' particular cases. It wants to be a 'philosophy' of the work of law and legal institutions and the craftsmen of the law. (Ms, 'The Low "Philosophy" of Law', K.L.P. B., III. 22,1 (1943).)

17 E.g. *Jurisprudence*, 152 (1940).

18 5–11 (infra. at 500ff). Basic to a 'horse-sense' approach is a refusal to see things in simple all-or-nothing terms. Thus, in respect of 'testable truth' there is a continuum ranging from pure guess to absolute certainty, with expert judgment backed by experience somewhere in the middle; in respect of technology Llewellyn was fond of reminding students that 'you don't need seven place logarithms for laying linoleum; jurisprudence is the art of laying linoleum' (lecture, 1958). Whereas ultimate goals and ideals are needed to give a general sense of direction, they cannot be expected to give detailed guidance in specific situations; despite the enormous diversity of opinions about values and priorities, he was often optimistic about the prospects for consensus; for example: 'Even [in respect of] non-testable truth, most Americans *can* agree on enough important goods to keep a "country" a working whole, with some recognized agreed machinery for handling most disagreements' (*Law in Our Society*, 34). On Llewellyn's optimism in respect of judicial processes, see below, pp. 224–6.

19 'In the first decades of this century American liberal thought was haunted by a fear of being remote. This was one of the sources of the revolt against formalism.' White, *Social Thought in America*, 128 (cf. 33) (1957).

20 There are several statements of the 'law-jobs theory' in addition to chapters 10 and 11 of *The Cheyenne Way*, notably: (i) 'The Normative, the Legal and the Law Jobs: The Job of Juristic Method', 49 *Yale L. J.*, 1355 (1940); (ii) *My Philosophy of Law* (ed. Kocoureck) 183 (1941); (iii) 'Law and The Social Sciences – Especially Sociology', 62 *Harv. L. Rev.*, 1286 (1949), reprinted in *Jurisprudence: Realism in Theory and Practice*, 352 (1962); (iv) *Law in our Society*. The most developed version is to be found in (iv) which differs in a number of points of detail from the earlier writings. The most important of these is the shift from 'the institution of law' to 'the institution of law-government' as his organising concept; see below, p. 179.

21 On the question whether this proposition is tautological see below, p. 180.

22 In some versions Llewellyn listed only five categories, (ii) and (iii) being combined. The most extensive elucidation of each of these categories is to be found in 49 *Yale L. J.*, 1375 *et seq.*

23 *My Philosophy of Law* (ed. Kocoureck), 187–8 (1941).

24 *Jurisprudence*, 356 (n).

25 8 *Enc. Soc. Sci.*, 84 (1932); see also Sumner, *Folkways, passim*.

26 *Ibid.*

27 *Law in Our Society*, 21.

28 *Folkways*, 61–2. Cp. *The Bramble Bush*, 40.

29 *The Bramble Bush*, 40. See Merton, *Social Theory and Social Structure*, especially ch. III (1949, 1967).

30 'A definition both excludes and includes. It marks out a field. It makes some matters fall inside the field; it makes some fall outside. And the exclusion is almost always rather arbitrary. I have no desire to exclude anything from matters legal. In one aspect law is as broad as life, and for some purposes one will have to follow life pretty far to get the bearings of the legal matters one is examining' (*Jurisprudence*, 4).

31 *My Philosophy of Law*, 185. The vagueness of 'institution' enabled Llewellyn to assemble a motley list of ingredients of the 'institution of law':

That whole is most fruitfully viewed as a going institution, and a necessary institution, in society. And a going institution is of course never made up of rules alone, nor of ideals alone. It may contain rules as one of its parts. In the case of our own law, the institution contains as one of its parts a tremendous and tremendously important body of rules, organized (quite loosely) around

concepts and shot through with principles. Indeed, companioning these rules
and principles of 'law' proper, there are other rules and other concepts: the
formulated techniques of 'precedent', of 'construction', and the like, to guide
manipulation of the first. But over and above these, the going institution of
our law contains an ideology and a body of pervasive and powerful ideals
which are largely unspoken, largely implicit, and which pass almost unmentioned in the books. It contains also a host of sometimes vagrant, sometimes rigid practices, of ways of doing what is done, without which such things
as rules would have no meaning in life. And it contains also a host of men, who
are an integral working portion of the whole, and are not simply persons
'subject' to some thing outside them which one can know as 'law' ('My
Philosophy of Law', 183–4).

Objection could be taken to the listing of such disparate phenomena
as rules, concepts, practices, and men as 'parts' of 'institution'. We may
concede that the passage is loosely worded. But Llewellyn's conception
of the subject-matter of jurisprudence may be restated in terms which,
while retaining the gist of what he was trying to say, may be less
vulnerable to criticism: a rounded approach to jurisprudential theory
must include a coherently related set of answers to a number of
different kinds of question. Some of these answers will take the form
of recommendations about the purposes of law; others will be statements about the values which are in fact pursued or assumed by
participants in the legal processes of a particular system; others will
be concerned with the nature of actual and possible instruments for
furthering these values; rules of law are among the most important
of such instruments, but they are not the only ones; other answers will
be concerned with the techniques of devising, improving and using
these instruments; others will be concerned with the actual effects on
human behaviour of particular measures and so on (see *Law in Our
Society*, 59, cited above, p. 184).

32 Above, p. 148.
33 Llewellyn to Hoebel, 24 January 1938.
34 *The Law of Primitive Man*, 28 (1954). Recently Hoebel has formulated a
new 'working general definition' of law. See his *Anthropology: The Study
of Man* 506 (1972).
35 49 *Yale L. J.*, 1355, 1364ff. (1940); *Law in Our Society*, 21–2.
36 H. L. A. Hart, *The Concept of Law* (1961). See also J. Raz, *The Concept
of a Legal System* (1970).
37 *Op. cit.* 1358.

Let me therefore put 'legal', and keep it, *in quotes* when the reference is to that
phase of life and problem and behavior of men in groups which is set against
the economic or religious or recreational. Let me *capitalize* it, as Legal, when the
reference may be to the content or system or correct consequences of our high
Rules of Law. This will not wholly do my work, for much of the time I shall
be dealing with incipient or half-way material which is beginning to be

distinctively 'legal', but has not yet taken on all the attributes which things 'legal' strain to acquire. I shall use some coinages to refer to one or another of the major incipient or part-way areas. For instance, in regard to the bare skeleton of authority and enforcement, where regularity and right are largely lacking, I shall speak of the 'skelegal'; and where felt right is present in a penumbra between recognizable Law and clear morality or etiquette or decency, I shall speak of the 'jurid'. And where an incipient practice is yet unpredictable in detail, and is interrupted, as is our own judicial practice of distinguishing a precedent which needs to be distinguished, which our judges waver between doing and not doing, I shall speak of 'law-wavers' which might be in process of becoming real law-ways. All of this part-way material, this penumbral stuff which does not answer to yes-or-no, but only to a how-much or intensity or regularity or clarity, I can then lump as the 'legaloid', and many things will be much easier to say clearly, and briefly, and without misconstruction.

Llewellyn in fact hardly used these terms, but the passage in the article does perform the function of stressing his concern to avoid seeing law and related phenomena in black-and-white terms (such as 'law' and 'not-law'), but rather in terms of the shades, suggested by such terms as 'incipient' and 'penumbra'. So, too, with the deliberately vague terms 'law-ways' and 'law-stuff', which he used quite frequently. ' "Law-ways" is used to indicate any behavior or practices distinctively legal in character, flavor, connotation, or effect; procedures for cleaning up trouble-cases, the use of tribunals, the enactment of legislation, the practice of policing. . . . A Rule of Law is not a law-way, not behavior, but a formulation with meaning and authority. Whereas using such a Rule, thinking in terms of such a Rule, observing it, applying it, construing it: these are law-ways' (*ibid.*, 1357–8). On rules, see below appendix B.

38 20ff.; Pound, *Outlines of Jurisprudence* 60ff (1943).
39 *Ibid.*
40 *Jurisprudence*, 357.
41 *Law in Our Society*, 112 (1956 ed.).
42 See below, p. 190.
43 See K.L.P. P.X. Some student papers were mimeographed and circulated as a supplement to *Law in Our Society*.
44 49 *Yale L. J.*, 1382.
45 However, it is possible to conceive of 'a group whose unification is achieved through the reciprocal interiorization by each of each other, in which neither a "common object" nor organizational or institutional structures etc., have a primary function as a kind of group "cement".' R. D. Laing, *The Politics of Experience*, ch. 4 (1967). This work contains an interesting analysis of the psychology of 'groupness', an aspect which Llewellyn tended to gloss over.
46 *Ex. rel.* Soia Mentschikoff Llewellyn.

47 For other claims made for the theory, see *49 Yale L. J.*, 1830. Some people (without giving reasons) dismiss as invalid analogies between simple groups, such as tribes, and modern industrial societies. Llewellyn himself glossed over the problem by maintaining that the difference was one of 'complexity'. Lévi-Strauss has suggested a possible difference which might have theoretical implications for jurisprudence:

> I would say that, in comparison with our own great society, with all the great modern societies, the societies studied by the anthropologist are in a sense 'cold' societies rather than 'hot' societies, or like clocks in relation to steam-engines. They are societies which create the minimum of that disorder which the physicists call 'entropy', and they tend to remain indefinitely in their initial state, and this explains why they appear to us as static societies with no history.
>
> Our modern societies are not only societies which make extensive use of the steam-engine; structurally, they resemble the steam-engine in that they work on the basis of a difference in potential, which finds concrete expression in different forms of social hierarchy. Whether we call it slavery, serfdom or class distinction is not of any fundamental importance, if we stand back and take a broad, panoramic view of the situation. Societies like these have managed to produce within themselves a kind of disequilibrium which they use to create, at one and the same time, much more order – we have mechanized societies – and greater disorder, greater entropy, on the level of human relations.

G. Charbonnier, *Conversations with Claude Lévi-Strauss* (trs. J. and D. Weightman), 33–4 (1969). For this suggestion I am indebted to Mr Adrian Taylor, who comments:

> For Lévi-Strauss's account of the dynamics of interaction of social structures and social functions forces upon our attention the question of the extent to which the doing of the law-jobs seen as consciously intended performances of legal systems *qua* systems simultaneously and by the same means and necessarily bring fresh problems for future solution.

48 The best discussion by Llewellyn is in 49 *Yale L. J.*, 1373ff. *Law in Our Society*, 24–6.
49 Above, ch. 8; see also the discussion of the 'parental' model of dispute-settlement (below, pp. 363–5).
50 Below, pp. 200–2, 488–96.
51 Below, pp. 199–200, 505–12.
52 But see 'The Constitution as an Institution', 34 *Col. L. Rev.*, 1 (1934).
53 See esp. 49 *Yale L. J.* 1355.
54 A good recent example is P. S. Atiyah, *Accidents, Compensation and the Law* (1970) which shows a number of traditional problems in a different light by looking at them in the context of 'the total compensation picture'.

55 49 *Yale L. J.*, 1381–2 (1940) (Llewellyn's italics).
56 *Law in Our Society*, 59.
57 *Law in Our Society*, 39–58; see also *Jurisprudence*, 201–10 (1941); the treatment of the topic in *Law in Our Society* shows some development in Llewellyn's ideas on justice. This probably occurred mainly in the period 1953–5, when he devoted quite a lot of thought to the subject.
58 *Ibid.*, 43.
59 *Ibid.*, 33.
60 O. W. Holmes, *Collected Legal Papers*, see below, p. 514.
61 See especially E. Cahn, *The Sense of Injustice* (1949).
62 F. R. Bienenfeld, *Rediscovery of Justice* (1947).
63 *Ibid.*, 18–55.
64 See J. Stone, *Human Law and Human Justice*, 317–8 (1965), and refs. there.
65 K.L.P.C. Series M. Lecture 6 (1955).
66 *Jurisprudence*, 203.
67 Lecture, *op. cit.* (n.65).
68 There are numerous references to natural law in Llewellyn's writings, especially in *Law in Our Society*, 59–65, *Jurisprudence* 111–5, 480–1; *The Common Law Tradition*, 122 and 422; 'On Philosophy in American Law', 82 *U. Pa. L. Rev.*, 205 (1934); Ms., 'Natural Law, Realism in Law and the Problems Ahead' (1946–9), K.L.P.B., II. 25. See also Garlan, *Legal Realism and Justice*, 103–8 (1941).
69 E.g., *Jurisprudence*, 55.
70 *Ibid.*, 114.
71 *Law in Our Society*, 64.
72 E.g., *Jurisprudence*, 55.
73 *Ibid.*, 114.
74 *Law in Our Society*, 64.
75 *Ibid.*
76 *Jurisprudence*, 500; *The Common Law Tradition*, 421–3; *Law in Our Society*, 60–5.
77 *Jurisprudence*, 115.
78 *Law in Our Society*, 85ᵃ.
79 Ms., 'Babel versus Teamwork: Jurisprudence since 1900', 5 K.L.P.B., III, 36 (d) (1942–3).
80 Published works include: (i) 'The Conditions for and the Aims and Methods of Legal Research' (1929); (ii) 'Legal Tradition and Social Science Method – A Realist's Critique' (1931); (iii) 'Behind the Law of Divorce' (1932–3); (iv) 'introduction to Jerome Hall, *Theft, Law and Society*, xv–xxxv (1935); (v) 'The Theory of Legal "Science" ' (1941). See below (n.81); (vi) 'Manpower for Research', in A. Conard (ed.), *Conference on Aims and Methods in Legal Research* (1955); (vii) 'Social Significance in Legal Problems', *ibid.* (1955); (viii) 'On What

498 NOTES TO CHAPTER 9

Makes Legal Research Worth-While?' (1956); (ix) Review of Michael and Adler, *Crime, Law and Social Science* (1934). See also bibliography, items 46, 72, 87, 98, 103, 138, 232.

Manuscripts include: (a) 'Behind the Law of Divorce III' (1933); (b) 'Jurisprudential "schools" at Columbia' (1939?); (c) 'Law and Social Science' (1930–35); (d) 'Loom of the Law: A Theory of Jural Sociology and Method' (1935–40); (e) 'On Robinson's Unscientific Science of Law' (1935); (f) 'Trends in Legal Sociology' (1933–38); (g) 'The Chicago Jury Project' (1955); (h) 'Memo. re plans for Michigan conference on The Aims and Methods of Legal Research' (1955).

81 20 *N. Carolina L. Rev.*, 1–23 (1941) (hereafter cited in this chapter as Cairns).

82 *Ibid.*, 6. Cf. *Jurisprudence*, 78:

> But one concerned with law as a social *science*, a science of *observation*, must center his thought on behavior, on the interactions between the behavior of law-officials and the behavior of laymen. The behavior which comes chiefly in question has two aspects: (a) the settling by somewhat regularized official action of disputes that do not otherwise get settled; and (b) the use of somewhat regularized official pressures to get people to do (or not to do) particular things, or to do (or not to do) what they do in particular ways – more briefly, the directing and channeling of the conduct of people.

83 Cairns, 7.

84 *Ibid.*, 8.

85 For Llewellyn's reservations about the uses made by some jurists of psychological and psychoanalytic theories, see *Jurisprudence*, 105–6, *The Common Law Tradition*, 12, *Law in Our Society*, 92–4.

86 *Op. cit.*, n.80.

87 Cairns, 13.

88 *Op. cit.*, n.80.

89 34 *Col. L. Rev.*, 286 *et seq.* (1934).

90 Cairns, 22.

91 *Ibid.*, 21.

92 E.g., Cairns, 20–1.

93 *Ibid.*, 21.

94 *Ibid.*, 14. Cf. *Jurisprudence*, 100.

95 Cairns, 13–4.

96 8 *Jo. Leg. Ed.*, 399, 421 (1956).

97 *Op. cit.*, n.80, (vi).

98 *Ibid.*, 411.

99 E.g., Ms. fragment. K.L.P. B. II. 6, 4 (1933).

100 See below, pp. 313–21.

101 See below, pp. 356–65.

102 See generally Currie, III, 28–38.

103 *Ibid.*, 32–4.

104 See n.80, items (iii) and (a).

105 *Ibid.*, 1281n.

106 *Ibid.*

107 R. Angell to Llewellyn, April 1933. K.L.P. A. 59.

108 Thurman Arnold to Llewellyn, *ibid.* On *Sartor Resartus*; see p. 421.

109 J. Hall, *Theft, Law and Society* (published 1955); E. A. Hoebel, *The Political Organization and Law-Ways of the Comanche Indians.* (Published 1940). See above, ch. 8; Paul W. Tappan, *Delinquent Girls in Court* (1947) with a foreword by Llewellyn.

110 See below, pp. 349–53.

111 Opinion of Professor Jerome Hall, interview December 1965; confirmed by a variety of other sources.

112 Llewellyn's main discussions of 'The Beautiful' in law are to be found in *Jurisprudence*, 171–96 (1942) and 389–94 (1960). *The Cheyenne Way*, 61–2, 307–9. Ms., K.L.P.B., III 30 (on Radbruch). See, further, P. Stein, 77 *L.Q.R.*, 242 (1961), A. Ehrenzweig *Psychoanalytic Jurisprudence* (1971).

113 *Jurisprudence*, 171; cf. 196.

114 Nor is literary aptness a primary value in Llewellyn's aesthetics (on which see Stein, *op. cit.* (n.112)). Stone, in *Legal System and Lawyers' Reasonings*, 256,n. errs in suggesting that Llewellyn equated 'elegantia' with beauty.

115 *Jurisprudence*, 172.

116 *Ibid.*

117 At 172–3.

118 See below, ch. 10.

119 *Jurisprudence*, 195.

120 *Ibid.*, 193.

121 Especially, *Jurisprudence*, 168–71. See further above, p. 120.

122 *My Philosophy of Law*, 188 (1941).

123 See below, pp. 505–12. His writings on the legal profession contain the basic ingredients from which the theory could be further developed.

124 Above, ch. 8.

125 Below, p. 260, 354.

126 *Ibid.*

127 Below, ch. 10.

128 See generally, Twining, 'Pericles and the Plumber', 83 *L.Q.R.*, 396 (1967).

129 T. Hayakawa, 18 *Rutgers L. Rev.*, 717, 732 (1964).

130 *My Philosophy of Law*, 188–9.

131 At 178–99.

132 K.L.P. B. II. 40 (1938–40?).

133 See above, p. 81.

134 See below, pp. 210–15, 493–6.

135 *The Common Law Tradition*, 179.
136 See above, 81.
137 *Ibid.*
138 Dias, *Jurisprudence* (2nd ed.), 477.
139 See, e.g., G. Gottlieb, *The Logic of Choice* (1968); J. Stone, *Legal System and Lawyers' Reasonings* (1964); H. L. A. Hart, *The Concept of Law* (1961); W. Twining, K. O'Donovan and A. Paliwala 'Ernie and the Centipede', in Jolowicz (ed.), *The Division and Classification of the Law* (1970).
140 *Jurisprudence*, 57.

10 THE COMMON LAW TRADITION

1 Lewis, O. C. *Llewellyn: Situational Sense and the Judicial Process*, New York (1962) (LL.M. thesis, Columbia Law School). Of the many published discussions of the book the following have been of particular assistance: Becht (1962), *Washington U.L.Q.*, 5; Clark and Trubek, 71 *Yale L.J.*, 255 (1961); Cooperrider, 60 *Mich. L. Rev.*, 119 (1961); Hayakawa, 18 *Rutgers L. Rev.*, 717, 725–34 (1964); Lasswell, 61 *Col. L. Rev.*, 940 (1961); Rohan, 32 *Fordham L. Rev.*, 51 (1963–4); Rumble, *American Legal Realism*, especially 145–54, and ch. 5; Shestack, 109 *U. Pa. L. Rev.*, 1051 (1961).

Two gaps in discussion are worth noting: first, *The Common Law Tradition* was not reviewed in a single British legal periodical; secondly, it is barely mentioned and is not discussed in Joel B. Grossman and Joseph Tanenhaus (eds.), *Frontiers of Judicial Research* (1969), which purports, *inter alia*, to survey work in this field. See, however, the remarks of Richard D. Schwartz at 490.

2 MS. Llewellyn's Inquiry into Appellate Judicial Deciding (1956–7).
3 An excellent detailed summary of the book in twenty-five pages is by Becht, *op. cit.* Teachers who would like their students to study *The Common Law Tradition* but who feel that it would be unreasonable to ask them to read the whole book could solve the problem by recommending Becht's summary and a selection of key passages from the original work.
4 See especially *The Common Law Tradition*, 3–18.
5 *Ibid.*, 4.
6 *Ibid.*
7 *Ibid.*
8 *Ibid.*
9 *Ibid.*, 28.
10 In some contexts it is not necessarily paradoxical or confused to assert: 'The rule is certain, but its application is doubtful'. For this could mean 'it is clear which rule is the applicable one, but the rule itself is not clear' or 'it is clear which rule is the applicable one and in what

words the rule is to be formulated, but some doubt arises as to its meaning'. But it may be paradoxical to say 'the meaning of the rule is certain/clear, but there is some doubt as to what situations it covers'.

11 *C.L.T.*, 19.

12 'Professor Llewellyn jumps off in mid-stream and neglects to extrapolate upon the nature of the interrelationship between these factors, the extent and nature of overlap, the probable varying degrees of importance between the elements, as well as many other problems raised by mere listing'. Theodore L. Becker, *Political Behavioralism and Modern Jurisprudence*, 63–4 (1964). See also Rumble, *op. cit.*, 173–4.

13 Becker, *Ibid.*

14 See *The Common Law Tradition*, index under 'Grand Tradition', 'Formal Style' and 'Style'. Other important discussions of 'style' include *Jurisprudence*, 176–92, 215–29, 305–8, 316–22.

15 519. Cf. 'In such matters, as in all other matters in this study, I preach neither revelation nor novelty, *I preach the neglected beauty of the obvious*' (339). This is a recurring theme of *The Common Law Tradition*, see e.g., 142, 156. See further the statement in 'On Reading and Using the Newer Jurisprudence' (1940) that: '. . . almost nothing the newer Jurisprudence has yet found, and little that it seems likely to find within the next few decades, will prove in any manner *new*, to the *best* lawyers'. *Jurisprudence*, 149. Lloyd considers that the English lawyer does not find this statement 'very encouraging'. (*Introduction to Jurisprudence* (2nd ed.), 262). With respect, this seems to place too high a premium on novelty in jurisprudence and to give insufficient weight to Llewellyn's stress on the *neglected* aspects of what the *best* lawyers know already. For a sceptical comment on Llewellyn's concern with the obvious, see Westwood, 61 *Col. L. Rev.*, 948–55, especially 954 (1961).

16 See especially 464–5, 519n.

17 *C.L.T.*, 36.

18 Llewellyn's discussion of the Grand Style in the nineteenth century is rather vague, except in connection with the work of specific judges. Contrast, for example, *The Common Law Tradition*, 35–41, with *Jurisprudence*, 178–92. On particular judges see esp. the dedication of *The Common Law Tradition* 'To the undying succession of the Great Commercial Judges whose work across the centuries has given living body, toughness and inspiration to the Grand Tradition of the Common Law', listing in the form of a dynastic succession, Holt, Mansfield, Stowell, Blackburn, Kennedy, Hamilton and Scrutton (England), Cowen, Hough and Learned Hand (U.S.).

19 *Jurisprudence*, 217 (formulated 1960).

20 *C.L.T.*, 38. Cf. *Jurisprudence*, 183, 303.

21 *Jurisprudence*, 124–6.

22 *C.L.T.*, 36, 291–309.

23 *Jurisprudence*, 183; cp. 171–2. On legal aesthetics see above, p. 197.

24 See generally 'Remarks on the Theory of Appellate Decision', 3 *Vanderbilt L. Rev.*, 395 (1950).

25 *C.L.T.*, 62–120.

26 *Ibid.*, 83.

27 *Ibid.*, 88.

28 *Ibid.*, 139, 440.

29 *Ibid.*, 139.

30 See, for example, the rationale for bigamy advanced by Cockburn C. J. in *Reg.* v. *Allen* (1873), L.R. 1 C.C.R., 367. Compare Glanville Williams, 'Bigamy and the Third Marriage', 13 *M.L.R.*, 417 (1950).

31 E.g., Lord Atkin's 'neighbour principle', in *Donoghue* v. *Stevenson* [1932] A.C., 562, discussed below, p. 236.

32 *C.L.T.*, 139.

33 *Ibid.*, 519n.

34 See *Jurisprudence*, 216–7.

35 See *ibid.*, 176–7.

36 [1932] A.C., 562.

37 217 N.Y. 382, 111 N.E. 1050 (1916).

38 217 N.Y. 391.

39 E.g., his treatment of *Langridge* v. *Levy* 2 M. and W. 519; 4 M. and W. 337 and *Winterbottom* v. *Wright* 10 M. and W. 109, 587–8.

40 For examples relating to Cardozo, J., see 430, 436–42.

41 Portia:

> Tarry a little, there is something else.
> This bond doth give thee here no jot of blood;
> The words expressly are 'a pound of flesh';
> Take then, thy bond, take thou thy pound of flesh;
> But, in the cutting of it, if thou dost shed
> One drop of Christian blood, thy land and goods
> Are, by the laws of Venice, confiscate
> Unto the State of Venice.

Merchant of Venice, Act IV, Scene 1. Cf. *Fisher* v. *Ruislip* [1945], 2 *All E.R.*, 458. Also, Twining in (1959) *Sudan Law Jo. and Reports* 112–39. Cf. S. Williston, *Life and Law*, 215–6 (1940). Ihering, *The Struggle for Law*, preface (1877).

42 Becht, *op. cit.*, n.1.

43 *C.L.T.*, 59.

44 Cahn, *The Sense of Injustice* (1949), cited by Llewellyn at 60.

45 *C.L.T.*, 60. Llewellyn, rather vaguely, continues: '*Wisdom* will serve well enough to indicate a goal of right decision, weighted heavily with and for the future'; see 60–1 and 46–7, and *The Cheyenne Way* at 308–9,

where the idea of adopting the viewpoint of the good of 'The Entirety' is associated with wisdom.

46 *C.L.T.*, 245, 268–77.

47 See above, pp. 185–8.

48 Rohan, 'The Common Law Tradition: Situation Sense, Subjectivism or Just-Result Jurisprudence?', 32 *Fordham L. Rev.*, 51, 56 (1963–4).

49 E.g., Mermin, *Jurisprudence and Statecraft*, 115 and 240 (1963).

50 *C.L.T.*, 60–1.

51 Quoted at 122; cf. 222:

> I remember the scorn which Konenkov, whose chisel woke in wood the beauty asleep in it, felt for Mestrović, who wreaked his will upon a block of wood as if it had been grainless granite. . . . Now as one reads the cases . . . it seems to me hard to miss this aura, this atmosphere not only of hesitance to upset the settled or to embark on an uncharted sea, *but of a desire to move in accordance with the material as well as within it, to carve with the grain like Konenkov, to reveal the latent rather than to impose new form, much less to obtrude* an outside will (italics added).

The quotation is said to be taken from Goldschmidt, preface to *Kritik des Entwurfs eines Handelsgesetzbuchs*. Cf. Sinzheimer, *Jews Who Were Classical Figures in German Legal Scholarship* (1938) (Extract on Goldschmidt, translated by Llewellyn and included in materials for *Law in Our Society*).

52 'Metaphysics' is used here in the sense of 'relating to what is conceived of as transcendent, supersensible or transcendental' (Webster's *Third New International Dictionary*). Mermin uses 'mystical' and 'metaphysical'; *op. cit.*, 115, 240

53 *C.L.T.*, 127 (Llewellyn's italics). Llewellyn's espousal of the terminology of 'immanent' and 'rightness' needs to be considered in the light of his general attitude to Natural Law (see above, pp. 123–6, 185–8).

54 71 *Yale L. J.*, 255 (1961).

55 61 *Col. L. Rev.*, 946 (1961).

56 On which see McDougal, *Studies in World Public Order* (1960).

57 See also Rohan, *op. cit.*, 56–60.

58 *C.L.T.*, 277.

59 See above, n.53.

60 See above, p. 188ff.

61 See, e.g., Llewellyn's discussion of Levi's *Introduction to Legal Reasoning* (1949), 125–6, and of *McPherson* v. *Buick*, *ibid.*, and 430–7.

62 *Ibid.* See also 452–3.

63 *C.L.T.*, 24–5, and 226–32.

64 *Ibid.*, 277.

65 See *Law in Our Society*, p. 85.

66 E.g., 492, 203, 504–5.

67 *C.L.T.*, 494.

68 *Ibid.*, 504.

69 *Ibid.*, 123.

70 *Ibid.*, 128.

71 *Ibid.*, see especially 121.

72 *Ibid.*, 151.

73 *Ibid.*, 157; cf. 207, 'new sense of and for the significant situation'.

74 *Ibid.*, 502.

75 E.g. *ibid.*, 431.

76 Rohan, *op. cit.*, 56–60.

77 *C.L.T.*, 57.

78 In Llewellyn's usage the terms 'principle' and 'policy' both refer to standards which are not 'rules of thumb' (see below, appendix B) and are not clearly differentiated. However, a distinction suggested by Dworkin is a useful starting-point for a more refined analysis and, where relevant, I have tried to observe this distinction.

I call a 'policy' that kind of standard that sets out a goal to be reached, generally an improvement in some economic, political or social feature of the community (though some goals are negative, in that they stipulate that some present feature is to be protected from adverse change). I call a 'principle' a standard that is to be observed, not because it will advance or secure an economic political or social situation deemed desirable but because it is a requirement of justice or fairness or some other dimension of morality.

R. Dworkin, 'Is Law a System of Rules?', in R. Summers (ed.), *Essays in Legal Philosophy*, 34–5 (1968).

79 At 210–2, 249–50, 430–7; *Legniti*, 186 App. Div. 105, 173 N.Y. Supp. 814 (1st Dept. 1919).

80 *C.L.T.*, 436, 432.

81 *Op. cit.*, at 59.

82 *C.L.T.*, 212 (Llewellyn's italics).

83 *Ibid.*

84 *Op. cit.*, 59.

85 *C.L.T.*, 54–6.

86 *Ibid.*, 277.

87 These distinctions can be re-stated as follows: There is no necessary inconsistency involved in (i) reporting that Judge X exhibited the use of situation sense in his opinion in that he: (a) articulated potentially relevant policies and (b) classified the facts under a general situational category; *and* (ii) expressing (a) approval *or* (b) disapproval of the policies articulated; *and* (iii) expressing the opinion that the articulated policies were (a) relevant *or* (b) irrelevant; *and* (iv) expressing the opinion that the general situational category was (a) appropriate *or* (b) inappropriate; *and* (v) expressing the view that a particular

precedent technique employed by Judge X was: (a) legitimate *or* (b) illegitimate; *and* (vi) expressing (a) approval *or* (b) disapproval of the result in the case (or Judge X's conclusion).

88 *C.L.T.*, 122, cited above, p. 217.

89 Above, p. 96.

90 (1914) *Yale Review* 250, cited above, p. 31.

91 The information about Goldschmidt in the text is derived from the unpublished translation by Llewellyn of a chapter of a work by Hugo Sinzheimer, the English title of which is *Jews who were Classical Figures in German Legal Scholarship* (1938). The passage from Goldschmidt is quoted by Sinzheimer; since the wording of Llewellyn's translation is different from the wording in *The Common Law Tradition*, and since this passage has occasioned more comment than any other part of the book, it is worth giving this version in full:

> Every problem situation of ordinary life, so far as it is accessible to the order of legal regulation, carries within itself its fitting natural rule of right law, its *jus aequum*. Thus there is a true natural law immanent in the conditions; it is not imaginary, it is not created out of empty reason, but it rests upon the real foundation of the nature of man when that is recognized by reason, and of his life conditions for the time being, so that it is of course not eternal and unchangeable and everywhere the same. The highest task of law-making rests in the discovery and implementation of this immanent right law. In this sense what we know as sources of law are never truly creative but on the contrary in essence only tools of discovery. For years I have been dominated by the conviction, and it has been constantly reinforced, that the controlling basic ideas of every body of legal doctrine have as their natural and necessary foundation the exploration of life conditions and problem situations whether economic or moral; I have therefore striven to find in commercial relations and in the needs of commerce a source for recognition of the law actually in force.
>
> (See above, n.51.)

92 At one stage Llewellyn tried to revive Mansfield's device of using juries of merchants; *Revised Uniform Sales Act, Second Draft*, 251–3 (1941).

93 *C.L.T.*, 245.

94 A further question might be: a dispute suggests a deviation from normality: what is normality in this kind of situation?

95 *C.L.T.*, 427–8. On 'narrow categories' see above, pp. 136–7.

96 *Ibid.*, 450.

97 *Ibid.*, 261; cf. 403.

98 *Ibid.*, 266.

99 *The Bramble Bush*, 125. Cf. *The Common Law Tradition*, 397.

100 E.g., *Jurisprudence*, 176–7. But in an obscure passage Llewellyn suggests that the Grand Style and the style of reason might sometimes be differentiated (at 465). He does not seem to have observed such a distinction himself.

101 *'Reason* I use to lap over both [wisdom and situation sense] and to include as well the conscious use of the court's best powers to be articulate, especially about wisdom and guidance in the result' (at 61).

102 *Ibid.*, 324. See also *Law in Our Society*; and an address on the Chicago Jury Project, K.L.P. B. IV. 1. (1955).

103 *C.L.T.*, 267.

104 Ibsen, *The Wild Duck.*

105 *C.L.T.*, 365; 52 *Harv. L. Rev.*, 703 (1939).

106 E.g., *C.L.T.*, 264, 268.

107 *Ibid.*, 266.

108 *Ibid.*, 268.

109 J. Bentham, *The Handbook of Political Fallacies*, I, ch. 2 (ed. Larrabee, 1952).

110 See generally, J. L. Montrose, 'The Language of, and a Notation for, the Doctrine of Precedent', 2 *W. Aust. Ann L. R.*, 301 and 504 (1952–3).

111 See, further, Gottlieb's distinction between rules of justification and rules of guidance, *The Logic of Choice* (1968).

112 *C.L.T.*, 131; also 56.

113 See *ibid.*, 26–7, 131–2, 289–91.

114 E.g., *ibid.*, 56.

115 Especially *ibid.*, 62–120, 521–35.

116 3 *Enc. Soc. Sci.*, 249 (1931).

117 *The Bramble Bush*, 48.

118 Julius Stone (i), 'The *Ratio* of the *Ratio Decidendi*', 22 *M.L.R.*, 597 (1959), (ii) *Legal System and Lawyers' Reasonings*, ch. 7 (1964).

119 *Ibid.* (ii) at 269–70; A. L. Goodhart, 'Determining the Ratio Decidendi of a Case', 40 *Yale L. J.*, 161 (1930), *Essays in Jurisprudence and the Common Law* (1931). For a recent discussion of this controversy see Gottlieb, *The Logic of Choice*, ch. VI (1968).

120 *The Bramble Bush*, 48.

121 Ch. V of the original Storrs Lectures was entitled 'Work with the Frozen Word'.

122 *The Bramble Bush*, 47.

123 [1932] A.C. 562, 578–9.

124 *Ibid.*, 599.

125 *Ibid.*, 583.

126 *Ibid.*, 580.

127 Discussed by Heuston, '*Donoghue* v. *Stevenson* in Retrospect', 20 *M.L.R.*, 1, 5–9 (1957).

128 See *ibid.*, 14–23.

129 See Twining, O'Donovan and Paliwala, 'Ernie and the Centipede', in Jolowicz (ed.), *The Classification and Division of the Law* (1970).

130 Especially 75–92.

131 *C.L.T.*, 77. Although the passage is headed 'A Selection of Available

Impeccable Precedent Techniques', it includes a number branded by Llewellyn as 'illegitimate' (85–6).

132 *Ibid.*, 87.

133 *Ibid.*, 99 (Llewellyn's italics).

134 *Ibid.*, 92.

135 Becht, *op. cit.*, 12.

136 *C.L.T.*, 76, 91.

137 See generally R. Cross, *Precedent in English Law* (2nd ed. 1968) *passim*. This work deals extensively with doctrine and somewhat erratically with techniques and practice.

138 [1966] 1 *W.L.R.*, 1234.

139 Lord Atkin cited *Oliver* v. *Saddler & Co.* [1929] A.C. 584 as supporting his view, and considered that 'I need only mention to distinguish' *Caledonian Ry. Co.* v. *Mulholland or Warwick* [1898] A.C. 216 and *Cavalier* v *Pope* [1906] A.C. 428.

140 E.g., *The Bramble Bush*, 78 ff.

141 Beem, 7 *U. Chi. L. Sch. Record*, 30 (1958).

142 Ms., K.L.P. B. VI. 2.

143 *The Bramble Bush*, 78–9.

144 *C.L.T.*, 371.

145 Llewellyn Lectures, 1958.

146 *The Bramble Bush*, 79.

147 On 'Dogmatics', see *Law in Our Society*, Lecture 14.

148 See, e.g., Bodenheimer, *Jurisprudence*, 140–3 (1962), Stone, *Legal System and Lawyers' Reasonings*, 254 (1964), Paton, *Jurisprudence* (3rd ed.), 218 (1964).

149 Appendix C, 529–30. This is an abbreviated version of 3 *Van. L. Rev.*, 395 (1950), one of Llewellyn's best articles (q.v.).

150 *C.L.T.*, 373–4.

151 *Ibid.*, 372.

152 Jurisprudence Lectures, 1958, lecture 5 (author's notes).

153 *The Bramble Bush*, 48–9. One of the basic flaws of some theories of the *ratio decidendi* (in the sense of the rule(s) that a case can be made to stand for) is that they assume that 'the' *ratio* can be extracted by reading the case in isolation. The weakness in this assumption is brought out if one considers the question: is the *ratio decidendi* of *Donoghue* v. *Stevenson* the same in 1972 as it was in 1932?

154 3 *Vand. L. Rev.*, 395, at 396 (1950).

155 *Ibid.*, 399. Cf. *The Common Law Tradition*, 267.

156 *C.L.T.*, 109. Cf. 99, quoted above at p. 237.

157 Especially 64–73, 91–120, 135–54, 158–77, 404–61, 469–507.

158 *Jurisprudence*, 82–3 (1931).

159 *Op. cit.*, ch. 1, n.4.

160 *C.L.T.*, 355.

161 Described at 264–8.

162 *C.L.T.*, 355, and see generally 355–62.

163 *Ibid.*

164 *Ibid.*, 357.

165 29 *U. Chi. L. Rev.*, 627, 629 (1962).

166 Cf., e.g., Levi, *Introduction to Legal Reasoning* (1949).

167 *C.L.T.*, 158.

168 *Jurisprudence*, 498–9 (criticising talk about '*the* administrative process').

169 E.g., 17–8.

170 *The Nature of the Judicial Process*, 164 (1921) cited, *C.L.T.*, 25n.

171 *The Growth of the Law*, 60 (1924), cited at *ibid*.

172 *C.L.T.*, 345.

173 *Ibid.*, 25n.

174 *Ibid.*, 21n. See also 189–90.

175 *The 'Theory of Rules'*, K.L.P. B. II. 40. Ch. V. 30 (1938–40).

176 See, e.g., 356–7. Cf. Mentschikoff:

> He read cases for their narrow holdings (the facts, precise legal issue and result), testing whether the courts were doing what doctrine seemingly required. The objectives of this analysis were, first, an accurate statement of the operative law; second, a testing of the relation between that law and the life situation it encompasses; third, an evaluation of the policy this reflected; and finally, a decision as to what the law ought to be, and its statement in a well-drafted legislative or judicial rule. 9 *Int. Enc. Soc. Sci* , 440 (1968).

177 *C.L.T.*, 470–2.

178 *Ibid.*, 403.

179 Cf. the strictures of Glendon Schubert on 'the legal realists' in 'The Future of Public Law', 34 *Geo. Wash. L. Rev.*, 593, 601 (1966):

> The realists, with rare exceptions, such as Walter Wheeler Cook and Underhill Moore, had neither theory nor methods; Llewellynisms about 'getting at' facts and 'polishing them' until they 'shone' were nothing more than the advocacy of barefoot empiricism. The contribution of the realists lay in the mood they created, through the attention attracted by the iconoclastic essays that some of them wrote; but lacking the technical training to do scientific research, they rarely followed through with the substantive findings to confirm (or refute) their often provocative, and sometimes brilliant, cues and hunches. Most of their work remained at the verbal level, in perfect harmony with the traditions of the profession of which they were a part.

> These remarks may have some justification when applied to Llewellyn, but, as Rumble pointed out (*op. cit.*, 170–5) they are somewhat overstated.

180 *C.L.T.*, 35–45. See also *Jurisprudence*, 178–80.

181 *Ibid.* See Pound, *The Formative Era of American Law* (1939).

182 Such generalizations need to be treated with caution; see Hurst, *The Growth of American Law: The Law Makers*, 185–9 (1950).
183 Wetter, *op. cit.*, 65.
184 S. Mermin, *Jurisprudence and Statecraft*, 100–1 (1963).
185 I. MacNeil to W. Rumble, quoted by Rumble, *op. cit.*, 212–3.
186 C. Breitel, 61 *Col. L. Rev.*, 931 (1961). P. Kurland, 28 *U. Chi. L. Rev.*, 580 (1961).
187 *C.L.T.*, 50.
188 *Ibid.*, 340–1.
189 *Ibid.*, 17–8.
190 See also *ibid.*, 180.
191 *Ibid.*, 37–8.
192 *Jurisprudence*, 70 (1931), *The Bramble Bush*, 68.
193 *C.L.T.*, 365.
194 The classic essay is Pollock, 'Judicial Caution and Judicial Valour', 45 *L.Q.R.*, 293 (1929); see also Denning and Asquith L.JJ., in *Candler* v. *Crane, Christmas* [1951] 2 K.B. 164.
195 *C.L.T.*, 25.
196 *Ibid.*
197 *Ibid.*
198 Dickinson, 79 *U. Pa. L. Rev.*, 1052, 1085 (1931). See Rumble, *op. cit.*, 90 *et seq.* Dickinson's criticism is specifically levelled against Frank's alleged view that every case is unique.
199 *C.L.T.*, 186.
200 *Ibid.*, 185.
201 *Ibid.*, 185–6.
202 *Wash. U.L.Q.*, 64, 71 (1962).
203 Once again this assumes a consensus about values; see above, p. 219.
204 *C.L.T.*, 352 ff.
205 *Ibid.*, 382 ff.
206 *Ibid.*, 236 ff.
207 *Ibid.*, 256 ff.
208 E.g. 191; cf. 29 *U. Chi. L. Rev.*, 627, 629–30.
209 Cf. 'Oral or written, shun the subtle. It *never persuades*. Subtle argument may do for justification; but *first* persuade!' (Llewellyn, 'Materials on Legal Argument', viii, K.L.P. N.2 (1957)).
210 *C.L.T.*, 241. Winning the case is the advocate's job, improving the law is for the court, but there is, and should be, a very high degree of compatibility between the two roles. Llewellyn considered it quite proper for a court to adopt part of an advocate's argument as its own; similarly he strongly commended the practice of a superior court adopting passages from a majority opinion of the lower court when affirming, or from a dissenting opinion when reversing: 'I say the device is deft. When a fitting occasion offers, it saves obvious time. It runs

flat free of cost. It capitalizes what is sometimes superb skill. *It builds morale below as does no other device available to a supreme tribunal . . .*' (318).

211 *C.L.T.*, 26–7, 289.

212 Prediction of likely outcome is, of course, an important part of deciding whether or not to pursue, or to contest, an appeal; analytically this is part of the counselling role, although in practice the person acting as advocate may be very much concerned with it.

213 *C.L.T.*, 383. Cf. *Jurisprudence*, 323–36.

214 *Ibid.*, 345–62.

215 *Ibid.*, 349.

216 *Ibid.*, 361–2.

217 See also *Jurisprudence*, 336–43, and 'A Lecture on Appellate Advocacy', 29 *U. Chi. L. Rev.*, 627 (1962).

218 *C.L.T.*, 239n.

219 *Ibid.*, 250, 258.

220 *Ibid.*, 237.

221 *Ibid.*, 238.

222 *Ibid.*

223 *Ibid.*

224 See especially K.L.P. N.I. 6 and II.

225 *Ibid.* The ABA's. Canons of Professional Ethics were adopted in 1908, but have been amended from time to time.

226 Materials on Legal Argument, K.L.P. N.1.b. at 1 (1957).

227 *Ibid.*

228 *C.L.T.*, 85–6, 450ff; above, p. 237.

229 *C.L.T.*, 559.

230 Llewellyn's principal references were to Wiener, *Effective Appellate Advocacy* (1950); see also works cited in 29 *U. Chi. L. Rev.*, 627, 628 (1962). Other books on advocacy which were found on Llewellyn's bookshelves included B.K. and W.F. Elliott, *The Work of the Advocate* (1911) and G. Rosman (ed.), *Advocacy and the King's English* (1960). E. A. Parry, *The Seven Lamps of Advocacy* (1923), at 76–7, makes statements strikingly similar to Llewellyn's, e.g., 'Judgment inspires a man to translate good sense into right action' (75).

An advocate of judgment has the power of gathering up the scattered threads of facts and weaving them into a pattern surrounding and emphasising the central point of the case. In every case there is one commanding theory, to the proof of which all the facts must be skilfully marshalled. An advocate with one point has infinitely greater chances than an advocate with twenty points (76–7)

Cf. also Sokol, *Language and Litigation* (1967): 'A properly phrased issue should meet three criteria: (1) it should be concrete and thus applicable to the case being argued and no other; (2) *it should suggest its own answer* and (3) it should produce an overall effect and thus have a tone' (157).

231 *C.L.T.*, 238.

232 *Ibid.*, 239.

233 *Ibid.*, 197, and 'Materials on Legal Argument', *passim.*

234 *C.L.T.*, 239.

235 E.g., C. Breitel, 61 *Col. L. Rev.*, 935 (1961); C. Desmond, 36 *N.Y.U.L. Rev.*, 529, 531 (1961); J. Shestack, 109 *U. Pa. L. Rev.*, 1051 (1961).

236 *C.L.T.*, 58.

237 On the need for caution in evaluating claims for new ventures in teaching, see Rita James Simon, 'An Evaluation of the Effectiveness of Some Curriculum Innovations in Law Schools', 2 *Jo. Applied Behavioral Science*, 219–37 (1966); extracts are reprinted in Simon, *The Sociology of Law* (1968) at 573 ff. Simon reports a lack of significant results discernible from a series of courses sponsored by the National Council of Legal Clinics.

238 E.g., 'What is . . . needed is men—a bench—right-minded, learned, careful, wise, to find and voice from among the still fluid materials of the legal sun the answer which will satisfy, and which will render semi-solid one more point, as a basis for further growth' (185).

239 It is worth noting that most of Llewellyn's models made their mark as commercial judges.

240 For a valuable exercise in analysing the use of authorities by a single court over a period of a year (California Supreme Court, 1950), see J. Merryman, 'The Authority of Authority', 6 *Stanford L. Rev.*, 613 (1954).

241 J. Gillis Wetter, *The Styles of Appellate Judicial Opinions* (1960), discussed by Llewellyn at 465ff.

242 It is outside the scope of the present discussion to summarise his conclusions, but it is interesting to note that his own research did not provide confirmation of Llewellyn's contention that there had been in American legal history a cycle of Grand Style followed by Formal Style followed by a resurgence of the Grand Style; Wetter suggests that systematic research would reveal a rather more complex picture. Furthermore, he hints that in his view American state appellate courts 'give the appearance of a prevalent judicial decadence', which is not easy to reconcile with Llewellyn's vision of a renaissance of the Grand Style. Wetter also reports:

My admittedly limited research has not substantiated the correctness of a theory of three successive 'styles' in American appellate courts possessing the characteristics ascribed to them by Llewellyn; yet I have found the idea interesting and worth exploring. A study of the California Supreme Court in the years 1855, 1905 and 1955 will show the prevalence of three radically different styles, and will reveal how within fifty year periods, new, uniform craft-traditions have become established in particular courts. But they do not all display the features described by Llewellyn (64–5).

243 *C.L.T.*, 75.

244 For Llewellyn's views on the value of signed opinions, see *C.L.T.*, 35, 429.

245 28 *U. Chi. L. Rev.*, 580 (1961).

246 Ex. rel. the late Professor Mark de Wolfe Howe, interview June 1964.

247 71 *Yale L. J.*, 240. This was a moderate substitute for the kind of critique that might have been expected of Frank, had he been alive to review the work. Some contemporary reactions to *The Common Law Tradition*, notably the discussion by Clark and Trubeck, reflect concern with 'the neutral principles' controversy which followed on the publication of Herbert Wechsler's article 'Toward Neutral Principles of Constitutional Law', 73 *Harv. L. Rev.*, 1 (1959). Whereas *The Common Law Tradition* was primarily oriented to private law disputes in the state courts, the 'neutral principles' debate was about the approach to public law issues by the federal courts. Judge Clark was an opponent of the 'neutral principles' idea and of the ideas of judicial restraint espoused by Mr Justice Frankfurter. He read *The Common Law Tradition* as providing support for the opposition (Ex. rel. Professor David Trubeck; this is confirmed by a letter from Clark to Llewellyn, 19 January 1962, K.L.P., A.II. 2. ee.). Llewellyn only touched on 'the neutral principles' debate very briefly (389) but it is unlikely that he would have sided with Wechsler. It is, however, fair to say that *The Common Law Tradition* does not face up to such questions as: is the Supreme Court an appropriate decision-making body to attempt to solve problems of desegregation or re-apportionment? When a judge of The Supreme Court feels that he is being asked to resolve issues which should be determined by some other institution, how should he behave? Llewellyn may not have stressed the extent to which Formal Style arguments have been used as a means of 'begging' questions by judges who wished, sometimes as a matter of deliberate policy, to limit their role (actual or apparent or both) as far as they could. For a recent discussion of 'judicial restraint', see L. Jaffe, *English and American Judges as Lawmakers* (1970).

248 Eg., Becker, Mermin, Moskowitz, Schubert, Hayakawa, and to a lesser extent Rumble, *op. cit.*

249 The book was also a vehicle for more personal self-expression, as this manuscript soliloquy confirms:

> I have been trying to get into words my own picture of the piece of me I like, as evidenced in the book. It is very hard to grapple onto.
> Maybe the first three pieces are three faiths: in goodness, in the need for drive, and in forgiveness. I think if you put these together they make a laboring craftsman who is as proud as he is humble.
> Maybe this is what the book has tried to do.
> But if the book is to convey its message, somebody from inside must echo

Loughran: 'It reads as if you had been present at the consultations' – or the like. Schaefer will say something of the kind; and Fuld may. But it would come best from someone completely outside the scope of the inquiry. . . .

I do think that in this book I have produced a new genre of literature: the work and flavor of an American Supreme Court in Action. This has never been done, and I think it as interesting a literary technique as Ibsen's beginning of a drama two-third's through (ms., K.L.P.).

250 One of Llewellyn's former pupils has underlined the point that to talk of 'the bar' is to conceal the enormous variety within the U.S. legal profession: Carlin, *Lawyers on Their Own* (1962).

251 E.g., the treatment of 'the steadying factors', and the overconcentration on cases 'worth appealing'.

252 *C.L.T.*, 179.

11   THE GENESIS OF THE UNIFORM COMMERCIAL CODE

1 The main sources of this chapter are the very extensive collection of papers in K.L.P., J, the 1962 text of the Uniform Commercial Code and the annual *Handbook of the National Conference of Commissioners on Uniform State Laws* (hereafter cited as *Handbook*). Only limited use has been made of the very extensive secondary literature on the Code. Where possible I have checked points of detail with individuals who were connected with the Code project, notably Professors Soia Mentschikoff, Allison Dunham, and Grant Gilmore. However, errors of fact and expressions of opinion are entirely my responsibility.

2 Article 1. General provisions
   2. Sales
   3. Commercial Paper
   4. Bank Deposits and Collections
   5. Letters of Credit
   6. Bulk Transfers
   7. Warehouse Receipts, Bills of Lading and Other Documents of Title
   8. Investment Securities
   9. Secured Transactions, Sales of Accounts, Contract Rights and Chattel Paper
   10. Effective Date and Repealer.

3 M. Ezer, *Uniform Commercial Code Bibliography* (1966). This has been kept up to date annually.

4 *Ibid.*, preface (1969).

5 See, e.g., W. Hawkland, *A Transactional Guide to the Uniform Commercial Code* (1964); S. Mentschikoff, *Cases on Commercial Transactions* (1968); G. Gilmore, *Security Interests in Personal Property* (1965).

6 Documentary sources on the Code, unpublished as well as published, give a very incomplete picture of this aspect of its history. This is largely because many disagreements were ironed out and decisions taken through informal oral communications of which no official record was kept. Indeed, sometimes the documentary sources can be quite misleading. It is to be hoped that some of the leading participants will record their reminiscences of the internal politics of the project for the benefit of posterity.

7 E.g., Gilmore, 'In Memoriam: Karl Llewellyn', 71 *Yale L.J.*, 813, 814 (1962).

8 F. Wallach, *Introduction to European Commercial Law*, 42 (1953).

9 Franklin, 16 *Law and Contemporary Problems*, 330 ff. (1951).

10 Mooney, 'Old Kontract Principles and Karl's New Kode', 11 *Villanova L. Rev.*, 213 (1966).

11 E.g., *Why should your state enact the Uniform Commercial Code?* (1958).

12 36 *A.B.A.J.*, 419 (1950).

13 E.g., 3 *American Business Law Journal*, 137 (1965) (editorial note to an article by Schnader entitled 'The Permanent Editorial Board for the Uniform Commercial Code: Can it Accomplish its Object?'). Allowance must be made for the public relations functions of some of these claims. See, further, below p. 286ff.

14 On the NCC and the ALI, see generally W. D. Lewis, 'History of the American Law Institute and The First Restatement of the Law', in American Law Institute, *Restatement in the Courts* (1945); The American Law Institute *Proceedings*, vol. I (1923); H. Goodrich, 'Story of the American Law Institute', *Wash. U.L.Q.*, 283 (1951); Annual *Handbook of the National Conference of Commissioners on Uniform Laws*; A. Dunham, 'A History of the National Conference of Commissioners on Uniform State Laws', 30 *L. and C.P.*, 233 (1965). W. Hurst, *The Growth of American Law: the Law Makers, passim* (1950). For further references see F. Klein, *Judicial Administration and the Legal Profession* (1963).

15 In its early years the scope of the work of the NCC was limited by the view that it should restrict itself to areas 'where Congress had no jurisdiction'; at that period the power of Congress to regulate interstate commerce was narrowly interpreted. Dunham, *op. cit.*, 236 *et seq.*

16 Adapted from R. Braucher, 58 *Col. L. Rev.*, 798, 799 (1958).

17 *Ibid.*

18 A.L.I., *Proceedings*, vol. I, part 1, 1–109 (1923). The reporters were Joseph Beale, Benjamin Cardozo, Albert Kales (who died shortly after appointment), Samuel Williston and William Draper Lewis. Among those appointed as 'critics' were Victor Morawetz, Roscoe Pound, Harlan F. Stone, John H. Wigmore and R. C. Leffingwell. *Ibid.*, part 2, 4–5.

19 In the foreword to the Account of the Proceedings at the organization of

the Institute in Washington D.C. on 23 February 1923 (A.L.I., *Proceedings* vol. 1, part 2), the history of the Institute is traced back directly to Hohfeld's paper, 'A Vital School of Jurisprudence and Law', read at the AALS meeting in 1914, and to a paper by Beale. The project for 'the betterment of law' is said to have emanated from Hohfeld's paper.

20 For a good critical discussion of realist attacks on the *Restatement*, see Merryman, 'The Authority of Authority', 6 *Stanford L. Rev.*, 613 (1954).

21 Lewis, *op. cit.* (note 14), (at 8 and 20) suggests that the policy of the *Restatement* was, when in doubt, to *predict* how the courts would decide in fact in a given situation. On the other hand, much of the discussion was in terms of 'betterment of the law', and Lewis suggests that the criterion was the most desirable solution. It may be that Lewis, like Llewellyn, was optimistic that the courts, if given the chance, would tend to choose the 'better' solution.

22 E.g., A.L.I., *Proceedings*, I, 26–8 (1923).

23 *Ibid.*, II, 112.

24 Election to individual membership of the ALI is widely regarded as a mark of distinction. Moreover, provision was made for *ex officio* membership for the chief justice of each state, for deans of recognised law schools, and for a number of other legal dignitaries. This ensured that a large number of holders of key positions were officially associated with, and made aware of, the Institute's activities.

25 See especially, *Report and Second Draft, The Revised Uniform Sales Act* (1941); *Handbooks* (1937–41); K.L.P. J. I–III (which includes an unfinished draft of a history of the RUSA by Llewellyn).

26 *Handbook*, 469 (1938).

27 H.R., 1619 (1937).

28 *Report of Special Committee on Federal Sales Bill of the Merchants' Association of New York* (18 February 1937). K.L.P., J. I.

29 H.R., 7824 (1937).

30 H.R., 8176 (1940).

31 'The Needed Federal Sales Act', 26 *Va. L. Rev.*, 558–71 (1940).

32 Report of Chairman of the section on Uniform Commercial Acts, 2, K.L.P., J. I. 4 (1938). Llewellyn was the chairman.

33 Schnader to Llewellyn, 27 October 1937, K.L.P., J. XXV 1.

34 *Ibid.*

35 *Handbook*, 58 (1940).

36 K.L.P., J. II, 1 (the most important of these is quoted at length below, Appendix E.)

37 *Revised Uniform Sales Act – Second Draft*, 4 (1941).

38 *Revised Uniform Sales Act – Second Draft (Text and Comments)*, 4 (1941). K.L.P., J, II, 2.

39 *Ibid.*

40 E.g., Nussbaum to Llewellyn, 5 May 1942. K.L.P., J. XXV, 6. Corbin, *loc. cit.* (below, note 41).

41 Corbin, 'A Tribute to Karl Llewellyn', 8 *Yale Law Report No. 2*, 10 (1962). Also MS, 'An Account by Arthur L. Corbin of his association with Karl N. Llewellyn', 8 (1965).

42 Memo. to Committee on Scope and Program. K.L.P., J, II, 1 (1940).

43 *Handbook*, 41 (1941). Schnader was, at the time, a Vice-President of the ALI as well as President of the NCC.

44 The matter was finally resolved in favour of continuing at the annual meeting in May 1944 when a decision of the executive committee to this effect was ratified.

45 K.L.P., J, VI (1944). 1, b, 14.

46 See below, p. 285ff.

47 K.L.P., J, V (1943). 2, K, 2.

48 William Draper Lewis in his annual report to the ALI said of the Revised Uniform Sales Act: 'In all my experience I have never seen an Act prepared with more thorough discussion of the problems dealt with and with greater care to express with clarity the conclusions reached.' K.L.P., J, VI, 2, K, 14 (1944).

49 Program for cooperative Preparation of the Proposed Uniform Commercial Code by the American Law Institute and the National Conference of Commissioners on Uniform State Laws, 1 December 1944. K.L.P., J, IX (1947). 1, b.

50 This board was subsequently enlarged. William F. Goodrich acted as chairman.

51 Up to 1949, in addition to Llewellyn the principal reporters and their main concerns were Charles Bunn (bulk transfers), Allison Dunham (secured transactions), Grant Gilmore (secured transactions), Friedrich Kessler (letters of credit and foreign banking), Fairfax Leary (bank collections and commercial paper), Soia Mentschikoff (sales and investment securities), William L. Prosser (commercial paper), Louis B. Schwartz (warehouse receipts and bills of lading).

52 K.L.P., J, VI, 1, h (1944) printed (with slight variations) in W. D. Lewis Report to ALI Council (1946) K.L.P., J, VIII, 1, c.

53 According to Soia Mentschikoff Llewellyn there was only one major disagreement between Schnader and Llewellyn in the period before the Editorial Board was enlarged. In 1952 Schnader was anxious to conclude the project, but Llewellyn insisted that the Code was not ready. Eventually, after a heated dispute, Llewellyn got his way.

54 Ex rel. Soia Mentschikoff Llewellyn.

55 *Ibid.*

56 S. Williston, 'The Law of Sales in the Proposed Uniform Commercial Code', 63 *Harv. L. Rev.*, 561 (1950). Williston was at first reluctant to express his opposition publicly. This reluctance might be attributed in

part to the fact that he could have been accused of having an emotional vested interest in the survival of the act which he had drafted. In his article he was careful to point out that he had no pecuniary interest. Williston was not reputed to be possessive about his ideas and the reasons he articulated were consistent with his general approach and attitudes.

57 Cf. R. Schlesinger, 1, *NYLRC Report*, 94–5 (1955).

58 *Op. cit.* (n.56), at 565.

59 'We are not drawing the statute for the experts themselves; we are trying to draw it for the unillumined, ordinary guy of the bar, and, as I said earlier, we find that he can read our statute while he has trouble with the other.' Llewellyn, Address to the Ohio State Bar Assoc., 27 May 1950, 24. K.L.P., J, XII, 1, q. In this address Llewellyn purported to answer Williston's principal criticisms. For Llewellyn's aspirations to make the Code, and law in general, more intelligible to ordinary practitioners, and sometimes laymen, see appendix E. How far this particular objective was achieved is debatable.

60 A. L. Corbin, 'The Uniform Commercial Code – Sales; Should it be Enacted?', 59 *Yale L.J.*, 821 (1950).

61 See especially 15 *NYUL Rev.*, 159, at 165 *et seq.* (1938).

62 *Op. cit.* n. 60, at 822n.

63 E.g., *Revised Uniform Sales Act – Second Draft*, 7ff (1941).

64 Letter Corbin to Twining, October 1965.

65 K.L.P., J, XXV (1949).

66 There were some individuals who were persistent critics of the U.C.C. The most notable of these was Professor Frederick K. Beutel of Nebraska (see, e.g., 61 *Yale L.J.*, 334 (1952), 16 *L and C.P.*, 141 (1951), 14 *Ohio St. L.J.*, 3 (1953)), from whom Emmett Smith derived most of his arguments. Beutel, like Williston, participated constructively in some of the Code discussions. At a later stage opposition from the Indiana State Bankers' Association led to the death of a bill to introduce the Code in the 1957 session of the Indiana State Legislature. *Handbook*, 172 (1957). However, the Code was enacted in Indiana in 1963. See also, John B. Waite, 'The Proposed New Uniform Sales Act', 48 *Mich. L. Rev.*, 603 (1950). See further below pp. 530–45.

67 See below, p. 528.

68 Ex rel. Soia Mentschikoff Llewellyn. On origins of Article 9, see Gilmore *Security Interests in Personal Property* 290 (1965) cp. above pp. 417–8.

69 K.L.P., J, XIII (1951), d, 50–2.

70 One incident illustrates his style. At a joint meeting of the ALI and the NCC in Washington in May 1951, a Mr Butler, representing the American Warehouseman's Association, Merchandise Division in Boston, gave evidence to the effect that his organisation favoured the indefinite postponement of the enactment of the Code. Since Mr Butler had no standing at the meeting, a member of the ALI, Mr Heineman,

undertook to move a motion in those terms on Mr Butler's behalf while making clear that he disagreed with it. Up jumped Karl Llewellyn: 'Solely on Mr Butler's behalf, I second it.' Not surprisingly, perhaps, the motion was defeated.

Llewellyn's faith in working for consensus was strengthened by his experience of the Code. He expressed some of his satisfaction in his evidence before the Pennsylvania Legislature Sub-Committee in June 1952. In discussing Article 6, he said: 'It is really amazing, gentlemen, when you take this ten-year haul that we have had, to find how many points of bitter conflict have splendidly worn themselves out as time has gone on and as frequently wisdom has come up in the form of some type of solution that satisfied both sides or by the process of dicker when an outfit insisting on one point was willing to give on that if something reasonable was given in return' (K.L.P., J, XIV (1952). j. 33). That Llewellyn was not always polite in responding to criticism is apparent from the record of the hearings of the NYLRC. See, for example, 2 *N.Y. Law Rev. Comm.*, 1437–8 (1954).

71 The part played by academic lawyers in the drafting of the Code is sometimes exaggerated. Llewellyn himself and Bunn were the only two of the original reporters who were, at the time of their appointment, established law teachers. Prosser and Mentschikoff were in practice at the time of appointment and Gilmore, Dunham, and Leary were young men at the outset of their careers. Except perhaps for Prosser, it is fair to say that this group made their names as legal scholars at a later stage.

72 *U. Ill. Law Forum*, 322 (1962).

73 See especially 61 *Yale L.J.*, 334 (1952), 16 *Law and Contemp. Prob.*, 141 (1951).

74 Gilmore, in an article replying to Beutel's general attack on the Code, felt that he must leave the answer to the allegations of a sell-out to the bankers 'to someone who can undertake it with a better heart'. 61 *Yale L.J.*, 364, 374 (1952). See generally, Kripke, *U. Ill. Law Forum*, 321, 322–8 (1962).

75 D. Caplowitz, *The Poor Pay More; Consumer practices of low-income families* (1963).

76 Uniform Consumer Credit Code, drafts (1966–9). See Helen Nelson (ed.), *Consumer Viewpoints* (1969).

77 Ex rel. Soia Mentschikoff Llewellyn. See also D. Murray, 'The Consumer and the Code: A Cross-sectional View', 23 *U. Miami L. Rev.*, 11 (1969).

78 The history of the New York Study is recounted in the Reports of the NYLRC for 1954 and 1956. See also Schnader, 'The Future of the Uniform Commercial Code' (MS), K.L.P., J, XVIII (1956). 1, c.

79 Adopted by ALI and NCC in 1955.

80 Published in edited form by NYLRC as Legislative Document (1954) No. 65 (A), Albany, 1955.

81 *Op. cit.*, note 78, at 67.

82 *Ibid.*, 68.

83 *Ibid.*

84 'Panel Discussion on the Uniform Commercial Code', 12 *The Business Lawyer*, 49 at 53–4 (1956). This discussion contains an excellent analysis of the areas of agreement and disagreement between the N.Y. Commission and the sponsors of the Code. Naturally it was in the interests of the latter to play down the extent of disagreement. See also R. Braucher, 58 *Col. L. Rev.*, 798 (1958).

85 *Ibid.*, 78. In fact, Article 5 was enacted in New York in a somewhat attenuated form.

86 Llewellyn was a member of the Editorial Board and the subcommittee on Article 2; Mentschikoff was on the subcommittees on Articles 5 and 8. Also by virtue of the treaty, the Chief Reporter and Associate Reporter could attend all subcommittee meetings, and nearly always did so.

87 *Handbook*, 100–1 (1957).

88 In fact the 1957 draft of Article 5 represented a return to conceptions which much more closely accorded with Llewellyn's views than the 1952 draft, which had been changed in an effort to placate some of the New York banking counsel. At several stages in the history of the code there were complicated political manoeuvrings about the retention of Articles 4 and 5.

89 R. Pasley, Panel Discussion, *op. cit.* (above, note 84), at 57.

90 NYLRC Report, 29.

91 See especially *ibid.*, 25.

92 71 *Yale L. J.*, 813 at 814–5 (1962). On the generally more iconoclastic approach of the drafting staff compared to their advisers, see H. Kripke, 'The Principles Underlying the Drafting of the Uniform Commercial Code', *U. Ill. Law Forum*, 321, at 322–3 (1962). Mentschikoff's opinion is that Gilmore's statement is more applicable to Articles 4 and 9 than to others.

93 For a brief account see R. Braucher, 'The Uniform Commercial Code – A Third Look?', 14 *W. Res. L. Rev.*, 7 (1962), and Schnader, 'The Permanent Editorial Board for the Uniform Commercial Code: Can it Accomplish its Object?', 3 *Am. Bus. Law. Jo.*, 137–44 (1965). Subsequently a number of studies of suggested amendments have been undertaken. See especially the first three *Reports of the Permanent Editorial Board* (1962, 1964, 1967). Schlesinger, in his report to the New York Law Revision Commission, had some shrewd observations to make on the difficulties of revising a code, once enacted, even in a single jurisdiction.

He concluded: 'No effort seems too great to keep such arteriosclerosis out of the law' (*op. cit.* 99–104).

94 Schnader, *id.*, at 143.

95 Permanent Editorial Board Report No. 3, X (1966). See further: 'UCC Annual Survey of Legal Developments', 26 *Bus. Law.* 1163 (1971), 27 *Bus. Law.* 709 (1972).

12 THE JURISPRUDENCE OF THE UNIFORM COMMERCIAL CODE

1 Corbin, 59 *Yale L. J.*, 835 (1950).

2 This version was drafted by Llewellyn; the 1962 official text contained some variations – see 1962 text 1–102(2): cf. Llewellyn to W. D. Lewis: 'Statement on value of Code for commercial and financial interests:
    (1) To bring the law abreast of modern need,
    (2) To clean out needless and expensive complexity and confusion,
    (3) To introduce throughout standards of commercial reasonableness and safety,
    (4) To provide a solid and clear basis for counselling and for informal adjustment of disputes.' K.L.P., J, V, 1, a (1943).

3 'Now what's to go into a uniform commercial code? Plainly you start with what you've got. If you've got a body of uniform commercial acts, you've got to pick up the uniform commercial acts that you have and start from there.' Llewellyn, at panel discussion of Code at Annual Meeting of the Ohio State Bar Association, 27 May 1950. K.L.P., J, XII, 1, q, p. 3 (1950).

4 Statement to N.Y. Law Revision Commission at p. 12 (below, p. 538).

5 Ex rel. Soia Mentschikoff Llewellyn.

6 Memo: 'Re Possible Uniform Commercial Code', addressed to executive committee on Scope and Program of NCC Section on Uniform Commercial Acts. K.L.P., J,II,1,b [reproduced in appendix E].

7 *Ibid.*, 2.

8 *Ibid.*

9 Mentschikoff, 27 *M.L.R.*, 167, 171 (1964), where she notes that in some places, primarily in Article 4, it tended to creep in during the process of amendment.

10 See, further, memo., *op. cit.* (n. 6) referring to ss. 63 and 59(3) and (4) of the RUSA draft (1940).

11 *Ibid.*, Llewellyn's italics.

12 *Ibid.*

13 For a sceptical view of this claim, see Gilmore, 'On Statutory Obsolescence', 39 *U. Colo. L. Rev.*, 461 (1967).

14 *Op. cit.*, above, ch. 11, n.57.

15 On the potential clash between uniformity and other values, see D. Mellinkoff, 77 *Yale L. Jo*, 185 (1967).

16 *Revised Uniform Sales Act, Second Draft*, 251–3 (1941).
17 This contained a number of rules of construction which could not be varied by agreement. The 1962 text reads:

> The effect of provisions of this Act may be varied by agreement, except as otherwise provided in this Act and except that the obligations of good faith, diligence, reasonableness and care prescribed by this Act may not be disclaimed by agreement but the parties may by agreement determine the standards by which the performance of such obligations is to be measured if such standards are not manifestly unreasonable (S.1–102(3)).

18 *Ibid.*
19 See above, p. 462, n.72–7. Kripke, *op. cit.* at p. 326, characterizes the Code as 'a fundamentally conservative piece of amendatory legislation'.
20 NYLRC, *op. cit.*, vol. I, at 37; cf. generally, Hawkland, 'The Uniform Commercial "Code" Methodology', 1962 *U. of Ill. Law Forum*, 291ff.
21 NYLRC, *op. cit.*, 12–13; memo: 'Re Possible Uniform Commercial Code (1940)', below, appendix E.
22 Lectures, K.L.P., C, series M, 12, 1 (1955).
23 Lobingier, Codification 3 *Enc. Soc. Sci.*, 606, 613.
24 *Op. cit.* (note 22 above).
25 Llewellyn: Carter, James Coolidge, 3 *Enc. Soc. Sci.*, 243, 244.
26 K.L.P., C, Series H. Cf. Llewellyn, 'Problems of Codifying Security Law', 13 *Law and Contemp. Problems*, 687 (1948).
27 Holmes 'Path of the Law' 10 *Harv. L. Rev.* 457 (1897).
28 *Op. cit.*, n.25 at 243.
29 *Ibid.*, at 244.
30 *Travaux de La Commission de Reforme du Code Civil 1948–49*, at 98, cited by Franklin, 16 *Law and Contemp. Problems*, 330, at 336 (1951).
31 S.1–103.
32 Mooney, 11 *Vill. L. R., passim*, esp. at 257–8 (1965–6).
33 Church, *Business Associations Under French Law*, 29–30 (1960); Schlesinger, *op. cit.* at 104ff.
34 See above, ch. 10.
35 Schlesinger, 1 *NYLRC*, at 96–7.
36 Rabel, Observations on Revised Uniform Sales Act, Final Draft No. 1 (memo: K.L.P., J, VIII, 2 June 1946); Rabel to Goodrich, 11 November 1946, referring to letter to Lewis. Llewellyn also held several informal meetings with Rabel (ex rel. Soia Mentschikoff Llewellyn).
37 Rabel mentions, for example, 'the kinds of sale contracts distinguished according to the place where the seller has to terminate his activity (ss. 73 *et seq*); unilateral appropriation to the contract by the seller (ss. 71, 72); the right of the seller to substitute conforming goods . . . ; the separation of risk of loss from title; the development of the rules for delivery in instalment contracts (s. 102); the merger of the remedies for breach of warranty with those for breach of contract and the improve-

ment of the rules for anticipatory breach (s. 100)', at 1–2, Memo by Rabel, dated 25 June 1946.

38 *Ibid.*, at 3.

39 *Ibid.*

40 See above (chapter 9).

41 *The Report of the Commission on Obscenity and Pornography* (1970) is an example of a recent trend of government-sponsored reports which have moved closer to the 'scientific model' in the United States. The Commission is estimated to have cost in the region of two and a half million dollars, yet the main empirical studies were admitted to be inconclusive and, at the end of 1970, it appeared unlikely that the Commission's recommendations would be implemented. The financing of the Code Project was on a much more modest scale.

42 L. Friedman, 'Contract Law and Contract Research: Past, Present and Future', 20 *Jo. Leg. Ed.*, 452, 455–6 (1968). See also F. Beutel, 16 *L. and C.P.*, 141, 142–5 (1951). Gilmore replied to Beutel, in 61 *Yale L.J.*, 364 at 366 (1952), but issue was not squarely joined in this debate.

43 'The Theory of Legal "Science",' 20 *N. Carolina L. Rev.*, 1, 13 (1941).

44 *Ibid.*, at 22.

45 *Ibid.*, at 13–4.

46 A questionnaire (relating to letters of credit) was sent out by members of the New York Law Revision Commission during their enquiry. In connection with Article 8 a request was sent to all commissioners to check what kinds of pieces of paper were being used in the local markets as investment securities. It is interesting to note that in their public relations the sponsors laid great stress on the theme that 'EXPERIENCE, NOT THEORY' should be the basis for evaluation of the Code. In a pamphlet which emphasised the theme, 'experience' is evidenced by resolutions and letters solicited by Schnader and Malcolm from leading law firms and commercial organizations in Pennsylvania and Massachusetts. This pamphlet appears to have been the nearest approach to an attempt by the sponsors to collect empirical data about the effects of the Code after enactment. It may represent shrewd public relations *vis a vis* state legislatures, but it is a far cry from the kind of evidence postulated by the scientific model. The full title of the pamphlet is *The Uniform Commercial Code in Pennsylvania 1956–1964 and in Massachusetts 1958–1964 – Experience – Not Theory – Some Interesting Letters and Resolutions . . . A Convincing Article by a Prominent Banker* (1964).

47 E.g., Lewis to Pepper, 25 September 1945, K.L.P.J., VII, I, C.

48 Ex rel. Soia Mentschikoff Llewellyn.

49 *Ibid.*

50 It has been suggested to me, by Mr Kirk Roose, that part of the puzzlement about the empirical base of the Code may be attributable

to differences between the way a commercial and, for instance, a penal law are designed to influence behavior. If I understand the suggestion correctly, it implies that whereas typically a penal law, for example, is primarily directed towards deterring or preventing certain classes of act on the part of the public at large, many rules of commercial law are designed to facilitate, to simplify or to give legal recognition to the practices of specialized groups, such as lawyers and businessmen. Thus to test the claim that the Code simplifies the law, it would be necessary, *inter alia*, to investigate how it has affected the behavior of teachers and students of the subject and whether it has appreciably reduced the time spent in research by lawyers in practice. This could be an interesting, but elusive, line of enquiry. Similarly it would not be easy to discover whose behaviour had been affected in what ways by making 'uniform the law among the various jurisdictions'. And, in so far as the Code recognized existing business practices or facilitated the development of new ones, it would be extraordinarily difficult to establish empirically a connection between the Code and changes in the behavior of businessmen. Of course there are specific sections of the Code which are designed to have a direct influence on the behavior not only of businessmen, but also of ordinary members of the public. Nevertheless the suggestion is an interesting one and, if elaborated, might provide the basis for elucidating such elusive concepts as 'merely technical reforms' and 'lawyers' law'.

Professor Robert Summers has commented:
I think the biggest and best reason for lack of empirical research is this: most of the Code is 'suppletive' law – it applies only when the parties have not agreed as to the matter in hand. It says what the law is when the parties don't say. It is therefore rather generalized stuff which courts must particularize in specific cases. How can we do good empirical research on such generalized stuff, or even on what constitutes rational particularization?
   Also, much of the Code deals with remedies (absent contractual specification again). It is relatively easy, without doing research, to decide in general terms what remedies are rational and just for what Llewellyn would have called 'type situations' (communication to author).

51 Professor Grant Gilmore, interview, April 1968.
52 Professor Gerhard Casper, interview, April 1968.
53 Doubt has been expressed about Llewellyn's assumptions (in *The Common Law Tradition*, pp. 370–71) concerning the behaviour and expectations of businessmen when they read the 'fine print' in standard form contracts. (A. Leff 115 U. Pa. L. Rev. 485, 506–8).
54 K.L.P., J, VI, 1, e, at 5 (1944).
55 The earlier drafts (esp. 1947, 1950, 1952) contained a number of other rules of construction drafted by Llewellyn which were subsequently dropped.

56 (1584) 3 Co. Rep., 7, A.
57 At 12.
58 At 13.
59 S. 1–106 (1). The comment states:

> Sub-Section (1) is intended to effect three things:
> 1. First, to negate the unduly narrow or technical interpretation of some remedial provisions of prior legislation by providing that the remedies in this Act are to be liberally administered to the end stated in the section. Second, to make it clear that compensatory damages are limited to compensation. They do not include consequential or special damages, or penal damages; and the Act elsewhere makes it clear that damages must be minimized. Cf. Sections 1–203, 2–706(1), and 2–712(2). The third purpose of sub-section (1) is to reject any doctrine that damages must be calculable with mathematical accuracy. Compensatory damages are often at best approximate: they have to be proved with whatever definiteness and accuracy the facts permit, but no more.

60 S.4–107 (1).
61 1 *NYLRC* Study of the Uniform Commercial Code, at 64, notes 74, 78 (1955).
62 Some early statements of reason in the text of the draft Sales Act were eliminated because of opposition from Learned Hand and Willard Luther. K.L.P.J., VI, 1 e, 6 (1944).
63 *The Common Law Tradition*, 183.
64 K.L.P.J., VI, 1, e, 6 (1944).
65 E.g., 2–204 (1), 2–237 (1), 2–603, 2–605, etc.
66 S.2–104 (1). Comment, 42–3.
67 S.2–201(2), 2–205, 2–207, 2–209.
68 At 43.
69 Mentschikoff, 27 *M.L.R.*, 167, 168 (1964).
70 *The Common Law Tradition*, 183.
71 S.2–104.
72 Skilton, 'Some Comments on the Comments to the Uniform Commercial Code', *Wis. L. Rev.*, 597, 599 (1966). This article was particularly helpful in the writing of this section.
73 See English and Scottish Law Commissions: Working Paper on Interpretation of Statutes (1967), app. D.
74 For refs see Merrill, 49 *A.B.A.J.*, 545, 546–7 (1963).
75 See esp. U.R.S.A., 1941 Draft, at 49, 1944 Draft, at 1 and 72.
76 Braucher, 58 *Col. L. Rev.*, 798, 809 (1958), *Handbook*, 149, 164 (1944).
77 Reproduced in Llewellyn, *Commercial Law Materials*, part 3. Mimeo., Spring 1948, K.L.P., K, II, 14.
78 K.L.P., J, V, 2, d, 1 (1943).
79 Braucher, *op. cit.*, 809. The purpose of the provision was to avoid confusion arising from the many changes made in the wording of different

drafts, when there was no intent to change substance (ex rel. Soia Mentschikoff Llewellyn).

80 S.1–102(3)(f), (1952 draft).

81 Judge Learned Hand is reported to have remarked that the dropping of these provisions involved no real sacrifice since the judges would use the comments anyway. (ex rel. Soia Mentschikoff Llewellyn.)

82 K.L.P., J, VII, 1, c. Lewis to Pepper, 25 September 1945.

83 See generally Skilton, *op. cit.*, 606 ff.

84 Honnold, *Sales and Sales Financing*, 18 (2nd ed., 1962).

85 Skilton, *op. cit.*, 598–605; Merrill, *op. cit.*, 546–7.

86 Skilton, *op. cit.*, 608.

87 *Ibid.*, 631.

88 For a more detailed discussion of the subject, see Donald B. King, *The New Conceptualism of the Uniform Commercial Code* (1969).

89 Llewellyn memo, Re. Possible Uniform Commercial Code (app. E). See also Mentschikoff, 27 *M.L.R.*, 167 (1964), and *Commercial Transactions, Cases and Materials*, introduction (1970).

90 Schlesinger, *op. cit.*

91 Mentschikoff, *op. cit.*, at 175n.

92 Schlesinger suggests (at 121–2) that it would have been difficult to achieve uniformity if agency had been included.

93 At 39.

94 Malcolm, 13 *The Business Lawyer*, 490, 499 (1958).

95 The effect of breach on risk of loss is also spelled out in detail in s. 2–510.

96 On Hohfeld's contribution to 'narrow issue' thinking, see p. 35 above. The draftsmen also kept Hohfeld's analysis very much in mind, but did not use his noun-form concepts (claim, no-right, etc), preferring for the most part the verb-form (may, must, can, etc.).

97 Malcolm, 'The U.C.C. as Enacted in Massachusetts,' 13 *Business Lawyer*, 490, at 505 (1958). Cf. Llewellyn, 'What is needed is clarity, simplicity, convenience, fairness, completeness, accessibility and uniformity', 13 *Law and C.P.*, 687 (1948).

98 Mentschikoff, *op. cit.*, 183.

99 Comment 1 on s.9–109.

100 S.9–307.

101 S.9–312.

102 S.9–401.

103 Another example of simplification is to be found in Article 5. This brings all letters of credit into a single category, governed by one set of rules.

104 Max Gluckman *The Judicial Process among the Barotse of Northern Rhodesia*, 160 (2nd ed. 1967).

105 E.g., Mentschikoff, 27 *M.L.R.*, at 171.

106 E.g., *NYLRC*, Report at 15–20 (1956).

107 An extended controversy has developed over the concept of 'unconscionability' in s.2–302 of The Uniform Commercial Code. The main difference has been between critics of the drafting of the section (who maintain, like Professor Leff, that the draftsmen erred in failing to give precise meaning to unconscionability), and those who believe that the code draftsmen were wise not to define 'unconscionability'. R. Speidel, R. Summers and J. White, *Commercial Transactions*, 466 (1969). See especially A. Leff, 'Unconscionability and the Code – The Emperor's New Clause', 115 *U. Pa. L. Rev.*, 485 (1967), M. P. Ellinghaus, 'In Defence of "Unconscionability",' 78 *Yale L.J.*, 757 (1969), and John E. Murray 'Unconscionability: Unconscionability', 31 *U. Pittsburgh L. Rev.*, 1 (1969); see further the symposium in 34 *Albany L. Rev.* 231 (1970). In so far as the main issue centres on a differences of opinion about the desirability of leaving a wide discretion to the courts in administering general standards, Llewellyn's position on the general point was quite clear: he believed that it was unwise to attempt to give precise legislative guidance in this area. However, as Leff points out, Llewellyn may himself have been uneasy about s.2–302.

108 S.1–201.

109 Ex rel. Soia Mentschikoff Llewellyn. For a critique of the definitions employed in the Code, see D. Mellinkoff, 'The Language of the Uniform Commercial Code', 77 *Yale L. J.*, 185 (1967).

110 See especially Bibliography, nos. 15, 21, 32, 53, 57, 59, 62, 63, 64, 65, 67, 76, 79, 88, 94, 102 and numerous reviews.

111 Above (note 110), nos. 57, 59, 64, 65.

112 47 *Yale L. J.*, 1243 (1938).

113 15 *NYUL Rev.* 159 (1938); see also *Cases and Materials on the Law of Sales*, ch. 6, especially 561–6 (1931).

114 44 *Col. L. Rev.*, 299 n. (1944).

115 *Jurisprudence*, 323.

116 See especially 'The Rule of Law in our Case Law of Contract', 47 *Yale L. J.*, 1243 (1938).

117 48 *Yale L. J.*, 779, 785 (1939).

118 Mooney, *op. cit.* (n.32) at 215.

119 48 *Yale L. J.*, at 32.

120 *Op. cit.*, at 223.

121 *Ibid.*, at 258.

122 *Ibid.*

123 Mooney acknowledges this, but nevertheless seems in some passages to exaggerate the importance of Llewellyn's contribution.

124 Mentschikoff, *Commercial Transactions, Cases, and Materials*, 4 (1970).

125 *Jurisprudence*, 217.

126 Mentschikoff, *op. cit.*, 7.

13   MISCELLANEOUS WRITINGS

1 The main sources for this account are (i) K.L.P., section G, which contains correspondence, memoranda, manuscripts, etc. which extensively document Llewellyn's activities; (ii) Joughin and Morgan, *The Legacy of Sacco and Vanzetti* (1948); Frankfurter, *The Case of Sacco and Vanzetti* (1961 ed.); Felix, *Protest: Sacco-Vanzetti and the Intellectuals* (1965).

2 See Felix, *op. cit., passim.*

3 *Jurisprudence*, 431 ff. (a section of the unfinished book discussed in the text, entitled 'Who are these Accused?'. The full passage is also to be found in Joughin and Morgan, *op. cit.*, and in Michael and Wechsler *Criminal Law and its Administration* (1940)).

4 Felix, *op. cit.*, n.1.

5 *Ibid.*, 247.

6 Joughin and Morgan, 385.

7 I.e., Joughin and Morgan, and Felix, *op. cit.*

8 MS. part I, 20–6. Thus Llewellyn's involvement began almost five years after the original conviction of the two accused.

9 See Joughin and Morgan, 255, Felix, 175.

10 Petition to Governor Fuller, dated 4 May 1927, K.L.P., G, II.

11 Delivered on Station WPCH, 20 August 1927. The full text is printed in Twining, *The Karl Llewellyn Papers*, at 105–10.

12 *Ibid.*, 110.

13 Joughin and Morgan, 314.

14 K.L.P., G, II (1938).

15 Of a total of approximately three hundred pages of typescript rather more than a third are by Llewellyn.

16 MS., citation mislaid.

17 MS., part I, 54. See A.B.A.J., 683–94 (1927).

18 Especially MS., part I, 68–77.

19 Letter to Dean Justin Miller of Duke University Law School, 6 August 1931. Cf. MS, part I, 152 ff.

20 Llewellyn formulated the question as follows: 'Is the accepted machinery of jury trial, party-presentation, and the technicality of our rules of evidence and criminal procedure an adequate method of determining disputed facts?' MS., part I, 77. See also *ibid.*, 152; on allegations about Llewellyn's indifference to such questions see Frank *Courts on Trial* (1963 ed.) at 73, discussed above p. 188ff.

21 *Jurisprudence*, 82–3.

22 MS., 68–77, 153. See also *Jurisprudence*, 434, 438.

23 MS., part I, 15–6.

24 MS., part II, 7, 1 (headed 'Stop!').

25 *Ibid.*

26 Felix, *op. cit.*, 166.

27 31 *Col. L. Rev.*, 1215, at 1217 (1931).

28 F. Klein, *Judicial Administration and the Legal Profession* (1963). Llewellyn's interest was stimulated by Morris Gisnet's *A Lawyer Tells the Truth* (1931), which he reviewed in 31 *Col. L. Rev.*, 1215. It is interesting to note that Carr-Saunders and Wilson's path-breaking work on *The Professions* was first published in England in 1933. The first report of the Committee on Professional Economics of the N.Y. County Lawyers' Association (May 1932) might be said to mark the start of systematic bar surveys in the United States.

29 See Twining *The Karl Llewellyn Papers*, Bibliography, items no. 26, 36, 40, 41, 44, 46, 51, 60, 61, 73, 82, 85, 89, 92, 94, 150, and 155.

30 See 8 *Am. L. Sch. Rev.*, 185 (1934), 751 (1936) and 1114 (1938) for reports of the committee.

31 See generally A. Blaustein and C. Porter, *The American Lawyer* (1954).

32 See generally L. K. Garrison (ed.), *The Economics of the Legal Profession;* ABA, *Special Committee on the Economic conditions of the Bar* (1938). This brings together some of the most important findings of the bar surveys conducted in the 1930s. On Llewellyn's contribution, see *ibid.*, at 71 and 108.

33 See K.L.P., H, II, *passim*.

34 See 'Bringing Legal Aid to the Little Man', 82 *Pittsburgh L. Jo.*, 10 (1934); see also 128 *American Magazine*, 41 (1939), an article on Weiss, which mentions Llewellyn's part in setting up the clinic.

35 K.L.P., H, III, 1.

36 These activities are extensively documented in K.L.P., H. See also works referred to in n. 33 above.

37 R. H. Smith to Llewellyn, 3 February 1947.

38 (i) 167 *Annals*, 177 (1933); (ii) 5 *Law and Contemp. Problems*, 104 (1938), reprinted *Jurisprudence*, 243.

39 Q. Johnstone and D. Hopson, *Lawyers and Their Work* (1967).

40 'The Bar specializes . . .,' at 343.

41 J. Carlin, *Lawyers and Their Work* (1962), *Lawyers' Ethics* (1966). The phrase quoted is from G. Hazard, preface to *Lawyer's Ethics*.

42 See generally Blaustein and Porter, *The American Lawyer* (1954).

43 'The Bar Specializes . . .', at 344.

44 Bentham, *The Handbook of Political Fallacies*, 34 (ed. Larrabee, 1962).

45 See especially 'The Bar Specializes . . .'.

46 'Bringing Legal Aid to the Little Man', *op. cit.* at 14.

47 See Abel-Smith and Stevens, *Lawyers and the Courts*, 191–2 (1967).

48 See G. Hazard, 'Reflections on Four Studies of the Legal Profession', in *Law and Society* (supplement to *Social Problems*, summer 1965).

49 See above, p. 199, below, Appendix C.

50 E.g., 'What is Wrong with so-called Legal Education', 35 *Col. L. Rev.*, 651 (1935).

51 Weber, *Law in Economy and Society*, ch. VII (ed. Rheinstein and Shils, 1954).
52 See above, p. 25.
53 A good idea of the bulk, if not of the quality, can be obtained from the series of bibliographies on legal education produced by the Library of N.Y.U. Law School; see Sullivan, *A Bibliography of Materials on Legal Education* (1961) and supplements.
54 Other members were Charles Bunn, Judson F. Falknor, Lester W. Feezor, Frederick J. Moreau.
55 45 *Col. L. Rev.*, 345–91 (1945).
56 See also *Jurisprudence*, 376–7.
57 See Sullivan's *Bibliography*, *op. cit.* A recent symposium is E. Kitch (ed.), *Clinical Education and the Future of the Law School* (1970).
58 On Advocacy, see above, pp. 260–4.
59 K.L.P., Q.
60 Irvin C. Rutter, 'A Jurisprudence of Lawyers' Operations', 13 *J. Leg. Ed.*, 301 (1961).
61 Charles D. Kelso, *A Programmed Introduction to the Study of Law* (1965); for a critique see O'Donovan, Twining and Mitchell, 'Legal Eagles or Battery Hens?', 10 *J.S.P.T.L.* (N.S.), 6 (1968).
62 The main sources for this section are as follows: (i) The Karl Llewellyn Papers, section I (II) and (V). (These include field notes, correspondence, memoranda and manuscript fragments, draft codes and some preliminary drafts of sections of a book on Pueblo Indian Law-Government.) (ii) Interviews with Professors E. A. Hoebel and S. Mentschikoff. (iii) E. A. Hoebel: (a) 'The Authority Systems of the Pueblos of the Southwestern United States', Akten des 34. Internationalen Amerikanisten-Kongresses (Wien, 1960); (b) 'Keresan Pueblo Law', in L. Nader (ed.), *Law in Culture and Society*, 92 (1969). (c) Correspondence with author. (iv) Ruth Benedict, *Patterns of Culture* (1934); W. Smith and J. M. Roberts, *Zuni Law: A Field of Values*; Papers of the Peabody Museum, Harvard University, vol. 43, no. 1 (1954); I. Goldman, 'The Zuni of New Mexico', in M. Mead (ed.), *Cooperation and Competition Among Primitive Peoples*, ch. 10, (1937); D. McNickle, *They Came Here First* (1949); Edward F. Dozier, 'Rio Grande Pueblos', in Edward H. Spicer (ed.), *Perspectives in American Indian Culture Change*, 94–180 (1961). The last cited is a most useful survey.
63 On the resistance of Pueblo culture to outside influences, see Dozier, *op. cit., passim.*
64 Benedict, *op. cit.*, esp. at 100, criticised by Llewellyn and Hoebel, draft MS., ch. I. at pp. 2–7, K.L.P., I, II, 20. See also Smith and Roberts, *op. cit.*, at n.62, Goldman (1937), *op. cit. id.*
65 Hoebel, MS., (K.L.P., I, II, 1).
66 Brophy to Mentschikoff, 27 February 1962. According to Hoebel the

Dean of the University of Colorado Law School had recommended *The Cheyenne Way* to Brophy and told him of Llewellyn's visit.

67 *Ibid.*

68 *Ibid.*

69 Llewellyn composed the following mnemonic on the limits of federal jurisdiction:

> Dangerous weapon, intent to kill,
>   Killing in either shape,
> robbery, burglary, larceny, will
>   go to the Feds., like rape
> and burning down a barn or house
>   or screwing family, like a louse.
> Embezzlement, fraud and fornication
>   are safe, within the reservation.

For a résumé of the legal position, see Hoebel, *op. cit.* (iii) (b), at 93 (1969).

70 Hoebel points out (*op. cit.* at (iii)(a)) that 'the repressive nature of Pueblo government induces some Pueblo Indians to seek relief in appeal for intervention by the Agency administration or by the state or federal courts. The Civil Rights Act of 1968 led to a crisis over the problem of jurisdiction.'

71 By this time (1941) Brophy had become Commissioner of Indian Affairs (i.e. Head of the Bureau of Indian Affairs). In this capacity he gave directions that official assistance should be given to Llewellyn and Hoebel. In any case several officials of the B.I.A. were already enthusiastic supporters of the project.

72 Notably Emma Corstvet (Llewellyn's second wife) and Thomas Gifford (then a law student at Columbia). The archives of the United Pueblo Agency were made available and proved to be a rich source of documentary material.

73 At the time anthropological research in the Keresan Pueblos was forbidden by the Indians; an exception was made in the case of Llewellyn and Hoebel only because they were giving practical assistance and in the case of Zia because they promised to publish nothing that would injure the Pueblo. Hoebel, *op. cit.* (iii) (b), (1969).

74 Some of the material has been used by Hoebel in the works referred to in no. 62.

75 See appendix F.

76 Llewellyn. Memo., 'The Individual and the Tribe,' K.L.P., I, II, 17 (also K.L.P., I, II, 15, 16 and 18).

77 Thus when some Protestant converts threatened the harmony of the Pueblos of Jemez and Zia the solution was to expel them; Dozier, *op. cit.*, 177.

78 See Twining, *The Place of Customary Law in the National Legal Systems of East Africa*, 32–53 (1964).

79 McNickle, *op. cit.*, 86. The preamble is reproduced in appendix F.

80 Memo. to Soc. Sci. Res. Council, entitled 'Project on Soviet Law', K.L.P., R, III, 14 (1947).

81 See above, 167.

82 Llewellyn, Memo., 'A Note on "Pueblo Soviet Parallels" '. This Memo. accompanied the application to the Soc. Sci. Res. Council (*op. cit.*).

83 See generally F. Hsu, *The Study of Literate Civilizations* (1969).

84 Hoebel, in summing up on the Pueblo system of law-government, concludes: 'Its basic ideology is rather different from that of the modern totalitarian state, but its collective emphasis produces striking parallels in the legal apparatus' (42).

85 E.g., Rheinstein, review of Berman, 'Justice in Russia', 64 *Harvard Law Rev.*, 1387, 1388 (1951).

86 Llewellyn MS., 'The Parental Pole of Law Government', K.L.P., B, IV, 15 (1960–2)?

87 K.L.P., B, IV, 6.

88 See above, n.80.

89 K.L.P., B, IV, 15, 5.

90 *Ibid.*, 3.

91 See *Law in Our Society* 45–50 (1950) and supplementary materials K.L.P., L,I, g and h.

92 See especially H. Berman, *Justice in Russia, passim*, especially 421–3 (2nd ed. 1963). Berman took Llewellyn's course on 'Law in Society' at Harvard in 1948–9, but claims that it was Eugen Rosenstock-Heussy who provided the main stimulus for his analysis of the Soviet system (Llewellyn was also an admirer of Rostenstock-Heussy, see K.L.P., R, XVIII). Professor Soia Mentschikoff developed the idea of the parental model in a seminar on 'dispute settlement' given in Chicago in 1964 and subsequent years.

15   THE SIGNIFICANCE OF REALISM

1 On Frank's qualities as a judge, see M. Schick, *Learned Hand's Court* (1970) and J. Mitchell Rosenberg, *Jerome Frank: Jurist and Philosopher* (1970).

2 *The Concept of Law*, 250 (1961).

3 *Law in Our Society*, 86–7.

4 See especially W. B. Kennedy, 'Functional Nonsense and the Transcendental Approach', 5 *Fordham L. Rev.*, 272 (1936); 'More Functional Nonsense', 6 *Fordham L. Rev.*, 75 (1937); 'Realism, What Next?', 7 *Fordham L. Rev.*, 203 (1938); and L. Fuller, *The Law in Quest of Itself* (1940).

5 E.g., J. Dickinson, 'Legal Rules: Their Function in the Process of Decision', 79 *U. Pa. L. Rev.*, 833 (1931); 'Legal Rules: their Application

and Elaboration', 79 *U. Pa. L. Rev.*, 1052 (1931); K. Olivecrona, *Law as Fact*, 213–5 (1962); H. L. A. Hart, 'Definition and Theory in Jurisprudence', 70 *L.Q.R.*, 37 (1954).

6 J. Dickinson, *op. cit.* (n. 5); see further his major work, *Administrative Justice and the Supremacy of Law in the United States* (1927). H. Wechsler, 'Toward Neutral Principles of Constitutional Law', 73 *Harv. L. Rev.*, 1 (1959); R. Dworkin, 'Is Law a System of Rules?', in R. Summers (ed.), *Essays in Legal Philosophy* (1968).

7 R. Stevens, 'The Role of a Final Appeal Court in a Democracy: The House of Lords Today', 28 *M.L.R.*, 509 (1968). L. Jaffe, *English and American Judges as Lawmakers* (1969).

8 Especially *Jurisprudence*, 57 (1931).

9 In 1954 he reasserted this view, while placing less emphasis on the systematic nature of their efforts. In a letter to G. B. J. Hughes, 10 August 1954, he said:

As I indicated back in 1931, the really important contributions of the Realist movement consist of the monograph jobs that get down under a sound, horse sense technology . . . In the main, I find the theoretical writing on the subject to have been rather useless since the original points were once made.

As examples of 'recent' material he cited Kessler and Sharp, *Contracts: Cases and Materials* (1953); Crosskey, *Politics and the Constitution* (1953) ('exaggerated but very effective'); the Chicago Arbitration Project; 'and above all . . . the really good articles and notes which appear in the major law reviews, gathering together significant factual inquiry as a basis for hard-eyed critique of existing doctrine and its effects and as a basis for suggesting more useful ways and means for handling the problems.

This relatively modest appraisal of the theoretical significance of 'realism' is acceptable if the ideas under consideration are those that were *common* to members of the movement. It is quite a separate issue whether some of the theoretical ideas of individual realists were original or significant: e.g. Llewellyn's 'law-jobs theory', Cook on the scientific analogy, Frank's 'fact-skepticism' (see Cahn, *Confronting Injustice*, 283), or Moore's methodological ideas on empirical research. In fact, Llewellyn was in the end not particularly impressed by most of the theoretical ideas of Frank, Cook and Moore.

10 E.g., 52 *Yale L. J.*, 203 (1943), 56 *Yale L. J.*, 1345 (1947); McDougal, *Law, Science and Policy* (forthcoming).

11 An interesting recent example is F. Deng, *Tradition and Modernization* (1971).

12 See, however, symposium in 54 *Virginia L. Rev.* (1968), especially articles by Stewart Macaulay (617–36) and John N. Moore (662–88).

13 Holmes 'The Path of the Law', 10 *Harv. L. Rev.*, 457, 477 (1896).

Appendices

Appendix A

The War Adventure[1]

Llewellyn's war adventure has become a legend among American law teachers. Although the main facts are not in dispute, several different accounts have survived which diverge on matters of detail. The version which is perhaps nearest to the historical truth and to the spirit of the legend can be made to read like the outline for a psychological novel: a young, articulate, somewhat romantic American student finds himself in Paris at the outbreak of the first world war. He has been at school in Germany, has German friends, a love of German culture, some sympathy with the German cause. He witnesses a surge of anti-German feeling in Paris; he is irritated by predictions in the English press that Germany will be defeated within three months; he is avid for experience; although he is troubled by the grimmer side of war, his predominating feelings are excitement and a sense of adventure; he is aware that war service will give him status back home. He decides to enlist on the German side. He has difficulty in getting out of France. Ironically, to get to Germany he has to cross to England and double back through Holland. He crosses the German border by train in the company of refugees. At each station he attempts to enlist, but is refused, until he reaches Osnabruck where he joins the 78th Prussian Infantry. He refuses to take the oath of allegiance to the Kaiser, as this would involve forfeiting his American citizenship, and so there is some doubt as to his eligibility for membership of the Kaiser's army. While a ruling on this is awaited, he undergoes basic training, the only member of the regiment in civilian clothes. Later at the front he acquires most of the uniform of a sergeant who has been shot, but throughout his career in the German army he has to be content with a pair of 'baggy zouave trousers' which he had removed from a dead French peasant.

Meanwhile in the United States worried parents are in touch

with the authorities and, eventually the American ambassador, Gerard, procures Llewellyn's discharge against his will.[2] On hearing this Llewellyn is incensed and writes to Gerard, saying that he is over twenty-one and that his father has no business to interfere. Gerard withdraws his request, but it is too late, for Llewellyn has already been discharged.

Soon after this the 78th Prussian Infantry is posted to the front. Llewellyn goes to the station to see his comrades off. As their train draws out of the station Llewellyn jumps aboard and is concealed by his friends; on arrival in France his presence is discovered. He is formally castigated by a captain, who says he will take the matter up with his colonel. Later on, during a rest pause on the march, an officer comes back down the line and is overheard saying to a sergeant: 'The captain says that the colonel says that if the fool American keeps quiet, no one will notice he is here.' Thereafter Llewellyn is generally known as 'the fool American'. The regiment stays near Reims for several weeks in 'comparative inaction' (which includes firing at Reims Cathedral). He has his first experience of being under fire; his reaction is 'an emptiness at the stomach and uncertainty at the knees'.[3] He soothes a nervous German companion by digging potatoes with a bayonet.

After a few weeks in Reims the regiment is summoned west. A day is spent in Turcoing 'to get rid of their pay'; then, after a rousing address by their general, on 17 November 1914, the regiment takes part in a series of attacks on the English lines near Ypres. Of the several surviving versions of the incident which won him the Iron Cross, the following, written on a postcard to a friend at Yale five days after the event, is the nearest in time:

Our regmt was transported in a rush from Reims to Tourcoing, to take part in the attacks on the 17th; aimed at cutting the whole English army off from the French and surrounding them. We only succeeded, however, in driving them out of their trenches (sounds like Jesse James, this post-card!) and in some places in occupying their second line as well. But little Karl was stung: just when the fun began and I was double-quicking it from our trenches to a house some 50 yds. ahead, they opened fire from the flank; it sounded just like heavy hail shooting by. And then somebody hit me in the small of the back with a hammer, & I fell half stunned. First thot: spine; but my legs could wiggle, so I was comforted & crawled on. Had to unsling my haversack. They scratcht my chin & ript up my clothes before I got to the house but couldn't hit me again. The shot hit neither spine nor kidneys – almost impossible luck – I'm nearly well and quite happy – except that I want to get back into it.[4]

According to one report, nicely ironical but of dubious reliability, the bullet that wounded him was made in Connecticut. There follows ten weeks in hospital in Nürtingen, near Stuttgart. During this period Llewellyn hears that his petition to be allowed to remain in the army without swearing allegiance to the Kaiser has been turned down; however, the disappointment is lessened by the news of the award of the Iron Cross (2nd class) and by his promotion to sergeant before discharge.[5] He returns to the United States in March and resumes his studies at Yale. There he is given his share of publicity. He addresses a packed hall of undergraduates about his experiences; according to the *Yale Daily News* his report is vivid and amusing, but 'did not throw any light on the serious aspects of the conflict'.[6] For a time he is invited by a number of pro-German groups to speak on behalf of the German cause, but his attitude to the issue strikes some of his friends as lukewarm and ambivalent. As anti-German feeling gathers force in the United States, Llewellyn understandably is less willing to talk about his experiences and when the United States joins the war he is quick to volunteer for the American army. However, to his great annoyance he is classified as 'morally unfit for military service', presumably because of his German escapade. He campaigns vigorously to have the decision reversed (according to one account the President of Yale made a special journey to Washington on Llewellyn's behalf), but he only succeeds in having his classification changed. To the unique honour of being the only American citizen to have won the Iron Cross is added the more bizarre distinction of being the first American to have been accorded the draft status of 4X.[7]

Such is the bare outline of the story that can be pieced together from the available sources, which are of varying reliability. The historical accuracy of the main facts is not in serious doubt, but different accounts conflict on some of the details. Llewellyn himself gave currency to a number of different versions as he cast himself in varying roles: the modest hero, the would-be artist trying to record his emotions during the event, the amusing, sometimes satirical raconteur, and the student of logistics and morale. Before anti-German feeling began to grow in the United States, he seems to have enjoyed his new-found prominence and he was not in the least reticent about his adventure. On his return, in addition to giving interviews to the press and the addresses that have been mentioned, he drew on his war experiences as raw material for a number of literary essays, some of which seem to have been done as academic assignments. Later, when adulation turned to suspicion, he rarely talked about the episode and when he did he tended to make light of it. These undergraduate essays are particularly revealing documents. They represent a series of attempts to record and to rationalize his feelings about one of the most important experiences of his life, before American involvement in the war made him defensive and reticent about the episode. Of those which survive, two are of particular interest in the present context.

The first, entitled 'Paris',[8] is a highly coloured, probably half-fictional account of the first few hours after the announcement that war had been declared. The theme is the contrast between Llewellyn's exhilaration and excitement at the news and the re-actions of three women at his lodgings: the wife of the concierge whose son wants to join up; Jeanne, an unidentified girl, who is worried about her brothers and cousins and boy friends, who will all go away and get themselves killed; and Madame, quiet, silver-haired, 'a charming talker', who works herself up into a frenzy of hatred against the Germans, as below in the street a crowd attacks a German shop. The story ends with Llewellyn mounting the stairs to his room to a chorus of weeping women ... 'somehow the jolly idea about war had all faded out'.

The central argument of the second piece, 'What (a) private thinks about the War',[9] is that the ordinary German soldier is just an ordinary human being, unrelated to the image of the 'brutal, soulless blackguard ravaging and ravishing wantonly', or to the shining hero of German opinion. Much of this essay is taken up with an evocation of the emotional atmosphere surrounding Llewellyn's adventures. Although he is ostensibly writing about the feelings of a German private soldier, Llewellyn identifies so closely with him that it can safely be taken as an account of his own feelings. The atmosphere is vividly depicted: the initial excitement of joining up; the heroes' welcome given to the recruits at each city they came to; the expression on the faces of the crowd in Cologne when Llewellyn's comrades started to sing the one song that German soldiers seem to know about Cologne and which had been sung by troops in every train that had passed through the city in previous months; the eagerness to get into the fight; the sensation of being one of fifteen thousand men singing 'A Mighty Fortress is Our God' as they wait for their general to address them before they go into battle for the first time; the mingled sense of anticipation and of anticlimax before action, the quick hardening to the sight of death and destruction; and then the first experience of being under fire:

The first shells have a remarkable effect. You have been marching, marching under tension, expecting you hardly know what – and suddenly the whine of a shrapnel breaks in on you – the crash of its explosion on the still air – and another, and another, and another. Whether you realize what they are or not, – whether they are near you or not – you duck, dodge – want to run anywhere, anyhow – and run fast. That this is WAR becomes a fact all vivid and threatening, the tension has snapped – there is the unexpectedness, the noise, the newness – the uncertainty of what will follow all in that one instant. You're in the trenches, the enemy is flying. – Then without warning comes the revulsion of feeling. You were very 'humanitarian' on the attack. You would have loved to carry your wounded neighbor back out of range, tho' it broke your back – purely out of pity for him, of course! Now there they are, running, running wildly – the men that were shooting at you! It isn't nice – it isn't civilized, but there is a fiendish joy in watching them drop or turn somersaults as you shoot – a joy the greater from your sense of new-gained safety after peril. That intoxication fades as quickly as does the glamor of war.[10]

Llewellyn then goes on to trace the replacement of glamour and excitement by drudgery. Long marches, burying dead men in shell holes, sanitary chores, digging trenches, the discomforts of living in trenches, but ever careful to present a balanced picture he introduces anecdotes about incidents which relieved the tedium and which revived the feeling of romance. Perhaps the most pervasive aspect of this experience was the sense of comradeship, conveyed quite well in his account of German soldiers singing:

You have heard a lot about the way the Germans sing; it's true all of it. Singing is a part of the German soldier's life; a part without which you cannot imagine him – how could he accomplish without it all that he has to do? The first thing we did when we were quartered in a village was to hunt the place over till we found some asthmatic old harmonium, to gather round it and sing – sing so that you could no longer hear the harmonium wheeze. Then just think of singing on the march. When men are tired and hungry – when the knapsack rides them like an old man of the sea – when the deadly monotony of Boots Boots Boots is torturing their very souls irregularity and they have neither the strength nor the will to look up and away – then you pull out your harmonica and pipe into 'Musketeers are happy fellows' or 'Lippe Detmold'. At first they scarcely notice it; but as the rhythm dins into their numbed consciousness you can see their drawn faces take on a trace of expression – to the right and left of you they are falling into step, unthinking, obedient to the instinct that tells them that rhythm means rest. The tune is ended; you take it up again, louder – and again – and again. And with the tune the words swing thro' their minds, with the beating of the words comes the desire – nay, the will, to sing – fighting its way up from the depths of consciousness, up thro' the crushing load of weariness – fighting its way free – and they do sing. That song and another and more – each one cheering them, giving them new strength. How could they have made those August marches without song![11]

It may be significant that Llewellyn attempted no serious political analysis of the issues of the war. In trying to provide a rationalization for joining up on the German side he mentioned, with varying emphasis on different occasions, such factors as his admiration for the Kaiser's army, his debt of gratitude to Germany, his thirst for experience, his desire for military training, and even sympathy for the underdog (for so he regarded Germany). The nearest approach to a political statement appears in a letter posted from the front:

I know now that the German Government did not provoke the war; neither by overt acts nor by covert intrigues. I know that the German Government was forced by circumstances over which no single nation had control to arm itself against attack during decades and to take up the war in 1914. . . . Result: The German Nation, all that is German, is in danger, in fearful danger, and without guilt. This summons me, who owe Germany so much, to do what I can to help. And so I have accepted the chance to serve in the best army in the world, and get what I have longed for so earnestly: military training and discipline. Furthermore, aside from gratitude and the chivalry of fighting against odds, aside from the purely selfish interest of military training, I shall be in the greatest epoch of the century. I shall see history made and see it in Germany with an understanding that few have had because I saw the beginning of the war in France. . . . Germany is undergoing a re-birth. The commercialism which threatened her had already begun serious inroads on her moral life and stamina, on her idealistic tendencies, and on all that is high and noble in her people.

The war has not uprooted this, but it has gone far towards so doing. The people have met the crisis and in meeting it have left much of the everyday dirt behind; and the sacrifice of blood and tears is none too great when such a result can be given to a whole nation. This new birth I can see, comparing my memories of three years ago with what I see today. And I can feel it. It is the sense of this that keeps me here now.[12]

It can readily be conceded that Llewellyn's motives for joining up and for changing sides could be quite easily explained in terms of adolescent impulsiveness or a desire for 'experience', and are in any case largely a matter for speculation; but there is an affinity between his legal writings and his writings about the war that should not be overlooked. There is a basic seriousness underlying his war essays. Whatever their literary defects, they are fascinating and revealing documents. When they are read as a group two themes stand out: the first is Llewellyn's concern to catch on paper the quality of his experiences—the atmosphere and what it was like to be there. It is a form of realism which takes as its standpoint the subjective view of individual participants. In a more subdued and less obvious way Llewellyn frequently adopted the same stand-point in his juristic writings. This is perhaps one important difference between him and the overwhelming majority of other jurists. His secret hope for *The Common Law Tradition* was that some judge would say that it read as if its author had been present at the deliberations; *The Cheyenne Way* is unusually evocative even for an anthropological work; in a more intellectualized way his concern with role, technique, perception of the situation and with daily work reflects his abiding interest in seeing things from the point of view of the participants themselves. This may help to explain the self-conscious and sometimes rather strained 'literary' quality of his legal writings. If one's object is to present the subjective reality of participants, it is not enough to talk detachedly in terms of 'role conception' and the like, one must also seek to catch the atmosphere of courtroom and office and the 'feel' of actually doing the work. Conventions of legal scholarship no doubt curbed Llewellyn's natural inclination to catch the ineffables of 'feel' and atmosphere; he had no such inhibitions when writing about his military experience and in some of his other non-legal writings.

A second recurrent theme in the war essays is no less apparent but is less easy to interpret. This is the idea that all the participants, the soldiers on both sides, the inhabitants of occupied territory, and Llewellyn himself, were all ordinary, for the most part decent, human beings caught up in events beyond their control. The suggestion that the ordinary soldier is not to be blamed for the horrors of war may be linked to Llewellyn's seeming indifference to what the war was about. There is a distinct note of apology underlying this theme, as if Llewellyn is trying to explain away some feelings of guilt, perhaps for having chosen the 'wrong' side, perhaps for having been involved in, and for having enjoyed, fighting, perhaps for some other reason. Some critics, who unfairly accused Llewellyn and other realists of being indifferent to questions of value, may have sensed in his legal writings a similar tendency to shy away from open discussion of great political or ideological issues and to concentrate on such matters as legal craftsmanship and juristic method, where technical proficiency can arguably be treated as being 'neutral' between competing ideologies in the way that a skilful engineer (mechanical or social) or an efficient bureaucrat or a machine can be an effective instrument for furthering various political or social ends.

[1] *A note on the sources.* The most detailed written accounts of Llewellyn's war adventure are to be found in *The History of the Class of Nineteen-Fifteen* (423–6); reports in the *Yale Daily News* (esp. 12 Feb., 17 March and 14 April 1915); James W. Gerard, *My Four Years in Germany*, 237-8 (1917); an interview with Llewellyn's mother by a correspondent of the *Brooklyn Eagle* (Literary Digest, vol. 15, 7 April 1915, 908-10); Drobnig's 'Karl Llewellyn and Germany'; and an unpublished 'Account by Arthur L. Corbin of his association with Karl N. Llewellyn', dated 26 September, 1965 and sent to Professor Eugene Rostow. None of these accounts is totally reliable; the class-book and the *Yale Daily News* are closest in time to the events and are based on Llewellyn's personal statements, written and oral. They are typical examples of undergraduate journalism. Gerard's account is brief and rather vague. Gerard does not mention Llewellyn by name and ends: 'What has since become of him I do not know.' By coincidence, Gerard became a partner of the law firm with which Soia Mentschikoff, Llewellyn's third wife, was associated for a time. The interview reported in the *Literary Digest*, besides being a report at third hand, contains some inaccuracies (for instance, Llewellyn is said to be half-German) and is written in sentimental journalese. It must accordingly be treated with suspicion. This is unfortunate in that it contains a number of details not found in other sources. Corbin's account, written out in long hand when he was nearly ninety, is based on old memories and contains a few minor errors of detail. Corbin even at that age had a remarkably consistent memory. Drobnig's version is based in part on the memories of Hans Lachmund, in part on an investigation of the few surviving official records in Germany and in part on some of the sources cited in this note. The account in the text has been pieced together from the above sources and checked against the memories of a number of informants who heard Llewellyn tell the story himself. There are a few discrepancies of detail between some of the versions, but there is general agreement on the main outline.

[2] Gerard, *op. cit.*
[3] Llewellyn, MS., K.L.P., V, 1.
[4] Quoted in *History of the Class of Nineteen-Fifteen, op. cit.*, 426.
[5] *Ibid.*, 248. Doubted by Drobnig.
[6] 14 April, 1915.

7 Ex rel. Soia Mentschikoff Llewellyn. According to an unconfirmed report this category designates an American citizen who has served with the armed forces of the enemy.

8 K.L.P., B,V, l, d.

9 *Ibid.*, V. l, i.

10 *Ibid.*, 13–4.

11 *Ibid.*, 9–10.

12 *History of the Class of Nineteen-Fifteen*, 424–5.

Appendix B

A Restatement of Llewellyn's Theory of Rules

INTRODUCTION

This is an attempt to assemble in one place some of Llewellyn's most important general statements about legal rules, their nature, their functions, their place in the institution of law-and-government, the values and dangers of making them the sole or main focus of attention, their role in American state appellate judicial decisions, and the kinds of rules which he considered to be the most desirable. It is only a 'theory' in the loose sense of a reasonably coherent collection of thoughts about a topic; these thoughts include some conceptual analysis, some broad factual generalizations, and some value judgments and recommendations.

Two principal sources have been used in this restatement: the manuscript of an unfinished book on *The Theory of Rules* and *The Common Law Tradition*, supplemented by a few passages from earlier writings. The manuscript is undated, but internal evidence suggests that it was probably written at some time during the period 1938–40 concurrently with or shortly before the preparation of the Storrs Lectures on 'The Common Law Tradition'. Most of what follows consists of verbatim quotations; where, for the sake of brevity or clarity, Llewellyn's own words have been paraphrased, references to relevant passages supporting this interpretation are given.

1. 'RULE' AND 'RULES OF LAW'

(i) *'Rule'*

   (a) 'A first working description of a *rule* could be: a form of words built to further the continuing organization and government of human conduct' (*New Bramble Bush*, ch. III,1).

(b) In ordinary usage 'a "rule" is general, and not limited to one person or occasion. A rule ought to be in clear explicit language, and if the rule is really clear, it is or can be put in such language' (*Theory of Rules*, ch. I, 1). Ordinary usage does not tell us how general or how precise a proposition must be to deserve to be called a 'rule' (*ibid.*, III, 19).

(c) In some contexts the term 'rule' is used to *describe* a practice, as in the statement: 'As a rule x behaves thus'. (Llewellyn termed these 'real rules' or 'rules *of* conduct'.) In other contexts a 'rule' *prescribes* how those subject to it must, ought or may behave (rules *for* conduct). ' "Paper rule" is a fair name for a rule to which no counterpart in practice is ascribed. (*Jurisprudence*, 12) In some contexts description and prescription are fused when 'rule' is used, as often happens in the use of the term 'custom' (*The Cheyenne Way*, ch. II). Here, unless otherwise stated, 'rule' is used in its prescriptive sense.

(d) 'What is true of "rules" is *a fortiori* true of "principles"—which, being conceived as broader, invite even more to looseness of thinking. Which of you has not seen books "on social *science*" in which the "principles" laid down were now descriptive of prevailing practices, now of prevailing aims or values, now the author's notion of what people ought to do to get where *they* wanted to go, and now *his* notion of where people ought to want to get to—with the reasoning proceeding as if all these were mud-pies of a single mud' (*Jurisprudence*, 85). Llewellyn sometimes quoted with approval Pound's distinction between precepts, concepts, standards, principles and ideals (e.g., *ibid.*, 3–7, 354).

(e) In the 'Theory of Rules', rules are not equated with 'commands' nor with 'predictions', rather 'rules' are chiefly considered as normative propositions (esp. *Theory of Rules*, ch. II, *passim*). The ideal type for such propositions is 'If X, then Y' (*ibid.*, VI, 1). (See below (ii) (b).)

(f) In this ideal type a rule is articulated in propositional form; in everyday life much human behaviour is in fact guided by 'rules' that have not been given verbal expression at all (see esp. *The Cheyenne Way*, ch. II, and below, (ii) (d.)

(ii) *Rules of Law*

(a) Rules of law 'are measurès, measures to be judged against their purposes' (*Theory of Rules*, I, 10). Seen thus the simple form of a legal rule is: to further this end (*purpose*) this legal consequence is prescribed (*means of effecting purpose*) in this type of situation (*scope*).

(b) A simple theoretical model (or 'ideal type') of a legal rule is 'a general proposition indicating a general situation of fact and prescribing for any concrete situation falling within the class a legal consequence of described and limited character' (III, 3). Thus in the simple proposition 'if X, then Y', X is 'a category or class of possible states of fact (as: "Dealers selling wares which contain a hidden defect through which a buyer suffers personal injury")' (VI, 1), and Y 'is a category or class of legal consequence ordained by the positive authority concerned to *follow* on due official perception that a state of fact duly presented for official action falls within the category X (as: "are to be made to pay damages to an injured buyer in the amount of the injury")' (VI, 1).

'The assumptions as to the nature of the categories are constant. What varies is either the sphere of application of the rule or the ordained legal consequences, or both, and nothing more' (*Ibid*).

(c) ' "Legal Concepts" are 'the categories *given* us by the legal order as the proper units *to have rules of law about*' (VI, 3). Some 'legal concepts' indicate the area of application of a rule, i.e. the factual situation (X); those may be termed 'situational concepts'; others refer to a legal consequence (Y), e.g. 'injunction' or 'execution'; other legal concepts, e.g. 'public utility', do not fit into the simple propositional scheme, because 'they range into the worlds of fact and legal consequence both at once' (straddle concepts) (VI, 4). Some legal concepts (like 'contract', 'sale') represent a major or minor classification of a whole body of related legal rules. In the *Theory of Rules* Llewellyn gave particular attention to situational concepts, especially in respect of problems of classification (ch. VI) and of what he later termed 'situation sense'. 'The problem of guidance by rules is the problem of guiding, by rules of law, the classification of emergent raw states of fact' (*Ibid.*, 8).

(d) The propositional form 'If X, then Y' is only a theoretical model. 'Current rules may be in that form or they may not' (III,18). Rules of law are in fact very varied in respect of degree of articulation, clarity, simplicity or complexity, quality, consistency with other rules, etc.; the 'purposes' of legal rules are similarly varied (I, 10); so also are the institutional contexts of the operation and use of legal rules (e.g. *Jurisprudence*, 19–21[12]); the propositional model is adopted as a tool for expressing certain relatively simple ideas.

(e) In the common law there are important differences between 'case law rules' and statutory rules. The principal difference is that statutory rules are expressed in fixed verbal form. (*Bramble Bush*, 47, *Theory of Rules*, ch. IV, see above, 240). Typically, case law rules are not expressed in fixed verbal form and 'can be found and recognized in or under seven divergent and only *more or less* co-extensive formulations. In our law, "the" rule rephrases of itself, almost, to adjust a notch or three, a compass point or four, to the call of sense, in what even when almost automatic is nonetheless highly *creative* "application" ' (*The Common Law Tradition*, 181). Even in the same judgment the 'same' rule may be restated at more than one level of generality (see above, 232ff).

(f) Despite the differences between case law rules and statutory rules, there are important similarities. For instance, 'the *range* of techniques correctly available in dealing with statutes is roughly equivalent to the range correctly available in dealing with case law materials' (*The Common Law Tradition*, 371).

2. THE PLACE OF LEGAL RULES IN THE INSTITUTION OF LAW

Rules of law occupy a central place in the institution of law (*The Theory of Rules*, I, 19). 'Any realistic worker in law must see [them] not only to be existent, but to be highly useful, indeed vital' (*Ibid*). But the institution of law is only part of the machinery of social control (or indeed, of the machinery for doing the 'law-jobs') and the rules of law 'are far from making up all that there is to law and the things of law' (*Ibid*). For example:

(a) To study 'law' should, and usually does, include the study of much beside rules of law.

(b) To practise 'law' involves dealing with much else beside legal rules and requires skills and knowledge beyond skills in handling and knowledge of legal rules.

(c) 'Legal research' should, and does, include not only the exposition and analysis and evaluation of positive rules of law, but also study of subjects in which actual behaviour rather than notional ideal behaviour of officials and others is the main focus of attention.

(d) In order to correct past imbalance, 'substantive rights and rules should be removed from their present position at the *focal point* of legal discussion, in favour of the *area of contact* between judicial (or official) *behavior* and the *behavior* of laymen; that the substantive rights and rules should be studied not as self-existent, nor as a major point of reference, but themselves with constant reference to that area of behavior contacts' (*Jurisprudence*, 16). (N.B. This, dated 1930, contains an element of over-statement, corrected in later writings).

3. THE PLACE OF RULES IN LEGAL SCIENCE

'A pre-science of behavior must deal with behavior as its center; and the Rules and Concepts have importance to it in so far as they are products or tools or causative factors in behavior' (*Law in our Society* , 79). (N.B. However, legal science is only one part of Jurisprudence.)

4. THE FUNCTIONS OF LEGAL RULES

Substantive rules of law are in fact used for various purposes, including:

(a) *guiding, or controlling or limiting*, the conduct of laymen (e.g., *Jurisprudence*, 17);

(b) *guiding, controlling or limiting*, the conduct of officials; in the case of appellate judicial decisions typically the rules guide rather than control decision (*The Common Law Tradition*, 179); however, 'where the rule rates high in wisdom and is also technically clear and neat, the guidance is indeed so cogent as, in effect, to be almost equivalent to control or dictation; so, also, when the measure is technically well designed and the rule is a legislative product of unmistakable policy and is too fresh off the griddle for modifying circumstances to have supervened' (*The Common Law Tradition*, 179).

(c) aiding the performance of the functions of 'the counsellor' — e.g. *predicting* the outcome of a dispute, *drafting* a 'court-proof' document, *shaping* a transaction (in all of these *prediction* is an element). N.B. Persons other than 'counsellors' are also concerned to predict—the counsellor's client, Holmes's 'bad man' etc. (esp. *Jurisprudence*, 323ff).

(d) *justifying* decisions, typically by judges,

(e) *supporting* a conclusion in argument advanced by an advocate,

(f) *describing* the practice of courts and other official agencies. Typically this use assumes that such practice 'conforms to the accepted oughts on the books' (*Jurisprudence*, 17, and 1(i) (c) above); such conformity should not be taken for granted (e.g. divorce, *Law in Our Society*, 37, and see generally Stone, *Social Dimensions of Law and Justice*, 728ff (1966).)

(g) *Generally* (i) as one of the principal instruments for performing the law-jobs; (ii) 'The rule phase of law-stuff is peculiarly well adapted to getting moderately similar results across space, time, and divergency of personnel' (*The Common Law Tradition*, 23) i.e. for promoting regularity and uniformity of behaviour of officials and laymen.

Llewellyn was aware that not all legal rules directly confer powers or duties; in his discussions of the functions of rules he seems to have had these types of rules in the forefront of his mind.

(h) Llewellyn, like many of his contemporaries, repeatedly emphasised that legal rights are of little value if they are not backed by effective remedies: e.g. 'if rules were results there would be little need of lawyers' (*The Bramble Bush*, 18; cf *ibid.*, 9).

5. GRAND STYLE AND FORMAL STYLE RULES

(i) *Rule-of-Thumb and Principle*

As a first distinction, then, within the field of rules of law to be expressed in the form of propositions prescribing the legal consequence of a described type of situation of fact, let us note as at one pole the rule-of-thumb, in which the flat result is articulated, leaving behind and unexpressed all indication of its reason; and let us note as at the other pole the way of principle, in which the reason is clearly and effectively articulated, and that articulation is made part of the very rule. Most current rules will be found mixed of the two elements; the one prevailing here, the other there; and we shall see that the two lines of approach call for differences in language machinery, and conceptual machinery, and in the structure of the rule. Rules-of-thumb, for instance, consort most happily with detail, with narrow range, with circumscribed as well as prescribed legal consequence, and with use of external signs to mark their application, whereas the vice of principle can be a vaporish vagueness, and the techniques of its effective formulation are not easy to isolate for communication and use. But of that hereafter. The point here is that a stable closed universe of states of fact, and concepts skilfully built to fit that world, and turned to use by formal logic of the schoolmen's type, is the ideal world to which the rule-of-thumb type of rule of law is perfectly adapted. A next point is that such an ideal and such a logic pulse through our own legal system as *one* of its main currents, and feed especially that part of legal work we know as 'legal reasoning'. The last point, to sum up this part of the discussion, is to repeat that the European attempts to cope with the problems of their law on such a basis have shattered of necessity upon the shifting character of modern conditions.

It is thus in regard to their emergent problems, their emergent groupings, their emergent new significances that we find the continentals developing their construction by analogy, or opening and widening their gaps-in-the-law (that is, in the *rules* of law) to fill up with what we should call judicial legislation, or construing 'as the legislat[or] would have meant it if he were speaking today and to this problem,' or sizing up and weighing the interests typically at stake, as a guide to 'interpretation' – that we find them, in a word, escaping limitation by the word, and using their rules rather as guides than as either compulsions or limitations. Thus, it seems a sound generalization from their experience to say that when the problems or the facts change form and meaning fast enough so that whatever reformulation machinery the system offers cannot be expected to keep up, then rule-of-thumb precision is no optimum for the relevant rule. Too much of it, under those conditions, invites – nay, seeks to force – a rule to work results which, though they fit its language, yet either shock its own implicit reason or, if its reason also be outdated, then just shock reason. Under such circumstances, even case-hardened literal-minded judges squirm; and experience shows that squirming judges mean uncertain and unpredictable results, as sense of general decency in result rolls in its wrestle with sense of legal decency in rule-work. Finally, we have seen that irregularity of result means imprecision in the *positive* rule of law. Its partial positivity then belies its certain form: no optimum there (*The Theory of Rules*, ch. IV. See further Twining, *The Karl Llewellyn Papers*, 81–96, where this chapter is printed *in toto*).

(ii) (a):

The quest becomes then one for guidance, first, as to when a court will use some particular one of such 'correct' techniques rather than any other; and second, as to when it ought to.

This discrimination between when it will and when it ought to, is the discrimination between rules for counselors and rules for judges. The counselor's basic need is accurate prediction; the judge's is clear guidance as to how to decide. A well-built rule can indeed under certain conditions serve both needs at one. First, if judges would abdicate their duty of serving justice, an accurate statement of past judicial practice could tell them how to decide. But judges will not ignore justice consistently, even if accepted jurisprudential theory tells them to – as once it did. Second, if there is a clear, and plainly wise, and plainly applicable rule, it can be followed by a court, and it will be, and a counselor can predict that rather accurately. But our prevailing stock of rules contains many which are either not so clear, or not so plainly wise, or far from plain as to when they apply (*My Philosophy of Law*, 189–90).

For counsellors and courts, at least, the most desirable kind of rule of substantive law is a 'rule with a singing reason': 'a rule which wears both a right situation-reason and a clear scope-criterion on its face yields regularity, reckonability and justice all together' (*The Common Law Tradition*, 183).

(b) The Grand Style tends to promote the creation of such rules:

... the future-directed quest for ever better formulations for guidance, which is inherent in the Grand Style, means the on-going production and improvement of rules which make sense on their face and which can be understood and reasonably well applied even by mediocre men. *Such* rules have a fair chance to get the same results out of very different judges, and so in truth to hit close to the ancient target of 'laws and not men'. Of the results of such rules, handled in such a manner, one can rightly say that Carter pungently but wrongly said of the common law of his own day: 'forefelt, if not foreseen' (*Ibid.*, 38).

(iii) (a): Apparently simple rules can give a misleading impression of 'certainty'. 'The sign-post of this in the law is the naive announcement so often met: "The principle is clear, but there is difficulty, there is uncertainty, in its application." This means that cases unlike in fact and outcome have been successfully verbalized into one jumbled pile' (*Jurisprudence*, 83).... 'the simple-seeming rules about the passing of title to chattels remind us, [as does] that extraordinary legal category "choses in action", forms of words which have a surface-simplicity can delude wise men by the thousands, over the generations, into overlooking a hundred sins and a thousand unreckonable uncertainties' (*The Common Law Tradition*, 429).

(b) The Formal Style, in taking 'rules-of-thumb' as a model, tends to promote such pseudo-simplicity (by inference: *Jurisprudence*, 304).

(iv) A major concern of Llewellyn's was to work for the increase in the incidence of Grand Style rules.

6. RULES IN AMERICAN STATE APPELLATE JUDICIAL PROCESSES

(i) 'That the *rules of law alone,* do not, because they cannot, decide any appealed case *which has been worth both an appeal and a response*' (*The Common Law Tradition,* 189).

(ii) Despite (i), 'effective', wise decisions are taken regularly by American state appellate courts (*Ibid.,* 561, Index: Rules of Law).

(iii) 'Rules are not to Control, but to Guide Decision' (*Ibid.,* 179. See above, 4(a) and (b).

(iv) '*The Law of Compatibility*':

If application of the seemingly apposite rule is compatible with sense, then the use in the deciding of *both* sense and the rule narrows the spread of possible decision and significantly increases the reckonability not only of the upshot but also of the direction which will be taken by the ground on which the decision will be rested. To know this both limits the field of doubt and sharpens the eyes of inquiry (*Ibid.,* 180).

(v) '*The Law of Incompatibility*'

If application of the seemingly apposite rule is incompatible with sense, then reckonability of either upshot or direction of the 'ground' of decision depends on factors apart from rule, sense, or both. To know this is to escape futile upset and to recognize instead the presence of danger and the need for exploration 'outside' the simpler areas of inquiry (*Ibid*).

(vi) 'The Law of the Singing Reason' (see above, 5(ii)).

There is a valuable discussion of Llewellyn's published writings on rules by Moskowitz in II *Villanova L. Rev.,* 480 (1966). Dr Moskowitz did not have access to Llewellyn's unpublished works at the time he did his research.

Appendix C

Extracts from Law in Our Society:

A Horse-Sense Theory of The Institution of Law
(unpublished course materials, 1950 edition)

The table of contents and three hitherto unpublished extracts from the Manuscript of *Law in Our Society* are reproduced here. The object is to give an indication of the nature and state of this document and to make available some of the more important passages which supplement Llewellyn's published writings. As much of it is in note-form it is neither elegant nor easy to understand; allowance must be made for the fact that Llewellyn did not consider the work to be complete or in publishable form. Permission to print these extracts has been given by his literary executrix, Professor Soia Mentschikoff Llewellyn. Except in a few places, which are indicated by square brackets, the original text is presented without emendation or comment.

(i) TABLE OF CONTENTS

III. The Traditional Lines of Approach

> Lecture 9. Right Law and Right Reason: the 'Natural Law' and 'Philosophical' Lines of Thinking
>
> Lecture 10. The Hard-head and the Ship-shape Thinker: 'Positive' and 'Analytical' Lines of Thinking; 'Science' in Law.
>
> Lecture 11. Law's People and the Law: 'Historical' and French and British 'Institutional' Lines of Thinking; Sociology of Law; 'Science' About Law
>
> Lecture 12. Theory of Imbalance, Exaggeration and the Generations. The Ideals of 'System' (philosophy) and of 'Objective Validity' (science). Synthesis and Balance.

IV. Theory of American Appellate Decision – Appellate Courts

> Lecture 13. Theory of Problem-Solution in General
>
> Lecture 14. Theory of Dogmatics in General
>
> Lectures 15-16. The American Appellate Court in Particular: Peculiarities, Craft-style, Period-style, Current Situation, Right Rules, Right Opinions, Right Methods.

V. Skills, Esthetics and Ethics of the Crafts

> Lectures 17-18. Appellate Advocacy
>
> Lectures 19-20. Counselling (over-advantage; negotiation; the need outside or against formal law, from persuasion through influence into 'law mcht')
>
> [Lecture 20: The whole problem other than 'legal' controls? Yes, as background.]

VI. Continued (i.e. seen as Crafts, primarily?)

> Lectures 21-22. Legislation (herein of Codes and of pressure-groups)
>
> Lectures 23-24. (Prob. trad)

VII. Ideals and Possibilities in Our System

> Lecture 25. The Liberties: Leeways and their urges as the very guts
>
> Lecture 26. Non-traditional Lines: T.V.A.
>
> Lecture 27. Soviet Challenge
>
> Lecture 28. The World

(ii) PART I. LECTURE I. THE COURSE IN GENERAL

1.1. *Three main themes of the course,* played in counterpoint:

(a) Necessity and functions of legal institutions, in the nature of man and of groups. 'Society', as a large and complex grouping, taken for discussion more or less as a single Entirety. The stress is on matters of continuing and current vitality.

(b) Operating machinery: the Law, the crafts, and the craftsmen, also the buttressing and companion work done by law's people – all in their relation to the eternal law-jobs and to one another. The stress is on current American conditions.

(c) Goals and critique. The stress is on current problems: craft, local, national, world, and personal.

1.2. Objective of the course:

1.2.(a) *Not 'Jurisprudence for the Hundred'*: i.e., not the more esoteric tradition of the writers about the writers and for the writers. Especially: not in the language or in the general tradition of professional philosophy. (T. R. Powell: 'jurisprudence on stilts'. E.g. Sidney Post Simpson on Jerome Hall on Hans Kelsen, 23 N.Y.U.L.R.:

'Jerome Hall, in his essay on "Integrative Jurisprudence," gives us one of the best critiques yet of the Pure Theory of Law. As Hall says:

". . . The particular incongruity of joining an idealistic epistemology with a naturalistic ethics in a legal philosophy should be evident. For on the dogmas of logical positivism, the propositions regarding and expressing rules of law, the basic legal conceptions, and the greatest part of the affirmative and important contributions of the Pure Theory are simply 'nonsense'. And, from the 'critical' standpoint, the naturalistic ethics of the Pure Theory is utterly indefensible. This basic incoherence of the Pure Theory is a certain index of its inadequacy."

'When men disagree about truth throughout generations, the issues have been misposed': e.g. 'What is the sole correct definition of "Law"?' (A *definition* not only takes in, but *thrusts out*). 'What is "pure" Law? What is the "Science" of Law?' (Note the conception of a *single* possible science. And 'science' means what?) 'What (meaning: what alone) gives Law its "Validity"?'

(*Note*: The major writers, and most of the minor ones who have stuff, have been much too good to hold their actual work within the confines of their own conscious – and always inadequate – definitions, much less within the frame of the pithy slogans of half-truth by which they have become known to their non-readers. Good writers have thus seen and felt and dealt with real stuff, but they have been for the most part as much hampered as helped by their conscious intellectual tool-kit. They are therefore always worth reading, and especially for what one may call their by-products, which make rich ore in the measure of the man's 'feel' for his material. Even the writers about the writers are likely to yield this type of good by-product, though they have been getting harder to read as the horrible tradition has grown up of borrowing the vocabulary of academic philosophy. What is here rejected as subject-matter of the course is thus not the great writers nor the good stuff they have written, but primarily the tradition of the last century or so about what *issues* are important. A crowning example is Kelsen – probably the most rigorously logical of all – as he developed his conscious and in my view sterile theory of 'pure' law, on which infra; yet shrewd and amazingly accurate and fruitful observations on the ways of things legal are scattered through Kelsen's writings like currants through a cake. Many are collected in Lauterpacht on Kelsen, in Modern Theories of Law (1933).)

1.2.(b) Instead, the subject matter of this course is '*Jurisprudence for the Hundred Thousand*': for the Bar in daily living, and for the citizen who is willing to take a moment off to ponder. 'Jurisprudence with hands and feet.' What questions bite in regard to what you, and your times, are up against, and what light is to be had on those questions? 'Good theory cuts ice'. And theory, as contrasted with rules of thumb based on other people's theory, is not 'good' to any man unless he can understand it and make it his own. Per contra, the wider and deeper a man's grasp of theory which does work, the more effective his own work can be, and the richer his life. – There are certainly times when theory must go deep. We shall not shun deep theory, at such times: compare Part II, especially Lect. 5. But we shall do our best to avoid abstruse theory: what cannot be discussed in ordinary language we shall leave to the specialist; that is what he is for.

Meantime, it is my conviction that all the fundamental, and most of the minor, problems of Jurisprudence have a level at which they can show themselves in simple terms and in simple relations with one another. Above this level are the layers of technical complexity of 'the Law' in any particular going legal system. Below it are the layers of metaphysics. (Is a 'fact' a *fact* when a legal Copernicus or an Einstein may come along tomorrow? What do we 'know'? How do we 'know'? Etc.) The game is to keep both top layers and lower layers from interfering with work and understanding in the place where an ordinary mortal can grasp meaning – while still keeping touch with the bearings of both the top and lower layers. 'Almost any rule of law can be put into language an ordinary man can understand.' The same is true of problems about law. Both jobs badly need doing.

1.2.(c) '*Jurisprudence for the Hundred Million*' is the next and needed step beyond. Men understand teamplay, in athletics, work, marriage, or government; then they can understand the guts of Jurisprudence. They need to. The question is the hard one of learning how to say simply what is in fact Simple. Law's people need this. They love it when they have it. It is their institution of the law, of which they are a major part and to which they give the major meaning. (The bank clerk and the Negotiable Instruments Law. The warehouseman and the Uniform Warehouse Receipts Act. The union and the Wagner Act. – The citizen in general?)

1.2.(d) Even for the layman, the institution of law – and government – is a *cultural* study of peculiar value. For the lawyer, law is also the most important of the fine arts (as will appear). Rightly seen, law, as the integrating discipline of all society, should serve also as an integration, for the individual man of law, of all his knowledge and experience, to gather, guide and enrich not only his professional but his personal living.

To this end, many ancient 'central' issues need to be reassessed and reposed. E.g. what is Sovereignty, and Where, in our system, does 'it' reside?

lacks body as against such issues as: Can we organize a World? How? Can even pieces of a world survive if we don't manage to? Again, What is Law? and What is A Law? are not central and crucial questions, but minor sub-questions capable of various workable answers, whereas a really fruitful line of questions is: what is a useful, or the most useful, material and way of organizing study about things legal, in order to get significant light on what needs knowing and doing? Again: Such pseudo-issues as Is Law certain? and should Law be certain? (Jerome Frank's obsession) and Do rules control the action of officials? prove, each one, to be a false issue which needs re-posing before any discussion of it can make sense. One thing badly needed is a childlike fresh look at What? and fresh question as to Why? and How? and Whither? ('But the King has no clothes on!' 'But what is law for?')

1.3. *Material and Approach of the Course:*

1.3.(a) Not '*Philosophy of Law*,' but philosophy *about* things legal. Not, that is, the contemporaneous polysyllabic professionalized academic discipline, applied to 'law', and all tied up with who derived how much from whom, and 'schools,' etc. (Cf. Pound's classifications in *Law & Morals*.) In contrast, what is here sought is old-fashioned non-professional 'philosophy': general serviceable life-wisdom about some body of material and its homely but basic meaning for life and for man. And not '*of*' law': i.e., no mere arrangement from within – but '*about*' law': i.e. a sizing-up from outside which only then moves on in for a resizing up from inside.

1.3.(b) Not '*history of thought*' or sequence of thinkers or our 'cultural heritage' in the matter. There will be little effort to meet or present any man's thinking as a whole, still less to place men in series. Adequate critical study of single great thinkers is most rewarding: but we lack time for it. See 1.3(f), below. The sequence of thinkers, especially when seen against their times, is also highly illuminating (cf. Pound's *Interpretations*); but again the problem is one of time if the job is to pay. Here the choice is, instead, to *select* from the literature, as from life, ideas and suggestions which help cope with what you and I and the country and the world are up against. (Literature and life are taken as a common stock, and 'credit' is given only by accident. There is nothing original here, that I know of. Even what, by chance, may not have been said once or a dozen times before has still been there for anybody to see if he would only look.)

1.3.(c) Not '*Science*': too little is known, in any Scientific fashion. Proper Science (even though undergoing constant development and change) has a significant degree of arrangement and order, with relationships sharply defined and approaching accurate statement by quantity; its results can be checked and agreed upon by skilled men with no ax to grind. In the disciplines dealing with man what we have is a sort of semi-Science, even on the more physical side (physiology, medicine), which moves as one approaches the study of man-in-groups into pre-Science—dotted with dubious, largely disconnected bits of more or less established quantitative relations. In the legal field, in the main, we do not even know the rawest of raw facts, let alone quantitative relations. E.g.: What percent of cases which come to lawyers get settled? Is there any relationship between size of case, or kind of case, and settlement (and is such relationship modified by such factors as incidence on a metropolitan-urban-rural scale or incidence by section of the country, etc.)? In the legal field what we 'know' is (1) partial and spotty: itching, growing pimples of near-knowledge here and there upon the otherwise unblemished skin of ignorance; (2) almost wholly uncoordinated, chunk of 'knowledge' by chunk of 'knowledge'; (3) 'known' quite differently to different people, according to whether they have observed at first hand (and that narrowly or widely, wisely or with eyes blind with prejudice), or have talked with a few (and with which?) people who have observed at first hand, or have 'read something somewhere', or just grew up with an idea, or 'had a case once' (*one* case, *once*), etc. (Consider the complete revolution in our general 'knowledge' about the D.A.'s office, about the quantitative incidence of jury trials in the criminal picture, and about the frequency of reversals of conviction on 'piddling technicality' which began with the Cleveland Crime Survey of 1919). Finally (4), as suggested by the Cleveland job, much of what we 'know' about things of law just isn't so.

In such a situation, the best approach to a *whole-view*, on the side of fact, and to some degree on the side of function (spotting, at least, certain lines of non-health or even disease) consists in mustering the various more careful and useful studies, carefully assessing the limitations but extracting their suggestive corrections of ordinary 'common sense' or common nonsense, trying with their help to build an imaginative working whole, and presenting it so to speak with the parts which have been somewhat investigated and checked painted in a different color from the parts which rest on the writer's personal but 'unproved' 'knowledge' as an expert, and these last painted in a different color from the parts about which the writer knows that he is reduced pretty well to guessing. (Kluckhohn's *Mirror for Man* is a recent popularizing but careful instance; Ogburn and Nimk [off], *Sociology*, is a more limited, and beautifully sustained job of the sort.) That is the kind of job which this one ought to be, but is not. The ten years which would have been needed for a proper full canvass and assessment of the dots of things which have been explored with some care, those years have gone instead into the Uniform Commercial Code. Hence what there is to be had, of semi-Science, is drawn on here only when I happen to have run across a piece of it. This does not mean that there has not been careful effort at substituting probable fact for prejudice and mere guess. See 1.3.(d). It does mean that the effort to present a working wholeview has consumed my powers.

Yet the presentation here, on the fact-side, aims at being pre-Science rather than mere opinion or random observation or the like, in that the effort to spot what seems to be really so has been sustained, and in that effort is made, in regard to stuff on the mere opinion-level, to mark it off as

APPENDICES 559

such. But all of it is non-Science in method, in so far as no effort at all is made to suggest *proof* of anything (except perhaps of the real nature of our system of precedent). Illustrations are used never as proofs, but only as means of making clear what is being said, and of calling up the reader's available experience for examination. If the propositions advanced on the side of what is there to look at are not obviously true as soon as thought about, that is just too bad.

The material is in part non-Science in a further and important aspect. It endeavors, throughout, to take account of values which are simply not open to verification or 'validation' by scientific means. A whole-view must wrestle with such problems of value, and must in so far move beyond the purview of Science. But here again, the effort is sustained, both to keep my views on values from obscuring my view of the facts, and to keep views on values from purporting to be other than what they are: fighting faiths.

1.3.(d) The essential method of the course, then, is the use of *Horse-sense* in an effort to get a Whole-view, and to maintain *Balance* in that view and in dealing with any particular aspect of the things of law. Horse-sense is not the sense of a horse. Horse-sense is the kind of highly informed, distinctly *un*common, better-than-common, expert but not scientifically demonstrable know-what and know-how which a David Harum had about horses and other horse-traders. In matters legal it is 'the forgotten obvious' that lies in the corner unnoticed. The job of horse-sense jurisprudence is the job of lyric poetry – to make the trite come alive, become real and vibrant with meaning; to make men take in and thrill to the what and the whither and the how of what is there and what is to be done.

1.3.(e) *Broad* truths, *not* 'general' or 'universal' truths, are the goal on the observation and description side; and roughly workable, not 'accurate' phrasing. Different times and cultures and individual persons show huge ranges of variation not only in particular behavior, but in manner of thought and manner of response, manner of selecting the significant. In things of law, in particular, the current legal system tends to strongly condition even perception of when and where there is a problem to be coped with. My own background of direct observation is dominantly American, Northern, urban, bourgeois, Protestant gentile, academic, liberal, 'private' rather than 'public' law, 'office' rather than 'litigation' – and of course contemporary. I have done what I could to become conscious of each such limitations and to develop corrective cross-bearings, both by direct contacts and by reading and conversation – as will appear. To a considerable degree I think I have learned to *see*, effectively, and to report fairly, facts which I do not at all enjoy seeing, and to spot when unfamiliar facts are significant and to go hunting for their significance. But 'horse-sense' remains conditioned by the man who thinks he has it. To persons of any other background I say only: do not junk my alleged observations of fact *merely* because they may seem at first blush prejudiced in the seeing. Thirty years have gone into trying to get them reasonably cross-lighted. They ought, at least, to cross-light your own. Frequently, I think they are reasonably close to 'general' truths.

1.3.(f) One main test I have used for judging of the accuracy of reports: of fact and of the completeness, typicality and significance of fact observed or reported, is whether and how the material fits into the *gestalt*, the general configuration, of things of law as I have come to see them. This is a line of testing which can be self-deceptive and essentially circular, new data being either left 'unseen' or so 'seen' as in the very seeing to be distorted into harmony with the apparatus of ideas that controls the eye. Nonetheless, a major test of any purported whole-view is its ability to accommodate new data without either distorting them or needing serious remodelling of itself. And a companion-test of any such whole-view is its adequacy in the weighting of new data, and especially the help it gives in making any new type of fact *signal its own incompleteness and the lines of profitable further inquiry* for further relevant *new* data. A *working* whole-view, one of a *functioning* institution as contrasted with a picture primarily of form, lends itself readily to this type of test; and one gains confidence in his 'feel' for the nature of the institution and for the gestalt of a process when that 'feel' has repeatedly proved out, on further inquiry.

1.3.(g) The 'law-crafts' is a concept to bridge between broad truths and the concrete problems which face the institution and its individual craftsmen. 'A sound discipline must feed into and be fed out of the daily problems of the practitioner.' (Compare natural science and technology: or the theory and practice of medicine.) Compare Lecture 2.

1.4. *Limitations of the Course*

In addition to what has been said, the course suffers especially from time-pressure. Jurisprudence means to me: any careful and sustained thinking about any phase of things legal, if the thinking seeks to reach beyond the practical solution of an immediate problem in hand. Jurisprudence thus includes any type at all of honest and thoughtful generalization in the field of the legal. It is, thus, the heart and body of any sound study of and for the law, and the parts of it which extend beyond 'the state of correct prevailing doctrine in this nation' should make out by far the better and greater 'half' of sound professional legal instruction. So that (granted effective teaching) a law school can be rated in adequacy by how much of its instruction is devoted to jurisprudence. And jurisprudence, as a field of study, is quite as bulky and complex as is any nation's 'law'. It is, however, the Cinderella of the law curriculum. 'Every course should be (or 'is') a course in jurisprudence' is a defensible slogan for many forward-looking schools; but what that slogan means in operation is: some crumbs from every table, but obscured by the fact that all the emphasis is on something else, on some *part*, some *aspect* – rarely on whole-view as such, never sustainedly on whole-view, never sustainedly on putting-together of a whole as a central and vital job.

To this last, grudgingly, a faculty *may* allocate two semester units, or three, out of seventy-six.

How, in that time, can the indispensable 30- or 40-unit job be 'done'? As I see it, only by treating the course as one in method, rather than in subject-matter. The problem is to learn and practice seeing and thinking from the vantage-point of a whole-view, which is a way of seeing and judging anything at all, including all the things this course will never get a chance to mention. The problem is, secondly, to draw together, to mobilize for action, the multitude of bits of jurisprudence now scattered all over any decent curriculum. I see no way of doing that directly; no instructor has accurate knowledge of the detail, though he can illustrate and stir the process by explicit treatment of some of his colleagues' more obvious – and neglected – contributions. But a sound framework to the functioning institution and a sound way of inquiring into its problems draws out of a student a mustering of his available experience, including precious things he has met in other courses 'but just didn't think about'. On such person-by-person contribution by the student a course like this depends utterly. It cannot in two or four or six semester hours provide subject-matter needing one or two solid years for study.

The topics chosen for fuller development claim to pay their way, but except for Lectures 1–4 and 9–11 they represent essentially arbitrary choices. One can illustrate by Lectures 6–8, on Justice, and by Part VII. Justice should certainly be cut into, but a single lecture could meet the bare bones need. Per contra, each of the four topics in Part VII would reward expansion into at least four lectures. Again, many vital lines of inquiry are touched at most in passing, either because I lack confidence in my available background of horse-sense about them, or because I do not feel that I have thought my way far enough into them, or just because 28 lectures are not 88. For example: the crucial problem of trial of fact, or that of bar organization, or that of the meaning of such particular major lines of institution as Contract, Property, Association or Taxation, or the interrelation of various types of control device (with particular attention to manners, ritual and 'imaginary environment'), or the pre-legislative and legislative processes. And so forth.

(iii) LECTURE 2. THEORY OF CRAFTS AND OF THE LAW CRAFTS, PRELIMINARY. WHAT LAWYERS ARE FOR

2.1.1. *What a craft is*: an organized, persisting body of skills and men to get some line of work done: e.g. carpentry; whaling; advertising; 'the practice of law'; advocacy. ('Craftsmanlike' is the adjective; 'crafty' reflects abuse by the craftsman unless, as in negotiation or war, manoeuvers and even deception are part of the craft. We shall here reserve 'art' for the 'fine art', for the quest-for-beauty aspects of craftsmanship as contrasted with just

getting the work done, or for the closely related extra and/non-communic-
able know-how of the better craftsman.) The fact and idea of *crafts focus as
nothing else does* (except the rearing of the young) *the homely daily processes of
interaction between individuals and the closer groups and larger society around them.*
Except for the fringes of genius and new experiment, the crafts include not
only all of technology but all of traditionally communicated life-wisdom
(e.g. husband-handling) and all of the organization of work and of management. The vital gains from use of the concept are that you can not think of a
craft, as such, apart from the line of work which that craft centers on: this
forces active critique. And you cannot think of a craft, as such, apart from
the craftsmen and their daily practice: this forces you down to people and
cases and results. Finally 'craft' opens up by necessity the picture of the
whole, because the organization and working of the whole move in any
persisting social grouping, almost exclusively by way of the set-up and
interlocking of the crafts. 'Craft' is a queerly neglected concept which we
propose to put to work.

2.1.2. *Make-up of a craft*: a craft is thus a small institution, and everything
true of either is true of the other, except perhaps in so far as it is rather rare
for a man of a craft not to be conscious of at least some part of what his
craft is for, whereas participants can grow into major institutions practically
without awareness [e.g. housewives and the market].

2.1.2.1. *The stuff of the craft.*

(a) A known goal or set of goals, function or functions, job or jobs to get
done. Where the specialization has been by drift, with no overall plan, one
finds frequently enough an amazing hodgepodge of diverse jobs: the
'lumber yard' stocks building materials in general, and fuel, the 'drug
store's' prescription department is hard to locate; 'the' 'private' 'practice of
law' (as the organization of any large firm shows) includes a considerable
number of crafts as diverse as those which once specialized out of, or
gathered in around, work in wood: carpenter generally: specializing e.g.
into sawyer, cooper, fletcher (with arrow-heads, string, feathers added),
wheelwright and cartwright (with smithy-work added), shipwright, cabinet-
maker. The lawyer, generally, has specialized e.g. into litigation 'department', estates, corporations, taxation, public relations, managing partner,
research (and see below for a more functional line of sub-division).

On the other hand, pressure of work and need for skill can lead, with or
without planned drive, into single-function specialization (diamond-cutting;
tea- or wine-tasting; negligence jury-practice – or in the older days, out of
the King-and-Council, treasury-administration (the Exchequer) and then
a Court.)

Some of the problems of a craft, as of any other institution, diverge
according to how far the job or function concerned approaches the single
('felt' operating correction of any muffs in articulate theory), or the conscious, or both. (Job-analysis.)

2.1.2.1.(b). *The ways and skills: Organized and interlocking*: as simple a process as sharpening a pencil calls for different treatment of wood and lead; how complicated a finger-job buttoning a button really is you will find by trying it out with the other hand. Team-skills of course call for timed gearing together. The degree of *complexity* and *organization* (and of *variation*) becomes clear only when one begins to break 'a' skill down for purposes of instruction or of substituting a mechanical or routine operation. (Thus 'the' art of correctly 'reading' a court decision, with various ways, e.g., (i) of distinguishing; (ii) of following, though distinguishable; (iii) of expanding or changing direction.) The ways and skills must, as a *body*, be relatively *lasting*, or we think of them not as constituting a craft but as individual achievement. A craft is something typically common to many people, and extending across generations, though in these days the technology may change with amazing speed.

2.1.2.1.(c). *An economic base* is normal to a craft, though I should include sport, dance and music for fun in with the crafts. The value may be in use (cooking for self) or in team or in exchange (household, restaurant, army cooking; canning, cooked foods for market). Crafts become socially important in any regime of divided labor, where some 'laymen' to the craft become dependent on the craftsman, and where the craftsman becomes more or less dependent on the laymen for a livelihood.

The foregoing represents a partial re-do of the following

(1) A *craft*: a body of skills and men for getting something done: carpentry; advertising; advocacy.
  (a) A known goal or set of goals: jobs and ideals.
  (b) A relatively stable body of complex and organized ways and skills – interlocking.
  (c) Partly teachable and taught: the rule of thumb; articulate theory. 'Taught Law' (which means not merely the verbalized Rules of Law, but also the *ways* of law, the whole going System so far as taught by 'breaking them in.') 'Taught Law is tough law' – even when it is bad law.
  (d) Partly learnable and learned: apprenticeship; 'practice'; 'breaking in.'
  (e) The extra 'art' element of intuition; of experienced know-how; of genius.
  (f) Men manning the craft; relied on; reliable?
  (g) The problem of reliable minimum competence and uprightness of the men.
  (h) The problem of organization and of leadership.

(2) *The Ways of Crafts*
  (a) A craft forms around a lasting line of work perceived as such.

(b) Bulking work means routine: 'rules' may emerge; it certainly means specialization and subspecialization.

(c) The craftsman is inescapably shaped – even in imagination – by his craft as given again: (apprenticeship; breaking in). (Become a lawyer and you will never be the same again. And our judges were lawyers.)

(d) The craftsman *may* also contribute to his craft; if so, his contribution *may* become common stock. (How far does the skilled lawyer's skill, today, die with him?)

(e) Craftsmanship as service and price v. What's in it for me? and What will get by? The problem of conscious craft-standards and ideals. The Old Man you learn under. Compare Jessup on Root.

(f) The monopoly-tendency of the craft (the campaign against un-authorized practice of the law; the policing of admission to the bar); how of the policing after admission? The monopoly tendency of the craftsman: the '*my* stock-in-trade' approach to knowledge and skill. The black-art, mumbo-jumbo approach to the layman v. modern counselling and drafting of documents. Monopoly, protected by law, connotes responsible, even-handed service to all, at a fair return. Well?

(g) Specialization by unplanned drift is typically a conglomerate (the drug store; the lumber yard; the practice 'of law'); specialization by way of planned drive can seem to approximate 'single'-function (machine-tools; diamond-cutting; negligence jury-practice or estate and probate practice).

(h) Production-engineering and effective instruction in the crafts: diagnosis of peculiarly significant lines of skill, for observation, for communication, for gathering and comparison of variants, for re-study and improvement of method. (How much of this is being done in legal education?)

(3) *Stability and change in crafts* (Addition: Degree of leeways? Death if ideals die out.)

('The job of the institution is to manage the job in hand: the "book" and the set-up, the staff-plan, the colonel's political judgment, the shavetail's ambition, the sergeant's experience, the private's pride in his outfit – any one or two may break down in the particular pinch, but a well-geared machine takes up the slack.')

(a) Without development and recurrence of patterns of performance we get neither large-scale operation nor relative similarity of results across time and space. Individuated artistry is rare, uncertain, fre-quently expensive and too frequently absent.

(b) All patterns tend into routine; routine tends into woodenness. Errors in initial design of pattern continue; needed adaptations fail of discovery or acceptance. To vested inertia is added vested interest, vested habit, vested emotion and vested conviction. 'Young man, you are asking me to rethink everything I know.' The trouble becomes greater if a vested defensive ideology has had time to form: 'It is best as it is because . . .' Or if the craft bulks large enough to pillow the impact of reform-drives.

(c) In a live craft, change comes constantly from within, via the craftsman's feeling for the changing needs of the felt job, and via invention followed by imitation (even though working frequently under the brake of attempted monopoly of secret knowhow: 'my' or 'my outfit's' trade secrets). In a deadened craft the pressure is more typically by revolt from without. The layman tests a craft by results, rarely understanding either craft-problems or craft-techniques. The layman can therefore rarely *engineer* a cure or reform. The *leeways* he allows the craftsman are correspondingly large. But he undercuts the craft's prestige by his grumbles. And he can, and has 'cut off the head.'

(d) Within the craft much of youth is typically in revolt (cf. Pinder's 'Problem of the Generations'). But the revolt is typically (i) revolt; the pseudo-radical mainly after his own slice of the pie; and (ii) pseudo-reform: the substitution of exaggeration No. 2 for exaggeration No. 1, leaving out of account the values actually underlying No. 1's exaggeration. (Typical: procedural 'reform' into pure looseness; or the first efforts to de-judicialize administrative procedure.) Meanwhile, growing into craftsmanship conditions the youth into tolerance, patience, satisfaction, smugness. (Look too often on that hideous face . . .) Finally, fighting-fire dies low; the fighting reforms of any day prove abortive or become slowly absorbed; and few men develop more than one set of fighting ideas in one lifetime.

(e) What is true of patterns, re technique, is true of 'lower motives' re motivation. A surge of idealism can kindle, but it cannot alone support an institution ('the law of kindling'); idealism burns out unless *machinery* is provided to supply patterns of work, to enlist habit, and to adequately satisfy drives for gain, prestige, power, etc. (Note the use, in wise institutions, of such drives as lust, envy, hate, etc.) Here lies a central engineering problem of any type of reform of any aspect of the institution of law or by way of it.

(f) A peculiar and peculiarly important aspect of change is the shift of 'period-style' in the work of a craft – akin to such shift in architecture, the drama, or music. This has been noted re the institution of law chiefly as an alternation of periods of relative growth and rigidity (e.g. Pound's 'stages of legal history'). The stress here is not on the substantive law, but on the craftsmen's manner of work, thought, ideals. Is the ideal and technique a Parke 'strong' opinion, arriving by reasoning no layman can follow at a result no layman could foresee? Is it direct, obvious soundness of result, reshaping the legal

566 APPENDICES

machinery as you go, as typified by Mansfield, Marshall, Cowen, Gibson, Parker, Shaw? Is it severe reverence for old form, even while readjusting to current need, as in the K. B. of the growth of assumpsit and the jurisdictional fictions? Is law-work to lord it or to listen, *or is law-work to labor to do each, as needed*? Why any contrast of *goal*? – The cause and process of change in dominant period-style is still largely unexplored. (Though the relation of such broad contrasts to contrasting types of human temperament ought to be obvious.)

(4) *The Law-Crafts*....
  (a) Their range (by tradition): chairing, client-getting and handling; office-management: general counsel as central corporate staff-man.
  (b) The basic functional law-crafts center on eternal human needs, in all human groups: spokesmanship, decision, advice: trouble-shooting, generally, in regard to the teamwork of people.
  (c) Acquaintance with the Rules of Law and with the nature and ways of tribunals and officials in a particular country, and the 'legal' background or context of many of the lawyer's activities, affect and heavily color his work in the law-crafts, but the essence of his work would continue even if all the Rules of Law (and even the courts) were abolished tomorrow. 'The Legislature can repeal my whole discipline (*Wissenschaft*) tomorrow' is a complete misconception; the discipline has in such an idea been misconceived as being merely the systematized Rules of Law and their doctrinally correct 'application.'

5. *Spokesmanship, as Illustrative of a Craft which Can Of Course Divide into Any Number of Sub-Crafts*
  (a) Sub-variants outside law-work: compare the union representative; the lobbyist; the majority leader; the introducer of a bill or of a motion in nomination; public relations counsel; the advertiser; John Alden. Inside law-work 'proper': jury advocacy, appellate advocacy, arbitration-advocacy; negotiation; the crystallizing of discussion-results; the drafting of the public statement. 'Lawyers' (meaning those many admitted persons who, though admitted, had never really learned any of their crafts, and had misdone much of their work) were anathema to F. H. La Guardia; 'lawyers' still are anathema to many business and many labor men. One can add, as to that unhappy kind of admitted persons, to many judges, and to me. But that has to do not with the *job* of spokesmanship, but with the mishandling of that job. Let me add, for the meditation of the critics, that I have seen lawyers' jobs *mishandled* as badly by non-lawyers as by any lawyers; and that I have seen even otherwise sweetly arranged jobs muffed by non-lawyers at times, for lack at the critical moment of a lawyer's proper experience. Of course anybody with sense knows that spokesmanship calls (along with general

technique) for full understanding of both the whole situation with all its unspoken implications, and of the nature of the interested parties, and of the nature of the particular tribunal.

(b) The 'speech'-need: experienced, ready, effective voicing for, and answering objections for, the shy, the slow of speech, or the over-truculent, the brash or the inexperienced, those with status-handicaps, etc. Cf. the oldest child or smartest child or favorite child, for the family child-group.

(c) The 'buffer'-need: elimination of direct emotion; more dispassionate 'outside' judgment. ('A lawyer who handles his own case has a fool for a client.') The buffer-need can arise anew in the middle of a negotiation which is breaking down.

(d) The 'knowledge'-need: familiarity with and access to needed stores of experience (in the Rules of Law, in the 'ropes,' in the nature of the situation, in the nature of the adversary or deciding personnel).

(e) The 'investigation'-need: spotting, getting, marshalling the significant facts.

(f) The 'judgment'-need: Skill to diagnose a trouble-situation, to spot what we need; then to spot and articulate the favorable *issue* that lines it all up our way, and to spot and phrase the appealing *solution*.

(g) The 'persuasion'-need: skill to find and ring the right bells, whether in an adversary (negotiation) or in a tribunal (court advocacy) or in the legal or lay public (the opinion-writer).

(h) The 'art' additions to the rule-of-thumb.

(i) Mediation as double-spokesmanship either for inexpert or face-involved parties; the Ifugao *monkalun*; the U. S. conciliator; the family friend.

(j) Spokesmanship need not be adversary. A man may become the voice of the whole. The judge; the war leader: Churchill; Brandeis as 'counsel for the situation.'

(k) Note how these same lines of skill, with different arrangement, weighting and flavor, recombine to produce much, even most, of what is needed in such other law-crafts as legislation, administrative policy-shaping, commercial counselling, negotiation, office-management, client-handling.

6. *The human prejudice against being a 'thing' – manipulated.*

(a) All crafts have to wrestle with people's sense of personal dignity, and those which like the law-crafts deal with direct approach to moving people into action become particularly suspect.

(b) But no lawyer should ever waste time 'defending' himself or his craft against any imputation of manipulation: *that is his function*, within the bounds of decency; and any layman can be made, in ten minutes, to see the value of spokesmanship.

(c) Hence, in regard to 'manipulation,' the problem comes up, head-on, of *purpose*, and of *character*. Of personal *uprightness*, and then of that *wisdom* which means vision for the Whole.

(iv) LECTURE 5. THEORY OF THEORIES, AND OF TRUTH

5.1. *What a theory is:*

5.1.1. First, on the 'fact' side (looking toward an ultimate Science) a theory is an attempt at significant and accurate observation of what is there and what happens and to state a significant working truth about it. The effort is to get at effective working relations general in their character. Among the difficulties are:

Seeing at all. It is hard to notice the too familiar (as a lawyer with a cause immediately 'sees' in an adverse case only its irreducible holding and the lines of distinction, but in a favorable case the true broad rule it announces). Or to notice the habitually neglected (as, that 'delivery' as a situation has two ends). Or to see the unwelcome, or the badly lighted. We 'see' not only in native *gestalt* but also with the spectacles of concept (in legal work we have *learned* gestalts: our legal concepts) and of unconscious conditioning about what to look for (you v. a Maine lobsterman, looking for weather signs), and of desire (selective observation, weighting and arrangement).

But a theory of fact has no business to imply, or to be read as implying, that the person announcing it either likes or approves or desires what he seeks to describe. (As: 'A government of laws *and not* of men is, as such, impossible.')

5.1.2. Second, on the 'value' side (looking toward or derived from a Philosophy): a theory is an attempt to state significant right goals, together, in matters legal, with conclusions regarding right action in a problem-situation. Here, approval is implicit in announcement.

5.1.3. Third, on the 'operating' side (looking toward or derived from a practical craft or practical policy): a theory is an attempt to state an effective working measure to deal with a problem-situation, or a type of situation. This may be either of the technological or cook-book variety (as, 'A brief gains in persuasive power in the measure of its simplicity and clarity' or: 'This brief will gain, etc.') in which case the operating theory rests on 'fact' theory under (a); or it may be a theory of practical desirability (as: 'What we need to do is . . .') in which case the theory contains a goal aspect which rests on 'value' theory under (b) and also an effectiveness aspect which rests on 'fact' theory under (a).

5.1.4. Nothing has standing to rate as a 'theory' unless it purports to have been seriously considered; and in the main men do not seriously consider anything unless they are bothered. A theory is therefore likely to be affected by the bother.

5.2. *Pareto's Theory of Theories* (superbly exemplified in Pound's description of the sequence of jurisprudential theories).

(a) What was there in the theory for the men who made it?

(b) What was there in the theory for the men who accepted it – (or else, why did men not accept it)?

(c) The cynic thinks the goal-aspect of the theory to generate and to distort the fact-aspect. Too often, it does, resulting in faulty fact-observation, fact-arrangement, fact-theory. The cynic also thinks acceptance or rejection of a fact-theory to depend not on its accuracy, but on the goal-desires or prejudices of the relevant public. The cynic also thinks the goal-desires in question to be commonly low and to be hidden under prettified allegations (lust under love, greed under honor, jealousy and hate under justice – and on down into the Freudian – sometimes enlightening – menagerie of motivations). Too often for comfort the cynic is right in any or all of this. But there are men whose motives are really high. And sound fact theory stands also on its own. And a louse may have a good eye, and a man pure in heart a poor one. Hence:

5.3. *Pareto's Theory Corrected.*

(a) On the observational side, what difference does it make whether the observer was a louse, if he saw straight? (Machiavelli's *Prince* is one of the shrewdest bodies of observation in print.) Pareto merely explains, psychologically, bad observation or reading of evidence, when it occurs, and warns that it keeps occurring.

(b) On the side of evaluation, if the particular goal-theory helps *you* see straight, it makes no difference that the other fellow got it because he was 'frustrated' or otherwise insane, or that *he* used it to cover dirty work nor yet that *he* linked it with seven other ideas which were insane or even vicious. (E.g. Napoleon, Hitler and Stalin have been thoroughly sound in perceiving a vital need for world-unification of government.) Which leads into the

5.4. *Theory of Truth.*

Two ultimate kinds of truth:

5.4.1. *Testable* truth: in any particular age, place and technology, all competent observers can agree, regardless of what they would like to find. This is the basis of any Scientific approach. (I deal with only 'empirical science' as Science, plus, by courtesy, so much of the logical branches as any competent students can agree on.)

(i) A constantly and usefully expanding realm, based on

(ii) prior recorded research and new labor and investigatory techniques and

(iii) with all data and results held always subject to correction; but

(iv) never in itself sufficient to produce a *whole* view of anything.

5.4.2. The time-variability of testable truth is of importance to legal work only in those fringe-areas which are both (a) in motion or uncertainty at the moment and (b) of practical impact. Even thinking *about* matters legal is, as *legal* philosophy, concerned with change in testable truth only in so far as the fact and nature of such change can hope, some day, of developing practical implications.

5.4.3. *Non-testable* truth is in my view also truth, though nobody can ever *test* whether he has it by the tail. Our beliefs about what truth is in this area are based on tradition, revelation, authority, intuition. Agreement is possible only among those who see it the same way. The area especially of ultimate meaning, of values, of man's goals; and also of the individual 'art'-factor in know-how or know-whither. Acceptance or recognition, not investigation, is the basic method as to *premises*. One can of course explore the bearings of premises by logic *and* experiment.

5.4.4. Results of any operations or work in the *testable*-truth field are always *partial*, in application to practical living: which always rests in part on goal-judgments. While results of any admixture of non-testable truth are always subject to irreconcilable disagreement. Both are needed, for any whole-view, and in actual application of theory to life. This leads into

5.4.5. The dilemma of life-philosophy and of the social disciplines, the would-be social 'sciences'. Cf. Holmes' 'Can't-Helps' by which men yet have to live. The Metaphysical Society. The conflict between the dogmatic and the free-opinion lines of organization of society. Dogmatism and tyrannical fanaticism are inherently logical. Against their premise stand only experience and the sense of human dignity.

5.5. *A working approach*:

5.5.1. Mark and remember which propositions lie in which area.

5.5.2. Re-testable truth, keep on the *level* of discussion appropriate to the material and the problem in hand. E.g. The 'new' 'revolutionary' laws of relativity and indeterminacy in metaphysical Physics are irrelevant to the solidity of rough-carpentry or of inlaid cabinet-work or good prefabricated houses. Almost all legal work resembles these last. (Contrast the practical effects of some people's theories of ultimate Justice, 6.2.) Even a Berkeley used chairs and police as did his neighbors. Even re non-testable truth, most Americans *can* agree on enough important goods to keep a 'country' a working whole, with some recognized agreed machinery for handling most disagreements.

5.5.3. Remember that we all live almost exclusively on faith, even re testable truth: How do *you* 'know' the acceleration of earth gravity; or that the earth is round; or that there is a Governor in California; or that atomic fission exists, or that a bona fide purchaser for value of the legal title to land takes free of a cestui's interest? *Tag every alleged 'fact' in your memory with its source*. What a lawyer does, re his propositions of law (which, on whether they prevail, are propositions of fact) is good practice with every other proposition of fact worth remembering. Indeed, most worthwhile aspects of a lawyer's work in office or court are worthwhile for use also in his life.

5.5.4.

(a) All practical judgments must of necessity move on such *working* bases: one seeks *enough* significant 'facts', accurately *enough*, with a measure *sufficiently* explored as to likely consequence as to be a worthwhile 'best' move into the confessedly uncertain future.

(b) It is at this point that discussion of 'certainty' of results in the work of law are so likely to go haywire. The certainty to be *expected* in human affairs is the certainty to be expected in *human* affairs. Where routine is available, the degree of certainty can be high; otherwise, the struggle is slow, to move from coin-flip chanciness into something we can recognize as skilled or expert judgment and which we then reward with pay, prestige, power or profit. J. Frank is a hardened sinner in misposing the issue in this connection.

Queer in Frank's writing is the treatment of lawyers' counselling as simply 'Guess,' while himself participating in the training of future lawyers. If they *simply* 'guess' when they are not 100% certain, then training them to prey upon the public is unconscionable.

5.5.5. *Ultimate goals and ideals* are like the stars to a mariner: they are the means of a consistent long-haul, overall course. But they say little if anything of current, or storm, or tide, or of the need to put in somewhere for fuel, water or repairs, or of sailing around Africa to get from Bombay to London. *Measures* must always be pragmatic. Ultimate goals guide pragmatic choice and use of pragmatic measures. Any 'either-or and-not-the-other' is here, as throughout almost all of Jurisprudence, a posing of false issues, headed for inadequacy.

5.5.6. Re other people's 'theories,' spot which kind they are, and distinguish the fact-phase from the value-phase for independent critique. (Measures can always be divided into purpose and machinery, which warrant separate study.) Re your own, you will gain clarity by spotting and marking the different aspects and gain somewhat, re effective communication. But most folk will still think you approve ('believe in' = desire) whatever you say is so ('believe in' = be convinced exists).

5.5.7. Excursus on analysis of institutions: Re *fact*-theories based on 'observation,' one useful idea is, along with factor-analysis, the idea of the manner of the working organization of the factors, together with the net-drive of the whole, as organized: the 'field of force' of physics, the 'ethos' of ethnology, the 'individual constitution' of medicine, Savigny's Volksgeist. Resort to such an idea always shows ignorance and vagueness about the 'what-else' which is at work, but it expresses also a sound perception that even a complete analysis of factors reaches only the isolated *parts* of a going whole, leaving still to be grasped their importance in quantity, in position, in quality, in function.

Similarly factors may be present, but submerged by more than countervailing factors, just as important values served by an institution may be hidden by its more explicit purposes. ('Professional ethics,' said a delegate to the A.B.A. House of Delegates, quoting a judge of a supreme court making a public address, 'are a device invented by old men to keep young men from getting at the old men's business.' The ethics against solicitation and the like serve other, obvious purposes. The problem here is one of a submerged function. We can now discuss: 'function' for whom?)

Note that in historical inquiry the question 'Why *not*?' is as important as '*Why*?' 'Why did this crucial case *not* become a leading case?' 'Why did Mansfield's great work in Commercial Law *not* reach the heart of Commercial Law: Sales?'

5.5.8. '*And-Not*' *is bad Jurisprudence*. In observation of any social scene, the complexity of material makes any *exclusively* single attribute or sequence highly improbable. 'And-not' is the traditional bane of sound Jurisprudence (and of lay thinking in general): 'Because it is A it is therefore *not* B' presupposes a thoroughly explored, exactly defined area of discussion, divided accurately and exhaustively into A and Not-A – which the current social scene almost never is. Examples: 'Good lawyers are born *and not* made.' (First half true sometimes; and *some* native capacity is indeed needed.) 'It is not law which shapes society, but society which shapes law.' (First half false; though much law has often failed to 'take'; but even then it may shape heavily in unforeseen directions: e.g. Volstead Act and gangsterism.) 'A craft is a mere way of earning a living, not a line of service to society.' (The 'mere' is true only of a craft or craftsman without the needed compass; the second half implies a *normal* incompatibility between earning and serving.)

[5.6 *Truth by fiat: Fiction* omitted.]

Appendix D

Llewellyn's Later
Interpretations of Realism

'Some Realism about Realism' was Llewellyn's most disciplined attempt to provide a coherent account of realism.[1] Despite its limitations, it remains one of the most important and illuminating discussions of the pre-1931 literature. On a number of subsequent occasions he was tempted to make further appraisals of the realist movement. In addition to many allusions scattered about his writings there are several unpublished items specifically about realism; however, the two most important sustained discussions appeared in print: an article 'On Reading and Using the Newer Jurisprudence' (1940) and Appendix B of *The Common Law Tradition*. None of these later writings was as painstaking as Part I of 'Some Realism about Realism'. Rather, they consist for the most part of detailed comments on particular works and of somewhat impressionistic general statements. 'On Reading and Using the Newer Jurisprudence'[2] was written in 1939–40 and was published simultaneously in the *American Bar Association Journal* and the *Columbia Law Review*. It was written principally for the benefit of readers of the former journal and set out to interpret the juristic antics of the 1930s in simple common-sense terms. The first half is largely devoted to a general analysis of judicial discretion and is more realistically treated as a statement of Llewellyn's views on the subject than as a serious analysis of the ideas of others. The second half takes the form of a review of a selection of books on jurisprudence by 'a few of the more striking writers' (especially Pound, Frank, Hutcheson, Michael and Adler, Arnold, Rodell), 'though much of the best material is in articles', many on specific legal topics.[3] It is interesting to note that of the seven writers who are accorded the most attention in this article only two, Frank and Hutcheson, featured in Llewellyn's sample of twenty 'realists' in 'Some Realism about Realism' and that, with the exception of Pound, the others were teaching either at Columbia or Yale. Llewellyn's article is still worth reading as a sane and perceptive appraisal of the work of some of his contemporaries, but it is generally too discursive and too selective to add more than a few loosely connected thoughts to his interpretations of the realist movement.

Although Llewellyn's perspective changed between 1931 and 1960 and his own thought continued to develop during this period, there is sufficient consistency in his discussions of realism to warrant treating them together as a group. Some of the recurrent themes of his other analyses are brought together in a single passage in *The Common Law Tradition*:

Realism was never a philosophy, nor did any group of realists as such ever attempt to present any rounded view, or *whole* approach. One or two – perhaps for instance Underhill Moore – may (though without companion or adherent) have conceived and even put forward his thinking as sufficiently complete to deserve description as a philosophy, as expressing views on those phases of the institution of law which reach beyond description and the techniques of operation. I know of no other such, however, unless Jerome Frank's faith in the unreachability of fact be deemed of this nature[3]. No. What realism was, and is, is a method, nothing more, and the only tenet involved is that the method is a good one. 'See it fresh,' 'See it as it works' – that was to be the foundation of any solid work, to *any* end. From there, one goes on into inquiry about e.g. What-it-is-for (function or goal), or e.g. to build a judgment on how far the measure fits the purpose, or e.g. on how far the particular purpose harmonizes with the Good Life, or e.g. on whether we do not then have to reexamine the original data about 'How it has been working' – a matter which often answers very differently to different questions.

Of all of these things, only 'see it fresh,' 'see it clean' and 'come back to make sure' are of the essence. They go to method. *That method is eternal.* That is point 1. The method may have come into first discussion among lawyers in relation to rules and judicial decision, but it is no more limited to that area than it is to matters legal. It applies to anything. That is point 2. But *the method* includes nothing at all about whither to go. That is point 3. *Realism* is *not* a philosophy, but a *technology*. That is why it is eternal. The fresh look is always the fresh hope. The fresh inquiry into results is always the needed check-up.

If any person caught up in the enthusiasms of the moment paraded a banner that suggested more than this, he was a parader, not a thinker, no *real* realist, certainly not one who had status to speak for any 'movement,' much less for any 'school.'[4]

This passage is rather loosely phrased and taken on its own could occasion difficulty; but if it is read in the light of Llewellyn's other writings it is possible to make sense of it and to treat it as a fair summary of his several attempts to interpret American legal realism. The key lies in the assertion '*Realism* is *not* a philosophy, but a *technology*'. This statement is as important as it is obscure. The two points are best treated as separate propositions for the purposes of elucidation.

(a) 'REALISM IS NOT A PHILOSOPHY'

What was Llewellyn trying to deny in this assertion? Probably in this context 'philosophy' is intended to mean 'ideology' or 'value system' as in the term 'philosophical jurisprudence', and the only point being made is that realism is morally neutral:

> If Jurisprudence of necessity includes a study of ideals for law, then realism is not [co-extensive with] jurisprudence. If, as I think, jurisprudence contains [seven] sub-disciplines, then realism deals with two out of the seven: craft techniques and descriptive sociology . . . Either or both are compatible with *any* philosophy about law's proper ultimate or immediate goals or about those of men in society. Realism in law is thus as ethically neutral as the science of mechanics or the art of bridge-building.[5]

This does not dispose of the matter, for 'philosophy' is often used in a much wider sense and in some contexts Llewellyn did not make clear that he was giving the word a restricted meaning. Thus Justice Charles Breitel was led to comment:

> . . . Llewellyn, in describing himself and others as realists, argued that the realism was not a philosophy, but a technology for the exploration of the law. As if technology or method could be separated from philosophy; as if one's view of the nature of things could be divorced from one's method of discovery and description of things.[6]

Whether or not Breitel's interpretation of the relevant passage from *The Common Law Tradition* is fair, he is making an important point. For there are good grounds for believing that Llewellyn did wish to put forward realism as a method which was neutral not only between competing sets of values but also between different political, epistemological or theological theories.[7] His answer to

Breitel would probably have been to the effect that while acceptance
of a method may be dependent upon one's view of the nature of
things, acceptance of the method of realism does not necessarily
presuppose any *particular* view of the nature of things. Shortly
before Llewellyn's death, one of his colleagues suggested to him
that he was *au fond* a 'realist in the Aristotelian sense'. His reported
reaction was 'Don't try to pin me down to an epistemology.'[8] He
might well have gone on to say that acceptance of a legal realist's
approach does not necessarily involve taking a stand on the traditional dispute between realists and nominalists.[9]

Another sense in which the word 'philosophy' might have been
used in this context is as a philosophical system or a *Weltanschauung*.
Llewellyn explicitly denied that realism *per se* is adequate as a
basis for such a system, he also doubted whether any members of
the realist movement put forward a sufficiently comprehensive set
of ideas to amount to a 'whole view'.[10] He omitted to mention that
in *Law in our Society* he was working towards such a statement.
Thus 'realism' for Llewellyn cannot be applied to any man's 'whole
view', if he has one. It can at best be only a part of a rounded
jurisprudential approach. As he developed his 'working whole view'
it became less and less appropriate to use 'realism' as a label for all
his legal thinking. It is dangerous to classify a thinker by reference
to a part of his thought only, for it may mislead people into mis-
taking a part for the whole. It is especially dangerous to do in the
case of 'realism'.[10]

(b) 'REALISM IS A METHOD' . . . 'REALISM . . . IS A TECHNOLOGY'

In *The Common Law Tradition* Llewellyn did not make it clear
whether he intended to equate 'method' and 'technology' or whether
he was making two separate points. The latter interpretation makes
more sense. It is reasonable to interpret exhortations to 'see it fresh',
'see it clean', 'see it as it works' as a colloquial way of advocating a
descriptive sociology of law for both observers and participants.
Only in a vague sense can they be said to be methodological
axioms in that they tell us to observe (and describe) legal processes,
but they do not tell us *how* to set about it. The shrewd practitioner
who relies on his impression of the 'realities', the systematic
participant observer and the perceptive but unmethodical com-

mentator have all adopted 'the method of realism' in this usage.

There is a danger of serious confusion if the proposition 'realism is a method' is equated with the proposition 'realism is a technology'. The latter statement can be given a meaningful interpretation if it is restated as follows: 'Realists are concerned to study and describe, among other things, juristic method, i.e., the techniques of participants in legal processes.' Legal technology (meaning the study of juristic techniques) in this sense was a particular concern of Llewellyn's and he was, perhaps, being unduly modest in attributing this concern to American legal realism generally. For, while there were other jurists who were interested in the subject, it is fair to say that some of Llewellyn's most distinctive contributions related to juristic method, for instance his 'Theory of the Crafts of Law', his analysis of judicial styles and his advocacy of the systematic teaching of certain skills in law school. Thus when Llewellyn says that 'realism is a technology' in that it deals with two parts of jurisprudence, 'craft techniques and descriptive sociology', (or that a major function of 'the newer jurisprudence' is to make the know-how of the best lawyers 'more explicit, and so more communicable, and so more teachable, and so more common'),[11] it is safer to treat this as an interpretation of his own ideas than as a reliable generalization about the concerns of all those he identified as realists.

(c) THE FRUITS OF REALISM

Llewellyn often complained that the critics of realism had overlooked the theoretical significance of some of the best works by realists because of a tendency to draw artificial distinctions between 'jurisprudential' and 'substantive' legal writings. Thus, Jerome Michael's 'work in *course books* in the fields of crime and procedure establish his standing as perhaps the most powerful and original thinker of his time in *jurisprudence*. Books on jurisprudence do not even mention him. Truly jurisprudence-in-English is still bound by the labels put not only on "schools" but on book covers.'[12]

In a letter to G. B. J. Hughes dated 10 August 1954, he was even more specific:

As I indicated back in 1931, the really important contributions of the Realist movement consist of the monograph jobs that get down under a sound, horse sense technology. . . . In the main, I find the theoretical writing on the subject to have been rather useless since the original points were once made.

Thus Llewellyn's final position appears to have been that the realist movement should be judged mainly by its influence on detailed work in various spheres of legal activity. Enquiry into the relationship between the operative ideas of judges, lawyers and legal scholars and the ideas of particular realists would be elusive, but could be illuminating. A general *post mortem* of this nature, combined with detailed studies of individual writers, offers the most promising basis for a sound appraisal of the realist movement.[13]

[1] Discussed above, ch. 5.

[2] Reprinted *Jurisprudence*, ch. 7 (1940).

[3] *Ibid.*, 145.

[4] *The Common Law Tradition*, 509–10.

[5] MS., 'Babel versus Teamwork: Jurisprudence since 1900', p. 5, K.L.P., B,III, 37(d), (1942–3).

[6] Breitel, 'Llewellyn: Realist and Rationalist', 18 *Rutgers L. Rev.*, 745, 746 (1964).

[7] *Op. cit.*, no. 5. In a letter Llewellyn made a similar point in discussing the relationship between American legal realism and Scandinavian realism. 'There is no historical link from this Swedish writing [Hargerstrom and Olivecrona] to the growth of Realism in this country. And I gravely doubt whether the Swedes were influenced in their thinking by us. There is something of a psychological similarity. Each of the two lines of thought represents reaction against an over-formalized body of doctrine which not only led repeatedly to unhappy results, but which obscured and made more unhappy and uncertain the working results of the legal system in which such doctrine prevailed. . . .

There is one other similarity between the Swedish thinkers and the Realistic thinkers: the effort of each to get down to what the thinker conceives as the real base of thinking rather than convention. But the Swedish drive, so far as I am acquainted with it, has been a type of philosophical enquiry into the nature of law. The drive of Realism, on the other hand, is to establish an effective legal technology. To this such a question as that of the nature of law is accidental, or incidental, or even immaterial. . . .' Letter to G. B. J. Hughes 10th August 1954. K.L.P. R. VIII 17. In this same letter Llewellyn doubted that there was any significant connection between the juristic and political views of Realists, except that some, but by no means all, who wanted reform within the field of law were also interested in political reform (id). Llewellyn suggested that Pound's dislike of Realism may have been politically motivated.

[8] Professor D. V. Cowen, interview, Chicago, 1963. Cf. Breitel, *op. cit.*, 755.

[9] *The Common Law Tradition*, 510, cited above.

[10] It is difficult to avoid the suspicion that Llewellyn's denial of the philosophical nature of 'realism' had an element of associational ambiguity. When he taught jurisprudence, 'philosophy' became almost a term of abuse. 'What the hell has Kant to do with my course in jurisprudence?' he asked angrily on one occasion (see above at p. 117). He explicitly excluded from his course 'the contemporaneous polysyllabic professionalized academic discipline' (but nevertheless gave students doses of Aquinas to read) and in other ways he made clear his dislike, in the jurisprudential context, of abstract discussions which had about them an aura of

'unreality' by virtue of their remoteness from everyday life of ordinary practice. His dislike of the esoteric Royal Tennis Tradition of jurisprudence has already been remarked (at p. 173). By asserting that 'realism is not a philosophy', Llewellyn may also have been hinting at a rejection of 'the esoteric tradition'.

[11] *Jurisprudence*, 149.
[12] *The Common Law Tradition*, 511–2.
[13] See further ch. 15.

Appendix E

Two Documents on the Uniform Commercial Code

THE KEYNOTE MEMORANDUM

From the mass of memoranda, letters, notes, articles and transcripts in which Llewellyn's thoughts on the Code are to be found, two documents stand out as having special significance: his general statement to the NYLRC in 1954, which is reproduced in full in the second part of this appendix. This is Llewellyn's most coherent apologia for the Code, but it must, of course, be taken for what it is —a powerful piece of advocacy. The other document, which is presented here, is less polished and more fragmentary, but is probably the most important single statement of the operative ideas of the Chief Reporter. This is a memorandum drafted by Llewellyn and addressed to the Executive Committee on Scope and Program of the NCC Section of Uniform Commercial Acts. Headed 'Re : Possible Uniform Commercial Code' it is undated, but was probably written in 1940, and circulated to the committee before Schnader's Presidential Address to the conference in September.

1. *The Reasons for a Uniform Commercial Code*

A Commercial Code, if successfully prepared, *and if accompanied by an adequate exposition of its reasons, its policies, and of the way its parts fit together*, has important values.

There is a very considerable body of commercial law which is very largely non-political in character, and which can be put into shape to be flexibly permanent. It affords, for use, a wide basis of case-law, and in many parts, a wide basis of good statutory material, together with experience under various Uniform Commercial Acts; also a wide basis of established commercial experience.

Those portions of the Negotiable Instruments Law which deal with presentment, notice, and protest, and material portions of the present Sales Act draft, show, moreover, that large portions of this body of law *can* be put into terms which afford material guidance to the layman in the *doing* of his commercial business. Law of which the interested layman becomes conscious, and which he seeks to put to work and to work under, is healthy law and helpful law. A democracy needs that kind of law, and needs to have citizens know they have it. A democracy needs law which is friendly to its people, law which is *known* to be friendly, even neighborly law. The legal profession needs to have the men of commerce think of law and legal work, not as a baffling intricacy of ununderstandable technicality, but as a helpful device which can be seen, directly, to be helpful though safety requires the use of a lawyer's skills in developing its help. The fact that the automobile is a friendly device has not reduced the need for mechanics; it has, on the other hand, increased the service rendered by mechanics. But that has depended on ready availability of the automobile to the public, on the public's understanding enough about it to use it – and so to learn when to consult the mechanic. So with commercial law.

The legal profession itself, moreover, needs a much greater *accessibility* of the base-lines of the semi-permanent portions of commercial law than is as yet available. Important as the work of the Restatement has been, the work lacks at once compactness and authority. One has only to compare a Restatement to a Negotiable Instruments Law to see the difference in their relative authority. One has only to compare one to the Uniform Act sections on documents to title to see the relative power possessed by the latter to clean up at once and for all old confusions on which a Restatement can move only by gentle persuasion. One has only to compare the bulk of an Act and a Restatement to see the advantages possessed by the Act as a filing system for law, and as a device for orientation. The Restatement work, moreover, is work for *lawyers'* consumption. Commercial law requires to be for consumption by commercial men, as well as lawyers. The needed work can profit by what has been done; but it is a separate task.

The Conference is the sole body both small enough and representative enough, both experienced enough and flexible enough, with enough prestige to accomplish that task. And it would crown the Conference's work. . . .

Harmonious arrangement, simplification of language, and thorough rethinking to eliminate all fine distinctions *which prove to have no adequate basis in policy and practice*, can tremendously ease access to commercial law, for lawyer and for layman.

I do not suggest any chasing of that will o' the wisp, 'business law made plain to every layman.' I do suggest that, for instance, the very layman who is today unable to find, anywhere, an exposition intelligible to him of what a 'C.I.F.' quotation will mean to him, can make reasonable sense out of Sections 63 and 59 (3) and (4) of the new Sales draft. He will still need a lawyer, to tell him what the effect will be, of a provision shifting the risk of an advance in freight rates to the buyer; but he will stand a much greater chance of seeing that he needs a lawyer for that purpose and also of understanding what his lawyer tells him. That is gain. I suggest, too, that with such sections to guide, a lawyer can marshall knowledge and thinking about the matter in a fraction of the time needed today. The Conference's greatest achievements along this line have been the 'secondary liability' provisions of the N.I.L., to which reference has been made, together with large portions of the Bills of Lading and Warehouse Receipts Acts.

2. *What Uniform Commercial Acts Do Not Commonly Accomplish*

What our Acts have, however, failed to accomplish, is several-fold.

A. In the first place, being prepared as they had to be, one by one, they have resulted in a wordiness and semi-duplication, and repeatedly in minor discrepancies, which cost labor to work through, and often are tricky. Where such discrepancies rest on needed shadings of policy, they are required; but then the discrepancies should be so gathered that they can be thought about together. Where discrepancies rest on accident or oversight, they need cure.

B. Related, but separate, is the tendency of Uniform Commercial Acts to be drawn as if they were ordinary legislation, and to be drawn *for lawyers*. By this I mean the heaping up of technical language and of qualifications. I speak with conviction of sin: no man working for the Conference has ever produced a more complex piece of wording than the Trust Receipts Act. It has worked well, and has stood up under heavy use; but I can now see that the same work *could* be done by a redrafting which would talk to others than those experts in the field who have been using that Act. What has made that Act work is the high and centralized skill of the counsel who use it. A Code chapter would not thus depend on so specialized a bar.

What is thus illustrated in extreme form in the Trust Receipts Act recurs among the Uniform Commercial Acts at large.

Technical language and complex statement cannot be wholly avoided. But they can be reduced to a minimum. *The essential presupposition of so reducing them is faith in the courts to give reasonable effect to reasonable intention of the language.*

Semi-permanent Acts must envisage and must encourage *development* by the courts.

(1) The first condition of such development is language which is clear as to direction, but which does not undertake too nicely to mark off the *outer* edges of its application. The language of principle, not that of 'rule drawn in derogation', is called for. Language drawn in distrust or anxiety about courts' understanding may accomplish its immediate purpose, but it paves the way with stumbling blocks within a decade.

(2) The second condition of sound development by courts is an *adequate* commentary which guides to the legal material concerned *as a whole*. Much of the over-detail of our Acts have been a device to discount the absence of

such a commentary. The Sales Act has been tremendously helped by having one.

For the fact is that our courts have not the time, in the disposition of single cases, to fathom the handling of a whole field by a whole uniform act or code chapter. They are courts of good will. But they are also courts of general, infinitely varied, jurisdiction, working under severe time pressure on a most heterogeneous assemblage of cases. The bearing of parts of an Act or Code on one another and on the whole the courts are willing to see, glad to see; but counsel do not show that full bearing, and the Conference has not undertaken to show it, either. The Conference has instead attempted to make particular sections do the work. And that means to cripple the long-range growth of the Act.

A commentary is thus an integral part of any thought about a Code.

C. The third thing which our Acts have not yet done, is to recanvass their own work, each in the light of the other and of all experience since the drafting. The very understandable and proper dislike of *Amendment*, however, has no need to stand in the way of *Consolidation*. Nor does redrafting accompanied by adequate statement of purpose have the dangers to fear, of 'implicit change', which accompanies mere redrafting.

At the same time, the preparation of Code chapters offers opportunities which the present Sales draft, for instance, illustrates peculiarly. There were strokes in the original Sales Act which, though thoroughly sound principle, seemed 'dangerously' bold in the climate of opinion thirty-four years ago – 'rescission for breach of warranty', e.g. – but which have proved so eminently satisfactory in general plan that what is now needed is to free them from the trammels which were originally placed on them only to keep them as little 'shocking' as possible. This, in a process of Consolidation, occurs, as of course, on the basis of the experience since the Act.

If one sets the pending Amendments to the Negotiable Instruments Act against such a background, he finds their whole theory to be unwise. They were intended as, and were prepared as, patchwork. But what was not seen as those Amendments were undertaken, and what I did not myself see when the Federal Sales Bill – a job of essentially similar character – appeared on the scene in 1937, was this: That if new sections represent real need, the need extends beyond patching. And, further, that new material is capable by hard work and thought of being *integrated* into an original structure very slightly revised;[4] indeed, that such integration can result in a materially more manageable and accessible whole than either the original Act plus the case-law, or the original Act plus any patchwork, can hope to afford. I submit that the present draft of the Sales Act demonstrates this; and I submit that the patchwork project on the N.I.L. requires to be promptly junked, and that a job like that done on the Sales Act should be undertaken. Both jobs *can* be carried through, as independent projects. Both jobs *should* be envisaged as prospective chapters in a Uniform Commercial Code.

3. *Scope of a Uniform Commercial Code*

The body of law of commerce which rests on a relatively permanent and non-political basis of experience is not a logically coherent body. 'Business Codes', for example, plainly belong in the subject-matter, integrally. Just as plainly, they have no business in a Commercial Code: We have too little experience with their regulation, and there is too much flux in regard to them. 'Business Corporations' belong, in many of their aspects, obviously; no less obviously, the divergent State policies and the unpredictabilities of development dictate their exclusion.

A. The heart of what can be seen as promising a solid field lies in the *movement of goods, the payment therefor, and the financing thereof.* This leads directly to such a line of material as:

Sales
Conditional Sales
Trust Receipts
Chattel Mortgages
Negotiable Paper (short term, and checks)
Current Banking Account: Deposits and Drawings and Collections
Certain Aspects of Contract and Agency affecting the above (cf. Sales Draft, Sec. 65)
Warehouse Receipts
Bills of Lading
Modern Commercial Letters of Credit

B. There would open for consideration a number of immediately related fields:

Short Term Suretyship and Guaranty
Aspects of Finance Company business which serve banking purposes.
Damage in Transit: both as to Carriers and as to 'marine' and 'inland-marine' insurers.
Bulk Sales and Transfers in Fraud
Partnership
Limited Partnership

C. To be avoided are aspects of Trust Law, other than such portions of the Fiduciaries Act as deal with bank deposits, etc., or as play into Trust Receipts.

To be avoided are problems of Small Loans and Small Purchasers ('Consumer Credit'), except as possible complementary material.

D. A serious question goes to the *Market for Securities*, which is often felt to be essentially commercial in character, and which is involved e.g. in the present N.I.L., Stock Transfer Act, and Trust Receipts Act. The answer may well lie in a separate portion of a Code, devoted to those problems. They will be noted to include the regulation of the transactions of Transfer Agents, with important overlaps into the Fiduciary field.

4. *General Procedure in Regard to a Code*

The bodies of material grouped under A have an internal unity and cross-relation which make them a useful initial group to attack. Two of the main bodies of the material concerned, the Conference is already engaged in reconsidering. The body of material is of itself both central, large, highly important, *and a working unit.* Unless it can be worked out to satisfaction, there is no point in tackling the other material mentioned.

The non-success of the Chattel Mortgage Act, together with the relative success of the Trust Receipts Act, point to two other measures of procedure. In the narrow field of Trust Receipts it has been possible not only to enlist support of the Act, and use of it, but to fight off, repeatedly, efforts at un-desirable amendment. The Chattel Mortgage Act, on the other hand, in-cluded some book accounts sections and a trust receipts section which have resulted in a continuously successful lobby against it.

The moral is clear. If matter is controversial, but needs regulation against abuse, and for the interest of harmonious development of the field, then there are two political steps which must go hand in hand with the general drafting job. First, the matter due to elicit opposition must be packed into a separate and separable portion, related and harmonious, but capable of individual act of legislation. Practicability demands severability. Second, there must be undertaken the type of conciliation and splitting of opposition which worked out so happily with Trust Receipts. Practically every field of business contains enough far-sighted, reasonable and public-minded persons in high position, to make this a practicable procedure.

On the other hand, more or less simultaneous work on the related aspects of the general field is highly desirable. Bank Collections and N.I.L. Amend-ments profited hugely from being canvassed together, as Trust Receipts from the Chattel Mortgage work. Trust Receipts were themselves dealt with against a background of prospective regulation of Commercial Letters of Credit and C.I.F. sales contracts, and could not have been handled effec-tively except with attention to these matters. The N.I.L. suffered materially from its divorce from the law of the current banking account, and from the law of collection.

Finally, another point of procedure is to be stressed. It is my firm belief that the putting of any Uniform Commercial Act into the form of a Code Chapter or part thereof cannot wisely be entrusted to the draftsman of the Act itself. That draftsman can be of tremendous assistance; but the revision of an Act is like operation on a child, and an outside surgeon's hand and judgment will prove steadier.

[5. Particular Procedure omitted.]

K. N. Llewellyn

STUDY OF UNIFORM COMMERCIAL CODE

STATEMENT TO THE LAW REVISION COMMISSION BY PROFESSOR KARL N. LLEWELLYN

A Simple Case on Behalf of the Code

When the New York Law Revision Commission, on behalf of the State of New York, undertook examination of the proposed Uniform Commercial Code, the Commission assumed a duty rare in our history. First and most, it had a truly judicial responsibility for fairness in both procedure and judgment. Second, it had a further-than-judicial responsibility. This latter was based upon long decades of careful inquiry by the Law Revision Commission into needed changes in the law, decades of skilled and impartial work which led to the choice of this Commission as the body to report upon the value of adopting the Uniform Commercial Code in New York. This second responsibility involved not only what judges can give: full and advertised hearings; it involved much more than that. The Commission's second responsibilty went into a whole world of independent gathering of material, and into independent research on a scale hardly matched even in its own path-finding studies on "Consideration", and went, in addition, into reducing results to available form.

With the Uniform Commercial Code, however, the New York Law Revision Commission approached for the first time a profound piece of legislation which had already received the benefit of ten years of expert study, labor and critique; of sustained section by section consideration in draft after successive draft, by two such bodies as the American Law Institute and that same Conference of Commissioners on Uniform State Laws which had produced the whole body of older uniform commercial acts which the Code will displace; the benefit of consultation and criticism by informed representatives of industry after industry and group upon group occupied in various areas of commerce or of commercial finance; and the general critique of bar association committees and of an extraordinary number of independent legal experts. What came before the New York Law Revision Commission for study was the result of all of this, backed by the strong and increasing approval of an overwhelming majority of those who had given careful study either to the Code as a whole or to specialized parts thereof.

It is against this background that the New York Law Revision

Commission did its work. With obvious wisdom, the Commission took the proponents' case as made, in major part, by history. The Commission called for objections and for adverse criticisms first, and what was heard first or presented first by memoranda was objections and adverse comment. In the limited time available—limited, despite the number of hearings—proponents of the Code had of necessity to devote most of their attention to showing the inaccuracy or unwisdom or unimportance of hollow objections put forward as solemnly as if they had body and value.

In the proceedings before the New York Law Revision Commission itself, this procedure caused no loss of perspective. The Commission was well along in its own independent and exhaustive study of the Uniform Commercial Code and of the case in favor of the Code. It had and used a full battery of independent resources to judge of the accuracy of the allegations of such witnesses as misstated the law. To the New York Law Revision Commission itself the positive case for the Uniform Commercial Code as a whole did not need to be made orally or by memorandum at the hearings themselves, because that Commission had already studied the proponents' case as made by the Code itself, its official Comments, its history, and the voluminous literature that has appeared over the years. What was needed before the New York Law Revision Commission was at no time and on no issue any opening statement for the proponent; what was needed was at most a brief reminder in summation.

When, however, the remarkable and extended proceedings before the New York Law Revision Commission go in published form before the country at large, it is respectfully submitted that the situation completely changes.

No new reader of these proceedings can be expected to know the Code. No reader can be expected to know the case for the Code. No reader can be expected to spot inaccuracies in regard to business fact or in regard to existing law; or even in regard to provisions of the Code itself, as such inaccuracies appear in the light-hearted language of so many of the adverse witnesses or memoranda.

Least of all can any reader, from the proceedings as they stand (to mention a few matters) be expected to gather any picture, even any inkling, of the utter multitude of details, unmentioned anywhere in the proceedings, in which the Uniform Commercial

Code will clarify confused present law, or clear away an existing mess, or settle a point now full of doubt, or simplify an unnecessary complexity, or accomplish a narrow but needed piece of modernization in the manner and tradition of the New York Law Revision Commission itself.

But without some inkling of such matters no perspective is possible. The result would be like examining the condition of a business by listening to an allegation of large numbers of alleged liabilities, one by one (totalling a possible hundred thousand dollars) with heavy discussion of whether any single one of the items is a real liability—while ten millions of assets go completely unmentioned.

As the Chief Draftsman ("Reporter") of the Uniform Commercial Code and as Chairman throughout its production of the Section on Uniform Commercial Acts which in months of sittings combed and revised each portion of the work before any such portion could come, in any draft, to the floor of the Conference of Commissioners, I beg leave to insert into this public edition of the proceedings some brief opening statements for the Code's proponents. The statements are inadequate, they are above all hopelessly incomplete. But they will do a little to enable the reader who has *not* first studied the Code to get some idea of the ten million dollar asset side before his attention is drawn off onto forty-nine or eighty-nine questions of the character of whether some one $27.50 item of February 17—or was it March 2?—was ever ordered, was ever delivered, was up to contract, has already been paid for, or by some accident represents one correct charge—of $27.50.

SOME REASONS FOR ADOPTING THE UNIFORM COMMERCIAL CODE

A. Because of Who Backs the Code

In the entire discussion of the Uniform Commercial Code not one person has appeared (outside of Louisiana) who has not applauded the Uniform Commercial Acts as being at least each in its own day a sound job, a wise job, and a useful job. These Uniform Commercial Acts were prepared for the country by the National Conference of Commissioners on Uniform State Laws. They were prepared one by one, in the period ranging from 1895 through 1934. These Acts include the Negotiable Instruments Law, the Uniform Sales Act, the Uniform Warehouse Receipts Act (in partnership with the Warehousemen's Association), the Uniform Bills of Lading Act, the Uniform Stock Transfer Act, the Uniform Trust Receipts Act. The National Conference of Commissioners— the members are officials appointed by the several States to prepare uniform laws—has also spent many sessions in work over piecemeal amendments, in sustained efforts to modernize the old Acts without changing their framework; and it has spent many, many sessions on problems of chattel security and of bank collection.

This is the body, with this now sixty-year record of careful work, with this record of unchallenged success whenever its product has been put to the test of being *enacted law at work*—this is the body which has prepared and which now stands behind the Uniform Commercial Code—a Code over which the Conference, beginning in 1940, worked for more than ten years before the appearance of even a first tentative final draft. What reason can there be for believing that this great law-preparing body has so changed its nature as to have lost either the competence or the wisdom demonstrated by its record? No single person, since discussion of the Code began, has suggested *any* reason for thinking that the skill which built the old Acts is not with us still, in modern form. No man has dared to!

This is the Conference which backs the Code with knowledge of it, and after years of labor over it and with it, and with enthusiasm.

The Conference of Commissioners on Uniform State Laws is not alone in this. A partnership was formed in 1943 between that Conference and the leading productive law-organization of these United States, the American Law Institute, the organization which had produced, by its own slow, sure and carefully tested methods, the famed Restatement of the Law. The Institute had previously left out of its labors the whole field of commercial law, as being a field already occupied, magnificently occupied, by the Conference.

In 1943 the two organizations put into partnership, in order to produce the Uniform Commercial Code, their resources, their slowly built-up know-how, their manpower. The American Law Institute also backs the Uniform Commercial Code. It also does so after years of labor with and over that Code.

B. *Because of How the Code was Built*

Article by Article there was one draftsman, or a team of two, preparing, presenting, revising. The drafter's work was under steady criticism and revision, typically in three-day sessions every six to ten weeks, by a group of advisors which included experts in the field of law concerned, experts in the field of business or finance concerned, and also lawyers or judges of general experience and *no* expertness whose important business was to see that it all made sense and that each part could be understood by men who were *not* experts. Results of any meeting were worked over, tested out, and brought in again for any misguess to be gone over afresh. There was constant correspondence and consultation with any outside experts in the business or law concerned who could be discovered and who would give the time. At all times the central planning and drafting staff were in on the drafting; in also on the discussions, to keep continuity, to add their own experience and expertness, and to keep the gears of the whole Code meshed; in on the presentations, to assure any group or floor that this was not only a whole-job but a whole-team job.

Each year's work (sometimes each half-year's) came for review in two- to four-day sessions before each of two singularly able general reviewing bodies : the Commercial Acts (or the Property Acts) Section of the Conference, each a group of 11 notable for its experienced down-to-earth practicing lawyer's approach to the text of any proposed law, and the Council of the Institute, a group of 30 notable especially for the membership of a large number of able judges who size up any proposed law as a court would. Only as the text of the year's work was shaped up by these bodies did it come to the floors of the organizations.

Floor discussion was again in detail, section by section, with the sustained attention of experienced lawyers from every section of the country, always including men who had represented various diverse interests, men of long experience in the details concerned, plus a most valuable range of men who had had one such case, or two or three (in the net an astounding range of experience), with many men also directing their attention in one large part to whether the text made general sense, and could be easily read. At this point let two further things be said : (a) The floor *worked,* in these sessions, over all the years. They gave attention, they followed text and debate, they did solid thinking. (b) Few votes, in any early stage, were 'binding,' save where the underlying plan of some piece of the work had to be determined. 'Suggestion' or 'recommendation for study' was the type of action. The work of one year's floor was thus *as a standard practice reviewed the next year,* after testing in between by the staff, by the advisors, by the Sections of the Conference, by the Council of the Institute.

As the work moved toward completion, it came further under the due attention and fire of critics of all kinds : experts from the law schools, representative committees of interested industries or other groups, bar association committees concerned peculiarly with the effect on the law of their particular State, and the like. All suggestions were worked over, often in detailed discussions which led to solutions of increased value and to satisfaction to all concerned.

This process of critique, and occasionally of real improvement in minor detail, has gone on even after the Code had come into seemingly final form.

Two things are notable about it :

(1) The criticisms which have proved to have bite have touched a very small portion of the Code indeed. In regard to any single area of the present law, the clear improvements made by the Code outnumber and outweigh between twentyfold and a hundredfold such minor errors as have been brought to light by even certain bitter chasers after error. And each real error or even semi-error which has been turned up *has been duly cured.*

(2) The men who have tested the Code in use and for use, by running it against the problems of a law course or against the problems of a daily practice : these men have become vigorous proponents of the Code. The men who have studied it carefully have found their study turning them into enthusiasts. Doubts vanish like haze on a summer morning.

The type of use-testing just referred to builds a foundation of peculiar confidence. Because a kit of tools, whether of rules of law or of anything else, if it is either ill-designed or ill-chosen turns up not only an occasional bug on the things in mind, but also an antheap of bugs on any job not consciously planned for. Whereas a well-designed and well-chosen kit of tools will handle in unplanned comfort any number of unforeseen jobs which may turn up.

The Code has proven, *in sharp contrast to the existing law,* to be a good and well-designed kit of legal tools.

In sum: a more carefully and fully *tested* piece of legislation has never been presented in these United States.

C. Because of Why it was Necessary to Build the Code

For a free economy, for soundly developing American enterprise and competition, it is of the essence that the rules of the game should be as simple as possible, and that those rules of the game should be readily known to all.

The first and best reason for the Code is that the law which governs our commerce and commercial finance is *substantially unknown to most lawyers,* whether they need to know it or not, and is almost wholly unknown to most business men.

The business men do not know even when they need to consult a lawyer. One major job which the old Uniform Commercial Acts did do was to cut down, so far as they went, the unknown character of the law by reducing parts of it to relatively clear language, easy to find. And that was both good and even then badly needed. It showed the way.

But first, those Acts covered much less than half of the most needed ground; and next, their text has now come to be overlaid by a mass of case-law which is almost as difficult to work through as was the law before those Acts; and again, new conditions have opened up new problems which in turn present new areas of unknown (or non-existent and therefore unknowable) law.

Law unknown is law which is uncomfortable, and which is expensive, and which is uncertain—and, which is indeed unfair. Important *general* areas of law have no business to be the monopoly of a relatively few experts, serving a relatively few clients. Business and finance are matters vital to all American enterprise, be that enterprise large or small, be it rural or metropolitan; sound, clear, legal advice at a reasonable rate is good for American business and finance: how else is competition to be fair and free? Such advice reduces risks, it reduces disputes, it makes for quick and fair adjustment.

Such advice, necessary to a free-running economy, cannot be had when the law is unknown or is hard to uncover or is confused when found. That difficulty the Code cures to a degree and on a scale hitherto almost unmatched in American law.

The fact that the law of commerce and commercial law is unknown did not become clear to me as a person until work on the Code had long begun; it took contacts on the subject with two thousand and more lawyers to really awaken me. But the fact itself is demonstrated independently by Mentschikoff and by Israels at this Commission's hearings on the Code as a whole held May 24, 25, 1954.

Yet, interestingly, that fact is not *historically* one of the reasons for undertaking the Code. No person associated with the undertaking had at the outset any remotest suspicion of how deep, how widespread was ignorance of our commercial law among both our bar and our business community; still less did any man have suspicion of how much of the 'knowledge' of many 'experts' was smug, flat ignorance—ignorance dangerous also to their clients. Yet the great fact of policy remains: if American enterprise is to develop as a free economy, then the rules of the game must be known, and they must therefore be made readily knowable. They must be made as simple (though adequate) and also as easy to know, as the best legal engineering can make them. That the Code does. That the present law does *not* do, in New York or any other of our States.

Thus, regardless of the history, the result is clear: With the Code, the law of commerce and commercial finance becomes relatively quick to find, to understand, and to use. This is a typical example of the point made above about the unplanned values of good tools.

The actual historical reasons for undertaking the Code have their own further and independent powerful punch.

(a) Much of the law, whether embodied in the original Uniform Commercial Acts or not, has become outmoded as the nature of business, of technology, and of financing has changed. Such law needs to be brought up to date.

(b) Akin to this is the continuing presence in the law of a large number of technical traps which can—in an era of bad times or in a situation of bad feeling—be used in bad faith to do outrage. These need cure.

(c) Both in areas of growth outside the old Uniform Acts and in wide troubling areas within them there is much case-law which is in conflict as between States and in confusion even within a State. These matters need to be cleared up.

(d) The existing law presents two lines of problems which involve one most needed quality : to wit, the best that we can do in regard to making law simple. On the one hand, we have areas in which almost unbelievable and almost utterly useless complexity has come since the first Elizabeth's time to make our transactions dubious and expensive. Here the Code has cut in clean (and with almost universal approval) to make 'Chattel Security,' in Article 9, an area that any thoughtful lawyer—not merely the veteran of many decades—can, under the Code, deal with in the course of his ordinary practice. The Code has eliminated the endlessly ragged-edged detailed difference between such institutions as conditional sale, chattel mortgage, trust receipt, and the like; the Code provides for any financier, in any financing which calls for security in movables or in intangibles, a legal machinery usefully stream-lined and well backed by people who really know the present law *and who therefore back the Code.*

On the other hand, the case-law welter of the existing law can sometimes point up clearly how *not* to make law, wherever simplicity has been sought by way of some mere *word-formula which does not fit the situation and the situation's set of problems.* The effort to settle questions between seller and buyer by way of the 'simple' idea of 'transfer of title' has, *e.g.,* led to unending uncertainty and confusion, and to frequent injustice. Equally, the effort to throw into a single basket the hugely varied situations generally classed as 'good faith purchase for value' has led again and again either to plain injustice or to the court's jumping whatever traces were sought to be imposed upon it—with a resulting complete uncertainty.

Where operation and results are today scrambled and unreliable even though the word-formula *looks* simple, then what is needed is to re-examine the problems and the material and to come out with language which *really fits the need.* This the Code has done in regard to 'good faith purchase for value,' and in regard to the questions between seller and buyer.

On the other hand, when useless complexity strews the path of work with thorns and traps, the Code's job has been to make things simpler, guiding action, giving safety. Article 9 illustrates this.

All of the above calls for re-examination and revision of commercial rules of law. But why in the form of a Code? In the first

place, experience has shown wide and unhappy gaps to exist between the existing Acts. Secondly, prior work over any type of
reform has turned up repeated problems which leaped across the
'boundaries' of the traditional 'fields' of law. Sound revision
anywhere proved to call for thinking through and for testing out
the bearings on all other sectors, even where the results then
proved to show no need for changing one piece in order to fit
better with another. (Such thinking through would never have
occurred save in the process of a whole-job. It gives partial guaranty on a point easy to overlook: that omissions from the Code
have also been checked for.)

Meanwhile the way and degree to which the revision demanded
large-scale work which *did* result in large-scale change can be
seen in quick illustration if one thinks about the (no longer uniform) Negotiable Instruments Law: plainly that law paid almost
no attention to payment-paper, to checks in process of being used
as 'the float' of payment and collection; the NIL's concept of
transfer, etc. was directed to credit paper—especially the note.
To revise such a statute into adaptation to modern conditions
required frequently a very different body of rules from those
proper to the transfer of credit paper. These revised rules have
become the Code's Article 4 on Bank Collections. But again, the
credit aspect on which the NIL is centered is the aspect of short
term paper: the note. Bonds have long been a constant worry
and disturbance. But to sever out investment paper for its needed
treatment without including the other major type of investment
paper, the certificate of stock, would make nonsense: hence Article
8 on Investment Securities.

Already one has here the subject-matter of half a Code. The
case is typical.

The Code, therefore, calls for adoption as an integrated whole,
whose parts supplement, support, mutually affect and balance
one another.

D. Because of How Much the Code Brings into Clear Form, Easy to Find

If all that the Uniform Commercial Code had done had been to
bring together, sort out, modernize and harmonize the old Uniform
Commercial Acts, together with a Bulk Sales Act and a new and
uniform version of the old laws on accounts receivable, and the
like—if that had been all the Code did, it still would be a tre-

mendously worthwhile job. This might be overlooked, because just as executives tend to underrate their secretaries, so do lawyers tend to underrate the provision—by somebody else—of a good filing system in the law. A good *statutory* filing system, moreover, runs free of any prejudices of any staff of any publisher: the framework is just there. Hence, even if this had been all, I find myself blind to why any person should do other than be glad to find the scattered patches of the older statutes made into a quilt that we can use. And the value of testing each single piece of law in any 'field' against the whole problem of movement of goods, and of financing the production and movement, and of payment and collection, has already been mentioned. Law that has grown by fits and starts and often enough by accident does need this kind of testing every fifty years.

But the Code does much more. The Code does not merely bring to suppliers from all over the nation *one* Bulk Sales Law instead of who-knows-how-many; it brings, in Article 6, the *best* which long experience has suggested. The Code does not merely make sure that a decision about transfer of a bill of lading will be indexed so that persons interested in transfer of warehouse receipts can find the decision—the Code also clears up doubts which have proved troublesome and provides (as with realization in case of mercantile storage) stream-lined procedures which do the job better than the present law.

And the Code really *covers* the commercial field in a way in which no present statute does. It is so queer to find no single one of the Code's opponents mentioning this fact. Where the present law is blank or else confused or else in conflict, the Code moves in, with competence based on net experience, to provide one single and very reasonable answer, which is so much more clear than the existing law that if a counsellor or business man really knew how unclear the existing law is *in the case of pinch,* he ought to be hailing the Code, again, for this cause alone. For it is true that even bad rules can be worked with (though unhappily) if they are rules clear to everyone, and if they are rules known or knowable to all. On rules clearly known, as Mr McCloy has soundly testified, a soundly free-running American economy depends. The Uniform Commercial Code provides such rules.

The present law does not provide the rules which Mr McCloy calls for as being necessary.

If you have any doubt, ask yourself or your client or your lawyer any one of the following questions under the present law. They are questions which any one can match by the hundred.

(a) You receive a 'check' 'payable through' another bank: can you become a holder in due course?

(b) You invite bids, for the known purpose of preparing your own bid, and you get a 'firm' sub-bid. Can you rely on it?

(c) You have what you think to be all the necessary papers, but the transfer agent wants more, and you are pressed for time. Can you force registration of transfer?

This is the kind of unnoticed thing which the Code *covers,* in one detail after another upon another, *for the effective guidance of any lawyer or businessman or financier.* The existing law does not.

Indeed, when one settles down to saying how much more the Uniform Commercial Code includes to guide the action of a commercial lawyer or of a business man or banker, it is queerly interesting how little of the huge new, rather clean, coverage fits into any big chunks with names. Of course there is the whole, freshly stated basic law of letters of credit, Article 5, approved, on my first hand information, by the relevant bankers and legal counsel of interested banking institutions in Boston, Chicago, New York, Philadelphia and San Francisco. There is the bothersome field of that 'open-term' type of sales contract which looks more to continuing business relations than to the fixed shifting of a market risk : a field covered by the Code in full accord with business need and understanding, and so much welcomed by lawyers such as the counsel for Bethlehem Steel. And there are other 'big-blocks' such as 'foreign terms,' so welcome to men like Wilbert Ward of the National City Bank of New York, and to the leaders of our import and export trade. There is in particular the making clear and stream-lining of the whole law of chattel security. There is also the very useful matter of simplifying and giving teeth to the rights of persons who need transfer of investment securities on the books.

And so on, throughout the Code. The opponents do not seem to understand a balance-sheet.

Meantime there is, here in the Uniform Commercial Code the heaping up, the bulking up, the towering up, in those hardly countable, those hardly observable, filing details which the Code—

without anybody mentioning or even suggesting any single detail
—proceeds to provide as seashells are provided on a seashore.

What do I do, *in any pitch,* if the bill or note is maybe not
'negotiable'? (About three hundred scattered and unfindable cases
handled clearly in one section.)

What do I do, *in any pinch,* when the draft carries a 'referee
in case of need'? (You find a case!)

What am I to do, *in any pinch,* with a check which comes in
among a hundred—or thousand—check batch, but is indorsed by
my correspondent's depositor "for acct," if I begin to worry
about my correspondent, which carries its account with me? (See
Soma v. Handrulis, 277 N.Y. 223 and see Memorandum by Professor Mentschikoff on 'good faith and commercial standards' in
re Article 3.

Or: to shift to the more commercial end: If my delivery is
off by a hair, can he, *in any pinch,* reject it?

Or: If I am a buyer: You mean I should pay a ten percent
advance, and then when I reject good goods I get a lien, and then
I can keep them out from his re-inspection and resell them to
make evidence of deficiency, and then ... ?? You mean ... ?

Under the present law, such things raise doubts or dangers.
Under existing law, they are tough. Under existing law, they are
either wide open or plain trouble, each, and all, and many more.

*The Uniform Commercial Code cuts down the doubts, and cuts
them down wisely, on literally hundreds of such things.*

*The friends of the Code have come to take that for granted.
They hardly mention it.*

But what is rather surprising, if you examine the attacks made
on the Code before the New York Law Revision Commission, is
the quiet and queer *assumption made by the attacks themselves:*

(a) that the Code is full of such unmentioned values;

(b) that only detail remains to be attacked; and, finally,

(c) that only by trying to distract attention from the Code's
huge and pervading merits is there any hope of keeping it from
its mission of helping business and banking and the country.

In sum, the Code gathers into a form quick and easy to find,
and to understand, and to use:

(1) the full subject-matter of all the present Uniform Commercial Acts, from the Negotiable Instruments Law through the

Sales and Warehouse Receipts and Stock Transfer Acts on into the Trust Receipts Act; and

(2) the full subject-matter of the related commercial acts: Bulk Transfer, Bank Collection, Factors, Accounts Receivable, and the like; and

(3) the judicial decisions which have come to overlie, obscure or supplement any of these statutes; and

(4) whole areas thus far left to scattered and often troubled case-law—such as open-term contracts, letters of credit, documentary collections, non-negotiable bills and notes, transfer on the books of stock and registered bonds, field warehouse rights, foreign trade terms; and especially

(5) literally *hundreds* of detailed matters spotted through the whole field of commercial law and finance which under our unhappy existing law still mean doubt or trouble to counsel and to operator.

And the solutions offered, in all of this, are wise solutions.

E. Because of the Nature of the Code Material

As compared with the existing law in New York or any other state:

(1) What the Code says is relatively clear. *The existing law is doubtful or empty throughout almost the whole area discussed by the Code's opponents.*

(2) What the Code says fits with modern business and finance. Where it changes existing law, the existing law will stand— if it gets appealed to, as it does in bad times—in the way of sense, and some honest operator will get stuck.

(3) What the Code says makes for fairness. Where it changes existing law it is where the existing law, as so often, makes trouble or sets traps for people who are acting in business good faith.

(4) What the Code says makes it relatively easy to set up transactions with fairness and with safety. Under the existing law this is a hard job, and unless a business or financing man happens by accident to draw an ace of counsel as he cuts the legal deck, the business man runs unnecessary risk or he incurs unnecessary expense, or both.

(5) What the Code says leads to relative simplicity plus safety, in action. No informed person can fairly claim any such thing for the existing law of New York or of any other State.

In sum: The Code makes business and financing sense. The

existing law makes neither, and is sought to be avoided by the commercial community by drafting (never wholly trustworthy, always expensive) and by arbitration (never wholly trustworthy, and in times of real hardship, a bending reed to lean on).

How can any honest critic, seriously, and for the supposed reading of intelligent persons, attack even a small portion of the Code without making clear the unbelievably awful condition of the existing commercial law which the Code so greatly improves?

F. The Code, although both large and new, is unbelievably easy to use

Never in American history has any statute, much less a large one such as the Code, been presented to bench, bar and public in form *so easy* and *so safe* for any man to use.

Accompanying the Code statutory sections are comments—the use of which is explicitly authorized by the Code itself—comments which give useful indication of the purposes of the section, and which do more: they cross-refer to almost everything else in the Code which bears upon the section in hand; they give clear cross-reference to the definition of any word of art whatever which the section may contain. To this add a thing: the captions of the sections have been worked over for years in order to make sure that they contain catchwords which will index all of the substance of any section.

If that were all, it would be enough to make use of this new Code easier than use of any ordinary, short, and simple statute.

But that is not all.

The job of the lawyer is not only to find the law; *the job of the lawyer goes on into the using of the law.*

The Uniform Commercial Code is a Code for use, not merely for the decision of rows over transactions which have gone dead, rows between one-time partners-in-enterprise who have become fighting enemies.

The Uniform Commercial Code comes, as no statute has ever come to these United States before, 'furnished.' The American Law Institute, and the Pennsylvania bankers, for example—with other outfits in full swing to follow—have put out *booklets which show what to do* under the Code, and how to do it.

You will have a hard time finding, anywhere, or at any price, equivalent advice as to how to handle your commercial or commercial financing transactions under the existing law of any State in these United States. You will indeed. *But the Code and the books which come with it make this whole branch of law right here and now a branch for every lawyer's easy use.*

G. Because the gains from the Code outweigh even uniformity

Suppose some other State, or thirty-seven other States, get chased into non-adoption of the Uniform Commercial Code. *It still is worth adoption* by any State large or small, 'commercial' or 'non-commercial.'

The proof of that has lain, now these ten years, in the law school classroom.

Present the Code to your class, and because it makes rather simple sense, they get it with three to four times the speed with which they 'get' the 'ordinary' law of any of the subject matter. With that background, they then proceed with equal speed to 'get' the ordinary law, in supplement and in comparison.

No lawyer in a Code State will ever have difficulty dealing with, or indeed in outmanoeuvring, his intellectual equal from an old-fashioned State. The Code State lawyer is—even in cross-State transactions—on the inside, looking out. He can hit, in quiet confidence, from an understanding which only about eighteen present experts in these United States can match.

At home, meanwhile, he has simpler, more workable, and fairer law.

Such is a preliminary case for the Uniform Commercial Code.

It is queer to watch the opponents chasing the mirror techniques around, each 'point' reflected from subcommittee to subcommittee and back and back again until it seems almost as if $27.50 (a doubtful charge to begin with) had become $2,750,000.00 with more to come. The assets side being, of course, always and still unmentioned.

But the assets side is solid. It is vital. It is great. And, *piece by piece,* inch by inch, section by section, *it* bears the scrutiny and study of any honest man.

KARL N. LLEWELLYN,
August 16, 1954.

Appendix F

The Pueblo Codes

The documents that follow may be of particular interest to those who are concerned with the recording, restatement or reform of tribal law especially where it survives within a 'modern' legal system. Llewellyn was invited to draft codes for three Pueblos: Zia, Santo Domingo and Santana. As far as I have been able to ascertain only one Pueblo, Santana, in fact formally adopted Llewellyn's draft code and it is doubtful if it was ever fully operative. The first document, which is addressed to 'White lawyers', throws some light on Llewellyn's conception of what he was doing. The second document, which is in the nature of a preamble or explanatory memorandum is a good example of Llewellyn's style in addressing the Pueblos. The excerpts from the draft code for the Santanas are taken from the General part and from the 'Bill of Rights'. The code contained less than one hundred sections, divided into eight parts.

(i) INTRODUCTORY NOTE ON PUEBLO CODES, FOR WHITE LAWYERS[1]

A Pueblo Code is written against a background of effective, working 'Common Law' of the Pueblo. A written provision is not like a statute which stands on its language alone (as does the act of a legislature which is intended to change the common law rule); it is more like the principle laid down in a well-reasoned leading decision, to be applied or extended in terms of its underlying reason, and the people who feel and know that reason are the men of the Pueblo Council.

Hence, when one puts down in English written rules for a Pueblo, one has to forget a good deal of his American legal technique. There are provisions in Sections 12 and 14, for instance, which on an American book of statutes or ordinances might well be just disregarded as being merely 'directory'. But in a Pueblo each provision has teeth, given by the background. Disrespect to an officer is an offense, a sort of contempt of office reminding one half of contempt of court, half of 'disrespect' inside the military establishment. But the insulted Pueblo officer does not punish by himself; he needs his court to advise, and, in the event of his personal grievance getting in the way, to moderate. Again, if the Pueblo officer fails to behave according to his office, the provision is not 'merely directory'. His staff will call him in for rebuke, and the rebuke can bite. But it would not, in a Pueblo Code, be seemly to set this down. Everybody knows that it can happen, how it is done, and that it will be done. But set it down in written words, for people of the Pueblo to contemplate, is as unseemly as to set down, for the Supreme Court of a State or of these United States, the manner in which proper judicial behavior is to be achieved, if some judge should start getting out of hand.

It is against this background that a Pueblo Court's interpretation of a Pueblo Code is to be read and understood. Reason and purpose of a provision are vital; machinery for enforcement is present and implicit; and the Pueblo common law supplements all provisions.

K. N. Llewellyn

(ii) DRAFT PREAMBLE FOR A CODE FOR THE PUEBLO OF ZIA[2]

It is well for our younger men to know our law. It is well for our older men and our younger men to agree about our law. It is not good to wait until trouble comes up before our law becomes clear to all. This is our law:

To hold membership and rights in this Pueblo, the member must do his community duties. The duties are known to everyone. Everyone is responsible for doing them. When the Governor cries in the plaza that there is spring ditch work three weeks or a month beforehand, or the War Captain cries in the plaza that there is plastering of public buildings two days beforehand, it is the duty of every one to know and report. We all know it is coming. We have waited to hear. Ours is a little pueblo; in three minutes any man can walk from any house to any other house.

In regard to the duties of peace, of not assaulting another member with a stock or a hand or a word, we have been trained, all of us, since we could talk. In regard to the duties of right conduct, of hard work, of respect to the people and respect to our officers, we have been trained since we could talk.

It is not the practice of our pueblo to put on any offender at any time the full penalty which the law makes possible. But the power is there to do that, when the good of the pueblo makes it necessary. Nineteen times out of twenty, the courts of this pueblo stay far inside the penalty which they have the power to order; half of the time the courts of this pueblo are content to make an offender swear on his knees that he will give up bad things and be a right member of the pueblo.

But when our courts fail to put the full penalty on an offender, or fail to go after an offender, that does not mean under our customary law that the offense is forgotten or washed out. It means that in the judgment of the court, or of the officers of the year, that there was more hope for the man and for the pueblo if things were made easy that time. Our officers know how to go easy some times; our officers also know how to wait. This often helps bring an offender to right ways.

These are all right parts of the customary law of our pueblo.

When a man just seems to forget his duties, it is the custom of this pueblo to warn him and advise him; and if he is within reach, he may be warned and advised several times, when he looks like a man who is likely to be reformed.

But when a man *refuses* to perform his duties, that tells his intention for all the future. It is then for the officers to decide whether to warn and advise him, and how often to do that. The man knows his duty. To 'forget' too often says 'I won't'.

It is the law and policy of this pueblo to recognize control and the right of control by parents over children. This is a question not of age, but of birth. Under our law children do not grow up to years in which they are free, without consent of their living parents. A widow of sixty-five, on her death bed, has still the power to say which of her thirty- or forty-year-old sons shall be head of the family and family-trustee of family property.

The law and policy of this pueblo show how great is the reliance of this pueblo on the right education of future members by the parents of the young. It is the parents who are relied on to raise the young in right ways, in ways of hard-working duty and clean living, in ways of quiet and peace with all of our close-living neighbors, in ways of respect for our constituted officers and institutions. It is a matter of shame if a child who has gotten into trouble requires to be advised not by the parents alone, but by the officers and the Council. Therefore, any conflict between the advice and commands of parents and the ways of this pueblo and the commands of its constituted officers, is a conflict which this pueblo cannot have. Such conflict cannot be permitted to continue.

Therefore, again, under the law and policy of this pueblo, if parents either leave the pueblo voluntarily or are expelled, the children must lose membership at the same time and by the same fact. Expulsion never happens quickly. It is a last resort, for peace and good order. Membership, even by birth, cannot continue when the relationship of birth itself produces a conflict in duties which the pueblo cannot have within it.

But if, when a member with children leaves or is expelled, that member gives up parental rights over children, then the case is different. Such rights can be surrendered to a responsible member of this pueblo in good standing, if the children are young; or, if the child is old enough to have judgment of his own, such rights can be surrendered by the parent to the child, by consent of the parent.

A child born into this pueblo, but taken out by a parent, remains in the eyes of the pueblo a child to be desired as a member, if that child ever desires to be readmitted. As in any other case of new admission, the Council must be careful. . . . It is not the policy of this pueblo to make children suffer for the faults of their parents; but it is the policy to make sure that its members have grown up with the respect and understanding for its officers and its laws and ways which this close community requires for its work together.

(iii) EXCERPTS FROM PUEBLO CODE OF LAW AND ORDER FOR SANTANA PUEBLO[3]

PART I. General Rules about this Code

(1) *The writing and intention control, so far as they go*

(a) This Code is intended to put down in writing some things which every officer and member of this Pueblo should know in regard to the authority and duties of officers and the duties of members inside the Pueblo and outside.

(b) This Code controls any case which falls within the language or intention of any rule stated in the Code.

(2) *This Code is not complete, and customary law is still in force, and cases of the same kind should be treated in the same way.*

It is understood that this Code does not cover fully and completely all the powers of the officers or all the duties of members or all the rights between members or families of this Pueblo. Therefore,

(a) Unwritten customary law is still in force in this Pueblo except where this Code or the Council has laid down a rule in writing.

(b) Unwritten customary law can be applied and interpreted by the Council to fit any new cases or conditions as new cases or conditions may arise.

(c) What has been done in any case is to be carefully considered in any later case of the same kind, and it is justice to do the same thing in the later case unless there is good reason for taking different action. Where different action is taken, the good reason for taking different action should be made clear.

(3) *The Council has the final say, and interprets according to the spirit and purpose of any rule.* In any case of doubt about the meaning of this Code or of an unwritten customary rule it is for the Council, when duly called, to decide

what rule applies and what the rule means in the case. The Council's duty is to decide according to the fair spirit and purpose of the rule, according to its heart. Written words are a guide and key to get at the heart.

(4) *General purpose of Code.* The general purpose of this Code is right and peaceful life in this Pueblo, and good faith and fairness in all dealings by officers and members of this Pueblo.

PART II. Powers, Rights and Duties of Officers

(11) ⁴ *An officer's duty is to the whole Pueblo.* Any officer who has a power or a right has a duty to the Pueblo to use his power or his right to help the whole Pueblo. Any officer has a duty to work for the whole Pueblo and a duty to put out of his mind his own interest and his own family or clan or society or kiva or friends and any other thing which might make him forget his duty to the whole Pueblo. The purpose of having officers is to have right government, and for right government it is needed that officers shall work only for the whole Pueblo. That is one reason why every officer is entitled to respect from every member of the Pueblo. Soldiers and veterans must respect the officers just as any other member of the Pueblo must.

(12) *Insulting or interfering with officers*

(a) An officer of this Pueblo has a duty to be slow to take offense, even if he is insulted. He must keep his dignity. The Pueblo is in his hands.

(b) The Governor or Lieutenant Governor, War Captain or Lt. War Captain, Fiscale or Lt. Fiscale, Ditch-boss or Lt. Ditch-boss, if he is insulted or interfered with in the exercise of his authority, has power to arrest the person who has insulted or interfered with him and hold that person for trial. The officer has a duty to have a trial within a reasonable time not more than (five) days from the arrest.

(13) *Purpose of Punishment; forgiveness of offense.* In regard to any offense against this Pueblo the duty of an officer is to correct the offender and to turn him into a good and right member if he can. This is the purpose of all punishment in this Pueblo. An officer or a court can forgive offenses that fall within the power of that officer or court whenever forgiveness seems to the officer to be the right way to help the offender become a good and decent citizen. But where the wrong done is also a wrong to a person or family, and damages are claimed, the damages can be forgiven only with consent of the person who has been wronged.

(14) *Respect to officer.* An officer in the exercise of his duty must always be listened to and spoken to with respect.

(15) *Where an officer's power reaches inside the Pueblo.* An officer's power in the exercise of his office covers any member of this Pueblo in any place on the reservation except a private house and covers a person in a private house in case of emergency or in case the officer has been duly invited to enter to exercise his authority. Once an officer has been invited into a house all his authority comes with him.

Note explaining Part IV, Bill of Rights

At the present time, it has become clear that the Pueblos have need for a strong government which will stand up under any kind of attack in the white courts.

The white courts have grown up in a tradition. No part of that tradition is deeper or more deeply felt than the idea that no government is a *right* and *proper* government unless there are some things which the government *cannot* do. Every citizen must have some definite protection against his government, if the government should ever stop being reasonable.

It is therefore important that a Pueblo Code should somewhere lay down, clearly, some limits on the powers of the government, in protection of the citizens.

Furthermore, the younger men ought to have some portion of the Code which they can rightly feel is for them.

This Bill of Rights, if accepted, will be very persuasive to any white court. It leaves full room for strong government. It ought to make the younger men feel that they also have been thought about.

PART IV. Bill of Rights

(41) *Reasonableness, fairness and evenness of rules.* Any law of this Pueblo, written or unwritten, is valid if it is reasonable and if it applies fairly and evenly. Under this section

(a) the appointment of officers in the old way is reasonable, fair and even, and any change in the method of appointing officers may take account of the old way as being reasonable, fair and even; and

(b) what is reasonable is what is reasonable for this whole Pueblo in the light of its history, its customs and its needs.

(42) *Trials and penalties.* Trials and penalties may follow the old and tested way of this Pueblo, unless this Code or the Council changes some part of that way. But

(a) trials must be fair and no man must be judged guilty because of spite or without reasonable grounds; and

(b) penalties must be fair and even; and

(c) any fines go to the Pueblo. No fine can go to any officer or other single person or group; and

(d) at any trial any party is entitled to know what the charge against him is and to call any witnesses whom he may need and to be heard in his own defense or to call a friend to speak in his defense. It is the duty of the officer presiding at the trial to call careful attention of the defendant to all of these rights; and

(e) A person is entitled to be satisfied with any serious judgment or penalty against him if there is any reasonable way of making him satisfied. If he remains unsatisfied even with a judgment by the Council, the Council must hear his case once more. But no man is entitled to hold up the business of the Pueblo by remaining stubborn after two judgments of the Council against him.

> [Note: This is probably the most important section in the Code (along with Section 45) to make a white court feel that the Pueblo way of justice is a right and just way.]

(43) *Sanctity of private house; searches.* Except in case of real emergency an officer must not without invitation enter a private house. Cases of real emergency include

(a) protection against impending fire;

(b) danger to life and limb because of an active fight going on in the house;

(c) reasonable suspicion that stolen goods are concealed in the house; and

(d) need to arrest a person accused of a serious offense and reasonably thought to be in the house.

But an officer should be slow to judge any case to be one of emergency if no invitation to enter has been given.

(44) *Rights in land and to membership.*

(a) All land even though in the possession and use of a particular person or family remains subject to the underlying general ownership-rights of the Pueblo. But land which is rightfully in the possession and also in the use of any person or family must not be taken from the user while the user remains a member of the Pueblo unless there is strong cause as judged by the Council. Any offense which is strong enough to make it right to take back land actually in the possession and use of the offender is strong enough to make it right to exclude the user from the Pueblo.

(b) Persistent refusal without good reason to perform community duties when properly ordered is sufficiently strong cause to justify exclusion from the Pueblo and the taking back of land.

(c) Even if land is taken back as a part of excluding a person from the Pueblo that person must be compensated for any improvements made on the land by him or by the people who have had the land before him.

(d) A person who voluntarily gives up his membership in the Pueblo gives up his rights to the use of land but retains a right to the value of improvements.

(e) Exclusion from the Pueblo for breach of communal duties requires three formal demands for performance of the duty and three failures to perform after such demand and two trials before the Council. The Agency should be consulted before the second trial.

(45) *Whipping and hanging up*

(a) No more than three strokes of whipping can be given at any one time, and no more than nine can be ordered for any offense. If there are to be more strokes, two full days must pass before further strokes can be given.

(b) If the offense is a civil offense which is a serious danger to the peace of the Pueblo (such as a beating up which results in serious injury); or if the offense is a serious civil offense which is willful and mean (such as serious damage to another's crops, done for spite); or if the offense is a serious offense against the civil government, and the offender remains stubborn and refuses after all due effort by the Council to repent (as where he refuses obedience to proper orders, insulting the civil officers in charge, and cannot be brought to repent), whipping may be ordered for a first offense.

(c) Hanging up cannot be ordered or done in this Pueblo.

(46) *Right of petition*

(a) Any member of this Pueblo is entitled to a hearing before any proper officer in regard to any grievance.

(b) Any members of this Pueblo are entitled to meet and discuss any grievance at any time and to present to the Council their request for remedy. Whether or not such a request is presented in writing, a spokesman is entitled to be heard in person before the Council.

PART V. Duties of members

(51) *General duties of members inside the Pueblo.* Each member of this Pueblo has a duty to keep the peace inside the Pueblo, to respect and aid all officers, to use no abusive language to other members of the Pueblo and to support the officers in the exercise of their authority.

(52) *General duties of members outside the Pueblo.* Each member of this Pueblo has a duty when he is outside the Pueblo to so act as to uphold the good name of the Pueblo.

(53) *Community work.* Each member of this Pueblo when duly called to community work has a duty to perform it as directed. Community duties are to be divided reasonably and evenly so far as possible. Private irrigation and any other work which requires use of community resources must be performed when assigned by the officer in charge.

[?(54) *Community work by person living and working outside.* If a member of the Pueblo is living and working outside, the Governor may give him permission not to return for any piece of community work. In such a case the person who is not doing his community work must pay the Pueblo a membership tax for the year of (? 5) dollars.?]

(55) *Duty to hold office.* A person appointed to office in this Pueblo may not refuse the office.

1 K.L.P. I. II. 18. Undated (circa 1947).
2 Cited in D'Arcy MacNickle, *They Came Here First* 86–9 (1949). Llewellyn was probably the draftsman. The most likely date is 1947.
3 K.L.P. I. II. 23 (second draft, 1947).
4 Paras 5–10, if they ever existed, are missing from the original typescript.

SELECT BIBLIOGRAPHY OF WORKS BY LLEWELLYN

(See Bibliographical Note, above p. xiv)

A. PUBLISHED WORKS

(Numbers in brackets refer to the Bibliography in Twining, *The Karl Llewellyn Papers*)

Books
Beach Plums (poems), New York, London, Century (1931), 8 pp. (28)
The Bramble Bush, Tentative Printing for the Use of Students at Columbia University School of Law, New York (1930), 160 pp.; New York, Oceana (1951), 158 pp. (23)
Cases and Materials on the Law of Sales, Chicago, Callaghan (1930), 1081 pp. (24)
The Cheyenne Way (with E. Adamson Hoebel), Norman, University of Oklahoma Press (1941), 360 pp. (77)
The Common Law Tradition—Deciding Appeals, Boston, Toronto, Little, Brown (1960), 565 pp. (115)
Jurisprudence: Realism in Theory and Practice, Chicago, University of Chicago Press (1962), 531 pp. (117)
Präjudizienrecht und Rechtsprechung in Amerika, Leipzig, Theodor Weicher (1933), 360 pp.; Sections 52–61 translated into English in John Dawson (ed.), *Comparative Law* 187–200, Ann Arbor, University of Michigan Law School (1951). (39)
Put in His Thumb (poems), New York, London, Century (1931), 119 pp. (30)
[*The Revised Uniform Sales Act,* Second Draft—1941.]

Articles
Across Sales on Horseback, 52 Harvard Law Review 725–746 (1939); reprinted by Harvard Law Review, with *The First Struggle To Unhorse Sales,* as *Horse-trade and Merchant's Market in Sales.* (64)

The Adventures of Rollo, 2 University of Chicago Law School Record, No. 1, pp. 3–4, 20–24 (1953). (107)

The American Common Law Tradition and American Democracy, 1 Journal of Legal and Political Sociology 14–45 (1942); Jurisprudence: Realism in Theory and Practice 282–315 (1962). (83)

The Bar Specializes–with What Results? 167 Annals of the American Academy of Political and Social Science 177–192 (1933); 39 Commercial Law Journal 336–343 (1934). (36)

The Bar's Troubles, and Poultices–and Cures? 5 Law and Contemporary Problems 104–134 (1938); Jurisprudence: Realism in Theory and Practice 243–281 (1962). (60)

Behind the Law of Divorce (Part 1), 32 Columbia Law Review 1281–1308 (1932). (35)

Behind the Law of Divorce (Part 2), 33 Columbia Law Review 249–294 (1933). (37)

Bringing Legal Aid to the Little Man, New York Times Magazine 7, 18 (March 25, 1934); 82 Pittsburgh Law Journal, No. 27, 10–15 (July 7, 1934). (41)

Carter, James Coolidge, 3 Encyclopedia of the Social Sciences 243–244 (1931). (194)

Case Law, 3 Encyclopedia of the Social Sciences 249–251 (1931). (195)

Case Method, 3 Encyclopedia of the Social Sciences 251–254 (1931). (196)

Commercial Transactions, New York, Practicing Law Institute (1946), 33 pp; revised version, *The Modern Approach to Counseling and Advocacy, Especially in Commercial Transactions,* 46 Columbia Law Review 167–195 (1946); Jurisprudence : Realism in Theory and Practice 323–351 (1962). (94)

The Conditions for and the Aims and Methods of Legal Research, Handbook of the Association of American Law Schools 35–47 (1929); 6 American Law School Review 670–678 (1930). (20)

The Constitution as an Institution, 34 Columbia Law Review 1–40 (1934); extracts reprinted as *On the Nature of an Institution,* Jurisprudence: Realism in Theory and Practice 233–242 (1962). (42)

On the Current Recapture of the Grand Tradition, 9 University of Chicago Law School Record, No. 1, pp. 6, 16–23 (Fall, 1960); Jurisprudence: Realism in Theory and Practice 215–229 (1962). (116)

The Effect of Legal Institutions upon Economics, 15 American Economic Review 665–683 (1925). (16)

Fictions, Encyclopaedia Britannica (1964). (244)

The First Struggle To Unhorse Sales, 52 Harvard Law Review 874–904 (1939); reprinted by Harvard Law Review, with *Across Sales on Horseback,* as *Horse-Trade and Merchant's Market in Sales.* (65)

On the Good, the True and the Beautiful in Law, 9 University of Chicago Law Review 224–265 (1942); Translated by José Brutan into Spanish as *Belleza y Estilo en el Derecho,* Barcelona, Bosch (1953), 80 pp.; Jurisprudence: Realism in Theory and Practice 167–213 (1962). (84)

Impressions of the Cincinnati Conference on the Status of Stare Decisis, 14 University of Cincinnati Law Review 343–355 (1940); Jurisprudence: Realism in Theory and Practice 116–127 (1962). (69)

Introduction, Jerome Hall, Theft, Law and Society xv–xxxv, Boston, Little, Brown (1935); reprinted as *Theft as a Behavior Problem,* Jurisprudence: Realism in Theory and Practice 412–430 (1962). (49)

On Law and Our Commerce, 1949 Wisconsin Law Review 625–633. (102)

Law and the Social Sciences, Especially Sociology, 62 Harvard Law Review 1266–1305 (1949); 14 American Sociological Review 451–462 (1949); translated by Enrique Vera Villalobos, *El Derecho y las Ciencas, Especialmente la Sociologia,* Lecciones y Ensayos, No. 4/5, pp. 29–44, University of Buenos Aires (1957); Jurisprudence: Realism in Theory and Practice 352–371 (1962). (101)

Legal Tradition and Social Science Method–A Realist's Critique, Essays on Research in the Social Sciences 89–120, Washington, Brookings Institution (1931), 194 pp. (29)

McDougal and Lasswell Plan for Legal Education, 43 Columbia Law Review 476–485 (1943). (87)

Meet Negotiable Instruments, 44 Columbia Law Review 299–329 (1944). (88)

Memoranda (presented to New York State Law Revision Commission Hearings on the Uniform Commercial Code), Report of the Law Revision Commission 21–34, 69, 106–126, 193–195, 284, 553–554, William Press, Albany (1954). (239)

My Philosophy of Law, A Kocourek (ed.), My Philosophy of Law 181–197, Boston, Boston Law Books Co. (1941). (78)

The Normative, the Legal and the Law-Jobs, 49 Yale Law Journal 1355–1400 (1940). (71)

The Place of Skills in Legal Education (report of Committee on Curriculum, drafted by Llewellyn), Handbook of the Association of American Law Schools 159–201 (1944); 45 Columbia Law Review 345–391 (1945). (89)

On Philosophy of American Law, 82 University of Pennsylvania Law Review 205–212 (1934). (45)

On the Problem of Teaching "Private" Law, 54 Harvard Law Review 772–810 (1941). (80)

On Reading and Using the Newer Jurisprudence, 40 Columbia Law Review 581–614 (1940); 26 American Bar Association Journal 300–307, 418–425 (1940); Jurisprudence: Realism in Theory and Practice 128–165 (1962). (72)

A Realistic Jurisprudence–The Next Step, 30 Columbia Law Review 431–465 (1930); Jurisprudence: Realism in Theory and Practice 3–41 (1962). (27)

Remarks on the Sacco-Vanzetti Case, Broadcast delivered at WPCH, Saturday, August 20, 1927; *The Karl Llewellyn Papers,* Twining, University of Chicago Law School, 105–110 (1968).

Remarks on the Theory of Appellate Decision and the Rules or Canons about How Statutes Are To Be Construed, 3 Vanderbilt Law Review 395–405 (1950). (105)

The Rule of Law in Our Case Law of Contract, 47 Yale Law Journal 1243–1271 (1938). (63)

The Sacco-Vanzetti Case (part of an unpublished study), Jerome Michael and Herbert Wechsler (eds.), Criminal Law and Its Administration 1085–1091, Chicago, Foundation (1940); Louis Joughin and Edmund Morgan, The Legacy of Sacco and Vanzetti 178–183, New York, Harcourt, Brace (1948); reprinted as *Who Are These Accused?* Jurisprudence: Realism in Theory and Practice 431–438 (1962). (75)

Social Significance in Legal Problems, A Conard (ed.), Conference on Aims and Methods of Legal Research 8–21, 27, 28–31, Ann Arbor, University of Michigan Law School (1955). (110)

Some Realism about Realism, 44 Harvard Law Review 1222–1264 (1931); Jurisprudence: Realism in Theory and Practice 42–76 (1962). (31)

Through Title to Contract and Beyond, 3 Law–a Century of Progress 80 (1937); amended version 15 New York University Law Review 159–209 (1938). (57)

On Warranty of Quality and Society (Part 1), 36 Columbia Law Review 699–744 (1936); reprinted by Columbia Law Review, with Part 2, as *Courts, Quality of Goods, and a Credit Economy.* (53)

On Warranty of Quality and Society (Part 2), 37 Columbia Law Review 341–409 (1937); reprinted by Columbia Law Review, with Part 1, as *Courts, Quality of Goods, and a Credit Economy.* (59)

Wesley Newcomb Hohfeld–Teacher (comment), 28 Yale Law Journal 795–798 (1919); Jurisprudence: Realism in Theory and Practice, 491–494 (1962). (9)

On What Is Wrong with So-Called Legal Education, 35 Columbia Law Review 651–678 (1935). (51)

On What Makes Legal Research Worthwhile? 8 Journal of Legal Education 399–421 (1956). (111)

What Price Contract–an Essay in Perspective, 40 Yale Law Journal 704–751 (1931). (32)

Reviews

Cairns, Huntington, *Law and the Social Sciences,* 36 Columbia Law Review 505–507 (1936). (159)

Campbell, Morton, *Cases on Mortgages of Real Property,* 40 Harvard Law Review 142–146 (1926). (139)

Frank, Jerome, *Law and the Modern Mind,* 31 Columbia Law Review 82–90 (1931); Jurisprudence: Realism in Theory and Practice 101–110 (1962). (148)

Gisnet, Morris, *A Lawyer Tells the Truth,* 31 Columbia Law Review 1215–1220 (1931). (150)

Michael, Jerome, and Adler, Mortimer, *Crime, Law and Social Science,* 34 Columbia Law Review 277–291 (1934). (157)

"The Modern Business Law Book," review of William Britton and Ralph Bauer, *Cases on Business Law;* Harold Perrin and Hugh Babb, *Commercial Law Cases;* Lincoln Schaub and Nathan Isaacs, *The Law in Business Problems;* William Spencer, *Law and Business,* 32 Yale Law Journal 299–307 (1923). (126)

Pound, Roscoe, *Jurisprudence,* 28 University of Chicago Law Review 174–182 (1960); Jurisprudence: Realism in Theory and Practice 495–504 (1962). (182)

Robinson, Edward, *Law and the Lawyers,* and Arnold, Thurman,

Symbols of Government, 5 Brooklyn Law Review 219–223 (1936). (161)

Weber, Max, *Law in Economy and Society* (edited with an Introduction and Annotations by Max Rheinstein), 24 University of Chicago Law Review 616–623 (1957); German version in 2 Zeitschrift für Äusländisches und Internationales Privatrecht, 22 Jahrgang 1957, Heft 4, pp. 720–721. (180)

Williston, Samuel, *Some Modern Tendencies in the Law*, 16 American Bar Association Journal 809–810 (1930). (146)

BIBLIOGRAPHY OF THE PUBLISHED WORKS OF DIOGENES
JONATHAN SWIFT TEUFELSDRÖCKH

Jurisprudence, The Crown of Civilization, 5 University of Chicago Law Review 171–183 (1938). (245)

The Universal Solvent of Jurisprudence, 8 Harvard Law Revue 1–2 (1940). (246)

B. UNPUBLISHED MANUSCRIPTS

'Behind the Law of Divorce' III (1933+).

'The Chicago Jury Project' (1955).

'The Common Law Tradition' (1941)

'Drama, Dramatics and Kids'.

'Elements of Law' (duplicated teaching materials) K.L.P. Section M.

'John Dewey and Our Law' (1949)

'Law and Language' (Symposium—Law and Humanities) (1961).

'Law and Social Science' (1930–35).

'Law in Crisis' (1940–1)

'Law in Our Society' (duplicated teaching materials) 1st Edition 1950, subsequent editions to 1958. K.L.P. Section L.

'Law in the Family' (193 —)

'Legal Argument' (duplicated teaching materials) K.L.P. Section N.

'Loom of the Law: A Theory of Jural Sociology and Method' (1935–40).

'The Low "Philosophy" of Law' (1943).

'Mechanisms of Group Control' (1932–4?).

Memoranda and other MSS. on Pueblos K.L.P. Section I.

Memoranda and papers on U.C.C. K.L.P. Section J.

The [New] Bramble Bush (1947–51).

'A Nonconformist Puzzles over Education' (1924).

'The Parental Pole of Law and Government' (1960–2?).

'Paris'.

'Position re Religion' (1943).

'Recht, Rechtsleben, und Gesellschaft' (1932).

'On Robinson's Unscientific Science of Law' (1935).

Sacco and Vanzetti v. The Commonwealth: An Indictment of the Workings of Our Judical Institutions (Started 1928—abandoned 1935?).

'Sales Law and Marketing 1800–1935' (1937+).

The Theory of Rules (1938–40?).

Transcripts of Lectures K.L.P. Section C.

'Trends in Legal Sociology' (1933–8?).

Unpublished Verse K.L.P. Section B. VI.

Weber, Max 'Sociology of Law' (translations) (1935 and later).

'What a Private Thinks About the War'.

'What's What in Jurisprudence' (including 'Babel Versus Teamwork : Jurisprudence Since 1900') (1942–3).

General Index

Adams, John, 126
Adler, Mortimer, 58, 190–1, 402, 517
  Crime, Law and Social Science, 191
advocates, advocacy, 257–64, 354, 355
aesthetics, *see* legal aesthetics
African customary law, 163–4, 431–3
agency, 331
Allen, C. K., 69
American Bankers Association, 287
American Bankers Institute, 101
American Bar Association (ABA), 6,
  272, 277, 287, 327, 351–2
  Canons of Ethics, 261–2
  Committee on Legal Service Bureaus,
  350
  Survey of the Legal Profession, 351
American Civil Liberties Union
  (ACLU), 110, 124, 344
American Indians, 111–12, 125, 126;
  see also Cheyenne Indians; Com-
  anche Indians; Pueblo Indians
American Law Institute, 6, 15, 23–4,
  272–4, 280–2, 286, 291, 299, 300,
  302–3, 317, 319, 459, 530, 533, 544
  Council, 285
American Philosophical Society, 113
American Warehousemen's Association,
  287, 461
Ames, J. B., 389
analysis of concepts, analytical
  jurisprudence, 34–6, 97, 136–7,
  177, 366, 397, 469; *see also*
  classification; narrow issue
  thinking
Anderson, Maxwell, *Winterset*, 344
'and-not', 515–16
Angell, Robert, 194, 195
anthropology, case method used in, 156,
  160–4, 166–7, 367, 433
appellate advocates, *see* advocates

Aquinas, St. Thomas, 124, 422
Arnold, Thurman, 25, 58, 67–8, 82,
  409, 517
  The Folklore of Capitalism, 67, 82
  The Symbols of Government, 67
Association of American Law Schools
  (AALS), 6, 36, 111–12, 124, 273,
  277, 350, 356
committee on curriculum, 354
Association of American Railroads, 287
Association of the Bar of the City of
  New York, 280, 293
Atiyah, P. S.,
  Accidents, Compensation and the Law, 384
Atkin, Lord, 214, 235–6, 239, 253–4
Austin, John, 22, 29, 35, 392, 397

Baldwin, Simeon, 32–3, 94
bank deposits and collections, 325, 330
bar surveys, 349–50, 351, 367, 472
Barton, R. F., 160
Beale, Joseph, 7, 14, 15, 38–9, 72, 172,
  389, 406
Beard, Charles, 8–9, 174
beauty in law, *see* legal aesthetics
Becht, A., 215, 237–8, 444
Becker, Theodore L.,
  *Political Behavioralism and Modern
  Jurisprudence*, 445
behavioural sciences, *see* social sciences
behaviourist psychology, 43, 63–4, 190,
  378, 380
Behrman, S. N., 344
Benedict, Ruth
  Patterns of Culture, 356, 433
Bentham, Jeremy, 8, 170, 308, 352, 378,
  385–7
Berle, Adolf A., 56, 58, 410
  *The Modern Corporation and Private
  Property*, 58

BOOKS IN THE SERIES (continued from page iii)

Lightning Source UK Ltd.
Milton Keynes UK
UKOW052331230113

205211UK00001BB/71/P